Stanley Gibbons

Great Britain

Specialised Stamp Catalogue

Volume 3

Seven designs produced in 1956 by C. P. Rang,
then Editor of *Gibbons Stamp Monthly*, to
promote the campaign for small-size definitives.

Stanley Gibbons

Great Britain

Specialised Stamp Catalogue

Volume 3
Queen Elizabeth II
Pre-decimal Issues

Eleventh Edition

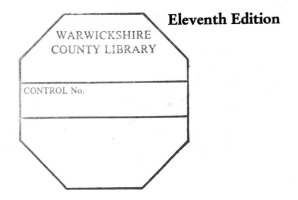

Stanley Gibbons Ltd
London and Ringwood

By Appointment to Her Majesty The Queen
Stanley Gibbons Limited, London
Philatelists

Published by **Stanley Gibbons Ltd.**
Editorial, Sales Offices and Distribution Centre:
7 Parkside, Christchurch Road, Ringwood,
Hants BH24 3SH

© **Stanley Gibbons Ltd 2006**

1st edition—August 1970
2nd edition—October 1971
3rd edition—February 1976
  Reprinted—October 1976
  Reprinted—April 1977
4th edition—November 1978
5th edition—November 1980

6th edition—June 1984
7th edition—November 1987
8th edition—September 1990
9th edition—October 1993
10th edition—October 1998
11th edition—March 2006

Item No. 2810 (08)

ISBN 0–85259–602–2

**Typeset and Printed in Great Britain by Piggott Black Bear Ltd,
Cambridge**

Contents

Preface . . . . *page* vii

Introductory Notes viii

The Wilding Issues (Sections S and T)

General Notes to Section S 1
Identification Table of Wilding Issues 7
Index to Wilding Coil Stamps 8
Section SA: Photogravure Low Values (1952–68) 9
Section SB: Booklet Panes in Photogravure (1952–68) 93
Index to Wilding Booklet Panes 94
Section T: Recess-printed High Values (1955–68) 141

The Machin £.s.d. Issues (Section U)

General Notes to Section U 153
Identification Table to Machin Low Values 157
Index to Machin Coil Stamps 158
Section UA: Photogravure Low Values (1967–70) 159
Section UB: Booklet Panes in Photogravure (1967–70) 184
Checklist of Machin Booklet Panes 185
Section UC: Recess-printed High Values (1969) 197

The Special Issues (Section W)

General Notes 202
Design Index 208

The Regional Issues (Section XA)

General Notes on Wilding Regional Issues in Photogravure 370
  A. Guernsey (1958–69) 372
  B. Jersey (1958–69) 377
  C. Isle of Man (1958–69) 382
  D. Northern Ireland (1958–70) 386
  E. Scotland (1958–70) 393
  F. Wales and Monmouthshire (1958–70) 404

The Postage Due Stamps (Section ZA)

General Notes 411
The Postage Due Issues (1954–71) 412

Appendices

Appendix G: Perforators 416
Appendix HA: Post Office Booklets of Stamps 426
  Wilding Issues 428
  Machin £.s.d. Issues 443
Appendix HB: Postage Rates 449

Further Reading 453

Stanley Gibbons Holdings Plc. Addresses

STANLEY GIBBONS LTD, STANLEY GIBBONS AUCTIONS
399 STRAND, LONDON, WC2R 0LX

Telephone 0207 836 8444 and Fax 0207 836 7342 for all departments.

Auction Room and Specialist Stamp Departments. Open Monday–Friday 9.30 a.m. to 5 p.m.

Shop. Open Monday–Friday 8.30 a.m. to 6 p.m. and Saturday 9.30 a.m. to 5.30 p.m.

STANLEY GIBBONS PUBLICATIONS
7 PARKSIDE, CHRISTCHURCH ROAD, RINGWOOD, HANTS BH24 3SH

Telephone 01425 472363 (24 hour answer phone service). Fax 01425 470247 and **E-mail info@stanleygibbons.co.uk**

Publications Mail Order. FREEPHONE 0800 611622. Monday–Friday 8.30 a.m. to 5 p.m.

Stanley Gibbons Publications has overseas licensees and distributors for Australia, Austria, Belgium, Canada, Denmark, Finland, France, Germany, Hong Kong, Israel, Italy, Japan, Luxembourg, Netherlands, New Zealand, Norway, Singapore, South Africa, Sweden, Switzerland, West Indies and Caribbean. Please contact the Ringwood address for details.

FRASER'S
(a division of Stanley Gibbons Ltd)
399 Strand, London WC2R 0LX
Autographs, photographs, letters and documents.
**Telephone 0207 836 8444
and Fax 0207 836 7342**
Monday–Friday 9 a.m. to 5.30 p.m. and Saturday 10 a.m. to 4 p.m.

Great Britain Philatelic Societies

Great Britain Philatelic Society. Hon. Membership Secretary: Debbie Harman "Greylands", Melton, Woodbridge, Suffolk IP12 1QE.

Modern British Philatelic Circle. Hon. Membership Secretary: A. J. Wilkins, 3 Buttermere Close, Brierley Hill, West Midlands, DY5 3SD.

The Great Britain Collectors' Club. Secretary: Mr. Parker A. Bailey, 17 Greenwood Road, Merrimack, NH 03054, U.S.A.

Preface

It is now 50 years since the Editor of *Gibbons Stamp Monthly*, C.P. Rang, published his proposed designs for small-size pictorial stamps bearing the Queen's head. The seven designs are reproduced on the frontispiece of this catalogue.

The designs received favourable press coverage and were referred to by Lord Elibank, a long-time advocate of pictorial definitive issues, in a speech to the House of Lords on 17 May 1956. As we know, the suggestion was not viewed favourably by the authorities, but on 18 July of the same year the Postmaster General announced the intention to issue regional stamps for Scotland, Wales, Northern Ireland, Jersey, Guernsey and the Isle of Man; a proposal which the Editor of GSM did not feel provided an adequate response!

Now, 50 years on, it might be said that most serious stamp collectors feel that there are far too many pictorial stamps being issued, but even the higher value definitives, which were pictorial until a few years ago, now share the same design as the 1p.

While the period covered by this catalogue may not have seen any radical departures in terms of definitive stamp design, it was hugely important in terms of the techniques of stamp production and mail handling, where the drive to mechanise the latter led to numerous developments in the former. Over the period between 1952 and 1971, definitive stamps went from plain, uncoated, watermarked paper, through graphites, various phosphors and paper changes to the coated, unwatermarked phosphor-banded stamps of the pre-decimal Machins. Meanwhile, the special issues were going through radical changes of their own – from eight stamps issued during the first years of the period in question to (ignoring ordinary/phosphor differences) 120 in the last five.

This new edition

The opportunity has been taken to completely redesign and re-set this catalogue. Improvements have been made to the presentation of the listings, with the small 6 point type completely abandoned in favour of a larger, more readable style. The illustrations have all been rescanned; where possible from original stamps and photographs, and we are sure that readers will welcome the opportunity to see clearly the varieties they are looking for!

Even after all these years, new discoveries continue to be made and are being added to the listings. As always, the provenance of such additions has had to be checked and additional notes have been included explaining the background to new listings and why other items which do appear on the market are not given catalogue status. It will be noted that some missing colour errors, previously shown in separate tables, are now given full listing and that prices are now given to National Postal Museum imprimaturs, hitherto listed but unpriced.

Prices

Values have been carefully reviewed and, with over seven years having elapsed since publication of the tenth edition, readers will not be surprised at the number and degree of movement of the increases. In the Wilding issues there have been significant increases to the booklet panes, which are becoming very hard to find with satisfactory perforations. Demand for the once-popular plate flaws and varieties is also beginning to revive and the first signs of price movement are evident in this catalogue. Who knows? the fact that they are now more clearly illustrated may result in steeper increases in the next edition!

Pre-decimal Machins remain 'quiet' but plate number blocks of the high values have increased way above the prices of singles which were somewhat 'oversubscribed' when issued.

Preface

Sufficient stocks of most of the special stamps are still widely held, so prices here are, again, stable. However, the same cannot be said for printing and perforation errors, which have risen in price very dramatically. We are grateful to all those who have assisted in ensuring that the prices given in this catalogue present an accurate picture of the market at the time of publication.

John Holman, the Editor of the *British Philatelic Bulletin*, advised us on the Bibliography and some dozen new titles have been added. Now that we have celebrated the 50th anniversary of the Dorothy Wilding portrait definitives, it is appropriate that this Catalogue should again be published with the latest prices and up-to-date information concerning these fascinating stamps.

Hugh Jefferies
Robert H. Oliver
Vince Cordell

Acknowledgements

We are grateful to the Great Britain Philatelic Society for allowing us to draw on information published in articles from *The GB Journal*, in particular *British Stamp Booklets* by Dr. Jean Alexander and the late Leonard F. Newbery. A special note of appreciation goes to J.R. Holman, Editor of the *British Philatelic Bulletin*. We thank Ross Candlish (Wildings), A.G. (Jim) Bond, Mike Holt (pre-decimal Machins), Tony Bellew, Richard Monteiro, Mark Brandon and many others for their contributions, expertise and advice.

Introductory Notes

The aim of this catalogue is to classify in specialised form the stamps of Great Britain, to give distinguishing numbers to them and to quote prices which are current with Stanley Gibbons Ltd. at the time of going to press and at which they will supply if in stock.

Detailed Introductory Notes

Before using the catalogue it is important to study the "General Notes" as these explain the technical background of the issues in question. They are to be found at the beginning of the relevant sections.

Arrangement of Lists

The Wilding, Machin £.s.d. and Regional issues are dealt with value by value. The order of listing is as follows:

- A. Basic listing of single stamps from sheets, booklets and coils according to paper, phosphor and gum with errors and varieties.
- B. Illustrations of listed cylinder and plate varieties.
- C. List of cylinder blocks according to paper, phosphor and gum combinations and priced according to perforation types.
- D. Details of constant minor sheet flaws without illustrations and prices but quoting positions on stamps.
- E. Information relating to coils.
- F. Ancillary data relating to withdrawal dates, and quantities issued or sold.

If there is a deliberate change in the number of phosphor bands this is treated as a separate issue which is then listed in the order shown above.

Booklet panes are listed separately in Sections SB and UB according to paper and gum, with errors and cylinder varieties, and all priced according to perforation types. These are followed by illustrations of cylinder varieties and lists of booklet pane cylinder numbers appear at the end of each listing.

The Special issues (Section W) are listed on the same basis, set by set, with the addition of ancillary information about sheet format, method of printing, a list of the sheet markings, quantities sold and withdrawal dates from information published by the Post Office.

Catalogue Numbering

All *Specialised Catalogue* numbers include a prefix letter or letters which denotes its Section in the Catalogue. This is followed by the related number in the 2005 edition of the *Stanley Gibbons Great Britain Concise Stamp Catalogue.*

Shades, where there is more than one, are denoted by bracketed numbers, e.g. (1) Green, (2) Deep green for No. S25, the Wildings 1½d., with watermark Tudor Crown.

Varieties have a letter identification, e.g. *a.* Watermark inverted; *b.* (short description of cylinder variety) and related varieties to item *b.* will be listed as *ba., bb.,* etc.

In Appendix HA the booklets have the same numbers and prefix letters as are used in the *G.B. Concise Catalogue.* Varieties of booklets listed in the *Specialised Catalogue* only are shown with number in brackets, thus "(*a*)".

Prices

Prices quoted in this Catalogue are the selling prices of Stanley Gibbons Ltd., at the time the book went to press. They are for stamps in fine condition for the particular issue, unless otherwise indicated: those of lesser quality may be offered at lower prices. All prices are subject to change without prior notice and no guarantee is given to supply all stamps priced, since it is not possible to keep every catalogued item in stock.

In the case of unused stamps, our prices are for unmounted mint. Prices for used stamps refer to postally used examples.

If a variety exists in more than one *shade* it is priced for the commonest shade and will be worth correspondingly more in a scarcer shade. Except where otherwise stated, varieties are priced for single examples and extra stamps required to make up positional blocks would be valued as normals. All *cylinder flaws* and other varieties listed under *booklet panes* are priced for the complete pane.

Cylinder blocks containing varieties are indicated by an asterisk against the price (which includes the cost of the variety).

Cases can exist where a particular stamp shows more than one listed variety. It might, for example, have an inverted watermark as well as a broad phosphor band, both of which are listed but priced separately. It is not practical to cover every possible combination, but the value of such items may be established by adding the difference between the price of the basic stamp and the dearest variety to the catalogue price of the cheapest variety.

The prices quoted for *booklet panes* are for panes with good perforations and complete with the binding margin. Prices for complete booklets are for those containing panes with average perforations as it is unusual for all panes in the booklet to show full perforations on the guillotined sides.

Cylinder blocks are priced according to the type of perforator used. This takes account of the state of the perforations on all four sides of the sheet, not just the corner where the cylinder number appears. Note that a full specification of a cylinder block should quote the basic number of the stamp; cylinder number; with or without dot; perforation type; cream or white paper; gum arabic or PVA, wherever such alternatives exist.

Guarantee

All stamps supplied by Stanley Gibbons Ltd., are guaranteed originals in the following terms:

If not as described, and returned by the purchaser, we undertake to refund the price paid to us in the original transaction. If any stamp is certified as genuine by the Expert Committee of the Royal Philatelic Society, London, or by B.P.A. Expertising Ltd., the purchaser shall not be entitled to make any claim against us for any error, omission or mistake in such certificate.

Consumers' statutory rights are not affected by the above guarantee.

Expertisation

We do not give opinions as to the genuineness of stamps. Expert Committees exist for this purpose and enquiry can be made of the Royal Philatelic Society, 41 Devonshire Place, London W1N 1PE, or B.P.A. Expertising Ltd., P.O. Box 137, Leatherhead, Surrey KT22 0RG. They do not undertake valuations under any circumstances and fees are payable for their services.

Correspondence

Letters should be addressed to the Catalogue Editor, Stanley Gibbons Publications, Parkside, Christchurch Road, Ringwood, Hants BH24 3SH, and return postage is appreciated when a reply is sought. New information and unlisted items for consideration are welcomed.

Please note we do not give opinions as to the genuineness of stamps, nor do we identify stamps or number them by our Catalogue.

To order from this Catalogue

Always quote the *Specialised Catalogue* number, mentioning *Volume 3, 11th Edition*, and where necessary specify additionally the precise item wanted.

National Postal Museum Archive Material, Sold 1984/5

During 1984 and 1985 surplus GB material from the National Postal Museum archives was included in three auction sales. The lots offered were mostly imprimaturs, which were handstamped on the reverse to indicate origin, and specimen overprints. In this catalogue items which are only known from the lots sold at these auctions are included in special entries, under headings clearly indicating their origin. Where items included in these sales had been previously listed a dagger is shown alongside the catalogue price.

Symbols and Abbreviations

†	(after date of issue) date of issue in sheet format, but available earlier from coil or booklet source. See Dates of Issue, under General Notes
†	(in price column) does not exist
—	(in price column) exists, but no market price is known
	(a blank conveys the same meading)
∗	(against the price of a cylinder block) price includes a listed variety
/	between colours means "on" and the colour following is that of the paper on which the stamp is printed.
Cyl.	Cylinder
GA	Gum arabic
mm.	Millimetres
No.	Number
OP	Ordinary and phosphor
Phos.	Phosphor
Pl.	Plate
PVA	Polyvinyl alcohol (gum)
R.	row (thus "R. 6/4" indicates the fourth stamp from the left in the sixth horizontal row from the top of a sheet of stamps)
Th.	Refers to the Stanley Gibbons "Thirkell" Position Finder. The letters and figures which follow (e.g. Th. E5) pinpoint the position of the flaw on the stamp according to the grid engraved on the Finder

Watermark Illustrations

The illustrations show watermarks as seen from the *front* of the stamp. This is important to remember when classifying sideways watermarks which also exist sideways inverted (i.e. Crown to right).

Quantities Sold

The figures for quantities issued or sold are those published by the Post Office. Some figures for the Regionals, however, came from an article by Mr. E. C. Ehrmann in *Stamp Collecting*.

Items Excluded

In dealing with *varieties* and *minor constant flaws* we record only those for which we can vouch, namely items we have seen and verified for ourselves. It should be recognised, however, that some flaws described as constant may be transient: they may develop in size to be sufficiently noticeable to be worth retouching.

Colour shifts due to faulty registration range from minor shifts to quite spectacular varieties. As it is very difficult to draw a line between major and minor shifts we have not listed any. We likewise exclude: doctor blade flaws; paper creases; partially omitted colours; negative offsets: and misplaced perforations.

We do not quote for traffic light blocks or positional blocks showing various sheet markings other than cylinder blocks, but when available they will be supplied at appropriate prices.

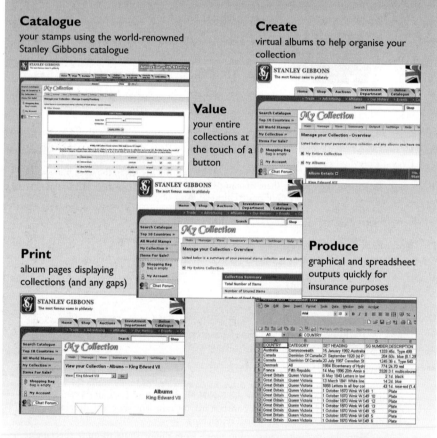

SECTION S
Dorothy Wilding Issues
1952–68. Sheet and Coil Stamps in Photogravure

General Notes

INTRODUCTION. Queen Elizabeth II came to the throne on 6 February, 1952. By contrast with the King George VI series there were five different basic designs from five artists with a common feature consisting of the portrait of the Queen by Dorothy Wilding Ltd. enclosed in an oval. The Queen is shown wearing the Crown Jewels, whilst the policy of embodying various emblems representative of the different parts of the United Kingdom was continued. These and the intricacies of the Crown Jewels produced many minor varieties and there are probably more varieties and flaws on this issue than on any other issue since the Victorian Line-engraved stamps.

The stamps were issued value by value over a period, the first, being the 1½d. and 2½d. which were placed on sale on the 5 December 1952 but it was not until February 1954 that the series was completed. During this period there was an interesting phase when booklets were issued containing panes of King George VI and Queen Elizabeth II stamps.

ARRANGEMENT. This section takes each value in turn and follows its history through the various watermarks, graphite lines, phosphors and papers taking in the coils and on page 7 there is a table setting out which values occurred in each state and quoting their catalogue numbers for easy reference.

The general arrangement of the catalogue is to show first the basic listing with errors and varieties, followed by illustrations of the listed cylinder flaws. These are priced whereas the minor constant flaws are not but they are included for reference. The sheet cylinder numbers and a record of the minor flaws follow. Where applicable the description of the coils and Imprimaturs and Specimens that were sold from the then National Postal Museum archives are dealt with. Quantities sold of the basic issue are included where known at the end of each listing although for the definitives this information was seldom available.

Booklet panes are dealt with in a similar manner in Section SB. For quantities issued or sold see under Appendix HA.

PAPER. For the first ten years the definitives were printed on a creamy paper but starting in April 1962 a whiter paper was gradually introduced. It is always a difficult matter to maintain successive supplies of paper in exactly the same colour and so it is not surprising that there is some variation in the degree of whiteness in the "whiter paper" which sometimes makes it difficult to identify. Sometimes knowledge of the cylinder used can be decisive. The whiter paper does not respond to the chalky test (that is applying silver to see if it will produce a black line) but a true coated chalk-surfaced paper was used for the 2s. Holiday Booklet issued in 1963 which affected the ½d. and 2½d. values in the Crowns watermark.

In 1964 an experimental paper was used for the 3d. non-phosphor Crowns watermark which was slightly thicker. It can be distinguished by the fact that an additional watermark letter "T" lying on its side occurred about four times in the sheet.

Variations can also be found in the thickness of the paper used, a notable example being the 3d. Tudor Crown watermark (No. S67) on thick paper. As weight standards were applied to complete reels only, such differences on individual stamps were within acceptable tolerances.

Paper Fluorescence. Stamps printed on unsurfaced paper may show a varying fluorescence when viewed under a short-wave ultra-violet lamp. This is due to the presence, in the rags used in paper making, of optical brightening agents. Such fluorescent properties are outside the scope of this catalogue.

WATERMARKS. In the Crowns watermark differences in the spacing of the Crowns have been noticed but it is believed that this is due to variations in the dandy roll and does not represent a different version of the watermark.

Errors, or replacement "bits", occur on most dandy rolls. For example during the period 1964 to 1966 the Crowns watermark can be found with one crown inverted. These errors have been seen on the ½d., No. S2b, and on various commemoratives.

Watermark Varieties. As the Wilding issues are all printed "on the web" inverted watermarks cannot occur on the sheet stamps, but they do occur on 50% of the booklet panes owing to the manner in which the sheets are arranged with some rows having the images inverted on the cylinders. The booklets are guillotined before issue resulting in some panes with the watermark inverted. Booklets are the only source of inverted watermarks in the Wilding issues.

Until 1961 all stamps with the watermark sideways came only from coils with left side delivery and these all show the top of the watermark pointing to left as seen from the front of the stamp. From 1961 all 2s. booklets on Crowns watermark had the watermark sideways and these, of course, have 50% of the panes with the crowns pointing to left and 50% to right and they are listed both ways.

SHEET PERFORATORS. The perforator types are described and illustrated in Appendix G. Definitive cylinder blocks are from the bottom left corner of the sheet and the following abbreviations relate to the margins at left and the bottom margin. The perforation type is given last and further details on the type of comb and perforation feed are in Appendix G.

(AE/I) Alternate extension holes in left margin and imperf bottom margin. Perf. Type E no dot pane

(E/I) On extension in left margin, each row and imperf. bottom margin. Perf. Types A both panes, E dot pane and H no dot pane

(E/P) As last but bottom margin perforated through. Perf. Type C no dot and dot also A(T) dot pane

(I/P) Imperf. left margin and bottom margin perforated through. Perf. Types B and J no dot panes only

(I/E) As last but extension holes in each row, bottom margin. Perf. Type F(L) no dot pane

(P/E) Left margin perforated through and extension holes in bottom margin. Perf. Types F no dot and dot panes and F(L) dot pane

(P/I) Left margin perforated and bottom margin imperf. Perf. Type H dot pane

EXPERIMENTAL GRAPHITE ISSUES. The first Automatic Letter Facing machine (known as ALF) was introduced experimentally at Southampton on 19 December 1957. The machine, which prepares letters for the sorting process, is fed with letters having their long edges parallel but with stamps in any of four possible positions. The letters are reorientated so that the stamps are in one of two possible positions on one long edge. These two positions, together with First and Second Class mail, are separated into stacks, and the stamps are cancelled. Items which cannot be faced, due for example to the absence of a stamp, are rejected to receive manual treatment.

The prototype facing machine looked in the stamp corner for an area of dense printing ink, having the characteristics of a stamp, as a means of stamp detection. This system was inefficient as the machine's performance was influenced by stamp design and the occasional presence of misleading writing on the envelope. However, facing machines were equipped with this method as a secondary means of stamp detection in order to deal with O.H.M.S. and Business Reply items.

To improve the efficiency of facing it was necessary to give these stamps some unmistakable identity. The first attempt used stamps which were printed with electrically conducting vertical black graphite lines on the back under the gum. One line on the 2d., then the printed paper rate, and two lines on the other values. The use of electrically conducting lines was not a complete success as failures were caused by metallic paper fasteners and damp mail.

There were two graphite issues. The first in November 1957 on the ½d., 1d., 1½d., 2d., 2½d. and 3d. sheet stamps with the St. Edward's Crown watermark and also on coils. The second issue came out during 1958–59 on the same values, plus the 4d. and 4½d. in sheets with the Crowns watermark and here there were also coils and booklets.

Stamps showing faked graphite lines are known especially on used samples.

PHOSPHOR-GRAPHITE ISSUES. In November 1959 existing graphite stamps were overprinted on the face with phosphorescent ink which, when exposed to ultra-violet (u.v.) light, releases energy in the form of visible light. The emission of visible light persists for some time after the exposure to u.v. light has ceased. These stamps were originally issued for further experiments at Southampton, November 1959 to February 1960, when the ALF operated with one electrical scanner and one phosphor scanner. Most countries which handle very large quantities of mail have followed the lead of Great Britain in the use of some form of luminescence on stamps to facilitate automatic facing.

The British Post Office used organic-resin phosphors containing an activator, the choice of activator affecting the optical properties.

Phosphor bands are not always easy to see, especially on used stamps, and it is usually necessary to hold the stamps up to the light at eye level when they become visible as broad bands.

The graphite lined stamps were overprinted with vertical phosphor bands on the face, again one band for the 2d. and two bands for the others. In sheets they appeared on the ½d., 1d., 1½d. and 2d. (in error) with St. Edward's Crown watermark and on the 2d., 2½d., 3d., 4d. and 4½d. with Crowns watermark. The substance used is commercially known as Lettalite B1 (the activator being Parahydroxydiphenyl) and it produces a greenish phosphorescence when reacting with u.v. light in the 2000 to 3000 Angstrom range.

As the phosphor treatment of stamps at Southampton was successful, residual stocks having graphite lines were distributed as normal stock to other areas and a notice was sent to Post Office clerks to say that they should disregard the black lines. This applied also to the 5s. booklet No. H46g (Sept. 1960).

PHOSPHOR ISSUES. The Southampton ALF was converted to scan phosphor only on 6 July 1960 and the ½d. to 4d. and 1s.3d. values with Crowns watermark with phosphor bands only were issued on 22 June 1960, the 6d. following on 27 June. Coils and booklets were issued later. The same phosphor reacting green was employed but in 1961 this was replaced as an interim measure by Lettalite B2

(Carbazole sulphonic acid being the activator) which reacts blue to u.v. in the 2000–4000 Ångstrom range. The advantage of this was that it gave a stronger signal.

At this time ALF machines were introduced into other areas and the "blue" phosphor was in use between 1961 and 1966 on the same values as for the "green" phosphor and with the addition of the $4\frac{1}{2}$d. value. This period covered the changeover to the whiter paper and also two changes in postal rates so that the 2d., $2\frac{1}{2}$d. and 3d. were each issued with one and two bands.

With the introduction of address coding and automatic letter sorting, at Norwich in 1965, it became necessary to use a phosphor for stamps which would not interfere with sorting. Thus another change was made, this time to Lettalite B3 (having Terephthalic acid as the activator) which was inert to the u.v. light of wavelength 3650 Ångstroms used in sorting machines but which has a bright visible light output when subjected to 2537 Ångstroms in the facing machine. This reacts violet under the lamp.

Identification of Phosphor Colours. Short wave ultra-violet lamps are available to enable collectors to identify the green, blue and violet phosphors. Please refer to the Stanley Gibbons Accessory list for information on these products currently available. Care should be taken when using such lamps as ultra-violet light can damage the eyes.

Phosphor Band Widths. Both the "green" and the "blue" bands normally measure 8 mm.
There are two widths of the "violet" phosphor bands, the 8 mm. bands, issued in 1965 ($\frac{1}{2}$d., 1d., $1\frac{1}{2}$d., 2d., 3d., 4d., 6d. and 1s.3d., plus coils and booklets) and the 9·5 mm. bands issued in 1966–67 (1d., 2d., 3d., 4d., 5d., 6d., 7d., 8d., 9d., 10d., 1s., 1s.3d. and 1s.6d. plus coils and booklets). As the bands overlap the stamps it is easier to distinguish these by measuring the space between the bands, this being approximately 12 mm. for the 8 mm. bands and 10·5 mm. for the 9·5 mm. bands. There is the further complication of identifying the 3d. value which has only one band but in the 8 mm. band series this is at the left or right of the stamp whilst in the 9·5 mm. band series it is in the centre.

Typographed 6 mm. and 8 mm. Phosphor Bands in Sheets. For values with the phosphor applied by typography the bands along the left and right margins were only 6 mm. wide, instead of the normal 8 mm. Where these varieties exist they have been listed, the prices being for stamps with the vertical margin attached. Some booklet panes of four from the watermark Crowns issue had the phosphor bands applied by typography. Examples with 6 mm. side bands, similar to those on sheets, have been identified on panes also showing shifted phosphor bands.

Phosphor Printed on Both Sides. Instances have been reported of stamps with phosphor bands on both the front and the back. These can be caused by offsets from normal phosphor bands, but where there is a sharp phosphor impression, these are listed. Offsets, which appear indistinct and weak, are outside the scope of this Catalogue.

Application of Phosphor Bands. The choice of method for applying the phosphor bands is a matter for the printer and three different methods have been used: photogravure, typography and flexography.
To apply bands in photogravure sometimes an additional printing cylinder is brought into use so that it is done in the same operation as printing the stamps. In the case of multicoloured special issues there may not be a spare cylinder available as this would depend upon the colour capacity of the press and the number of colours to be used. The bands may then be applied by typography or photogravure as a separate operation on a sheet-fed press.
Typography was used to apply the bands to cut sheets on the phosphor-graphite issue; and for various later "emergency" printings.
Flexography is a typographic process but using a rubber cylinder (which does not indent the paper) to pick up the impression from a photo-etched inking cylinder. The screen pattern is usually blurred, although some traces of it remain. This method is usually employed for applying bands to stamps already printed "on the web" before being cut into sheets.
Photogravure bands do not indent the paper, are screened (either 150 or 250 lines to the inch, but occasionally occur mixed), extend through the top and bottom sheet margins and cause a glazed appearance on unsurfaced paper, due to the pressure of the cylinder. Bands applied by typography generally indent the paper, as can be seen from the back, are solid and stop short of the edges of the sheet.
It is rather difficult to distinguish with certainty flexography phosphor bands from those printed by photogravure, and for this reason they are not listed separately. Flexography is known to have been used to apply phosphor bands to special issues, and was also used for some printings of the 9·5 mm. violet phosphor series; it may also have been used on earlier definitive issues.

Phosphor Reaction. The "green" phosphor was overprinted by typography on the graphite stamps but in photogravure only on the first phosphor only issue. The "blue" phosphor was normally applied in photogravure but some values also exist with typographic overprint. The "violet" 8 mm. bands are normally applied in photogravure but again some values exist with them typographed, but the 9·5 mm. series exist with them only in photogravure or flexography.

Misplaced Bands on Sheets, Coils and Booklet Panes. Phosphor bands frequently appear misplaced but such varieties are outside the scope of this Catalogue except where the misplacement affects the number of bands, i.e. one band instead of two or two narrow bands over the vertical perforations, instead of one centre or side band.

CYLINDER VARIETIES.   Most of the more prominent varieties are listed and illustrated but we have restricted ourselves to those we have actually seen. Others will be added to future editions as specimens become available for illustration.

The position is always indicated by stating first the cylinder number (and where no full stop is shown this means the "no dot" cylinder, whereas a full stop means the "dot" cylinder) followed by the position indicated first by the horizontal row and then the position in it. Thus "Cyl. 15, R. 10/3" means cylinder 15 no dot, the third stamp in the tenth row down. Where the same cylinder is used on stamps with different watermark, paper or type of phosphor, etc. the varieties on that cylinder will recur, unless corrected by retouching, and these are then listed again with footnotes referring back to its first appearance where it is illustrated.

Unless otherwise stated the prices are for single stamps and extra copies needed to make positional blocks will be charged as normals.

TÊTE-BÊCHE ERRORS.   These derive from booklets due to faulty making-up; this is described in the introductory notes to Appendix HA.

MINOR CONSTANT FLAWS.   These are so numerous that they are merely recorded without illustrations. Their location on the stamp is indicated, where helpful, by reference to the S.G. "Thirkell" Position Finder, an essential tool for identifying flaws. The recording of these flaws, often insignificant in themselves, will prove an aid in identifying a particular cylinder and will also serve to show that the flaw has been considered for listing as a variety but rejected as being too minor. Again we have only recorded what we have actually seen but the picture is necessarily incomplete as we have not been able to view full sheets from every cylinder.

COILS.   Coils are generally printed from double cylinders. In identifying their position the roll number is quoted (this is the number printed on the outer wrapper of the coil which corresponds to the row in the sheet before reeling) but where double cylinders are used only half the coils bearing the roll numbers will contain the variety. Hence there are twelve rolls (vertical delivery) and ten rolls (sideways delivery) from every sheet and varieties will be repeated on every 21st stamp on vertical rolls and on every 25th stamp on sideways delivery rolls.

SHADES.   Intended changes of colour such as the 2d. red-brown and light red-brown, the 6d. reddish purple and deep claret and the 4d. ultramarine and deep ultramarine are given full numbers and some of the more marked shades which were not made by design are shown as alternatives. In some cases, however, there is a whole range of shades which it would be meaningless to attempt to list.

The colour descriptions given are based on the Stanley Gibbons Colour Key.

DATES OF ISSUE.   The dates given in bold type in the headings are those on which stamps in normal Post Office *sheets* were first issued, notwithstanding the fact that they may have appeared earlier in booklet form. A dagger is added to the sheet date where stamps were issued at an *earlier* date in booklets or coils. Stamps with inverted or sideways watermarks which appeared either earlier or later than those from ordinary sheets have the dates given after the listing of each item, and for stamps from booklets we have taken the earliest possible dated booklet, i.e. taking into account booklets containing panes with mixed watermarks.

Where there is a change of watermark or type of phosphor or to the whiter paper, the dates given are generally those on which they were first issued by the Supplies Department to Postmasters.

WITHDRAWAL DATE.   All the low value Wilding stamps not previously sold out were withdrawn from issue at the Philatelic Bureaux on 27 February 1970, and were invalidated as from 1 March 1972.

POST OFFICE TRAINING SCHOOL STAMPS.   Examples of most low value stamps exist overprinted with two thick vertical bars. Some values on Tudor Crown watermark paper are also known overprinted "SCHOOL SPECIMEN". Stamps cancelled with either of these overprints were for use in Post Office Training Schools, and their issue to the public was unauthorised, although most values appear to be quite common.

SHEET MARKINGS.   Compared with the King George VI period a wide variety of markings of various kinds have been introduced in Elizabethan issues to facilitate new elements such as registration of multicoloured stamps, ensuring that the cylinders are applied in the correct sequence, aids to registration of perforation, colour dots to ease checking for omission of colours and so on. We give below notes and illustrations of the markings which were used in the Wilding issues and those which apply to other issues are described in the General Notes relating to the other Sections. They are particularly helpful in establishing the position of varieties in the case of marginal blocks and can also help in identifying the type of perforator used or the type of machine employed for printing, etc.

Cylinder Number

Cylinder Number. This always occurs in the left-hand margin opposite Row 18 No. 1. In double pane cylinders the no dot pane is on the left and the dot pane on the right. Booklet cylinder numbers are described in Appendix HA.

Varieties in Cylinder Blocks. Where a cylinder block contains a listed variety the price is adjusted accordingly and bears an asterisk.

"V" shaped
Hand engraved

"W" shaped Photo etched

Marginal Arrows. These occur against the middle rows of the sheet as an aid to Post Office Clerks when breaking up the sheets. They may be hand engraved or photo-etched. The earlier cylinders were "V" shaped (hand engraved) at the top and bottom of the sheet and "W" shaped (photo-etched) at both sides. Later cylinders were often "W" shaped (photo-etched) at top, bottom and sides but a number of combinations exist. In some cases they are accidentally missing from the cylinder and where these are known this is stated under the cylinder number listing. The $2\frac{1}{2}$d. on Crowns watermarked paper, cylinder 55, exists with "V" shaped arrow in the correct position below rows 6/7 and a faint outline to the right, below rows 8/9, where the mark had been placed in error.

Narrow Rule   Wide Rule   Damaged Rule

Marginal Rules. These are the solid bands of colour which appear below the bottom row of the sheet and which used to be called "Jubilee Lines" because they were first introduced in the so-called "Jubilee" issue of 1887. These are invariably co-extensive (with breaks between each stamp) and come in various widths.

5

Unboxed   Boxed   In Double Box   Black Bar

Perforation Guide Holes on Sheets. These large circular punched holes occur on reel-fed printings usually boxed opposite rows 14/15 at left (no dot) or right (dot) or unboxed opposite rows 1 and 7/8 at both sides. They are an indication of the type of perforator used and further reference to these is made in Appendix G. They also occur in double boxes, those illustrated being representative. They are liable to be trimmed off almost completely.

See also General Notes for Section W.

Black Bar. This was used alongside the marginal arrows at left on no dot sheets and at right on dot sheets on green and early blue phosphor printings. It was intended for easy recognition of phosphor stocks in the Post Office Supplies Department.

Sheet Numbers. Most sheets are serially numbered in black after printing for checking purposes but the numbers are liable to be placed anywhere in the margins and so are of no use for identifying a position. They are not of much help in establishing whether a sheet occurred early or late in a printing either, as a particular printing was not necessarily numbered from 1 and several machines may have been used.

Checkers Marks. These are small encircled numbers applied with a rubber stamp in a variety of colours. They are applied by Post Office checkers when counting the sheets delivered by the printer. As with sheet numbers they are liable to be placed anywhere in the sheet margins.

Table of Wilding Issues

	½d.	1d.	1½d.	2d.	2d.	2d.	2½d.	2½d.	2½d.	2½d.	3d.	4d.	4d.	4½d.	5d.	6d.	6d.	7d.	8d.	9d.	10d.	11d.	1s.	1s.3d.	1s.6d.
				Red-brown	Light red-brown	2 bands	Type I	Type II	Type II 1 band	Type I 1 band		Ultramarine	Deep ultramarine			Reddish purple	Deep claret								
Tudor Crown	S1	S13	S25	S36			S50	S51			S67	S81			S99	S104		S114	S119	S124	S129	S134	S136	S141	S150
St. Edward's Crown	S2	S14	S26	S37			S52	S53			S68	S82			S100	S105	S106	S115	S120	S125	S130	S135	S137	S142	S151
Graphite. St. Edward's Crown	S3	S15	S27		S38			S54			S69														
Crown	S4	S16	S28		S39						S70	S83		S93	S101		S107	S116	S121	S126	S131		S138	S143	S152
Crowns. Cream Paper	S5	S17	S29		S40		S56	S55			S71	S84	S85	S94	S102		S108	S117	S122	S127	S132		S139	S144	S153
Crowns. Whiter Paper					S41		S56c	S57																	
Crowns. Chalky Paper	S6	S18	S30					S58			S72	S86		S95											
Graphite. Crowns	S7	S19	S31		S42			S59			S73	S87		S96											
Phosphor-graphite	S8	S20	S32		S43			S60			S74	S88												S145	
Green Phosphor	S9	S21	S33		S44			S61	S63		S75	S89		S97			S109							S146	
Blue Phosphor. Cream Paper					S45	S46		S62		S64							S110								
Blue Phosphor. Whiter Paper	S10	S22	S34			S47		S66	S65		S76		S90	S98			S111							S147	
Violet Phosphor. 8 mm.	S11	S23				S48					S80		S91		S103		S112	S118	S123	S128	S133		S140	S148	S154
Violet Phosphor. 9.5 mm.	S12	S24				S49							S92				S113							S149	
1 Side Band. Blue Phosphor											S77														
1 Side Band. Violet Phosphor											S78														
1 Centre Band. Violet Phosphor											S79														

Presentation Packs .. .. At end of Section SA

Face Value	Watermark	Further description	Delivery		Stamp No.
½d.	Tudor Crown	....	V	S	S1
½d.	St. Edward's Crown	....	V	S	S2
½d.	St. Edward's Crown	Graphite lines	V		S3
½d.	Crowns	Cream or whiter paper	V	S	S6
½d.	Crowns	Graphite lines	V		S7
½d.	Crowns	Green phosphor		V	S9
½d.	Crowns	Blue phosphor, cream or whiter paper ...	V		S11
½d.	Crowns	Violet phosphor, 8 mm.	V		S12
1d.	Tudor Crown	....	V	S	S13
1d.	St. Edward's Crown	....	V	S	S14
1d.	St. Edward's Crown	Graphite lines	V		S15
1d.	Crowns	Cream or whiter paper	V	S	S17
1d.	Crowns	Graphite lines	V		S18
1d.	Crowns	Green phosphor		V	S20
1d.	Crowns	Blue phosphor, cream or whiter paper	V		S22
1d.	Crowns	Violet phosphor, 8 mm.	V		S23
1d.	Crowns	Violet phosphor, 9·5 mm.	V		S24
1½d.	Tudor Crown	....	V		S25
1½d.	Tudor Crown, sideways	....		S	S25
1½d.	St. Edward's Crown	....	V		S26
1½d.	St. Edward's Crown, sideways	....		S	S26
1½d.	St. Edward's Crown	Graphite lines	V		S27
1½d.	Crowns	Cream paper	V		S29
1½d.	Crowns	Whiter paper		S	S29
2d.	Tudor Crown	Red-brown	V		S36
2d.	Tudor Crown, sideways	Red-brown		S	S36
2d.	St. Edward's Crown	Red-brown	V		S38
2d.	St. Edward's Crown, sideways	Red-brown		S	S38
2d.	St. Edward's Crown	Light red-brown	V		S38
2d.	St. Edward's Crown, sideways	Light red-brown		S	S38
2d.	St. Edward's Crown	Graphite lines	V		S39
2d.	Crowns	Cream or whiter paper	V		S41
2d.	Crowns, sideways	Cream or whiter paper		S	S41
2d.	Crowns	Graphite lines	V		S42
2d.	Crowns	Green phosphor	V		S44
2d.	Crowns	Blue phosphor, 1 left band	V		S45
2d.	Crowns	Blue phosphor, cream or whiter paper, 2 bands .	V		S47
2d.	Crowns	Violet phosphor, 8 mm.	V		S48
2d.	Crowns	Violet phosphor, 9·5 mm.	V		S49
2d.	Crowns, sideways	Violet phosphor, 9·5 mm.		S	S49
2½d.	Tudor Crown	Type I	V		S50
2½d.	Tudor Crown, sideways	Type I		S	S50
2½d.	St. Edward's Crown	Type I	V		S52
2½d.	St. Edward's Crown, sideways	Type I		S	S52
2½d.	St. Edward's Crown	Type II, Graphite lines		S	S54
2½d.	Crowns	Type I. Cream or whiter paper	V		S56
2½d.	Crowns, sideways	Type I. Cream or whiter paper		S	S56
2½d.	Crowns, sideways	Type II. Whiter paper		S	S57
3d.	Tudor Crown	....	V	S	S67
3d.	St. Edward's Crown	....	V	S	S68
3d.	St. Edward's Crown, sideways	....		S	S68
3d.	St. Edward's Crown	Graphite lines		S	S69
3d.	Crowns	Cream or whiter paper	V		S71
3d.	Crowns, sideways	Cream or whiter paper		S	S71
3d.	Crowns	Graphite lines	V	S	S72
3d.	Crowns	Blue phosphor, cream or whiter paper, 2 bands .	V		S77
3d.	Crowns	Blue phosphor, whiter paper, 1 side band	V		S77
3d.	Crowns	Violet phosphor, 1 side band	V		S80
3d.	Crowns	Violet phosphor, 1 centre band	V		S80
3d.	Crowns, sideways	Violet phosphor, 1 centre band		S	S80
4d.	Tudor Crown	Ultramarine		S	S81
4d.	St. Edward's Crown	Ultramarine	V	S	S82
4d.	Crowns	Ultramarine, cream or whiter paper	V	S	S85
4d.	Crowns	Deep ultramarine, whiter paper	V		S85
4d.	Crowns, sideways	Deep ultramarine, whiter paper		S	S85
4d.	Crowns, sideways	Violet phosphor, 9·5 mm.		S	S92
6d.	Tudor Crown	....	V		S104
6d.	St. Edward's Crown	Reddish purple	V		S106
6d.	St. Edward's Crown	Deep claret	V		S106
6d.	Crowns	Cream or whiter paper	V		S108
6d.	Crowns	Violet phosphor, 9·5 mm.	V		S113

PRINTERS. All the Wilding issues were printed in photogravure by Harrison & Sons. They were printed on continuous reels of paper "on the web" generally in double pane width, i.e. 480 stamps consisting of two panes (no dot and dot) each of 240 stamps arranged in twenty rows of twelve stamps, the panes being guillotined before issue. However, some printings were made from single cylinders printing sheets of 240 stamps (i.e. no dot panes only). Exceptionally, the 1963 2s. Holiday Booklet (No. NR1) stamps were printed on a sheet-fed machine.

PAPER AND WATERMARK

All the following issues are printed on unsurfaced paper, except the ½d. and 2½d. values (Nos. S6 and S58) printed on chalk-surfaced paper.

The illustrations of the watermarks are as seen from the *front* of the stamp. The "Tudor Crown" was in use from 1952 to 1954, the "St. Edward's Crown" from 1955 to 1958 and the Multiple Crowns from 1958 onwards. No Wilding issues appeared on paper without watermark.

GUM. Only gum arabic has been used for the Wilding issues as PVA gum was not introduced until the Machin series.

PERFORATION. All stamps are comb perforated 15 × 14 as the King George VI issues. However, the horizontal perforation is very close to the three-quarters mark and so is sometimes described as 14½ × 14.

Perforation varieties such as double or misplaced perforations are not listed in this Catalogue.

Tudor Crown
W.22

St. Edward's Crown
W.23

Crowns
W.24

S1

S2

S3

S4

S5

S6

S7

Portraits of Queen Elizabeth II and National Emblems

(Des. Miss Enid Marx (S1), Michael C. Farrar Bell (S2/3), George T. Knipe (S4), Miss Mary Adshead (S5), Edmund Dulac (S6/7))

(Portrait by Dorothy Wilding Ltd.)

1953–65 ½d. Orange-red, Type S1

1953 (AUGUST 31). ½d. WATERMARK TUDOR CROWN, TYPE W.22

			Mint	Used
S1 (=S.G.515)	½d.	Orange-red	10	15
	a.	Watermark inverted (3.54)	60	60
	b.	Coil join (horiz. pair)	4·00	
	c.	"A" flaw (Vert. coil, Roll 3)	5·50	
	d.	Spot on "d" (Vert. coil, Roll 5)	5·00	
	f.	Rose flaw (Cyls 1 & 3 Dot, R. 19/12)	4·25	

S1c, S2g, S4k   S1d, S2h, S4l   S1f, S2f
Retouched on Crowns
watermark

Cylinder Numbers (Blocks of Six)

Perforation Type B (I/P no dot) and C (E/P dot)			Perforation Type A (E/I)		
Cyl. No.	No dot	Dot	Cyl. No.	No dot	Dot
1	6·50	6·50	1	3·00	3·00
			3	3·50	3·50

Minor Constant Sheet Flaws

Cyl. 1   4/4 White smudge at left of upper left rose (Th. B1)
         5/6 White spot at end of stem of upper right shamrock (Th. C6)
       13/1 Large concealed retouch on Queen's cheek (Th. D3–4)
Cyl. 1.   1/7 Background retouch below upper left rose (Th. B1)
      1/10 Orange spot at top right of centre cross in crown (Th. A–B3–4)
      15/4 Retouched background between OS of POSTAGE
      18/8 Coloured dot in P of POSTAGE
Cyl. 3   4/4 As cyl. 1
         5/6 As cyl. 1
Cyl. 3.   18/8 As cyl. 1.

Coils

All coils have the watermark upright and Cylinder A1 or A2 was used. Vertical delivery printed in continuous reels

Code No.	Number in roll	Face value
AA	240	10/-
G	480	£1
W	960	£2
D	960	£2
Y	1920	£4

Sideways delivery made up from sheets with sheet margin joins

P	480	£1

Imprimaturs from the National Postal Museum Archives

Imperforate, watermark Type W.22

Watermark upright
Watermark inverted
Tête-bêche pair

1955 (DECEMBER 12).†   ½d. WATERMARK ST. EDWARD'S CROWN, TYPE W.23

			Mint	Used
S2 (=S.G.540)	½d.	Orange-red	15	15
	b.	Watermark inverted (9.55)	20	30
	c.	Coil join (horiz. pr.)	3·50	
	d.	Flaw on shamrock stem (Cyl. 2 Dot, R. 18/8)	5·50	
	e.	Major retouch (Cyl. 2 Dot, R. 19/2)	8·00	
	f.	Rose flaw (Cyl. 2 Dot, R. 19/12)	5·50	
	g.	"A" flaw (Vert. coil, Roll 3)	5·50	
	h.	Spot on "d" (Vert. coil, Roll 5)	5·00	
	i.	Shamrock flaw (Vert. coil, Roll 11)	5·75	
	j.	"R" flaw (Vert. coil, Roll 11)	6·00	

For illustrations of Nos. S2*f*/*h*, see Nos. S1*c*/*d* and S1*f*.

S2*d*, S4*g*

S2*e*, S4*h*

Shows as retouched area
to design edge

S2*i*, S4*m*, S5*g*, S9*b*,
S10*g*, S11*f*

S2*j*, S4*n*, S5*i*, S9*c*, S10*h*, S11*g*

Cylinder Numbers (Blocks of Six)

Perforation Type B (I/P no dot) and C (E/P dot)			Perforation Type A (E/I)		
Cyl. No.	No dot	Dot	Cyl. No.	No dot	Dot
1	3·25	3·25	2	3·25	10·00*
			3	4·00	4·00

Minor Constant Sheet Flaws

Cyl. 1 no dot and dot. As for No. S1, cyl. 1.
Cyls. 2 and 3 no dot and dot. As for No. S1, cyl. 3 except that flaw on 4/4 is retouched on cyl. 3 no dot.
Cyl. 2.   20/2 Retouch by lower right thistle and rose (Th. F5–6).

Coils

All coils have the watermark upright and it is believed that the cylinder numbers used were A3 in double panes as well as cylinder A1 or A2.

Vertical delivery printed in continuous reels

Code No.	Number in roll	Face value
AA	240	10/-
G	480	£1
W	960	£2
D	960	£2
Y	1920	£4

Sideways delivery made up from sheets with sheet margin joins

P	480	£1

Imprimaturs from the National Postal Museum Archives

Imperforate, watermark Type W.23

Watermark upright
Watermark inverted
Tête-bêche pair

GRAPHITE-LINED ISSUES

The graphite lines were printed in black on the back, beneath the gum. Two lines per stamp, except for the 2d. value which have one line.

S8

1957 (NOVEMBER 19). ½d. WITH GRAPHITE LINES, TYPE S8. WMK. ST. EDWARD'S CROWN

			Mint	Used
S3 (=S.G.561)	½d.	Orange-red	25	25
	a.	"E" flaw (Cyl. 5 No dot, R. 17/9)	4·50	
	b.	Extra stem to thistle (Cyl. 5 No dot, R. 18/10)	4·50	

S3*a*, S8*b*

S3*b*, S8*c*

Cylinder Numbers (Blocks of Six)

	Single pane cylinders				Single pane cylinders	
Cyl. No.	Perforation Type	No dot		Cyl. No.	Perforation Type	No dot
4	B (I/P)	4·50		5	B (I/P)	5·50
4	C (E/P)	4·50		5	C (E/P)	5·50

Minor Constant Sheet Flaw

Cyl. 4   12/8 Orange spot in top thistle (Th. A4)

Coils

All have watermark upright, sheet cylinder 4 having been converted to a 21-row cylinder Vertical delivery printed in continuous reels

Code No.	Number in roll	Face value
G	480	£1
W	960	£2
Y	1920	£4

Imprimatur from the National Postal Museum Archives

Imperforate, watermark Type W.23

Watermark upright

Quantity Issued   22,508,400

1958 (NOVEMBER 25). ½d. WATERMARK CROWNS, TYPE W.24

A. Cream Paper   Mint   Used
S4		½d.	Orange-red	15	10
	c.		Watermark inverted (11·58)	40	40
	d.		Watermark Crown to left (26.5.61)	2·00	1·00
	e.		Watermark Crown to right	2·00	1·00
	f.		Coil join (horiz. pair)	3·50	
	g.		Flaw on shamrock stem (Cyl. 2 Dot, R. 18/8)	4·25	
	h.		Major retouch (Cyl. 2 Dot, R. 19/2)	8·00	
	k.		"A" flaw (Vert. coil, Roll 3)	5·00	
	l.		Spot on "d" (Vert. coil, Roll 5)	5·00	
	m.		Shamrock flaw (Vert. coil, Roll 11)	4·00	
	n.		"R" flaw (Vert. coil, Roll 11)	4·00	

B. Whiter Paper (27 July 1962)†
S5 (=S.G.570)		½d.	Orange-red	10	10
	a.		Watermark Crown to left (5.6.62)	30	40
	b.		Watermark Crown to right	30	40
	c.		Watermark inverted (29.7.62)	75	60
	f.		Large dot by daffodil (Vert. coil, Roll 4)	5·50	
	g.		Shamrock flaw (Vert. coil, Roll 11)	5·50	
	h.		"d" joined to shamrock (Vert. coil, Roll 11)	6·00	
	i.		"R" flaw (Vert. coil, Roll 11)	5·50	

Tête-bêche. No. S5 exists *tête-bêche* from booklet sheets which were not issued. (*Price* £1750 *pair.*)

C. Chalky Paper. Booklets only (15 July 1963)
S6 (=S.G.570k)		½d.	Orange-red	2·50	2·75
	a.		Watermark inverted	2·75	3·00

†The earliest issue was in vertical coils on 30 April 1962.

For illustrations of No. S4g, see No. S2d; for No. S4h, see No. S2e; for No. S4k, see No. S1c; for No. S4l, see No. S1d; for Nos. S4m/n and S5g, S5i, see Nos. S2i/j.

S5f, S12e

S5h, S12f

Cylinder Numbers (Blocks of Six)

A. Cream Paper. (No. S4)

Perforation Type B (I/P no dot) and C
(E/P dot)   Perforation Type A (E/I)

Cyl. No.	No dot	Dot	Cyl. No.	No dot	Dot
1	3·50	3·50	2	5·00	10·00*
3	3·50	3·50	3	5·00	5·00

B. Whiter Paper. (No. S5).

Perforation Type A (E/I)

Cyl. No.	No dot	Dot
1	2·75	2·75
3	2·75	2·75

Minor Constant Sheet Flaws

Cyl. 1   4/4 White smudge at left of upper left rose (Th. B1)
          5/6 White spot at end of stem of upper right shamrock (Th. C6), rather faint on this cylinder
          13/1 Large concealed retouch on Queen's cheek (Th. D3–4)
Cyl. 1.   1/10 Orange spot at top right of centre cross in crown (Th. A–B3–4)
Cyl. 2.   18/8 Coloured dot in P of POSTAGE (later retouched)
          20/2 Retouch by lower right thistle and rose (Th. F5–6)
Cyl. 3   5/6 White spot at end of stem of upper right shamrock (Th. C6)
Cyl. 3.   18/8 Coloured dot in P of POSTAGE

Coils

All have watermark upright and cylinder numbers A1, A2 and A3 were used for cream paper printings and numbers A3 and A4 for whiter paper issues.

Vertical delivery printed in continuous reels. Cream or whiter paper.

Code No.	Number in roll	Face value
AA	240	10/-
G	480	£1
W	960	£2
D	960	£2
Y	1920	£4

Sideways delivery made up from sheets with sheet margin joins. Cream paper

P	480	£1

Imprimaturs from the National Postal Museum Archives

Imperforate, watermark Type W.24. Cream or whiter paper

Watermark upright
Watermark inverted
Tête-bêche pair

1959 (JUNE 15). ½d. WITH GRAPHITE LINES, TYPE S8. WATERMARK CROWNS

			Mint	Used
S7 (=S.G.587)	½d.	Orange-red	9·00	9·00
	a.	Watermark inverted (4.8.59)	3·25	4·00

No. S7/*a* was only issued in booklets and coils. For panes, see Section SB, Nos. SB14/a.

Coils

All have watermark upright, sheet cylinder 4 having been converted to a 21-row cylinder.

Code No.	Number in roll	Face value
W	960	£2
Y	1920	£4

Imprimaturs from the National Postal Museum Archives

Imperforate, watermark Type W.24

Watermark upright
Watermark inverted
Tête-bêche pair

Quantity Issued   4,161,840

1959 (NOVEMBER 18). ½d. PHOSPHOR-GRAPHITE ISSUE. WMK. ST. EDWARD'S CROWN

			Mint	Used
S8 (=S.G.599)	½d.	Orange-red	4·00	3·75
	a.	Narrow band at left or right (stamp with vert. margin)	7·50	
	b.	"E" flaw (R. 17/9)	10·00	
	c.	Extra stem to thistle (R. 18/10)	10·00	

This has two graphite lines, Type S8, on the back and two phosphor bands, applied by typography, on the front, which react green under the lamp.

The listed flaws are as illustrated for Nos. S3*a/b*.

Cylinder Numbers (Blocks of Six)

	Single pane cylinder	
Cyl. No.	Perf. Type	No dot
5	B (I/P)	27·00
5	C (E/P)	27·00

Imprimatur from the National Postal Museum Archives

Perf. 15 × 14, watermark Type W.24

Watermark upright

Quantity Issued   707,040

1960 (JUNE 22). ½d. TWO PHOSPHOR BANDS REACTING GREEN. WMK. CROWNS

			Mint	Used
S9	½d.	Orange-red	1·75	1·50
	a.	Watermark inverted (14.8.60)	6·00	6·00
	b.	Shamrock flaw (Coil, Roll 11)	6·00	
	c.	"R" flaw (Coil, Roll 11)	6·00	
	d.	Coil join (vert. pair)	9·00	
	e.	One 8 mm. phosphor band	£140	

The bands were applied in photogravure.
For illustrations of Nos. S9*b/c* see Nos. S2*i/j*.

Cylinder Numbers (Blocks of Six)

Perforation Type B (I/P no dot) and C (E/P dot)		
Cyl. No.	No dot	Dot
1	14·00	14·00

Minor Constant Sheet Flaws

Cyl. 1	4/4	White smudge at left of upper left rose (Th. B1)
	5/6	White spot at end of stem of upper right shamrock (Th. C6), rather faint on this cylinder
	13/1	Large concealed retouch on Queen's cheek (Th. D3–4)
Cyl. 1.	1/10	Orange spot at top right of centre cross in crown (Th. A–B3–4), later retouched
	19/12	White bulge on upper right sepal of lower right rose (Th. E5–6)

Coils

All have watermark upright and cylinder number A3 was used in double panes. Vertical delivery printed in continuous reels

Code No.	Number in roll	Face value
G	480	10/-
W	960	£2
Y	1920	£4

Vertical delivery. Made up from sheets with sheet margin joins.

Y	1920	£4

Imprimatur from the National Postal Museum Archives

Imperforate, watermark Type W.24

Watermark upright

1961 (JUNE 5).†   ½d. TWO PHOSPHOR BANDS REACTING BLUE. WMK. CROWNS

A. Cream Paper

			Mint	Used
S10	½d.	Orange-red	25	20
	a.	Watermark inverted (3.61)	90	90
	b.	Watermark Crown to left (14.7.61)	10·00	10·00
	c.	Watermark Crown to right	10·00	10·00
	d.	One band (wmk. sideways)	20·00	
	da.	One band (wmk. upright or inverted)	70·00	
	g.	Shamrock flaw (Coil, Roll 11)	3·25	
	h.	"R" flaw (Coil, Roll 11)	3·50	

B. Whiter Paper (21 June 1965)†

S11 (=S.G.610)	½d.	Orange-red	10	15
	a.	Watermark Crown to left (15.8.62)	12·00	12·00
	b.	Watermark Crown to right	12·00	12·00
	c.	Watermark inverted (3.6.63)	1·50	1·50
	f.	Shamrock flaw (Coil, Roll 11)	3·00	
	g.	"R" flaw (Coil, Roll 11)	4·00	

The bands were applied in photogravure on the stamps with upright watermark and by typography on those with watermark sideways.

For illustrations of Nos. S10g and S11f see No. S2i and for S10h and S11g see No. S2j.

Cylinder Numbers (Blocks of Six)

Perforation Type A (E/I)

Cream paper. (No. S10)				Whiter paper. (No. S11)		
Cyl. No.	No dot	Dot		Cyl. No.	No dot	Dot
1	3·50	3·50		1	2·75	2·75

Minor Constant Sheet Flaws

As for No. S9

Coils

All have watermark upright and cylinder number A3 was used in double panes. Vertical delivery printed in continuous reels. Cream or whiter paper.

Code No.	Number in roll	Face value
G	480	10/-
W	960	£2 (cream paper only)
Y	1920	£4

Imprimaturs from the National Postal Museum Archives

Imperforate, watermark Type W.24. Cream or whiter paper

Watermark upright
Watermark inverted
Tête-bêche pair

1965 (AUGUST 13). ½d. TWO 8 mm. PHOSPHOR BANDS REACTING VIOLET. WMK. CROWNS

			Mint	Used
S12	½d.	Orange-red	55	45
	a.	One 6 mm. band at left or right (stamp with vert. margin)	3·50	
	b.	Typo. bands omitted*	25·00	
	c.	One 8 mm. band (typo.)	4·50	
	ca.	As c. but 6 mm. band	3·00	
	d.	Bands applied photo. (15.10.65)	1·25	50
	e.	Large dot by daffodil (Coil, Roll 4)	4·50	
	f.	"d" joined to shamrock (Coil, Roll 11)	4·50	

The bands were applied by typography on the sheets and in photogravure on the coils.

*No S12b can be distinguished from a non-phosphor stamp by the fact that this shows a clear impression of the typo. plate with no reaction under the lamp.

For illustrations of Nos. S12e/f, see Nos. S5f/h.

Cylinder Numbers (Blocks of Six)

Perforation Type A (E/I)

Cyl. No.	No dot	Dot
1	7·00	16·00

Minor Constant Sheet Flaws

As for No. S9

Coils

All have the watermark upright and it is believed a new double pane cylinder number A4 was used.

Vertical delivery printed in continuous reels

Code No.	Number in roll	Face value
G	480	10/–
W	960	£2
Y	1920	£4

1953–67 1d. Ultramarine, Type S1

1953 (AUGUST 31). 1d. WATERMARK TUDOR CROWN, TYPE W.22

			Mint	Used
S13 (=S.G.516)	1d.	Ultramarine	20	20
	a.	Watermark inverted (3.54)	4·50	2·75
	b.	Coil join (horiz. pair)	10·00	
	c.	Shamrock flaw (Cyl. 2 No dot, R. 18/2)	15·00	

S13*c*, S14*d*, also
SB22*a*, SB28*a*, see Section SB

White flaw on top shamrock,
later retouched on St.
Edward's Crown watermark

Cylinder Numbers (Blocks of Six)

Perforation Type B (I/P no dot) and
        C (E/P dot)

				Perforation Type A (E/I)		
Cyl. No.		No dot	Dot	Cyl. No.	No dot	Dot
1		3·50	3·50	2	20·00*	5·00

Minor Constant Sheet Flaws

Cyl. 2.   19/8 White flaw between thistle stem and lower right rose (Th. E6)

Coils

Single pane cylinders B1 or B2 were used for the Tudor Crown watermark. The watermark is always upright.
    Vertical delivery printed in continuous reels

	Code No.	Number in roll	Face value
	AB	240	£1
	E	480	£2
	X	960	£4
	Z	1920	£8

Sideways delivery made up from sheets with sheet margin joins

	O	480	£2

Imprimaturs from the National Postal Museum Archives

Imperforate, watermark Type W.22

Watermark upright
Watermark inverted
Tête-bêche pair

1955 (SEPTEMBER 19).† 1d. WATERMARK ST. EDWARD'S CROWN, TYPE W.23

			Mint	Used
S14 (=S.G.541)	1d.	Ultramarine	30	15
	a.	Tête-bêche (horiz. pair)	£5500	
	b.	Watermark inverted (8.55)	65	60
	c.	Coil join (horiz. pair)	10·00	
	d.	Shamrock flaw (Cyl. 2 No dot, R. 18/2)	12·00	

†The earliest issue was from E coils in August 1955.
For illustration of No. S14*d* see No. S13*c*.

Cylinder Numbers (Blocks of Six)

Perforation Type A (E/I)

Cyl. No.		No dot	Dot
1	. . . .	3·50	3·50
2	. . . .	15·00*	3·50
4	. . . .	3·50	3·50

Perforation Type B (I/P no dot) and C (E/P dot)

Cyl. No.		No dot	Dot
4	. . . .	6·00	6·00

Minor Constant Sheet Flaws

Cyl. 2   19/8 White flaw between thistle stem and lower right rose (Th. E6)
Cyl. 4   11/9 Blue spot in E of POSTAGE
           19/8 As cyl. 2
Cyl. 4.   14/11 White spur to bottom leaf of shamrock above diadem (Th. A3)

Coils

Single pane cylinders B1 or B2 were again used for the St. Edward's Crown watermark. The watermark is always upright.
    Vertical delivery printed in continuous reels

Code No.	Number in roll	Face value
AB	240	£1
E	480	£2
B	960	£4
X	960	£4
Z	1920	£8

Sideways delivery made up from sheets with sheet margin joins

O	480	£2

Imprimaturs from the National Postal Museum Archives

Imperforate, watermark Type W.23

Watermark upright
Watermark inverted
Tête-bêche pair

1957 (NOVEMBER 19). 1d. WITH GRAPHITE LINES, TYPE S8. WMK. ST. EDWARD'S CROWN

				Mint	Used
S15 (=S.G.562)	1d.	Ultramarine		40	40
	a.	Flaw on thistle head (Cyls. 7 and 8 No dot, R. 6/1 and Coil, Roll 1)		5·50	
	b.	Daffodil stem flaw (Cyls. 7 & 8 No dot, R. 15/2 and Coil, Roll 2)		6·00	
	c.	Extra stop (Coil, Roll 2)		15·00	
	d.	Stop omitted (Coil, Roll 3)		15·00	
	e.	White flaw on shamrock leaf (Coil, Roll 8)		7·50	

Flaw on top thistle occurs on sheets (Nos. S15*a* and S19*b*) or coils (Nos. S16*n*, S18*i*, S20*g* and S21*g*)

S15*a*, S16*n*, S18*i*, S19*b*, S20*g*, S21*g*

S15b, S19c	S15c	S15d	S15e
	Later retouched	White stop omitted	

Cylinder Numbers (Blocks of Six)

Single pane cylinders

Cyl. No.	Perf. Type		No dot
7	B (I/P)	....	5·00
7	C (E/P)	....	5·00
8	B (I/P)	....	10·00
8	C (E/P)	....	10·00

Coils

Single pane cylinder B4 was used and all have the watermark upright. Vertical delivery printed in continuous reels

Code No.	Number in roll	Face value
E	480	£2
X	960	£4
Z	1920	£8

Imprimatur from the National Postal Museum Archives

Imperforate, watermark Type W.23

Watermark upright

Quantity Issued   29,620,080

1959 (MARCH 24).†   1d. WATERMARK CROWNS, TYPE W.24

A. Cream Paper   Mint   Used

			Mint	Used
S16	1d.	Ultramarine	25	20
	a.	Imperf. (vert. pair from coil)	£700	
	d.	Watermark inverted (11.58)	25	20
	e.	Watermark Crown to left (26.5.61)	1·50	1·25
	f.	Watermark Crown to right	1·50	1·25
	g.	Coil join (horiz. pair)	6·50	
	h.	Daffodil flaw (Cyl. 5 No dot, R. 10/11)	4·00	
	n.	Flaw on thistle head (Coil)	4·00	

B. Whiter Paper (7 May 1962)

			Mint	Used
S17 (=S.G.571)	1d.	Ultramarine	10	10
	a.	Watermark Crown to left (5.6.62)	1·50	1·25
	b.	Watermark Crown to right	1·50	1·25
	c.	Watermark inverted (29.7.62)	40	30
	d.	Coil join (horiz. pair)	3·00	
	e.	Daffodil flaw (Cyl. 5 No dot, R. 10/11)	3·50	
	f.	Tête-bêche (horiz. pair)	£8000	

For illustration of No. S16n, see No. S15a.

S16*h*, S17*e*, S20*c*, S21*e*
Later retouched

Cylinder Numbers (Blocks of Six)

A. Cream Paper (No. S16)

	Perforation Type A (E/I)			Perforation Type B (I/P no dot) and C (E/P dot)		
Cyl. No.		No dot	Dot	Cyl. No.	No dot	Dot
4	. . . .	3·75	3·75	4	5·00	5·00
5	. . . .	3·75	3·75			

B. Whiter Paper (No. S17)

	Perforation Type A (E/I)		
4	. . . .	2·75	2·75
5	. . . .	2·75	2·75

Minor Constant Sheet Flaws

Cyl. 4	11/9	Blue spot on E of POSTAGE
	19/8	White flaw between thistle stem and lower right rose (Th. E6)
Cyl. 4.	14/11	White spur to bottom leaf of shamrock above diadem (Th. A3)
Cyl. 5	3/5	Dark patch below bottom right rose (Th. E5)
	19/8	White flaw between thistle stem and lower right rose (Th. E6)
Cyl. 5.	1/12	Small white flaw on top of top left daffodil (Th. A2)

Coils

Double pane cylinder B1 was used for cream paper printings and cylinder B3 was used for both cream and whiter paper issues with the watermark always upright.
Vertical delivery printed in continuous reels. Cream or whiter paper

Code No.	Number in roll	Face value
AB	240	£1
E	480	£2
B	960	£4
X	960	£4
Z	1920	£8

Sideways delivery made up from sheets with sheet margin joins. Cream or whiter paper

O	480	£2

Imprimaturs from the National Postal Museum Archives

Imperforate, watermark Type W.24. Cream or whiter paper

Watermark upright
Watermark inverted
Tête-bêche pair

1958 (DECEMBER 18). 1d. WITH GRAPHITE LINES, TYPE S8. WATERMARK CROWNS

				Mint	Used
S18 (=S.G.588)	1d.	(1)	Ultramarine (coils)	1·50	1·50
		(2)	Bright ultramarine (booklets)	3·00	2·00
	a.		Watermark inverted (4.8.59)	1·25	2·00
	b		Two lines at left or right (7.61)	80	1·25
	c.		One line at left or right	80	1·25
	d.		Three lines	20·00	18·00
	i.		Flaw on thistle head (Coil, Roll 1)	10·00	

No. S18 was only issued in booklets and coils. For panes, see Section SB, Nos. SB39/a.

The misplaced graphite lines (varieties *b*/*d*) came from Z coils. They were printed after the graphite line experiment had ended to use up residual stock of graphite-lined paper which had been prepared for booklets.

For illustration of No. S18*i*, see No. S15*a*.

Coils

Double pane cylinder B3 was used only for the Z coils with misplaced lines (issued July 1961); other coils were from cylinder B4. The watermark is always upright.

Vertical delivery printed in continuous reels

Code No.	Number in roll	Face value
E	480	£2
X	960	£4
Z	1920	£8

Imprimaturs from the National Postal Museum Archives

Imperforate, watermark Type W.24

Watermark upright
Watermark inverted
Tête-bêche pair

Quantity Issued   12,428,880 including 3,400 Z coils with misplaced lines

1959 (NOVEMBER 18). 1d. PHOSPHOR-GRAPHITE ISSUE. WMK. ST. EDWARD'S CROWN

				Mint	Used
S19 (=S.G.600)	1d.	Ultramarine		11·00	11·00
	a.	One 6 mm. band at left or right (stamp with vert.			
		margin)		14·00	
	b.	Flaw on thistle head (Cyl. 8, R. 6/1)		15·00	
	c.	Daffodil stem flaw (Cyl. 8, R. 15/2)		15·00	

This has two graphite lines, Type S8, on the back and two phosphor bands on the front, (applied typo.), which react green under the lamp.

For illustrations of Nos. S19*b*/*c*, see Nos. S15*a*/*b*.

Cylinder Numbers (Blocks of Six)

Single pane cylinder

Cyl. No.	Perf. Type		No dot
8	B (I/P)		70·00
8	C (E/P)		70·00

Imprimatur from the National Postal Museum Archives

Perf. 15 × 14, watermark Type W.24
Watermark upright

Quantity Issued   709,680

1960 (JUNE 22). 1d. TWO PHOSPHOR BANDS REACTING GREEN. WMK. CROWNS

				Mint	Used
S20	1d.	Ultramarine		1·50	1·50
	a.	Watermark inverted (14.8.60)		5·50	5·50
	b.	Single 8 mm. band (wmk. upright or inverted)		25·00	
	ba.	As *b* but 6 mm. band			
	c.	Daffodil flaw (Cyl. 5 No dot, R. 10/11		6·50	
	g.	Flaw on thistle head (Coil, Roll I)		6·00	

The bands were applied in photogravure.

For illustrations of No. S20*c*, see No. S16*h* and for No. S20*g*, see No. S15*a*.

Cylinder Numbers (Blocks of Six)

Perforation Type B (I/P no dot) and
C (E/P dot)

Cyl. No.	No dot	Dot
5	10·00	10·00

Minor Constant Sheet Flaws

Cyl. 5   3/5 Dark patch below bottom right rose (Th. E5)
          19/8 White flaw between thistle stem and lower right rose (Th. E6)
Cyl. 5.   1/12 Small white flaw on top of top left daffodil (Th. A2)

Coils

Double pane cylinder B3 was used with the watermark always upright.
    Vertical delivery printed in continuous reels

Code No.	Number in roll	Face value
E	480	£2
X	960	£4
Z	1920	£8

Imprimatur from the National Postal Museum Archives

Imperforate, watermark Type W.24

Watermark upright

1961 (JUNE 5).† 1d. TWO PHOSPHOR BANDS REACTING BLUE. WMK. CROWNS

A. Cream Paper

			Mint	Used
S21	1d.	Ultramarine	90	90
	a.	Watermark inverted (3.61)	90	90
	b.	Watermark Crown to left (14.7.61)	3·00	3·00
	c.	Watermark Crown to right	3·00	3·00
	d.	One band (wmk. sideways)	15·00	
	e.	Daffodil flaw (Cyl. 5 No dot, R. 10/11)	4·00	
	g.	Flaw on thistle head (Coil, Roll 1)	10·00	

B. Whiter Paper (21 June 1965)†

S22	1d.	Ultramarine	80	80
	a.	Watermark Crown to left (15.8.62)	3·00	3·00
	b.	Watermark Crown to right	2·75	2·75
	c.	Watermark inverted (3.6.63)	90	90
	d.	One band (wmk. sideways)	30·00	
	da.	One band (wmk. upright or inverted)	40·00	

The bands were applied in photogravure on the stamps with upright watermark and by typography
on those with watermark sideways.
    For illustrations of No. S21*e*, see No. S16*h* and for No. S21*g*, see No. S15*a*.

Cylinder Numbers (Blocks of Six)

A. Cream paper. (No. S21)

Perforation Type B (I/P no dot) and C (E/P
dot)

Cyl. No.	No dot	Dot
5	7·00	7·00

B. Whiter paper. (No. S22)

Perforation Type A (E/I)

Cyl. No.	No dot	Dot
4	5·50	5·50

Minor Constant Sheet Flaws

Cyl. 4   11/9 Blue spot on E of POSTAGE
          19/8 White flaw between thistle stem and lower right rose (Th. E6)
Cyl. 5   3/5 Dark patch below bottom right rose (Th. E5)
          19/8 As for cyl. 4
Cyl. 5.   1/12 Small white flaw on top of top left daffodil (Th. A2)

Coils

Double pane cylinder B3 was used with the watermark always upright.
Vertical delivery printed in continuous reels. Cream or whiter paper

Code No.	Number in roll	Face value
E	480	£2
X	960	£4
Z	1920	£8

Imprimaturs from the National Postal Museum Archives

Imperforate, watermark Type W.24. Cream or whiter paper

Watermark upright
Watermark inverted
Tête-bêche pair

1965 (AUGUST 13). 1d. TWO 8 mm. PHOSPHOR BANDS REACTING VIOLET. WMK. CROWNS

			Mint	Used
S23	1d.	Ultramarine	22·00	12·00
	a.	One 6 mm. band at left or right (stamp with vert. margin)	90·00	
	b.	Bands applied photo. (1966)	50	50
	c.	Watermark inverted (9.65)	25	30
	ca.	One 8 mm. band (wmk. inverted)		
	d.	Watermark Crown to left (10.65)	1·50	1·50
	e.	Watermark Crown to right	1·50	1·50
	f.	One band (wmk. sideways)	20·00	

The bands were originally applied by typography on sheets and 2s. Booklets and later in photogravure on sheets, coils and booklets.

Cylinder Numbers (Blocks of Six)

Perforation Type A (E/I)

Bands typo. (No. S23)			Bands photo. (No. S23*b*)		
Cyl. No.	No dot	Dot	Cyl. No.	No dot	Dot
5	£325	£400	5	5·00	5·00

Minor Constant Sheet Flaws

Cyl. 5   3/5 Dark patch below bottom right rose (Th. E5)
             19/8 White flaw between thistle stem and lower right rose (Th. E6)
Cyl. 5.   1/12 Small white flaw on top of top left daffodil (Th. A2)

Coils

Double pane cylinder B3 was used with the watermark always upright. Bands photo.
Vertical delivery printed in continuous reels

Code No.	Number in roll	Face value
E	480	£2
X	960	£4
Z	1920	£8

1967 (EARLY). 1d. TWO 9·5 mm. PHOSPHOR BANDS REACTING VIOLET. WMK. CROWNS

			Mint	Used
S24 (=S.G.611)	1d.	Ultramarine	10	10
	a.	Watermark inverted (2.67)	85	85
	b.	Watermark Crown to left (4.67)	90	90
	c.	Watermark Crown to right	90	90
	e.	One 9·5 mm. band (wmk. sideways)	10·00	

The bands were mainly applied in photogravure, but the 2s. Booklets had the bands applied by typography or flexography.

Cylinder Numbers (Blocks of Six)

	Perforation Type F (L)*			Perforation Type A (E/I)	
Cyl. No.	No dot (I/E)	Dot (P/E)	Cyl. No.	No dot	Dot
4	1·90	1·90	5	1·90	1·90

Minor Constant Sheet Flaws

Cyl. 4   11/9 Blue spot on E of POSTAGE
          19/8 White flaw between thistle stem and lower right rose (Th. E6)
Cyl. 5   3/5 Dark patch below bottom right rose (Th. E5)
          19/8 As for Cyl. 4
Cyl. 5.   1/12 Small white flaw on top of top left daffodil (Th. A2)

Coils

Double pane cylinder B3 was used with the watermark always upright.
    Vertical delivery printed in continuous reels

Code No.	Number in roll	Face value
E	480	£2
X	960	£4
Z	1920	£8

1952–65 1½d. Green, Type S1

1952 (DECEMBER 5). 1½d. WATERMARK TUDOR CROWN, TYPE W.22

				Mint	Used
S25 (=S.G.517)	1½d.	(1)	Green	10	20
		(2)	Deep green	90	50
	b.		Imperf. between stamp and top margin	£350	
	c.		Watermark inverted (5.53)	60	70
	d.		Watermark sideways (15.10.54)	50	70
	e.		"Butterfly" flaw (Cyl. 6 Dot, R. 19/1) (*Cyl.*		
			block of 6)	£650	
	f.		Flaw on daffodil stem (Cyl. 9 Dot, R. 18/1 . . .	5·00	
	g.		Extra dot (Cyl. 13 Dot, R. 17/10)	10·00	
	h.		Rose and thistle joined at right (Cyl. 13 Dot,		
			R. 19/1)	15·00	
	i.		Scratch on neck (Cyl. 13 Dot, R. 20/3)	9·00	
	m.		Flaw over "O" of "POSTAGE" (Sideways coil,		
			Roll 2)	8·00	
	n.		Dot over rose (Sideways coil, Roll 10)	8·00	
	o.		Daffodil flaw (Sideways coil, Roll 8)	6·50	

Stamps with sideways watermark are from N coils with sideways delivery.

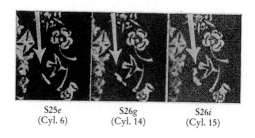

S25*e*	S26*g*	S26*i*
(Cyl. 6)	(Cyl. 14)	(Cyl. 15)

The first and later states of the "butterfly" flaw. All on dot panes only.

Of the first thirteen cylinders used, numbered 1 to 15 (with the exception of Nos. 3 and 7 which were not used), the following is a record of the development of the above illustrated flaws:

Cyl. 1.   No flaws
Cyls. 2, 4 and 5. Disturbed background
Cyls. 6.   This is found in two states. One with disturbed background and the other with a short white flaw as illustrated, the latter being the first of the clear defects in this position
Cyls. 8 to 13. Disturbed background
Cyl. 14.   Found in two states, one with disturbed background and the other with a long white flaw as illustrated
Cyl. 15.   Also found in two states, one with disturbed background and the other with a larger white flaw as illustrated, the latter only occurring on the St. Edward's Crown watermark

The most plausible explanation of the development of this flaw is that prior to the making of cylinder 2, the multipositive was damaged and imperfectly retouched with the result that cylinders 2, 4 and 5 show an uneven background. Before the making of cylinder 6 the opaque retouching medium appears to have partly peeled off from the multipositive leaving a transparent area which produced the small white flaw on the stamp. This was evidently discovered during the run and the cylinder retouched with the result that we have cylinder 6 with uneven background.

The multipositive was again retouched and this time continued to be used uneventfully for cylinders 8 to 13. After this the retouching medium appears to have peeled off again before making cylinders 14 and 15, each time being discovered and retouched during the printing run. Cylinder 22 is normal, showing no trace of the flaw or a retouch, possibly being from a new multipositive.

Prices are for cylinder blocks of six. The cylinder blocks showing the disturbed background are priced without an asterisk.

S25f, SB61a

S25g, S26d
Later retouched on
St. Edward's Crown
watermark

S25h, S26e

S25i, S26f
White vertical line
from ear to shoulder

S25m, S26q

S25n, S26r
From sideways delivery
N coils

S25o, S26s

Cylinder Numbers (Blocks of Six)

Perforation Type A (E/I)		
Cyl. No.	No dot	Dot
1	1·90	1·90
2	1·90	1·90
4	1·90	1·90
5	1·90	1·90
6	3·00	3·50
8	4·00	4·00
9	1·60	12·00*
10	1·60	1·60
11	1·60	1·60
12	1·60	1·60
13	3·00	22·00*

Perforation Type B (I/P no dot) and C (E/P dot)		
Cyl. No.	No dot	Dot
1	3·50	3·50
2	7·00	7·00
6	3·50	3·50
9	3·50	15·00*

Coils

Printed in continuous reels

Double pane cylinders C1 or C2 were used for the vertical delivery coils and single pane cylinder number C3 for the sideways delivery coils.

	Code No.	Number in roll	Face value
(a) Vertical delivery.		Watermark upright	
	L	480	£3
	K	960	£6
(b) Sideways delivery.		Watermark sideways	
	N	480	£3

Imprimaturs from the National Postal Museum Archives

Imperforate, watermark Type W.22

Watermark upright
Watermark inverted
Tête-bêche pair

1955 (OCTOBER 11).† 1½d. WATERMARK ST. EDWARD'S CROWN, TYPE W.23

				Mint	Used
S26 (=S.G.542)	1½d.	(1)	Green	25	30
		(2)	Deep green	40	20
	a.		Tête-bêche (horiz. pair)	£2500	
	b.		Watermark inverted (8.55)	60	60
	c.		Watermark sideways (7.3.56)	35	70
	d.		Extra dot (Cyl. 13 Dot, R. 17/10)	9·00	
	e.		Rose and thistle joined at right (Cyl. 13 Dot, R. 19/1)	8·50	
	f.		Scratch on neck (Cyl. 13 No dot, R. 20/3) . . .	8·50	
	g.		"Butterfly" flaw (Cyl. 14 Dot, R. 19/1) (*cyl. block of 6*)	50·00	
	h.		Bud on shamrock stem (Cyl. 14) No dot, R. 8/6)	4·50	
	i.		"Butterfly" flaw (Cyl. 15 Dot, R. 19/1) (*cyl. block of 6*)	40·00	
	j.		Spot between rose and shamrock (Cyl. 15 No dot, R. 20/3)	5·50	
	q.		Flaw over "O" of "POSTAGE" (Sideways coil, Roll 2)	5·00	
	r.		Dot over rose (Sideways coil, Roll 10)	5·00	
	s.		Daffodil flaw (Sideways coil, Roll 8)	4·50	

Stamps with sideways watermark are from N coils with sideways delivery.

For illustrations of Nos. S26*d/f* see Nos. S25*g/i*; for Nos. S26*g* and S26*i* see No. S25*e*; and for Nos. S26*q/s* see Nos. S25*m/o*.

S26*h*

S26*j*, S28*e*, S32*b*
Later retouched on whiter paper
with Crowns watermark

Cylinder Numbers (Blocks of Six)

Perforation Type A (E/I)

Cyl. No.	No dot	Dot	Cyl. No.	No dot	Dot
11	2·50	3·00	14	2·50	3·00
13	2·50	12·00*	15	2·50	3·00

See note below No. S25 on the butterfly flaw which occurs on some examples of cylinders 14 and 15 dot. Prices are for normals with disturbed background.

Minor Constant Sheet Flaws

Cyl. 15   17/9 Nick in frame bottom right (Th. G6)
           20/9 Speck opposite left 1 (Th. G1)
Cyl. 15.   1/4 Green dot in lower half of 1 of left ½ (Th. G1)

Coils

Printed in continuous reels

Double pane cylinders C1 or C2 were again used for the vertical delivery coils and single pane cylinder number C3 for the sideways delivery coil.

	Code No.	Number in roll	Face value
(a) Vertical delivery. Watermark upright			
	L	480	£3
	K	960	£6
(b) Sideways delivery. Watermark sideways			
	N	480	£3

Imprimaturs from the National Postal Museum Archives

Imperforate, watermark Type W.23

Watermark upright
Watermark inverted
Tête-bêche pair

1957 (NOVEMBER 19). 1½d. WITH GRAPHITE LINES, TYPE S8. WMK. ST. EDWARD'S CROWN

				Mint	Used
S27 (=S.G.563)	1½d.	Green	. . . .	1·20	1·40
	a.	Both lines at left	£1200	£450
	b.	Horiz. pair, one stamp with only one line . . . . *pair*	£1000	
	c.	Coil join (horiz. pair)	15·00	
	d.	Green stroke below "E" (Cyl. 21 No dot, R. 13/8) .	8·00	

Nos. S27*a*/*b* result from a misplacement of the graphite lines.

Diagonal green stroke below middle "E" of "REVENUE" in bottom margin of stamp

S27*d*, S31*b*

Cylinder Numbers (Blocks of Six)

Single pane cylinder

Cyl. No.	Perf. Type	No dot
21	B (I/P)	8·50
21	C (E/P)	8·50

Coil

Sideways delivery made up from sheets with sheet margin joins

Code No.	Number in roll	Face value
N	480	£3

Quantity Issued   10,506,720

Imprimatur from the National Postal Museum Archives

Imperforate, watermark Type W.23

Watermark upright

1960 (AUGUST 30).† 1½d. WATERMARK CROWNS, TYPE W.24

A. Cream Paper   Mint   Used

S28	1½d.	(1)	Green	40	25
		(2)	Deep green	90	70
	a.		Watermark inverted (12.58)	1·50	80
	b.		Watermark Crown to left (26.5.61)	10·00	5·00
	c.		Watermark Crown to right	10·00	5·00
	d.		Coil join (vert. pair)	6·00	
	e.		Spot between rose and shamrock (Cyl. 15 No dot, R. 20/3)	6·00	

B. Whiter Paper (7 May 1962)

S29 (=S.G.572)	1½d.	(1)	Green	10	15
		(2)	Deep green	60	60
	a.		Imperf. three sides (horiz, strip of 3)	£5500	
	b.		Watermark Crown to left (5.6.62)	9·00	6·00
	c.		Watermark Crown to right	9·00	6·00
	d.		Watermark inverted (18.9.62)	4·00	4·00
	e.		Coil join (horiz. pair)	5·00	
	g.		Thistle flaws (Cyl. 22 Dot, R. 12/1)	6·00	
	h.		Daffodil flaw (Cyl. 22 Dot, R. 1/12)	6·00	
	i.		Tête-bêche (horiz. pair)	£8000	

For illustration of No. S28*e* see No. S26*j.*

S29*g,* S34*f*
White flaws in and around
thistle at upper left

S29*h,* S34*g*
White spot by upper
left daffodil

Cylinder Numbers (Blocks of Six)

A. Cream paper. (No. S28)

Perforation Type A (E/I)

Cyl. No.		No dot	Dot
15	. . . .	3·50	3·50

B. Whiter paper. (No. S29)

Perforation Type A (E/I)

Cyl. No.		No dot	Dot
15	. . . .	1·90	1·90
22	. . . .	2·50	2·50

Marginal arrows: Cylinder 15 "V" shaped, hand-engraved, at top and bottom; "W" shaped, photo-etched, at both sides

Cylinder 22 "W" shaped, hand-engraved, at top; "W" shaped, photo-etched at bottom and at both sides

Marginal rule: Cylinder 15 At bottom of sheet (1½ mm. wide)

Cylinder 22 At bottom of sheet (2 mm. wide)

Minor Constant Sheet Flaws

Cyl. 15   13/9 White spur on top left daffodil stem (Th. A2)
Cyl. 15.   1/4 Green dot in lower half of 1 of left ½ (Th. G1)

Coils

Made up from sheets with sheet margin joins. Watermark upright

Code No.	Number in roll	Face value	
L	480	£3	Vertical delivery (Cream paper)
N	480	£3	Sideways delivery (Whiter paper)

Imprimaturs from the National Postal Museum Archives

Imperforate, watermark Type W.24. Cream or whiter paper

Watermark upright
Watermark inverted
Tête-bêche pair

1959 (AUGUST 4). 1½d. WITH GRAPHITE LINES, TYPE S8. WATERMARK CROWNS

			Mint	Used
S30 (=S.G.589)	1½d.	Green	90·00	80·00
	a.	Watermark inverted (4.8.59)	60·00	48·00

This was only issued in 3s. Booklets. See Section SB, Nos. SB70/a.

Imprimaturs from the National Postal Museum Archives

Imperforate, watermark Type W.24

Watermark upright
Watermark inverted
Tête-bêche pair

Quantity Issued   1,862,400

1959 (NOVEMBER 18). 1½d. PHOSPHOR-GRAPHITE ISSUE. WMK. ST. EDWARD'S CROWN

			Mint	Used
S31 (=S.G.601)	1½d.	Green	4·00	4·00
	a.	One 6 mm. band at left or right (stamp with vert. margin)	10·00	
	b.	Green stroke below "E" (Cyl. 21 No dot, R. 13/8) .	10·00	

No. S31 has two graphite lines, Type S8, on the back and two phosphor bands on the front, applied typo., which react green under the lamp.
For illustration of No. S31*b* see No. S27*d.*

Cylinder Numbers (Blocks of Six)

Single pane cylinder

Cyl. No.	Perf. Type	No dot
21	B (I/P)	28·00
21	C (E/P)	28·00

Imprimatur from the National Postal Museum Archives

Perf. 15 × 14, watermark Type W.24

Watermark upright

Quantity Issued   704,160

1960 (JUNE 22). 1½d. TWO PHOSPHOR BANDS REACTING GREEN. WMK. CROWNS

			Mint	Used
S32	1½d.	Green	2·00	1·50
	a.	Watermark inverted (14.8.60)	12·00	9·50
	b.	Spot between rose and shamrock (Cyl. 15 No dot,		
		R. 20/3)	5·50	

The bands were applied in photogravure.

For illustration of No. S32*b* see No. S26*j*.

Cylinder Numbers (Blocks of Six)

Perforation Type B (I/P no dot) and C (E/P dot)

Cyl. No.	No dot	Dot
15	14·00	14·00

Minor Constant Sheet Flaws

Cyl. 15   13/9 White spur on top left daffodil stem (Th. A2)
Cyl. 15.   1/4 Green dot in lower half of 1 of left ½ (Th. G1)

Imprimaturs from the National Postal Museum Archives

Imperforate, watermark Type W.24

Watermark upright
Watermark inverted
Tête-bêche pair

1961 (JUNE 5).† 1½d. TWO PHOSPHOR BANDS REACTING BLUE. WMK. CROWNS

A. Cream Paper

			Mint	Used
S33	1½d.	Green	85	85
	a.	Watermark inverted (4.61)	12·00	10·00
	b.	Watermark Crown to left (14.7.61)	10·00	10·00
	c.	Water Crown to right	10·00	10·00
	d.	One broad band (wmk. sideways)	25·00	
	da.	One broad band (wmk. upright or inverted)	40·00	

B. Whiter Paper (Sept. 1964)†

			Mint	Used
S34 (=S.G.612)	1½d.	Green	15	15
	a.	Watermark Crown to left (15.8.62)	12·00	12·00
	b.	Watermark Crown to right	12·00	12·00
	c.	Watermark inverted (7.64)	22·00	15·00
	d.	One broad band (wmk. upright or inverted)	75·00	
	f.	Thistle flaws (Cyl. 22 Dot, R. 12/1)	6·00	
	g.	Daffodil flaw (Cyl. 22 Dot, R. 1/22)	6·00	
	h.	White bulge on clover (Cyl. 22 No dot, R. 7/2) . . .	5·00	

The bands were applied in photogravure on the stamps with upright watermark and by typography on those with watermark sideways.

For illustrations of Nos. S34*f/g*, see Nos. S29*g/h*.

S34*h*

Cylinder Numbers (Blocks of Six)

A. Cream paper. (No. S33)

Perforation Type B (I/P no dot) and C (E/P dot)

Cyl. No.	No dot	Dot
15	7·00	7·00

B. Whiter paper. (No. S34)

Perforation Type A (E/I)

Cyl. No.	No dot	Dot
15	2·00	2·00
22	3·00	3·00

The notes on the marginal arrows below No. S29 also apply here.

Minor Constant Sheet Flaws

Cyl. 15   13/9 White spur on top left daffodil stem (Th. A2)
Cyl. 15.   1/4 Green dot on lower half of 1 of left ½ (Th. G1)

Imprimaturs from the National Postal Museum Archives

Imperforate, watermark Type W.24. Cream or whiter paper

Watermark upright
Watermark inverted
Tête-bêche pair

1965 (AUGUST 13). 1½d. TWO 8 mm. PHOSPHOR BANDS REACTING VIOLET. WMK. CROWNS

				Mint	Used
S35	1½d.	Green	1·50	1·50
	a.	One 6 mm. band at left or right (stamp with vert. margin)	5·00	
	b.	One 8 mm. band	10·00	
	ba.	As *b* but 6 mm. band	15·00	

The bands were applied by typography.

Cylinder Numbers (Blocks of Six)

Perforation Type A (E/I)

Cyl. No.	No dot	Dot
15	11·00	11·00

Marginal arrows as for Cylinder 15 under Nos. S28/9.

1953–67 2d. Red-brown, Type S1

1953 (AUGUST 31). 2d. WATERMARK TUDOR CROWN, TYPE W.22

			Mint	Used
S36 (=S.G.518)	2d.	Red-brown	20	20
	a.	Watermark inverted (3.54)	25·00	18·00
	b.	Watermark sideways (8.10.54)	1·25	2·00
	c.	Rose petal flaw (Cyl. 3 No dot, R. 4/8)	15·00	
	d.	"Tadpole" flaw (Cyl. 4 Dot, R. 17/6)	22·00	
	e.	Retouched (Cyl. 3 Dot, R. 17/6)	20·00	
	g.	Extra leg to "R" (Sideways coil, Roll 2)	5·00	
	h.	Retouched left "2" (Sideways coil, Roll 5)	6·00	
	i.	Dot on rose (Sideways coil, Roll 1)	4·50	

Stamps with sideways watermark are from T coils with sideways delivery.

S36c, S37e

S36d, S37f, S38f
White flaw resembles a
tadpole below thistle

S36e, S37g, S38g, S40d
Later retouched state of
the "tadpole" flaw

S36g, S37l, S38s,
S40i, S41b, S49c

Normal

S36h, S37m, S38t,
S40j, S41c, S49d

S36i, S37k, S38w

From sideways delivery T coils

Cylinder Numbers (Blocks of Six)

Perforation Type A (E/I)

Cyl. No.		No dot	Dot	Cyl. No.		No dot	Dot
1	. . . .	6·00	6·00	3	. . . .	3·50	3·50
2	. . . .	6·00	6·00	4	. . . .	3·50	3·50

Sheets from cylinder 2 No dot are known with the marginal arrows omitted from top and bottom selvedge.

Coils

Double pane cylinder number D1 was used for vertical delivery coils and single pane cylinder D3 for sideways delivery coils.

Printed in continuous reels

         Code No.   Number in roll   Face value

         (a) Vertical delivery. Watermark upright

             R   480   £4

             Q   960   £8

             V   960   £8

         (b) Sideways delivery. Watermark sideways

             T   480   £4

Imprimaturs from the National Postal Museum Archives

Imperforate, watermark Type W.22

Watermark upright
Watermark inverted
Tête-bêche pair

1955 (SEPTEMBER 6). 2d. WATERMARK ST. EDWARD'S CROWN, TYPE W.23

A. Red-brown

			Mint	Used
S37 (=S.G.543)	2d.	Red-brown	25	35
	a.	Imperf. between pair (from vert. coil)	£3500	
	aa.	Imperf. between pair (from sdwys. wmk. horiz. coil) .	£3500	
	ad.	Imperf. between vert. pair (from sheet)		
	c.	Watermark inverted (9.55)	11·00	9·00
	d.	Watermark sideways (31.7.56)	55	70
	e.	Rose petal flaw (Cyl. 3 No dot, R. 4/8)	5·00	
	f.	"Tadpole" flaw (Cyl. 4 No Dot, R. 17/6)	10·00	
	g.	Retouched (R. 17/6 on Cyls. 3, 6, 7 all Dot. Vertical coil, Roll 6)	5·00	
	h.	"Tadpole" flaw with shamrock flaw (Cyl. 9 Dot, R. 17/6)	8·00	
	i.	Flaw between shamrock and diadem (Cyl. 7 Dot, R. 1/6)	6·00	
	j.	White spot by daffodil (Cyl. 9 Dot, R. 18/8)	4·50	
	k.	Dot on rose (Sideways coil, Roll 1)	3·50	
	l.	Extra leg to "R" (Sideways coil, Roll 2)	5·00	
	m.	Retouched left "2" (Sideways coil, Roll 5)	4·50	
	n.	Extended stem on daffodil (Sideways coil, Roll 9) . .	3·50	

Stamps with sideways watermark are from T coils with sideways delivery.

No. S37*ad* came from the second vertical row of a sheet affected by a paper fold. One pair exists from this source being in a perforated block of 18 (6 × 3) with left sheet margin. Perforations at left and right of the vertical rows were severed during perforating when several stamps were folded under the sheet.

For illustrations of Nos. S37*e/g*, see Nos. S36*c/e* and for Nos. S37*k/m*, see Nos. S36*g/i.* No. S37*h* comprises the variety shown for No. S36*d* but in addition there is a white flaw to the left of the adjoining shamrock; see also Nos. S40*f*, S41*e* and S49*e.*

S37*i*, S38*j*
This was a multipositive flaw
which was retouched on
other cylinders

S37*n*, S38*u*,
S40*k*, S41*d*

S37*j*, S38*k*

B. Light red-brown (17 October 1956)   Mint   Used
S38 (=S.G.543*b*)   2d.   Light red-brown   20   20
         a.   Tête-bêche (horiz pair) £1800
         c.   Imperf. between stamp and top margin £275
         d.   Watermark inverted (1.57) . . . .   9·00   7·00
         e.   Watermark sideways (5.3.57) . . . .   8·00   7·00
         f.   "Tadpole" flaw (R. 17/6 on Cyls. 8, 10 and 11 Dot) . .   9·00
         g.   Retouched (R. 17/6 on Cyls. 6, 7, 8, 11, 12, 13 & 15 all
                 dot, Vertical coil, Row 6) . . . .   5·00
         h.   "Tadpole" and shamrock flaws (R. 17/6 on Cyls. 9 &
                 12 Dot) . . . .   8·00
         i.   "Tadpole" flaw retouched with shamrock flaw
                 (R. 17/6 on Cyls. 14 and 16 Dot . . . .   8·00
         j.   Flaw between shamrock and diadem (Cyl. 7 dot,
                 R. 1/6) . . . .   6·00
         k.   White spot by daffodil (Cyl. 9 Dot, R. 18/8) . . . . .   4·50
         l.   Extended leaf on shamrock (Cyl. 10 No dot, R. 8/6) .   4·00
         m.   "Double trumpet" flaw (Cyl. 10 No dot, R. 11/1) . .   7·50
         n.   Dot on shamrock (Cyl. 10 No dot, R. 20/1) . . . . . .   5·00
         o.   White flaw on crown (Cyl. 11 No dot, R. 9/11) . . . .   8·00
         p.   White flaw on shamrock (Cyl. 12 dot, R. 20/3) . . . .   8·00
         q.   White spot by right thistle (Cyl. 14 Dot, R. 11/10) . .   10·00
         r.   Dot over rose stem (Cyl. 14 No dot, R. 1/1) . . . . . .   8·00
         s.   Extra leg to "R" (Sideways coil, Roll 2) . . . .   12·00
         t.   Retouched left "2" (Sideways coil, Roll 5) . . . . . .   12·00
         u.   Extended stem on daffodil (Sideways coil, Roll 9) . .   12·00
         w.   Dot on rose (Sideways coil, Roll 1) . . . .   12·00

Stamps with sideways watermark are from T coils with sideways delivery.

In December 1956 a completely imperforate sheet was noticed by clerks in a Kent post office, one of whom purchased it against P.O. regulations. In view of this irregularity we do not consider it properly issued. (*Price* £375 *pair.*)

Tadpole flaws: Nos. S38*f/h* are as Nos. S37*f/h*. The first printings from cylinder 12 show No. S38*h* larger, but on later printings both flaws appear to have been retouched. No. S38*i* is a fourth state which combines the shamrock flaw (small on cyl. 14, larger on cyl. 16) with the retouched state of the tadpole flaw.

For illustrations of Nos. S38*j/k*, see Nos. S37*i/j*, and for Nos. S38*s/w*, see Nos. S36*g/i* and S37*n*.

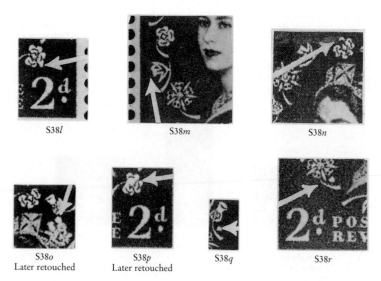

S38*l*   S38*m*   S38*n*

S38*o*   S38*p*   S38*q*   S38*r*
Later retouched   Later retouched

Cylinder Numbers (Blocks of Six)

(a) Red-brown (No. S37)

Perforation Type A (E/I)

Cyl. No.	No dot	Dot	Cyl. No.	No dot	Dot
3	3·50	3·50	7	3·50	3·50
4	3·50	3·50	9	15·00	15·00
6	3·50	3·50			

(b) Light red-brown (No. S38)

Perforation Type A (E/I)

Cyl. No.	No dot	Dot	Cyl. No.	No dot	Dot
6	3·00	3·00	12	3·00	3·00
7	3·00	3·00	13	3·00	3·00
8	3·00	3·00	14	3·00	3·00
9	3·00	3·00	15	3·00	3·00
10	8·00*	3·00	16	3·00	3·00
11	3·00	3·00			

Perforation Type E

	No dot (AE/I)	Dot (E/I)		No dot (AE/I)	Dot (E/I)
7	24·00	3·00**	9	24·00	3·00**

**Both light red-brown same appearance and same prices as perforation type A with extension holes in left margin.

Minor Constant Sheet Flaws

Cyl. 7	14/8	White dot above T of POSTAGE
Cyl. 9	20/1	White spur on lower daffodil (Th. G3)
Cyl. 10	14/12	Nick in R of REVENUE
Cyl. 10.	9/6	Dark spot on necklace (Th. E/F3)
Cyl. 16.	20/12	"REVENUE" retouched (Th. G2–5)

Coils

Double pane cylinder number D1 was used for vertical delivery coils of No. S37, cylinder D2 for No. S38; single pane cylinder D3 was used for the sideways delivery coils of No. S37d and cylinders D3 or D4 for No. S38e.

Printed in continuous reels

Code No.	Cat. No.	Number in roll	Face value
(a) Vertical delivery.		Watermark upright	
R	S37	480	£4
Q	S37	960	£8
V	S37	960	£8
R	S38	480	£4
Q	S38	960	£8
V	S38	960	£8
(b) Sideways delivery.		Watermark sideways	
T	S37d	480	£4
T	S38e	480	£4

Imprimaturs from the National Postal Museum Archives

A. Red-brown. Imperforate, watermark Type W.23

Watermark upright
Watermark inverted
Tête-bêche pair

B. Light red-brown. Imperforate, watermark Type W.23

Watermark upright
Watermark inverted
Tête-bêche pair

GRAPHITE-LINED ISSUES

On the 2d. value, Nos. S39, S42/3 the single graphite line normally appeared at the right when viewed from the back. It was printed in black under the gum.

S9

1957 (NOVEMBER 19). 2d. WITH GRAPHITE LINE, TYPE S9. WMK. ST. EDWARD'S CROWN

		Mint	Used
S39 (=S.G.564)	2d. Light red-brown	1·60	2·25
	a. Line at left (as seen from back)	£650	£225
	b. Horiz. pair, one with line omitted	£1400	
	c. Coil join (vert. pair)	15·00	
	d. Coil join (horiz. pair)	15·00	

Nos. S39a/b result from a misplacement of the line.

Cylinder Numbers (Blocks of Six)

Single pane cylinder

Cyl. No.	Perf. Type	No dot
17	B (I/P)	16·00
17	C (E/P)	16·00

Minor Constant Sheet Flaws

Cyl. 17   11/2 White flaw on tail of left d
16/1 White flaw in centre of upper left rose (Th. B1)

Coils

Made up from sheets with sheet margin joins

Code No.	Number in roll	Face value	
V	960	£8	Vertical delivery
T	480	£4	Sideways delivery

Imprimatur from the National Postal Museum Archives

Imperforate, watermark Type W.23

Watermark upright

Quantity Issued   37,686,480

1958 (DECEMBER 4).†   2d. WATERMARK CROWNS, TYPE W.24

A. Cream Paper

			Mint	Used
S40	2d.	Light red-brown	40	25
	a.	Imperf. between stamp and top margin	£450	
	b.	Watermark sideways (3.4.59)	1·25	1·25
	c.	Watermark inverted (10.4.61)	£140	70·00
	d.	"Tadpole" retouch (R. 17/6 on Cyls. 15 Dot and others)	5·50	
	e.	"Swan's head" flaw (Cyl. 24 Dot, R. 19/10)	6·50	
	f.	"Tadpole" flaw retouched with shamrock flaw (Cyl. 27 Dot, R. 17/6)	7·00	
	i.	Extra leg to "R" (Sideways coil, Roll 2)	5·00	
	j.	Retouched left "2" (Sideways coil, Roll 5)	5·00	
	k.	Extended stem on daffodil (Sideways coil, Roll 9) . .	5·00	

B. Whiter Paper (5 September 1963)†

S41 (=S.G.S73)	2d.	Light red-brown	10	10
	a.	Watermark sideways (27.7.62)	50	1·00
	b.	Extra leg to "R" (Sideways coil, Roll 2)	5·00	
	c.	Retouched left "2" (Sideways coil, Roll 5)	5·00	
	d.	Extended stem on daffodil (Sideways coil, Roll 9) . .	5·00	
	e.	"Tadpole" flaw retouched with shamrock flaw (Cyl. 27 Dot, R. 17/6)	6·00	

†No. S40 was issued in November 1958 in V coils and No. S41 appeared on 20 September 1962 in V coils.

Stamps with sideways watermark are from T coils with sideways delivery.

Tadpole flaw: No. S40d is as No. S38g. For illustrations of Nos. S40i/j and S41b/c, see Nos. S36g/h; for Nos. S40k and S41d, see No. S37n. For description of Nos. S40f and S41e see below No. S37.

S40e

Cylinder Numbers (Blocks of Six)

A. Cream paper. (No. S40)

Perforation Type A (E/I)			Perforation Type A (E/I)		
Cyl. No.	No dot	Dot	Cyl. No.	No dot	Dot
15	3·50	3·50	24	3·50	3·50
19	3·50	3·50	25	3·50	3·50
20	3·50	3·50	27	3·50	3·50
21	3·50	3·50	29	3·50	3·50
22	3·50	3·50	30	3·50	3·50
23	3·50	3·50			

B. Whiter paper. (No. S41)

Perforation Type A (E/I)			Perforation Type A (E/I)		
Cyl. No.	No dot	Dot	Cyl. No.	No dot	Dot
23	2·25	2·25	27	2·25	2·25
25	2·25	2·25	30	2·25	2·25

Coils

Double cylinder D2 was used for vertical delivery coils and cylinders D3 and D4 (single pane) for sideways delivery coils.

Printed in continuous reels. Cream or whiter paper

	Code No.	Number in roll	Face value
(a) Vertical delivery. Watermark upright			
	R	480	£4
	Q	960	£8
	V	960	£8
(b) Sideways delivery. Watermark sideways			
	T	480	£4

Imprimaturs from the National Postal Museum Archives

Imperforate, watermark Type W.24. Cream or whiter paper

Watermark upright
Watermark inverted
Tête-bêche pair

1958 (NOVEMBER 24). 2d. WITH GRAPHITE LINE, TYPE S9. WATERMARK CROWNS

				Mint	Used
S42 (=S.G.590)	2d.	Light red-brown	....	9·00	3·50
	a.	Line at extreme left (as seen from back)	....	£700	
	ab.	Horizontal pair, one stamp as S42*a* and one without			
		line	....	£2250	
	b.	Coil join (vert. pair)	....	30·00	

Cylinder Numbers (Blocks of Six)

Single pane cylinder

Cyl. No.	Perf. Type	No dot
17	B (I/P)	65·00
17	C (E/P)	65·00

Minor Constant Sheet Flaw

Cyl. 17   11/2 White flaw on tail of left d

Coil

Vertical delivery. Made up from sheets with sheet margin joins

	Code No.	Number in roll	Face value
	V	960	£8

Imprimatur from the National Postal Museum Archives

Imperforate, watermark Type W.24

Watermark upright

Quantity Issued   48,419,520

1959 (NOVEMBER 18). 2d. PHOSPHOR-GRAPHITE ISSUE. WATERMARK CROWNS

				Mint	Used
S43 (=S.G.605)	2d.	Light red-brown	....	5·00	4·25
	a.	Error. Watermark St. Edward's Crown Type W.23			
		(3.60)	....	£180	£150

This has one graphite line (Type S9), on the back and one phosphor band on the front, applied typo., which reacts green under the lamp.

Cylinder Numbers (Blocks of Six)

Single pane cylinder

Watermark Crowns (No. S43)			Watermark St. Edward's Crown (No. S43*a*)		
Cyl. No.	Perf. Type	No dot	Cyl. No.	Perf. Type	No dot
17	B (I/P)	40·00	17	B (I/P)	£1250
17	C (E/P)	40·00	17	C (E/P)	£1250

Minor Constant Sheet Flaws

Cyl. 17   11/2 White flaw on tail of left d
            16/1 White flaw in centre of upper left rose (Th. B1) (on St. Edward's Crown wmk. only)

Imprimatur from the National Postal Museum Archives

Perf. 15 × 14, watermark Type W.24

Watermark upright

Quantity Issued   4,509,120 (including both watermarks)

1960. (JUNE 22). 2d. ONE PHOSPHOR BAND AT LEFT REACTING GREEN. WMK. CROWNS

			Mint	Used
S44 (=S.G.613)	2d.	Light red-brown	16·00	18·00
	a.	Coil join (vert. pair)	45·00	

The band was applied in photogravure.

Cylinder Numbers (Blocks of Six)

Single pane cylinder

Cyl. No.	Perf. Type	No dot
17	B (I/P)	£130
17	C (E/P)	£150

Minor Constant Sheet Flaw

Cyl. 17   11/2 White flaw on tail of left d

Coil

Vertical delivery. Made up from sheets with sheet margin joins

Code No.	Number in roll	Face value
V	960	£8

Imprimatur from the National Postal Museum Archives

Imperforate, watermark Type W.24

Watermark upright

1961 (JUNE 5). 2d. ONE PHOSPHOR BAND AT LEFT REACTING BLUE. WMK. CROWNS

			Mint	Used
S45	2d.	Light red-brown	35·00	28·00

This exists on cream paper only and the phosphor band was applied in photogravure or flexo. See General Notes—Application of Phosphor Bands.

Cylinder Numbers (Blocks of Six)

	Perforation Type A (E/I)			Perforation Type B (I/P no dot) and C (E/P dot)		
Cyl. No.		No dot	Dot	Cyl. No.		No dot	Dot
29	. . . .	£250	£250	29	. . . .	£250	£250

Minor Constant Sheet Flaw

Cyl. 29.   17/6 There is only a slight shading to the background where the tadpole and shamrock flaws were

Coil

Double pane cylinder D2 was used.

Printed in continuous reels. Vertical delivery with watermark upright

Code No.	Number in roll	Face value
V	960	£8

1961 (OCTOBER 4). 2d. TWO PHOSPHOR BANDS REACTING BLUE. WMK CROWNS

A. Cream Paper Bands typographed

				Mint	Used
S46	2d.	Light red-brown	10·00	7·00
	a.	Imperf. three sides*	£8500	
	b.	One 6 mm. band at left or right (stamp with vert. margin)	16·00	
	c.	Error. One 8 mm. band (typo)	20·00	
	ca.	As c. but 6 mm. band	25·00	
	d.	Bands applied photo. (3.4.62)	2·00	2·00
	da.	Error. One 8 mm. band (photo)	25·00	

B. Whiter Paper (5 November 1964)† Bands applied in photogravure

			Mint	Used
S47	2d.	Light red-brown	7·00	7·00
	a.	Error. Single 8 mm. band	£110	

*This comes from the bottom row of a sheet which is imperf. at bottom and both sides. From cyl. 29 no dot with bands applied photo.

†No. S47 appeared earlier from V coils on 21 January 1963.

Cylinder Numbers (Blocks of Six)

Cream paper
Two bands applied typo. (No. S46)
Perforation Type A (E/I)

Cyl. No.		No dot	Dot
25	. . . .	70·00	†
27	. . . .	†	70·00
29	. . . .	70·00	70·00
30	. . . .	70·00	70·00

Two bands applied photo. (No. S46d)
Perforation Type B (I/P no dot) and C (E/P dot)

29	. . . .	16·00	16·00

Whiter paper
Two bands applied photo. (No. S47)
Perforation Type A (E/I)

Cyl. No.		No dot	Dot
25	. . . .	50·00	50·00

As the typographed bands were applied on individual sheets and not in the reel, it is possible that the items marked with a dagger may exist.

Minor Constant Sheet Flaw

Dot cyls.   17/6 There remains only a slight disturbance to the background where the tadpole and shamrock flaws were

Coil

Double pane cylinder D2 was used.

Printed in continuous reels. Vertical delivery with watermark upright. Cream or whiter paper.

Code No.	Number in roll	Face value
V	960	£8

Imprimatur from the National Postal Museum Archives

Imperforate, watermark Type W.24. Cream or whiter paper

Watermark upright

1965 (AUGUST 17). 2d. TWO 8 mm. PHOSPHOR BANDS REACTING VIOLET. WMK. CROWNS

			Mint	Used
S48	2d.	Light red-brown	90	60

The bands were applied in photogravure only.

Cylinder Numbers (Blocks of Six)

Perforation Type A (E/I)

Cyl. No.	No dot	Dot
30	7·50	7·50

Minor Constant Sheet Flaw

Cyl. 30.   17/6 There remains only a slight disturbance under the thistle of the original tadpole and shamrock flaws

Coil

Double pane cylinder D2 was used.
Printed in continuous reels. Vertical delivery with watermark upright

Code No.	Number in roll	Face value
V	960	£8

1967 (SEPTEMBER).† 2d. TWO 9·5 mm. PHOSPHOR BANDS REACTING VIOLET. WMK. CROWNS

			Mint	Used
S49 (=S.G.613*a*)	2d.	Light red-brown	10	15
	a.	Watermark Crown to left (6.4.67)	30	60
	b.	One band (wmk. sideways ex. T coil)	15·00	
	c.	Extra leg to "R" (Sideways coil, Roll 2)	5·50	
	d.	Retouched left "2" (Sideways coil, Roll 5)	5·50	
	e.	"Tadpole" flaw retouched with shamrock flaw (Cyl. 27 Dot, R. 17/6)	6·00	

The bands were applied in photogravure only.
Stamps with sideways watermark are from T coils with sideways delivery.
For illustrations of Nos. S49*c/d*, see Nos. S36*g/h*. No. S49*e* is described below No. S37.

Cylinder Numbers (Blocks of Six)

Perforation Type F (L)*			Perforation Type A (E/I)		
Cyl. No	No dot	Dot	Cyl. No.	No dot	Dot
	(I/E)	(P/E)			
25	2·00	2·00	27	2·00	2·00

Minor Constant Sheet Flaw

Dot panes.   17/6 There remains only a slight disturbance to the background where the tadpole and shamrock flaws were

Coils

Double pane cylinder D2 was used for the vertical delivery coils and cylinder D3 (single pane) for sideways delivery coils.
Printed in continuous reels

Code No.	Number in roll	Face value
	(a) Vertical delivery. Watermark upright	
R	480	£4
V	960	£8
	(b) Sideways delivery. Watermark sideways	
T	480	£4

1952–65 2½d. Carmine-red, Type S2

Two Types

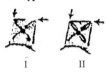

I   II

Type I   In the frontal cross of the diadem, the top line is only half the width of the cross.

Type II   The top line extends to the full width of the cross and there are signs of strengthening in other parts of the diadem.

Variations in the Multipositives

The original multipositive became damaged and had to be replaced. The original negative consisted of two negatives placed in contact against each other, one for the frame and one for the Queen's head and oval setting. When these two pieces of glass were placed together the position of the two was not exactly the same as when the first multipositive was made, resulting in a slight tilting of the portrait.

The second multipositive (Type B) was used for making cylinder 46 which was employed for No. S53 and the third multipositive (Type C) was used for all later cylinder numbers, i.e. Nos. 49 onwards.

Multipositive A was used for the booklets listed under Nos. S53, S55, S57, S59, S61/2 and S65, and, in consequence, stamps from these sections showing multipositive A and upright watermark are worth the same as inverted watermark varieties from booklets

A   B   C

Type A. At the shoulder lines above "E" of "POSTAGE" the line dividing the light from the dark material of the dress, if projected, runs level with the top of the two diagonal lines of the ribbon on the wreath.
Type B. The line runs between the first and second diagonal line of the ribbon.
Type C. The line runs level with the first diagonal line of the ribbon.

These are not listed as separate varieties because the stamps printed from the cylinders made from the three variations in the multipositives differed in other respects. It was, however, a most interesting development which also applied to the 3d. value.

1952 (DECEMBER 5). 2½d. WATERMARK TUDOR CROWN, TYPE W.22. TYPE I

			Mint	Used
S50 (=S.G.519)	2½d.	Carmine-red	15	15
	a.	Watermark sideways (15.11.54)	7·00	8·00
	b.	Broken value circle (Cyl. 8 No dot, R. 20/2)	7·50	
	c.	Extended broken top of diadem (Cyl. 16 Dot, R. 20/5)	7·50	
	d.	Frame retouch (Sideways coil, Roll 7)	15·00	

Stamps with sideways watermark are from M coils with sideways delivery.

S50*b*   S50*c*   S50*d*, S52*e*, S56*ba*, S56*da*

Cylinder Numbers (Blocks of Six)

Perforation Type A (E/I)

Cyl. No.		No dot	Dot	Cyl. No.		No dot	Dot
2	. . . .	2·50	2·50	16	. . . .	2·50	2·50
4	. . . .	2·50	2·50	17	. . . .	2·50	2·50
5	. . . .	2·50	2·50	18	. . . .	2·50	2·50
6	. . . .	2·50	2·50	19	. . . .	2·50	2·50
7	. . . .	2·50	2·50	22	. . . .	2·50	2·50
8	. . . .	10·00*	2·50	23	. . . .	2·50	2·50
9	. . . .	2·50	2·50	24	. . . .	2·50	2·50
10	. . . .	2·50	2·50	25	. . . .	4·00	4·00
11	. . . .	2·50	2·50	27	. . . .	2·50	2·50
12	. . . .	2·50	2·50				
13	. . . .	4·00	4·00	Perforation Type B (I/P no dot) and C (F/P dot)			
14	. . . .	2·50	2·50	14	. . . .	9·00	9·00
15	. . . .	2·50	2·50	24	. . . .	9·00	9·00

Minor Constant Sheet Flaws

Multipositive flaws
No dot   1/4 Red dot over left of crown (Th. A3)
           12/4 Red spot in leaf of shamrock (Th. G1)
           18/1 Diagonal scratch from chin to neck (Th. E3–F4)
Dot   11/9 White spot in R of E R (Cyls. 23, onwards)

Cylinder flaws
Cyl. 2.   16/1 Smudge line across top of REVENUE
Cyl. 8.   19/1 Red spot in 1 of fraction
Cyl. 10. 20/1 Extended top of 2 in value

Coils

Single pane cylinder L1 was used for the vertical delivery coils and L3 for the sideways delivery coils.
   Printed in continuous reels

	Code No.	Number in roll	Face value
(a) Vertical delivery. Watermark upright			
	F	960	£10
	U	1920	£20
(b) Sideways delivery. Watermark sideways			
	M	480	£5

Imprimatur from the National Postal Museum Archives

Imperforate, watermark Type W.22

Watermark upright

1953 (MAY). 2½d. WATERMARK TUDOR CROWN, TYPE W.22. TYPE II

				Mint	Used
S51 (=S.G.519b)	2½d.	Carmine-red	. . . .	1·25	1·25
	a.	Watermark inverted (5.53)	. . . .	30	75

This issue appeared from booklets only. See Section SB, Nos. SB80/a.

1955 (SEPTEMBER 28). 2½d. WATERMARK ST. EDWARD'S CROWN, TYPE W.23. TYPE I

			Mint	Used
S52 (=S.G.544)	2½d.	Carmine-red	20	25
	a.	Imperf. between stamp and top margin	£500	
	b.	Watermark sideways (23.3.56)	1·50	1·75
	c.	"b" for "D" in value (Cyl. 30 Dot, R. 19/11)	8·00	
	d.	White flaw below oval (Cyl. 44 Dot, R. 1/4)	5·00	
	e.	Frame retouch (sideways coil, Roll 7)	8·00	

Stamps with sideways watermark are from M coils with sideways delivery.

S52c

S53d

For illustration of No. S52e, see No. S50d.

Cylinder Numbers (Blocks of Six)

Perforation Type A (E/I)

Cyl. No.		No dot	Dot	Cyl. No.		No dot	Dot
22	....	3·25	3·25	43	....	3·25	3·25
24	....	3·25	£900	44	....	3·25	3·25
25	....	3·25	3·25	45	....	60·00	60·00
27	....	3·25	3·25				

Perforation Type E

Cyl. No.		No dot (AE/I)	Dot (E/I)
32	....	15·00	3·25**
37	....	15·00	3·25**

Perforation Type A (E/I) (continued):

Cyl. No.		No dot	Dot
30	....	3·25	3·25
32	....	3·25	3·25
33	....	3·25	3·25
34	....	†	15·00
37	....	3·25	3·25
38	....	3·25	3·25
39	....	3·25	3·25
40	....	3·25	3·25
42	....	3·25	3·25

**Same price and appearance as perforation type A with extension holes in left margin.

In cylinder 42, both panes, the marginal arrows at the top and bottom were omitted at first, but added later.

Minor Constant Sheet Flaws

Multipositive flaws as for No. S50

Cylinder flaw
Cyl. 43 18/5 Red spot on Queen's lip (Th. D3)

Coils

Single pane cylinders L1 or L2 were used for the vertical delivery coils and L3 for the sideways delivery coils.

Printed in continuous reels

Code No.	Number in roll	Face value
(a) Vertical delivery. Watermark upright		
F	960	£10
U	1920	£20
(b) Sideways delivery. Watermark sideways		
M	480	£5

Imprimatur from the National Postal Museum Archives

Imperforate, watermark Type W.23

Watermark upright

1957.† 2½d. WATERMARK ST. EDWARD'S CROWN, TYPE W.23. TYPE II

				Mint	Used
S53 (=S.G.544b)	2½d.	Carmine-red		45	45
	a.	Tête-bêche (horiz. pair)		£2000	
	d.	Imperf. between stamp and top margin		£500	
	e.	Watermark inverted (9.55)		25	70

Cylinder Numbers (Blocks of Six)

Perforation Type A (E/I)

Cyl. No.		No dot	Dot
46	....	4·00	4·00

Imprimaturs from the National Postal Museum Archives

Imperforate, watermark Type W.23

Watermark upright
Watermark inverted
Tête-bêche pair

1957 (NOVEMBER 19). 2½d. WITH GRAPHITE LINES, TYPE S8. WMK. ST. EDWARD'S CROWN. TYPE II

				Mint	Used
S54 (=S.G.565)	2½d.	Carmine-red		8·50	7·00
	a.	Coil join (horiz. pr.)		30·00	

Cylinder Numbers (Blocks of Six)

Single pane cylinder

Cyl. No.	Perf. Type		No dot
49	B (I/P)		55·00
49	C (E/P)		55·00

Coil

Made up from sheets with sheet margin joins. Sideways delivery

Code No.	Number in roll	Face value
M	480	£5

Imprimatur from the National Postal Museum Archives

Imperforate, watermark Type W.23

Watermark upright

Quantity Issued   20,578,800

1959 (SEPTEMBER 15).† 2½d. WATERMARK CROWNS, TYPE W.24

A. Type II Cream Paper

				Mint	Used
S55	2½d.	Carmine-red		60	30
	a.	Tête-bêche (horiz. pair)		£4250	
	b.	Imperf. strip of 3			
	c.	Imperf. between stamp and bottom margin			
	d.	Watermark inverted (11.58)		3·75	1·50
	e.	State 1. Leaf and extra rose stem flaws (Cyl. 50 Dot, R. 9/4)		8·50	
	ea.	State 2. Extra rose stem. Leaf flaw retouched (Cyl 50 Dot, R. 9/4)		8·00	
	f.	White emblems (Cyl. 52 No dot, R. 12/4)		8·00	

B. Type I. Cream Paper (4 October 1961)   Mint   Used
S56   2½d.   Carmine-red . . . .   3·50   2·00
                 b.   Watermark sideways (10.11.60) . . . .   1·25   70
                 ba.   Imperf, strip of 6 . . . .
                 bb.   Frame retouch (Sideways coil, Roll 7) . . . .   9·00

C. Type I. Whiter Paper (30 October 1963)
S56c (=S.G.574e) 2½d.   Carmine-red   70   70
                 d.   Watermark sideways (3.8.62)   25   40
                 da.   Frame retouch (Sideways coil, Roll 7) . . . .   7·00

D. Type II. Whiter Paper (7 May 1962)
S57 (=S.G.574)   2½d.   Carmine-red   10   20
                 a.   Watermark inverted (29.7.62) . . . .   4·50   3·00
                 b.   Imperf. between stamp and top margin . . . .
                 c.   Watermark Crown to left (coils, 9.65 and booklets,
                        1.7.64)   70   1·25
                 d.   Watermark Crown to right   70   1·25
                 e.   State 2. Extra rose stem. Leaf flaw retouched (Cyl.
                        50 Dot, R. 9/4) . . . .   8·00
                 f.   Serif to "A" (Cyl. 55 No dot, R. 11/8) . . . .   7·00

E. Type II. Chalky Paper. Booklets only (15 July 1963)
S58 (=S.G.574k) 2½d.   Carmine-red   50   80
                 a.   Watermark inverted (15.7.63)   75   1·25

Imperf. stamps, No. S55b comes from a booklet with watermark upright and No. S56ba is from an M coil with sideways watermark.

Sideways watermark. Nos. S56b, S56d and S57c came from M coils with sideways delivery and Nos. S57c/d are from 2s. Holiday Booklets No. NR2.

For illustration of Nos. S56bb and S56da, see No. S50d. No. S56da is known in a second state showing a vertical line adjoining the right-hand frame not filled in with colour.

State 1. Triangular white flaw adjoining left leaf and extra stem to rose.
State 2. Later printings exist with the leaf flaw retouched (Nos S55ea, S57e, S61c, S62b, S63e).
State 3. Both flaws retouched (S65d).

S55e

S55f   Normal
Later retouched

S57f

Cylinder Numbers (Blocks of Six)

Type II. (No. S55) Cream Paper.

Perforation Type A (E/I)			Perforation Type B (I/P no dot) and C (E/P dot)		
Cyl. No.	No dot	Dot	Cyl. No.	No dot	Dot
50	4·75	4·75	50	8·00	8·00
51	4·75	4·75	51	8·00	8·00
52	4·75	4·75	52	7·50	7·50
53	4·75	4·75			
54	4·75	4·75			

Type I. (No. S56). Cream Paper

Perforation Type A (E/I)

	No dot	Dot
42	24·00	24·00

Perforation Type B (I/P no dot) and C (E/P dot)
Cream paper

42	£750	£750

Type II. (No. S57). Whiter Paper

Perforation Type A (E/I)

50	1·75	1·75
51	1·75	1·75
52	1·75	1·75
53	1·75	1·75
54	1·75	1·75
55	1·75	1·75
56	1·75	1·75

Type I. (No. S56c). Whiter Paper

Perforation Type A (E/I)

	No dot	Dot
42	5·75	5·75

Perforation Type A (E/I)

57	1·75	1·75
58	1·75	1·75
59	1·75	1·75

Perforation Type B (I/P no dot) and C (E/P dot)

51	7·00	7·00
52	7·00	7·00

Marginal arrows. In Type II these exist hand-engraved at left as well as photo-etched. Also sheets are known with the arrows omitted at bottom. On cylinder 55 the faint outline of the "V" shaped arrow is below rows 8/9 in addition to the etched arrow below vertical rows 6/7.

Minor Constant Sheet Flaws

Cyl. 42   1/4 Red spot over left of crown (Th. A3)
             12/4 Red spot in leaf of shamrock (Th. G1)
Cyl. 42.   4/1 Red and white dots in oval (Th. B2)
             5/8 Red dot in thistle (Th. G2)
             11/9 White spot in R of E R
             14/5 Slight retouch in forehead above Queen's right eye (Th. C2)
             16/3 White dot between thistle and leaf (Th. G2)
             17/2 Small white flaw on tail of R of E R
             18/10 Red dot between Queen's lip and nose (Th. D3). Later partially removed
             20/10 White flaw by oval at left (Th. D1–2)
Cyl. 50.   6/10 Background retouched behind P of POSTAGE and R of REVENUE
Cyl. 51.   7/5 Retouch to left of hair (Th. C2)
             9/6 White dot at bottom left of R of REVENUE
Cyl. 55.   11/8 Spur on A of POSTAGE (Th. G4)

Coils

Single pane cylinder L2 was used for the vertical delivery coils and cylinders L3 for sideways delivery Type I coils and L5 for Type II coils.

Printed in continuous reels

	Code No.	Number in roll	Face value	
(a) Vertical delivery. Watermark upright				
	F	960	£10	Type I. Cream or whiter paper
(b) Sideways delivery. Watermark sideways				
	M	480	£5	Type I. Cream or whiter paper
	M	480	£5	Type II. Whiter paper

Imprimaturs from the National Postal Museum Archives

Type II. Imperforate, watermark Type W.24. Cream or whiter paper

Watermark upright
Watermark inverted
Tête-bêche pair

1959. (JUNE 9). 2½d. WITH GRAPHITE LINES, TYPE S8. WATERMARK CROWNS. TYPE II

			Mint	Used
			10·00	10·00
S59 (=S.G.591)	2½d.	Carmine-red	10·00	10·00
	a.	Watermark inverted (21.8.59)	65·00	50·00

Cylinder Numbers (Blocks of Six)

Single pane cylinder

Cyl. No.	Perf. Type		No dot
49	B (I/P)	. . . .	75·00
49	C (E/P)	. . . .	75·00

Imprimaturs from the National Postal Museum Archives

Imperforate, watermark Type W.24

Watermark upright
Watermark inverted
Tête-bêche pair

Quantity Issued   10,012,800

1959 (NOVEMBER 18). 2½d. PHOSPHOR-GRAPHITE ISSUE. WATERMARK CROWNS. TYPE II

				Mint	Used
S60 (=S.G.606)	2½d.	Carmine-red	. . . .	22·00	18·00
	a.	One 6 mm. band at left or right (stamp with vert. margin)	. . . .	25·00	
	b.	One 8 mm. band	. . . .	£150	
	ba.	As *b* but 6 mm. band	. . . .		

No. S60 has two graphite lines (Type S9), on the back and two phosphor bands on the front, applied typo., which react green under the lamp.
    This phosphor-graphite value is known with St. Edward's Crown watermark Type W.23, but this was not officially issued.

Cylinder Numbers (Blocks of Six)

Single pane cylinder

Cyl. No.	Perf. Type		No dot
49	B (I/P)	. . . .	£160
49	C (E/P)	. . . .	£160

Imprimatur from the National Postal Museum Archives

Perf. 15 × 14, watermark Type W.24

Watermark upright

Quantity Issued   689,280

1960 (JUNE 22). 2½d. TWO PHOSPHOR BANDS REACTING GREEN. WMK. CROWNS. TYPE II

				Mint	Used
S61	2½d.	Carmine-red	. . . .	1·75	1·40
	a.	Watermark inverted (14.8.60)	. . . .	£170	£120
	b.	One broad band (wmk. upright)	. . . .	45·00	
	c.	State 2. Extra rose stem. Leaf flaw retouched (Cyl. 50 Dot, R. 9/4)	. . . .	8·00	

The bands were applied in photogravure.
For illustration of No. S61*c*, see No. S55*e*.

Cylinder Numbers (Blocks of Six)

Perforation Type B (I/P no dot) and C (E/P dot)

Cyl. No.		No dot	Dot
50	. . . .	14·00	14·00

Minor Constant Sheet Flaw

Cyl. 50.   6/10 Background retouch behind P of POSTAGE and R of REVENUE

Imprimaturs from the National Postal Museum Archives

Imperforate, watermark Type W.24

Watermark upright
Watermark inverted
Tête-bêche pair

1961 (JUNE 5). 2½d. PHOSPHOR BANDS REACTING BLUE. WATERMARK CROWNS.

			Mint	Used
A. Two 8 mm. Bands (applied photo.). Type II. Cream Paper				
S62	2½d.	Carmine-red	6·00	3·00
	a.	Watermark inverted (3.61)	£170	75·00
	b.	State 2. Extra rose stem. Leaf flaw retouched (Cyl. 50 Dot, R. 9/4)	10·00	

B. One Band at left (applied typo.). Type II. Cream Paper (4 October 1961)				
S63	2½d.	Carmine-red	4·00	4·00
	a.	Band applied photo. (3.11.61)	12·00	12·00
	b.	Watermark inverted (photo.) (3.62)	40·00	38·00
	c.	Error. Two bands (photo.)*	80·00	
	ca.	Error. Band (photo.) omitted in pair with one band at right	£150	
	d.	Error. Band (typo.) omitted in pair with one band at right	£180	
	e.	State 2. Extra rose stem. Leaf flaw retouched (Cyl. 50 Dot, R.9/4)	12·00	

C. One Band at left (applied typo.). Type I. Cream Paper (4 October 1961)				
S64 (=S.G.614*b*)	2½d.	Carmine-red	45·00	40·00
	b.	Error. Band omitted, in pair with one band at right .	£180	
	c.	Error. Two bands (typo.)*	90·00	

D. One Band at left (applied photo.). Type II. Whiter Paper (22 June 1962)				
S65 (=S.G.614*a*)	2½d.	Carmine-red	60	75
	a.	Band applied typo.	£225	90·00
	b.	Watermark inverted (3.6.63)	40·00	38·00
	d.	State 3. Rose stem and leaf flaws retouched (Cyl. 50 Dot, R, 9/4)	6·00	
	e.	Horiz. pair ex. pane. Band at right and one stamp missing phosphor		

*Two Band Errors. These can be identified by the distance between the bands. This is 12 mm. on No. S62, but 16 mm. on the two band errors, Nos. S63*c* and S64*c*. These two varieties have the 4 mm. left band applied in error over the vertical perforations at each side of the stamp.

E. Two Bands (applied photo.). Type II. Whiter Paper (20 September 1964)				
S66 (=S.G.614)	2½d.	Carmine-red	40	30
	a.	Bands applied typo.		
	b.	One 8 mm. band (photo.)	15·00	

No. S66 was a reissue of No. S62 but from cylinder 57 and on whiter paper. The shade is slightly more carmine. It was first released in error in the S.E. London area in September 1964 and then put on sale in Birmingham in December 1964 as electronic sorting machines were not in use there at that time. To prepare for the alteration in postal rates on 17 May 1965 when the 2½d. ceased to be the second class mail rate, it was released in the phosphor areas on 3 May 1965 in place of the single band stamps. However, as there was no longer a postal need for this value it was not reprinted.

For description of Nos. S62*b*, S63*e* and S65*d*, see illustration No S55*e*.

Cylinder Numbers (Blocks of Six)

Two bands (No. S62). Type II Cream paper. Perforation Type A (E/I)

Cyl. No.	No dot	Dot
50	40·00	40·00

One band at left. Type II. Cream paper

	Perforation Type A (E/I) Applied typo. (No. S63)			Perforation Type B (I/P no dot) or C (E/P dot) Applied photo. (No. S63a)	
50	. . . . 28·00	28·00	50	. . . . 85·00	85·00
			53	. . . . 85·00	85·00

One band at left. Type I. Cream paper. Perforation Type A (E/I)
Applied typo. (No. S64)

42	. . . . £300	£300

Type II. Whiter paper, Perforation Type A (E/I)

	One band. Applied photo. (No. S65)			One band. Applied typo. (No. S65a)	
51	. . . . 4·75	4·75	50	. . . . —	—
52	. . . . 4·75	4·75			
54	. . . . 4·75	4·75			
56	. . . . 4·75	4·75			
57	. . . . 4·75	4·75			

Two bands. Applied photo. (No. S66)

57	. . . . 3·25	3·25

Minor Constant Sheet Flaws

As recorded for Nos. S55/7

Imprimaturs from the National Postal Museum Archives

One band at left. Type II. Imperforate, watermark Type W.24. Cream or whiter paper

Watermark upright
Watermark inverted
Tête-bêche pair

1954–67 3d. Deep lilac, Type S2

Variations in the Multipositives

There are similar variations in the tilt of the portrait in the multipositives used as occurred in the 2½d. value (see notes and illustration at the beginning of the 2½d. list).

The second multipositive, corresponding to Type B, was used for cylinders 25 to 33 and the third multipositive, corresponding to Type C, was employed for cylinders 36 and 37. A fourth multipositive, also Type C, was introduced for cylinders 41 onwards.

1954 (JANUARY 18). 3d. WATERMARK TUDOR CROWN, TYPE W.22

			Mint	Used
S67 (=S.G.520)	3d.	Deep lilac	1·50	90
	a.	Imperf. between stamp and top margin	£500	
	b.	Coil join (horiz. pair)	4·00	
	c.	Coil join (vert. pair)	12·00	

See General Notes under Paper—this stamp exists on very thick paper for this issue. (*Price* £75 *mint*)

Cylinder Numbers (Blocks of Six)

Perforation Type A (E/I)			Perforation Type B (I/P no dot) and C (E/P dot)		
Cyl. No.	No dot	Dot	Cyl. No.	No dot	Dot
3	8·00	8·00	3	8·00	8·00

Minor Constant Sheet Flaws

Multipositive flaws
No dot   1/3 White scratch to bottom right of R of large E R (Th. A–B6)
Dot   9/8 Dark patch to left of central cross of tiara (Th. B3)

Coils

Made up from sheets with sheet margin joins. Watermark upright

Code No.	Number in roll	Face value	
C	960	£12	Vertical delivery
S	480	£6	Sideways delivery

Imprimatur from the National Postal Museum Archives

Imperforate, watermark Type W.22

Watermark upright

1956 (JULY 17). 3d. WATERMARK ST. EDWARD'S CROWN, TYPE W.23

			Mint	Used
S68 (=S.G.545)	3d.	Deep lilac	25	25
	a.	Tête-bêche (horiz. pair)	£2000	
	b.	Imperf. three sides (pair)	£1500	
	c.	Imperf. between stamp and bottom margin	£500	
	d.	Watermark inverted (1.10.57)	1·00	1·00
	e.	Watermark sideways (22.11.57)	18·00	17·00
	f.	Coil join (horiz. pair)	7·00	
	g.	Coil join (vert. pair)	14·00	
	h.	White flaw over Queen's eye (Cyl. 2 Dot, R. 13/7) . .	7·00	

Stamps with sideways watermark are from S coils with sideways delivery.

No. S68*b* comes from a partly perforated booklet pane of six. No complete panes showing this error have been recorded.

S68h

Cylinder Numbers (Blocks of Six)

Perforation Type A (E/I)

Cyl. No.	No dot	Dot	Cyl. No.	No dot	Dot
2	2·50	2·50	10	2·50	2·50
3	2·50	2·50	15	2·50	2·50
4	2·50	2·50	16	2·50	2·50
5	2·50	2·50	17	2·50	2·50
9	2·50	2·50			

Perforation Type B (I/P no dot) and C (E/P dot)

2	8·00	8·00	3	8·00	8·00

Perforation Type F (L) (I/E)

5	70·00	†

Marginal arrows:

"V" shaped, hand engraved at top and bottom

"W" shaped, photo-etched at both sides

Early printings from cylinder 2 had the "V" shaped arrow omitted from the bottom of the sheet on no dot and dot panes

(*Price for positional block showing arrow omitted £15 no dot £25 dot*)

Minor Constant Sheet Flaws

Multipositive flaws
No dot   1/3 White scratch to bottom right of R of large E R (Th. A–B6)
Dot   9/8 Dark patch to left of central cross of tiara (Th. B3)

Cylinder flaw
Cyl. 17   17/3 Coloured scratches through E of large E R (Th. A1)

Coils

(a) Made up from sheets with sheet margin joins. Watermark upright

Code No.	Number in roll	Face value	
C	960	£12	Vertical delivery
S	480	£6	Sideways delivery

(b) Printed in continuous reels. Double pane cylinders M1 or M2 were used for the vertical delivery coils and cylinder M9 for the sideways delivery coil.

Code No.	Number in roll	Face value
(a) Vertical delivery. Watermark upright		
C	960	£12
U	1920	£24
(b) Sideways delivery. Watermark sideways		
S	480	£6

Imprimaturs from the National Postal Museum Archives

Imperforate, watermark Type W.23

Watermark upright
Watermark inverted
Tête-bêche pair

1957 (NOVEMBER 19). 3d. WITH GRAPHITE LINES, TYPE S8. WMK. ST. EDWARD'S CROWN

			Mint	Used
S69 (=S.G.566)	3d.	Deep lilac	80	50
	a.	Coil join (horiz. pair)	2·50	

Cylinder Numbers (Blocks of Six)

Single pane cylinders

Cyl. No.	Perf. Type	No dot
7	B (I/P)	6·00
7	C (E/P)	6·00
11	B (I/P)	6·00
11	C (E/P)	6·00

Coils

Made up from sheets with sheet margin joins. Watermark upright

Code No.	Number in roll	Face value	
S	480	£6	Sideways delivery

Imprimatur from the National Postal Museum Archives

Imperforate, watermark Type W.23

Watermark upright

Quantities Issued   91,466,400

1958 (DECEMBER 8).†   3d. WATERMARK CROWNS, TYPE W.24

			Mint	Used
A. Cream Paper				
S70	3d.	Deep lilac	25	25
	c.	Imperf. between stamp and top margin	£325	
	d.	Watermark Crown to left (Coils, 24.10.58 and		
		booklets, 26.5.61)	1·25	75
	e.	Watermark inverted (11.58)	25	40
	f.	Watermark Crown to right (Booklets, 26.5.61)	1·25	65
	g.	Spot on "T" of "POSTAGE" (Cyl. 37 No dot,		
		R. 19/11)	5·00	
	h.	Phantom "R" (Cyl. 37 No dot, below R. 20/12) . . .	45·00	
	i.	Do. Retouch	12·00	
	j.	Phantom "R" (Cyl. 41 No dot, below R. 20/12) . . .	£350	
	k.	Do. First retouch	20·00	
	l.	Do.Second or third retouch	20·00	
B. Whiter Paper (30 April 1962)				
S71 (=S.G.575)	3d.	Deep lilac	10	20
	a.	Watermark Crown to left (Coils, 30.4.62 and		
		booklets, 5.6.62)	25	35
	b.	Watermark Crown to right (Booklets, 5.6.62)	25	35
	c.	Watermark inverted (16.7.62)	20	20
	d.	Experimental "T" watermark* (*marginal block of* 6) .	20·00	
	e.	Serif on "E" (Cyl. 68 Dot, R. 16/5)	5·00	
	f.	Flaw on "E" (R. 14/11 on Cyls. 60 No dot and others)	5·50	
	g.	White spur on thistle left of "P" (Cyl. 70 No dot,		
		R. 4/2)	3·50	

*In 1964 No. S71 was printed from Cylinder 70 no dot and dot on an experimental paper which is distinguished by an additional watermark letter "T" lying on its side, which occurs about four times in the sheet, usually in the side margins where it is easiest to see. It is difficult to see when it occurs on the stamps themselves. 48,000 sheets were issued.

Variations in the Multipositives. See the notes at the beginning of the 3d. list about the variations in the tilt of the portrait on the different multipositives used.

Tête-bêche. No. S70 exists *tête-bêche*, also separated by gutters. These are from booklet sheets which were not issued.

Imperforate. Examples of No. S71 are known imperforate; these come from uncut booklet sheets which were not issued.

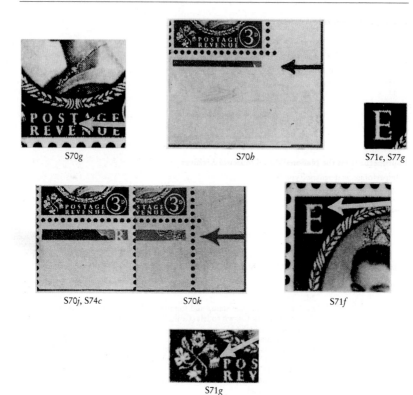

S70g

S70h

S71e, S77g

S70j, S74c

S70k

S71f

S71g

An incomplete masking of the stamp image beneath the marginal rule revealed an "R" on cyls. 37 and 41 no dot. It is more noticeable on the latter because of the wider marginal rule. The retouch on cyl. 37 is not easily identified. There is no trace of the "R" but the general appearance of that part of the marginal rule is uneven. However, the retouch can be confirmed in a positional block by the presence of the "Spot on T" variety on R. 19/11, No. S70g.

The "R" on cyl. 41 was retouched three times, the first being as illustrated here (No. S70k) and traces of the "R" can still be seen in the others.

Cylinder Numbers (Blocks of Six)

A. Cream Paper. (No. S70)

Perforation Type A (E/I)

Cyl. No.		No dot	Dot	Cyl. No.		No dot	Dot
15	. . . .	4·00	4·00	46	. . . .	3·25	3·25
16	. . . .	40·00	40·00	47	. . . .	3·25	3·25
22	. . . .	3·25	3·25	49	. . . .	3·25	3·25
25	. . . .	3·25	3·25	51	. . . .	3·25	3·25
26	. . . .	3·25	3·25	52	. . . .	3·25	3·25
28	. . . .	3·25	3·25	53	. . . .	3·25	3·25
29	. . . .	3·25	3·25	54	. . . .	3·25	3·25
30	. . . .	3·25	3·25	55	. . . .	3·25	3·25
31	. . . .	3·25	3·25	58	. . . .	3·25	3·25
33	. . . .	3·25	3·25	60	. . . .	3·25	3·25
36	. . . .	3·25	3·25	61	. . . .	3·25	3·25
37	. . . .	3·25	3·25	62	. . . .	3·25	3·25
41	. . . .	3·25	3·25	64	. . . .	3·25	3·25

Perforation Type B (I/P no dot) and C (E/P dot)

Cyl. No.		No dot	Dot	Cyl. No.		No dot	Dot
28	. . . .	5·00	5·00	52	. . . .	6·00	6·00
41*	. . . .	28·00	†	54	. . . .	6·00	6·00
51	. . . .	5·00	5·00				

*This has been seen Perf. Type B (I/P no dot) and may be an example of No. S74 with phosphor bands omitted.

Perforation Type H

		(E/I)	(P/I)			(E/I)	(P/I)
31		3·25**	30·00	37	. . . .	3·25**	35·00
36	. . . .	3·25**	30·00	41	. . . .	3·25**	35·00

**Same price and appearance as perforation type A with extension holes in left margin.

B. Whiter Paper. (No. S71)

Perforation Type   A (E/I)

Cyl. No.		No dot	Dot	Cyl. No.		No dot	Dot
51	. . . .	1·60	†	69	. . . .	1·60	1·60
52	. . . .	1·60	1·60	70	. . . .	1·60	1·60
54	. . . .	1·60	1·60	71	. . . .	1·60	1·60
58	. . . .	1·60	1·60	72	. . . .	1·60	1·60
60	. . . .	1·60	1·60	73	. . . .	1·60	1·60
61	. . . .	1·60	1·60	75	. . . .	1·60	1·60
62	. . . .	1·60	1·60	78	. . . .	1·60	1·60
63	. . . .	1·60	1·60	79	. . . .	1·60	1·60
64	. . . .	1·60	1·60	80	. . . .	1·60	1·60
66	. . . .	1·60	1·60	81	. . . .	1·60	1·60
67	. . . .	1·60	1·60	82	. . . .	1·60	1·60
68	. . . .	1·60	1·60				

Marginal arrows: These vary from cylinder to cylinder. The following combinations are known:—
   (a) All hand engraved. "V" shaped at top and bottom; "W" shaped at both sides
   (b) "V" shaped, hand engraved at top and bottom; "W" shaped, photo-etched at both sides
   (c) All photo-etched. "W" shaped at top and bottom and at both sides

Minor Constant Sheet Flaws

Multipositive flaws (Cyls. 15, 16 and 22 only)
No dot   1/3 White scratch to bottom right of R of large E R (Th. A-B6)
Dot   9/8 Dark patch to left of central cross of tiara (Th. B3)
Cylinder flaws
Cyl. 46.   20/2 White flaw on leaves of oval at left (Th. E-FI)
Cyl. 52.   17/9 White spur to circle around 3d. by D (Th. G6)
Cyl. 52.   18/2 Coloured line from Queen's hair to top of oval (Th. B2)
Cyl. 60.   4/11 Coloured flaw on thistle leaf (Th. G2)
Cyl. 63.   4/11 White flaw on leaf (Th. G2)
Cyl. 69.   5/10 White flaw on wreath (Th. F6)
Cyl. 70.   10/4 White flaw above PO of POSTAGE (Th. G3)
              10/11 White flaw on daffodil stem giving appearance of thick stalk (Th. G-H2)
              19/8 Coloured scratch from tiara to oval (Th. C5)

Coils

   Printed in continuous reels. Double pane cylinders M1 or M2 were used for the vertical delivery coils and cylinders M9, M10 and M11 for the sideways delivery coils. Cylinders M9 and M10 were used on cream paper and M10 and M11 on the whiter paper.

Code No.	Number in roll	Face value
(a) Vertical delivery. Watermark upright.Cream or whiter paper		
C	960	£12
U	1920	£24
AC	480	£6
AD	960	£12
(b) Sideways delivery. Watermark sideways. Cream or whiter paper		
S	480	£6

Imprimaturs from the National Postal Museum Archives

Imperforate, watermark Type W.24. Cream or whiter paper

Watermark upright
Watermark inverted
Tête-bêche pair

1958 (NOVEMBER 24). 3d. WITH GRAPHITE LINES, TYPE S8. WATERMARK CROWNS

			Mint	Used
S72 (=S.G.592)	3d.	Deep lilac	50	65
	a.	Watermark inverted (4.8.59)	45	75
	b.	Two lines at left (5.61)	£450	£380
	c.	Three lines	32·00	22·00
	d.	One line	£600	£200
	e.	Coil join (horiz. pair)	12·00	

The misplaced graphite lines (varieties *b*/*d*) came from sheets from cyls. 51 no dot and dot printed after the graphite line experiment had ended to use up residual stock of graphite-lined paper. (*Price for cylinder block of* 6, from £250.)

Examples of No. S72*b* have both graphite lines printed clear of the perforations. Stamps showing lines cutting the perforations are common and worth a fraction of the price of the genuine variety. This applies particularly to cylinder blocks.

Cylinder Numbers (Blocks of Six)

Single pane cylinder

Cyl. No.	Perf. Type		No dot
11	B (I/P)		6·00
11	C (E/P)		6·00

Coils

Printed in continuous reels. Double-pane cylinders M1 or M2 were used. Watermark upright.

	Code No.	Number in roll	Face value	
	C	960	£12	Vertical delivery

Made up from sheets with sheet margin joins. Watermark upright.

	S	480	£6	Sideways delivery

Imprimaturs from the National Postal Museum Archives

Imperforate, watermark Type W.24

Watermark upright
Watermark inverted
Tête-bêche pair

Quantity Issued   57,222,960

1959 (NOVEMBER 18). 3d. PHOSPHOR-GRAPHITE ISSUE. WATERMARK CROWNS

			Mint	Used
S73 (=S.G.607)	3d.	Deep lilac	10·00	8·00
	a.	One 6 mm. band at left or right (stamp with vert. margin)	17·00	

No. S73 has two graphite lines, Type S8, on the back and two phosphor bands on the front, applied typo., which react green under the lamp.

Cylinder Numbers (Blocks of Six)

Single pane cylinder

Cyl. No.	Perf. Type		No dot
11	B (I/P)		70·00
11	C (E/P)		70·00

Imprimatur from the National Postal Museum Archives

Perf. 15 × 14, watermark Type W.24

Watermark upright

Quantity Issued   4,625,040

1960 (JUNE 22). 3d. TWO PHOSPHOR BANDS REACTING GREEN. WMK. CROWNS

			Mint	Used
S74	3d.	Deep lilac	1·75	1·75
	a.	Watermark inverted (14.8.60)	1·75	1·75
	b.	One band (wmk. upright)	40·00	
	c.	Phantom "R" (Cyl. 41 No dot, below R. 20/12) . . .	40·00	
	d.	One 8 mm. band (wmk. inverted)		
	da.	As d but 6 mm. band		

The bands were applied in photogravure.

For illustrations of No. S74c, see No S70j.

Cylinder Numbers (Blocks of Six)

Perforation Type B (I/P no dot) and C (E/P dot)

Cyl. No.	No dot	Dot
41	14·00	14·00

1961 (JUNE 5).† 3d. PHOSPHOR BANDS REACTING BLUE. WATERMARK CROWNS

A. Two Bands. Cream Paper

			Mint	Used
S75	3d.	Deep lilac	1·25	1·25
	a.	Watermark inverted (3.61)	1·25	1·25
	b.	Watermark Crown to left (14.7.61)	3·00	3·00
	c.	Watermark Crown to right	3·00	3·00
	d.	One 8 mm. band (wmk. sideways)	28·00	

B. Two Bands. Whiter Paper (24 October 1962)†

			Mint	Used
S76 (=S.G.615)	3d.	Deep lilac	60	55
	a.	Watermark Crown to left (15.8.62)	2·50	1·75
	b.	Watermark Crown to right	2·50	1·75
	c.	Watermark inverted (25.9.62)	50	90
	d.	Error. One band on each stamp (horiz. pair)	£100	

The 8 mm. bands on *both* stamps of No. S76d prove that the bands were displaced for this issue in addition to No. S77 (see No. S77fa). *Price for single with one 8 mm. band, £45 mint.*

C. One Side Band*. Whiter Paper (29 April 1965)

			Mint	Used
S77	3d.	Deep lilac (side band at left)	2·75	2·50
	a.	Side band at right	2·75	2·50
	ab.	Nos. S77/a (horiz. pair)	7·00	5·00
	b.	Watermark Crown to left, band at left (16.8.65)	25·00	15·00
	c.	Watermark Crown to left, band at right	25·00	15·00
	d.	Watermark Crown to right, band at left	30·00	20·00
	e.	Watermark Crown to right, band at right	30·00	20·00
	f.	Error. Pair, left-hand stamp with phosphor omitted, right-hand stamp with one 8 mm. band	90·00	
	g.	Serif on "E" (Cyl. 68 Dot, R. 16/5)	10·00	

The bands were all applied in photogravure on the stamps with upright watermark and by typography on those with watermark sideways.

*The one side band stamps were produced by an 8 mm. band applied down alternate vertical rows of the sheet over the perforations so that alternate stamps have the band at left (No. S77) or right (No. S77a). In theory the width of the band on a single stamp should be 4 mm. but this will vary if the bands have not been perfectly positioned.

For illustration of No. S77g see No. S71e.

Cylinder Numbers (Blocks of Six)

Two bands (No. S75). Cream paper. Perforation Type B (I/P no dot) and C (E/P dot)

Cyl. No.	No dot	Dot	Cyl. No.	No dot	Dot
52	8·00	8·00	60	8·00	8·00

Whiter paper. Perforation Type A (E/I)

Two bands. (No. S76)			One side band. (No. S77)		
60	5·00	5·00	67	24·00	24·00
61	5·00	5·00	68	24·00	24·00
62	5·00	5·00	71	24·00	24·00
64	5·00	5·00	72	24·00	24·00
67	5·00	5·00			
71	5·00	5·00			

Minor Constant Sheet Flaws

Cyl. 52   17/9 White spur to circle around 3d. by D (Th. G6)
Cyl. 52.   18/2 Coloured line from Queen's hair to top of oval (Th. B2)
Cyl. 60.   4/11 Coloured flaw on thistle leaf (Th. G2)

Coils

Double pane cylinders M1 or M2 were used. Watermark upright.
Two bands. Vertical delivery in continuous reels. Cream or whiter paper.

Code No.	Number in roll	Face value
AC	480	£6
AD	960	£12
U	1920	£24

One side band (left or right). Vertical delivery in continuous reels. Whiter paper

AC	480	£6
AD	960	£12
U	1920	£24

Imprimaturs from the National Postal Museum Archives

Two Bands. Imperforate, watermark Type W.24. Cream or whiter paper

Watermark upright
Watermark inverted
Tête-bêche pair

One Side Band. Imperforate, watermark Type W.24. Whiter paper

Watermark sideways
Vertical *tête-bêche* pair with sideways watermark

1965 (AUGUST 13). 3d. PHOSPHOR BANDS REACTING VIOLET. WATERMARK CROWNS

A. One Side Band*

			Mint	Used
S78 (=S.G.615c)	3d.	Deep lilac (side band at left)	60	70
	a.	Side band at right	60	55
	ab.	Nos. S78/a (horiz. pair)	1·25	1·25
	b.	One 8 mm. band (wmk. sideways)	10·00	
	ba.	Pair, left-hand stamp with phosphor omitted, right-hand stamp with one band (wmk. upright) (*pair*) . . .	45·00	
	bb.	One 8 mm. band (wmk. upright)	15·00	
	c.	Watermark Crown to left, band at left (10.65)	5·50	5·00
	d.	Watermark Crown to left, band at right	5·50	5·00
	e.	Watermark Crown to right, band at left	5·50	5·00
	f.	Watermark Crown to right, band at right	5·50	5·00
	g.	Watermark inverted (band at left) (2.67)†	50·00	45·00
	h.	Watermark inverted (band at right)†	2·25	2·25
	ha.	Nos. S78g/h (horiz. pair)†	60·00	

B. One 4 mm. Centre Band (8 December 1966)			Mint	Used
S79 (=S.G.615e)	3d.	Deep Lilac	40	45
	a.	Watermark sideways (19.6.67)	70	50
	b.	Watermark inverted (8.67)	2·25	2·25

C. Two 9·5 mm. Bands. *Se-tenant* 2s. Booklets only (November 1967)				
S80 (=S.G.615b)	3d.	Deep lilac (Watermark Crown to left)	1.75	1.75
	a.	Watermark Crown to right	1·75	1·75
	b.	One 9·5 mm. band (wmk. sideways)	20·00	

The bands applied in photogravure, except for stamps with sideways watermark where they were applied by typography or flexography.

*The one side band stamps were produced by an 8 mm. band applied down alternate vertical rows of the sheet over the perforations so that alternate stamps have the band at left (No. S78) or right (No. S78a). In theory the width of the band on a single stamp should be 4 mm. but this will vary if the bands have not been perfectly positioned. In addition, one side band stamps with *sideways watermark* were produced by applying a 9·5 mm. band over the perforations but these only came in the April 1967 and October 1967 2s. Booklets (N28p(b) and N30p(b)) *se-tenant* with the 1d. value. As it is not possible to distinguish these from the 8 mm. bands (Nos. S78c/f) *in singles*, the complete panes only are listed under No. SB50.

†*Inverted watermark.* Nos. S78g/h only come from the 10s. Booklet of February 1967 (X15p(a/b)). Each pane, No. SB103a comprises two stamps with band at left and four stamps with band at right.

Sideways watermark. Nos. S78c/f come from 2s. Booklets N22p(b), N23p(b), N24p/28p(a), N29p/30p(a), N31p(c) and N32p(c). No. S79a comes from S coils with sideways delivery and Nos. S80/a come from 2s. Booklets N31p(a/b) and N32p(a/b).

Cylinder Numbers (Blocks of Six)

Perforation Type A (E/I)

One side band. (No. S78)				One centre band. (No. S79)		
Cyl. No.		No dot	Dot	Cyl. No.	No dot	Dot
67	. . . .	4·75	4·75	78	3·50	3·50
71	. . . .	4·75	4·75	79	3·50	3·50
72	. . . .	4·75	4·75	81	3·50	3·50
81	. . . .	4·75	4·75	82	3·50	3·50
82	. . . .	4·75	4·75			

Coils

Double pane cylinder M12 was used for the vertical delivery coils and cylinder M11 for the sideways delivery coils.

(a) One side band. Vertical delivery printed in continuous reels with the watermark upright

Code No.	Number in roll	Face value
AC	480	£6
AD	960	£12
U	1920	£24

(b) One centre band. Printed in continuous reels

	Code No.	Number in roll	Face value
(a) Vertical delivery. Watermark upright			
	AC	480	£6
	AD	960	£12
(b) Sideways delivery. Watermark sideways			
	S	480	£6

1953–67 4d. Ultramarine, Type S3

1953 (NOVEMBER 2). 4d. WATERMARK TUDOR CROWN, TYPE W.22

				Mint	Used
S81 (=S.G.521)	4d.	Ultramarine		3·25	1·25
	a.	Coil join (horiz. pair)		14·00	
	b.	Dotted "R" (Cyl. 1 No dot, R. 10/8		15·00	

The blue dot is of varying size and was eventually touched out on the St. Edward's Crown watermark.

S81*b*, S82*c*

Cylinder Numbers (Blocks of Six)

Perforation Type A (E/I)			Perforation Type B (I/P no dot) and C (E/P dot)		
Cyl. No.	No dot	Dot	Cyl. No.	No dot	Dot
1	25·00	25·00	1	28·00	28·00

Minor Constant Sheet Flaws

Cyl.1   1/4 Retouch on cheek left of ear (Th. D4)

       16/9 Scar on neck. This was later the object of a major retouch (see No. S82*d*) but the original flaw is not available for illustrating and listing here

Coil

Made up from sheets with sheet margin joins. Sideways delivery with the watermark upright

Code No.	Number in roll	Face value
H	480	£8

Imprimatur from the National Postal Museum Archives

Imperforate, watermark Type W.22

Watermark upright

1955 (NOVEMBER 14). 4d. WATERMARK ST. EDWARD'S CROWN, TYPE W.23

				Mint	Used
S82 (=S.G.546)	4d.	Ultramarine		1·25	45
	a.	Coil join (vert. pair)		12·00	
	b.	Coil join (horiz. pair)		10·00	
	c.	Dotted "R" (Cyl. 1 No dot, R. 10/8		9·00	
	d.	Retouched neck (Cyl. 1 No dot, R. 16/9)		8·00	

For illustration of No. S82*c*, see No. S81*b*.

This is the major retouch of the flaw described in this position on No. S81 under Minor Constant Sheet Flaws. The blue line joining the Queen's neck to the frame is also constant.

S82*d*, S83*c*

Cylinder Numbers (Blocks of Six)

	Perforation Type A (E/I)				Perforation Type B (I/P no dot) and C (E/P dot)		
Cyl. No.		No dot	Dot		Cyl. No.	No dot	Dot
1	. . . .	15·00	15·00		1	10·00	10·00
3	. . . .	17·00	17·00				

Minor Constant Sheet Flaws

Cyl. 1   1/4 Retouch on cheek left of ear (Th. D4)
            16/9 Scar on neck before retouch as No. S82d

Coils

Made up from sheets with sheet margin joins with the watermark always upright

Code No.	Number in roll	Face value	
A	960	£16	Vertical delivery
H	480	£8	Sideways delivery

Imprimatur from the National Postal Museum Archives

Imperforate, watermark Type W.23

Watermark upright

1958 (OCTOBER 29). 4d. WATERMARK CROWNS, TYPE W.24

A. Ultramarine. Cream Paper

			Mint	Used
S83	4d.	Ultramarine	1·60	90
	a.	Coil join (vert. pair)	10·00	
	b.	Coil join (horiz. pair)	10·00	
	c.	Retouched neck (Cyl 1 No dot, R. 16/9)	6·00	
	d.	Imperf. between stamp and top margin	£450	

B. Ultramarine. Whiter Paper (18 October 1962)

S84 (=S.G.576)	4d.	Ultramarine	45	35
	a.	Coil join (vert. pair)	9·00	
	b.	Coil join (horiz. pair)	9·00	

C. Deep Ultramarine†. Whiter Paper (28 April 1965)

S85 (=S.G.576a)	4d.	Deep ultramarine	15	15
	b.	Double impression	£1800	
	c.	Imperf. between stamp and top margin	£190	
	d.	Wmk. Crown to left (Coils, 31.5.65 and booklets,		
		16.8.65)	70	55
	e.	Watermark inverted (21.6.65)	60	50
	f.	Watermark Crown to right (Booklets only, 16.8.65) .	70	55

†This "shade" was brought about by making more deeply etched cylinders from a new multipositive, resulting in apparent depth of colour in parts of the design but there is no difference in the colour
of the ink. The change was made deliberately and coincided with the change in the first class letter rate
from 3d. to 4d. on 17 May 1965.

Examples of No. S85b were the result of slight paper movement during printing rather than the sheet
actually being presented twice in the press.

For illustration of No. S83c, see No. S82d.

Cylinder Numbers (Blocks of Six)

Perforation Type A (E/I)

(a) Ultramarine

	Cream Paper. (No. S83)				Whiter Paper. (No. S84)		
Cyl. No.		No dot	Dot		Cyl. No.	No dot	Dot
1	. . . .	12·00	12·00		8	4·50	4·50
6	. . . .	12·00	12·00				
8	. . . .	12·00	12·00				

(b) Deep Ultramarine, Whiter paper. (No. S85)

12	. . . .	2·10	2·10	23	. . . .	2·10	2·10
13	. . . .	2·10	2·10	25	. . . .	2·10	2·10
16	. . . .	2·10	2·10	26	. . . .	2·10	2·10
18	. . . .	2·10	2·10	27	. . . .	2·10	2·10
20	. . . .	2·10	2·10				

Minor Constant Sheet Flaws

Cyl. 1   1/4 Retouch on cheek left of ear (Th. D4)
                10/8 Darker shading to right of and below large R caused by retouching the dot variety
Cyl. 18   18/11 Two patches of retouching by frame at left (Th. C1)

Coils

(a) Ultramarine. Cream or whiter paper
Made up from sheets with sheet margin joins. Watermark upright

Code No.	Number in roll	Face value	
A	960	£16	Vertical delivery
H	480	£8	Sideways delivery

(b) Deep ultramarine
    Printed in continuous reels. It is believed that cylinder P1 was used for the vertical delivery coil and that it was a double pane cylinder but that cylinder P2 was used for the sideways delivery coil and that this was a single pane cylinder.

(a) Vertical delivery. Watermark upright
A   960   £16
(b) Sideways delivery. Watermark sideways
H   480   £8

Imprimatur from the National Postal Museum Archives

Imperforate, watermark Type W.24. Cream or white paper

Watermark upright

1959 (APRIL 29). 4d. WITH GRAPHITE LINES, TYPE S8. WATERMARK CROWNS

			Mint	Used
S86 (=S.G.593)	4d.	Ultramarine	5·50	5·00
	a.	Two lines at left	£1800	

The misplaced graphite lines listed as No. S86a result in two lines at left (with the left line down the perforations) and traces of a third line down the opposite perforations.

Cylinder Numbers (Blocks of Six)

Perforation Type A (E/I)

Cyl. No.	No dot	Dot
6	40·00	40·00

Imprimatur from the National Postal Museum Archives

Imperforate, watermark Type W.24

Watermark upright

Quantity Issued   6,891,600

1959 (NOVEMBER 18). 4d. PHOSPHOR-GRAPHITE ISSUE. WATERMARK CROWNS

			Mint	Used
S87 (=S.G.608)	4d.	Ultramarine	20·00	16·00
	a.	One 6 mm. band at left or right (stamp with vert.		
		margin)	15·00	

No. S87 has two graphite lines (Type S8) on the back and two phosphor bands on the front, applied typo., which react green under the lamp.

Cylinder Numbers (Blocks of Six)

Perforation Type A (E/I)

Cyl. No.	No dot	Dot
6	£140	£120

Imprimatur from the National Postal Museum Archives

Perf. 15 × 14, watermark Type W.24

Watermark upright

Quantity Issued   490,560

1960 (JUNE 22). 4d. TWO PHOSPHOR BANDS REACTING GREEN. WATERMARK CROWNS

			Mint	Used
S88	4d.	Ultramarine	9·00	8·00

The bands were applied in photogravure.

Cylinder Numbers (Blocks of Six)

Perforation Type B (I/P no dot) and C (E/P dot)

Cyl. No.	No dot	Dot
8	70·00	70·00

Imprimatur from the National Postal Museum Archives

Imperforate, watermark Type W.24

Watermark upright

1961 (JUNE 5). 4d. TWO PHOSPHOR BANDS REACTING BLUE. WATERMARK CROWNS

A. Ultramarine. Cream Paper			Mint	Used
S89 (=S.G.616)	4d.	Ultramarine	3·50	3·50
	a.	Error. One 8 mm. band	£150	

B. Deep Ultramarine †. Whiter Paper (28 April 1965)				
S90	4d.	Deep ultramarine	70	60
	b.	Watermark inverted (21.6.65)	1·40	1·00
	c.	Watermark Crown to left (16.8.65)	2·00	2·00
	d.	Watermark Crown to right (16.8.65)	2·00	2·00
	e.	One broad band (wmk. sideways)	50·00	

The bands were applied in photogravure on the stamps with upright watermark and by typography on those with watermark sideways.

†The note below No. S85 concerning deep ultramarine applies here.

Cylinder Numbers (Blocks of Six)

(a) Ultramarine. (No. S89)

Perforation Type B (I/P no dot) and C (E/P dot)

Cyl. No.	No dot	Dot	Cyl. No.	No dot	Dot
8	28·00	28·00			

(b) Deep ultramarine. (No. S90)

Performation Type A (E/I)

	No dot	Dot		No dot	Dot
12	5·75	5·75	18	5·75	5·75
13	5·75	5·75	20	5·75	5·75

Minor Constant Sheet Flaw

Cyl. 18   18/11 Two patches of retouching by frame at left (Th. C1)

1965 (AUGUST 13). 4d. TWO 8 mm. PHOSPHOR BANDS REACTING VIOLET. WMK. CROWNS

			Mint	Used
S91	4d.	Deep ultramarine	60	60
	a.	Watermark inverted (9.65)	45	45
	b.	Wmk. Crown to left (photo.) (1.67)	60	60
	c.	Wmk. Crown to right (photo.) (1.67)	60	60
	d.	One 8 mm. band (photo.) (wmk. sideways)	10·00	
	e.	Wmk. Crown to left (typo.) (10.65)	15·00	
	f.	Wmk. Crown to right (typo.) (10.65)	15·00	

The bands were applied in photogravure, except for the sideways watermark stamps from 2s. Booklets which also had them applied by typography.

No. S91 is known with a very wide "phantom" band in addition to the normal two bands. This was probably due to a weak mixture of the phosphor ink, which leaked under the doctor blade. This occurred in the first and second vertical rows in a sheet.

Cylinder Numbers (Blocks of Six)

Perforation Type A (E/I)

Cyl. No.		No dot	Dot	Cyl. No.		No dot	Dot
18	. . . .	5·00	5·00	20	. . . .	5·00	5·00

Minor Constant Sheet Flaw

Cyl. 18   18/11 Two patches of retouching by frame at left (Th. C1)

1967 (EARLY). 4d. TWO 9·5 mm. PHOSPHOR BANDS REACTING VIOLET. WMK. CROWNS

			Mint	Used
S92 (=S.G.616*a*)	4d.	Deep ultramarine	25	25
	a.	Watermark inverted (2.67)	40	40
	b.	Wmk. Crown to left Booklets, 4.67 and Coils, 24.4.67)	35	50
	c.	Wmk. Crown to right (Booklets, 4.67)	35	50
	e.	One 9·5 mm. band (wmk. sideways)	12·00	

The bands were applied in photogravure, except for the 2s. Booklets which had them flexo.

Cylinder Numbers (Blocks of Six)

Perforation Type A (**E/I**)

Cyl. No.		No dot	Dot	Cyl. No.		No dot	Dot
16	. . . .	2·75	2·75	26	. . . .	2·75	2·75
18	. . . .	2·75	2·75	27	. . . .	2·75	2·75
23	. . . .	2·75	2·75				

Minor Constant Sheet Flaw

Cyl. 18   18/11 Two patches of retouching by frame at left (Th. C1)

Coil

Printed in continuous reels. It is believed that cylinder P2 was used and that it was a single pane cylinder.

Sideways delivery. Watermark sideways

Code No.	Number in roll	Face value
H	480	£8

1959–66 4½d. Chestnut, Type S3

1959 (FEBRUARY 9). 4½d. WATERMARK CROWNS, TYPE W.24

A. Cream Paper

			Mint	Used
S93	4½d.	Chestnut	55	55

B. Whiter Paper (29 May 1962)

S94 (=S.G.577)	4½d.	Chestnut	10	25
	a.	Phantom frame (Cyl. 8 No dot below R. 20/12) . . .	7·50	

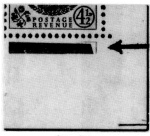

S94*a*, S98*c*

An incomplete marginal rule revealed a right-angled shaped frame-line on cylinder 8 no dot below R. 20/12. Later retouched on No. S98.

Cylinder Numbers (Blocks of Six)

Perforation Type A (E/I)

Cream paper. (No. S93)			Whiter paper. (No. S94)		
Cyl. No.	No dot	Dot	Cyl. No.	No dot	Dot
2	7·50	7·50	7	1·75	1·75
6	4·50	4·50	8	1·75	1·75
7	4·50	4·50			

Minor Constant Sheet Flaws

Multipositive flaw:

No dot   5/6 Pale top half of rose in bottom left corner (Th. F1–2)

Cylinder flaws

Cyl. 2	1/9 White spot on cheek level with mouth (Th. D3)
	1/11 Break in bottom frame line at left corner
	5/5 Three dots to right of curve in S of POSTAGE
	10/8 White dot in laurel oval (Th. E6)
	16/2 Dotted line in bottom right corner (Th. H6)
	19/10 White dot on tail of R of E R
Cyl. 6	5/5 Nick in laurel oval at left (Th. D1)
	16/9 Extra jewel on dress above O of POSTAGE
Cyl. 7	18/6 White flaw in thistle flower (Th. G2)

Imprimatur from the National Postal Museum Archives

Imperforate, watermark Type W.24. Cream or whiter paper

Watermark upright

1959 (JUNE 3). 4½d. WITH GRAPHITE LINES, TYPE S8. WATERMARK CROWNS

			Mint	Used
S95 (=S.G.594)	4½d.	Chestnut	6·50	5·00

Cylinder Numbers (Blocks of Six)

Perforation Type A (E/I)

Cyl. No.	No dot	Dot
6	45·00	45·00

Minor Constant Sheet Flaw

Cyl. 6   5/6 Pale top half of rose in bottom left corner (Th. F1–2)

Imprimatur from the National Postal Museum Archives

Imperforate, watermark Type W.24

Watermark upright

Quantity Issued   5,388,480

1959 (NOVEMBER 18). 4½d. PHOSPHOR-GRAPHITE ISSUE. WATERMARK CROWNS

			Mint	Used
S96 (=S.G.609)	4½d.	Chestnut	30·00	20·00
	a.	One 6 mm. band at left or right (stamp with vert. margin)	42·00	
	b.	One 9·5 mm. band		

This has two graphite lines (Type S8), on the back and two phosphor bands on the front, applied typo., which react green under the lamp.

Cylinder Numbers (Blocks of Six)

Perforation Type A (E/I)

Cyl. No.	No dot	Dot
6	£210	£210

Minor Constant Sheet Flaw

Cyl. 6   5/6 Pale top half of rose in bottom left corner (Th. F1–2)

Imprimatur from the National Postal Museum Archives

Perf. 15 × 14, watermark Type W.24

Watermark upright

Quantity Issued   696,000

1961 (SEPTEMBER 13). 4½d. TWO PHOSPHOR BANDS REACTING BLUE. WATERMARK CROWNS

A. Cream Paper. Bands by Typography

			Mint	Used
S97	4½d.	Chestnut	3·50	2·50
	a.	One 6 mm. band at left or right (stamp with vert. margin)	10·00	
	b.	One 8 mm. band	15·00	
	ba.	As b but 6 mm. band	20·00	
	c.	Bands applied photo. (3.4.62)	22·00	15·00

B. Whiter Paper. Bands applied in Photogravure (24 January 1963)

			Mint	Used
S98 (=S.G.616b)	4½d.	Chestnut	25	30
	a.	Bands applied typo. (6.65)	2·00	2·00
	ab.	One 6 mm. band at left or right (stamp with vert. margin)	10·00	
	b.	One 8 mm. band (typo.)	15·00	
	ba.	As b but 6 mm. band	20·00	
	c.	Phantom frame (Cyl. 8, below R. 20/12)	15·00	

For illustration of No. S98c., see No. S94a.

Cylinder Numbers (Blocks of Six)

A. Cream Paper

Applied typo. (No. S97)
Perforation Type A (E/I)

Cyl. No.	No dot	Dot
7	30·00	30·00

Applied photo. (No. S97c)
Perforation Type B (I/P no dot) and C (E/P dot)

Cyl. No.	No dot	Dot
7	£140	£140

B. Whiter Paper

	Applied photo. (No. S98) Perforation Type A (E/I)				Applied typo. (No. S98a) Perforation Type A (E/I)	
7	. . . .	3·00	3·00	8	. . . . 20·00	20·00
8	. . . .	2·50	2·50			

Minor Constant Sheet Flaws

Cyls. 7/8   5/6 Pale top half of rose in bottom left corner (Th. F1–2)
Cyl. 7   18/6 White flaw in thistle flower (Th. G2). Later retouched

Imprimatur from the National Postal Museum Archives

Imperforate, watermark Type W.24. Cream or whiter paper
Watermark upright

1953–67 5d. Brown, Type S4

1953 (JULY 6). 5d. WATERMARK TUDOR CROWN, TYPE W.22

			Mint	Used
S99 (=S.G.522)	5d.	Brown	75	3·50
	a.	Spot by "E" of "POSTAGE" (No dot, R. 4/8)	6·00	
	b.	Spot on daffodil (No dot, R. 10/12)	6·00	
	c.	Neck retouch (Cyl. 1 Dot, R. 2/12)	6·00	

S99/103a   S99/103b   S99/103c

These two varieties occur on the multipositive

Cylinder Numbers (Blocks of Six)

Perforation Type A (E/I)

Cyl. No.	No dot	Dot
1	7·50	7·50

Imprimatur from the National Postal Museum Archives

Imperforate, watermark Type W.22

Watermark upright

1955 (SEPTEMBER 21). 5d. WATERMARK ST. EDWARD'S CROWN, TYPE W.23

			Mint	Used
S100 (=S.G.547)	5d.	Brown	6·00	6·00
	a.	Spot by "E" of "POSTAGE" (No dot, R. 4/8)	12·00	
	b.	Spot on daffodil (No dot, R. 10/12)	12·00	
	c.	Neck retouch (Cyl. 1 Dot, R. 2/12)	12·00	

For illustrations of Nos. S100a/c, see Nos. S99a/c.

Cylinder Numbers (Blocks of Six)

Perforation Type A (E/I)

Cyl. No.	No dot	Dot
1	45·00	45·00

Imprimatur from the National Postal Museum Archives

Imperforate, watermark Type W.23

Watermark upright

1958 (NOVEMBER 10). 5d. WATERMARK CROWNS, TYPE W.24

A. Cream Paper

			Mint	Used
S101	5d.	Brown	3·00	1·50
	a.	Spot by "E" of "POSTAGE" (No dot, R. 4/8)	7·50	
	b.	Spot on daffodil (No dot, R. 10/12)	7·50	
	c.	Neck retouch (Cyl. 1 Dot, R. 2/12)	7·50	

B. Whiter Paper (1 May 1963)   Mint   Used
S102 (=S.G.578)   5d.   Brown   40   30
                          a.   Spot by "E" of "POSTAGE" (No dot, R. 4/8) . . . .   4·00
                          b.   Spot on daffodil (No dot, R. 10/12) . . . .   4·00
                          c.   Neck retouch (Cyl. 1 Dot, R. 2/12) . . . .   3·50

    For illustrations of Nos. S101/2a, S101/2b and S101/2c, see Nos. S99a, S99b and S99c respectively.

Cylinder Numbers (Blocks of Six)

Cream Paper. (No. S101) Perforation Type A (E/I)			Whiter Paper. (No. S102) Perforation Type A (E/I)		
Cyl. No.	No dot	Dot	Cyl. No.	No dot	Dot
1	20·00	20·00	1	3·00	3·00
2	20·00	20·00			

Perforation Type F(L)* (I/E no dot and P/E dot)
    1* . . . .
    *This is probably No. S103 but with phosphor omitted.

Imprimatur from the National Postal Museum Archives

Imperforate, watermark Type W.24. Cream or whiter paper

Watermark upright

1967 (JUNE 9). 5d. TWO 9·5 mm. PHOSPHOR BANDS REACTING VIOLET. WMK. CROWNS

                                                 Mint   Used
S103 (=S.G.616c)   5d.   Brown   25   35
                          a.   Spot by "E" of "POSTAGE" (No dot, R. 4/8) . . . .   4·50
                          b.   Spot on daffodil (No dot, R. 10/12) . . . .   4·50
                          c.   Neck retouch (Cyl. 1 Dot, R. 2/12) . . . .   4·50

The bands were applied in photogravure.
For illustrations of Nos. S103a/c, see Nos S99a/c.

Cylinder Numbers (Blocks of Six)

Perforation Type A (E/I)			Perforation Type F (L)*		
Cyl. No.	No dot	Dot	Cyl. No.	No dot	Dot
1	3·00	3·00		(I/E)	(P/E)
			1	3·00	3·00

1954–67 6d. Purple, Type S4

1954 (JANUARY 18). 6d. WATERMARK TUDOR CROWN, TYPE W.22

				Mint	Used
S104 (=S.G.523)	6d.	Reddish purple		4·00	1·00
	a.	Imperforate at top and sides (pair)		£750	
	b.	Imperf. between stamp and bottom margin		£425	
	c.	Coil join (vert. pair)		15·00	

Cylinder Numbers (Blocks of Six)

Single pane cylinder

Perforation Type B		Perforation Type C		Perforation Type F (L)	
Cyl. No.	No dot (I/P)	Cyl. No.	No dot (E/P)	Cyl. No.	No. dot (I/E)
1 . . . . 32·00		1 . . . . 32·00		1 . . . . 32·00	

Minor Constant Sheet Flaws

Multipositive flaws used for cylinders 1, 2 and 3
8/8 Small purple flaw joining C of PENCE to inner frame line
19/6 Small dark flaw on daffodil stem (Th. G2)
20/3 Coloured dot in top leaf of thistle (Th. A6)

Coil

Made up from sheets with sheet margin joins. Vertical delivery with the watermark upright

Code No.	Number in roll	Face value
J	480	£12

Imprimatur from the National Postal Museum Archives

Imperforate, watermark Type W.22

Watermark upright

1955 (DECEMBER 20). 6d. WATERMARK ST. EDWARD'S CROWN, TYPE W.23

A. Reddish Purple

				Mint	Used
S105 (=S.G.548)	6d.	Reddish purple		4·50	1·25
	a.	Imperforate three sides (pair)		£3000	
	b.	Imperf. between stamp and left margin			
	c.	Coil join (vert. pair)		24·00	
	d.	Pink tinted paper††		75·00	

B. Deep Claret† (8 May 1958)

				Mint	Used
S106 (=S.G.548a)	6d.	Deep claret		4·50	1·40
	a.	Imperforate three sides (pair)		£3000	
	b.	Coil join (vert. pair)		15·00	

†This was a deliberate change of colour although shade variations exist. See footnote after No. S108.

††This is known from cylinder 1 perforation Type C (E/P).

Cylinder Numbers (Blocks of Six)

Single pane cylinders

Reddish Purple. (No. S105)
Perforation Type B (I/P)

Cyl. No.	No dot
1	35·00
2	35·00

Perforation Type C (E/P)

Cyl. No.	No dot
1	32·00
2	32·00

Deep Claret. (No. S106)
Perforation Type B (I/P)

Cyl. No.	No dot
2	35·00
3	35·00

Perforation Type C (E/P)

Cyl. No.	No dot
2	32·00
3	32·00

Perforation Type F (L) (I/E)

Cyl. No.	No dot
3	45·00

Minor Constant Sheet Flaws

Multipositive flaws as shown for No. S104

Coils

Made up from sheets with sheet margin joins. Vertical delivery with the watermark upright

Code No.	Number in roll	Face value	
J	480	£12	Reddish purple
J	480	£12	Deep claret

Imprimatur from the National Postal Museum Archives

A. Reddish Purple. Imperforate, watermark Type W.23
Watermark upright

B. Deep Claret. Imperforate, watermark Type W.23
Watermark upright

1958 (DECEMBER 23). 6d. WATERMARK CROWNS, TYPE W.24

A. Cream Paper

			Mint	Used
S107	6d.	Deep claret*	1·25	70
	a.	Imperforate three sides (pair)	£1250	
	b.	Imperf. (pair)	£1500	
	c.	Coil join (vert. pair)	15·00	

B. White Paper (29 June 1962)

S108 (=S.G.579)	6d.	Deep claret*	30	25
	a.	Coil join (vert. pair)	12·00	
	b.	Spur to frame (Cyl. 10 No dot. R. 17/2)	4·50	

*This colour is unstable and a range of shades exists which also vary according to the colour of the paper. One of the more marked variations is a purple-claret on the cream paper from cylinder 8.

S108*b*

Cylinder Numbers (Blocks of Six)

A. Cream Paper. (No. S107)
Single pane cylinders

Perforation Type B (I/P)			Perforation Type C (E/P)	
Cyl. No.		No dot	Cyl. No.	No dot
2	. . . .	10·00	2	10·00
3	. . . .	10·00	3	10·00

Double pane cylinders

Perforation Type B (I/P no dot) and C (E/P dot)			Perforation Type A (E/I)		
Cyl. No.	No dot	Dot	Cyl. No.	No dot	Dot
5	16·00	16·00	7	10·00	10·00
7	10·00	10·00	8	10·00	10·00

B. Whiter Paper. (No. S108)

	Perforation Type A (E/I)			Perforation Type F (L)*		
Cyl. No.		No dot	Dot	Cyl. No.	No dot	Dot
					(I/E)	(P/E)
8	. . . .	3·25	3·25			
10	. . . .	3·25	3·25	10	5·00	5·00
11	. . . .	32·00	32·00			

The marginal rule is damaged in most positions on cyl. 8

Minor Constant Sheet Flaws

Multipositive flaws on cylinders 2 and 3 as shown for No. S104
   A second multipositive was used for cylinder 5 and a third for cylinders 7 onwards.

Coils

(a) Made up from sheets with sheet margin joins. Vertical delivery with the watermark upright

Code No.	Number in roll	Face value	
J	480	£12	Cream paper
J	480	£12	Whiter paper

(b) Printed in continuous reels. Single pane cylinder Q1 was used. Vertical delivery. Watermark upright

J	480	£12	Whiter paper

Imprimatur from the National Postal Museum Archives

Imperforate, watermark Type W.24. Cream or whiter paper

Watermark upright

1960 (JUNE 27). 6d. TWO PHOSPHOR BANDS REACTING GREEN. WATERMARK CROWNS

				Mint	Used
S109	6d.	Deep claret	. . . .	2·75	2·25

The bands were applied in photogravure.

Cylinders Numbers (Blocks of Six)

Single pane cylinder

	Perforation Type B (I/P)			Perforation Type C (E/P)	
Cyl. No.		No dot	Cyl. No.		No dot
2	. . . .	22·00	2	. . . .	22·00

Minor Constant Sheet Flaws

Multipositive flaws as shown for No. S104

Imprimatur from the National Postal Museum Archives

Imperforate, watermark Type W.24

Watermark upright

1961 (JUNE 5). 6d. TWO PHOSPHOR BANDS REACTING BLUE. WATERMARK CROWNS

A. Cream Paper. Bands applied in Photogravure				Mint	Used
S110	6d.	Deep claret	. . . .	4·50	3·50
	a.	Bands applied typo.	. . . .		

B. White Paper. Bands applied in Photogravure (3 October 1963)					
S111	6d.	Deep claret	. . . .	1·00	80
	a.	Bands applied typo.	. . . .	£450	
	ab.	Narrow band at left or right (stamp with vert. margin)		£500	

Cylinder Numbers (Blocks of Six)

Perforation Type A (E/I)
Bands applied photo.

Cream Paper. (No. S110)			Whiter Paper. (No. S111)		
Cyl. No.	No dot	Dot	Cyl. No.	No dot	Dot
7	35·00	35·00	8	9·00	9·00
			10	9·00	9·00

Bands applied typo.

Cream Paper (No. S110a)		Whiter Paper (No. S111a)
8	†	8 . . . .

The marginal rule is damaged in most positions on cyl. 8

1965 (AUGUST 13). 6d. TWO 8 mm. PHOSPHOR BANDS REACTING VIOLET. WMK. CROWNS

			Mint	Used
S112	6d.	Deep claret	12·00	9·00
	a.	One 6 mm. band at left or right (stamp with vert. margin)	20·00	
	b.	One 8 mm. band	25·00	

The bands were applied by typography.

Cylinder Numbers (Blocks of Six)

Perforation Type A (E/I)
Applied typo.

Cyl. No.	No dot	Dot
8	75·00	75·00

1967 (EARLY). 6d. TWO 9·5 mm. PHOSPHOR BANDS REACTING VIOLET. WMK. CROWNS

			Mint	Used
S113 (=S.G.617)	6d.	Deep claret	30	30

The bands were applied in photogravure only.

Cylinder Numbers (Blocks of Six)

Perforation Type A (E/I)			Perforation Type F (L)*		
Cyl. No.	No dot	Dot	Cyl. No.	No dot	Dot
10	10·00	10·00		(I/E)	(P/E)
11	5·00	5·00	10	5·00	5·00

Coils

Printed in continuous reels. It is believed that cylinder Q1 was used and that it was a single pane cylinder.

Vertical delivery. Watermark upright

Code No.	Number in roll	Face value
J	480	£12

1954–67 7d. Bright green, Type S4

1954 (JANUARY 18). 7d. WATERMARK TUDOR CROWN, TYPE W.22

		Mint	Used
S114 (=S.G.524)	7d. Bright green	9·50	5·50

Cylinder Numbers (Blocks of Six)

Perforation Type A (E/I)			Perforation Type B (I/P no dot) and C (E/P dot)		
Cyl. No.	No dot	Dot	Cyl. No.	No dot	Dot
2	70·00	70·00	2	70·00	70·00

Imprimatur from the National Postal Museum Archives

Imperforate, watermark Type W.22

Watermark upright

1956 (APRIL 23). 7d. WATERMARK ST. EDWARD'S CROWN, TYPE W.23

		Mint	Used
S115 (=S.G.549)	7d. Bright green	50·00	10·00

Cylinder Numbers (Blocks of Six)

Perforation Type A (E/I)		
Cyl. No.	No dot	Dot
2	£300	£300

Imprimatur from the National Postal Museum Archives

Imperforate, watermark Type W.23

Watermark upright

1958 (NOVEMBER 26). 7d. WATERMARK CROWNS, TYPE W.24

A. Cream Paper		Mint	Used
S116	7d. Bright green	2·50	70

B. Whiter Paper (3 July 1962)			
S117 (=S.G.580)	7d. Bright green	50	45

Cylinder Numbers (Blocks of Six)

Cream Paper. (No. S116)			Whiter Paper. (No. S117)		
Perforation Type A (E/I)			Perforation Type A (E/I)		
Cyl. No.	No dot	Dot	Cyl. No.	No dot	Dot
1	18·00	18·00	1	4·50	4·50
2	18·00	18·00	2	4·50	4·50
Perforation Type B (I/P no dot) and C (E/P dot)			Perforation Type F(L)*		
2	18·00	18·00		No dot	Dot
				(I/E)	(P/E)
			1*	£400	£400

*This is probably No. S118 but with phosphor omitted.

Imprimatur from the National Postal Museum Archives

Imperforate, watermark Type W.24. Cream or whiter paper

Watermark upright

1967 (FEBRUARY 15). 7d. TWO 9·5 mm. PHOSPHOR BANDS REACTING VIOLET. WMK. CROWNS

			Mint	Used
S118 (=S.G.617a)	7d.	Bright green	55	50
	a.	Imperf. between stamp and top margin		

The bands were applied in photogravure.

No. S118a came from the top row of twelve examples of which six were defective.

Cylinder Numbers (Blocks of Six)

	Perforation Type F (L)*				Perforation Type A (E/I)	
Cyl. No.		No dot	Dot	Cyl. No.	No dot	Dot
		(I/E)	(P/E)			
1	. . . .	8·00	8·00	2	5·00	5·00

Imprimatur from the National Postal Museum Archives

Imperforate, watermark Type W.24

Watermark upright

1953–67 8d. Magenta, Type S5

1953 (JULY 6). 8d. WATERMARK TUDOR CROWN, TYPE W.22

	Mint	Used
S119 (=S.G.525) 8d. Magenta	75	85

Cylinder Numbers (Blocks of Six)

Perforation Type A (E/I)			Perforation Type B (I/P no dot) and C (E/P dot)		
Cyl. No.	No dot	Dot	Cyl. No.	No dot	Dot
3	7·50	7·50	3	7·50	7·50

Minor Constant Sheet Flaw

Cyl. 3   20/1 Coloured dot between rose at top left and A of POSTAGE (Th. B2)

Imprimatur from the National Postal Museum Archives

Imperforate, watermark Type W.22

Watermark upright

1955 (DECEMBER 21). 8d. WATERMARK ST. EDWARD'S CROWN, TYPE W.23

	Mint	Used
S120 (=S.G.550) 8d. Magenta	7·00	1·25

Cylinder Numbers (Blocks of Six)

Perforation Type A (E/I)		
Cyl. No.	No dot	Dot
3	50·00	50·00

Minor Constant Sheet Flaw

Cyl. 3   20/1 Coloured dot between rose at top left and A of POSTAGE (Th. B2). Later retouched

Imprimatur from the National Postal Museum Archives

Imperforate, watermark Type W.23

Watermark upright

1960 (FEBRUARY 24). 8d. WATERMARK CROWNS, TYPE W.24

A. Cream Paper

	Mint	Used
S121 8d. Magenta	4·00	1·00

B. Whiter Paper (6 July 1962)

			Mint	Used
S122 (=S.G.581)	8d.	Magenta	60	40
	a.	Diadem flaw (Cyls. 4 No dot, R. 18/2)	5·00	
	b.	Extra pearl (Cyl. 4 Dot, R. 16/2)	5·00	

S122*a*, S123*a*
Multipostive white flaw on diadem,
lower left of "E" of "POSTAGE"
Exists as a minor flaw on Cyl. 3

S122*b*, S123*b*

Cylinder Numbers (Blocks of Six)

	Cream Paper. (No. S121) Perforation Type A (E/I)				Whiter Paper. (No. S122) Perforation Type A (E/I)		
Cyl. No.		No dot	Dot	Cyl. No.		No dot	Dot
3	. . . .	27·00	27·00	3	. . . .	7·50*	5·50
				4	. . . .	7·50*	5·50

Perforation Type F(L)* (I/E, no dot and P/E dot)

4* . . . .

*This is probably No. S123 but with the phosphor omitted.

Marginal arrows:
"V" shaped, hand engraved at top and bottom of sheet (Cyls. 3 and 4)
"W" shaped, photo-etched at both sides (Cyl. 3) or photo-etched at left and hand engraved at right (Cyl. 4)

Imprimatur from the National Postal Museum Archives

Imperforate, watermark Type W.24. Cream or whiter paper

Watermark upright

1967 (JUNE 28). 8d. TWO 9·5 mm. PHOSPHOR BANDS REACTING VIOLET. WMK. CROWNS

			Mint	Used
S123 (=S.G.617*b*)	8d.	Magenta	40	45
	a.	Diadem flaw (Cyl. 4 No dot, R. 18/2)	5·00	
	b.	Extra pearl (Cyl. 4 Dot, R. 16/2)	5·50	
	c.	Petal joined to frame (Cyl. 4 Dot, R. 13/11)	5·50	

The bands were applied in photogravure.
For illustrations of Nos. S123*a/b*, see Nos. S122*a/b*.

S123*c*

Cylinder Numbers (Blocks of Six)

	Perforation Type A (E/I)				Perforation Type F (L)*		
Cyl. No.		No dot	Dot	Cyl. No.		No dot (I/E)	Dot (P/E)
4	. . . .	6·00*	3·25	4	. . . .	6·00*	3·25

Marginal arrows:
"V" shaped, hand engraved at top and bottom of sheet
"W" shaped, photo-etched at left and hand engraved at right

Imprimatur from the National Postal Museum Archives

Imperforate, watermark Type W.24

Watermark upright

1954–66 9d. Bronze-green, Type S5

1954 (FEBRUARY 8). 9d. WATERMARK TUDOR CROWN, TYPE W.22

			Mint	Used
S124 (=S.G.526)	9d.	Bronze-green	23·00	4·75
	a.	Frame break at upper right (Cyl. 1 No dot, R. 8/6) . .	30·00	
	b.	Imperf. between stamp and top margin*		

*No. S124*b* was caused by a paper fold.

Frame broken at upper right and shading below it missing. Later retouched on Crowns watermark. A very similar variety occurs on Cyl. 2, R. 11/11; see Nos. S126*c.* etc.

S124*a*, S125*a*, S126*a*

Cylinder Numbers (Blocks of Six)

	Perforation Type A (E/I)			Perforation Type B (I/P no dot) and C (E/P dot)		
Cyl. No.		No dot	Dot	Cyl. No.	No dot	Dot
1	. . . .	£145	£145	1	£145	£145

Imprimatur from the National Postal Museum Archives

Imperforate, watermark Type W.22

Watermark upright

1955 (DECEMBER 15). 9d. WATERMARK ST. EDWARD'S CROWN, W.23

			Mint	Used
S125 (=S.G.551)	9d.	Bronze-green	20·00	2·75
	a.	Frame break at upper right (Cyl. 1 No dot, R. 8/6) . .	20·00	

For illustration of No. S125*a*, see No. S124*a*.

Cylinder Numbers (Blocks of Six)

	Perforation Type A (E/I)			Perforation Type B (I/P no dot) and C (E/P dot)		
Cyl. No.		No dot	Dot	Cyl. No.	No dot	Dot
1	. . . .	£140	£140	1	£140	£140

Imprimatur from the National Postal Museum Archives

Imperforate, watermark Type W.23

Watermark upright

1959 (MARCH 24). 9d. WATERMARK CROWNS, TYPE W.24

A. Cream Paper

			Mint	Used
S126	9d.	Bronze-green	4·00	1·00
	a.	Frame break at upper right (Cyl. 1 No dot, R. 8/6) . .	10·00	
	b.	Broken daffodil (Cyl. 2 No dot, R. 7/2)	9·00	
	c.	Frame break at upper right (Cyl. 2 No dot, R. 11/11)	10·00	
	d.	Frame flaw (Cyl. 2 Dot, R. 12/5)	9·00	

B. Whiter Paper (4 June 1962)

			Mint	Used
S127 (=S.G.582)	9d.	Bronze-green	60	40
	a.	Broken daffodil (Cyl. 2 No dot, R. 7/2)	5·00	
	b.	Frame break at upper right (Cyl. 2 No dot, R. 11/11) .	5·50	
	c.	Frame flaw (Cyl. 2 Dot, R. 12/5)	5·00	

For illustration of No. S126*a*, see No. S124*a*.

S126*b*, S127*a*, S128*b*
Stem of daffodil
is broken

S126*c*, S127*b*, S128*c*
A very similar variety to
the one on Cyl. 1, R. 8/6
but more pronounced

S126*d*, S127*c*, S128*d*
Flaw on frame
at lower left

Cylinder Numbers (Blocks of Six)

	Cream Paper. (No. S126) Perforation Type A (E/I)			Whiter Paper. (No. S127) Perforation Type A (E/I)	
Cyl. No.	No dot	Dot	Cyl. No.	No dot	Dot
1	27·00	27·00	2	4·75	4·75
2	27·00	27·00			

Imprimatur from the National Postal Museum Archives

Imperforate, watermark Type W.24. Cream or whiter paper

Watermark upright

1966 (DECEMBER 29). 9d. TWO 9·5 mm. PHOSPHOR BANDS REACTING VIOLET. WMK. CROWNS

				Mint	Used
S128 (=S.G.617*c*)	9d.	Bronze-green		60	55
	a.	Imperf. between stamp and top margin		£500	
	b.	Broken daffodil (Cyl. 2 No dot, R. 7/2)		5·00	
	c.	Frame break at upper right (Cyl. 2 No dot, R. 11/11)		6·00	
	d.	Frame flaw (Cyl. 2 Dot, R. 12/5)		6·00	

The bands were applied in photogravure.
For illustrations of Nos. S128*b/d*, see Nos. S126*b/d*.

Cylinder Numbers (Blocks of Six)

	Perforation Type A (E/I)	
Cyl. No.	No dot	Dot
2	5·00	5·00

Imprimatur from the National Postal Museum Archives

Imperforate, watermark Type W.24

Watermark upright

1954–66 10d. Prussian blue, Type S5

1954 (FEBRUARY 8). 10d. WATERMARK TUDOR CROWN, TYPE W.22

			Mint	Used
S129 (=S.G.527)	10d.	Prussian blue	18·00	4·75

Cylinder Numbers (Blocks of Six)

Perforation Type A (E/I)			Perforation Type B (I/P no dot) and C (E/P dot)		
Cyl. No.	No dot	Dot	Cyl. No.	No dot	Dot
1	£120	£120	1	£120	£120

Minor Constant Sheet Flaws

Cyl. 1   3/3 White spur on right fork of V of REVENUE
10/12 White flaw on thistle shows as a cut into the left-hand side of the flower (Th. A6)
13/10 White flaw on rim of diadem below emblems (Th. B4)

Imprimatur from the National Postal Museum Archives

Imperforate, watermark Type W.22

Watermark upright

1955 (SEPTEMBER 22). 10d. WATERMARK ST. EDWARD'S CROWN, TYPE W.23

			Mint	Used
S130 (=S.G.552)	10d.	Prussian blue	20·00	2·75

Cylinder Numbers (Blocks of Six)

Perforation Type A (E/I)		
Cyl. No.	No dot	Dot
1	£150	£150

Minor Constant Sheet Flaws

Cyl. 1   3/3 White spur on right fork of V of REVENUE
10/12 White flaw on thistle shows as a cut into the left-hand side of the flower (Th. A6)
13/10 White flaw on rim of diadem below emblems (Th. B4)

Imprimatur from the National Postal Museum Archives

Imperforate, watermark Type W.23

Watermark upright

1958 (NOVEMBER 18). 10d. WATERMARK CROWNS, TYPE W.24

A. Cream Paper			Mint	Used
S131	10d.	Prussian blue	3·75	1·00

B. Whiter Paper (13 November 1962)				
S132 (=S.G.583)	10d.	Prussian blue	1·00	50

Cylinder Numbers (Blocks of Six)

Cream Paper. (No. S131)			Whiter Paper. (No. S132)		
Perforation Type A (E/I)			Perforation Type A (E/I)		
Cyl. No.	No dot	Dot	Cyl. No.	No dot	Dot
1	27·00	27·00	1	7·50	7·50
Perforation Type B (I/P no dot) and C (E/P dot)			Perforation Type F (L)* (I/E no dot and P/E		
1	27·00	27·00	dot)		
			1*	£2250	
			*This is probably No. S133 but with the phosphor omitted.		

Minor Constant Sheet Flaws

Cyl. 1   3/3 White spur on right fork of V of REVENUE. Later retouched

          10/12 White flaw on thistle shows as a cut into the left-hand side of the flower (Th. A6). Later retouched

          13/10 White flaw on rim of diadem below emblems (Th. B4). Later retouched

           14/3 Retouch on Queen's nose (Th. D3)

Imprimatur from the National Postal Museum Archives

Imperforate, watermark Type W.24. Cream or whiter paper

Watermark upright

1966 (DECEMBER 30). 10d. TWO 9·5 mm. PHOSPHOR BANDS REACTING VIOLET. WMK. CROWNS

			Mint	Used
S133 (=S.G.617*d*)	10d.	Prussian blue	70	60
	a.	One 9·5 mm. band	£200	

The bands were applied in photogravure.

Cylinder Numbers (Blocks of Six)

Perforation Type A (E/I)			Perforation Type F (L)*		
Cyl. No.	No dot	Dot	Cyl. No.	No dot	Dot
				(I/E)	(P/E)
1	5·50	5·50	1	5·50	5·50

Minor Constant Sheet Flaws

Cyl. 1   3/3 White spur on right fork of V of REVENUE. Later retouched

          14/3 Retouch on Queen's nose (Th. D3)

Imprimatur from the National Postal Museum Archives

Imperforate, watermark Type W.24

Watermark upright

1954–65 11d. Brown-purple, Type S5

1954 (FEBRUARY 8). 11d. WATERMARK TUDOR CROWN, TYPE W.22

		Mint	Used
S134 (=S.G.528)	11d. Brown-purple	35·00	15·00

Cylinder Numbers (Blocks of Six)

Perforation Type B (I/P no dot) and C (E/P dot)

Cyl. No.	No dot	Dot
1	£225	£225

Minor Constant Sheet Flaw

Cyl. 1   19/3 White flaw in frame pattern at left by O of POSTAGE (Th. D1)

Imprimatur from the National Postal Museum Archives

Imperforate, watermark Type W.22

Watermark upright

1955 (OCTOBER 28). 11d. WATERMARK ST. EDWARD'S CROWN, TYPE W.23

		Mint	Used
S135 (=S.G.553)	11d. Brown-purple	50	1·10

Cylinder Numbers (Blocks of Six)

Perforation Type A (E/I)			Perforation Type B (I/P no dot) and C (E/P dot)		
Cyl. No.	No dot	Dot	Cyl. No.	No dot	Dot
1	4·50	4·50	1	4·50	4·50

Minor Constant Sheet Flaw

Cyl. 1   19/3 White flaw in frame pattern at left by O of POSTAGE (Th. D1)

Imprimatur from the National Postal Museum Archives

Imperforate, watermark Type W.23

Watermark upright

1953–67 1s. Bistre-brown, Type S6

1953 (JULY 6). 1s. WATERMARK TUDOR CROWN, TYPE W.22

				Mint	Used
S136 (=S.G.529)	1s.	Bistre-brown	. . . .	80	50

Cylinder Numbers (Blocks of Six)

Perforation Type A (E/I)			Perforation Type B (I/P no dot) and C (E/P dot)		
Cyl. No.	No dot	Dot	Cyl. No.	No dot	Dot
1	8·00	8·00	1	12·00	12·00
2	22·00	22·00			

Minor Constant Sheet Flaws

Cyl. 1.   3/10 Coloured flaw between left-hand leaves of thistle (Th. B6)
5/10 Coloured spur to top of lacing at right of value (Th. G5)
Cyl. 2.   3/10 As on Cyl. 1. (multipositive flaw)

Imprimatur from the National Postal Museum Archives

Imperforate, watermark Type W.22

Watermark upright

1955 (NOVEMBER 3). 1s. WATERMARK ST. EDWARD'S CROWN, TYPE W.23

				Mint	Used
S137 (=S.G.554)	1s.	Bistre-brown	. . . .	22·00	65
	a.	Thistle flaw (Cyl. 3 Dot, R. 4/5)	. . . .	30·00	

S137a, S138b, S139a

Cylinder Numbers (Blocks of Six)

Perforation Type A (E/I)					
Cyl. No.	No dot	Dot	Cyl. No.	No dot	Dot
2	£150	£150	4	£180	£180
3	£150	£150			

Minor Constant Sheet Flaws

Cyl. 2.   3/10 Coloured flaw between left-hand leaves of thistle (Th. B6). Later retouched leaving a pale mark
Cyl. 3.   3/10 As on Cyl. 2, but flaw is retouched and appears much smaller (multipositive flaw)
Cyl. 4.   3/10 As for Cyl. 3.
11/12 Coloured spur to foot of first E of REVENUE

Imprimatur from the National Postal Museum Archives

Imperforate, watermark Type W.23

Watermark upright

1958 (OCTOBER 30). 1s. WATERMARK CROWNS, TYPE W.24

A. Cream Paper

			Mint	Used
S138	1s.	Bistre-brown	3·75	80
	a.	Double impression	£200	
	b.	Thistle flaw (Cyl. 3 Dot, R. 4/5)	8·00	

B. Whiter Paper (22 July 1962)

			Mint	Used
S139 (=S.G.584)	1s.	Bistre-brown	45	30
	a.	Thistle flaw (Cyl. 3 Dot, R. 4/5)	4·50	

The note below No. S85 4d. deep ultramarine concerning paper movement applies to No. S138*a*. For illustration of Nos. S138*b* and S139*a*, see No. S137*a*.

Cylinder Numbers (Blocks of Six)

Cream Paper. (No. S138) Perforation Type A (E/I)			Whiter Paper. (No. S139) Perforation Type A (E/I)		
Cyl. No.	No dot	Dot	Cyl. No.	No dot	Dot
2	26·00	26·00	2	4·50	4·50
3	26·00	26·00	3	4·50	4·50
4	26·00	26·00	4	4·50	4·50

Minor Constant Sheet Flaws

Multipositive flaw
Dot   3/10 Coloured flaw between left-hand leaves of thistle (Th. B6) now only exists retouched. Cyls. 2. and 3. show as a smudge and Cyl. 4. as a much smaller flaw
Cyl. 4.   11/12 Coloured spur to foot of first E of REVENUE

Imprimatur from the National Postal Museum Archives

Imperforate, watermark Type W.24. Cream or whiter paper

Watermark upright

1967 (JUNE 28). 1s. TWO 9·5 mm. PHOSPHOR BANDS REACTING VIOLET. WMK. CROWNS

			Mint	Used
S140 (=S.G.617*e*)	1s.	Bistre-brown	40	35

The bands were applied in photogravure.

Cylinder Numbers (Blocks of Six)

	Perforation Type F (L)*	
Cyl. No.	No dot	Dot
	(I/E)	(P/E)
4	4·25	4·25

Minor Constant Sheet Flaws

Cyl. 4.   3/10 Coloured flaw between left-hand leaves of thistle (Th. B6) is now retouched leaving a much smaller flaw
11/12 Coloured spur to foot of first E of REVENUE

Imprimatur from the National Postal Museum Archives

Imperforate, watermark Type W.24

Watermark upright

1953–67 1s.3d. Green, Type S7

1953 (NOVEMBER 2). 1s.3d. WATERMARK TUDOR CROWN, TYPE W.22

			Mint	Used
S141 (=S.G.530)	1s.3d.	Green	4·75	3·25
	a.	White flaw in Queen's hair (Dot, R. 2/9)	12·00	
	b.	"P" flaw (Dot, R. 6/10)	10·00	

S141*a*, S142*a*, S143*a*, S144*a*,
S145*a*, S146*a*, S147*b*

S141*b*, S142*b*, S143*b*, S144*b*,
S145*b*, S146*b*, S147*c*

Cylinder Numbers (Blocks of Six)

Perforation Type A (E/I)			Perforation Type B (I/P no dot) and C (E/P dot)		
Cyl. No.	No dot	Dot	Cyl. No.	No dot	Dot
1 .... 35·00		35·00	1 .... 35·00		35·00

Imprimatur from the National Postal Museum Archives

Imperforate, watermark Type W.22

Watermark upright

1956 (MARCH 27). 1s.3d. WATERMARK ST. EDWARD'S CROWN, TYPE W.23

			Mint	Used
S142 (=S.G.555)	1s.3d.	Green	30·00	1·60
	a.	White flaw in Queen's hair (Dot, R. 2/9)	40·00	
	b.	"P" flaw (Dot, R. 6/10)	38·00	

For illustrations of Nos. S142*a/b*, see Nos. S141*a/b*.

Cylinder Numbers (Blocks of Six)

Perforation Type A (E/I)		
Cyl. No.	No dot	Dot
1 .... £200		£200

Imprimatur from the National Postal Museum Archives

Imperforate, watermark Type W.23

Watermark upright

1959 (JUNE 17). 1s.3d. WATERMARK CROWNS, TYPE W.24

A. Cream Paper

			Mint	Used
S143	1s.3d.	Green	3·00	1·25
	a.	White flaw in Queen's hair (Cyl. 1 Dot, R. 2/9) ..	9·00	
	b.	"P" flaw (Cyl, 1, Dot, R. 6/10)	9·00	

B. Whiter Paper (29 August 1962)

			Mint	Used
S144 (=S.G.585)	1s.3d.	Green	45	30
	a.	White flaw in Queen's hair (Cyl. 1 Dot, R. 2/9) ..	4·75	
	b.	"P" flaw (Cyl. 1 Dot, R. 6/10)	4·75	

For illustrations of Nos. S143*a/b* and S144*a/b*, see Nos. S141*a/b*.

Cylinder Numbers (Blocks of Six)

Cream Paper. (No. S143) Perforation Type A (E/I)			Whiter Paper. (No. S144) Perforation Type A (E/I)		
Cyl. No.	No dot	Dot	Cyl. No.	No dot	Dot
1	21·00	21·00	1	3·75	3·75
			2	3·75	3·75

Imprimatur from the National Postal Museum Archives

Imperforate, watermark Type W.24. Cream or whiter paper

Watermark upright

1960 (JUNE 22). 1s.3d. TWO PHOSPHOR BANDS REACTING GREEN. WATERMARK CROWNS

				Mint	Used
S145	1s.3d.	Green	. . . .	7·00	4·50
	a.	White flaw in Queen's hair (Dot, R. 2/9)	. . . . . .	12·00	
	b.	"P" flaw (Dot, R. 6/10)	. . . .	12·00	

The bands were applied in photogravure.
For illustrations of Nos. S145a/b, See Nos. S141a/b.

Cylinder Numbers (Blocks of Six)

Perforation Type B (I/P no dot) and C (E/P dot)

Cyl. No.	No dot	Dot
1	50·00	50·00

Imprimatur from the National Postal Museum Archives

Imperforate, watermark Type W.24

Watermark upright

1961 (JUNE 5). 1s.3d. TWO PHOSPHOR BANDS REACTING BLUE. WATERMARK CROWNS

A. Cream Paper

				Mint	Used
S146	1s.3d.	Green	. . . .	22·00	10·00
	a.	White flaw in Queen's hair (Cyl. 1 Dot, R. 2/9)	. .	30·00	
	b.	"P" flaw (Cyl. 1 Dot, R. 6/10)	. . . .	30·00	

The bands were applied in photogravure.

B. Whiter Paper (21 January 1963)

				Mint	Used
S147 (=S.G.618)	1s.3d.	Green	. . . .	1·90	2·50
	a.	One 8 mm. band	. . . .	10·00	
	b.	White flaw in Queen's hair (Cyl. 1 Dot, R. 2/9)	. .	4·75	
	c.	"P" flaw (Cyl. 1 Dot, R. 6/10)	. . . .	4·75	

For illustrations of Nos. S146a/b and S147b/c, see Nos. S141a/b.

Cylinder Numbers (Blocks of Six)

Cream Paper. (No. S146) Perforation Type A (E/I)			Whiter Paper. (No. S147) Perforation Type A (E/I)		
Cyl. No.	No dot	Dot	Cyl. No.	No dot	Dot
1	£140	£140	1	15·00	15·00
			2	15·00	15·00

Imprimatur from the National Postal Museum Archives

Imperforate, watermark Type W.24. Cream or whiter paper

Watermark upright

1965 (AUGUST 13). 1s.3d. TWO 8 mm. PHOSPHOR BANDS REACTING VIOLET. WMK. CROWNS

			Mint	Used
S148	1s.3d.	Green	18·00	4·50
	a.	One 6 mm. band at left or right (stamp with vert. margin)	27·00	
	b.	Bands applied photo. (1966)	7·50	3·50
	c.	Error. One 8 mm. band (photo.)	30·00	
	d.	Error. One 8 mm. band (typo.)	25·00	
	da.	Error. As *d* but 6 mm. band (typo.)	40·00	

The bands were originally applied by typography.

Cylinder Numbers (Blocks of Six)

Perforation Type A (E/I) Applied typo (No. S148)			Applied photo. (No. S148*b*)		
Cyl. No.	No dot	Dot	Cyl. No	No dot	Dot
2	£150	£150	2	48·00	48·00

1967 (EARLY). 1s.3d. TWO 9·5 mm. PHOSPHOR BANDS REACTING VIOLET. WMK. CROWNS

			Mint	Used
S149	1s.3d.	Green	9·00	5·00

The bands were applied in photogravure only.

Cylinder Numbers (Blocks of Six)

Perforation Type A (E/I)		
Cyl. No.	No dot	Dot
2	65·00	65·00

1953–66 1s.6d. Grey-blue, Type S6

1953 (NOVEMBER 2). 1s.6d. WATERMARK TUDOR CROWN, TYPE W.22

			Mint	Used
S150 (=S.G.531)	1s.6d.	Grey-blue	14·00	3·75
	a.	White flaw in Queen's hair below diadem (Dot, R. 20/1)	22·00	
	b.	White flaw in Queen's hair opposite "N" of "REVENUE" (Dot, R. 20/2)	22·00	

S150*a*, S151*a*, S152*a*, S153*a*, S154*a*

S150*b*, S151*b*, S152*b*, Later retouched on Crowns watermark

Cylinder Numbers (Blocks of Six)

	Perforation Type A (E/I)			Perforation Type B (I/P no dot) and C (E/P dot)		
Cyl. No.		No dot	Dot	Cyl. No.	No dot	Dot
1	. . . .	95·00	£110*	1	. . . . 95·00	£110*

Imprimatur from the National Postal Museum Archives

Imperforate, watermark Type W.22

Watermark upright

1956 (MARCH 27). 1s.6d. WATERMARK ST. EDWARD'S CROWN, TYPE W.23

			Mint	Used
S151 (=S.G.556)	1s.6d.	Grey-blue	23·00	1·60
	a.	White flaw in Queen's hair below diadem (Dot, R. 20/1)	32·00	
	b.	White flaw in Queen's hair opposite "N" of "REVENUE" (Dot, R. 20/2)	32·00	

For illustrations of Nos. S151*a/b*, see Nos. S150*a/b*.

Cylinder Numbers (Blocks of Six)

	Perforation Type A (E/I)			Perforation Type B (I/P no dot) and C (E/P dot)		
Cyl. No.		No dot	Dot	Cyl. No.	No dot	Dot
1	. . . .	£140	£160*	1	. . . . £140	£160*

Imprimatur from the National Postal Museum Archives

Imperforate, watermark Type W.23

Watermark upright

1958 (DECEMBER 16). 1s.6d. WATERMARK CROWNS, TYPE W.24

A. Cream Paper

			Mint	Used
S152	1s.6d.	Grey-blue	15·00	4·00
	a.	White flaw in Queen's hair below diadem (Cyl. 1 Dot, R. 20/1)	22·00	
	b.	White flaw in Queen's hair opposite "N" of "REVENUE" (Cyl. 1 Dot, R. 20/2)	22·00	

B. Whiter Paper (14 November 1962)

			Mint	Used
S153 (=S.G.586)	1s.6d.	Grey-blue	4·00	40
	a.	White flaw in Queen's hair below diadem (Cyl. 1		
		Dot, R. 20/1)	10·00	

For illustrations of Nos. S152*a/b* and S153*a*, see Nos. S150*a/b*.

Cylinder Numbers (Blocks of Six)

Cream Paper. (No. S152) Perforation Type A (E/I)			Whiter Paper. (No. S153) Perforation Type A (E/I)		
Cyl. No.	No dot	Dot	Cyl. No.	No dot	Dot
1	90·00	£110*	1	30·00	35·00*
3	90·00	90·00			
Perforation Type B (I/P no dot) and C (E/P dot)					
1	90·00	£110*			
3	90·00	90·00			

Imprimatur from the National Postal Museum Archives

Imperforate, watermark Type W.24. Cream or whiter paper

Watermark upright

1966 (DECEMBER 12). 1s.6d. TWO 9·5 mm. PHOSPHOR BANDS REACTING VIOLET. WMK. CROWNS

			Mint	Used
S154 (=S.G.618*a*)	1s.6d.	Grey-blue	2·00	2·00
	a.	White flaw in Queen's hair below diadem (Cyl. 1		
		Dot, R. 20/1)	6·00	

The bands were applied in photogravure.
For illustration of No. S154*a*, see No. S150*a*.

Cylinder Numbers (Blocks of Six)

Perforation Type A (E/I)			Perforation Type F (L)*		
Cyl. No.	No dot	Dot	Cyl. No.	No dot (I/E)	Dot (P/E)
1	15·00	20·00*	8	20·00	20·00

Imprimatur from the National Postal Museum Archives

Imperforate, watermark Type W.24

Watermark upright

Presentation Packs

SPP1 (issued 1960)   Eighteen values   £275
The issued pack contained one of each value. The 1½d. and 11d. were with St. Edward's Crown watermark (Nos. S26 and S135) and the remainder were Crowns watermark all on cream paper, ½d. (No. S4), 1d (S16), 2d. (S40), 2½d. (S55), 3d. (S70), 4d. (S83), 4½d. (S93), 5d. (S101), 6d. (S107), 7d. (S116), 8d. (S121), 9d. (S126), 10d. (S131), 1s. (S138), 1s.3d. (S144), 1s.6d. (S152).

Two forms of the pack exist:
(a) Inscribed "10s 6d" for sale in the U.K. and
(b) Inscribed "$1·80" for sale in the U.S.A.

SPP2 (issued 1960)   Sixteen values   £300
The issued pack contained two of each value of the Phosphor-Graphite experimental issue, ½d. (No. S8), 1d. (S19), 1½d. (S31), 2d. (S43), 2½d. (S60), 3d. (S73), 4d. (S87), 4½d. (S96). The ½d., 1d. and 1½d. were with St. Edward's Crown watermark and the remainder with Crowns watermark. Although the details printed on the pack erroneously describe the stamps as all having Crowns watermark, the packs usually bear a sticker inscribed "CORRECTION. The ½d., 1d., & 1½d. stamps bear the St. Edward Crown Royal Cypher watermark".

Two forms of the pack exist:
(a) Inscribed "3s 8d" for sale in the U.K. and
(b) Inscribed "50c" for sale in the U.S.A.

SECTION SB
Dorothy Wilding Issues
1953–68. Booklet Panes in Photogravure

General Notes

INTRODUCTION.   All panes were printed in photogravure by Harrison & Sons. See the detailed notes under Section S for information on printing, paper, gum and phosphor application.

ARRANGEMENT.   The panes are listed in face value order of the stamps they include (for *se-tenant* panes under the lowest denomination). The main listing is followed by errors and varieties.

PERFORATION.   Wilding booklet stamps exist in panes of two, four and six and details together with illustrations of the perforation types will be found in Appendix G, section 4. The type abbreviations found above the pane prices refer to the appearance of the binding margin, i.e. I = imperforate, AP = alternate perf., P = perforated and E = extension hole.

BOOKLET ERRORS.   Those listed as "Imperf. pane" show one row of perforations either at top or bottom of booklet pane. Those listed as "part perf. pane" have one row of three stamps imperforate on three sides. The tête-bêche errors derive from booklets but these are listed in Section SA.

BOOKLET CYLINDER NUMBERS.   These are listed for panes where most of the number is visible. Some panes of four had the number engraved wide of the stamps and such examples are priced in a footnote. Information on the cylinders used is given in most cases. Phosphor cylinder numbers have not been found on Wilding panes. The cylinder numbers being hand-engraved varied slightly as to their position in relation to the stamp so that some were invariably trimmed. A pane showing a complete cylinder number placed away from the stamp will only exist with trimmed perforations on the opposite side.

BOOKLET CYLINDER FLAWS.   Cylinder flaws on booklet stamps are listed under the panes in which they occur. Prices are for the variety in a complete pane with its binding margin intact. In cases where a 21-row cylinder has been used both possible positions in the pane are given.

  When quoting the position on booklet panes no attention is paid to the labels. In a pane of six, stamp 3 would be the third stamp in the row counting from left to right. Again "R. 1/3" refers to row one, third stamp from the left margin. Panes of four from 1s. and 2s. booklets contain panes with a top binding margin and other booklets have panes of six with the binding margin at left.

PHOSPHOR BAND WIDTHS AND MISPLACEMENT.   See notes in Section S; the booklet stamps being similar to those printed in Post Office counter sheets. The 6 mm. bands were printed in typo on panes of four, but these can only be identified when the bands are slightly misplaced. Likewise panes of six showing 8 mm. bands have the 6 mm. band printed *over the first vertical row of perforations at the left*. Major shifts result in stamps from the first column having one 6 mm. wide band and the other four stamps a misplaced band of 8 mm. This, in effect, changes the numbers of bands on a single stamp and these have always been popular with collectors. A different kind of error exists where the phosphor cylinder printed one band instead of two but this only occurred on a small printing of the 1d./3d. *se-tenant* panes in 2s. booklets.

  See Section SA for phosphor bands misplaced on singles derived from panes. Although complete panes with full perforations showing listable band shifts are included some remain unpriced due to their scarcity. It is possible that such panes were split up later especially if the perforations were no better than average. Prices quoted in this Section are for good perfs all round.

PHOSPHOR APPLICATION.   It is appropriate to mention here that we do not list separately panes with bands applied in photogravure and flexography. Refer to the notes in Section S under "Phosphor Issues" for information on the types of phosphor employed.

STAMPS OVERPRINTED "SPECIMEN".   Panes exist with a handstamped overprint in two sizes. These derive from the National Postal Archive sales mentioned in the Introductory Notes. The handstamp can be found inverted or overlapping the perforations but these are not listed as varieties.

SB No.	Face Value	Watermark	Size of Pane	Further description	Page
1	½d.	Tudor Crown	6	. . . .	96
2	½d.	Tudor Crown	4	. . . .	96
3	½d.	Tudor Crown	2	. . . .	97
4	½d.	St. Edward's Crown	6	. . . .	97
5	½d.	St. Edward's Crown	4	. . . .	98
6	½d.	St. Edward's Crown	2	. . . .	98
7	½d.	Crowns	6	Cream paper	98
8	½d.	Crowns	6	Whiter paper	98
9	½d.	Crowns	4	Cream paper	99
10	½d.	Crowns, sideways	4	Cream paper	100
11	½d.	Crowns, sideways	4	Whiter paper	100
12	3×½d. +2½d.	Crowns	4	Chalky paper	101
13	2×½d. +2 × 2½d.	Crowns, sideways	4	Whiter paper	101
14	½d.	Crowns	6	Graphite lines	103
15	½d.	Crowns	6	Green phosphor	103
16	½d.	Crowns	6	Blue phosphor, cream paper	103
17	½d.	Crowns	6	Blue phosphor, whiter paper	103
18	½d.	Crowns, sideways	4	Blue phosphor, cream paper	104
19	½d.	Crowns, sideways	4	Blue phosphor, whiter paper	104
20	1d.	Tudor Crown	6	. . . .	104
21	1d.	Tudor Crown	4	. . . .	105
22	1d.	Tudor Crown	2	. . . .	105
23	1d.	Tudor Crown	6	Including 3 labels: "MINIMUM INLAND PRINTED PAPER RATE 1½d."	106
24	1d.	Tudor Crown	6	Including 3 labels: "PLEASE POST EARLY IN THE DAY"	107
25	1d.	Tudor Crown	6	Including 3 different labels	108
26	1d.	St. Edward's Crown	6	. . . .	108
27	1d.	St. Edward's Crown	4	. . . .	109
28	1d.	St. Edward's Crown	2	. . . .	110
29	1d.	St. Edward's Crown	6	Including 3 different labels	110
30	1d.	Crowns	6	Cream paper	110
31	1d.	Crowns	6	Whiter paper	111
32	1d.	Crowns	4	Cream paper	111
33	1d.	Crowns, sideways	4	Cream paper	112
34	1d.	Crowns, sideways	4	Whiter paper	112
35/8	2 × 1d. +2 × 3d.	Crowns, sideways	4	Whiter paper 112/3
39	1d.	Crowns	6	Graphite lines	113
40	1d.	Crowns	6	Green phosphor	113
41	1d.	Crowns	6	Blue phosphor, cream paper	114
42	1d.	Crowns	6	Blue phosphor, whiter paper	114
43	1d.	Crowns, sideways	4	Blue phosphor, cream paper	114
44	1d.	Crowns, sideways	4	Blue phosphor, whiter paper	115
45/8	2 × 1d. +2 × 3d.	Crowns, sideways	4	Blue phosphor, whiter paper	115
49	1d.	Crowns	6	Violet phosphor, 8 mm.	116
50/3	2 × 1d. +2 × 3d.	Crowns, sideways	4	3d. with 1 side violet 8 mm. band	116
54	1d.	Crowns	6	Violet phosphor, 9·5 mm.	117
55/58	2 × 1d. +2 × 3d.	Crowns	4	3d. with 2 violet 9·5 mm. bands	117
59	1½d.	Tudor Crown	6	. . . .	118
60	1½d.	Tudor Crown	4	. . . .	118
61	1½d.	Tudor Crown	2	. . . .	119
62	1½d.	St. Edward's Crown	6	. . . .	119
63	1½d.	St. Edward's Crown	4	. . . .	120
64	1½d.	St. Edward's Crown	2	. . . .	120
65	1½d.	Crowns	6	Cream paper	121
66	1½d.	Crowns	6	Whiter paper	121
67	1½d.	Crowns	4	Cream paper	121
68	1½d.	Crowns, sideways	4	Cream paper	122
69	1½d.	Crowns, sideways	4	Whiter paper	122
70	1½d.	Crowns	6	Graphite lines	122
71	1½d.	Crowns	6	Green phosphor	122
72	1½d.	Crowns	6	Blue phosphor, cream paper	123
73	1½d.	Crowns	6	Blue phosphor, whiter paper	123
74	1½d.	Crowns, sideways	4	Blue phosphor, cream paper	123
75	1½d.	Crowns, sideways	4	Blue phosphor, whiter paper	123
76	2d.	Tudor Crown	6	. . . .	124

SB No.	Face Value	Watermark	Size of Pane	Further description	Page
77	2d.	St. Edward's Crown	6	Red-brown	124
78	2d.	St. Edward's Crown	6	Light red-brown	124
79	2d.	Crowns	6	Cream paper	126
80	2½d.	Tudor Crown	6	Type II	126
81	2½d.	St. Edward's Crown	6	Type II	127
82	2½d.	Crowns	6	Type II. Cream paper	128
83	2½d.	Crowns	6	Type II. Whiter paper	128
84	2½d.	Crowns	4	Type II. Chalky paper	129
85	2½d.	Crowns	6	Type II. Graphite lines	129
86	2½d.	Crowns	6	Type II. Green phosphor	129
87	2½d.	Crowns	6	Type II. Blue phosphor, 2 bands, cream paper .	130
88	2½d.	Crowns	6	Type II. Blue phosphor, 1 band, cream paper .	130
89	2½d.	Crowns	6	Type II. Blue phosphor, 1 band, whiter paper .	130
90	3d.	St. Edward's Crown	6	. . . .	131
91	3d.	St. Edward's Crown	4	. . . .	131
92	3d.	Crowns	6	Cream paper	132
93	3d.	Crowns	6	Whiter paper	132
94	3d.	Crowns	4	Cream paper	133
95	3d.	Crowns, sideways	4	Cream paper	133
96	3d.	Crowns, sideways	4	Whiter paper	133
97	3d.	Crowns	6	Graphite lines	134
98	3d.	Crowns	6	Green phosphor	134
99	3d.	Crowns	6	Blue phosphor, cream paper	134
100	3d.	Crowns	6	Blue phosphor, whiter paper	134
101	3d.	Crowns, sideways	4	Blue phosphor, cream paper	135
102	3d.	Crowns, sideways	4	Blue phosphor, whiter paper	135
103	3d.	Crowns	6	Violet phosphor, 1 side band	136
104	3d.	Crowns	6	Violet phosphor, 1 centre band	136
105	4d.	Crowns	6	Deep ultramarine	137
106	4d.	Crowns, sideways	4	Deep ultramarine	137
107	4d.	Crowns	6	Deep ultramarine. Blue phosphor	138
108	4d.	Crowns, sideways	4	Deep ultramarine. Blue phosphor	138
109	4d.	Crowns	6	Violet phosphor, 8 mm.	138
110	4d.	Crowns, sideways	4	Violet phosphor, 8 mm.	139
111	4d.	Crowns	6	Violet phosphor, 9·5 mm.	139
112	4d.	Crowns, sideways	4	Violet phosphor, 9·5 mm.	140

> **BOOKLET PANE PRICES.** The prices quoted are for panes with good perforations all round and with binding margin attached. Panes showing some degree of trimming will be worth less than the published prices in this Catalogue. It should be appreciated that some panes are scarce with full perforations and the prices shown in the Catalogue reflect this. Panes from the 2s. booklets are particularly difficult to find with full perforations on the three sides.
>
> Prices in Appendix HA are for booklets containing panes described as having average perforations (i.e. full perforations on two edges of the pane only).

½d. BOOKLET PANES OF SIX
6 × ½d. Tudor Crown
From 2s.6d. Booklets F14/34 and 5s. Booklets H6/16

A. Watermark upright
    SB1   Pane of 6 × ½d.   (containing No. S1 × 6) (3.54) . . . . 3·75

B. Watermark inverted
    SB1a   Pane of 6 × ½d.   (containing No. S1a × 6) (3.54) . . . . 6·00

Booklet Cylinder Numbers

Panes of six (20-row cylinders)

Cyl. No.	No dot	Dot	Cyl. No.	No dot	Dot
E1	25·00	25·00	E4*	20·00	20·00
E2	15·00	15·00			

*The no dot pane of cylinder E4 originally had a dot inserted in error. This can be distinguished from the true dot cylinder in which the "4" is broader and further from the "E", and the dot is more circular than the erroneous dot.

The erroneous dot was not noticed until the Crowns watermark which exists in three states: I with the erroneous dot; II with dot removed leaving a smudge; and III with smudge removed. These are shown in the following illustration:—

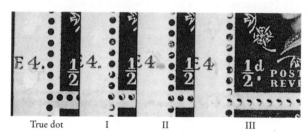

       True dot   I   II   III

½d. BOOKLET PANES OF FOUR
4 × ½d. Tudor Crown
From 1s. Booklet K1/a for use in "E" machines.

A. Watermark upright

                                                   Perf. Type P
    SB2   Pane of 4 × ½d.   (containing No. S1 × 4) (22.7.54) . . . . 6·00

B. Watermark inverted
    SB2a   Pane of 4 × ½d.   (containing No. S1a × 4) (22.7.54) . . . . 8·00

Booklet Cylinder Numbers

Cylinder No. E3 was used, but it does not appear in the finished booklets.

Imprimaturs from the National Postal Museum Archives

Booklet pane of four. Imperforate, watermark Type W.22

Two panes arranged vertically *tête-bêche* with a 12 mm. horizontal gutter margin between

½d. BOOKLET PANES OF TWO

2 × ½d. Tudor Crown
From 1s. Booklet E1 for use in experimental "D" machines.

Watermark upright

		Perf. Type	
		E	E(½v)
SB3	Pane of 2 × ½d. (containing No. S1 × 2) (2.9.53)	4·00	8·00

Made up from vertical rows 1 and 2 from sheets.

Booklet Cylinder Numbers

Panes of two (from sheets). Perf. Type E

Cyl. No.	No dot	Dot	Cyl. No.	No dot	Dot
1	35·00	35·00	3	25·00	25·00

½d. BOOKLET PANES OF SIX

6 × ½d. St. Edward's Crown
From 2s.6d. Booklets F34/61, 3s. Booklets M1/10 and 5s. Booklets H17/37

A. Watermark upright

SB4	Pane of 6 × ½d. (containing No. S2 × 6) (9.55)	2·50
	b.	Part perf. pane*	£4000
	c.	White flaw in Queen's hair (R. 1/3 or 2/3)	15·00

B. Watermark inverted

SB4a	Pane of 6 × ½d. (containing No. S2b × 6) (9.55)	4·00

*Booklet error—see General Notes.

SB4c, SB7e, SB14b
(Cyl. E4 dot)

Booklet Cylinder Numbers

Panes of six (20/21-row cylinders)

Cyl. No.	No dot	Dot	Cyl. No.	No dot	Dot
E4*	15·00	15·00	E4 T*	25·00	15·00

*See notes after booklet panes of No. SB1.

The ½d. double pane cylinders E1, E2 and E4 contained 20 rows and the cylinder number always occurred opposite row 18 so that it always appears next to the bottom row of the pane.

Cylinder E4 was later modified by adding another row of 24. In this and later 21-row cylinders, which are printed continuously on the web, the perforated web is cut at every 20th row to make sheets of 480. Consequently on successive sheets the cylinder number appears one row lower and thus a pane can have it adjoining the top or bottom row. Where the cylinder number adjoins the top row of the pane it is designated by the letter "T".

½d. BOOKLET PANES OF FOUR
4 × ½d. St. Edward's Crown
From 1s. Booklets K2/*b* for use in "E" machines and 2s. Booklet N1

A. Watermark upright

			Perf. Type	
			AP	P
SB5	Pane of 4 × ½d.	(containing No. S2 × 4) (5.7.56)	10·00	8·00

B. Watermark inverted
| SB5a | Pane of 4 × ½d. | (containing No. S2*b* × 4) (5.7.56) . . . . | 10·00 | 8·00 |

Booklet Cylinder Numbers

Cylinder No. E3 was used, but it does not appear in the finished booklets.

Imprimaturs from the National Postal Museum Archives

Booklet pane of four. Imperforate, watermark Type W.23

Two panes arranged vertically *tête-bêche* with a 12 mm. horizontal gutter margin between

½d. BOOKLET PANES OF TWO
2 × ½d. St. Edward's Crown
From 1s. Booklet E2 for use in experimental "D" machines.

Watermark upright

			Perf. Type	
			E	E(½v)
SB6	Pane of 2 × ½d.	(containing No. S2 × 2) (11.57)	15·00	20·00

Made up from vertical rows 1 and 2 from sheets.

Booklet Cylinder Numbers

Panes of two (from sheets). Perf. Type E

Cyl. No.	No dot	Dot
3	. . . . 35·00	£100

½d. BOOKLET PANES OF SIX
6 × ½d. Crowns. Cream or whiter paper
From 3s. Booklets M9(*a*)/74, 5s. Booklets H35(*a*) and H37/74 and 10s. Booklets X1/2

Cream Paper
A. Watermark upright
SB7		Pane of 6 × ½d.	(containing No. S4 × 6) (11.58)	5·50
	b.	Part perf. pane*	£3000
	c.	Dot on left fraction bar (R. 1/1 or R. 2/1)	15·00
	d.	Extended right fraction bar (R. 1/1 or R. 2/1)	15·00
	e.	White flaw in Queen's hair (R. 1/3 or R. 2/3)	15·00

B. Watermark inverted
| SB7a | Pane of 6 × ½d. | (containing No. S4*c* × 6) (11.58) . . . . | 5·50 |

Whiter Paper
A. Watermark upright
SB8		Pane of 6 × ½d.	(containing No. S5 × 6) (6.62)	7·50
	b.	Dot on left fraction bar (R. 1/1 or R. 2/1)	15·00
	c.	Extended right fraction bar (R. 1/1 or R. 2/1)	15·00

B. Watermark inverted
| SB8a | Pane of 6 × ½d. | (containing No. S5*c* × 6) (6.62) . . . . | 7·50 |

*Booklet error—see General Notes.

For illustration of No. SB7*e* see No. SB4*c*.

SB7*c*, SB8*b*,   SB7*d*, SB8*c*,
SB16*c*, SB17*c*   SB16*b*, SB17*b*
(Cyl. E12 no dot)   (Cyl. E12 no dot)

Booklet Cylinder Numbers

Panes of six (21-row cylinders)

Cream paper			
Cyl. No.		No dot	Dot
E4* With erroneous dot . . .		20·00	18·00
E4* No dot with smudge . .		30·00	†
E4* Smudge removed		25·00	†
E4 T* With erroneous dot . .		25·00	25·00
E4 T* No dot with smudge .		25·00	†
E4 T* Smudge removed . . .		20·00	†
E11		20·00	20·00
E11 T		20·00	20·00
E12		30·00	30·00
E12 T		30·00	30·00

Whiter paper			
Cyl. No.		No dot	Dot
E11		30·00	30·00
E11 T		30·00	30·00
E12		25·00	25·00
E12 T		25·00	25·00

*For explanation see notes below No. SB1.

Specimen overprints from the National Postal Museum Archives

Booklet pane of six. Perf. 15 × 14, watermark Type W.24 inverted

Each stamp handstamped "Specimen" (15 × 2½ mm.)

½ d. BOOKLET PANES OF FOUR

4 × ½ d. Crowns. Cream paper

From 1s. Booklets K3/*a* for use in "E" machines and 2s. Booklets N2/3. Perf. Type AP

A. Watermark upright
   SB9   Pane of 4 × ½ d.   (containing No. S4 × 4) (13.8.59) . . . .   4·00

B. Watermark inverted
   SB9a   Pane of 4 × ½ d.   (containing No. S4*c* × 4) (13.8.59) . . . .   4·00

Booklet Cylinder Numbers

Cylinder No. E3 was used, but it does not appear in the finished booklets.

Imprimaturs from the National Postal Museum Archives

Booklet pane of four. Imperforate, watermark Type W.24

Two panes arranged vertically *tête-bêche* with a 12 mm. horizontal gutter margin between

Specimen overprints from the National Postal Museum Archives

Booklet pane of four. Perf. 15 × 14, watermark Type W.24 inverted

Each stamp handstamped "Specimen" (13 × 2 mm.)

½d. BOOKLET PANES OF FOUR. SIDEWAYS WATERMARK
4 × ½d. Crowns. Cream or whiter paper
From 2s. Booklets N4/20

Cream Paper
A. Watermark Crown to left

	Perf. Type		
	I	I(½v)	AP
SB10 Pane of 4 × ½d. (containing No. S4d × 4) (26.5.61)	15·00	35·00	10·00

B. Watermark Crown to right
SB10a   Pane of 4 × ½d.   (containing No. S4e × 4) (26.5.61) . . . . 15·00 35·00 10·00

Whiter Paper
A. Watermark Crown to left
SB11   Pane of 4 × ½d.   (containing No. S5a × 4) (5.6.62)   . . . . 9·00 35·00 7·50

B. Watermark Crown to right
SB11a   Pane of 4 × ½d.   (containing No. S5b × 4) (5.6.62)   . . . . 9·00 35·00 7·50

Booklet Cylinder Number

Cylinder No. E13 was used, but it was partly trimmed off. (*Price for pane showing* (E13), *from* £85.)

Specimen overprints from the National Postal Museum Archives

Booklet pane of four. Perf. 15 × 14, watermark Type W.24

Each stamp handstamped "Specimen" (13 × 2 mm.)

SB12   SB13

SE-TENANT PANES OF FOUR FROM HOLIDAY BOOKLETS

Crowns watermark. Chalky paper. 3 × ½d. with 2½d. from 2s. Booklet NR1/1a

A. Watermark upright

			Perf. Type		
			I	I(½v)	AP
SB12	Pane of ½d./2½d.	(containing No. S6 × 3, S58) (15.7.63)	15·00	25·00	9·00
	b.	Screen damage on 2½d.	†	†	30·00

B. Watermark inverted

SB12a	Pane of ½d./2½d.	(containing No. S6a × 3, S58a) (15.7.63)	15·00	25·00	9·00
	ab.	Daffodil flaw on ½d.	†	†	35·00
	ac.	Daffodil trumpet flaw on ½d.	†	†	30·00

SB12b   SB12ab   SB12ac
Later retouched   Bottom left stamp of pane   Upper right
                       (2½d. to right)   stamp of pane

Whiter paper. Crowns sideways watermark
Pair of ½d. with pair of 2½d. from 2s. Booklet NR2

A. Watermark Crown to left

			Perf. Type		
			I	I(½v)	AP
SB13	Pane of 2 × ½d./2½d.	(containing Nos. S5a × 2, S57c × 2) (1.7.64) .	5·00	20·00	2·25
	b.	Comma flaw (R. 1/2)	25·00	†	†
	c.	Spot to right of d (R. 1/1)	20·00	†	†
	d.	Rose flaw (R. 1/2)	†	†	15·00
	e.	"P" for "D" (R. 2/1)	†	†	15·00
	f.	Wreath flaw (R. 2/1)	†	†	12·00
	g.	White spot above 2 (R. 2/1)	†	†	12·00

101

B. Watermark Crown to right

SB13a	Pane of 2 × ½d./2½d.	(containing Nos. S5*b* × 2, S57*d* × 2) (1.7.64) .	5·00	20·00	2·25
ab.	Rose stem flaw (R. 1/2)	†	†	15·00
ac.	Frame flaw (R. 1/2)	†	†	20·00
ad.	White spot by daffodil (R. 1/1)	†	†	15·00

SB13*b*
Right stamp of pane

SB13*c*
Left stamp of pane

SB13*d*
Upper right stamp
of pane

SB13*e*
Left stamp of pane

SB13*f*
Left stamp of pane

SB13*g*
Left stamp of pane

SB13*ab*
Upper right
stamp of pane

SB13*ac*
Upper right
stamp of pane

SB13*ad*
Upper left stamp
of pane

Booklet Cylinder Numbers

Panes of four (20-row single pane cylinder of 480 stamps).
Cylinder numbers are not known from Booklets NR1/1*a* but the following exists from the Holiday Booklet NR2 on whiter paper

Cyl. Nos.	No dot
E14 (½d.), J15 (2½d.)	45·00

Imprimaturs from the National Postal Museum Archives

Se-tenant booklet panes of four. Imperforate, watermark Type W.24

Two panes as No. SB12 arranged vertically *tête-bêche* with binding margin at top and bottom
Two panes as No. SB13 arranged sideways *tête-bêche* with binding margin at top and bottom

½d. BOOKLET PANES OF SIX WITH GRAPHITE LINES

6 × ½d. Crowns. Graphite lines as Type **S8**, shown above No. S3 on page 12.
From 3s. Booklets M13g/15g, M19g/21g and 5s. Booklets H39g, H43g and H46g

A. Watermark upright
    SB14   Pane of 6 × ½d. (containing No. S7 × 6) (4.8.59) . . . . 65·00
                b.   White flaw in Queen's hair (R. 1/3 or 2/3) . . . . 85·00

B. Watermark inverted
    SB14a Pane of 6 × ½d. (containing No. S7a × 6) (4.8.59) . . . . 21·00
For illustration of No. SB14b, see No. SB4c.

Booklet Cylinder Numbers

Panes of six (21-row cylinder)

Cyl. No.	No dot	Dot	Cyl. No.	No dot	Dot
E4	85·00	85·00	E4 T	85·00	85·00

½d. BOOKLET PANES OF SIX WITH TWO PHOSPHOR BANDS REACTING GREEN

6 × ½d. Crowns. Two phosphor bands applied in photogravure
From 3s. Booklets M25p, M28p/29p and M37p(a) and 5s. Booklet H46p

A. Watermark upright
    SB15   Pane of 6 × ½d. (containing No. S9 × 6) (14.8.60) . . . . 20·00

B. Watermark inverted
    SB15a Pane of 6 × ½d. (containing No. S9a × 6) (14.8.60) . . . . 40·00

Booklet Cylinder Numbers

Panes of six (21-row cylinder)

Cyl. No.	No dot	Dot	Cyl. No.	No dot	Dot
E11	65·00	65·00	E11 T	65·00	65·00

½d. BOOKLET PANES OF SIX WITH TWO PHOSPHOR BANDS REACTING BLUE

6 × ½d. Crowns. Two phosphor bands applied in photogravure. Cream or whiter paper
From 3s. Booklets M33p, M36p, M37p(b), M38p/39p, M43p/47p, M49p/53p, M55p/61p, M64p/74p,
and 5s. Booklets H49p, H51p/52p and H54p/74p

Cream Paper
A. Watermark upright
    SB16   Pane of 6 × ½d. (containing No. S10 × 6) (3.61) . . . . 5·00
                b.   Extended right fraction bar (R. 1/1 or 2/1) . . . . 15·00
                c.   Dot on left fraction bar (R. 1/1 or 2/1) . . . . 15·00
                d.   One band on each stamp £450

B. Watermark inverted
    SB16a Pane of 6 × ½d. (containing No. S10a × 6) (3.61) . . . . 8·00

Whiter Paper
A. Watermark upright
    SB17   Pane of 6 × ½d. (containing No. S11 × 6) (3.6.63) . . . . 9·00
                b.   Extended right fraction bar (R. 1/1 or 2/1) . . . . 20·00
                c.   Dot on left fraction bar (R. 1/1 or 2/1) . . . . 20·00

B. Watermark inverted
    SB17a Pane of 6 × ½d. (containing No. S11c × 6) (3.6.63) . . . . 15·00
For illustrations of Nos. SB16b/c and SB17b/c, see Nos. SB7c/d.

Booklet Cylinder Numbers

Panes of six (21-row cylinder)

Cyl. No.	Cream paper	No dot	Dot	Cyl. No.	Whiter paper	No dot	Dot
E12	. . . .	30·00	30·00	E12	. . . .	35·00	35·00
E12 T	. . . .	30·00	30·00	E12 T	. . . .	35·00	35·00

Specimen overprints from the National Postal Museum Archives

Booklet pane of six. Perf. 15 × 14, watermark Type W.24 upright

Each stamp handstamped "Specimen" (13 × 2 mm.)
Each stamp handstamped "Specimen" (15 × 2½ mm.)

½d. BOOKLET PANES OF FOUR WITH TWO PHOSPHOR BANDS REACTING BLUE. SIDEWAYS WATERMARK

4 × ½d. Crowns. Two phosphor bands applied by typography. Cream or whiter paper
From 2s. Booklets N4p, N8p/10p, N12p/20p

Cream Paper
A. Watermark Crown to left

			Perf. Type		
			I	I(½v)	AP
SB18	Pane of 4 × ½d.	(containing No. S10*b* × 4) (14.7.61)	70·00	85·00	40·00
	b.	Error. One band on each stamp	£180	—	£100

B. Watermark Crown to right

			I	I(½v)	AP
SB18a	Pane of 4 × ½d.	(containing No. S10*c* × 4) (14.7.61)	70·00	85·00	40·00
	ab.	Error. One band on each stamp	—	—	£100

Whiter Paper
A. Watermark Crown to left

			Perf. Type		
			I	I(½v)	AP
SB19	Pane of 4 × ½d.	(containing No. S11*a* × 4) (15.8.62)	75·00	95·00	50·00

B. Watermark Crown to right

			I	I(½v)	AP
SB19a	Pane of 4 × ½d.	(containing No. S11*b* × 4) (15.8.62)	75·00	95·00	50·00

Booklet Cylinder Numbers

Panes of four (20-row single pane cylinder of 480 stamps)
In the 2s. Booklets the cylinder numbers were partly trimmed off, but No. E13 was the cylinder used. (*Price for pane showing* (E13), *from* £95).

Imprimaturs from the National Postal Museum Archives

Booklet pane of four. Imperforate, watermark Type W.24

Two panes arranged sideways *tête-bêche*

Specimen overprints from the National Postal Museum Archives

Booklet pane of four. Perf. 15 × 14, watermark Type W.24

Each stamp handstamped "Specimen" (13 × 2 mm.)

1d. BOOKLET PANES OF SIX
6 × 1d. Tudor Crown
From 5s. Booklets H7/16

A. Watermark upright

SB20	Pane of 6 × 1d.	(containing No. S13 × 6) (3.54)	25·00
	b.	Hair flaw (R. 1/1)	35·00

B. Watermark inverted

SB20a	Pane of 6 × 1d.	(containing No. S13*a* × 6) (3.54)	40·00
	ab.	Extended leaf on shamrock (R. 2/1)	55·00

This is a multipostive flaw from booklet panes.
All watermarks and phosphors
(Cyls. F3, F4 and F10
from the no dot pane)

SB20*b*, SB26*d*   SB20*ab*, SB26*ad*, SB30*ac*, SB31*ad*,
(Cyl. F4 no dot)   SB39*ac*, SB40*ac*, SB41*ab*, SB42*ab*,
                         SB49*ab*, SB54*ab*

Booklet Cylinder Numbers

Panes of six from 5s. Booklets

Cyl. No.	No dot	Dot
F4	35·00	50·00*

*Contains the dot in serif flaw (R. 1/3).

1d. BOOKLET PANES OF FOUR
4 × 1d. Tudor Crown
From 1s. Booklet K1/*a* for use in "E" machines.

A. Watermark upright

Perf. Type P

SB21   Pane of 4 × 1d.   (containing No. S13 × 4) (22.7.54) . . . .   9·00

B. Watermark inverted
SB21a   Pane of 4 × 1d.   (containing No. S13*a* × 4) (22.7.54) . . . .   30·00

Booklet Cylinder Numbers

Cylinder No. F7 was used, but it does not appear in the finished booklets.

Imprimaturs from the National Postal Museum Archives

Booklet pane of four. Imperforate, watermark Type W.22

Two panes arranged vertically *tête-bêche* with a 12 mm. horizontal gutter margin between

1d. BOOKLET PANES OF TWO
2 × 1d. Tudor Crown
From 1s. Booklet E1 for use in experimental "D" machines.
Watermark upright

			Perf. Type		
		I	I($\frac{1}{2}$v)	E	E($\frac{1}{2}$v)
SB22 Pane of 2 × 1d. (containing No. S13 × 2) (2.9.53)		3·00	9·00	3·00	—
a. Shamrock flaw (as on No. S13*c*)		†	†	20·00	†

Made up from vertical rows 1 and 2 from sheets.

Booklet Cylinder Numbers

Panes of two (from sheets)

	Perf. Type				Perf. Type	
	I	E			E	
Cyl. No.	No dot	Dot	Cyl. No.		No dot	Dot
1	25·00	25·00	2		25·00	50·00

SB23

1d. SE-TENANT WITH PRINTED LABELS—"MINIMUM INLAND PRINTED PAPER RATE 1½d."

3 × 1d. Tudor Crown
From 2s.6d. Booklet F15

A. Watermark upright
    SB23   Pane of 3 × 1d.   (containing S13 × 3) (3.54) £250
                b.   "RATE" and "1½d." 16 mm. apart (on cyl. pane) £350
                c.   Dot in serif (R. 1/3) £285

B. Watermark inverted
    SB23a   Pane of 3 × 1d.   (containing S13*a* × 3) (3.54) £250

In the label inscription the distance between "RATE" and "1½d." is usually 15 mm. However, on the cylinder pane of No. SB23, F5 dot and F6 no dot and dot only, the right-hand label shows a spacing of 16 mm.

SB23*c*, SB24*ba*, SB24*c*, SB25*b*, SB26*b*, SB29*b*,
SB30*e*, SB31*b*, SB41*b*, SB42*b*, SB49*b*, SB54*b*

Dot in serif of "1". Right-hand stamp

This is a multipositive flaw which is found only in booklet panes, stamp 3 in either the first or second horizontal rows; all watermarks and phosphors on the dot cylinder panes F3, F4 and F10 also on the ordinary panes from cylinders F3, F4, F5, F6, F9 and F10. On cylinder F3 dot the flaw exists as a retouched state leaving the dot as a blemish and later the mark was removed. The later state occurs only in the position R. 2/3 and is not listed separately. Note that the flaw is present on all panes of six (R. 1/3) with cylinder number in bottom position.

Booklet Cylinder Numbers

Panes with printed labels from 2s.6d. Booklet F15

Cyl. No.	No dot	Dot
F5	†	£1200
F6	£375	£375

SB24

1d. SE-TENANT WITH PRINTED LABELS—"PLEASE POST EARLY IN THE DAY"
3 × 1d. Tudor Crown
From 2s.6d. Booklets F16/25

A. Watermark upright
SB24	Pane of 3 × 1d.	(containing S13 × 3) (4.54)	35·00
b.		Modified setting	55·00
ba.		Do. Dot in serif (R. 1/3)	75·00
c.		Dot in serif (R. 1/3)	45·00

B. Watermark inverted
SB24a	Pane of 3 × 1d.	(containing S13*a* × 3) (4.54)	35·00
ab.		Modified setting	55·00

In the modified setting the distance between "IN THE" is 1 mm. and this is only found on the majority of the Jan. 1955 edition (Booklet F25). The normal spacing is 1½ mm.

Booklet Cylinder Numbers
Panes with printed labels from 2s.6d. Booklets F16/25

Cyl. No.	No dot	Dot
F6	75·00	60·00
F6 (modified setting)	£150	£150

From cylinder F6 onwards the labels were printed in photogravure instead of typography.

SB25, SB29

**1d. SE-TENANT WITH PRINTED LABELS—"PACK YOUR PARCELS SECURELY"
(1st label), "ADDRESS YOUR LETTERS CORRECTLY" (2nd label) and "AND POST EARLY
IN THE DAY" (3rd label)**
3 × 1d. Tudor Crown
From 2s.6d. Booklets F26/34

A. Watermark upright
  SB25   Pane of 3 × 1d.   (containing No. S13 × 3) (1.55) . . . .   45·00
            b.   Dot in serif (R. 1/3) . . . .   55·00
            c.   Daffodil flaw (R. 1/1) . . . .   55·00

B. Watermark inverted
  SB25a   Pane of 3 × 1d.   (containing No. S13*a* × 3) (1.55) . . . .   45·00

SB25*c*, SB29*c*
(Cyl. F6 no dot)

Booklet Cylinder Numbers

Panes with printed labels from 2s.6d. Booklets F26/34

Cyl. No.   No dot   Dot
  F6 . . . .   75·00   75·00

Imprimaturs from the National Postal Museum Archives

Booklet pane with printed labels. Imperforate, watermark Type W.22

Two panes as No. SB25 arranged *tête-bêche*

1d. BOOKLET PANES OF SIX
6 × 1d. St. Edward's Crown
From 3s. Booklets M1/9 and 5s. Booklets H17/36

A. Watermark upright
  SB26   Pane of 6 × 1d.   (containing No. S14 × 6) (8.55) . . . .   4·00
            b.   Dot in serif (R. 2/3, F3 dot)) . . . .   15·00
            c.   "Dew drop" (R. 1/1 or 2/1) . . . .   15·00
            d.   Hair flaw (R. 1/1) . . . .   15·00

B. Watermark inverted
  SB26a   Pane of 6 × 1d.   (containing No. S14*b* × 6) (8.55) . . . .   6·50
            ab.   Spot on "d" (R. 1/1 or 2/1) . . . .   15·00
            ac.   White flaw by rose (R. 1/2 or 2/2) . . . .   15·00
            ad.   Extended leaf on shamrock (R. 1/1 or 2/1) . . . .   15·00
            ae.   Rose flaw (R. 1/1 or 2/1) . . . .   15·00

  For illustrations of No. SB26*b*, see No. SB23*c*, for No. SB26*d*, see No. SB20*b* and for No. SB26*ad*,
see No. SB20*ab*.

| SB26*c*, SB30*d*, SB39*b* Later retouched on Crowns and phosphor (Cyl. F3 dot) | SB26*ab*, SB30*ab*, SB31*ac* SB39*ab*, SB40*ab* (Cyl. F3 dot) | SB26*ac* (Cyl. F3 dot) | SB26*ae*, SB30*ad*, SB39*ad*, SB40*ad* (Cyl. F3 no dot) |

Booklet Cylinder Numbers

Panes of six

Cyl. No.	Cat. No	No dot	Dot
F3	SB26	25·00	25·00*
F3 T . . .	SB26	20·00	20·00
F4	SB26	30·00	25·00*

Cylinder F3 contained 21 rows so that cylinder numbers adjoin either the top (T) or the bottom row. It was used in all 5s. Booklets H31/36. Cylinder F4 was a 20-row cylinder and used for the 5s. Booklets H17/30.

1d. BOOKLET PANES OF FOUR
4 × 1d. St. Edward's Crown
From 1s. Booklets K2/*b* for use in "E" machines and 2s. Booklet N1

A. Watermark upright

			Perf. Type	
			AP	P
SB27	Pane of 4 × 1d.	(containing No. S14 × 4) (5.7.56)	10·00	8·00
	b.	Spur to shamrock (R. 2/1)	25·00	†

B. Watermark inverted
| SB27a | Pane of 4 × 1d. | (containing No. S14*b* × 4) (5.7.56) . . . . | 10·00 | 8·00 |

SB27*b*, SB32*b*
Later retouched on Crowns wmk.

Booklet Cylinder Numbers

Cylinder Nos. F7 and F8 were used, but they do not appear in the finished booklets.

Imprimaturs from the National Postal Museum Archives

Booklet pane of four. Imperforate, watermark Type W.23

Two panes arranged vertically *tête-bêche* with a 12 mm. horizontal gutter margin between

1d. BOOKLET PANES OF TWO
2 × 1d. St. Edward's Crown
From 1s. Booklet E2 for use in experimental "D" machines.

Watermark upright

			Perf.Type	
			E	E($\frac{1}{2}$v)
SB28	Pane of 2 × 1d.	(containing No. S14 × 2) (11·57)	15·00	20·00
	a.	Shamrock flaw (as on No. S14*d*)	25·00	†

Made up from vertical rows 1 and 2 from sheets.

Booklet Cylinder Numbers
Panes of two (from sheets). Perf. Type E

Cyl. No.	No dot	Dot
1	95·00	95·00

1d. SE-TENANT WITH PRINTED LABELS—"PACK YOUR PARCELS SECURELY" (1st label), "ADDRESS YOUR LETTERS CORRECTLY" (2nd label) and "AND POST EARLY IN THE DAY" (3rd label)
3 × 1d. St. Edward's Crown
From 2s.6d. Booklets F34/52

A. Watermark upright

SB29	Pane of 3 × 1d.	(containing No. S14 × 3) (8.55)	16·00
	b.	Dot in serif (R. 1/3)	25·00
	c.	Daffodil flaw (R. 1/1)	25·00

B. Watermark inverted

SB29a   Pane of 3 × 1d.   (containing No. S14*b* × 3) (8.55) . . . .   16·00

For illustration of No. SB29*b* see No. SB23*c* and for No. SB29*c* see No. SB25*c*.

Booklet Cylinder Numbers
Panes with printed labels from 2s.6d. Booklets F34/52

Cyl. No.	No dot	Dot
F6	35·00	35·00
F9	65·00	65·00

Cylinder F6 was used for the 2s.6d. Booklets F34/40 and part of F41/52 and F9 for 2s.6d. Booklets F41/52. Both cylinders were 20-row.

Imprimaturs from the National Postal Museum Archives
Booklet pane with printed labels. Imperforate, watermark Type W.23

Two panes as No. SB29 arranged *tête-bêche*

1d. BOOKLET PANES OF SIX
6 × 1d. Crowns. Cream or whiter paper
From 3s. Booklets M9(*b*)/(*c*), M10/74, 4s.6d. Booklets L59/65, 5s. Booklets H35(*b*)/(*c*), H36(*a*) and H37/74 and 10s. Booklets X1/14

Cream Paper
A. Watermark upright

SB30	Pane of 6 × 1d.	(containing No. S16 × 6) (11.58)	6·00
	b.	Imperf. pane*	£4500
	c.	Part perf. pane*	£3500
	d.	"Dew drop" (R. 1/1 or 2/1)	15·00
	e.	Dot in serif (R. 2/3)	15·00

B. Watermark inverted

SB30a	Pane of 6 × 1d.	(containing No. S16*d* × 6) (11.58)	6·00
	ab.	Spot on "d" (R. 1/1 or 2/1)	15·00
	ac.	Extended leaf on shamrock (R. 1/1 or 2/1)	15·00
	ad.	Rose flaw (R. 1/1 or 2/1)	15·00

Whiter Paper

A. Watermark upright

SB31	Pane of 6 × 1d.	(containing No. S17 × 6) (29.7.62)	6·00
	b.	Dot in serif (R. 2/3)	20·00

B. Watermark inverted

SB31a	Pane of 6 × 1d.	(containing No. S17*c* × 6) (29.7.62)	7·00
	ab.	Part perf. pane*	£3500
	ac.	Spot on "d" (R. 1/1 or 2/1)	20·00
	ad.	Extended leaf on shamrock (R. 1/1 or 2/1)	20·00

*Booklet errors—See General Notes.

For illustrations of No. SB30*d* see No. SB26*c*; for Nos. SB30*ab* and SB31*ac* see No. SB26*ab*; for Nos. SB30*ac* and SB31*ad* see No. SB20*ab* and for No. SB30*ad* see No. SB26*ae*.

On the cream paper the dot in serif flaw (Cyl. F3 dot) was removed by retouching but a smudged state exists. For illustration of No. SB30*e*, see No SB23*c*. On white paper the flaw exists from Cyl. F10 dot.

Booklet Cylinder Numbers

Panes of six (21-row cylinders)

	Cream paper				Whiter paper		
Cyl. No.		No dot	Dot	Cyl. No.		No dot	Dot
F3		20·00	20·00*	F3		35·00	35·00
F3 T		20·00	20·00	F3 T		35·00	35·00
F10		35·00	25·00*	F10		35·00	25·00*
F10 T		35·00	25·00	F10 T		35·00	25·00

Specimen overprints from the National Postal Museum Archives

Booklet pane of six. Perf. 15 × 14, watermark Type W.24.

Each stamp handstamped "Specimen" (13 × 2 mm.) wmk. upright
Each stamp handstamped "Specimen" (15 × 2½ mm.) wmk. inverted

1d. BOOKLET PANES OF FOUR

4 × 1d. Crowns. Cream paper

From 1s. Booklets K3/*a* for use in "E" machines and 2s. Booklets N2/3. Perf. Type AP

A. Watermark upright

SB32	Pane of 4 × 1d.	(containing No. S16 × 4) (13.8.59)	5·00
	b.	Spur to shamrock (R. 2/1)	15·00

B. Watermark inverted

SB32a	Pane of 4 × 1d.	(containing No. S16*d* × 4) (13.8.59)	5·00

For illustration of No. SB32*b* see No. SB27*b*.

Booklet Cylinder Numbers

Cylinder No. F8 was used, but it does not appear in the finished booklets.

Imprimaturs from the National Postal Museum Archives

Booklet pane of four. Imperforate, watermark Type W.24

Two panes arranged vertically *tête-bêche* with a 12 mm. horizontal gutter margin between

Specimen overprints from the National Postal Museum Archives

Booklet pane of four. Perf. 15 × 14, watermark Type W.24 upright

Each stamp handstamped "Specimen" (13 × 2 mm.)

1d. BOOKLET PANES OF FOUR WITH SIDEWAYS WATERMARK
4 × 1d. Crowns. Cream or whiter paper
From 2s. Booklets N4/20

Cream paper
A. Watermark Crown to left

			Perf. Type		
			I	I($\frac{1}{2}$v)	AP
SB33	Pane of 4 × 1d.	(containing No. S16*e* × 4) (26.5.61)	18·00	35·00	10·00

B. Watermark Crown to right

SB33a	Pane of 4 × 1d.	(containing No. S16*f* × 4) (26.5.61)	18·00	35·00	10·00

Whiter Paper
A. Watermark Crown to left

SB34	Pane of 4 × 1d.	(containing No. S17*a* × 4) (5.6.62)	12·00	30·00	10·00

B. Watermark Crown to right

SB34a	Pane of 4 × 1d.	(containing No. S17*b* × 4) (5.6.62)	12·00	30·00	10·00

Booklet Cylinder Numbers
Cylinder No. F12 was used, but it was partly trimmed off. (*Price for pane showing* (F12) *from* £65).

Specimen overprints from the National Postal Museum Archives
Booklet pane of four. Perf. 15 × 14, watermark Type W.24

Each stamp handstamped "Specimen" (13 × 2 mm.)

SB35, SB37, SB45, SB47,
SB50, SB52, SB55, SB57
(1d. values at left)

SB36, SB38, SB46, SB48,
SB51, SB53, SB56, SB58
(1d. values at right)

1d. AND 3d. SE-TENANT BOOKLET PANES OF FOUR. SIDEWAYS WATERMARK
Pair of 1d. with pair of 3d. Crowns, Whiter paper
From 2s. Booklets N21/27

Panes SB35 and SB37   Panes of four with 1d. at left
Panes SB36 and SB38   Panes of four with 1d. at right

A. Watermark Crown to left

			Perf. Type		
			I	I($\frac{1}{2}$v)	AP
SB35	Pane of 2 × 1d./3d.	(containing Nos. S17*a* × 2, S71*a* × 2) (16.8.65) .	15·00	45·00	10·00
SB36	Pane of 2 × 3d./1d.	(containing Nos. S71*a* × 2, S17*a* × 2) (16.8.65) .	15·00	45·00	11·00
	a.	Thistle flaw on 1d. (R. 2/2)	†	45·00	†

B. Watermark Crown to right

SB37	Pane of 2 × 1d./3d.	(containing Nos. S17b × 2, S71b × 2) (16.8.65)	.	15·00	40·00	10·00
SB38	Pane of 2 × 3d./1d.	(containing Nos. S71b × 2, S17b × 2) (16.8.65)	.	15·00	40·00	11·00
	a.	"R" flaw on 1d. (R. 2/2)		†	†	15·00

SB36a, SB46c, SB51c, SB56a, SB56ba
Large white flaw to right of left thistle.
Occurs on bottom right stamp of
pane with 3d. at left

SB38a, SB48c, SB53c, SB58a, SB58ba
Flaw on "P" which appears as "R" and
occurs on bottom right stamp of
pane with 3d. at left

Booklet Cylinder Numbers

Panes of four (24-row single pane cylinder of 480 stamps, sideways).
From *se-tenant* pane booklets on whiter paper

Cyl. Nos.	No dot
F13 (1d.), K22 (3d.)	50·00

1d. BOOKLET PANES OF SIX WITH GRAPHITE LINES

6 × 1d. Crowns. Graphite lines as Type **S8** (page 12)
From 3s. Booklets M13g/15g, M19g/21g and 5s. Booklets H39g, H43g and H46g

A. Watermark upright

SB39	Pane of 6 × 1d.	(containing No. S18 × 6) (4.8.59)	18·00
	b.	"Dew drop" (R. 1/1 or 2/1)	25·00

B. Watermark inverted

SB39a	Pane of 6 × 1d.	(containing No. S18a × 6) (4.8.59)	16·00
	ab.	Spot on "d" (R. 1/1 or 2/1)	25·00
	ac.	Extended leaf on shamrock (R. 1/1 or 2/1)	25·00
	ad.	Rose flaw (R. 1/1 or 2/1)	25·00

For illustrations of No. SB39b see No. SB26c; for Nos. SB39ab/ad see Nos. SB26ab, SB20ab and SB26ae.

Booklet Cylinder Numbers

Panes of six (21-row cylinder)

Cyl. No.	No dot	Dot	Cyl. No.	No dot	Dot
F3	55·00	55·00	F3 T	55·00	55·00

1d. BOOKLET PANES OF SIX WITH TWO PHOSPHOR BANDS REACTING GREEN

6 × 1d. Crowns. Two phosphor bands applied in photogravure
From 3s. Booklets M25p, M28p/29p and M37p(a) and 5s. Booklet H46p

A. Watermark upright

SB40	Pane of 6 × 1d.	(containing No. S20 × 6) (14.8.60)	25·00
	b.	One band on each stamp	

B. Watermark inverted

SB40a	Pane of 6 × 1d.	(containing No. S20a × 6) (14.8.60)	38·00
	ab.	Spot on "d" (R. 1/1 or 2/1)	55·00
	ac.	Extended leaf on shamrock (R. 1/1 or 2/1)	55·00
	ad.	Rose flaw (R. 1/1 or 2/1)	55·00
	ae.	One band on each stamp	

For illustrations of Nos. SB40ab/ad see Nos. SB26ab, SB20ab and SB26ae.

Booklet Cylinder Numbers

Panes of six (21-row cylinder)

Cyl. No.		No dot	Dot	Cyl. No.		No dot	Dot
F3	. . . .	75·00	75·00	F3 T	. . . .	75·00	75·00

1d. BOOKLET PANES OF SIX WITH TWO PHOSPHOR BANDS REACTING BLUE

6 × 1d. Crowns. Two phosphor bands applied in photogravure. Cream or whiter paper
From 3s. Booklets M33p, M36p, M37p(*b*), M38p/9p, M43p/7p, M49p/53p, M55p/61p, M64p/74p,
4s.6d. Booklets L59p/60p(*a*), L61p(*a*), L62p(*a*) and 5s. Booklets H49p, H51p/2p, H54p/74p

Cream Paper
A. Watermark upright

SB41	Pane of 6 × 1d.	(containing No. S21 × 6) (3.61)	6·00
	b.	Dot in serif (R. 2/3)	20·00

B. Watermark inverted

SB41a	Pane of 6 × 1d.	(containing No. S21*a* × 6) (3.61)	6·00
	ab.	Extended leaf on shamrock (R. 1/1 or 2/1)	20·00

Whiter Paper
A. Watermark upright

SB42	Pane of 6 × 1d.	(containing No. S22 × 6) (3.6.63)	7·00
	b.	Dot in serif (R. 2/3)	25·00
	c.	One band on each stamp	

B. Watermark inverted

SB42a	Pane of 6 × 1d.	(containing No. S22*c* × 6) (3.6.63)	7·00
	ab.	Extended leaf on shamrock (R. 1/1 or 2/1)	25·00
	ac.	One band on each stamp	

For illustrations of Nos. SB41*b* and SB42*b* see No. SB23*c*; for Nos. SB41*ab* and SB42*ab* see No.
SB20*ab*.

Booklet Cylinder Numbers

Panes of six (21-row cylinders).

	Cream paper				Whiter paper		
Cyl. No.		No dot	Dot	Cyl. No		No dot	Dot
F10	. . . .	30·00	30·00*	F10	. . . .	30·00	30·00*
F10 T	. . . .	30·00	30·00	F10 T	. . . .	30·00	30·00

Specimen overprints from the National Postal Museum Archives

Booklet pane of six. Perf. 15 × 14, watermark Type W.24 inverted

Each stamp handstamped "Specimen" (13 × 2 mm.)

1d. BOOKLET PANES OF FOUR WITH TWO PHOSPHOR BANDS REACTING BLUE. SIDEWAYS WATERMARK

4 × 1d. Crowns. Two phosphor bands applied by typography. Cream or whiter paper
From 2s. Booklets N4p, N8p/10p, N12p/20p

Cream Paper
A. Watermark Crown to left

			Perf. Type		
			I	I($\frac{1}{2}$v)	AP
SB43	Pane of 4 × 1d.	(containing No. S21*b* × 4) (14.7.61)	16·00 40·00		9·00
	b.	One band on each stamp	—	—	65·00

B. Watermark Crown to right

SB43a	Pane of 4 × 1d.	(containing No. S21*c* × 4) (14.7.61)	16·00 40·00		9·00
	ab.	One band on each stamp	—	—	65·00

Whiter Paper
A. Watermark Crown to left
  SB44 Pane of 4 × 1d. (containing No. S22a × 4) (15.8.62) . . . . 18·00 40·00 9·00
        b. One band on each stamp . . . . £160 — £160

B. Watermark Crown to right
  SB44a Pane of 4 × 1d. (containing No. S22b × 4) (15.8.62) . . . . 18·00 40·00 9·00
        ab. One band on each stamp . . . . £160 — £150

Booklet Cylinder Numbers

Panes of four (20-row single pane cylinder of 480 stamps).
In the 2s. Booklets the cylinder numbers were partly or completely trimmed off, but No. F12 was the cylinder used. (*Price for pane showing* (F12), *from* £75.)

Imprimaturs from the National Postal Museums Archives

Booklet pane of four. Imperforate, watermark Type W.24

Two panes arranged vertically *tête-bêche*

Specimen overprints from the National Postal Museum Archives

Booklet pane of four. Perf. 15 × 14, watermark Type W.24

Each stamp handstamped "Specimen" (13 × 2 mm.)

1d. AND 3d. SE-TENANT BOOKLET PANES OF FOUR WITH PHOSPHOR BANDS REACTING BLUE. SIDEWAYS WATERMARK

Pair of 1d. (two bands) with pair of 3d. (1 side 8 mm. blue band) applied by typography. Crowns.

Whiter paper

From 2s. Booklets N21p/22p(a) and N23p(a)

Panes SB45 and SB47 Panes of four with 1d. (two bands) at left; 3d. side band at left
Panes SB46 and SB48 Panes of four with 1d. (two bands) at right; 3d. side band at right

A. Watermark Crown to left

				Perf. Type	
			I	I(½v)	AP
SB45	Pane of 2 × 1d./3d.	(containing Nos. S22a × 2, S77b × 2) (16.8.65) .	90·00	†	70·00
SB46	Pane of 2 × 3d./1d.	(containing Nos. S77c × 2, S22a × 2) (16.8.65) .	90·00	£120	70·00
	a.	One band on each stamp	—	—	—
	b.	One band on 1d. and no bands on 3d.	—	—	—
	c.	Thistle flaw on 1d. (R. 2/2)	†	£120	†

B. Watermark Crown to right

SB47	Pane of 2 × 1d./3d.	(containing Nos. S22b × 2, S77d × 2) (16.8.65) .	90·00	£110	70·00
	a.	One band on each stamp	†	†	
SB48	Pane of 2 × 3d./1d.	(containing Nos. S77e × 2, S22b × 2) (16.8.65) .	90·00	†	70·00
	a.	One band on each stamp	—	†	—
	b.	One band on 1d. and no bands on 3d.	—	†	—
	c.	"R" flaw on 1d. (R. 2/2)	†	†	80·00

For illustrations of Nos. SB46c and SB48c see Nos. SB36a and SB38a.
The following illustration shows how the *se-tenant* stamps with one phosphor band on 3d. are printed and the arrows indicate where the guillotine falls. The result gives 1d. stamps with two bands and 3d. stamps with one band, either at left or right.
The stamps were printed sideways, as indicated by the position of the watermark.

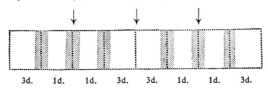

3d. 1d. 1d. 3d. 3d. 1d. 1d. 3d.

Booklet Cylinder Numbers

Panes of four (24-row single pane cylinder of 480 stamps sideways).
From *se-tenant* pane booklets on whiter paper

Cyl. Nos.	No dot
F13 (1d.), K22 (3d.)	£120

1d. BOOKLET PANES OF SIX WITH TWO 8 mm. PHOSPHOR BANDS REACTING VIOLET

6 × 1d. Crowns. Two phosphor bands applied in photogravure
From 4s.6d. Booklets L60p(*b*), L61p(*b*) and L62p(*b*)/65p(*a*) and 10s. Booklet X15p(*a*)

A. Watermark upright

SB49	Pane of 6 × 1d.	(containing No. S23*b* × 6) (9.65)	6·00
	b.	Dot in serif (R. 2/3)	8·50

B. Watermark inverted

SB49a	Pane of 6 × 1d.	(containing No. S23*c* × 6) (9.65)	6·00
	ab.	Extended leaf on shamrock (R. 1/1 or 2/1)	8·50

For illustrations of Nos. SB49*b* and SB49*ab* see Nos. SB23*c* and SB20*ab*.

Booklet Cylinder Numbers

Panes of six (21-row cylinder). Bands photo.

Cyl. No.	No dot	Dot		Cyl. No.	No dot	Dot
F10	25·00	25·00*		F10 T	25·00	25·00

1d. AND 3d. SE-TENANT BOOKLET PANES OF FOUR WITH 8 mm. PHOSPHOR BANDS REACTING VIOLET. SIDEWAYS WATERMARK

Pair of 1d. (two bands) with pair of 3d. (1 side 8 mm. violet band) applied by typography. Crowns.
From 2s. Booklets N22p(*b*), N23p(*b*)/28p(*a*), N29p, N30p(*a*), N31p(*c*) and N32p(*c*)

Panes SB50 and SB52 Panes of four with 1d. (two bands) at left; 3d. side band at left
Panes SB51 and SB53 Panes of four with 1d. (two bands) at right; 3d. side band at right

A. Watermark Crown to left

			Perf. Type		
			I	I(½v)	AP
SB50	Pane of 2 × 1d./3d.	(containing Nos. S23*d* × 2, S78*c* × 2) (10.65) . .	20·00	†	15·00
SB51	Pane of 2 × 3d./1d.	(containing Nos. S78*d* × 2, S23*d* × 2) (10.65) . .	20·00	35·00	15·00
	a.	One 8 mm. band on each stamp	60·00	—	50·00
	b.	One 8 mm. band on 1d. and no bands on 3d. .	60·00	†	50·00
	c.	Thistle flaw on 1d. (R. 2/2)	†	35·00	†

B. Watermark Crown to right

SB52	Pane of 2 × 1d./3d.	(containing Nos. S23*e* × 2, S78*e* × 2) (10.65) . .	20·00	30·00	15·00
SB53	Pane of 2 × 3d./1d.	(containing Nos. S78*f* × 2, S23*e* × 2) (10.65) . .	20·00	†	15·00
	a.	One 8 mm. band on each stamp	60·00	—	50·00
	b.	One 8 mm. band on 1d. and no bands on 3d. .	60·00	—	50·00
	c.	"R" flaw on 1d. (R. 2/2)	†	†	30·00

For illustrations of Nos. SB51*d* and SB53*d* see Nos. SB36*a* and SB38*a*.

Booklet Cylinder Numbers

Panes of four (24-row single pane cylinder of 480 stamps sideways).
From *se-tenant* pane booklets. Bands printed in typography.

Cyl. Nos.	No dot
F13 (1d.), K22 (3d.)	50·00

1d. BOOKLET PANES OF SIX WITH TWO 9·5 mm. PHOSPHOR BANDS REACTING VIOLET

6 × 1d. Crowns. Two phosphor bands applied in photogravure
From 4s.6d. Booklets L65p(b)/71p and 10s. Booklets X15p(b) and X16p/17p

A. Watermark upright

SB54	Pane of 6 × 1d.	(containing No. S24 × 6) (2.67)	6·00
	b.	Dot in serif (R. 2/3)	10·00

B. Watermark inverted

SB54a	Pane of 6 × 1d.	(containing No. S24a × 6) (2.67)	6·00
	ab.	Extended leaf on shamrock (R. 1/1 or 2/1)	10·00

For illustrations of Nos. SB54b and SB54ab see Nos. SB23c and SB20ab.

Booklet Cylinder Numbers

Panes of six (21-row cylinder)

Cyl. No.	No dot	Dot	Cyl. No.	No dot	Dot
F10	35·00	35·00	F10 T	35·00	35·00

Specimen overprints from the National Postal Museum Archives

Booklet pane of six. Perf. 15 × 14, watermark Type W.24 inverted

Each stamp handstamped "Specimen" (15 × 2½ mm.)

1d. AND 3d. SE-TENANT BOOKLET PANES OF FOUR WITH 9·5 mm. PHOSPHOR BANDS REACTING VIOLET. SIDEWAYS WATERMARK

Pair of 1d. (two bands) with pair of 3d. (two 9·5 mm. violet bands) applied by flexography.
Crowns
From 2s. Booklets N31p(a/b) and N32p(a/b)

Panes SB55 and SB57 Panes of four with 1d. (two bands) at left; 3d. (two bands) at right
Panes SB56 and SB58 Panes of four with 1d. (two bands) at right; 3d. (two bands) at left

A. Watermark Crown to left

			Perf. Type		
			I	I(½v)	AP
SB55	Pane of 2 × 1d./3d.	(containing Nos. S24b × 2, S80 × 2) (11.67) . .	12·00	†	8·00
	a.	As SB55 but one 9·5 mm. band on 3d.	£170	—	£160
SB56	Pane of 2 × 3d./1d.	(containing Nos. S80 × 2, S24b × 2) (11.67) . .	12·00	25·00	8·00
	a.	Thistle flaw on 1d. (R. 2/2)	†	25·00	†
	b.	As SB56 but one 9·5 mm. band on 3d.	£170	—	£160
	ba.	Do. with thistle flaw	†	—	†
	c.	One 9·5 mm. band on each stamp	80·00	£110	65·00
	d.	One 9·5 mm. band on 1d. and no bands on 3d.	70·00	—	60·00

B. Watermark Crown to right

SB57	Pane of 2 × 1d./3d.	(containing Nos. S24c × 2, S80a × 2) (11.67) . .	12·00	25·00	8·00
	a.	As SB57 but one 9·5 mm. band on 3d	£170	—	£160
SB58	Pane of 2 × 3d./1d.	(containing Nos. S80a × 2, S24c × 2) (11.67) . .	12·00	†	8·00
	a.	"R" flaw on 1d. (R. 2/2)	†	†	25·00
	b.	As SB58 but one band on 3d	£190	—	£180
	ba.	Do. with "R" flaw	†	†	£190
	c.	One 9·5 mm. band on each stamp	80·00	—	65·00

Part of the October 1967 2s. Booklets (N30p(a)) had 8 mm. bands and part 9·5 mm. bands (N30p(b)) which had only a single line band on the 3d. value at right or left as listed above. As these bands are applied across the perforations and are liable to shift, it is not possible to distinguish the 3d. one-band 9·5 mm. bands from the 8 mm. bands of Nos. SB50, etc. *in singles*, and hence these are not listed as varieties under the 3d. value. Two examples of the April 1967 2s. Booklet (N28p(b)) are also known with a single 9·5 mm. band on the 3d.

For illustrations of the cylinder flaws, see Nos. SB36a and SB38a.

Booklet Cylinder Numbers

Panes of four (24-row single pane cylinder of 480 stamps sideways). From *se-tenant* pane booklets. Bands in typography.

Cyl. Nos.   No dot
  F13 (1d.), K22 (3d.) . . . . . . 35·00

1½d. BOOKLET PANES OF SIX
6 × 1½d. Tudor Crown
From 2s.6d. Booklets F1/36 and 5s. Booklets H1/17

A. Watermark upright
  SB59   Pane of 6 × 1½d.   (containing No. S25 × 6) (5.53) . . . . 3·00
          b.   Extra jewel (R. 1/1) . . . . 25·00
          c.   Extra bud on daffodil stem (R. 2/1) . . . . 25·00

B. Watermark inverted
  SB59a   Pane of 6 × 1½d.   (containing No. S25*c* × 6) (5.53) . . . . 4·00
          ab.   Imperf. pane* . . . .

  *Booklet error.—This pane of six stamps is completely imperf. (cf. General Notes).

SB59*b*, SB62*c*
Multipositive flaw on Tudor
and Edward Crown watermarks   SB59*c*

Booklet Cylinder Numbers

Panes of six (20-row cylinders)

Cyl. No.	No dot	Dot	Cyl. No.	No dot	Dot
G2	20·00	20·00	G6	55·00	55·00
G3	20·00	20·00			

1½d. BOOKLET PANES OF FOUR
4 × 1½d. Tudor Crown
From 1s. Booklet K1/*a* for use in "E" machines.

A. Watermark upright
                                                                      Perf. Type P
  SB60   Pane of 4 × 1½d.   (containing No. S25 × 4) (22.7.54) . . . . 7·50
          b.   Rose petal flaw (R. 1/1) . . . . 25·00

B. Watermark inverted
  SB60a   Pane of 4 × 1½d.   (containing No. S25*c* × 4) (22.7.54) . . . . 9·00

SB60*b*, SB63*b*, SB67*b*

Booklet Cylinder Numbers

Cylinder No. G5 was used, but it does not appear in the finished booklets.

Imprimaturs from the National Postal Museum Archives

Booklet pane of four. Imperforate, watermark Type W.22

Two panes arranged vertically *tête-bêche* with a 12 mm. horizontal gutter margin between

1½d. BOOKLET PANES OF TWO

2 × 1½d. Tudor Crown
From 1s. Booklet E1 for use in experimental "D" machines.

Watermark upright

			Perf. Type			
			I	I(½v)	E	E(½v)
SB61	Pane of 2 × 1½d.	(containing No. S25 × 2) (2.9.53)	4·00	12·00	4·00	12·00
	a.	Flaw on daffodil stem (as on No. S25*f*) . .	†	†	25·00	†

Made up from vertical rows 1 and 2 from sheets.
No. SB61*a* was later retouched on cylinder 9 dot.

Booklet Cylinder Numbers

Panes of two (from sheets)

	Perf. Type				Perf. Type	
	I	E			E	
Cyl. No.	No dot	Dot	Cyl. No.		No dot	Dot
2	75·00	50·00	6		50·00	50·00
			9		50·00	30·00*
			12		50·00	30·00

Panes from cylinder 4 have been reported.

1½d. BOOKLET PANES OF SIX

6 × 1½d. St. Edward's Crown
From 2s.6d. Booklets F33(*b*) and F34/52, 3s. Booklets M1/11 and 5s. Booklets H17/31

A. Watermark upright
SB62	Pane of 6 × 1½d.	(containing No. S26 × 6) (8.55)	3·00
	b.	"Rabbit's ears" (R. 2/2)	15·00
	c.	Extra jewel (R. 1/1 or 2/1)	15·00
	d.	Large dot by daffodil (R. 1/1)	15·00
	e.	Major retouch around emblems (R. 2/2)	30·00
	f.	Flaw on rose at right (R. 1/2)	15·00

B. Watermark inverted
SB62a	Pane of 6 × 1½d.	(containing No. S26*b* × 6) (8.55)	4·00
	ab.	Flaw on rose at top left (R. 1/2 or 2/2)	15·00

For illustration of No. SB62*c* see No. SB59*b*

SB62*b*
Two white dots extending upwards
from shamrock at left appearing as
rabbit's ears (Cyl. G7 no dot)

SB62*d* (Cyl. G7)

119

SB62*e*	Normal	SB62*f*	SB62*ab*
Major retouch affecting a pair with weak shading in the emblems. (Cyl. G7 dot)		(Cyl. G10 dot)	White flaw on rose at top left (Cyl. G10 dot)

Booklet Cylinder Numbers

Panes of six (G6 and G7 20-row cylinders, others 21-row cylinders)

Cyl. No.	No dot	Dot	Cyl. No.	No dot	Dot
G6	35·00	25·00	G9 T	50·00	50·00
G7	35·00	25·00	G10	50·00	40·00
G9	45·00	45·00	G10 T	50·00	40·00

1½d. BOOKLET PANES OF FOUR

4 × 1½d. St. Edward's Crown
From 1s. Booklet K2/*b* for use in "E" machines and 2s. Booklet N1

A. Watermark upright

			Perf. Type	
			AP	P
SB63	Pane of 4 × 1½d.	(containing No. S26 × 4) (5.7.56)	12·00	8·00
b.	Rose petal flaw (R. 1/1)	25·00	25·00

B. Watermark inverted

| SB63a | Pane of 4 × 1½d. | (containing No. S26*b* × 4) (5.7.56) . . . . | 12·00 | 8·00 |

For illustration of No. SB63*b* see No. SB60*b*.

Booklet Cylinder Numbers

Cylinder No. G5 was used, but it does not appear in the finished booklets.

Imprimaturs from the National Postal Museum Archives

Booklet pane of four. Imperforate, watermark Type W.23

Two panes arranged vertically *tête-bêche* with a 12 mm. horizontal gutter margin between

1½d. BOOKLET PANES OF TWO

2 × 1½d. St. Edward's Crown
From 1s. Booklet E2 for use in experimental "D" machines.

Watermark upright

			Perf. Type	
			E	E(½v)
SB64	Pane of 2 × 1½d.	(containing No. S26 × 2) (11.57)	15·00	20·00

Made up from vertical rows 1 and 2 from sheets

Booklet Cylinder Numbers

Panes of two (from sheets)

	Perf. Type E	
Cyl. No.	No dot	Dot
13	—	†
14	65·00	45·00

1½d. BOOKLET PANES OF SIX
6 × 1½d. Crowns. Cream or whiter paper
From 3s. Booklets M9/74 and 10s. Booklets X1/9

Cream Paper
A. Watermark upright
    SB65   Pane of 6 × 1½d.   (containing No. S28 × 6) (12.58) . . . . 10·00
               b.   Dot on thistle (R. 1/3 or 2/3) . . . . 25·00

B. Watermark inverted
    SB65a Pane of 6 × 1½d.   (containing No. S28a × 6) (12.58) . . . . 12·00

Whiter Paper
A. Watermark upright
    SB66   Pane of 6 × 1½d.   (containing No. S29 × 6) (18.9.62) . . . . 22·00
               b.   Dot on thistle (R. 1/3 or 2/3) . . . . 35·00

B. Watermark inverted
    SB66a Pane of 6 × 1½d.   (containing No. S29d × 6) (18.9.62) . . . . 30·00

SB65*b*, SB66*b*
Dot on thistle
Retouched on cream paper (Cyl. G15 dot)

Booklet Cylinder Numbers
Panes of six (21-row cylinders)

Cream paper			Whiter paper		
Cyl. No.	No dot	Dot	Cyl. No.	No dot	Dot
G10	40·00	40·00	G15	65·00	65·00
G10 T	40·00	40·00	G15 T	65·00	65·00
G11	40·00	40·00	G16	85·00	85·00
G11 T	40·00	40·00	G16 T	85·00	85·00
G15	35·00	35·00			
G15 T	35·00	35·00			

Specimen overprints from the National Postal Museum Archives
Booklet pane of six. Perf. 15 × 14, watermark Type W.24 upright

Each stamp handstamped "Specimen" (13 × 2 mm.)

1½d. BOOKLET PANES OF FOUR
4 × 1½d. Crowns. Cream paper
From 1s. Booklet K3/a for use in "E" machines and 2s. Booklets N2/3. Perf. Type AP

A. Watermark upright
    SB67   Pane of 4 × 1½d.   (containing No. S28 × 4) (13.8.59) . . . . 5·00
               b.   Rose petal flaw (R. 1/1) . . . . 25·00

B. Watermark inverted
    SB67a Pane of 4 × 1½d.   (containing No. S28a × 4) (13.8.59) . . . . 8·00
    For illustration of No. SB67*b* see No. SB60*b*.

Booklet Cylinder Numbers
    Cylinder No. G5 was used, but it does not appear in the finished booklets.

Imprimaturs from the National Postal Museum Archives

Booklet pane of four. Imperforate, watermark Type W.24

Two panes arranged vertically *tête-bêche* with a 12 mm. horizontal gutter margin between

Specimen overprints from the National Postal Museum Archives

Booklet pane of four. Perf. 15 × 14, watermark Type W.24 inverted

Each stamp handstamped "Specimen" (13 × 2 mm.)

1½d. BOOKLET PANES OF FOUR WITH SIDEWAYS WATERMARK
4 × 1½d. Crowns. Cream or white paper
From 2s. Booklets N4/20

Cream Paper
A. Watermark Crown to left

			I	I(½v)	AP
				Perf.Type	
SB68	Pane of 4 × 1½d.	(containing No. S28*b* × 4) (26.5.61)	60·00	85·00	50·00

B. Watermark Crown to right

| SB68a | Pane of 4 × 1½d. | (containing No. S28*c* × 4) (26.5.61) . . . . | 60·00 | 85·00 | 50·00 |

Whiter Paper
A. Watermark Crown to left

| SB69 | Pane of 4 × 1½d. | (containing No. S29*b* × 4) (5.6.62) . . . . | 45·00 | 80·00 | 35·00 |

B. Watermark Crown to right

| SB69a | Pane of 4 × 1½d. | (containing No. S29*c* × 4) (5.6.62) . . . . | 45·00 | 80·00 | 35·00 |

Booklet Cylinder Numbers

Cylinder No. G17 was used, but it was partly trimmed off. (*Price for pane showing* (G17), *from* £100).

Specimen overprints from the National Postal Museum Archives

Booklet pane of four. Perf. 15 × 14, watermark Type W.24

Each stamp handstamped "Specimen" (13 × 2 mm.)

1½d. BOOKLET PANES OF SIX WITH GRAPHITE LINES
6 × 1½d. Crowns. Graphite lines as Type **S8**
From 3s. Booklets M13g/15g and M19g/21g

A. Watermark upright

| SB70 | Pane of 6 × 1½d. | (containing No. S30 × 6) (4.8.59) . . . . | £600 |

B. Watermark inverted

| SB70a | Pane of 6 × 1½d. | (containing No. S30*a* × 6) (4.8.59) . . . . | £375 |

Booklet Cylinder Numbers

Panes of six (21-row cylinder)

Cyl. No.		No dot	Dot	Cyl. No.		No dot	Dot
G11	. . . .	£850	£850	G11 T	. . . .	£850	£850

Imprimaturs from the National Postal Museum Archives

Booklet pane of six. Imperforate, watermark Type W.24

Two panes as No. SB70 arranged *tête-bêche*

1½d. BOOKLET PANES OF SIX WITH TWO PHOSPHOR BANDS REACTING GREEN
6 × 1½d. Crowns. Two phosphor bands applied in photogravure
From 3s. Booklets M25p, M28p/29p and M37p(*a*)

A. Watermark upright

| SB71 | Pane of 6 × 1½d. | (containing No. S32 × 6) (14.8.60) . . . . | 25·00 |

B. Watermark inverted
    SB71a Pane of 6 × 1½d. (containing No. S32a × 6) (14.8.60) . . . . 75·00

Booklet Cylinder Numbers

Panes of six (21-row cylinders)

Cyl. No.	No dot	Dot	Cyl. No.	No dot	Dot
G11	85·00	85·00	G11 T	85·00	85·00

1½d. BOOKLET PANES OF SIX WITH TWO PHOSPHOR BANDS REACTING BLUE

6 × 1½d. Crowns. Two phosphor bands applied in photogravure. Cream or whiter paper
From 3s. Booklets M33p, M36p, M37p(b), M38p/9p, M43p/7p, M49p/53p, M55p/61p and M64p/74p

Cream Paper
A. Watermark upright
    SB72   Pane of 6 × 1½d. (containing No. S33 × 6) (4.61) . . . . 10·00
                b.   One broad band on each stamp £350

B. Watermark inverted
    SB72a Pane of 6 × 1½d. (containing No. S33a × 6) (4.61) . . . . 70·00
              ab. One broad band on each stamp £350

Whiter Paper
A. Watermark upright
    SB73   Pane of 6 × 1½d. (containing No. S34 × 6) (7.64) . . . . 32·00
                b.   One broad band on each stamp £500

B. Watermark inverted
    SB73a Pane of 6 × 1½d. (containing No. S34c × 6) (7.64) £150
              ab. One broad band on each stamp £500
              ac. Phosphor displaced with marginal stamps showing
                   a left and centre band, others with 8 mm. band in
                   centre . . . . —

Booklet Cylinder Numbers

Pane of six (21-row cylinders)

	Cream paper				Whiter paper		
Cyl. No.		No dot	Dot	Cyl. No.		No dot	Dot
G15		45·00	45·00	G16		95·00	95·00
G15 T		45·00	45·00	G16 T		95·00	95·00

1½d. BOOKLET PANES OF FOUR WITH TWO PHOSPHOR BANDS REACTING BLUE. SIDEWAYS WATERMARK

4 × 1½d. Crowns. Two phosphor bands applied by typography. Cream or whiter paper
From 2s. Booklets N4p, N8p/10p, N12p/20p

Cream Paper
A. Watermark Crown to left

					Perf. Type		
					I	I(½v)	AP
SB74	Pane of 4 × 1½d.	(containing No. S33b × 4) (14.7.61)			60·00	90·00	42·00
	b.	One band on each stamp			£120	—	£100

B. Watermark Crown to right

SB74a	Pane of 4 × 1½d.	(containing No. S33c × 4) (14.7.61)			60·00	90·00	42·00
	ab.	One band on each stamp			£120	—	£100

Whiter Paper
A. Watermark Crown to left
    SB75   Pane of 4 × 1½d. (containing No. S34a × 4) (15.8.62) . . . . 60·00 90·00 42·00

B. Watermark Crown to right
    SB75a Pane of 4 × 1½d. (containing No. S34b × 4) (15.8.62) . . . . 60·00 90·00 42·00

Booklet Cylinder Numbers

Panes of four (20-row single pane cylinder of 480 stamps)

In the 2s. Booklets the cylinder numbers were partly trimmed off, but No. G17 was the cylinder used. (*Price for pane showing (G17), from* £150.)

Imprimaturs from the National Postal Museum Archives

Booklet pane of four. Imperforate, watermark Type W.24

Two panes arranged vertically *tête-béche*

Specimen overprints from the National Postal Museum Archives

Booklet pane of four. Perf. 15 × 14, watermark Type W.24

Each stamp handstamped "Specimen" (13 × 2 mm.)

2d. RED-BROWN BOOKLET PANES OF SIX
6 × 2d. Tudor Crown
From 5s. Booklets H8/16

A. Watermark upright
SB76   Pane of 6 × 2d.   (containing No. S36 × 6) (3.54) . . . . 30·00

B. Watermark inverted
SB76a   Pane of 6 × 2d.   (containing No. S36a × 6) (3.54) £225

Booklet Cylinder Numbers

Panes of six (20-row cylinder)

Cyl. No.   No dot   Dot
H1   . . . . 85·00* 75·00

*Includes retouched face variety (R. 2/1). Two states exist showing as a small retouch to left of ear and in state two the retouched area includes the forehead and cheek. Same price for either state included in the cylinder pane with upright watermark.

2d. RED-BROWN BOOKLET PANES OF SIX
6 × 2d. St. Edward's Crown
From 5s. Booklets H17/25

A. Watermark upright
SB77   Pane of 6 × 2d.   (containing No. S37 × 6) (9.55) . . . . 24·00

B. Watermark inverted
SB77a   Pane of 6 × 2d.   (containing No. S37c × 6) (9.55) . . . . 90·00

Booklet Cylinder Numbers

Panes of six (20-row cylinder)

Cyl. No.   No dot   Dot
H1   . . . . 95·00* 85·00

*Includes the second state of the retouched face variety (R. 2/1).

2d. LIGHT RED-BROWN BOOKLET PANES OF SIX
6 × 2d. St. Edward's Crown
From 2s.6d. Booklets F53/61 and 5s. Booklets H26/31

A. Watermark upright
SB78   Pane of 6 × 2d.   (containing No. S38 × 6) (1.57) . . . . 15·00
          b.   Imperf. pane* £4500
          ba.   Part perf. pane* £4000
          c.   Daffodil flaw (R. 1/3 or 2/3) . . . . 55·00
          d.   Shamrock flaw (R. 1/3 or 2/3) . . . . 50·00
          e.   Bud on thistle stem (R. 1/3 or 2/3) . . . . 40·00
          f.   White flaw on thistle (R. 1/1 or 2/1) . . . . 40·00
          g.   Daffodil stem flaw (R. 2/2) . . . . 40·00

B. Watermark inverted
SB78a   Pane of 6 × 2d.   (containing No. S38d × 6) (1.57) . . . . 50·00
      ac.   "D" for "P" (R. 1/2 or 2/2) . . . . 60·00
      ad.   Spot after "2" (R. 1/2 or 2/2) . . . . 60·00
      ae.   "Dew drop" (R. 1/2 or 2/2) . . . . 55·00
      af.   Diadem flaw (R. 1/3 or 2/3)   . . . . 55·00
      ag.   White flaw at top of thistle (R. 1/2 or 2/2) . . . . . . 55·00
      ah.   Accent on first "2" and spot on shamrock (R. 1/3 or
         2/3) . . . . 55·00
      aha.   Retouched state. Spot on shamrock (R. 1/3 or 2/3) . . . 55·00

  *Booklet error—see General Notes.

SB78c
Later retouched
(Cyl. H6 no dot)

SB78d
Later retouched
(Cyl. H6 no dot)

SB78e, SB79b
Later retouched
(Cyl. H6 dot)

SB78f
(Cyl. H6 dot)

SB78g
Later retouched
(Cyl. pane H6 and on
ordinary pane)

SB78ac, SB79ab
(Cyl. H6 dot)

SB78ad, SB79ac
(Cyl. H6 no dot)

SB78ae
Later retouched
(Cyl. H6 no dot)

SB78af
Later retouched
(Cyl. H6 dot)

SB78ag
Later retouched
(Cyl. H6 no dot)

SB78ah
The flaw on value
was later
retouched but the
spot on shamrock
remained.
(Cyl. H6 no dot)

Booklet Cylinder Numbers

Panes of six (21-row cylinder)

Cyl. No.	No dot	Dot
H6	75·00	65·00
H6 T	75·00	65·00

Early printings of the Cyl. H6 pane show a white dot below the daffodil stem at left (R. 1/2). This was later removed by retouch. *Cylinder No. H6 no dot with variety price £75.*

2d. LIGHT RED-BROWN BOOKLET PANES OF SIX
6 × 2d. Crowns. Cream paper
From 10s. Booklets X1/2

A. Watermark upright
SB79	Pane of 6 × 2d.	(containing No. S40 × 6) (10.4.61)	85·00
	b.	Bud on thistle stem (R. 1/3 or 2/3)	£125

B. Watermark inverted
SB79a	Pane of 6 × 2d.	(containing No. S40c × 6) (10.4.61)	£850
	ab.	"D" for "P" (R. 1/2 or 2/2)	£900
	ac.	Spot after "2" (R. 1/2 or 2/2)	£900

For illustration of No. SB79*b*, see No. SB78e and for Nos. SB79*ab/ac* see Nos. SB78*ac/ad*.

Booklet Cylinder Numbers

Panes of six (21-row cylinder). Cream paper

Cyl. No.	No dot	Dot	Cyl. No.	No dot	Dot
H6	£350	£350	H6 T	£350	£350

All stamps in the 2½d. panes show the frontal cross of the diadem with the top line extending the full width of the cross (Type II).

2½d. BOOKLET PANES OF SIX
6 × 2½d. Tudor Crown.
From 2s.6d. Booklets F1/34, 3s.9d. Booklets G1/10 and 5s. Booklets H1/16

A. Watermark upright
SB80	Pane of 6 × 2½d.	(containing No. S51 × 6) (5.53)	7·50
	b.	Jewels flaw (R. 2/2)	30·00

B. Watermark inverted
SB80a	Pane of 6 × 2½d.	(containing No. S51a × 6) (5.53)	3·75
	ab.	"R" flaw (R. 1/1)	30·00

SB80*b*
(Cyl. J1 or J3 no dot)

SB80*ab*, SB81*ad*
(Cyl. J5 no dot)

Booklet Cylinder Numbers

Panes of six (20-row cylinders)

Cyl. No.	No dot	Dot	Cyl. No.	No dot	Dot
J1	22·00	22·00	J5	26·00	26·00
J3	22·00	22·00			

2½d. BOOKLET PANES OF SIX

6 × 2½d. St. Edward's Crown
From 2s.6d. Booklets F34/6(a) and F37/61, 3s.9d. Booklets G9(a) and G10(a)/21 and 5s. Booklets H17/36

A. Watermark upright

SB81	Pane of 6 × 2½d.	(containing No. S53 × 6) (9.55)	3·50
	b.	Imperf. pane*	£3500
	d.	"Swan's head" (R. 1/1 or 2/1)	40·00
	e.	Wreath flaw (R. 1/3 or 2/3)	25·00
	f.	Damaged "P" (R. 1/3 or 2/3)	25·00
	g.	Dot by shamrock (R. 1/1 or 2/1)	25·00
	h.	Forehead retouch R. 1/2 or 2/2)	25·00
	i.	White flaw below thistle (R. 1/2 or 2/2)	25·00

B. Watermark inverted

SB81a	Pane of 6 × 2½d.	(containing No. S53e × 6) (9.55)	3·50
	ac.	Part perf. pane*	£3250
	ad.	"R" flaw (R. 1/1)	25·00
	ae.	Dotted "R" (R. 1/3 or 2/3)	25·00
	af.	Spur to "1" (R. 1/1 or 2/1)	25·00

For illustration of No. SB81ad, see No. SB80ab.

SB81d, SB82d
Top of figure 2 is extended
and curled (Cyl. J8 no dot)

SB81e, SB82e
(Cyl. J9 no dot)

SB81f, SB82f
Red flaw almost obliterates the
loop on "P". St. Edward's
and Crown wmks., (Cyl. J8 dot)

SB81g
Retouched later
(Cyl. J9 dot)

SB81h, SB82g
(Cyl. J9 no dot)

SB81i, SB82h
(Cyl. J8 no dot)

SB81ae
Later retouched on Crowns
wmk. (Cyl. J9 no dot)

SB81af, SB82ac, SB85ab
(Cyl. J9 dot)

Booklet Cylinder Numbers

Panes of six (J5 20-row cylinder, others 21-row cylinders)

Cyl. No.	No dot	Dot	Cyl. No.	No dot	Dot
J5	20·00	20·00	J8 T	40·00	30·00
J6	40·00	40·00	J9	50·00	50·00
J6 T	40·00	20·00	J9 T	50·00	50·00
J8	40·00	30·00			

2½d. BOOKLET PANES OF SIX

6 × 2½d. Crowns. Cream or whiter paper
From 5s. Booklets H36(*b*)/(*c*), (*e*) and H37/74 and 10s. Booklets X3/9

Cream Paper
A. Watermark upright

SB82	Pane of 6 × 2½d.	(containing No. S55 × 6) (11.58)	11·00
	d.	"Swan's head" (R. 1/1 or 2/1)	35·00
	e.	Wreath flaw (R. 1/3 or 2/3)	25·00
	f.	Damaged "P" (R. 1/3 or 2/3)	25·00
	g.	Forehead retouch (R. 1/2 or 2/2)	25·00
	h.	White flaw below thistle (R. 1/2 or 2/2)	25·00

B. Watermark inverted

SB82a	Pane of 6 × 2½d.	(containing No. S55*d* × 6) (11.58)	25·00
	ac.	Spur to "1" (R. 1/1)	30·00

Whiter Paper
A. Watermark upright

SB83	Pane of 6 × 2½d.	(containing No. S57 × 6) (29.7.62)	15·00
	b.	Imperf. pane*	£3250

B. Watermark inverted

SB83a	Pane of 6 × 2½d.	(containing No. S57*a* × 6) (29.7.62)	42·00

*Booklet error—see General Notes.

For illustrations of Nos. SB82*d/f*, see Nos. SB81*d/f*, for Nos. SB82*g/h*, see Nos. SB81*h/i* and for No. SB82*ac* see No. SB81*af*.

Booklet Cylinder Numbers

Panes of six (21-row cylinders)

	Cream paper				Whiter paper		
Cyl. No.		No dot	Dot	Cyl. No.		No dot	Dot
J6		50·00	50·00	J13		50·00	50·00
J6 T		50·00	50·00	J13 T		50·00	50·00
J8		60·00	60·00	J14		65·00	65·00
J8 T		60·00	60·00	J14 T		65·00	65·00
J9		50·00	50·00				
J9 T		50·00	50·00				
J13		50·00	50·00				
J13 T		50·00	50·00				

Specimen overprints from the National Postal Museum Archives

Booklet pane of six. Perf. 15 × 14, watermark Type W.24 inverted

Each stamp handstamped "Specimen" (13 × 2 mm.)

2½d. BOOKLET PANES OF FOUR
4 × 2½d. Crowns. Chalky paper
From 2s. Booklet NR1/1a

A. Watermark upright

			Perf. Type		
			I	I(½v)	AP
SB84	Pane of 4 × 2½d.	(containing No. S58 × 4) (15.7.63)	5·50	14·00	3·50

B. Watermark inverted

SB84a	Pane of 4 × 2½d.	(containing No. S58a × 4) (15.7.63)	5·50	14·00	3·50

Booklet Cylinder Numbers
Panes of four (20-row single pane cylinder of 480 stamps).
Cylinder numbers are not known from Booklets NR1/1a.

Imprimaturs from the National Postal Museum Archives
Booklet pane of four. Imperforate, watermark Type W.24

Two panes arranged vertically *tête-bêche*

2½d. BOOKLET PANES OF SIX WITH GRAPHITE LINES
6 × 2½d. Crowns. Graphite lines as Type S8
From 5s. Booklets H39g, H43g and H46g

A. Watermark upright

SB85	Pane of 6 × 2½d.	(containing No. S59 × 6) (21.8.59)	75·00
	b.	Forehead retouch (R. 1/2 or 2/2)	85·00

B. Watermark inverted

SB85a	Pane of 6 × 2½d.	(containing No. S59a × 6) (21.8.59)	£400
	ab.	Spur to "1" (R. 1/1 or 2/1)	£450

For illustration of No. SB85b, see No. SB81h and for No. SB85ab, see No. SB81af.

Booklet Cylinder Numbers
Panes of six (21-row cylinders)

Cyl. No.	No dot	Dot	Cyl. No.	No dot	Dot
J6	£375	£375	J9	£375	£375
J6 T	£375	£375	J9 T	£375	£375

2½d. BOOKLET PANES OF SIX WITH TWO PHOSPHOR BANDS REACTING GREEN
6 × 2½d. Crowns. Two phosphor bands applied in photogravure
From 5s. Booklet H46p

A. Watermark upright

SB86	Pane of 6 × 2½d.	(containing No. S61 × 6) (14.8.60)	80·00
	b.	One band on each stamp	£300

B. Watermark inverted

SB86a	Pane of 6 × 2½d.	(containing No. S61a × 6) (14.8.60)	£1100

Booklet Cylinder Numbers
Panes of six (21-row cylinder)

Cyl. No.	No dot	Dot	Cyl. No.	No dot	Dot
J13	£275	£275	J13 T	£275	£275

2½d. BOOKLET PANES OF SIX WITH TWO PHOSPHOR BANDS REACTING BLUE

6 × 2½d. Crowns. Two phosphor bands applied in photogravure. Cream paper
From 5s. Booklets H49p, H51p/52p and H54p

A. Watermark upright
  SB87   Pane of 6 × 2½d. (containing No. S62 × 6) (3.61) . . . . 85·00

B. Watermark inverted
  SB87a   Pane of 6 × 2½d. (containing No. S62a × 6) (3.61) £1100

Booklet Cylinder Numbers

Panes of six (21-row cylinders)

Two bands. Cream paper

Cyl. No.	No dot	Dot	Cyl. No.	No dot	Dot
J13	£275	£275	J13 T	£275	£275

Specimen overprints from the National Postal Museum Archives

Booklet pane of six. Perf. 15 × 14, watermark Type W.24 upright
Each stamp handstamped "Specimen" (13 × 2 mm.)

2½d. BOOKLET PANES OF SIX WITH ONE PHOSPHOR BAND AT LEFT REACTING BLUE

6 × 2½d. Crowns. Band at left applied in photogravure. Cream or whiter paper
From 5s. Booklets H55p/74p

Cream Paper
A. Watermark upright
  SB88   Pane of 6 × 2½d. (containing No. S63 × 6) (3.62) . . . . 80·00

B. Watermark inverted
  SB88a   Pane of 6 × 2½d. (containing No. S63b × 6) (3.62) £250

Whiter Paper
A. Watermark upright
  SB89   Pane of 6 × 2½d. (containing No. S65 × 6) (3.6.63) . . . . 60·00
        b.   One 8 mm. band at right but omitted on stamps 3
              and 6 . . . .

B. Watermark inverted
  SB89a   Pane of 6 × 2½d. (containing No. S65b × 6) (3.6.63) £250
  No. SB89b was the source of No. S65e.

Booklet Cylinder Numbers

Pane of six (21-row cylinders)

One band. Cream paper	No dot	Dot		No dot	Dot
J13	£350	£350	J13 T	£350	£350

One band. Whiter paper					
J13	£125	£125	J13 T	£125	£125
J14	£125	£125	J14 T	£125	£125

Specimen overprints from the National Postal Museum Archives

Booklet pane of six. Perf. 15 × 14, watermark Type W.24 upright
Each stamp handstamped "Specimen" (15 × 2½ mm.)

3d. BOOKLET PANES OF SIX
6 × 3d. St. Edward's Crown
From 3s. Booklets M1/10, 4s.6d. Booklets L1/17 and 5s. Booklets H32/36

A. Watermark upright
    SB90   Pane of 6 × 3d.   (containing No. S68 × 6) (1.10.57) . . . .   4·25
                  b.   White dot on laurel leaf (R. 1/2 or 2/2) . . . . 25·00

B. Watermark inverted
    SB90a Pane of 6 × 3d.   (containing No. S68*d* × 6) (1.10.57) . . . .   9·00

SB90*b*
(Cyl. K2 no dot)

Booklet Cylinder Numbers

Panes of six (K8 20-row cylinder, others 21-row cylinders)

Cyl. No.	No dot	Dot	Cyl. No.	No dot	Dot
K1	30·00	30·00	K7	30·00	30·00
K1 T	30·00	30·00	K7 T	30·00	30·00
K2	30·00	30·00	K8 T	30·00	30·00
K2 T	30·00	30·00			

K8 was engraved in the middle of the sheet by row 11 and only occurs at the top of the pane.

3d. BOOKLET PANES OF FOUR
4 × 3d. St. Edward's Crown
From 2s. Booklet N1. Perf. Type AP

A. Watermark upright
    SB91   Pane of 4 × 3d.   (containing No. S68 × 4) (22.4.59) . . . . 20·00

B. Watermark inverted
    SB91a Pane of 4 × 3d.   (containing No. S68*d* × 4) (22.4.59) . . . . 30·00

Booklet Cylinder Numbers

Cylinder numbers did not appear in the finished booklets, but it is known that K12 and one other cylinder were used.

Imprimaturs from the National Postal Museum Archives

Booklet pane of four. Imperforate, watermark Type W.23

Two panes arranged vertically *tête-bêche* with a 12 mm. horizontal gutter margin between

3d. BOOKLET PANES OF SIX
6 × 3d. Crowns. Cream or whiter paper
From 3s. Booklets M10/74, 4s.6d. Booklets L8/58, 5s. Booklets H36(*d*)/(*e*) and H37/74 and 10s. Booklets X1/14

Cream Paper
A.Watermark upright

SB92	Pane of 6 × 3d.	(containing No. S70 × 6) (11.58)	3·50
	b.	Imperf. pane*	£3250
	c.	Part perf. pane*	£3000

B. Watermark inverted

SB92a	Pane of 6 × 3d.	(containing No. S70*e* × 6) (11.58)	4·00
	ab.	Long tailed "R" (R. 1/1)	25·00
	ac.	Background retouch (R. 1/1)	25·00
	ad.	Part perf. pane*	£3000

Whiter Paper
A. Watermark upright

SB93	Pane of 6 × 3d.	(containing No. S71 × 6) (16.7.62)	3·50

B. Watermark inverted

SB93a	Pane of 6 × 3d.	(containing No. S71*c* × 6) (16.7.62)	3·75
	ab.	Long tailed "R" (R. 1/1)	25·00
	ac.	Background retouch (R. 1/1)	25·00

*Booklet errors—see General Notes.

SB92*ab*, SB93*ab*,
SB97*ab*, SB99*ab*, SB100*ab*
(Cyl. K15 no dot)

SB92*ac*, SB93*ac*, SB97*ac*,
SB99*ac*, SB100*ac*
Retouched area of fine dots behind
Queen's head (Cyl. K15 no dot)

Booklet Cylinder Numbers

Panes of six (K13, K15 and K16 20-row cylinders, others 21-row cylinders)

Cream paper			Whiter paper		
Cyl. No.	No dot	Dot	Cyl. No.	No dot	Dot
K7	40·00	40·00	K15	25·00	25·00
K7 T	40·00	40·00	K16	£125	£125
K13	25·00	25·00	K18	25·00	25·00
K15	35·00	35·00	K18 T	25·00	25·00
K17	20·00	20·00	K20	25·00	25·00
K17 T	20·00	20·00	K20 T	25·00	25·00
K18	20·00	20·00	K21	—	—
K18 T	20·00	20·00	K21 T	—	—
K20	20·00	20·00			
K20 T	20·00	20·00			

Specimen overprints from the National Postal Museum Archives

Booklet pane of six. Perf. 15 × 14, watermark Type W.24 upright

Each stamp handstamped "Specimen" (13 × 2 mm.)
Each stamp handstamped "Specimen" (15 × 2½ mm.)

3d. BOOKLET PANES OF FOUR
4 × 3d. Crowns. Cream paper
From 2s. Booklets N2/3. Perf. Type AP

A. Watermark upright
SB94   Pane of 4 × 3d.   (containing No. S70 × 4) (2.11.60) . . . . 15·00

B. Watermark inverted
SB94a   Pane of 4 × 3d.   (containing No. S70e × 4) (2.11.60)   . . . . 15·00
           ab.   Break in bottom ribbon (R. 1/2) . . . . 30·00

SB94*ab*

Booklet Cylinder Numbers
Cylinder No. K14 was used, but it does not appear in the finished booklets.

Specimen overprints from the National Postal Museum Archives
Booklet pane of four. Perf. 15 × 14, watermark Type W.24 inverted
Each stamp handstamped "Specimen" (13 × 2 mm.)

3d. BOOKLET PANES OF FOUR WITH SIDEWAYS WATERMARK
4 × 3d. Crowns. Cream or whiter paper
From 2s. Booklets N4/20 and NX1

Cream Paper
A. Watermark Crown to left

		Perf. Type		
		I	I($\frac{1}{2}$v)	AP
SB95	Pane of 4 × 3d. (containing No. S70d × 4) (26.5.61)	12·00	30·00	8·00

B. Watermark Crown to right
SB95a   Pane of 4 × 3d.   (containing No. S70f × 4) (26.5.61)   . . . . 12·00 30·00 8·00

Whiter Paper
A. Watermark Crown to left
SB96   Pane of 4 × 3d.   (containing No. S71a × 4) (5.6.62) . . . . 7·50 25·00 3·25

B. Watermark Crown to right
SB96a   Pane of 4 × 3d.   (containing No. S71b × 4) (5.6.62) . . . . 7·50 25·00 3·25

Booklet Cylinder Numbers
Cylinder No. K19 was used, but it was partly trimmed off. (*Price for pane showing* (K19), *from* £85.)

Imprimaturs from the National Postal Museum Archives
Booklet pane of four. Imperforate, watermark Type W.24
Two panes arranged vertically *tête-bêche* with a 12 mm. horizontal gutter margin between

Specimen overprints from the National Postal Museum Archives
Booklet pane of four. Perf. 15 × 14, watermark Type W.24
Each stamp handstamped "Specimen" (13 × 2 mm.)

3d. BOOKLET PANES OF SIX WITH GRAPHITE LINES

6 × 3d. Crowns. Graphite lines as Type S8
From 3s. Booklets M13g/15g, M19g/21g, 4s.6d. Booklets L11g, L15g/16g, L18g/19g and 5s. Booklets
H39g, H43g and H46g

A. Watermark upright
   SB97   Pane of 6 × 3d.   (containing No. S72 × 6) (4.8.59) . . . . 6·00

B. Watermark inverted
   SB97a Pane of 6 × 3d. (containing No. S72a × 6) (4.8.59) . . . . 7·00
            ab. Long tailed "R" (R. 1/1) . . . . 40·00
            ac. Background retouch (R. 1/1) . . . . 40·00

For illustrations of Nos. SB97ab/ac, see Nos. SB92ab/ac.

Booklet Cylinder Numbers

Panes of 6 (K7 21-row cylinder, others 20-row cylinders)

Cyl. No.	No dot	Dot	Cyl. No.	No dot	Dot
K7	40·00	40·00	K13	65·00	65·00
K7 T	40·00	40·00	K15	50·00	50·00

3d. BOOKLET PANES OF SIX WITH TWO PHOSPHOR BANDS REACTING GREEN

6 × 3d. Crowns. Two phosphor bands applied in photogravure
From 3s. Booklets M25p, M28p/9p and M37p(a), 4s.6d. Booklets L21p, L24p, and L27p(a) and 5s.
Booklet H46p

A. Watermark upright
   SB98   Pane of 6 × 3d.   (containing No. S74 × 6) (14.8.60) . . . . 16·00

B. Watermark inverted
   SB98a Pane of 6 × 3d. (containing No. S74a × 6) (14.8.60) . . . . 16·00

See No. S74b,d for the 8 mm. phosphor band variety.

Booklet Cylinder Numbers

Panes of six (21-row cylinders)

Cyl. No.	No dot	Dot	Cyl. No.	No dot	Dot
K17	50·00	50·00	K17 T	50·00	50·00

3d. BOOKLET PANES OF SIX WITH PHOSPHOR BANDS REACTING BLUE

6 × 3d. Crowns. Two phosphor bands applied in photogravure. Cream or whiter paper
From 3s. Booklets M33p, M36p, M37p(b), M38p/9p, M43p/7p, M49p/53p, M55p/61p, M64p/74p,
4s.6d. Booklets L25p, L27p(b), L28p, L30p/42p, L44p/56p and 5s. Booklets H49p, H51p/2p and
H54p/74p

Cream Paper
A. Watermark upright
   SB99   Pane of 4 × 3d.   (containing No. S75 × 6) (3.61) . . . . 7·50

B. Watermark inverted
   SB99a Pane of 4 × 3d. (containing No. S75a × 6) (3.61) . . . . 7·50
            ab. Long tailed "R" (R. 1/1) . . . . 30·00
            ac. Background retouch (R. 1/1) . . . . 30·00

Whiter Paper
A. Watermark upright
   SB100 Pane of 4 × 3d. (containing No. S76 × 6) (25.9.62) . . . . 7·50

B. Watermark inverted
   SB100a Pane of 4 × 3d. (containing No. S76c × 6) (25.9.62) . . . . 7·50
            ab. Long tailed "R" (R. 1/1) . . . . 30·00
            ac. Background retouch (R. 1/1) . . . . 30·00

For illustrations of Nos. SB99ab/ac and SB100ab/ac, see Nos. SB92ab/ac.

Booklet Cylinder Numbers

Panes of six (K15 20-row cylinder, others 21-row cylinders). Two bands.

Cream paper			Whiter paper		
Cyl. No.	No dot	Dot	Cyl. No.	No dot	Dot
K15	35·00	35·00	K15	35·00	35·00
K18	55·00	55·00	K18	35·00	35·00
K18 T	55·00	55·00	K18 T	35·00	35·00
			K20	40·00	40·00
			K20 T	40·00	40·00

Specimen overprints from the National Postal Museum Archives

Booklet pane of six. Perf. 15 × 14, watermark Type W.24 upright

Each stamp handstamped "Specimen" (13 × 2 mm.)
Each stamp handstamped "Specimen" (15 × 2½ mm.)

3d. BOOKLET PANES OF FOUR WITH TWO PHOSPHOR BANDS REACTING BLUE. SIDEWAYS WATERMARK

4 × 3d. Crowns. Two phosphor bands applied by typography. Cream or whiter paper
From 2s. Booklets N4p, N8p/10p, N12p/20p

Cream Paper

A. Watermark Crown to left

				Perf. Type		
				I	I($\frac{1}{1}$v)	AP
SB101	Pane of 4 × 3d.	(containing No. S75*b* × 4) (14.7.61)		25·00	60·00	20·00
	b.	One broad band on each stamp		—	—	£120

B. Watermark Crown to right

SB101a	Pane of 4 × 3d.	(containing No. S75*c* × 4) (14.7.61)		25·00	60·00	20·00
	ab.	One broad band on each stamp		—	—	£120

Whiter Paper

A. Watermark Crown to left

SB102	Pane of 4 × 3d.	(containing No. S76*a* × 4) (15.8.62)		25·00	50·00	20·00

B. Watermark Crown to right

SB102a	Pane of 4 × 3d.	(containing No. S76*b* × 4) (15.8.62)		25·00	50·00	20·00

Booklet Cylinder Numbers

Cylinder No. K19 was used, but it was partly or completely trimmed off. (*Price for pane showing* (K19), *from* £85).

Imprimaturs from the National Postal Museum Archives

Booklet pane of four. Imperforate, watermark Type W.24

Two panes arranged vertically *tête-bêche*

Specimen overprints from the National Postal Museum Archives

Booklet pane of four. Perf. 15 × 14, watermark Type W.24

Each stamp handstamped "Specimen" (13 × 2 mm.)

SB103

3d. BOOKLET PANES OF SIX WITH 8 mm. PHOSPHOR BANDS REACTING VIOLET

2× 3d. (band at left) and 4 × 3d. (band at right). Crowns. Phosphor bands applied in photogravure
From 10s. Booklet X15p(*a/b*)

A. Watermark upright
    SB103   Pane of 6 × 3d.   (containing Nos. S78 × 2, S78*a* × 4) (2.67) . . . . 25·00

B. Watermark inverted
    SB103a Pane of 6 × 3d.   (containing Nos. S78*g* × 2, S78*h* × 4) (2.67) £100

Booklet Cylinder Numbers

    Panes of six (21-row cylinder)

	One side band	
Cyl. No.	No dot	Dot
K18	£100	£100
K18 T	£100	£100

3d. BOOKLET PANES OF SIX WITH 4 mm. PHOSPHOR BANDS REACTING VIOLET

6 × 3d. (centre band). Crowns. The centre phosphor bands were applied in photogravure using a mixed screen.
From 10s. Booklets X16p/17p

A. Watermark upright
    SB104   Pane of 6 × 3d.   (containing No. S79 × 6) (8.67) . . . . 8·00

B. Watermark inverted
    SB104a Pane of 6 × 3d.   (containing No. S79*b* × 6) (8.67) . . . . 20·00

Booklet Cylinder Numbers

    Panes of six (21-row cylinder)

	One centre band	
Cyl. No.	No dot	Dot
K18	45·00	45·00
K18 T	45·00	45·00

4d. DEEP ULTRAMARINE BOOKLET PANES OF SIX
6 × 4d. Crowns
From 4s.6d. Booklets L59/65, 6s. Booklets Q1/23 and 10s. Booklets X10/14

A. Watermark upright

SB105	Pane of 6 × 4d.	(containing No. S85 × 6) (21.6.65)	6·00
b.	Imperf. pane*	. . . .	£4000
c.	Part perf. pane*	. . . .	£3000
d.	Line through diadem (R. 1/1 or 2/1)	35·00
e.	Dot below top frame (R. 1/1 or 2/1)	30·00
f.	"Y" flaw (R. 1/2 or 2/2)	20·00

B. Watermark inverted

SB105a	Pane of 6 × 4d.	(containing No. S85e × 6) (21.6.65)	6·00
ab.	Retouch over "4" (R. 1/1 or 2/1)	30·00

SB105d
Later retouched (Cyl. N1 no dot)

SB105e, SB107c,
SB109b, SB111b
(Cyl. N1 dot)

SB105f, SB107d, SB109c, SB111c
Multipositive flaw from panes showing
N1, N2 (T), N3 also without cylinder no.

SB105ab, SB107ab,
SB109ab, SB111ab
(Cyl. N1 no dot)

Booklet Cylinder Numbers (Deep ultramarine)

Panes of six (21-row cylinders N1/2 or 20-row cylinder N3)

Cyl. No.	No dot	Dot	Cyl. No.	No dot	Dot
N1	30·00*	30·00	N1 T	30·00	30·00
N2	30·00	30·00	N2 T	30·00*	30·00
N3	45·00*	45·00			

Specimen overprints from the National Postal Museum Archives

Booklet pane of six. Perf. 15 × 14, watermark Type W.24 inverted

Each stamp handstamped "Specimen" (13 × 2 mm.)

4d. DEEP ULTRAMARINE BOOKLET PANES OF FOUR. SIDEWAYS WATERMARK
4 × 4d. Crowns
From 2s. Booklets N21/27

A. Watermark Crown to left

			Perf. Type		
			I	I($\frac{1}{2}$v)	AP
SB106	Pane of 4 × 4d.	(containing No. S85d × 4) (16.8.65)	6·00	25·00	3·25

B. Watermark Crown to right

SB106a	Pane of 4 × 4d.	(containing No. S85f × 4) (16.8.65)	6·00	25·00	3·25

Booklet Cylinder Numbers

Panes of four (20-row single pane cylinder of 480 stamps). Sideways watermark

Cyl. No.	No dot
N4 (Wmk. Crown to left)	65·00
N4 (Wmk. Crown to right)	65·00

4d. DEEP ULTRAMARINE BOOKLET PANES OF SIX WITH TWO PHOSPHOR BANDS REACTING BLUE

6 × 4d. Crowns. Two phosphor bands applied in photogravure
From 4s.6d. Booklets L59p, L60p(*a*)/(62p(*a*) excl. (*b*) nos. and 6s. Booklets Q1p/3p, Q4p(*a*)/8p(*a*) excl. (*b*) nos.

A. Watermark upright
SB107	Pane of 6 × 4d.	(containing No. S90 × 6) (21.6.65)	10·00
	c.	Dot below top frame (R. 1/1 or 2/1)	30·00
	d.	"Y" flaw (R. 1/2 or 2/2)	20·00

B. Watermark inverted
SB107a	Pane of 6 × 4d.	(containing No. S90*b* × 6) (21.6.65)	15·00
	ab.	Retouch over "4" (R. 1/1 or 2/1)	30·00

For illustrations of Nos. SB107*c/d* and SB107*ab*, see Nos. SB105*e/f* and SB105*ab*.

Booklet Cylinder Numbers

Panes of six (21-row cylinder)

Cyl. No.	No dot	Dot	Cyl. No.	No dot	Dot
N1	30·00*	30·00	N1 T	30·00	30·00

4d. DEEP ULTRAMARINE BOOKLET PANES OF FOUR WITH TWO PHOSPHOR BANDS REACTING BLUE. SIDEWAYS WATERMARK

4 × 4d. Crowns. Two phosphor bands applied by typography
From 2s. Booklets N21p, N22p(*a*) and N23p(*a*)

A. Watermark Crown to left

			Perf. Type		
			I	I($\frac{1}{2}$v)	AP
SB108	Pane of 4 × 4d.	(containing No. S90*c* × 4) (16.8.65)	25·00	45·00	15·00
	b.	One band on each stamp	—	—	—

B. Watermark Crown to right
SB108a	Pane of 4 × 4d.	(containing No. S90*d* × 4) (16.8.65)	25·00	45·00	15·00
	ab.	One band on each stamp	—	—	—

Booklet Cylinder Numbers

Panes of four (20-row single pane cylinder of 480 stamps). Sideways watermark

Cyl. No.	No dot
N4 (Wmk. Crown to right) .	85·00

4d. DEEP ULTRAMARINE BOOKLET PANES OF SIX WITH TWO 8 mm. PHOSPHOR BANDS REACTING VIOLET

6 × 4d. Crowns. Two phosphor bands applied in photogravure
From 4s.6d. Booklets L60p(*b*), L61p(*b*) and L62p(*b*)/65p(*a*), 6s. Booklets Q4p(*b*)/8p(*b*) excl. (*a*) nos. and Q9p/20p and 10s. Booklet X15p(*a*)

A. Watermark upright
SB109	Pane of 6 × 4d.	(containing No. S91 × 6) (9.65)	5·50
	b.	Dot below top frame (R. 1/1 or 2/1)	30·00
	c.	"Y" flaw (R. 1/2 or 2/2)	20·00

B. Watermark inverted

SB109a Pane of 6 × 4d. (containing No. S91a × 6) (9.65) . . . . 5·50

                 ab. Retouch over "4" (R. 1/1 or 2/1) . . . . 30·00

For illustrations of Nos. SB109*b/c* and SB109*ab*, see Nos. SB105*e/f* and SB105*ab*.

Booklet Cylinder Numbers

Panes of six (21-row cylinders N1 and N2 or 20-row cylinder N3)

Cyl. No.	No dot	Dot	Cyl. No.	No dot	Dot
N1	40·00*	30·00	N1 T	30·00	30·00
N2	30·00	30·00	N2 T	30·00*	30·00
N3	50·00*	50·00			

4d. DEEP ULTRAMARINE BOOKLET PANES OF FOUR WITH TWO 8 mm. PHOSPHOR BANDS REACTING VIOLET. SIDEWAYS WATERMARK

4 × 4d. Crowns. Two phosphor bands applied in photogravure or typography
From 2s. Booklets N22p(*b*), N23p(*b*)/28p(*a*), N29p, N30p(*a*), N31p(*b*) and N32(*b*)

A. Watermark Crown to left

			Perf. Type		
			I	I($\frac{1}{2}$v)	AP
SB110	Pane of 4 × 4d.	(containing No. S91*b* × 4) (1.67)	8·50	25·00	6·00
	b.	One broad band on each stamp	—	—	—
	c.	Bands typo. (10.65)	70·00	—	60·00

B. Watermark Crown to right

SB110a	Pane of 4 × 4d.	(containing No. S91*c* × 4) (1.67)	8·50	25·00	6·00
	ab.	One broad band on each stamp	—	—	—
	ac.	Bands typo. (10.65)	70·00	—	60·00

Booklet Cylinder Numbers

Panes of four (20-row single pane cylinder of 480 stamps).
Sideways watermark

	Photo. bands			Typo. bands	
Cyl. No.		No dot	Cyl. No.		No dot
N4 (Wmk. Crown to left)		55·00	N4 (Wmk. Crown to left) . .		†
N4 (Wmk. Crown to right)	.	45·00	N4 (Wmk. Crown to right) .		—

4d. DEEP ULTRAMARINE BOOKLET PANES OF SIX WITH TWO 9·5 mm. PHOSPHOR BANDS REACTING VIOLET

6 × 4d. Crowns. Two phosphor bands applied in photogravure
From 4s.6d. Booklets L65p(*b*)/71p, 6s. Booklets Q21/27p and 10s. Booklet X15p(*b*), X16p/17p

A. Watermark upright

SB111	Pane of 6 × 4d.	(containing No. S92 × 6) (2.67)	3·50
	a.	Part perf. pane*	£4000
	b.	Dot below frame (R. 1/1 or 2/1)	25·00
	c.	"Y" flaw (R. 1/2 or 2/2)	15·00

B. Watermark inverted

SB111a	Pane of 6 × 4d.	(containing No. S92*a* × 6) (2.67)	3·50
	ab.	Retouch over "4" (R. 1/1 or 2/1)	25·00

*Booklet error—see General Notes.
For illustrations of Nos. SB111*b/c* and SB111*ab*, see Nos. SB105*e/f* and SB105*ab*.

Booklet Cylinder Numbers

Panes of six (21-row cylinders)

Cyl. No.	No dot	Dot	Cyl. No.	No dot	Dot
N1	25·00*	25·00	N1 T	25·00	25·00
N2	25·00	25·00	N2 T	30·00*	30·00
N2 (Wmk. inverted)			N2 T (Wmk. inverted)	£250	£250

Cylinder panes showing watermark inverted (Cyl. No. N2) come from Booklet X17p.

Specimen overprints from the National Postal Museum Archives

Booklet pane of six. Perf. 15 × 14, watermark Type W.24 inverted

Each stamp handstamped "Specimen" (13 × 2 mm.)

4d. DEEP ULTRAMARINE BOOKLET PANES OF FOUR WITH TWO 9·5 mm. PHOSPHOR BANDS REACTING VIOLET. SIDEWAYS WATERMARK

4 × 4d. Crowns. Two phosphor bands applied by photogravure
From 2s. Booklets N28p(*b*), N30p(*b*), N31p(*a*), N31p(*c*), N32p(*a*) and N32p(*c*)

A. Watermark Crown to left

		Perf. Type		
		I	I($\frac{1}{2}$v)	AP
SB112	Pane of 4 × 4d. (containing No. S92*b* × 4) (4.67)	5·00	20·00	2·50
b.	One 9·5 mm. band on each stamp	60·00	—	50·00

B. Watermark Crown to right

SB112a	Pane of 4 × 4d. (containing No. S92*c* × 4) (4.67)	5·00	20·00	2·50
ab.	One 9·5 mm. band on each stamp	60·00	—	50·00

Booklet Cylinder Numbers

Panes of four (20-row single pane cylinder of 480 stamps).
Sideways watermark

Cyl. No.	No dot
N4 (Wmk. Crown to right) .	55·00

SECTION T
Dorothy Wilding Issues
1955–68. High Values. Recess-printed

General Notes

CROWNS WATERMARK. The Crowns are slightly smaller than in the low values.

PAPER. The stamps are all on unsurfaced paper except the *2s.6d.*, No. T6 which is on chalky paper.
Bradbury, Wilkinson printings are found with a degree of fluorescence when viewed under a short-wave u.v. lamp. This is due to the use of optical brightening agents in the rags used for paper making.
Stamps printed by Waterlow and De La Rue tend to curl from top to bottom while Bradbury, Wilkinson printings curl at the sides.

PERFORATION. All stamps in this Section are comb perforated 11 × 12 and the sheet perforation is always Type A.

PLATE NUMBERS. All plates were made from the original Waterlow Die. All stamps were printed from double plates producing left and right panes which were guillotined to make Post Office sheets of 40 (4 × 10). Plate numbers were used both by Waterlow and De La Rue but they appeared between the panes and were trimmed off. The Bradbury, Wilkinson plate numbers appear below stamps 3/4 in the bottom margin, the whole numbers on the left pane and the "A" numbers on the right pane. All three printers used rotary sheet-fed machines.

Bradbury, Wilkinson Plate No.

DE LA RUE PLATE DOTS. De La Rue printed on paper with St. Edward's Crown watermark and with Crowns watermark and as a control to distinguish the two papers during the changeover period, dots were inserted in the bottom margin below the first stamp in the bottom row.

In the case of the 2s.6d. the first printings on St. Edward's Crown paper were without dot, but later a single dot appeared on this paper, whilst early printings of stamps on the Crowns paper had two dots.

In the 10s. the dots are 7 mm. from the design and 5 mm. apart and in the other values they are 6 mm. from the design and 2½ mm. apart.

The number of sheets printed with double dots were:—

| 2s.6d. | 93,630 | 10s. | 37,510 |
| 5s. | 60,158 | £1 | 18,660 |

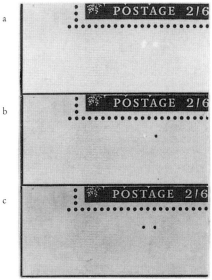

a. No dot   b. One dot   c. Two dots

DISTINGUISHING THE WORK OF THE THREE PRINTERS. Waterlow printed the stamps up to 31 December 1957 and then De La Rue held the contract until 31 December 1962, after which all printings were made by Bradbury, Wilkinson. The following characteristics will help to distinguish their work:—

Paper

Waterlow	De La Rue	Bradbury, Wilkinson
(a) Wmk. W.**23** Creamy	(a) Wmk. W.**23** Light cream	(a) Wmk. W.**24** Whiter
(b) Wmk. W.**23** Light cream	(b) Wmk. W.**24** Light cream	(b) Wmk. W.**24** Chalky
(From Feb., '57)	(c) Wmk. W.**24** Whiter	(2s.6d. only)
	(From 1962)	(c) No wmk. White

Shades

	Waterlow	De La Rue
2s.6d.	Blackish brown	More chocolate
5s.	Rose-carmine	Lighter red, less carmine
10s.	Ultramarine	More blue
£1	Black	Less intense

The shade variations result in part from the differences in paper.

Gutters. The width of gutters between the stamps varies, particularly the horizontal, as follows:—

Waterlow	De La Rue
3.8 to 4.0 mm.	3.4 to 3.8 mm.

Later De La Rue plates were less distinguishable in this respect.

Perforation. The vertical perforation of the Bradbury, Wilkinson is 11.9 to 12 as against 11.8 for the De La Rue.

Impression. The individual lines of the De La Rue impression are cleaner and devoid of the whiskers of colour of Waterlow's, and the whole impression is lighter and softer. The Bradbury, Wilkinson stamps are generally more deeply engraved than the De La Rue, showing more of the diadem detail and heavier lines on the Queen's face.

Waterlow Sheet Markings

Perforation Markings. As a check for the alignment of the perforations the following marks occur between the stamps in the Waterlow printings only:—
 (a) 3 mm. cross in the centre of the sheet.
 (b) 2½ mm. vertical lines in centre at top and bottom of sheet
 (c) 2½ mm. horizontal lines in centre at each side of sheet

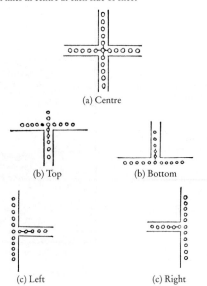

(a) Centre

(b) Top   (b) Bottom

(c) Left   (c) Right

Perforation Pin-holes. Coloured circles appear at left and right with a pin-hole through the opposite row six at left and right, although one is usually trimmed off.

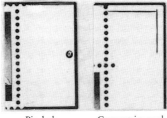

Pin-hole   Corner trim mark

Corner Trim Marks. These occur in the corners but naturally one or both sides may be trimmed off.

De La Rue Sheet Markings

Guide Marks. The only markings on De La Rue sheets are the guide marks which appear in the side margins between rows 5 and 6 which also serve to distinguish the left and right panes. Their position varies with each value and also in some cases in format between the different plates used from time to time. The circles or crosses also have pin-holes.

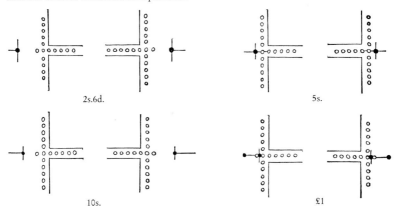

2s.6d.   5s.

10s.   £1

St. Edward's Crown Watermark

2s.6d., 5s., 10s. Type 1. £1 Type 1a

Multiple Crowns Watermark

2s.6d. Types 1, 2, 2a, 2b, 2c, 4. 5s. Types 1, 2c, 2d, 3. 10s. Types 1, 2, 2d. £1 Types 1, 1b, 2, 4a.

Specialists recognise four basic types of guide marks which are described as seen from left panes. Reverse for right.

Type 1 Horizontal "T" shaped mark with spot at intersection
    a As above but dot added to left extremity of horizontal arm
    b As above but with "target" added between the two dots

The "target" mark is small, circular with open centre which was pierced by the perforating machine.

Type 2 This is as type 1 but with the addition of a "target" between the horizontal "T" and stamp
    a As type 2 but intersection dot to right of cross over point
    b As type 2 but intersection dot to left of cross over point
    c As type 2 but no dot
    d As type 2c but "target" *joined* to "T"

Type 3 This is as type 1 but "target" is added first followed by "T"

143

Type 4 "Target" centred on "T" and without dot at intersection
> a As type 4 but arms partly erased (south and east arms erased left pane; north and west arms for right pane).

Bradbury, Wilkinson Sheet Markings

Guide Holes. These appear in a coloured circle opposite row 6, at left on left-hand panes and at right on right-hand panes.

Lay Dots. On the 2s.6d. plates 1/1A to 7/7A small "lay" dots appear in the top sheet margin, above the first vertical row on the left-hand pane and on the right-hand pane above the fourth vertical row. Only one copy of the 5s. is known but examples may exist on the other values. These were guide marks to check any movement of the plate.

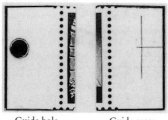

Guide hole   Guide cross

Guide Crosses. These occur in the region of rows 5 and 6 at right on left-hand panes and at left on right-hand panes. However, these do not appear on all plates, being omitted for instance on plates 8/8A, 9/9A of the 2s.6d. and 4/4A of the 5s.

TINTED SHEET MARGINS.   Some sheets show a background wash or tint of the colour in which the stamps are printed. This is an indication of a new state of a plate or a plate that has been rechromed. The explanation for this is that in wiping off the excess ink from the surface of the plate a small amount may be left at the edge of the plate and this will continue until the plate is sufficiently smooth for the surface to be thoroughly wiped clean of ink. These marginal tints stop short of the edge of the sheet as the extremities of the plate do not come into contact with the inking roller.

DATES OF ISSUE.   Where a change of watermark or paper occurs the date given is generally that on which the stamps were first issued by the Suppliers Department to Postmasters.

POST OFFICE TRAINING SCHOOL STAMPS.   All values of the Waterlow printings exist over-printed with thick vertical bars and stamps from the other printings with thin vertical bars. These were supplied to Post Office Training Schools, and their issue to the public was unauthorised.

"CANCELLED" OVERPRINT.   Nos. T5, T17 and T24 come overprinted "CANCELLED" (size 40 × 5 *mm*) as part of the test programme carried out by the Forensic Department of the Post Office.
    The values overprinted "CANCELLED" (size 24 × 3 *mm*) from the De La Rue archive are listed below No. T2.

WITHDRAWAL DATES.   It is known that the following went off sale at the Philatelic Bureau in the months shown:

Mar. 1968	£1 No. T24
Nov. 1968	2s.6d. No. T6
Nov. 1968	5s. No. T12
Jan. 1969	2s.6d. No. T5
Mar. 1970	10s. No. T18

The 2s.6d., 5s., 10s. and £1 no watermark, white paper (Nos. T7, T13, T19 and T25) were all withdrawn on 15 May 1970.

All 2s.6d., 5s. and 10s. stamps were invalidated as from 1 March 1972.

T1. Carrickfergus Castle

T2. Caernarvon Castle

T3. Edinburgh Castle

T4. Windsor Castle

(Des. Lynton Lamb. Portrait by Dorothy Wilding, Ltd.)

1955–68. 2s.6d., Type T1

1955 (SEPTEMBER 23).   2s.6d. WATERMARK ST. EDWARD'S CROWN, TYPE W.23

(a) Waterlow Printings

				Mint	Used
T1 (=S.G.536)	2s.6d.	Black-brown		9·00	2·00
	a.	Re-entry (R. 2/2)		50·00	

(b) De La Rue Printings (17 July 1958)

T2 (=S.G.536a)	2s.6d.	Black-brown		30·00	2·50
	a.	Watermark inverted		†	£2500
	b.	With one plate dot in bottom margin (R. 10/1) . .		75·00	

Imprimatur from the National Postal Museum Archives

No. T1 imperforate, watermark Type W.23

Watermark upright

Cancelled Overprints from the De La Rue Archives

Nos. T2, T9, T15 and T21 overprinted "CANCELLED" (24 × 3 mm) . . . . *Set of four* £600.

The overprint was handstamped in violet and impressions vary slightly in position.
   The above were from surplus registration sheets used by the printer for colour matching. They were placed on the market in 1990.

Plates. Plates numbered 47001, 47145 and 47316, each double pane, are known to have been used by Waterlow. These plates were later destroyed and it is possible that others could have been created. The De La Rue plates were made using the original Waterlow dies. No plate numbers were found on the issued sheets, but from study of the stamps it is likely that there were six double pane plates.

T1*a*
The doubling occurs down the left-hand margin

1959 (JULY 22). 2s.6d. WATERMARK CROWNS, TYPE W.24
(a) De La Rue Printings
A. Light Cream Paper

			Mint	Used
T3	2s.6d.	Black-brown	15·00	1·00
	a.	With two plate dots in bottom margin (R. 10/1) . .	35·00	

B. Whiter Paper (13 July 1962)

T4 (=S.G.595)	2s.6d.	Black-brown	10·00	75
	a.	Watermark inverted	—	£1500

No. T4*a*. Probably no more than five used examples exist.

(b) Bradbury, Wilkinson Printings
A. Whiter Paper (1 July 1963)

T5 (=S.G.595a)	2s.6d.	Black-brown	35	40
	a.	Watermark inverted	£1750	£175
	b.	Weak entry (Pl. 5A, R. 5/4 or 6/4)	10·00	
	c.	Re-entry (Pl. 9A, R. 8/4)	12·00	
	d.	Re-entry (Pl. 9, R. 10/2)	10·00	

B. Chalky Paper (30 May 1968)

T6 (=S.G.595k)	2s.6d.	Black-brown	50	1·50
	a.	Re-entry (Pl. 9A, R. 8/4)	15·00	
	b.	Re-entry (Pl. 9, R. 10/2)	10·00	

Imprimatur from the National Postal Museum Archives

No. T6 imperforate, watermark Type W.24

Watermark upright

T5*b*

Lines of shading weak or
omitted at base of collar,
on dress and at foot of
background
Occurs on R. 5/4 and
6/4 (the illustration is of
R. 6/4)

T5*c*, T6*a*

Re-entry shows in the
form of brown dots over
battlements
The re-entry on Nos.
T5*d* and T6*b* occurs in
the same place but is less
marked

Plates Numbers (Blocks of Four)

Bradbury, Wilkinson Printings
Whiter Paper. (No. T5)

Pl. No.		Pl. No.		Pl. No.		Pl. No.	
1	22·00	1A	22·00	6	5·50	6A	5·50
2	22·00	2A	22·00	7	5·50	7A	5·50
3	22·00	3A	22·00	8	5·00	8A	5·00
4	£300	4A	£500	9	4·00	9A	4·00
5	9·00	5A	9·00				

Chalky Paper. (No. T6)

9	6·00	9A	6·00

A "trial" perforation exists on plates 5 and 6, of which 21,000 sheets were reported to come with double extension holes in the side margins.

Minor Constant Flaws

On Plate 9 there are a number of faint scratch marks in the top and bottom margins and these are particularly noticeable on the chalky paper. They occur in the top margin on R. 10/3 and in the bottom margin on R. 1/1, 1/2, 2/1, 3/3, 3/4, 7/2, 7/4 and 8/2.

Plates 8A, 10 and 10A all show evidence of progressive wear around the guide hole. On plates 10 and 10A this takes the form of a crack extending from the guide hole towards the stamps. Plate 13A R. 1/2 shows a 2 cm. long scratch on the left-hand side of the bottom margin.

1968 (JULY 1). 2s.6d. NO WATERMARK. WHITE PAPER
Bradbury, Wilkinson Printings

			Mint	Used
T7 (=S.G.759)	2s.6d.	Black-brown	30	45

Plate Numbers (Blocks of Four)

Pl. No.		Pl. No.		Pl. No.		Pl. No.	
10	4·00	10A	4·00	12	3·00	12A	3·00
11	4·00	11A	4·00	13	3·00	13A	3·00

Imprimatur from the National Postal Museum Archives

No. T7 imperforate

No watermark

1955–68. 5s., Type T2

1955 (SEPTEMBER 23).   5s. WATERMARK ST. EDWARD'S CROWN, TYPE W.23
(a) Waterlow Printings

				Mint	Used
T8 (=S.G.537)	5s.	Rose-carmine	....	35·00	4·00
	a.	Re-entry (R. 8/1)	....	90·00	

(b) De La Rue Printings (30 April 1958)

T9 (=S.G.537a)	5s.	Rose-carmine	....	80·00	10·00

T8*a*

Major re-entry showing doubling of vertical lines of background above the diadem, and in the diadem along the left edge of the frontal cross, both sides of the side cross and the diagonals

Imprimatur from the National Postal Museum Archives

No. T8 imperforate, watermark Type W.23

Watermark upright

Plates. It is known that a double pane plate numbered 46726 was used by Waterlow. De La Rue created a further four plates, all double pane. Plate numbers did not occur on the issued sheets.

1959 (JUNE 15).   5s. WATERMARK CROWNS, TYPE W.24
(a) De La Rue Printings
A. Light Cream Paper

				Mint	Used
T10	5s.	Scarlet-vermilion	....	65·00	3·00
	a.	Watermark inverted	....	£2750	£275
	b.	With two plate dots in bottom margin (R. 10/1)	....	£100	

B. Whiter Paper (7 May 1962)

T11 (=S.G.596)	5s.	Scarlet-vermilion	....	55·00	2·00

(b) Bradbury, Wilkinson Printings
Whiter Paper (3 September 1963)

T12 (=S.G.596a)	5s.	(1)	Red	2·50	70
		(2)	Brownish red (Plates 3, 4)	1·20	50
	a.		Watermark inverted	£275	75·00
	b.		Printed on the gummed side	£800	

Plate Numbers (Blocks of Four)

Bradbury, Wilkinson Printings. (No. T12)

Pl. No.		Pl. No.		Pl. No.		Pl. No.	
1	. . . . . 45·00	1A	. . . . . 45·00	3	. . . . . 6·00	3A	. . . . . 6·00
2	. . . . . 45·00	2A	. . . . . 45·00	4	. . . . . 8·50	4A	. . . . . 8·50

1968 (APRIL 10). 5s. NO WATERMARK. WHITE PAPER
Bradbury, Wilkinson Printings

		Mint	Used
T13 (=S.G.760) 5s. Brownish red		70	75

Plate Numbers (Blocks of Four)

Pl. No.		Pl. No.		Pl. No.		Pl. No.	
4	. . . . . 7·00	4A	. . . . . 7·00	6	. . . . . 9·00	6A	. . . . . 9·00
5	. . . . . 7·00	5A	. . . . . 7·00				

Imprimatur from the National Postal Museum Archives

No. T13 imperforate

No watermark

1955–68. 10s., Type T3

1955 (SEPTEMBER 1).   10s. WATERMARK ST. EDWARD'S CROWN, TYPE W.23
(a) Waterlow Printings

				Mint	Used
T14 (=S.G.538)	10s.	(1)	Ultramarine	85·00	14·00
		(2)	Pale ultramarine	85·00	14·00
	a.		Weak entry (R. 1/2)	£160	25·00

(b) De La Rue Printings (25 April 1958)

			Mint	Used
T15 (=S.G.538a)	10s.	Dull ultramarine	£225	22·00
	a.	Weak frame (R. 4/1)	£250	

Other weak frames have been found on this design in different positions but always on the right-hand side of the stamp

T14*a*
Weak entry to right of lower panel gives ragged appearance

T15*a*, T17*a*

Minor Sheet Flaws

In rows 8, 9 and 10 there are blue marks on the extremity of the white letters and figures of "POSTAGE" and value which are more marked on the bottom two rows. These may not be fully constant but could be helpful for purposes of identification.

Imprimatur from the National Postal Museum Archives

No. T14 imperforate, watermark Type W.23

Watermark upright

Plates. It is known that Waterlow used a double pane plate numbered 46728. De La Rue are stated to have created three more, but study of the stamps suggests that four were made.

1959 (JULY 21).   10s. WATERMARK CROWNS, TYPE W.24
(a) De La Rue Printings
A. Light Cream Paper

			Mint	Used
T16	10s.	Blue	70·00	8·00
	a.	With two plate dots in bottom margin (R. 10/1) . . .	£125	

B. Whiter Paper (30 April 1962)

			Mint	Used
T17 (=S.G.597)	10s.	Blue	55·00	5·00
	a.	Weak frame (R. 4/1)	70·00	

(b) Bradbury, Wilkinson Printings
Whiter Paper (16 October 1963)

			Mint	Used
T18 (=S.G.597a)	10s.	Bright ultramarine	4·50	4·50
	a.	Watermark inverted	—	£1500

No. T18*a*. Three used examples have been confirmed.

Plate Numbers (Blocks of Four)

Bradbury, Wilkinson Printings. (No. T18)

Pl. No.		Pl. No.		Pl. No.		Pl. No.	
1	65·00	1A	65·00	2	23·00	2A	23·00

1968 (APRIL 10). 10s. NO WATERMARK. WHITE PAPER
Bradbury, Wilkinson Printings

			Mint	Used
T19 (=S.G.761)	10s.	Bright ultramarine	4·75	6·25

Plate Numbers (Blocks of Four)

Pl. No.		Pl. No.	
2	. . . . . 30·00	2A	. . . . . 30·00

Imprimatur from the National Postal Museum Archives

No. T19 imperforate

No watermark

1955–67. £1, Type T4

1955 (SEPTEMBER 1). £1 WATERMARK ST. EDWARD'S CROWN, TYPE W.23
(a) Waterlow Printings

			Mint	Used
T20 (=S.G.539)	£1	Black	£130	35·00

(b) De La Rue Printings (28 April 1958)

T21 (=S.G.539a)	£1	Black	£350	65·00

Minor Re-entries
Waterlow Printings

1/2 Slight doubling (Th. B1 and D–F1)
4/4 Slight doubling (Th. B1)
5/2 Slight doubling (Th. B1 and D–E1)
6/1 Slight doubling (Th. A–C13)
7/1 Slight doubling (Th. A–C13)
Other minute signs of doubling of left frame line occur on R. 7/2 and of right frame line on R. 1/1, 2/1, 3/3, 4/1, 4/2 and 9/2.

Imprimatur from the National Postal Museum Archives

No. T20 imperforate, watermark Type W.23

Watermark upright

Plates. It is known that the double pane plate used by Waterlow was numbered 46727. A further two plates were created by De La Rue. No plate numbers appeared on the issued sheets.

1959 (JUNE 23). £1 WATERMARK CROWNS, TYPE W.24
(a) De La Rue Printings
A. Light Cream Paper

			Mint	Used
T22	£1	Black	£130	15·00
	a.	With two plate dots in bottom margin (R. 10/1)	£175	

B. Whiter Paper (30 April 1962)

T23 (=S.G.598)	£1	Black	£120	12·00
	a.	Watermark inverted	—	£1750

No. T23a. No more than three or four examples, all used, have been reported.

(b) Bradbury, Wilkinson Printings
Whiter Paper (14 November 1963)

T24 (=S.G.598a)	£1	Black	11·00	8·00
	a.	Watermark inverted	£7000	£2500

Plate Numbers (Blocks of Four)

Bradbury, Wilkinson Printings. (No. T24)

Pl. No.		Pl. No.	
1 . . . . . 60·00		1A . . . . . 60·00	

1967 (DECEMBER 4). £1 NO WATERMARK. WHITE PAPER

Bradbury, Wilkinson Printings

			Mint	Used
T25 (=S.G.762)	£1	Black	4·50	6·00

Plate Numbers (Blocks of Four)

Pl. No.		Pl. No.	
1 . . . . . 25·00		1A . . . . . 25·00	

Imprimatur from the National Postal Museum Archives

No. T25 perf. 11 × 12

No watermark

Presentation Pack

TPP1 (issued 1960)	Four values	£1100

The issued pack contained one of each value in the De La Rue printing with Crowns watermark on the light cream paper (Nos. T3, T10, T16 and T22).

Three forms of the pack exist:

(a) Inscribed "$6·50" for sale in the U.S.A. (*Price* £550)

(b) Without price for sale in the U.K.

(c) With "£1.18s." for sale at 1960 Festival Hall, Int. Stamp Exhibition

SECTION U
Machin £.s.d. Issues
1967–70. Sheet and Coil Stamps in Photogravure

General Notes

INTRODUCTION. In February 1965, after twelve years of the Wilding portrait issue, the Queen granted permission for the preparation of studies for a new definitive series. Designs from several artists were submitted and Arnold Machin was eventually selected. His preferred approach, with the aim of emulating the simplicity of the Penny Black of 1840, was to present the Queen's head in profile by the medium of a plaster cast or plaque. He progressively worked upon this cast through most of 1966, for instance by adding a corsage at the Queen's request, until he was satisfied that his aim had been fulfilled.

Photographs by Lord Snowdon and later Professor John Hedgecoe were taken of the cast in various conditions of light, of which one was finally approved. The first version came to be used for values with a solid background, but it was found to be unsatisfactory for other values with a light or gradated background. Accordingly an earlier version of the cast was also selected which gave an improved sculptured appearance to the image. There were small differences between these two casts, which, as is explained under Machin Heads on page 154, led to two different series of Head Types.

Of the original casts used by Arnold Machin, one is in the National Postal Museum and the other is said to have been lost.

The first three values, 4d., deep sepia, 1s. and 1s.9d., of the sterling Machin definitives appeared on 5 June 1967. The remaining values were issued in stages during the following thirteen months and the low value series was completed on 1 July 1968, although subsequent changes of stamp colours and variations in the number of phosphor bands on some values introduced further additions to the basic series. Uniquely this was the first definitive issue to be printed on paper without watermark, thus eliminating some of the factors which complicated the listing for previous issues.

PRINTERS. All the low value Machin issues £.s.d. were printed in photogravure by Harrison & Sons. They were printed on continuous reels of paper "on the web" generally in double pane width, i.e. 480 stamps consisting of two panes (no dot and dot) each of 240 stamps arranged in twenty rows of twelve stamps, the panes being guillotined before issue. The 10d., 1s.6d., 1s.9d. and part of the 1s. printings were made from single cylinders printing sheets of 240 stamps (i.e. no dot panes only).

The phosphor bands were applied at the same operation. The bi-coloured 1s.6d. and 1s.9d. were printed by the three-colour (including the phosphor cylinder) Halley machine and the remainder by the two-colour Timson machine. The multi-value coils and se-tenant panes from the £1 "Stamps for Cooks" booklet were printed by the five-colour Thrissell machine.

MASTER NEGATIVES and MULTIPOSITIVES. The process of preparing a new Machin definitive photogravure cylinder started with a master negative from photographs (sometimes referred to as master positives) of one of the two casts of the Queen's head in profile. Further master negatives are taken as needed and there is evidence that these can be retouched. The next step is the transfer of the image on this master negative by means of a step-and-repeat camera onto a photographic plate known as a multipositive. This is normally rather larger than the pane size of 200 or double pane size of 400. This multipositive of the head and background is then combined with a second multipositive for the face value, added to the previously screened carbon tissue. The relative positioning of these two multipositives is not always uniformly precise and can result in tiny variations of distance between head and value digits described under Machin Heads in these notes. Finally this carbon tissue forms the medium by means of which each new cylinder is etched. After an application of a thin layer of chrome the cylinder is ready for use.

PAPER. Unwatermarked chalk-surfaced paper was used for all values. Exceptionally, examples of all four panes from the £1 "Stamps for Cooks" booklet and the 3d. and 10d. from sheets exist on uncoated paper. It does not respond to the chalky test (that is applying silver to see if it will produce a black line) and may be further distinguished from the normal chalk-surfaced paper by the fibres which clearly show on the surface, resulting in the printing impression being rougher, and by the screening dots which are not so evident.

Paper Thickness and Fluorescence. Variation in the thickness of paper sometimes occurs in the making and is undetected where the finished reel conforms to the prescribed weight. Within the reel there may be sections where the paper is unusually thick or thin. A particular example is the 2s. booklet of March 1970 which is known with panes UB15 and UB18 on very thick paper. This has an effect on the thickness of the booklet and could cause jamming in the vending machine. Such varieties are not listed. Certain coil issues were on translucent paper, the design showing clearly on the back of the stamps.

On some printings the fluorescent reaction varies. This is best seen on marginal examples, but the difference is not sufficient or consistent to warrant separate listing and, indeed, the brighter paper can be made to appear dull by exposure to sunlight. Stamps cannot be made to appear brighter, however, and none of the pre-decimal paper is as bright under u.v. as the fluorescent coated paper which was introduced in 1971.

GUM. Polyvinyl alchohol (PVA) was introduced by Harrison & Sons in place of gum arabic in 1968. It is almost invisible except that a small amount of pale yellowish colouring matter was introduced to make it possible to see that the stamps had been gummed. Although this can be distinguished from gum arabic in unused stamps there is, of course, no means of detecting it in used copies. Where the two forms of gum exist on the same value they are listed separately.

It should be further noted that gum arabic is normally shiny in appearance, and that, normally, PVA has a matt appearance. However, depending upon the qualities of the paper ingredients and the resultant absorption of the gum, occasionally, PVA has a slightly shiny appearance, and in cases of severe under-gumming gum arabic may appear matt. In such cases it is sometimes impossible to be absolutely sure which gum has been used except by testing the stamps with a very expensive infra-red spectrometer. Chemical tests unfortunately destroy the stamps. Therefore, whilst very shiny gum is gum arabic it does not follow that all matt gum is PVA. A few late printings of stamps originally issued on PVA were made on gum arabic paper, either in error or to use up stocks.

Paper treated with gum arabic is passed over a fracture bar before printing to reduce its tendency to curl. This results in a "crazy paving" appearance, often visible under magnification, not present on PVA.

The term PVA is used because it is generally accepted, but the official abbreviation is PVAl to distinguish it from PVAc, polyvinyl acetate, another adhesive which has not so far been used for stamps, although it does occur on postal stationery. De La Rue use the term PVOH, polyvinyl hydroxyl, to describe the same adhesive.

MACHIN HEADS. Basically two master negatives were used for preparing the multipositive for each value comprising (*a*) head with background and (*b*) value. The portrait negative used for the initial releases had a three-dimensional effect only in the 10d. and 1s. values where a light background was used. On the other values, for which a different portrait master negative was used, the darker background merged with the outline and much of the relief effect was lost.

Beginning with coils and booklets in March 1968 a modified portrait negative was used giving greater contrast at those points where it had been lost. Thus there are three clearly different portraits; the original Head A with a flatter bust, Head B with a curved "shadow" and Head C the three-dimensional version from the light background stamps.

These differences are listed and, for ease of reference, appear in tabulated form, together with details of the phosphor screens, at the beginning of the catalogue list.

As a result of the combination of two master negatives described above the position of the value in relation to the frame varies from one multipositive to another. The 2d. Types I and II show an extreme case of this, where the change was made deliberately. Taking the 4d. for example the distance to the left frame varies from 0·9 mm. on the early sheet cylinders to 1·2 mm. on the multi-value coils, while the spacing to the bottom is normally 0·9 mm. but decreases to 0·6 mm. in the £1 "Stamps for Cooks" booklet.

PHOSPHOR BANDS. See the General Notes for Section S for a detailed description of these. The Machin definitives were normally issued with "violet" phosphor bands only. Most values have appeared with the phosphor omitted in error and these are listed separately.

The 1s.6d. (No. U29) was issued as an experiment in 1969 with violet phosphor incorporated into the coating.

PHOSPHOR SCREENS. The phosphor bands were applied in photogravure, some of the cylinders having a 150-line screen and others a 250-line screen. The absence of a screen on parts of a printing is due to the cylinder becoming clogged.

The phosphor screen used for the single centre band on the 3d., 4d. sepia and 4d. vermilion booklet panes of six is unique in having a mixed screen. Continuous 21-row cylinders are normally produced from two pieces of carbon tissue, thus giving two joins. On this particular phosphor cylinder, the pieces of carbon tissue had different screens. Thus four types of booklet panes can be found—(1) 150 screen; (2) screen join 150/250; (3) 250 screens; (4) screen join 250/150. It is calculated that out of 100 panes the proportions are 67 150 screen, 14 250 screen and 19 screen joins.

It is not easy to distinguish the different screens but we include them in the following check list of the Machin Head Types.

PERFORATION. Harrisons used the same 15 × 14 comb perforation as for the previous Wilding definitives. A number of different perforators were used for both sheets and booklets and these are described and illustrated in Appendix G. The cylinder numbers are listed and priced according to the type of perforator used.

BOOKLET PANES.   In Section UB we list separately the booklet panes and the varieties on them and priced according to perforator types. See General Notes to that Section.

COIL VARIETIES.   See General Notes for Section S for detailed notes on these.

SHADES.   There are numerous shades in these issues and we have restricted our listing to the most marked ones and related them to the cylinder number blocks where possible.

DATES OF ISSUE.   The dates given are those announced by the Post Office, except in the case of dates for changes of gum or in the number of phosphor bands when we have quoted either the dates of release by the Philatelic Bureau or the earliest dates known. As in Section S the dates given in bold type in the headings are those on which stamps first appeared in sheet form. Where a date is followed by a dagger it means that the stamp appeared earlier in coils or booklets as indicated in footnotes.

FIRST DAY COVERS.   They are listed after the Presentation Pack but we only quote for official covers, prepared and issued by the Post Office, cancelled by "FIRST DAY OF ISSUE" circular postmarks.

PRESENTATION PACKS.   See General Notes under Section W.

"UNPRINTED STAMPS".   Widely trimmed sheet margins may produce the effect of unprinted stamps as illustrated above. The blank paper has the phosphor bands printed as on the normal stamps. In the Machin and Regional issues they come from either the left or right-hand margins; in the special issues they are known from the top of the sheet.

INVALIDATION.   All £.s.d. Machin definitives were withdrawn from sale on 25 November 1971, and were, with the exception of the £1 value, invalidated as from 1 March 1972. They ceased to be valid in Guernsey and Jersey from 1 October 1969 when these islands each established their own independent postal administrations and introduced their own stamps.

SHEET MARKINGS.   Reference should be made to the descriptions of sheet markings given in the General Notes for Section S, as most of these apply to this Section and the information given there is not repeated here. In the case of the 1s.6d. and 1s.9d. bicoloured Machin definitives reference should be made to the descriptions of sheet markings in Section W as many of them also apply to these two values. Additional information to that provided in Sections S and W is given here.

Cylinder Numbers.   In the Machin definitives $\frac{1}{2}$d. to 1s. values they appear in the left-hand margin opposite Row 18 No. 1 in the style as illustrated in Section S. In the case of the 1s.6d. and 1s.9d. values the cylinder numbers appear boxed in the left-hand margin opposite Row 19 No. 1 in the style as illustrated in Section W.

Phosphor Cylinder Numbers.   As with the 1970 General Anniversaries, special issue in Section W, phosphor cylinder numbers were introduced during 1970, "Ph 1" appearing on the Machin issues. It only occurs on the dot panes and appears in the right-hand margin and therefore not on the cylinder block. Moreover it is not synchronised with the ink cylinders and so can appear anywhere in the margin, and the "1" is often trimmed off. Its existence is recorded under the sheet markings.

Varieties in Cylinder Blocks.   Where a cylinder block contains a listed variety the price is adjusted accordingly and bears an asterisk.

Marginal Arrows. In the Machin definitives these are "W" shaped (photo-etched) at top, bottom and sides, unless otherwise stated.

Perforation Guide Holes. A number of different styles of guide hole box have been used for the Machin definitives and these are fully illustrated as for Sections S and W.

In addition to guide hole boxes of one type or another opposite rows 14/15 (used for perforation Type A), the earlier cylinders of nearly all the values from $\frac{1}{2}$d. to 1s. also show a single "traffic light" type box above and below the eighth vertical row in the no dot panes. This latter type would only be used in conjunction with perforation Type F (L)* and it is illustrated here to explain its presence on the sheets. When Type F (L)* is used the circular central part of the box is either partly or completely removed.

CHECK LIST OF MACHIN HEADS AND PHOSPHOR SCREENS

For fuller explanations see General Notes.

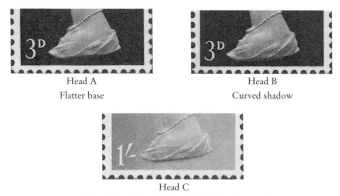

Head A   Head B

Flatter base   Curved shadow

Head C

Three-dimensional effect with light background

Abbreviations

Phosphor bands: 1C = one centre; 1L = one left side; 1R = one right side

Booklet panes: s/t = stamps *se-tenant*; s/t labels = stamps *se-tenant* with labels

Coils: MV = multi-value; S = sideways delivery; V = vertical delivery

Face Value	Cat. No.	Description	Phosphor Bands	Gum	Head	Screen	Sheet Cylinders	Sources Booklet Panes	Coils
½d.	U 1		2	PVA	A	150	2, 3	—	—
1d.	U 2		2	PVA	A	150	2	—	—
	U 2		2	PVA	B	150	4, 6	6	V
	U 2		2	PVA	B	250	—	s/t, 6 s/t 15 s/t	—
	U 3		1C	PVA	B	250	—	6 s/t	—
	U 4		1C	GA	B	250	—	—	MV
2d.	U 5	Type I	2	PVA	A	150	1	—	—
	U 6	Type II	2	PVA	B	150	5, 6	—	V
	U 6	„	2	PVA	B	250	—	—	V, S
	U 7	„	1C	GA	B	250	—	—	MV
3d.	U 8		1C	GA	A	150	1	—	V
	U 8		1C	GA	A	250	—	—	S
	U 8		1C	GA	B	250	—	—	MV
	U 9		1C	PVA	A	150	1, 3, 4	—	—
	U 9		1C	PVA	A	250	—	—	S
	U 9		1C	PVA	B	150	—	6	—
	U 9		1C	PVA	B	Join	—	6	—
	U 9		1C	PVA	B	250	—	6	—
	U10		2	PVA	A	150	3, 4	—	V
	U10		2	PVA	B	150	—	—	V
	U10		2	PVA	B	250	—	4 s/t	—
4d.	U11	Sepia	2	GA	A	150	4, 8	6	V
	U11	„	2	GA	A	250	—	—	S
	U11	„	2	GA	B	250	14	—	—
	U12	„	2	PVA	A	150	4, 10, 12, 13	6	—
	U12	„	2	PVA	B	250	14, 15	4	—
	U13	„	1C	PVA	A	150	4, 12, 13	6	V
	U13	„	1C	PVA	A	Join	—	6	—
	U13	„	1C	PVA	A	250	—	6	S
	U13	„	1C	PVA	B	250	14, 15	4, 4 s/t labels 6 s/t	—

Face Value	Cat. No.	Description	Phosphor Bands	Gum	Head	Screen	Sheet Cylinders	Sources Booklet Panes	Coils
4d.	U14	Vermilion	1C	PVA	A	150	4, 10, 13	6	V
	U14	„	1C	PVA	A	Join	—	6	—
	U14	„	1C	PVA	A	250	—	6	S
	U14	„	1C	PVA	B	150	—	6	—
	U14	„	1C	PVA	B	Join	—	6	—
	U14	„	1C	PVA	B	250	15, 16, 17	4, 4 s/t labels 6, 15	S
	U15	„	1C	GA	B	250	—	—	MV
	U15	„ Feb/Mar	1C	GA	A	150	—	6	—
	U15	„ '69 6s. &	1C	GA	A	Join	—	6	—
	U15	„ May '69 10s	1C	GA	A	250	—	6	—
	U16	„	1L	PVA	B	250	—	6 s/t, 15 s/t	—
	U16A	„	1R	PVA	B	250	—	15 s/t	—
5d.	U17		2	PVA	A	150	1	—	—
	U17		2	PVA	B	150	7, 10, 15	6	V
	U17		2	PVA	B	250	11, 13	15, 15 s/t	S
6d.	U18		2	PVA	A	150	2, 3, 4, 5	—	—
	U18		2	PVA	B	150	—	—	V
	U18		2	PVA	B	250	—	—	V
7d.	U19		2	PVA	B	150	3, 4	—	—
8d.	U20	Vermilion	2	PVA	A	150	2	—	—
	U21	Turquoise-blue	2	PVA	B	150	3	—	—
9d.	U22		2	GA	A	150	2	—	—
	U23		2	PVA	A	150	2	—	—
10d.	U24		2	PVA	C	150	1	—	—
	U24		2	PVA	C	250	1	—	—
1s.	U25		2	GA	C	150	3, 11	—	—
	U26		2	PVA	C	150	11	—	—
	U26		2	PVA	C	250	11	—	—
1s.6d.	U27		2	GA	A	150	2A–2B, 3A–2B	—	—
	U27	(3) Phosphor omitted	—	GA	A	—	5A–2B	—	—
	U28		2	PVA	A	150	3A–2B, 5A–2B	—	—
	U28		2	PVA	A	250	3A–1B	—	—
	U29	"All-over" phos.	—	PVA	A	—	5A–2B	—	—
1s.9d.	U30		2	GA	A	150	1A–1B	—	—
	U31		2	PVA	A	250	1A–1B	—	—

INDEX TO COIL STAMPS

Face Value	Phosphor Bands	Gum	Head	Further description	Delivery		See stamp No.
1d.	2	PVA	B	. . . .	V		U2
2d.	2	PVA	B	Type II	V	S	U6
3d.	1C	GA	A	. . . .	V	S	U8
3d.	1C	PVA	A	. . . .		S	U9
3d.	2	PVA	A	. . . .	V		U10
3d.	2	PVA	B	. . . .	V		U10
4d.	2	GA	A	Deep olive-brown	V	S	U11
4d.	1C	PVA	A	Deep olive-brown	V	S	U13
4d.	1C	PVA	A	Bright vermilion	V	S	U14
4d.	1C	PVA	B	Bright vermilion		S	U14
5d.	2	PVA	B	. . . .	V	S	U17
6d.	2	PVA	B	. . . .	V		U18
2 × 2d. + 3d. + 1d. + 4d.	1C	GA	B	Multi-value coil. 4d. Bright vermilion		S	U32

PAPER AND WATERMARK

All the following issues are printed on chalk-surfaced paper, except for the uncoated errors, and are without watermark.

U1
Value at left

U2
Value at right

Queen Elizabeth II

(Des. after plaster cast by Arnold Machin)

½d., Type U1 (1968)

1968 (FEBRUARY 5).   ½d. TWO 9·5 mm. PHOSPHOR BANDS. PVA GUM. HEAD A

			Mint	Used
U1 (=S.G.723)	½d.	Orange-brown	10	20
	a.	Phosphor omitted	30·00	
	b.	Dot in 1 of ½ (Cyl. 3 No dot, R. 20/2)	4·50	

U1*b*

Cylinder Numbers (Blocks of Six)

Perforation Type A

Cyl. No.	No dot	Dot
2	2·00	2·00
3	6·00*	5·00

*Includes variety U1*b*.

Minor Constant Sheet Flaws

Cyl. 2.   5/12 Small retouch at base of Queen's hair (Th. E4–5)
          9/5 Dark horizontal strip of shading behind Queen's neck (Th. F5–6)
Cyl. 3   12/9 Dark patch below Queen's chin (Th. E2–3)

A number of stamps from cylinder 2 dot display irregularities of the background in the form of dark patches and lines. This is most prominent on R. 9/5 recorded above; others occur on R. 2/2, 7/6, 8/6, 9/11, 10/1, 13/2–5, 14/5, 17/4–5 and 18/1.

Sheet Markings

Guide holes: In double "SON" box opposite rows 14/15, at left (no dot) or right (dot). In addition a single "traffic light" type box appears above and below the eighth vertical row in the no dot pane only. These would only be used in conjunction with perforation Type F (L)*).

Others: As given in General Notes

Sold Out   10.2.70.

1d., Type U1 (1968–70)

1968 (FEBRUARY 5). 1d. YELLOWISH OLIVE
A. Two 9·5 mm. 1d. Phosphor Bands. PVA Gum.

				Mint	Used
U2 (=S.G.724)	1d.	(1)	Light olive (A) Head A	60	15
		(2)	Yellowish olive (B) Head B	10	10
		(3)	Greenish olive	20	15
	a.		Imperf. (coil strip)*	£2000	
	b.		Uncoated paper (1970)**	90·00	
	c.		Phosphor omitted	1·00	
	d.		Phosphor omitted on front but printed on the gummed side	£250	
	e.		Error. One 9·5 mm. phosphor band	5·00	
	g.		Neck retouches (Cyl. 4 No dot, R. 20/3)	4·50	
	h.		Flaw by Queen's chin (Vertical Coil)	5·50	
	i.		Thick "1 D" (Vertical coil)	12·00	
	k.		Imperforate at bottom (Vertical coil)	—	£300
	s.		Optd. "Specimen" (14 mm.)	£200	

B. One 4 mm. Centre Phosphor Band. PVA Gum.
Se-tenant Booklet pane only (16 September 1968)

U3 (=S.G.725)	1d. Yellowish olive (Head B)	30	35

C. One 4 mm. Centre Phosphor Band. Gum Arabic.
Multi-value coil only (27 August 1969)

U4 (=S.G.725Eg)	1d. Yellowish olive (Head B)	30	

*No. U2*a* occurs in a vertical strip of four, top stamp perforated on three sides, bottom stamp imperf. three sides and the two middle stamps completely imperf.

**Uncoated paper. No. U2*b* comes from the *se-tenant* pane of 15 in the £1 "Stamps for Cooks" Booklet (see No. UB2*ab*); see also General Notes.

No. U3 only comes from the 10s. Booklet of September 1968 (XP6). It also occurs with the phosphor omitted but since a single stamp would be difficult to distinguish from No. U2*c* it is only listed when in a complete *se-tenant* booklet pane (see No. UB3*a*).

No. U4 only comes from the multi-value coil strip which is listed as No. U32.

A single used example is known of No. U2*k*.

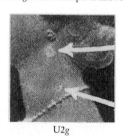

U2*g*	U2*h*	Normal U2

Cylinder Numbers (Blocks of Six)

Two bands. Perforation Type A

Cyl. No.	No dot	Dot
2 (Shade 1) (Head A)	7·00	7·00
4 (Shade 2) (Head B)	2·00	2·00
6 (Shade 3) (Head B)	2·00	2·00

Minor Constant Sheet Flaws

Cyl. 2.   5/11 Small flaw at back of Queen's collar (Th. F5)
Cyl. 4   6/9 White flaw at top of Queen's hair (Th. B3)
Cyl. 6.   11/7 Horizontal line of coloured dots across Queen's shoulder (Th. F3–5)
        12/10 Vertical lines of coloured dots through Queen's forehead and cheek (Th. B2, C2–3 and D2)

Coils

Two bands. Vertical delivery printed in continuous reels from double pane cylinder B1

Head B

Code No.	Number in roll	Face value
E	480	£2
X	960	£4
Z	1920	£8

One centre band. Multi-value coil, see No. U32.

Sheet Markings

Guide holes:
  Cyl. 4, in single "SN" box opposite rows 14/15, at left (no dot) or right (dot)
  Cyls. 2 and 6, in double "SON" box opposite rows 14/15, at left (no dot) or right (dot)

Marginal arrows:
  Cyls. 2 and 6, "W" shaped, photo-etched at top, bottom and sides
  Cyl. 4, "W" shaped, hand engraved at top, bottom and sides

Marginal rule:
  Cyl. 2, at bottom of sheet, 2 mm. wide
  Cyls. 4 and 6, at bottom of sheet, $2\frac{1}{2}$ mm. wide

Others: As given in General Notes

2d., Type U1 (1968–69)

Two Types

I   II

Type I. Value spaced away from left side of stamp (Cyls. 1 no dot and dot)

Type II. Value closer to left side from new multipositive (Cyls. 5 no dot and dot onwards). The portrait appears in the centre, thus conforming to the other values.

1968 (FEBRUARY 5). 2d. TYPE I. TWO 9·5 mm. PHOSPHOR BANDS. PVA GUM. HEAD A

			Mint	Used
U5 (=S.G.726)	2d.	Lake-brown	10	15
	a.	Phosphor omitted	30·00	

Cylinder Numbers (Blocks of Six)

Perforation Type A

Cyl. No.	No dot	Dot
1	1·75	1·75

Minor Constant Sheet Flaws

Cyl. 1   3/11 Small white spot in band of diadem (Th. C5)
          8/8 Dark spot by emblems at rear of diadem (Th. B5)
          12/9 Retouching in Queen's hair just by ear (Th. C–D4)

Sheet Markings

Guide holes: In double "S O N" box opposite rows 14/15, at left (no dot) or right (dot)

Others: As given in General Notes

1969 (FEBRUARY).† 2d. CHANGE TO TYPE II. HEAD B
A. Two 9·5 mm. Phosphor Bands. PVA Gum

			Mint	Used
U6 (=S.G.727)	2d.	Lake-brown	15	20
	a.	Phosphor omitted	1·00	
	b.	Error. One 9·5 mm. phosphor band	55·00	

B. One 4 mm. Centre Phosphor Band. Gum Arabic.

Multi-value coil only (27 August 1969)

U7 (=S.G.728)	2d.	Lake-brown	70	90

†No. U6 was issued on 4 April 1968 in sideways delivery coils, and on 19 March 1969 in vertical delivery coils.

No. U7 only comes from the multi-value coil strip which is listed as No. U32.

Cylinder Numbers (Blocks of Six)

Two bands. Perforation Type A

Cyl. No.	No dot	Dot
5	4·50	4·00
6	4·00	4·00

Minor Constant Sheet Flaws

Cyl. 5.   6/8 Dark area above 2 (Th. F1)
          8/1 Small flaw on Queen's shoulder (Th. F3)
          10/1 Coloured line through Queen's nose and upper lip (Th. C–D2)
          10/3 Dark spot below Queen's chin (Th. E2)
          19/5 Retouch to background to left of diadem (Th. A2–3). There are two states of this

Cyl. 6.   18/4 Small retouch at top of Queen's neck and vertical scratch extending to her dress (Th. E3–G3). Several states exist

Coils

Two bands. Printed in continuous reels from double pane cylinders D2 (vertical) or single pane D1 (sideways)

Code No.	Number in roll	Face value	
T	480	£4	Sideways delivery
V	960	£8	Vertical delivery

One centre band. Multi-value coil, see No. U32

Sheet Markings

Phosphor cylinder number: "Ph 1" found on a later printing of cyl. 6 dot, right margin (*price* £25 *in block of* 6).

Guide holes: In double "S O N" box opposite rows 14/15, at left (no dot) or right (dot). In addition a single "traffic light" type box appears above and below the eighth vertical row in the no dot pane only (These would only be used in conjunction with perforation Type F (L)*).

Others: As given in General Notes

3d., Type U1 (1967–69)

1967 (AUGUST 8). 3d. ONE 4 mm. CENTRE PHOSPHOR BAND
A. Gum Arabic

				Mint	Used
U8 (=S.G.729)	3d.	(1)	Violet (A) Head A	15	10
		(2)	Bluish violet (sideways coils)	2·50	50
		(1)	Violet (multi-value coils) (B) Head B	60	15
	a.		Imperf (vertical pair)	£700	
	b.		Phosphor omitted	1·25	
	c.		Spot on nose (Sideways coil, Roll 10)	4·50	
	d.		Gash on diadem (Multi-value coil, Roll 1)	5·50	

B. PVA Gum (12 March 1968)

U9 (=S.G.729Ev)	3d.	(1)	Violet (A) Head A	15	
		(2)	Bluish violet (sideways coils)	45·00	
		(1)	Violet (booklets) (B) Head B	5·00	
	a.		Phosphor omitted	2·00	
	b.		Spot on nose (Sideways coil, Roll 10)	4·50	

No. U8 is known pre-released on 7 August at Bournemouth, Hyde (Cheshire), in South London and at Torquay.

U8*c*, U9*b*	U8*d*
From sideways delivery coils	Occurs in sideways delivery multi-value GS and GL coils on every fifth 3d. stamp

Cylinder Numbers (Blocks of Six)

Gum Arabic Perforation Type A			PVA Gum Perforation Type A		
Cyl. No.	No dot	Dot	Cyl. No.	No dot	Dot
1	25·00	28·00	1	2·50	2·50
			3	2·50	2·50
Perforation Type F (L)*			4	8·00	8·00
1	2·50	2·50	Perforation Type F(L)*		
			1	†	—

There are two states of cyl. 1 no dot: (a) "1" is hatched, the bottom part lacks colour and the serifs are short (gum arabic printings); (b) "1" is solid and the serifs are long (gum arabic perf. type F(L)* and PVA).

Cylinder blocks from the no dot pane of Cylinder 3 show a phantom "3", slightly smaller and just below and to the right of the normal cylinder number. This occurred on part of the printing.

Minor Constant Sheet Flaws

Cyl. 1	1/9 Vertical scratch on Queen's neck (Th. E3–4)
	3/9 Pale patch in background around D of value
	7/1 Small white flaw inside cross of diadem (Th. B5)
Cyl. 1.	1/4 Small retouch on Queen's neck below ear (Th. D4). PVA only
	1/7 White scratch in Queen's hair below diadem at right (Th. C5). PVA only
	4/11 Small retouch on Queen's neck (Th. E3).
	12/4 Retouch at front of Queen's collar (Th. G3)
	19/6 Small retouch by Queen's mouth (Th. D3)
Cyl. 3.	8/3 Scratch on Queen's temple (Th. C3)
	12/7 Retouch on Queen's neck below necklace (Th. F4)
	16/4 Flaw on Queen's shoulder (Th. F4). Later retouched

Coils

Printed in continuous reels from double pane cylinder M1 (vertical) or single pane M2 (sideways).
Head A

Gum Arabic.

Code No.	Number in roll	Face value	
S	480	£6	Sideways delivery
AC	480	£6	Vertical delivery
AD	960	£12	do.
U	1920	£24	do.

PVA Gum

S*	480	£6	Sideways delivery

*Stamps from this coil can be distinguished from all other PVA centre-band stamps in singles. The coil stamps have Machin Head Type A and 250-line phosphor screen. The sheet stamps have Head Type A and 150-line screen, whilst the booklet stamps have Head Type B.

One centre band. Multi-value coil, see No. U32

Sheet Markings

Guide holes:
Perf. Type A, in double "S O N" box opposite rows 14/15, at left (no dot) or right (dot). In addition a single "traffic light" type box appears above and below the eighth vertical row in the no dot pane from cyl. 1 (latter only used in conjunction with perforation Type F (L)*).
Perf. Type F (L)*, boxed above and below the eighth vertical row in the no dot pane only. The usual "S O N" boxes opposite rows 14/15 remain.

Others: As given in General Notes

1969 (AUGUST 20).† 3d. CHANGE TO TWO 9·5 mm. PHOSPHOR BANDS. PVA GUM

			Mint	Used
U10 (=S.G.730)	3d.	Violet (A) Head A	30	35
		(B) Head B	50	40
	a.	Uncoated paper*	£2000	
	b.	Error. One 9·5 mm. phosphor band	2·50	

*Uncoated paper—see General Notes.
†Issued on 6.4.68 in 2s. Booklets dated May 1968, on 26 September 1968 in vertical delivery coils.

Cylinder Numbers (Blocks of Six)

Perforation Type A

Cyl. No.		No dot	Dot
3 (Head A)	. . . .	3·75	3·75
4 (Head A)	. . . .	6·50	6·50

The note about the phantom "3" mentioned under No. U9 also applies here and the whole of the printing was affected.

Minor Constant Sheet Flaws

Cyl. 3.   8/3 Scratch on Queen's temple (Th. C3)
12/7 Retouch on Queen's neck below necklace (Th. F4)

Coil

Vertical delivery printed in continuous reels from double pane cylinders M1 (Head A) or M4 (Head B)

Code No.	Number in roll	Face value
AD	960	£12

Sheet Markings

Guide holes: In double "S O N" box opposite rows 14/15, at left (no dot) or right (dot)

Others: As given in General Notes

4d. Deep Sepia, Type U1 (1967–68)

1967 (JUNE 5).   4d. TWO 9.5 mm. PHOSPHOR BANDS
A. Gum Arabic

				Mint	Used
U11 (=S.G.731/*Ea*)	4d.	(1)	Deep sepia (A) Head A	10	10
		(2)	Deep olive-brown	10	15
		(2)	Deep olive-brown (B) Head B £1400		
	a.		Phosphor omitted. Shade (1)	1·00	
	ab.		Phosphor omitted. Shade (2)	2·00	
	b.		Error. One 9·5 mm. phosphor band	50·00	

B. PVA Gum (22 January 1968)

				Mint	Used
U12 (=S.G.731Eav)	4d.	(2)	Deep olive-brown (A) Head A	10	
		(3)	Deep olive-sepia	10	10
		(2)	Deep olive-brown (B) Head B	25	10
		(3)	Deep olive-sepia	25	10
	a.		Error. One 9·5 mm. phosphor band	5·00	
	b.		Phosphor omitted	2·00	
	c.		White patch (Cyl. 13 No dot, R. 20/12)	4·50	
	d.		Nick in hair (Cyl. 15 Dot, R. 16/5)	4·50	

No. U11 (1) in shades of washed out grey are colour changelings which we understand are caused by the concentrated solvents used in modern dry-cleaning methods.

No. U11 (1) is known pre-released on 25 May at Gravesend.

U12c, U13b, U14e
White patch over
eye and hair

U12d, U13c, U14f
Reported as
being later retouched

Cylinder Numbers (Blocks of Six)

Gum Arabic
Perforation Type F (L)*

Cyl. No.	No dot	Dot
(a) Shade (1) Deep sepia		
4 (Head A)	5·50	5·50
8 (Head A)	6·75	6·75
(b) Shade (2) Deep olive-brown		
4 (Head A)	12·00	12·00
8 (Head A)	12·00	12·00
Perforation Type A		
14 (Head B)	—	—

PVA Gum
Perforation Type F (L)*

Cyl. No.	No dot	Dot
(a) Shade (2) Deep olive-brown		
4 (Head A)	24·00	20·00
Perforation Type A		
4 (Head A)	12·00	12·00
10 (Head A)	4·00	4·00
12 (Head A)	12·00	12·00
13 (Head A)	20·00	20·00
14 (Head B)	3·00	3·00
15 (Head B)	70·00	70·00
(b) Shade (3) Deep olive-sepia		
Perforation Type A		
14 (Head B)	3·00	3·00
15 (Head B)	70·00	70·00

Stamps from cylinder 12 show traces of screening dots within the white area of the face value. Cylinder 15 has the number close to the stamp resulting in the dot often being removed by the perforations. The dot pane has a tiny dot on the horizontal rule below R. 20/1 whilst in the no dot pane the marginal rule below R. 20/1 is damaged and there is a line in the margin below R. 20/2.

Minor Constant Sheet Flaws

Cyl. 4.	1/1 Nick in neck (Th. F5)
	1/13 Nick in neck (Th. F5)
	2/9 Dark flaw in Queen's hair (Th. C4)
	20/8 Scar on Queen's forehead (Th. C2–3)
Cyl. 8	18/12 Diagonal line through back of Queen's hair (Th. C5)
Cyl. 8.	9/9 White spot in band of diadem (Th. B3–4)
	15/3 Diagonal coloured line on Queen's shoulder and dress (Th. F–G4)
	15/5 Prominent retouch on Queen's neck just below jawline (Th. E3–4)
Cyl. 10	18/12 As Cyl. 8
Cyl. 10.	3/4 Coloured flaw on Queen's shoulder (Th. F3)
	3/6 Two coloured flaws on Queen's shoulder (Th. F3)
	10/8 Pale patch in background to left of Queen's throat (Th. E2)
	11/7 Dark flaw at back of Queen's neck, just above necklace (Th. E4)
	12/5 Dark flaw on Queen's shoulder, just below necklace (Th. F3)
	15/3 As Cyl. 8
	15/5 As Cyl. 8
	19/2 Dark coloured vertical line in lower right-hand stamp margin (Th. G7)
Cyl. 12	18/12 As Cyl. 8.
Cyl. 12.	15/3 As Cyl. 8
	15/5 As Cyl. 8
Cyl. 13	9/12 Large area of retouching behind Queen's head (Th. C5–6 and D5–6)
	18/12 As Cyl. 8
Cyl. 13.	15/3 As Cyl. 8
	15/5 As Cyl. 8 but more prominent
Cyl. 14	6/11 Vertical white scratch on Queen's neck (Th. E–F4)
	18/7 White flaw at back of Queen's dress (Th. F5)

Coils

Printed in continuous reels from double pane cylinder P3 (vertical) or single pane P1 (sideways). Head A

Gum Arabic. Shade (2) Deep olive-brown

Code No.	Number in roll	Face value	
H	480	£8	Sideways delivery
A	960	£16	Vertical delivery

Sheet Markings

Guide holes:
Perf. Type A, in double "S O N" box opposite rows 14/15, at left (no dot) or right (dot). In addition a single "traffic light" type box appears above and below the eighth vertical row in the no dot pane only (latter only used in conjunction with perforation Type F (L)*).
Perf. Type F (L)*, boxed above and below the eighth vertical row in the no dot pane only. The usual "S O N" boxes opposite rows 14/15 remain.

Others: As given in General Notes

1968 (SEPTEMBER 16).   4d. CHANGE TO ONE 4 mm. CENTRE PHOSPHOR BAND. PVA GUM

				Mint	Used
U13 (=S.G.732)	4d.	(2)	Deep olive-brown (A) Head A	10	10
		(2)	Deep olive-brown (B) Head B	25	10
		(3)	Deep olive-sepia	25	10
	b.		White patch (Cyl. 13 No dot, R. 20/12)	5·00	
	c.		Nick in hair (Cyl. 15 Dot, R. 16/5)	4·50	

For illustrations of Nos. U13b/c see Nos. U12c/d.

No. U13 also occurs with the phosphor omitted but since a single stamp would be indistinguishable from No. U12b it is only listed when in a complete *se-tenant* booklet pane (see No. UB3a).

Cylinder Numbers (Blocks of Six)

Perforation Type A

(a) Shade (2) Deep olive-brown			(b) Shade (3) Deep olive-sepia		
Cyl. No.	No dot	Dot	Cyl. No.	No dot	Dot
4 (Head A)	2·50	2·50	14 (Head B)	3·00	3·00
12 (Head A)	2·50	2·50	15 (Head B)	3·00	3·00
13 (Head A)	70·00	70·00			
14 (Head B)	3·00	3·00			
15 (Head B)	3·00	3·00			

The notes, concerning cylinders 12 and 15, under No. U12 also apply here.

Minor Constant Sheet Flaws

Cyl. 4.	1/1 Nick in neck (Th. F5)
	1/13 Nick in neck (Th. F5)
	2/9 Coloured flaw in Queen's hair (Th. C4)
	19/1 Flaw on lower rim of Queen's diadem shows as "missing pearls" (Th. C5)
	20/8 Scar on Queen's forehead (Th. C2–3)
Cyl. 12	18/12 Diagonal line through back of Queen's hair (Th. C5)
Cyl. 12.	15/3 Diagonal coloured line on Queen's shoulder and dress (Th. F–G4)
	15/5 Prominent retouch on Queen's neck just below jawline (Th. E3–4)
Cyl. 13	9/12 Large area of retouching behind Queen's head (Th. C5–6 and D5–6)
	18/12 As Cyl. 12
Cyl. 13.	15/3 As Cyl. 12
	15/5 As Cyl. 12, but more prominent
Cyl. 15.	5/12 Two small white dots on Queen's shoulder (Th. F–G4). Later retouched
	17/12 White scratch in background above value, extending to Queen's shoulder. Later retouched but flaw still shows on Queen's shoulder

Coils

Printed in continuous reels from double pane cylinder P3 (vertical) or single pane P5 (sideways). Head A

Code No.	Number in roll	Face value	
H	480	£8	Sideways delivery
A	960	£16	Vertical delivery

Sheet Markings

Guide holes: As for perf. Type A under Nos. U11/12

Others: As given in General Notes

4d. Bright Vermilion, Type U1 (1969)

1969 (JANUARY 6). 4d. COLOUR CHANGED. ONE 4 mm. CENTRE PHOSPHOR BAND
A. PVA Gum

			Mint	Used
U14 (=S.G.733)	4d.	Bright vermilion (A) Head A	25	25
		(B) Head B	10	10
	a.	Tête-bêche (horiz. pair)	£3500	
	b.	Uncoated paper ('70)**	6·00	
	c.	Phosphor omitted	1·25	
	d.	Red nick in D (Cyl. 4 Dot, R. 1/4)	4·50	
	e.	White patch (Cyl. 13 Dot, R. 20/12)	5·50	
	f.	Nick in hair (Cyl. 15 Dot, R. 16/5)	4·50	
	g.	Imperf. between stamp and top margin	£125	
	h.	Error. Two bands*	60·00	
	s.	Opt. "Specimen" (14 mm.)	40·00	

B. Gum Arabic. (20 February 1969)

U15 (=S.G.733Eg)	4d.	Bright vermilion (A) Head A (booklets)	27·00	
		(B) Head B (multi-value coil)	10	
	a.	Phosphor omitted	£1500	
	b.	Diagonal scratch in background (Multi-value coil) . .	7·50	

**Uncoated paper. No. U14b comes from the £1 "Stamps for Cooks" Booklet (see Nos. UB16ab and UB17ab); see also General Notes.

Nos. U14 and U16/A from the £1 "Stamps for Cooks" Booklet (ZP1) show slight differences compared with stamps from normal sheets and all other booklets. The main stem of the "4" is thicker and it is only 0·6 mm. from its foot to the base of the design compared with 0·9 mm. on stamps from sheets and all other booklets. Also, the cross-bar of the "4", normally opposite the point of the Queen's gown, is lower on the £1 booklet stamps. See under "Machin Heads" in General Notes.

Misplaced Phosphor Bands. *No. U14h comes from "Method" pane UB17af which has the central phosphor bands printed over the vertical perforations at each side.

No. U15B comes from the multi-value coil strip, issued 27 August 1969, which is listed as No. U32 and U15A from the February and part of March 1969 6s. Barn Owl and Jay Booklets (QP46/7) and also part of May 1969 10s. Mary Kingsley Booklets (XP8).

For illustrations of Nos. U14e/f, see Nos. U12c/d.

U14d
Believed later retouched

U15b

Cylinder Numbers (Blocks of Six)

PVA Gum. Perforation Type A

Cyl. No.	No dot	Dot	Cyl. No.	No dot	Dot
4 (Head A)	2·00	2·00	15 (Head B)	2·50	2·50
10 (Head A)	2·00	2·00	16 (Head B)	5·50	5·50
13 (Head A)	2·00	2·00	17 (Head B)	2·50	2·50

The note about the cylinder number being close to the stamp on Cylinder 15 mentioned under No. U12 also applies here.

169

Minor Constant Sheet Flaws

Cyl. 4.   1/1 Nick in neck (Th. F5)
             1/13 Nick in neck (Th. F5)
             19/1 Flaw on lower rim of Queen's diadem shows as "missing pearls" (Th. C5)
             20/8 Scar on Queen's forehead (Th. C2–3)
Cyl. 10   18/12 Diagonal line through back of Queen's hair (Th. C5).
Cyl. 10.   15/3 Diagonal coloured line on Queen's shoulder and dress (Th. F–G4)
             15/5 Prominent retouch on Queen's neck just below jawline (Th. E3–4)
Cyl. 13   9/12 Large area of retouching behind Queen's head (Th. C5–6 and D5–6)
             18/12 As Cyl. 10
Cyl. 13.   15/3 As Cyl. 10
             15/5 As Cyl. 10, but more prominent
Cyl. 15.   17/12 Scratch on Queen's shoulder at left (Th. F3)
Cyl. 17   4/7 Small coloured spot in band of diadem (Th. B4)
             7/3 Small retouch on Queen's shoulder (Th. F3)
             18/4 Small flaw in band of diadem (Th. B4)
Cyl. 17.   19/10 White scratch at back of Queen's shoulder (Th. F5)

Coils

PVA Gum. Printed in continuous reels from double pane cylinder P3 (vertical) or single pane P5 (Head A) and P7 (Head B) (sideways)

Code No.	Number in roll	Face value	
H	480	£8	Sideways delivery Head A or Head B
A	960	£16	Vertical delivery Head A

One centre band, gum arabic. Multi-value coil, see No. U32

Sheet Markings

Guide holes: As for perf. Type A under Nos. U11/12

Others: As given in General Notes

1969 (JANUARY 6)   4d. BRIGHT VERMILION
A. One Side Phosphor Band at Left*. PVA Gum. Head B
From 10s. Booklets XP7/12 and £1 Booklet ZP1

			Mint	Used
U16 (=S.G.734)	4d.	Bright vermilion	1·50	1·90
	b.	Uncoated paper ('70)**	£250	
	c.	Error. One 9·5 mm. phosphor band	£200	
	d.	Phosphor omitted on front but printed at left on the gummed side	£300	
	s.	Optd. "Specimen" (14 mm.)	£250	

B. One Side Phosphor Band at Right*. PVA Gum. Head B
From £1 Booklet ZP1 only (1 December 1969)

U16A (=S.G.734Eb)	4d.	Bright vermilion	1·75	2·50
	b.	Uncoated paper ('70)**	£250	
	c.	Phosphor omitted on front but printed at right on the gummed side	£300	
	s.	Optd. "Specimen" (14 mm.)	£250	

*The one side band stamps were produced by applying a 9·5 mm. band over the vertical perforations between the 4d. and its adjoining stamp in the booklet panes. In theory the width of the band on a single stamp should be 4¾ mm. but this will vary if the band has not been perfectly positioned.

**Uncoated paper. Nos. U16b and U16Ab came from the *se-tenant* pane of 15 in the £1 "Stamps for Cooks" Booklet (see No. UB2ab.); see also General Notes.

No. U16 also occurs with the phosphor omitted but since a single stamp would be indistinguishable from No. U14c it is only listed when in a complete *se-tenant* booklet (see No. UB4a).

No. U16Ac came from the *se-tenant* pane No. UB2ad of which three examples are believed to exist.

See note after No. U15 describing the differences between 4d. stamps in the £1 Booklet (ZP1) and those in sheets and all other booklets.

5d., Type U1 (1968–70)

1968 (JULY 1). 5d. TWO 9·5 mm. PHOSPHOR BANDS. PVA GUM.

				Mint	Used
U17 (=S.G.735)	5d.	(1)	Royal blue (A) Head A	10	10
		(2)	Deep blue (B) Head B	10	15
	a.		Imperforate (pair)†	£250	
	ab.		Imperf. between stamp and top margin		
	b.		Uncoated paper ('70)**	20·00	
	c.		Two bands and phosphor coating (Cyl. 15)	£300	
	d.		Phosphor omitted. Shade (1)	2·00	
	da.		Phosphor omitted. Shade (2)	3·00	
	db.		Right-hand band omitted		
	e.		Phosphor omitted on front but printed on the gummed side	£300	
	f.		Error. One 9.5 mm. phosphor band	55·00	
	g.		Neck retouch (Cyls. 7, 10, 11, 13 No dot, R. 18/1 and Cyl. 15 R. 19/1)	3·75	
	h.		Scratch severing neck (Cyl. 13 No dot, R. 19/4) .	20·00	
	s.		Optd. "Specimen" (14 mm.)	50·00	

†No. U17*a* comes from the original state of cylinder 15 which is identifiable by the screening dots in the gutters (see note after cylinder number list). This must not be confused with imperforate stamps from cylinder 10, a large quantity of which was stolen from the printers early in 1970.

**Uncoated paper. No. U17*b* comes from the £1 "Stamps for Cooks" Booklet (see Nos. UB2*ab* and UB20*ab* and *b*); see also General Notes.

No. U17*c* is thought to result from the issue, in error, of stamps on phosphor-coated paper, intended for experiments only. Examples were purchased from various sources in 1972.

No. U17 from the £1 "Stamps for Cooks" Booklet (ZP1) and cylinders 7, 10 and 11 (no dot and dot panes) show slight differences compared with stamps from cylinder 1 (no dot and dot) and all other booklet panes. The "5D" is slightly thicker and is positioned fractionally lower than on stamps from cylinder 1 and all other booklet panes. See under "Machin Heads" in the General Notes.

No. U17 is known postmarked at Trafalgar Square (London) on 29 June and at Dorking and Guildford on 30 June 1968.

Tête-Bêche Pairs. Examples of No. U17 in *tête-bêche* pairs were not issued.

U17*g*

This variety is due to damage on the multipositive. Cyl. 1 is normal and the most marked retouch is on cyl. 11. Cyl. 15 was formed by moving up one row of the multipositive (which is 28 rows by 31 columns) and the variety occurs on R. 19/1. All on no dot panes.

U17*h*

Cylinder Numbers (Blocks of Six)

Perforation Type A

Cyl. No.	No dot	Dot	Cyl. No.	No dot	Dot
1 (Shade 1) (Head A)	2·50	2·50	11 (Shade 2) (Head B)	10·00*	8·50
7 (Shade 2) (Head B)	4·75*	2·00	13 (Shade 2) (Head B)	£800*	£450
10 (Shade 2) (Head B)	4·75*	2·00	15 (Shade 2) (Head B)	6·00*	3·50

Cyl. 15 dot has a smudge so that it looks like "151".

Original printings of cylinder 15 (no dot and dot) had screening dots extending through the gutters of the stamps and into the margins of the sheet. Later the cylinder was cleaned and re-chromed.

Minor Constant Sheet Flaws

Cyl. 1	7/1 Coloured spot in band of diadem (Th. C5)
	7/5 Short white flaw in Queen's hair (Th. C4)
	12/2 White flaw in band of diadem (Th. B4)
Cyl. 1.	1/11 Pale patch in background below top bar of 5 (Th. G1)
	20/4 White spot in band of diadem (Th. C5)
Cyl. 7	18/2 Scratch on Queen's shoulder (Th. F4)
Cyl. 7.	1/10 White flaw on Queen's forehead (Th. C3)
	14/12 Small retouch on Queen's shoulder (Th. G4)
Cyl. 10	15/8 Coloured flaw below Queen's earring (Th. D4)
	18/2 Scratch on Queen's shoulder (Th. F4)
	20/5 Two diagonal scratches on Queen's neck (Th. E3–4, F4 and G4)
	20/6 Retouch on Queen's neck (Th. E4)
Cyl. 13	5/6 White flaw in Queen's hair (Th. C3)
	12/4 White ring flaw on Queen's forehead (Th. C2)
	13/3 Flaw on Queen's shoulder (Th. G3)
	14/5 Necklace flaw (Th. E4)
	18/2 Coloured flaw on Queen's neck (Th. F5)
Cyl. 15	16/8 Coloured flaw below Queen's earring (Th. D4)
	19/2 Scratch on Queen's shoulder (Th. F4)
Cyl. 15.	1/10 Scratch on Queen's nose (Th. C2)

Coils

Printed in continuous reels from double pane cylinder S1 (vertical) or single pane S2 (sideways). Head B

Code No.	Number in roll	Face value	
AF	480	£10	Sideways delivery
AE	960	£20	Vertical delivery

Sheet Markings

Phosphor cylinder number "Ph 1" found on the later printings of cyl. 15 dot, right margin (*price* £30 *block of 6*).

Guide holes: In double "S O N" box (or "S O" box cyl. 10) opposite rows 14/15, at left (no dot) or right (dot). In addition a single "traffic light" type box appears above and below the eighth vertical row in the no dot pane only. (These would only be used in conjunction with perforation Type F (L)*.)

Others: As given in General Notes.

6d., Type U1 (1968)

1968 (FEBRUARY 5). 6d. TWO 9·5 mm. PHOSPHOR BANDS. PVA GUM

				Mint	Used
U18 (=S.G.736)	6d.	(1)	Bright reddish purple (*shades*) (A) Head A	20	25
		(2)	Bright magenta	8·00	6·00
		(3)	Claret	50	45
		(1)	Bright reddish purple (B) Head B (coils)	15·00	6·00
		(3)	Claret	80·00	35·00
	a.		Phosphor omitted. Shade (1)	6·50	
	ab.		Phosphor omitted. Shade (3)	15·00	
	b.		Hair flaws (Cyl. 2 No dot, R. 18/1)	6·00	
	c.		Background retouch (Cyl. 2 Dot, R. 11/1)	5·50	
	d.		Diadem flaw (Cyl. 3 No dot, R. 2/3)	5·00	
	e.		Two spots in front of neck (Vert. coil, Roll 12) ((1) Head B)	15·00	
	f.		Retouch above "6 D" (Vert. coil) ((1) Head B) . .	16·00	

U18*b*
Two coloured lines
crossing base of
diadem, one extending
in curves through
the hair

U18*c*
Large circular
retouch above
value

U18*d*
Coloured flaw
in band of
diadem

U18*e*
Two spots in front of neck

U18*f*

Cylinder Numbers (Blocks of Six)

Perforation Type A

(a) Shade (1) Bright reddish purple

Cyl. No.	No dot	Dot
2	7·00	5·50
3	3·50	3·50
4	45·00	45·00
5	4·00	4·00

(b) Shade (2) Bright magenta

Cyl. No.	No dot	Dot
3	55·00	55·00

(c) Shade (3) Claret

	No dot	Dot
5	8·50	8·50

Minor Constant Sheet Flaws

Cyl. 2.   2/4   White flaw in band of diadem (Th. B4)
          4/4   Coloured line in band of diadem (Th. B3–4)
          4/11 Small retouch on Queen's collar (Th. G4)
          10/11 Vertical flaws in Queen's hair and in band of diadem (Th. B–C4)

Cyl. 3   13/5 Two small white flaws on Queen's neck above necklace (Th. F3)
          19/9 Small coloured dot in band of diadem (Th. B3)
Cyl. 3.   5/3 Line of white dashes on Queen's collar (Th. G3–4)
          11/5 Small retouch on Queen's collar (Th. G4)
Cyl. 4   11/10 Small background retouch left of Queen's forehead (Th. B2)
Cyl. 5   18/1 White tail below "D"

Coil

Vertical delivery printed in continuous reels from cylinder Q2. Head B

Code No.	Number in roll	Face value
J	480	£12

Sheet Markings

Phosphor cylinder number: "Ph 1" found on a later printing from cyl. 5 dot, right margin (*price* £140, *block of 6*).

Guide holes: In double "S O N" box opposite rows 14/15, at left (no dot) or right (dot). In addition a single "traffic light" type box appears above and below the eighth vertical row in the no dot pane only (These would only be used in conjunction with perforation Types F (L)*.)

Others: As given in General Notes

7d., Type U2 (1968)

1968 (JULY 1).   7d. TWO 9.5 mm. PHOSPHOR BANDS. PVA GUM. HEAD B

			Mint	Used
U19 (=S.G.737)	7d.	Bright emerald	40	35
	a.	Phosphor omitted . . . . 85·00		

No. U19 is known postmarked at Dorking and at Guildford on 30 June 1968.

Cylinder Numbers (Blocks of Six)

Perforation Type A

Cyl. No.		No dot	Dot
3	. . . .	4·50	4·50
4	. . . .	15·00	12·00

Minor Constant Sheet Flaws

Cyl. 3   8/6 Flaw in background by Queen's collar (Th. F5)
         12/6 Dark flaw on jewel in band of diadem (Th. C5)

Sheet Markings

Phosphor cylinder number: "Ph 1" found on all sheets from cyl. 4 dot, right margin (*Price* £55, *block of 6*)

Guide holes: in single hand engraved box opposite rows 14/15, at left (no dot) or right (dot)

Marginal arrows: "W" shaped, hand engraved at top, bottom and sides on cyl. 3, photo-etched on cyl. 4

Others: As given in General Notes

8d. Bright Vermilion, Type U2 (1968)

1968 (JULY 1). 8d. TWO 9·5 mm. PHOSPHOR BANDS. PVA GUM. HEAD A

			Mint	Used
U20 (=S.G.738)	8d.	Bright vermilion	20	45
	a.	Phosphor omitted	£400	

No. U20 is known postmarked at Dorking and at Guildford on 30 June 1968.

Cylinder Numbers (Blocks of Six)

Perforation Type A

Cyl. No.	No dot	Dot
2	2·50	2·50

Sheet Markings

Guide holes: In double "S O N" box opposite rows 14/15, at left (no dot) or right (dot). In addition a single "traffic light" type box appears above and below the eighth vertical row in the no dot pane only. (These would only be used in conjunction with perforation Type F (L)*.)

Other: As given in General Notes

8d. Light Turquoise-blue, Type U2 (1969)

1969 (JANUARY 6). 8d. COLOUR CHANGED. TWO 9·5 mm. PHOSPHOR BANDS. PVA GUM. HEAD B

			Mint	Used
U21 (=S.G.739)	8d.	Light turquoise-blue	50	60
	a.	Phosphor omitted	60·00	
	b.	Left band omitted		
	c.	Missing pearls (Cyl. 3 No dot, R. 19/2)	5·50	

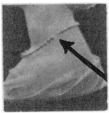

U21c

Cylinder Numbers (Blocks of Six)

Perforation Type A

Cyl. No.	No dot	Dot
3	10·00*	7·00

Minor Constant Sheet Flaw

Cyl. 3. 19/2 White flaw by Queen's mouth (Th. D2)

Sheet Markings

Guide holes: In single "S N" box opposite rows 14/15, at left (no dot) or right (dot). In addition a single "traffic light" type box appears above and below the eighth vertical row in the no dot pane only. (These would only be used in conjunction with perforation Type F (L)*.)

Others: As given in General Notes.

9d., Type U2 (1967–68)

1967 (AUGUST 8).   9d. TWO 9·5 mm. PHOSPHOR BANDS. HEAD A
A. Gum Arabic

			Mint	Used
U22 (=S.G.740)	9d.	Myrtle-green	40	25
	a.	Phosphor omitted	35·00	
	b.	Dots below necklace (Cyl. 2 Dot, R. 9/6)	5·00	

B. PVA Gum (29 November 1968)

U23 (=S.G.740Ev)	9d.	Myrtle-green	50	
	a.	Phosphor omitted	65·00	

No. U22 is known pre-released on 7 August at Bournemouth and Torquay.

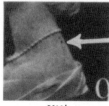

U22*b*

Cylinder Numbers (Blocks of Six)

	Gum Arabic				PVA Gum		
	Perforation Type F (L)*				Perforation Type A		
Cyl. No.		No dot	Dot	Cyl. No.		No dot	Dot
2	. . . .	6·00	6·00	2		5·50	5·50
	Perforation Type A						
2	. . . .	35·00	30·00				

Cylinder 2 has the number close to the stamp resulting in the dot often being removed by the perforations. The no dot cylinder can be distinguished by a horizontal line below R. 20/2, although this may be trimmed off if the margin is narrow.

Minor Constant Sheet Flaws

Cyl. 2   2/7 Coloured line in gutter above stamp (Th. above A4–6)
3/12 Retouch on Queen's shoulder (Th. F4)
6/2 Pale area on Queen's shoulder (Th. F4). Retouched on PVA
6/7 Dark patches on Queen's neck (Th. E–F3). Less noticeable on PVA
7/3 Dark spot over D of value (Th. F6)
Cyl. 2.   6/10 Coloured line across Queen's shoulder and dress (Th. F–G4)
8/11 Retouch on Queen's forehead (Th. B–C2)
10/4 Coloured spot at rear of diadem (Th. C5)
14/8 Two white flaws on Queen's neck by hair (Th. D–E4). Retouched on PVA
14/11 Retouch on Queen's neck by necklace (Th. E4)
15/11 Retouch on Queen's dress at front (Th. G3)
19/10 Retouch on Queen's shoulder (Th. F4)

Sheet Markings

Phosphor cylinder number: "Ph 1" found on a later printing from cyl. 2 dot, right margin (*Price* £850 *block of* 6)

Guide holes:

Perforation Type A, in double "S O N" box opposite rows 14/15, at left (no dot) or right (dot). In addition a single "traffic light" type box appears above and below the eighth vertical row in the no dot pane only (latter only used in conjunction with perforation Type F (L)*).

Perforation Type F (L)*, boxed above and below the eighth vertical row in the no dot pane only. The usual "S O N" boxes opposite rows 14/15 remain.

Others: As given in General Notes

10d., Type U1 (1968)

1968 (JULY 1).   10d. TWO 9·5 mm. PHOSPHOR BANDS. PVA GUM. HEAD C

			Mint	Used
U24 (=S.G.741)	10d.	Drab	50	50
	a.	Uncoated paper ('69)*	25·00	
	b.	Phosphor omitted	50·00	
	c.	Neck flaw (Cyl 1, R. 2/12)	4·50	

*Uncoated paper—see General Notes.

No. U24 is known postmarked at Dorking and at Guildford on 30 June 1968.

Flaw comprises dark spots surrounded by white "halo" caused by lack of screening dots

U24c

Cylinder Number (Block of Six)

Single pane cylinder

Perforation Type F (L)

Cyl. No.	No dot
1	6·00

Minor Constant Sheet Flaw

Cyl. 1   20/5 Coloured flaw in Queen's hair (Th. B3)

Sheet Markings

Guide holes: Through marginal arrow above vertical rows 6/7 and below vertical row 10

Others: As given in General Notes

1s., Type U1 (1967–68)

1967 (JUNE 5). 1s. TWO 9·5 mm. PHOSPHOR BANDS. HEAD C
A. Gum Arabic

				Mint	Used
U25 (=S.G.742/E*a*)	1s.	(1)	Light bluish violet	45	25
		(2)	Pale bluish violet	2·25	50
	a.		Phosphor omitted	75·00	
	b.		Background retouches (Cyl. 3 No dot, R. 20/5) .	5·50	

B. PVA Gum (26 April 1968)

U26 (=S.G.742Ea*v*)	1s.	Pale bluish violet	45
	a.	Phosphor omitted	3·50

No. U25(1) is known pre-released on 25 May at Gravesend.

Retouching extends from behind the Queen's neck to the base of the design where it is most noticeable. There are also minor retouches on the Queen's shoulder and on her dress

U25*b*

Cylinder Numbers (Blocks of Six)

Gum Arabic

Double pane cylinder

Perforation Type F (L)*
Shade (1) Light bluish violet

Cyl. No.	No dot	Dot
3	5·50	5·50

Single pane cylinder

Perforation Type F (L)
Shade (2) Pale bluish violet

Cyl. No.	No dot
11	11·00

PVA Gum
Single pane cylinder

Perforation Type F (L)

Cyl. No.	No dot
11	5·50

Minor Constant Sheet Flaws

Cyl. 3   1/10 Retouch in background above diadem (Th. A5)
2/2 Light diagonal line extending from lowest point of Queen's hair to bottom right-hand corner (E5 through to G6)
2/3 White spot in background left of Queen's shoulder (Th. G2)
9/12 White spot in background to right of Queen's necklace (Th. E5)
11/11 Coloured spot in band of diadem (Th. B4)
17/2 As 11/11 but Th. B3
18/12 Coloured spot in hyphen of value
19/10 Coloured scratch through Queen's neck and background below portrait
20/4 Horizontal scratch through Queen's neck and into background at right

Cyl. 3.   1/8 White spot in background at top of stamp (Th. A4)
7/8 Coloured flaw in Queen's hair to right of earring (Th. D4)
8/4 Coloured flaw in Queen's hair (Th. B3)
9/7 Retouch to background to right of Queen's ear (Th. D5)
19/8 Coloured spot in background above diadem emblems (Th. B5)

Cyl. 11   7/8 Coloured spot by band of diadem, also small spot in background at rear of diadem (Th. B4 and C5)
7/9 Diagonal coloured line in background behind Queen's neck (Th. F5)
15/4 Disturbed area in background at rear of diadem (Th. C–D5)

Cyl. 11 continued

    16/9 Diagonal coloured scratches extending the depth of the stamp behind the Queen's portrait

    18/7 Diagonal coloured scratch about 10 mm. long at left of Queen's portrait

    19/2 White flaw in Queen's hair to right of ear (Th. D4)

Sheet Markings

Guide holes:

Perforation Type F (L)*, boxed above and below the eighth vertical row in the no dot pane only. In addition double "S O N" box appears opposite rows 14/15, at left (no dot) or right (dot). (These would only be used in conjunction with perforation Type A.)

Perforation Type F (L), through marginal arrow above vertical rows 6/7 and below vertical row 10

Others: As given in General Notes

1s.6d., Type U1 (1967–69)

1967 (AUGUST 8).   1s.6d. TWO 9·5 mm. PHOSPHOR BANDS. HEAD A

A. Gum Arabic

				Mint	Used
U27 (=S.G.743)	1s.6d.	(1)	Greenish blue and deep blue	50	50
		(2)	Prussian blue and indigo (phosphor omitted) .	11·00	
	a.		Greenish blue omitted	80·00	
	b.		Phosphor omitted. Shade (1)	6·00	
	c.		Retouch on dress (Cyl. 2A, R. 7/12)	7·00	
	d.		Neck retouch (Cyl. 2A, R. 19/4)	6·50	
	e.		Neck retouch (Cyl. 2A, R. 20/3)	6·50	

B. PVA Gum (28 August 1968)

U28 (=S.G.743Ev)	1s.6d.	(1)	Greenish blue and deep blue	75	
		(2)	Prussian blue and indigo	2·25	1·50
	a.		Greenish blue omitted	£125	
	b.		Imperf. top margin. Shade (2)	80·00	
	c.		Phosphor omitted. Shade (1)	14·00	
	d.		Error. One 9·5 mm. phosphor band	20·00	
	e.		Greenish blue omitted and one 9·5 mm.		
			phosphor band	£150	

No. U27 is known pre-released on 7 August at Bournemouth and Torquay.

U27c

U27d

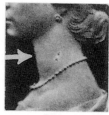
U27e

Cylinder Numbers (Blocks of Four)

Single pane cylinders.
Perforation Type A

Cyl. Nos.	No dot
Gum Arabic	
2A (deep blue)—2B (greenish blue)	7·50
3A (deep blue)—2B (greenish blue)	15·00
5A (indigo)—2B (Prussian blue) (phosphor omitted)	£170
PVA Gum	
3A (deep blue)—2B (greenish blue)	7·50
3A (indigo)—1B (Prussian blue)	20·00
5A (indigo)—2B (Prussian blue)	18·00

Minor Constant Sheet Flaws

Cyls. 2A–2B   3/12 Coloured spot in band of diadem (Th. B4)
                7/8 Coloured spots on Queen's collar (Th. G3)
                14/1 Coloured spot on Queen's shoulder (Th. F4–5)
                17/3 Coloured spot on Queen's temple (Th. C3)
                18/4 Coloured spot on Queen's shoulder (Th. F5)
                20/2 Pale patch on Queen's neck (Th. E3–4)
                20/7 Retouch on Queen's neck (Th. E4)
Cyls. 3A–2B   3/12 As for cyls. 2A–2B
Cyls. 5A–2B   19/1 Retouch on Queen's shoulder (Th. F5)

Sheet Markings

Cylinder numbers: Boxed, opposite R. 19/1

Guide holes: In single "traffic light" type box opposite rows 14/15, at both sides

Colour register marks: Opposite rows 3/4 and 17/18, at both sides

Autotron marks (solid): Deep blue and greenish blue opposite rows 7/8, left margin

Colour designations: "G1" (greenish blue) opposite rows 7/8 and "G2" (deep blue) opposite rows 5/6 both reading up in right margin

Traffic lights (boxed): Deep blue and greenish blue opposite row 19, right margin

Others: As given in General Notes

1969 (DECEMBER 10).   1s.6d. CHANGE TO PHOSPHORISED PAPER. PVA GUM. HEAD A

			Mint	Used
U29 (=S.G.743c)	1s.6d.	Prussian blue and indigo	80	80
	a.	Prussian blue omitted	£400	

No. U29 was an experimental issue and the small printing represented approximately three months normal issue. After the supply was exhausted No. U28 again became the normal issue.

Cylinder Numbers (Block of Four)

Single pane cylinders.

Cyl. Nos. (No dot)	Perf. Type A
5A (indigo)—2B (Prussian blue)	12·00

Minor Constant Sheet Flaws

Cyls. 5A–2B   12/5 Two white spots on Queen's dress (Th. G3)
19/1 Retouch on Queen's shoulder (Th. F5)

Sheet Markings

All the same as for Nos. U27/8

1s.9d., Type U1 (1967–70)

1967 (JUNE 5).   1s.9d. TWO 9·5 mm. PHOSPHOR BANDS. HEAD A
A. Gum Arabic

				Mint	Used
U30 (=S.G.744)	1s.9d.	(1)	Dull orange and black	50	45
		(2)	Bright orange and black	1·75	70
	a.		Phosphor omitted	50·00	

B. PVA Gum (16 November 1970)

U31 (=S.G.744Ev)	1s.9d.	Bright orange and black	75

No. U30 is known pre-released on 25 May at Gravesend.
The bright orange shade occurs on whiter paper and may be due to this.

Cylinder Numbers (Blocks of Four)

Single pane cylinders

Cyl. Nos. (No dot)	Perforation Type A	
	Gum Arabic	PVA Gum
1A (black)—1B (dull orange)	14·00	†
1A (black)—1B (bright orange)	20·00	20·00

Minor Constant Sheet Flaws

Cyls. 1A–1B   4/6 White spot in Queen's ear (Th. D4)
5/7 Coloured spots on Queen's upper lip (Th. D2)
5/10 White patch in Queen's hair (Th. B4)
8/1 Coloured flaw on Queen's neck (Th. E4)
13/1 Retouch on Queen's shoulder (Th. F3–4)
20/1 Pale patch in Queen's hair (Th. C4)

Sheet Markings

Cylinder numbers: Boxed, opposite R. 19/1

Guide holes: In single "traffic light" type box opposite rows 14/15, at both sides

Colour register marks: Opposite rows 3/4 and 17/18, at both sides

Autotron marks (solid): Black and orange opposite rows 7/8, left margin

Colour designations: "G1" (orange) opposite rows 7/8 and "G2" (black) opposite rows 5/6 both reading up in right margin

Traffic lights (boxed): Black and orange opposite row 19, right margin

Others: As given in General Notes

Multi-value Coil Strip (1969)

1969 (AUGUST 27). STRIP OF FIVE (2d. + 2d. + 3d. + 1d. + 4d. SE-TENANT) EACH WITH ONE 4 mm. CENTRE PHOSPHOR BAND. GUM ARABIC. HEAD B

	Mint	Used
U32 (=S.G.725m) (Strip of 5) 1d. Light olive (No. U4), 2d. lake-brown (No. U7 × 2), 3d. violet (No. U8) and 4d. bright vermilion (No. U15)	1·25	

No. U32 was issued in strips from stamp vending machines taking a shilling or a five pence piece. Complete coils only were available from the Philatelic Bureau in Edinburgh.

For listed varieties, see Nos. U4*a*, U8*d* and U15*b*.

A new type of perforation was adopted for these coils. The paper was drawn, gum upwards, over a cylinder containing short points pushing up pimples from the undersurface which were then shaved off.

It is understood that gum arabic was used for these coils, as also for the next decimal multi-value coil, because it is more brittle than PVA and facilitates the clean removal of the perforations.

Coils

Sideways delivery printed in continuous reels from cylinders B5–D3–M3–P6

Code No.	Number in roll	Face value
GS	1500 (300 strips)	£15
GL	3000 (600 strips)	£30

Presentation Pack

UPP1 (issued 5 March 1969) Fourteen values	7·00	
a. With German text	90·00	

The issued Pack contained one each of the low value definitive stamps (½d. to 1s.9d.). The 4d. and 8d. were in the changed colours (Nos. U14 and U21 respectively).

UPP1 also exists with a Japanese insert card.

First Day Covers

On official covers prepared and issued by the Post Office and stamps franked with circular "FIRST DAY OF ISSUE" postmarks.

UFC1 (5.6.67)	4d., 1s, 1s. 9d.	3·00
UFC2 (8.8.67)	3d., 9d., 1s. 6d.	3·00
UFC3 (5.2.68)	½d., 1d., 2d., 6d.	3·00
UFC4 (1.7.68)	5d., 7d., 8d., 10d.	3·00
UFC5 (1.12.69)	"Stamps for Cooks" pane stamps, four covers	20·00*

There was no F.D.C. service for the 4d. red and 8d. turquoise-blue values.

*The price is for covers with complete panes with recipe attached. The Milk Marketing Board issued a special handstamp cancellation reading "Visit the Stamps for Cooks Exhibition, Milk Marketing Board, Thames Ditton, Surrey".

183

SECTION UB
Machin £.s.d. Issues
1967–70. Booklet Panes in Photogravure

General Notes

INTRODUCTION. All panes were printed in photogravure by Harrison & Sons. See the detailed notes under Section U for information on printing, paper and gum. Reference to the note, "Booklet Cylinder Flaws", at the beginning of Section SB describes the panes which were printed from 21-row cylinders. These panes are found with varieties and the cylinder number in either the top or bottom row of the pane. In this Section the panes of six of the 1d., 3d., 4d. (both colours) and 5d. were printed from 21-row cylinders.

BOOKLET ERRORS. Those listed as "Part perf. pane" have one row of three stamps imperforate on three sides.

Booklet Cylinder Number

BOOKLET CYLINDER NUMBERS. These are listed for the panes of six only and the other panes had cylinder numbers engraved so that they did not occur in the finished booklet. The cylinders employed are recorded for reference. The cylinder numbers being hand-engraved varied as to their position in relation to the stamp so that some were invariably trimmed. A pane which shows a complete cylinder number placed away from the stamp will only exist with badly trimmed perforations on the opposite side.

BOOKLET CYLINDER FLAWS. Cylinder flaws on booklet stamps are listed under the panes in which they occur as in Section SB. The flaws are priced in panes since this is the preferred method of collecting wherever possible. In consequence when checking varieties on single stamps it will be necessary to look at the lists of the sheet and coil stamps as well as the booklet panes.

When quoting the position on booklet panes no attention is paid to the labels. Therefore a flaw on the first stamp in the pane No. UB13 (4d. (2) and pair of labels) will be described as being on "R. 1/1". Since this Catalogue is primarily concerned with stamps we do not list flaws which sometimes occur in the wording of the labels from booklet panes.

BOOKLET PANE PRICES. The prices quoted are for panes in mint condition, good perforations all round and complete with binding margin. Prices for complete booklets in Appendix HA are for booklets with average perforations.

CHECKLIST OF MACHIN £.s.d. BOOKLET PANES

UB No.	Face Value	Phos. Bands	Gum	Head	Size of Pane	Further description	Page
1	1d.	2	PVA	B	6	Yellowish olive	186
2	6 × 1d. 3 × 4d. 3 × 4d. 3 × 5d.	2 1L 1R 2	PVA	B	15	"Baked Stuffed Haddock" recipe	186
3	4 × 1d. 2 × 4d.	1C 1C	PVA	B	6	4d. in sepia	188
4	4 × 1d. 2 × 4d.	2 1L	PVA	B	6	4d. in bright vermilion	188
5	2 × 1d. 2 × 3d.	2 2	PVA	B	4	1d. at left	189
5a	2 × 1d. 2 × 3d.	2 2	PVA	B	4	1d. at right	189
6	3d.	1C	PVA	B	6	Violet	189
7	4d.	2	GA	A	6	Deep sepia	189
8	4d.	2	GA	A	6	Deep olive-brown	190
9	4d.	2	PVA	A	6	Deep olive-brown	190
10	4d.	2	PVA	B	4	Deep olive-brown	190
11	4d.	1C	PVA	A	6	Deep olive-brown	191
12	4d.	1C	PVA	B	4	Deep olive-sepia	191
13	4d.	1C	PVA	B	4	Deep olive-sepia, including 2 labels	192
14 (A)	4d.	1C	PVA	A	6	Bright vermilion	192
14 (B)	4d.	1C	PVA	B	6	Bright vermilion	192
14 (b)	4d.	1C	GA	A	6	Bright vermilion	192
15	4d.	1C	PVA	B	4	Bright vermilion	192
16	4d.	1C	PVA	B	15	"Stuffed Cucumber" and "Method" recipe .	193
17	4d.	1C	PVA	B	15	"Method" for Braised Shoulder of Lamb recipe	194
18	4d.	1C	PVA	B	4	Bright vermilion, including 2 labels	194
19	5d.	2	PVA	B	6	Deep Blue	195
20	5d.	2	PVA	B	15	"Method" for Cream of Potato Soup recipe .	196

1d. BOOKLET PANES OF SIX

6 × 1d. (two bands). Head B.
Shade (2) Yellowish olive
From 4s.6d. Booklets LP45/59 and 10s. Booklets XP4/5

UB1   Pane of 6 × 1d.   (containing No. U2 × 6) (25.3.68) . . . . 2·00
           a.   Part perf. pane* . . . .
           b.   Imperf. pane* £4250
           c.   Phosphor omitted . . . . 32·00
   *Booklet error—see General Notes.

Booklet Cylinder Numbers

Panes of six (21-row cylinders)

Pane No.	Cyl. No.	Perf. Type I No dot	Dot	Pane No.	Cyl. No.	Perf. Type I No dot	Dot
UB1	F1	65·00	65·00	UB1	F3	5·50	5·50
UB1	F1 T	65·00	65·00	UB1	F3 T	5·50	5·50

In the above and all other 21-row cylinders, which are printed continuously on the web, the perforated web is cut at every 20th row to make sheets of 480. Consequently on successive sheets the cylinder number appears one row lower and thus a pane can have it adjoining the top or bottom row. Where the cylinder number adjoins the top row of the pane it is designated by the letter "T".

Examples of Cyl. No. pane F1 (lower position) are known with forged cylinder number.

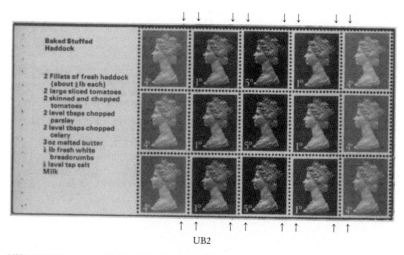

UB2

"STAMPS FOR COOKS" SE-TENANT BOOKLET PANE WITH RECIPE LABEL

Pane of fifteen comprising 6 × 1d. (two bands) with 3 × 4d. (one side band at left), 3 × 4d. (one side band at right), 3 × 5d. and *se-tenant* recipe label. Head B
"Baked Stuffed Haddock" recipe from £1 "Stamps for Cooks" Booklet ZP1

A. Stapled

UB2   Pane of 3 × 4d./1d./5d./1d./4d.   (containing Nos. U2 × 6, U16 × 3,
                                     U16A × 3, U17 × 3) (1.12.69) . . . . . . 35·00
           b.   Phosphor omitted £500
           c.   One 9·5 mm. phosphor band on each
                 stamp, except first vertical row which
                 has phosphor omitted £700
           d.   Mole on cheek (R. 1/2) . . . . 40·00
           s.   Optd. "Specimen" (14 mm.) £1900

B. Stitched

UB2a Pane of 3 × 4d./1d./5d./1d./4d. (containing Nos. U2 × 6, U16 × 3,
U16A × 3, U17 × 3) . . . . 8·50

ab. Uncoated paper* £900
ac. Phosphor omitted £150
ad. Phosphor omitted from front, but
shown on gummed side £2250
ae. Mole on cheek (R. 1/2) . . . . 12·00
ag. One 9·5 mm. phosphor band on each
stamp except for first vertical row which
has phosphor omitted £750
ah. As ag but phosphor omitted from first
two vertical rows and one 9·5 mm. band
at left on rows containing 5d., 1d., 4d. . £2250
aj. One 9·5 mm. band at right on first row
at left and phosphor omitted from
vertical rows 1d., 5d., 1d., 4d. . . . . . .

*Uncoated paper—see General Notes for Section U.

UB2d, UB2ae(1d.)

Booklet Cylinder Numbers

In the £1 Booklet (ZP1) the cylinder numbers were always trimmed off, however, the cylinders
known to have been used were F7 (1d.), N8 (4d.) and R5 (5d.).

UB3

1d. AND 4d. SEPIA SE-TENANT BOOKLET PANES OF SIX

4 × 1d. (centre band) with vertical pair 4d. sepia (centre band). Head B
From 10s. Booklet XP6

		Perf. Type		
		I	I($\frac{1}{2}$v)	P
UB3 Pane of 2 × 1d./1d./4d.	(containing Nos. U3 × 4, U12 × 2) (16.9.68)	4·00	14·00	5·00
a.	Phosphor omitted	30·00	65·00	45·00
b.	Centre band on second and third vert. rows and missing phosphor on first row (2 × 1d.)			
c.	Centre band on first and second vert. rows and missing phosphor on third row (2 × 4d.)			
d.	Centre band on second vert. row only . .	—	†	†

Booklet Cylinder Numbers

Se-tenant pane of six (20-row cylinder)
One centre band

		Perf. Type	
		I	P
Pane No.	Cyl. Nos.	No dot	Dot
UB3	F4 (1d.), N5 (4d. sepia)	28·00	30·00

UB4

1d. AND 4d. BRIGHT VERMILION SE-TENANT BOOKLET PANES OF SIX

4 × 1d. (two bands) with vertical pair 4d. bright vermilion (one left side band). Head B
From 10s. Booklets XP7/12

		Perf. Type P
UB4 Pane of 2 × 1d./1d./4d.	(containing Nos. U2 × 4, U16 × 2) (6.1.69)	3·50
a.	Phosphor omitted	£160

Booklet Cylinder Numbers

Se-tenant pane of six (20-row cylinder)
Two bands

		Perf. Type P
		No Dot
Pane No.	Cyl. Nos.	
UB4	F4 (1d.), N5 (4d. vermilion)	15·00

UB5 UB5a

1d. AND 3d. SE-TENANT BOOKLET PANES OF FOUR

Pair 1d. (two bands) with pair 3d. (two bands). Head B
From 2s. Booklets N P27/9

Pane UB5 Pane of four with 1d. at left
Pane UB5a Pane of four with 1d. at right

			Perf. Type		
			I	I($\frac{1}{2}$v)	AP
UB5	Pane of 2 × 1d./3d.	(containing Nos. U2 × 2, U10 × 2) (6.4.68) . . .	7·00	£275	3·00
	b.	One 9·5 mm. phosphor band on each stamp . .	22·00	£250	15·00
	c.	Phosphor omitted	£100	†	75·00
UB5a	Pane of 2 × 3d./1d.	(containing Nos. U2 × 2, U10 × 2) (6.4.68) . . .	7·00	18·00	3·00
	ab.	One 9·5 mm. phosphor band on each stamp . .	22·00	50·00	15·00
	ac.	Phosphor omitted	£100	£150	75·00

Booklet Cylinder Numbers

Se-tenant panes of four
In the 2s. Booklets (NP27/9) the cylinder numbers were always trimmed off, but cylinders F2 and K3 were used.

3d. BOOKLET PANES OF SIX

6 × 3d. (centre band). PVA gum. Head B
From 10s. Booklets XP4/5

UB6	Pane of 6 × 3d.	(containing No. U9 × 6) (25.3.68)	25·00
	a.	Phosphor omitted	

Booklet Cylinder Numbers

Panes of six (21-row cylinder)

Pane No.	Cyl. No.	No dot	Dot	Pane No.	Cyl. No.	No dot	Dot
UB6	K2	60·00	60·00	UB6	K2 T	60·00	60·00

4d. DEEP OLIVE-BROWN BOOKLET PANES OF SIX

6 × 4d. (two bands). Gum Arabic. Head A
(a) Shade (1) Deep sepia
From 6s. Booklets QP28/32

UB7	Pane of 6 × 4d.	(containing No. U11 × 6) (21.9.67)	10·00
	a.	Phosphor omitted	28·00

189

(b) Shade (2) Deep olive-brown
From 6s. Booklets QP33/6

UB8	Pane of 6 × 4d.	(containing No. U11 × 6) (1.68)	12·00
	a.	Part perf. pane*	£2500
	b.	Phosphor omitted	32·00

*Booklet error—see General Notes.

6 × 4d. (two bands). PVA gum. Head A
From 4s.6d. Booklets LP45/6, 6s. Booklets QP37/40 and 10s. Booklets XP4/5

UB9	Pane of 6 × 4d.	(containing No. U12 × 6) (25.3.68)	1·50
	a.	One 9·5 mm. phosphor band on each stamp	£190
	b.	Phosphor omitted	25·00
	c.	Patch on cheek (R. 1/2 or 2/2)	6·00

UB9*c*, UB11*b*
From 10s. Booklet

Booklet Cylinder Numbers

Panes of six (21-row cylinders)

	Gum Arabic					PVA Gum		
Pane No.	Cyl. No.	No dot	Dot		Pane No.	Cyl. No.	No dot	Dot
(a) Shade (1) Deep sepia								
UB7	N1	22·00	22·00					
UB7	N1 T	22·00	22·00		UB9	N1	6·75	6·75
(b) Shade (2) Deep olive-brown					UB9	N1 T	6·75	6·75
UB8	N1	22·00	22·00		UB9	N2	6·00	6·00
UB8	N1 T	22·00	22·00		UB9	N2 T	6·00	6·00

4d. DEEP OLIVE-BROWN BOOKLET PANES OF FOUR

4 × 4d. (two bands). PVA gum. Head B
From 2s. Booklets NP27/31

			Perf. Type		
			I	I($\frac{1}{2}$v)	AP
UB10	Pane of 4 × 4d.	(containing No. U12 × 4) (6.4.68)	4·00	15·00	2·50
	a.	One 9·5 mm. phosphor band on each stamp	25·00	38·00	22·00
	b.	Phosphor omitted	25·00	70·00	18·00
	c.	Dot on "D" (R. 1/2)	18·00	†	—
	ca.	Retouched state	7·00	†	—

Later retouched and shows as a
pale triangular patch on Nos.
UB10, 12 and 15.

UB10*c*

Booklet Cylinder Numbers

In the 2s. Booklets (NP27/31) the cylinder numbers were always trimmed off, however, the cylinder known to have been used was N3.

4d. DEEP OLIVE-BROWN BOOKLET PANES OF SIX

6 × 4d. (centre band). PVA gum. Head A
From 4s.6d. Booklets LP47/8, 6s. Booklets QP41/5 and 10s. Booklet XP6

UB11	Pane of 6 × 4d. (containing No. U13 × 6) (16.9.68)	2·50
	a. Part perf. pane*	£1750
	b. Patch on cheek (R. 1/2 or 2/2)	6·50

No. UB11 also occurs with the phosphor omitted but since a single pane would be indistinguishable from No. UB9*b* it is only listed there.

*Booklet error—see General Notes.

Booklet Cylinder Numbers

Panes of six (21-row cylinders)

Pane No.	Cyl. No.	No dot	Dot	Pane No.	Cyl. No.	No dot	Dot
UB11	N1	6·00	6·00	UB11	N2	6·00	6·00
UB11	N1 T	6·00	6·00	UB11	N2 T	6·00	6·00

4d. DEEP OLIVE-SEPIA BOOKLET PANES OF FOUR

4 × 4d. (centre band). PVA gum. Head B
From 2s. Booklets NP31*a*/33

	Perf. Types			
	I	I($\frac{1}{2}$v)	AP	P
UB12 Pane of 4 × 4d. (containing No. U13 × 4) (16.9.68)	24·00	35·00	2·50	2·50
a. Phosphor omitted	*	*	*	50·00
b. Dot on "D" retouched	26·00	†	—	—

*Phosphor omitted errors exist from these booklets in Perf. Types I and AP, but the panes are identical with No. UB10*b*.

Booklet Cylinder Numbers

In the 2s. Booklets (NP31/3) the cylinder number was always trimmed off, however, the cylinder known to have been used was N3.

UB13, UB18

4d. DEEP OLIVE-SEPIA SE-TENANT WITH PRINTED LABELS
2 × 4d. (centre band). with two labels. PVA gum. Head B
"£4,315 FOR YOU AT AGE 55" (1st label) and "SEE OTHER PAGES" (2nd label) from 2s. Booklets
NP30/3

			I	I($\frac{1}{2}$v)	Perf. Types AP	P
UB13	Pane of 2 × label/4d.	(containing No. U13 × 2) (16.9.68) ..	3·50	12·00	1·00	2·75
	a.	Phosphor omitted	75·00	—	60·00	†
	b.	Damaged pearls in crown (R. 1/2) . . .				

UB13*b*, UB18*b*

Booklet Cylinder Numbers

In the 2s. Booklets (NP30/3) the cylinder number was always trimmed off, however, the cylinder known to have been used was N6.

4d. BRIGHT VERMILION BOOKLET PANES OF SIX
6 × 4d. (centre band). PVA gum.
From 4s.6d. Booklets LP49/59, 6s. Booklets QP46/55 and 10s. Booklets XP7/12

UB14	Pane of 6 × 4d.	(containing No. U14 × 6) (6.1.69) (A) Head A	1·75
		(B) Head B	2·50
	a.	Phosphor omitted	35·00
	b.	Gum arabic (Head A)	£150
	ba.	Gum arabic (Head A). Phosphor omitted	£600

Booklet Cylinder Numbers
Panes of six (21-row cylinders)

Pane No.	Cyl. No.	No dot	Dot	Pane No.	Cyl. No.	No dot	Dot
UB14 (A)	N1 (Head A)	7·00	7·00	UB14 (A)	N2 (Head A) . . .	7·00	7·00
UB14 (A)	N1 T	7·00	7·00	UB14 (A)	N2 T	7·00	7·00
UB14*b*	N1 (gum arabic) . .	£325	£325	UB14 (B)	N7 (Head B) . . .	10·00	10·00
UB14*b*	N1 T (gum arabic) .	£325	£325	UB14 (B)	N7 T	10·00	10·00

Stamps from booklet cylinder N7 show screening dots within the face value and in the margins.

4d. BRIGHT VERMILION BOOKLET PANES OF FOUR
4 × 4d. (centre band). PVA gum. Head B
From 2s. Booklets NP34/45

			I	I($\frac{1}{2}$v)	Perf.Types AP	P
UB15	Pane of 4 × 4d.	(containing No. U14 × 4) (3.3.69)	3·50	16·00	£750	90
	a.	Phosphor omitted	60·00	£150	†	55·00
	b.	Dot on "D" retouched	6·00	†	—	—

Booklet Cylinder Numbers

In the 2s. Booklets (NP34/45) the cylinder number was always trimmed off, however, the cylinder known to have been used was N3.

UB16

4d. BRIGHT VERMILION BOOKLET PANE OF FIFTEEN WITH RECIPE LABEL

15 × 4d. (centre band). Panes of fifteen *se-tenant* with recipe label. PVA gum. Head B "Stuffed Cucumber" recipe and "Method" from £1 "Stamps for Cooks" Booklet ZP1

A. Stapled
UB16	Pane of 15 × 4d.	(containing No. U14 × 15) (1.12.69)	18·00
	b.	Broken necklace (R. 1/1)	22·00
	c.	Tail on 4 (R. 1/4)	24·00
	s.	Opt. "Specimen" (14 mm.)	£650

B. Stitched
UB16a	Pane of 15 × 4d.	(containing No. U14 × 15)	3·00
	ab.	Uncoated paper ('70)*	£150
	ac.	Phosphor omitted	£110
	ad.	Broken necklace (R. 1/1)	5·50
	ae.	Tail on 4 (R. 1/4)	8·00

UB17

"Method" only for Braised Shoulder of Lamb from £1 "Stamps for Cooks" Booklet ZP1

A. Stapled

UB17   Pane of 15 × 4d.   (containing No. U14 × 15) (1.12.69) . . . . 18·00
        b.   Broken necklace (R. 1/1) . . . . 22·00
        c.   Spot over eye (R. 2/2) . . . . 24·00
        s.   Opt. "Specimen" (14 mm.) £650

B. Stitched

UB17a Pane of 15 × 4d.   (containing No. U14 × 15) . . . . 3·00
        ab.   Uncoated paper ('70)* £130
        ac.   Phosphor omitted £160
        ad.   Broken necklace (R. 1/1) . . . . 5·50
        ae.   Spot over eye (R. 2/2) . . . . 7·50
        af.   Two narrow bands on each stamp £600

*Uncoated paper—see General Notes for Section U.
The note below No. U15, describing No. U14*b*, also applies to pane UB17*af*.

UB16*b*, UB16*ad*,
UB17*b*, UB17*ad*

UB16*c*, UB16*ae*

UB17*c*, UB17*ae*
Later retouched on
UB17 and exists
retouched only on UB16

Booklet Cylinder Numbers

In the £1 Booklet (ZP1) the cylinder number was always trimmed off, however, the cylinder known to have been used was N9.

4d. BRIGHT VERMILION SE-TENANT WITH PRINTED LABELS

2 × 4d. (centre band). PVA gum. Head B
"£4,315 FOR YOU AT AGE 55" (1st label) and "SEE OTHER PAGES" (2nd label) from 2s. Booklets NP34/45

		Perf. Types			
		I	I($\frac{1}{2}$v)	AP	P
UB18 Pane of 2 × label/4d.	(containing No. U14 × 2) (3.3.69) . . .	3·25	20·00	£800	1·00
a.	Phosphor omitted	90·00	£160	†	70·00
b.	Damaged pearls in crown (R. 1/2) . . .				

Booklet Cylinder Numbers

In the 2s. Booklets (NP34/45) the cylinder number was always trimmed off, however, the cylinder known to have been used was N6.

For illustration of No. UB18*b*, see No. UB13*b*.

5d. BOOKLET PANES OF SIX

6 × 5d. (two bands). PVA gum. Head B
From 5s. Booklets HP26/38 and 10s. Booklets XP6/12

UB19	Pane of 6 × 5d.	(containing No. U17 × 6) (27.11.68)	1·75
	a.	Imperf. pane*	£2500
	b.	Part perf. pane*	£1300
	c.	Phosphor omitted	40·00
	ca.	Third and fourth phosphor bands from left omitted . .	£120
	d.	White flaw on diadem (R. 1/2 or 2/2)	5·00
	e.	Scratch through hair (R. 1/1 or 2/1)	8·00

*Booklet errors—see General Notes.
No. UB19*ca* is known with cylinder number R3T. Single variety is No. U17*db*.

UB19*d*

UB19*e*

Booklet Cylinder Numbers

Panes of six (21-row cylinders)

Pane No.	Cyl. No.	No dot	Dot	Pane No.	Cyl. No.	No dot	Dot
UB19	R2	4·75	4·75	UB19	R3	4·75	4·75
UB19	R2 T	4·75	4·75	UB19	R3 T	4·75	4·75

UB20

5d. BOOKLET PANE OF FIFTEEN WITH RECIPE LABEL

15 × 5d. (two bands). Panes of fifteen *se-tenant* with recipe label. PVA gum. Head B "Method" only for Cream of Potato Soup from £1 "Stamps for Cooks" Booklet ZP1

A. Stapled

UB20	Pane of 15 × 5d.	(containing No. U17 × 15) (1.12.69) . . . . 25·00
b.		Uncoated paper ('70)* £300
c.		White flaw below collar (R. 1/2) . . . . 30·00
d.		Flaw on shoulder (R. 1/2) . . . . 30·00
s.		Opt. "Specimen" (14 mm.) £650

B. Stitched

UB20a	Pane of 15 × 5d.	(containing No. U17 × 15) . . . . 4·00
ab.		Uncoated paper ('70)* £350
ac.		Phosphor and recipe omitted £750
ad.		One 9·5 mm. band on each stamp £800
ae.		Phosphor omitted £200
af.		White flaw below collar (R. 1/2) . . . . 6·50
ag.		Flaw on shoulder (R. 1/2) . . . . 6·50

*Uncoated paper—see General Notes for Section U.

UB20c, UB20*af*   UB20*d*, UB20*ag*

Booklet Cylinder Numbers

In the £1 Booklet (ZP1) the cylinder number was always trimmed off, however, the cylinder known to have been used was R6 for UB20.

SECTION UC
Machin £.s.d. Issues
1969. High Values. Recess-printed

General Notes

INTRODUCTION. The four high values, in similar design to the low values, were issued on 5 March, 1969 thus completing the Machin definitive series.

PRINTERS. The Machin high values were recess-printed by Bradbury, Wilkinson & Co. Ltd. on rotary sheet-fed machines.

PAPER. Unwatermarked lightly coated paper was used for all values. Several types of coated paper appear to have been used and generally there is only a slight response to the chalky test. Variations in the thickness of the paper also exist. Shades are known but it is probable that they are due to the variations in the coating and thickness of the paper rather than to the use of different inks.

GUM. Only PVA gum was used for the Machin high values.

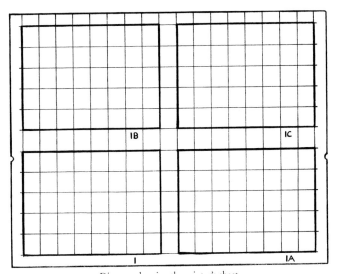

Diagram showing the printer's sheet
comprising four Post Office panes, the
method of perforation, and the positions of the
plate numbers and perforation guide holes

SHEET DETAILS. The printer's sheets comprised 160 stamps in four panes of 40 each arranged in five rows of eight stamps (see diagram above), the sheet being guillotined into four before issue.

Perforation. All values are comb perforated 12. The printer's sheet was perforated as a complete sheet with perforation Type A*; therefore, the characteristics of each individual pane are different as is clearly shown in the diagram above. Perforator Type A* is described in Appendix G.

Plate Numbers. See the General Notes for Section T for an illustration of these. Each printer's sheet produces four plate numbers comprising a "whole number" and "A", "B" and "C" numbered panes and these appear below stamp 7 in the bottom row of each pane, as shown in the diagram above. The arrangement of the panes is the same for all plates of all the values.

Guide hole and plugged impression

Perforation Guide Holes.   The Machin high values have a single guide hole opposite the first row of stamps, in the left-hand margin of the "whole" number panes and in the right-hand margin of the "A" plates as shown in the diagram of the printer's sheet. Additionally for plate 2 of the 2s.6d., and 5s., and plate 1 of the 10s., there are "blind" perforation guide holes slightly below the punched holes.

The punched holes are usually heavily rimmed with colour and may be either partly or completely trimmed off. The appearance of the "blind" holes ranges from a thin outline to being completely coloured in.

U3. Queen Elizabeth II
(Des. after plaster cast by Arnold Machin)

1969. Type U3

1969 (MARCH 5). 2s.6d. BROWN

				Mint	Used
UC1 (=S.G.787)	2s.6d.	Brown	. . . .	35	30

Plate Numbers (Blocks of Four)

Pl. No.		Pl. No.		Pl. No.	
2	7·00	3	7·00	6	10·00
2A	7·00	3A	7·00*	6A	10·00
2B	7·00	3B	7·00	6B	10·00
2C	7·00	3C	7·00	6C	48·00

*This contains the recorded minor constant flaw.

Minor Constant Flaw

Pl. 3A 5/8 Dot to right of Queen's eye (Th. D–E4)

Quantities Printed. Pl. 2/2C 7,840,000; Pl. 3/3C 27,200,000; Pl. 6/6C 9,360,000

1969 (MARCH 5). 5s. CRIMSON-LAKE

				Mint	Used
UC2 (=S.G.788)	5s.	Crimson-lake	. . . .	1·75	60

Plate Numbers (Blocks of Four)

Pl. No.		Pl. No.	
2	16·00	3	15·00
2A	16·00	3A	15·00
2B	16·00	3B	15·00
2C	16·00	3C	15·00

Quantities Printed. Pl. 2/2C 8,480,000; Pl. 3/3C 15,200,000

1969 (MARCH 5). 10s. DEEP ULTRAMARINE

			Mint	Used
UC3 (=S.G.789)	10s.	Deep ultramarine	6·00	7·00

Plate Numbers (Blocks of Four)

Pl. No.		Pl. No.	
1	45·00	1B	45·00
1A	45·00	1C	45·00

Quantities Printed. Pl. 1/1C 8,880,000

1969 (MARCH 5). £1 BLUISH BLACK

					Mint	Used
UC4	£1	(1)	Bluish black		3·00	2·00
		(2)	Indigo		£750	

The indigo shade, from plate 3B, was due to a faulty ink mix and has been confirmed by analysis.

Plate Numbers (Blocks of Four)

Pl. No.			Pl. No.	
3	35·00		4	48·00
3A	35·00		4A	48·00
3B	35·00		4B	48·00
(3C)*	†		4C	48·00

*This plate number block is not known as there was a fault on the plate and only the left half of this pane was issued.

New plates were made for the decimal £1 in 1970, but in single pane settings of 100 (10 × 10) in place of the plates of four panes each of 40 (8 × 5). Plate blocks of four from Plate 3 of the decimal issue (No. UC11 in Vol. 4 of this catalogue) can easily be distinguished from Plate 3 blocks of the pre-decimal issue as they show part of the "TOTAL SHEET VALUE" inscription in the margin opposite R. 9/10.

However, specialists may also recognise single stamps by studying the background shading under a strong magnifying glass, particularly in the top left and bottom right corners. The pre-decimal issue has thicker horizontal lines of shading whilst the decimal issue has thicker vertical lines, each caused by the direction in which the transfer roller was rocked, both plates being produced by the conventional process of rocking in impressions from the die. (Illustrations taken from top left corner)

 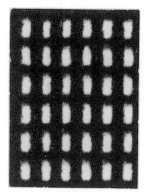

UC4	UC11
Pre-decimal issue	Decimal issue
Thicker horizontal lines	Thicker vertical lines

Quantities Printed. Pl. 3/3C 3,760,000; Pl. 4/4C 2,800,000

Proofs

Imperforate in the £1 design TYPE U3 each mounted on a Bradbury Wilkinson card and marked "Approved by the Queen" signed and dated "14 Jan/Feb. 1968" in blue. The stamps are printed in the approved colours of Nos. UC1 to 4

Card inscribed in red "A1" with £1 in brown as No. UC1
Card inscribed in red "A2" with £1 in crimson-lake as No. UC2
Card inscribed in red "A3" with £1 in deep ultramarine as No. UC3
Card inscribed in red "A4" with £1 in issued colour as No. UC4

As above but 2s.6d., 5s., 10s., and £1 imperforate proofs in the issued colours mounted on Bradbury Wilkinson card

Card with four values imperforate inscribed "AS SUBMITTED 20.3.68"

The above were originally in the Bradbury Wilkinson archive later acquired by De La Rue and sold by them in 2000.

Presentation Pack

UPP2 (issued 5 March 1969)   Four values . . . .   16·00
                              a. With German text . . . .   60·00

The issued Pack contained one each of Nos. UC1/4.

UPP2 also exists with a Japanese insert card.

First Day Cover

UFC6 (5.3.69)   2s.6d., 5s., 10s., £1 . . . .   9·50

SECTION W
Special Issues
(1953–70)

General Notes

SPECIAL ISSUES. Until 1966 it had been the policy of the Post Office to restrict commemorative issues to celebrating particular events, such as anniversaries or exhibitions, conferences and festivals, etc. The introduction of the Landscape series in May 1966 heralded a new departure as this was followed by pictorial sets showing British Birds, Paintings, Bridges, Cathedrals, etc. and Technological Achievements. These cannot be described as being commemorative stamps, yet it is obviously convenient and logical for them to be listed here and so we have headed this Section Special Issues.

SE-TENANT COMBINATIONS. *Se-tenant* means "joined together". Some sets include stamps of different design arranged *se-tenant* as blocks or strips and, in mint condition, these are usually collected unsevered as issued. Where such combinations exist, the individual stamps are priced normally as mint and used singles.

PRINTERS. All the £.s.d. special issues were printed in photogravure by Harrison & Sons with the exception of the 1964 2s.6d. Shakespeare and 1966 2s.6d. Westminster Abbey which were recess-printed by Bradbury, Wilkinson & Co. and the 1969 Post Office Technology and 1970 Commonwealth Games issues which were printed by De La Rue & Co. by lithography.

Generally, the double-sized stamps were printed on continuous reels of paper "on the web" in double pane width, i.e. 240 stamps consisting of two panes (no dot and dot) each of 120 stamps arranged in twenty rows of six stamps, the panes being guillotined before issue. However, the higher values were often printed in single panes, either on reel or sheet-fed machines. After the listing of each issue we give the sheet arrangement and state whether printed in the reel or in sheets.

QUEEN'S PORTRAIT. The portrait from the photograph by Dorothy Wilding Ltd. was used from the 1953 Coronation to the 1966 Westminster Abbey issues. This was replaced on the 1966 Landscapes to 1967 Christmas by the profile coinage design by Mrs. Mary Gillick, adapted by David Gentleman. The third, and final, change was made on the 1968 Bridges issue with the introduction of design from a plaster cast by Arnold Machin. The Machin head can be distinguished from the Gentleman adaptation of the Gillick profile by two, instead of one, laurel leaves on top of the Queen's head.

PAPER. The same type of paper as for the definitive issues was used up to the 1960 General Letter Office issue and thereafter chalk-surfaced paper was used.

SCREEN. The 200-line screen as used for the Wilding definitives was employed up to the 1960 Europa issue but thereafter Harrisons used a finer 250-line screen.

WATERMARKS. These are illustrated in Section SA and were used as follows:

Tudor Crown	1953 Coronation issue
St. Edward's Crown	1957 World Scout Jubilee and Inter-Parliamentary Union and 1958 Commonwealth Games
Crowns	All later issues until 1967 Wild Flowers and British Discovery and Invention
No watermark	1967 Paintings and Sir Francis Chichester and all issues from 1967 Christmas onwards

The watermark normally appears sideways on upright designs. On certain stamps, the 2½d. and 3d. 1962. Productivity Year, and the 1963 Freedom from Hunger and Paris Postal Conference issues, the watermark is normally inverted. These stamps were printed "on the web" and for technical reasons the paper had to be re-reeled and, to save time and expense, it was decided to print on the paper wound in the reverse direction to normal, thus resulting in the watermark being inverted. A large proportion of the printing for the 1967 Wild Flowers 9d. was similarly treated. Other inverted watermark varieties on commemorative issues are normally from sheet-printed issues where the paper has been accidentally fed the wrong way and these are often quite scarce.

GUM. The distinction between gum arabic and PVA gum is explained in the General Notes relating to Section UA. It is sufficient to state here that gum arabic was used for all commemorative stamps up to the 1967 Christmas issue and thereafter Harrisons and De La Rue only used PVA gum.

PERFORATION. Harrisons used the same 15 × 14 comb perforation as for the Wilding definitives but some of the upright designs are perforated 14 × 15. The 1964 2s.6d. Shakespeare and 1966 2s.6d. Westminster Abbey were comb perforated 11 × 12 by Bradbury, Wilkinson and the 1969 Post Office Technology and 1970 Commonwealth Games issues were comb perforated 13½ × 14 by De La Rue.

Cylinder and plate blocks are listed according to the perforator type as described in Appendix G together with abbreviations for the side and horizontal margins of the listed block. These are usually from the bottom left corner, therefore the first letter refers to the left margin and the second to the bottom margin. For details see page 2 in Section S.

PHOSPHOR BANDS.   See the General Notes for Section S for a detailed description of these. In the special issues they were applied as follows:

"Blue": From 1962 N.P.Y. to 1965 Salvation Army and 1965 L.T.U. Generally 8 mm. but occasionally 9·5 mm. bands.

"Violet" 8 mm. bands: Other 1965 issues to 1966 Christmas.

"Violet" 9·5 mm. bands: 1967 E.F.T.A. to 1970 Christmas.

From 1962 until the 1967 Wild Flowers set the special issues appeared both with and without phosphor bands. From the 1967 British Paintings set onwards it was intended that all special issues should appear only with phosphor bands. However, it is quite common practice for sheets to be issued with the phosphor accidentally omitted and these are listed as varieties.

Methods of Application.   All three methods, photogravure, flexography and typography were utilised to apply the phosphor bands to £.s.d. special issues (for the characteristics of each method see Section S Notes).

In the light of considerable research it now appears that from 1962 until 1969 the bands were applied either by flexography or photogravure, the only exceptions being the two special issues printed by De La Rue which had the bands applied by typography. These two issues used a slightly different substance known as SA, sulphanilic acid being the activator.

It is known that the first phosphor issue, 1962 National Productivity Year set, had the bands printed on the web by flexography and the following reel-fed issues used the same process or photogravure. Flexography was used for the few sheet-fed issues. Since 1970 Harrisons have only used photogravure to apply the bands, and phosphor cylinder numbers were introduced.

Some difficulty can arise in distinguishing between phosphor bands applied by photogravure and those printed by flexography. The latter often do not run to the bottom of the sheet or show a break in the bottom margin. They also show, in some instances, a vertical split in the centre of the band.

In some instances the cylinders or stereos used to apply the bands were made-up with a narrow band at one side or both sides, of the sheet. These narrow bands vary in size, as do the normal bands, but most are 6 mm. wide. Where such varieties occur they are included, listing being for a single stamp with vertical margin attached.

PHOSPHOR CYLINDER NUMBERS.   Starting with the 1970 Anniversaries issue cylinder numbers were introduced on the phosphor cylinders as an additional check on tracing errors in applying the bands.

CYLINDER VARIETIES AND MINOR CONSTANT FLAWS.   We have only listed or recorded those we have actually seen and know to be constant in the position given. Others have been reported and may be added in future editions as specimens become available for inspection. To pinpoint the position of the flaws we give the reference according to the S.G. "Thirkell" Position Finder where this is appropriate. Please note that for designs which lack outer frame lines the position finder should be placed over the outside of the perforation. For further information see the General Notes to Section S under **"Varieties"** and **"Varieties in Cylinder Blocks"**.

Flaws on Phosphor Issues.   In the recorded lists of flaws on stamps which come both ordinary and phosphor, "O" means that the flaw occurs only on the ordinary stamp, "P" phosphor only and "OP" on ordinary and phosphor.

MULTICOLOURED STAMPS.   Colour descriptions are taken from the traffic lights to identify the colours of the cylinder numbers and also missing colour errors. Where colours are superimposed one over another, the colours that result will be different from those described. So far as possible we have followed the normal practice giving the colours starting first with the most prominent one in the centre of the stamp and then moving outwards, usually ending with the colours of the inscriptions, background and Queen's head.

PRESENTATION PACKS.   Special Packs comprising slip-in cards with printed commemorative inscriptions and descriptive notes on the back and with protective covering, were introduced in 1964 with the Shakespeare issue. These are listed and priced.

Issues of 1968–69 (British Paintings to the Prince of Wales Investiture) were also issued in packs with text in German for sale through the Post Office's German Agency and these are also listed.

Subsequently, the packs sold in Germany, Japan and the Netherlands were identical to the normal English version with the addition of a separate printed card in German, Japanese or Dutch. These are noted where they exist.

Spelling errors on insert cards exist, but these are outside the scope of this catalogue.

REPRINTED INSERT CARDS.   In 1988 permission was granted to a British stamp dealer by the Post Office to reproduce, from an original, 1,000 sets of the Dutch insert cards for the 1969 Ships to the 1970 Literary Anniversaries issues.

"SPECIMEN" AND "CANCELLED" STAMPS. The former practice of distributing these ceased during the reign of King George VI but occasionally such overprints were applied to Elizabethan Special Issues for advance publicity or exhibition purposes and these are listed.

Various issues of 1964, 1965 and 1966 are known overprinted "CANCELLED", usually without gum. These were for use in trials carried out by the Forensic Department of the Post Office, and should not have reached the general public.

Issues of 1969/70 are known with "CANCELLED" applied with a violet *rubber* handstamp (26 × 3½ mm.), generally across a corner of the stamps. This practice was introduced in an attempt to defeat the postal use of the stamps prior to their first day of issue and which could be obtained from advance publicity material distributed to shops supplied by the Post Office Agency in West Germany. When it was realised that the use of the rubber handstamp created material of a collectable nature the practice was discontinued but the following are known to exist, Nos. W159/97. The Machin 1969 high values, Nos. U33/6 were similarly obliterated. Later stamps were cancelled by a red pen line across the corner. Such publicity material is outside the scope of this catalogue.

WITHDRAWAL DATES. The earlier commemorative issues were left on sale until exhaustion and definite withdrawal dates are not always known, but starting with 1963 Red Cross issue the Post Office announced a standard practice to keep commemorative stamps on sale at the Philatelic Bureau for twelve months from date of issue unless sold out before. All £.s.d. stamps were invalidated as from 1 March 1972.

QUANTITIES. Up to the end of the 1962 issues (N.P.Y.) it is believed that stamps were sold to exhaustion except where a definite withdrawal date was announced, and so the printing figures are quoted as being the *quantities sold*. Starting with the 1963 Freedom from Hunger issue the quantities are stated as being the number *sold, issued* or *printed*. These are defined as follows:

Sold   Actual quantities sold after accounting for undistributed stocks and unsold stocks returned to stores for destruction.

Issued   Quantities issued from Post Office Stores Department to post offices, including the Philatelic Bureau. These figures are given for the 1965 issues (Churchill to I.T.U.) and for which we do not have actual sales figures. Some may have been withdrawn and destroyed.

Printed   Quantities actually supplied by the printers. These often differ from advance announcements of quantities ordered, owing to spoilage, etc.

We also quote figures for sales of Presentation Packs and these were only made available after the total quantities sold, etc., had been announced. The quantities for Packs are not additional as they have already been included in the figures for the numbers sold, issued or printed.

We have noticed slight variations in the figures given for quantities sold, etc., stated in other publications and would point out that the figures we have given are those furnished to us by the Post Office. However, the differences are insignificant. See note above Type No. **W 178**.

SHEET MARKINGS. Reference should be made to the descriptions of sheet markings given in the General Notes for Section S, as most of these apply to this section and the information given there is not repeated here. In the commemorative issues the markings are most interesting as they begin with the same basic markings as for the definitives for the first monocoloured issues but as more colours were introduced other markings began to appear. They are described here in the order of their appearance.

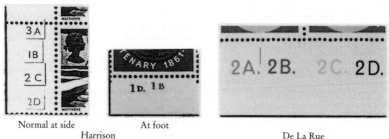

Normal at side   At foot
        Harrison   De La Rue
                    Cylinder Numbers

Cylinder Numbers. These are described in Section S but we show above how they occur on stamps printed in more than one colour. In the listing of cylinder number blocks for stamps printed in more than one colour we give the colour of each cylinder number in order, reading downwards. The information is sometimes helpful in connection with varieties and flaws where more than one cylinder has been used for the same colour in combination with others.

Plate Numbers. The Plate Numbers used by Bradbury, Wilkinson for the 2s.6d. Shakespeare and the 2s.6d. Westminster Abbey are as shown in our notes on the sheet markings for Section T. It should be stated that some of the sheet-fed commemorative stamps were printed by Harrisons on a Linotype and Machinery No. 4 press which uses curved plates and on these the "cylinder numbers" are, strictly speaking, plate numbers. However, as they appear just like the cylinder numbers they are referred to as such.

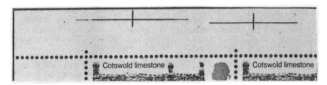

Colour Register Marks. These are coloured crosses of very fine lines, one for each colour superimposed as illustrated. They appear on all sheets of stamps printed in more than one colour, starting with the 1960 Europa issue.

Photo-etched Solid

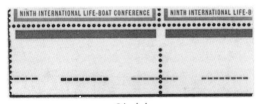

Stippled

Autotron Marks. Coloured bars which may be photo-etched solid or stippled (dotted lines). They serve as an electronic control on colour registration and were first used on the 1961 C.E.P.T. issue.

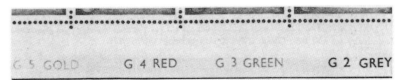

Colour Designations. These consist of colour names usually preceded by a figure and the letter "G" which stands for "Gear". They are usually trimmed off but sometimes appear on extra wide right-hand margins on double and single pane reel-fed printings. They are to indicate which side the cylinder should be fitted and aligned with the colour gear in the press. They are not always shown in the colour indicated. They began to be used on the 1961 C.E.P.T. issue, but do not appear on correctly trimmed sheets of £.s.d. stamps after the 1969 Notable Anniversaries issue.

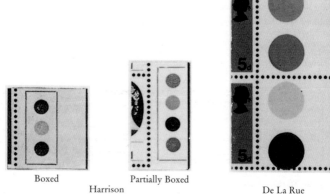

Boxed   Partially Boxed

Harrison   De La Rue

"Traffic Lights".   This term is used to denote coloured check dots which were first introduced on the 1962 N.P.Y. issue. They are intended as a means of checking sheets for missing colours before delivery to the Post Office. They may be fully boxed or partially boxed as shown but we have not distinguished between these. We quote the colours in the order of their appearance reading downwards. Sometimes they are in the same order as the cylinder numbers in which case we state this to save space. Rather larger dots were used by De La Rue.

Coloured Crosses.   These are most usually found on sheet-fed printings and they serve as trimming lines and as an additional check on colour registration. They are often trimmed off. They first appeared on the 1s.3d. 1964 Botanical stamp.

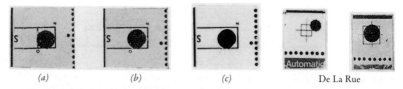

(a)   *(b)*   *(c)*   De La Rue

Perforation Guide Holes.   At first the styles as shown in the General Notes for Section S were used but the types illustrated above were introduced as follows:—
   (a) Double "S O N" box for the 6d. 1965 Parliament
   (b) Single "S O N" box for the 4d. 1966 Landscapes
   (c) Single "S N" box for the 4d. 1966 World Football Cup
   The letters stand for "Selvedge", "Off-side" and "Near-side" and they appear in the reverse order on the other side of the sheet. The "S" or "S O" and part of the box are liable to be trimmed off. We also show the styles used by De La Rue for the 1969 Post Office Technology set and 1970 Commonwealth Games issue respectively.

TOTAL SHEET VALUE   £ 4. 10. 0.

Total Sheet Values.   As an aid to counter clerks in stocktaking and in selling stamps by the sheet, the "TOTAL SHEET VALUE" and amount was printed in the margin. This practice was introduced with the 1969 Anniversaries issue and this was presumably found to be necessary with the introduction of stamps of unusual size and sheet make-up.

EMBOSSED HEAD.   Starting with the 1968 British Paintings set the Queen's head was sometimes embossed over the gold printing. This gives rise to missing embossing varieties which are listed, although we do not list misplaced embossing. Provision is also made for an embossed dot in the traffic lights.

DESIGN INDEX

This index gives an easy reference to the inscriptions and designs of the Special Stamps 1953 to 1970. Where a complete set shares an inscription or type of design, then only the catalogue number of the first stamp is given. Paintings, inventions, etc., are indexed under the name of the artist or inventor, where this is shown on the stamp.

Aberfeldy Bridge W131
Alcock, John W154
Antrim W86
Arbroath Declaration, 650th
   Anniversary W182
Architecture: Cathedrals W159
           Rural W178
Atlantic Flight, 50th Anniversary W154
Automatic Sorting W174

Battle of Britain, 25th Anniversary W67
Battle of Hastings, 900th Anniversary ...W101
Blackbird W95
Black Headed Gull W92
Blue Tit W93
Bridges W130
Brown, Arthur W154
Burns, Robert W81

Cairngorms W88
Canterbury Cathedral W162
C.E.P.T. W14, W21
Christmas 1966, Children's Paintings (3d.,
           1s.6d.) W109
      1967, Paintings (3d., 4d., 1s.6d.)W127
      1968, Children's Toys (4d., 9d.,
           1s.6d.) W142
      1969, Traditional Religious
        Themes (4d., 5d., 1s.6d.) W175
      1970, Lisle Psalter (4d., 5d.,
           1s.6d.) W198
Churchill, Winston W56
Commonwealth Arts Festival W65
Commonwealth Cable W40
Commonwealth Games (1958) W9
Commonwealth Games (1970) W192
Commonwealth Parliamentary
   Conference W24
"Concorde" W151
Constable, John W141
Cook's First Voyage of Discovery, 200th
   Anniversary W137
Coronation W1
Cotswold Limestone W179
Cutty Sark W148

Dickens, Charles, Death Centenary W187
Durham Cathedral W159

East Indiaman W147
E.F.T.A. W111
Elizabethan Galleon W146
"Elizabeth I" W138
England Winners World Cup Football
   Championships, 1966 ....W96
Europa, C.E.P.T., 1st Anniversary W14
Europa, C.E.P.T., 10th Anniversary W155

Fife Harling W178

First England-Australia Flight, 50th
   Anniversary W158
Flowers W113
Forth Road Bridge W54
Freedom from Hunger W29

Gandhi, Mahatma, Birth Centenary W170
General Letter Office, Tercentenary W12
Gipsy Moth W122
Great Britain W149

Harlech Castle W87
Hovercraft W99

International Botanical Congress W50
International Co-operative Alliance W184
International Geographical Congress W46
International Labour Organisation,
   50th Anniversary W156
International Lifeboat Conference W34
International Telecommunications
   Union, Centenary W79

Jet Engine W125
Jubilee Jamboree (1957) W5

Landscapes W85
Lawrence, Thomas W119, W139
Le Nain, Louis W129
Lister, Joseph W63
Liverpool Metropolitan Cathedral W164
Lowry, L. S. W121

Mauretania W150
Mayflower, 350th Anniversary of
   Voyage W185
Menai Bridge W132
Montfort's Parliament, 700th Anniversary W59
Motor Cars W98
Murillo W128
M4 Viaduct W133

National Giro W171
National Nature Week W32
National Productivity Year W26
Nightingale, Florence, 150th Birth
   Anniversary W183
North Atlantic Treaty Organisation
   (NATO), 20th Anniversary W157
Nuclear Power W100

Paris Postal Conference, Centenary W31
Parliamentary Conference W8
Parliament, 700th Anniversary W59
Penicillin W124
Philympia 1970 ....W195
Piper, John W140
Post Office Savings Bank, Centenary W16
Post Office Tower W75

DESIGN INDEX

Prince of Wales, Investiture W165

Queen Elizabeth 2 . . . . .W145

Radar W123
Radio Telescope .W97
Red Cross Centenary Congress W37
Robin W94
Royal Air Force, 50th Anniversary W136
Royal Astronomical Society, 150th
    Anniversary W186

St. Giles' Edinburgh W161
St. Paul's Cathedral W163
Salvation Army Centenary W61
Seville School W127
Shakespeare Festival W41
Stubbs, George W120
Sussex W85

Tarr Steps W130
Telecommunications W172
Television W126
Trades Union Congress, Centenary W134

Ulster Thatch W181
United Nations, 20th Anniversary W77

Votes for Women, 50th Anniversary W135

Welsh Stucco W180
Westminster Abbey, 900th Anniversary . .W83
World Cup Football Championships,
    1966 . . . . .W89
Wordsworth, William, 200th Birth
    Anniversary W191

York Minster W160

*PRICES FOR CYLINDER BLOCKS WITH ASTERISKS

These denote cylinder blocks containing a listed flaw.

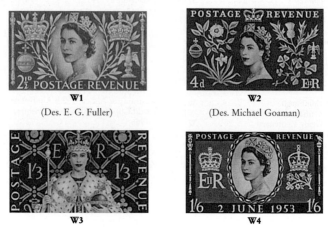

W1	**W2**
(Des. E. G. Fuller)	(Des. Michael Goaman)
W3	**W4**
(Des. Edmund Dulac)	(Des. M. C. Farrar-Bell)

(Portrait by Dorothy Wilding Ltd (except 1s.3d.))

1953 (JUNE 3).   CORONATION OF QUEEN ELIZABETH II

Celebrating the Coronation of Queen Elizabeth II.

Watermark Tudor Crown, Type W.22

				Mint	Used
W1 (=S.G.532) **W1**	2½d.	carmine-red	. . . .	20	25
	a.	Missing pearl (Cyl. 3 Dot, R. 1/4)	. . . .	22·00	
	b.	Pearls retouched	. . . .	15·00	
W2 (=S.G.533) **W2**	4d.	ultramarine	. . . .	1·10	1·90
	a.	Daffodil leaf flaw (Cyl. 1 No dot, R. 19/1)	. . . .	5·50	
W3 (=S.G.534) **W3**	1s.3d.	deep yellow-green	. . . .	5·00	3·00
	a.	Clover leaf flaw (Cyl. 2 No dot, R. 20/1)	. . . . . .	7·00	
W4 (=S.G.535) **W4**	1s.6d.	deep grey-blue	. . . .	10·00	4·75
	a.	Mis-shapen emblems (Cyl. 1 Dot, R. 1/6)	. . . . . .	16·00	
	b.	Thistle flaw (Cyl. 1 Dot, R. 16/5)	. . . .	20·00	

First Day Cover (W1/4) . . . .   75·00

Nos. W1/4 are known used from an Army Post Office in Egypt and Lambeth, London S.W. on 2 June 1953. The latter example was an error as the U.K. offices were closed on 2 June.

Reprints, in black, of these four stamps were included in the *Penrose Annual* for 1954. These reprints were printed in photogravure by Harrisons, on ungummed paper, but were perforated. They were inscribed on the reverse "Reproduction only—no postal or philatelic value".

For a £1 value as Type **W3** see No. **MS**2147 Concise Catalogue.

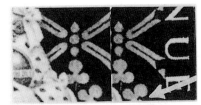

W1*a*	W1*b*		Normal	W3*a*

W2*a*	W4*a*	W4*b*

Cylinder Numbers (Blocks of Six)

Perforation Type A (E/I)

Cyl. No.		No dot	Dot	Cyl. No.		No dot	Dot
2½d.	1	5·50	5·50	4d.	1	12·00*	7·50
	2	1·75	1·75	1s.3d.	2	35·00*	32·00
	3	1·75	1·75	1s.6d.	1	70·00	70·00
	4	1·75	1·75				

Minor Constant Flaws

2½d. Cyl. 1 no dot
   19/2 Spur to top of A of POSTAGE

2½d. Cyl. 3 dot
   13/2 Bulge on left-hand fraction bar

2½d. Cyl. 4 no dot
   1/3 White flaw in diadem (Th. A7)
   1/4 White spur on left-hand crown (Th. B2)
   7/1 Red spot behind hair level with earring (Th. D8–9)
   14/2 Red spot on face level with earring (Th. D7)
   17/1 White spot on branch below left-hand crown (Th. C3)

4d. Cyl. 1 dot
   1/4 Retouched stem of daffodil (Th. F2–3)

1s.3d. Cyl. 2 dot
   2/6 Retouch behind upper part of E of E R and white flaw at top of sceptre (Th. B4)

1s.6d. Cyl. 1 no dot
   18/2 Malformed foot to R of REVENUE

1s.6d. Cyl. 1 dot
   19/1 White flaw on wreath below R of REVENUE (Th. B9)

Sheet Details

Sheet size: 120 (6 × 20). Double pane reel-fed
Sheet markings:
   Cylinder numbers: Opposite R. 18/1
   Guide holes: Boxed opposite rows 14/15, at left (no dot) or right (dot)
   Marginal arrows:
      "V" shaped, hand engraved at top and bottom of sheet
      "W" shaped, photo-etched at both sides
   Marginal rule: At bottom of sheet

Imprimaturs from the National Postal Museum Archives
Nos. W1/4 imperforate, watermark Type W.22
Watermark upright (*set of* 4) £4000

Quantities Sold
2½d. 415,034,000; 4d. 19,816,000; 1s.3d. 8,012,000; 1s.6d. 5,987,200

W5. Scout Badge and   **W6.** "Scouts coming
"Rolling Hitch"   to Britain"
(Des. Mary Adshead)   (Des. Pat Keely)

W7. Globe within a Compass
(Des. W. H. Brown)

1957 (AUGUST 1). WORLD SCOUT JUBILEE JAMBOREE
Commemorating the 50th Anniversary of the founding of the Boy Scout Movement. The Jubilee
Jamboree was held at Sutton Coldfield.

Watermark St. Edward's Crown, Type W.23

				Mint	Used
W5 (=S.G.557) **W5**	2½d.	carmine-red		50	50
	a.	Broken rope strand (Cyl. 4 Dot, R. 1/1)		5·00	
	b	Neck retouch (Cyl. 5 No dot, R. 11/5)		7·00	
W6 (=S.G.558) **W6**	4d.	ultramarine		75	1·50
	a.	Solid pearl at right (Cyl. 1 No dot, R. 14/5)		8·00	
W7 (=S.G.559) **W7**	1s.3d.	green		4·50	4·50
	a.	Major retouch (Cyl. 1 Dot, R. 2/4)		14·00	

First Day Cover (W5/7) . . . . 25·00

W5*a*   W5*b*

W6*a*   W7*a*

Cylinder Numbers (Blocks of Six)

Perforation Type A (E/1)

	Cyl. No.	No dot	Dot		Cyl. No.	No dot	Dot
2½d.	4	4·50	4·50	4d.	1	18·00	18·00
	5	4·50	4·50	1s.3d.	1	30·00	30·00

	Perforation Type B (I/P)				Perforation Type C (E/P)		
4d.	1	5·75	5·75	4d.	1	†	5·75

Minor Constant Flaws

2½d. Cyl. 4 dot
  11/2 Red spot over Queen's left eyebrow, later retouched (Th. C9)
  14/1 Red spot in rope between L E (Th. G5)
  16/5 White spot in rope at junction with fifth line at left (Th. C1)
  17/3 Red spot in large 2 just left of curve
  19/2 White dot after small 2
  20/4 White stop after M

2½d. Cyl. 5 dot
  13/4 Red spot in top of A

1s.3d. Cyl. 1 dot
  18/2 Green spot in compass point above badge (Th. E2)

Coils

Special rolls were prepared of this issue for servicing first day covers mechanically. They were produced from different cylinders and printed on continuous reels of paper. The cylinders bore 126 impressions in 21 rows of six. The cylinders were numbered J1 for the 2½d. and 4d. and J2 for the 1s.3d. The reels were cut so as to provide single rolls of 4800 stamps, numbered 1 to 6. Some very minor flaws have been noted on these coil stamps.

The rolls were put on sale at the London Chief Office but as the quantities were too large for stamp collectors, some were rewound into smaller rolls of 480 for the 2½d. and 4d. and 240 for the 1s.3d. and put on sale there on 2 September.

Sheet Details

Sheet size: 120 (6 × 20). Double pane reel-fed
Sheet markings:
  Cylinder numbers: Opposite R. 18/1
  Guide holes: Opposite rows 14/15, at left (no dot) or right (dot)
  Marginal arrows:
    "V" shaped, hand engraved at top and bottom of sheet
    "W" shaped, hand engraved on both sides
  Marginal rule: At bottom of sheet

Imprimaturs from the National Postal Museum Archives

Nos. W5/7 imperforate, watermark Type W.23

Watermark upright (*set of* 3) £3000

Quantities Sold

Sheets and coils: 2½d. 137,235,286; 4d. 9,318,477; 1s.3d. 3,820,478

Coils:

Value	Size	Printed	Sold	Size	Printed	Sold
2½d.	4800	487	23	480	100	49
4d.	4800	480	21	480	100	37
1s.3d.	4800	482	20	240	100	33

Total number of coil stamps sold or used on covers:

2½d. 133,920; 4d. 118,560; 1s.3d. 103,920

Only 60,632 covers were serviced and 14 large rolls of each value were used for this purpose.

Withdrawn 11.9.57

W8

(Des. M. C. Farrar-Bell and adopted by Frank Langfield with added lettering)

1957 (SEPTEMBER 12). 46th INTER-PARLIAMENTARY UNION CONFERENCE

To mark the 46th Conference held at Church House, Westminster. The Union was founded in 1889.

Watermark St. Edward's Crown, Type W.23

				Mint	Used
W8 (=S.G. 560) **W8**	4d.	ultramarine		1·00	1·00
	a.	Broken wreath (R. 2/6)		8·00	
	b.	Broken frame (R. 12/5)		7·00	
	c.	Partial double frame line (R. 17/3, 17/6 and 18/6) . .		7·00	

> First Day Cover (W8) £140

W8*a*

W8*b*

W8*c*

Cylinder Numbers (Blocks of Six)

	Cyl. No.	Perf. Type B (I/P)	Perf. Type C (E/P)
4d.	2	7·00	7·00

Minor Constant Flaws

4d. Cyl. 2 no dot

    1/5 Blue blob in frame over last N of CONFERENCE (Th. E6)

    1/6 Outline of left-hand jewel of diadem incomplete (Th. A/B3)

    2/1 Line joining shamrock leaf to bottom frame (Th. G–H1)

3/2   Blue scratch on right frame near bottom (Th. H6)
8/7   Small break in frame opposite last E in CONFERENCE
14/6   Fine scratch from ear right across neck (Th. E4)
15/8   Blue blob in bottom right corner (Th. H6)
18/1   Blue spot below A of POSTAGE

Sheet Details

Sheet size: 240 (12 × 20). Single pane reel-fed
Sheet markings:
    Cylinder number: Opposite R. 18/1
    Guide holes: Six. Opposite rows 1 and 7/8 at both sides and also boxed opposite rows 14/15 at both
sides
    Marginal arrows:
      "V" shaped, hand engraved at top and bottom of sheet
      "W" shaped, etched in photogravure at both sides
    Marginal rule: At bottom of sheet

Imprimatur from the National Postal Museum Archives

No. W8 imperforate, watermark Type W.23
Watermark upright £1000

Quantity Sold   10,472,160

Withdrawn   13.10.57

W9. Welsh Dragon

(Des. Reynolds Stone)

W10. Flag and Games Emblem

(Des. W. H. Brown)

W11. Welsh Dragon

(Des. Pat Keely)

SPECIMEN

A

1958 (JULY 18).   SIXTH BRITISH EMPIRE AND COMMONWEALTH GAMES

The 1958 Empire and Commonwealth Games were held at Cardiff.

Watermark St. Edward's Crown, Type W.23

				Mint	Used
W9 (=S.G. 567) **W9**	3d.		deep lilac	20	20
	a.	Short scale (Cyl. 2 Dot, R. 1/1)	4·50	
	b.	Shoulder flaw (Cyl. 2 Dot, R. 12/2)	5·50	
	c.	Shoulder flaw retouched	4·50	
	d.	Body flaw. State II (Cyl. 2 Dot, R. 20/3)	5·50	
	e.	Body flaw. State III	4·50	
	f.	Retouched face (Cyl. 7 Dot, R. 10/6)	4·50	
	g.	"H" flaw (Cyl. 7 Dot, R. 11/2)	15·00	
	h.	"H" flaw retouched	4·50	
	s.	"Specimen", Type A	20·00	

W10 (=S.G. 568) **W10**	6d.	reddish purple	. . . .	40	45
	s.	"Specimen", Type A	. . . .	20·00	
W11 (=S.G. 569) **W11**	1s.3d.	green	. . . .	2·25	2·40
	s.	"Specimen" Type A	. . . .	20·00	

First Day Cover (W9/11) . . . . 75·00

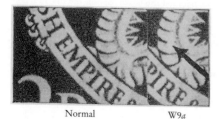

Part of the shading is missing on the scale near "M" of "EMPIRE".

Normal   W9*a*

White flaw on shading of dragon's body above shoulder. Later retouched with an irregular pattern of dots.

W9*b*   W9*c*

W9*d*   W9*e*   W9*f*

Flaw on body above second "E" of "EMPIRE". This is a progressive flaw. Initially normal, the first stage showed the faintest outline of a flaw. State II shows the flaw solid and state III with a dark outline and pale centre.

The retouches across the Queen's cheek and below the chin are quite marked on Cyl. 7 dot, R. 10/6 but there are other minor retouches in this position in stamp No. 6 in rows 2 to 13.

White flaw crossing line behind dragon's left foreleg shows as a letter "H". After retouching there is a light vertical line across the flaw.

W9g

Cylinder Numbers (Blocks of Six)

Perforation Type A (E/I)

	Cyl. No.		No dot	Dot		Cyl. No.		No dot	Dot
3d.	2	. . . .	1·75	1·75	6d.	6	. . . .	4·25	4·25
	7	. . . .	3·50	3·50	1s.3d.	3	. . . .	16·00	16·00

Minor Constant Flaws

3d. Cyl. 2 no dot
    13/1 Dark diagonal line across last two fins of dragon's tail; later the upper line was touched out (Th. F–G9)
    19/3 Dots to left of right stroke of H in BRITISH (Th. D2)

3d. Cyl. 7 no dot
    8/4 White spot on M in EMPIRE; later retouched (Th. E2)

3d. Cyl. 7 dot
    3/4 White flaw on fin of dragon's tail above E of COMMONWEALTH (Th. F8)
    4/5 Break in left frame by top of 3 (Th. E1)
    20/3 White flaw on dragon's ankle above N of COMMONWEALTH (Th. F7)

6d. Cyl. 6 no dot
    18/6 Dot between O and N of COMMONWEALTH (Th. A6)

6d. Cyl. 6 dot
    10/1 BRI thicker than normal and retouch under left corner of flag (Th. G3)
    11/1 IRE thicker than normal
    16/1 IR thicker than normal
    20/3 Dent in bottom frame below Queen (Th. H10–11)

1s.3d. Cyl. 3 no dot
    12/3 Retouched background above RE of EMPIRE (Th. G5)

1s.3d. Cyl. 3 dot
    16–19/5 Vertical scratch of varying length in left-hand margin, petering out in rows 18/19

Sheet Details

Sheet size: 120 (6 × 20). Double pane reel-fed

Sheet markings:
    Cylinder numbers: Opposite R. 18/1
    Guide holes: Boxed opposite rows 14/15, at left (no dot) or right (dot)
    Marginal arrows:
      "V" shaped, hand engraved at top and bottom of sheet
      "W" shaped, photo-etched at both sides
      In the early printings of the 6d. the arrow was omitted in the right margin on the no dot pane, and in the left margin on the dot pane. Later they were inserted by hand engraving and appear quite rough
    Marginal rule: At bottom of sheet

Imprimaturs from the National Postal Museum Archives

Nos. W9/11 imperforate, watermark Type W.23
Watermark upright (*set of 3*) £3000

Quantities Sold   3d. 320,400,000; 6d. 28,595,880; 1s.3d. 9,870,000

W.24

CROWNS WATERMARK

The Multiple Crowns watermark, Type **W.24**, was used for all the following special issues up to the 1967 Wild Flowers issue.

W12. Postboy of 1660   **W13.** Posthorn of 1660
(Des. Reynolds Stone)   (Des. Faith Jaques)

1960 (JULY 7).   TERCENTENARY OF ESTABLISHMENT OF "GENERAL LETTER OFFICE"

Charles II Act of 1660 establishing the G.P.O. "legally settled" the Post Office and was the first of a long series of laws for the regulation of postal matters.

The watermark is sideways on the 1s.3d.

				Mint	Used
W12 (=S.G.619) **W12**	3d.	deep lilac		50	50
	a.	Broken mane (Cyl. 1 No dot, R. 17/2)		5·50	
	b.	Face scratch (Cyl. 1 Dot, R. 17/3)		4·25	
W13 (=S.G.620) **W13**	1s.3d.	green		3·75	4·25

First Day Cover (W12/13) .... 55·00

Part of the printing of the 3d. was on chalk-surfaced paper.

W12*a*

W12*b*
Scratch extends from eye to hair

Cylinder Numbers (Blocks of Six)

	Cyl. No.	Perforation Type A (E/I)	
		No dot	Dot
3d.	1	4·50	4·50

		Perf. Type B (P/I)	Perf. Type C (P/E)
1s.3d.	1	25·00	25·00

For Types B and C the 1s.3d is with sheet orientated showing head to right.

Minor Constant Flaws

3d. Cyl. 1 no dot
    1/2 White dot in bottom of large C (Th. B1)
  10/5 White notch in bottom frame below r of Letter (Th. H7)
  13/1 r of Letter weak (Th. G7)
  15/6 White patch on left foreleg of horse (Th. E5)

3d. Cyl. 1 dot
  11/6 White dot in hair near top of ear (Th. D12)
  20/5 White nick in back of boy (Th. D4)

1s.3d. Cyl. 1 no dot
  1/18 White bulge inside 0 of 1960 (Th. E7)
  2/20 White bulge on stem of acorn under horn (Th. L3)
  5/19 White spot in centre of leaf on right of portrait (Th. G6)
  6/5 White dot at junction of two acorns under Queen's shoulder (Th. G5)

Sheet Details

Sheet sizes:
    3d. 120 (6 × 20). Double pane reel-fed; 1s.3d. 120 (20 × 6). Single pane reel-fed
Sheet markings:
    Cylinder numbers: 3d. opposite R. 18/1; 1s.3d. opposite R. 4/1
    Guide holes:
    3d. opposite rows 14/15, at left (no dot) or right (dot)
    1s.3d. Six. Above and below vertical rows 1, 7/8 and boxed above and below 14/15
Marginal arrows (hand engraved):
    3d. "V" shaped at top and bottom of sheet; "W" shaped on both sides
    1s.3d. "V" shaped on both sides: "W" shaped at top and bottom of sheet.
Marginal rule: 3d. at bottom of sheet and 1s.3d. at right-hand side

Imprimaturs from the National Postal Museum Archives

Nos. W12/13 imperforate, watermark Type W.24
Watermark upright (3d.) or sideways (1s.3d.) (*set of 2*) £2000

Quantities Sold   3d. 143,390,520; 1s.3d. 6,090,840

Withdrawn   31.12.60

CHALKY PAPER

All the following special issues are on chalk-surfaced paper, unless otherwise stated.

W14. Conference Emblem
(Des. Reynolds Stone, emblem by P. Rahikainen)

Miniature Sheets

On the occasion of the EUROSTAMP—1962 London Stamp Exhibition, organised with the help of the Council of Europe, a miniature sheet, size 114 × 124 mm., was produced comprising three each of Nos.

W14/15 *se-tenant* in a block of six (2 × 3) printed in grey-blue, imperforate and surrounded by a brown frame and inscriptions in black on white unwatermarked gummed paper. The stamps were printed by Harrison & Sons in photogravure and the rest of the sheet was printed by Wm. Clowes & Sons by letterpress. The sheet had no franking value.

A similar sheet exists, size 110 × 125 mm., but with the stamps printed in black and surrounded by a green frame and inscription giving details of the issue in red. The stamps were printed in photogravure and the rest of the sheet by letterpress by Harrison & Sons. The sheet had no franking value.

1960 (SEPTEMBER 19).   FIRST ANNIVERSARY OF EUROPEAN POSTAL AND TELE-COMMUNICATIONS CONFERENCE
Celebrating the first Anniversary of the Conference of European Postal and Telecommunications Administrations.

				Mint	Used
W14 (= S.G.621) **W14**	6d.	bronze-green and purple	....	1·50	50
	a.	Broken diadem (R. 1/2)	....	8·00	
	b.	Blurred E (R. 13/5)	....	5·50	
W15 (=S.G.622) **W14**	1s.6d.	brown and blue	....	8·50	5·00
	a.	Broken diadem (R. 1/2)	....	20·00	
	b.	Major retouch (R. 9/2)	....	20·00	
	c.	Blurred E (R. 13/5)	....	16·00	

> First Day Cover (W14/15) .... 55·00

Printing Screen. Nos. W14/15 were the last photogravure commemoratives from Harrisons to utilise the 200-line screen. On the 1s.6d. a 200-line screen was used for the portrait and the new 250-line version for the background.

W14/15*a*	W14*b*, W15*c*	W15*b*

Cylinder Numbers (Blocks of Four)

	Cyl. Nos. (No dot)	Perf. Type B (E/P)	Perf. Type C (I/P)
6d.	1 (purple)–1A (green)	7·50	7·50
1s.6d.	2 (blue)–1A (brown)	40·00	40·00

The same cylinder 1A was used for both values.

Minor Constant Flaws

6d. Cyls. 1–1A no dot
  1/4 Pale purple spots in bottom of oval and below bottom frame (Th. G9–10 and H10)
  6/2 Two short lines in scroll above T of TELECOMMUNICATIONS (Th. E2)
  9/3 Small coloured line in scroll above E of EUROPEAN (Th. B1)
  12/2 Dot in M of ADMINISTRATION
  19/1 Vertical seratch left of scroll containing EUROPEAN (Th. B–D1)
  20/5 Two scratches in scroll left of C of CONFERENCE (Th. A1–2)

1s.6d. Cyls. 2–1A no dot
  10/4 Retouch to spine of P of EUROPA
  12/2 Dot in M of ADMINISTRATION
  17/4 Dotted retouch above CO (Th. F4)
  18/5 Retouch in background above first M of TELECOMMUNICATIONS

Sheet Details

Sheet size: 120 (6 × 20). Single pane reel-fed
Sheet markings:
    Cylinder numbers: Bottom margin below R. 20/5
    Guide holes: Opposite rows 1 and 7/8, at both sides and boxed opposite rows 14/15, at both sides
    Marginal arrows (hand engraved):
        "V" shaped at top and bottom and "W" shaped at both sides
    Marginal rule: At bottom of sheet
    Colour register marks: Opposite rows 2 and 19 at both sides

Imprimaturs from the National Postal Museum Archives

Nos. W14/15 imperforate, watermark Type W.24
Watermark upright (*set of 2*) £2000

Quantities Printed   6d. 16,990,320; 1s.6d. 7,682,520

Withdrawn   31.12.60, but placed on sale again during "Stampex" exhibition in March 1961

W15. Thrift Plant   **W16.** "Growth of Savings"   **W17.** Thrift Plant

(Des. Peter Gauld)   (Des. Michael Goaman)   (Des. Michael Goaman)

1961 (AUGUST 28).   POST OFFICE SAVINGS BANK CENTENARY

    To mark the centenary of the establishment of the P.O. Savings Bank.

The watermark is sideways on the 2½d.

A. "TIMSON" Machine

    2½d.   Cyls. 1E–1F no dot. Deeply shaded portrait (dull black)
    3d.   Cyls. 3D–3E no dot. Sharp portrait with good contrast and bright highlights

			Mint	Used
W16 (=S.G.623A) **W15** 2½d.	dull black and red		25	25
	a.	Dull black (Queen's Head) omitted	£16000*	
	b.	Forehead retouch (R. 4/19)	4·00	
W17 (=S.G.624A) **W16** 3d.	orange-brown and violet		20	20
	a.	Orange-brown omitted	£170	
	b.	Perf. through right sheet margin	28·00	30·00
	ba.	Do. and orange-brown omitted	£450	
	c.	Extension hole in top or bottom sheet margin	6·00	
	d.	Nick in "S" (R. 9/3)	15·00	
	e.	Nick retouched	5·50	
W18 (=S.G.625A) **W17** 1s.6d.	red and blue		2·50	2·25
	a.	Phantom oval in light blue (R. 19/3)	16·00	

> First Day Cover (W16/18) . . . . 65·00

B. "THRISSELL" Machine

2½d. Cyls. 1D–1B no dot or dot. Lighter portrait (grey-black)
3d. Cyls. 3C–3B no dot or dot. Dull portrait, lacking in contrast

		Mint	Used
W19 (=S.G.623B) **W15** 2½d. grey-black and red		2·25	2·25

W20 (=S.G.624B) **W16**	3d.	orange-brown and violet	40	40
	a.	Orange-brown omitted	£850	
	b.	Notch in flower (No dot, R. 7/1)	4·25	
	c.	Notch in leaf (No dot, R. 14/4)	4·25	

A very small quantity of all values was pre-released at the Chorley, Lancs., P.O. on 21 August, 1961.
*No. W16a dull black omitted. The price is for certificated examples without the grey ghosting present on same stamps.

W16*b*

W17*d*
Nick in S

W17*e*
Nick filled in but centre
of S is narrower

W18*a*

W20*b*

W20*c*

Cylinder Numbers (Blocks of Four)

A. "Timson" printings. Single pane cylinders only (no dot). Nos. W16/18

Cyl. Nos.		Perforation Types		
		B	C	F(L)
2½d.	1E (black)–1F (red)*	2·50 (P/I)	2·50 (P/E)	†
3d.	3D (violet)–3E (brown)	1·50 (E/P)	1·50 (I/P)	70·00 (P/E)
1s.6d.	2E (blue)–2C (red)	14·00 (E/P)	14·00 (I/P)	†

*The black number is superimposed over the red.

B. "Thrissell" printings. Double pane cylinders. Nos. W19/20

Cyl. Nos.		Perforation No dot	Type A Dot
2½d.	1D (black)–1B (red)†	10·00 (I/E)	10·00 (I/E)
3d.	3C (violet)–3B (brown)‡	10·00 (E/1)	2·50 (E/I)

†In the 2½d. dot pane the dot was omitted in error after 1B.
‡In the 3d. no dot pane "3E" was wrongly inserted and the "C" was engraved over the "E".

Two blocks of four are needed to show both cylinders in the 3d. no dot "Thrissell" printing as the numbers are below R. 20/2 and R. 20/5 on the bottom margin.

For Types B and C the 2½d. is with sheet orientated showing head to right.

Minor Constant Flaws

2½d. Cyls. 1E–1F no dot
1/13 Two white dots on right curve below last S of SAVINGS
1/16 Two black dots right of Queen's left eye (Th. D4)
1/17 State I. Dark red patch left of top thrift flower (Th. H3)
     State II. Later printings show whitish patch

2/3   White horizontal line from Queen's hair to OF of OFFICE (Th. C3)
5/3   White spot on top of right arm of V of SAVINGS

3d. Cyls. 3D–3E no dot
   8/1   Diagonal retouch across Queen's cheek from right of her left eye to nose (Th. D9–10)
   11/5   Brown spot on squirrel's neck (Th. D5)
   17/1   Retouch on Queen's chin (Th. E9)
   17/2   Retouch on neck (Th. E10)
   19/2   Retouch above necklace (Th. E–F10)
   20/1   Vertical violet line on branch in bottom right corner (Th. F–G13)

3d. Cyls. 3C–3B no dot
   1/4   Additional serif at top of K of BANK
   3/3   Notch in upper right leaf on lowest right-hand branch of tree (Th. E7)
   4/2   Retouch on neck below earring (Th. E10)
   4/6   Dot in B of BANK
   7/3   Retouch above necklace (Th. E10)

Sheet Details

	Timson	Thrissell
Sheet sizes:		
2½d. 120 (20 × 6)	Single pane reel-fed	Double pane reel-fed
3d. 120 (6 × 20)	Single pane reel-fed	Double pane reel-fed
1s.6d. 120 (6 × 20)	Single pane reel-fed	
Sheet markings:		
Cylinder numbers:		
2½d.	Bottom margin below R. 6/19	Bottom margin below R. 6/19
3d.	Bottom margin below R. 20/5	Bottom margin below R. 20/2
1s.6d.	As 3d.	and R. 20/5
Guide holes:		
2½d.	Above and below vertical rows 1, 7/8 and (boxed) 14/15	Below vertical rows 14/15 (no dot) or above (dot), boxed
3d.	Opposite rows 1, 7/8 and (boxed) 14/15, both sides	Opposite rows 14/15, at left (no dot) or right (dot), boxed
1s.6d.	As 3d.	
Marginal arrows (hand engraved):		
2½d.	"V" shaped on both sides; "W" shaped at top and bottom	As Timson
3d.	"V" shaped, all round	"V" shaped, at top and bottom; "W" shaped at both sides
1s.6d.	"V" shaped, at top and bottom; "W" shaped, at both sides	
Marginal rule:		
2½d.	At right-hand side	As Timson
3d.	At bottom	As Timson
1s.6d.	At bottom	
Colour register marks:		
2½d.	Above and below vertical rows 2/3 and 17/18	Below vertical rows 2/3 and 17/18 (no dot) or above (dot)
3d.	Opposite rows 3/4 and 17/18 at both sides	Opposite rows 3/4 and 17/18 at left (no dot) or right (dot)
1s.6d.	Opposite rows 2/3 and 18/19 at left (no dot) or right (dot)	
Colour designations (usually trimmed off):		
2½d.	None	
3d.	"BROWN" opposite row 11 and "BLUE" opposite row 12, right margin, dot pane	
1s.6d.	"RED" opposite row 15 and "BLUE" opposite row 16, right margin	

In the case of marginal copies the differences in sheet markings, in conjunction with the different types of perforators used, provide helpful clues for identifying the printing machine used.

Autotron markings were engraved on the Thrissell cylinders during the printing run.

Imprimaturs from the National Postal Museum Archives

Nos. W16/18 imperforate, watermark Type W.24

Watermark upright (3d., 1s.6d.) or sideways (2½d.) *(set of* 3) £3000

Quantities Sold   2½d. 24,720,000; 3d. 114,360,000; 1s.6d. 7,560,000

W18. C.E.P.T. Emblem   **W19.** Doves and Emblem

W20. Doves and Emblem

(All values des. Michael Goaman, doves by T. Kurpeschoek)

1961 (SEPTEMBER 18). EUROPEAN POSTAL AND TELECOMMUNICATIONS (C.E.P.T.) CONFERENCE

Representatives of nineteen countries met at Torquay on 11 September for the Second Anniversary Conference of the European Postal and Telecommunications Administrations.

These were the first stamps of Great Britain to be printed in three colours

				Mint	Used
W21 (=S.G.626) **W18**	2d.		orange, pink and brown	15	20
	a.		Orange omitted	£12000	
	b.		White ear (Dot, R. 11/2)	3·50	
W22 (=S.G.627) **W19**	4d.		buff, mauve and ultramarine	15	25
W23 (=S.G.628) **W20**	10d.		turquoise, pale green and Prussian blue	15	80
	a.		Pale green omitted	£9000	
	b.		Turquoise omitted	£2750	

> First Day Cover (W21/3) . . . . 6·00

W21*b*

Cylinder Numbers (Blocks of Four)

	Cyl. Nos.	Perforation Type A (E/I)	
		No dot	Dot
2d.	1A (brown)–1B (orange)–1C (pink)	1·50	1·50
4d.	2E (ultramarine)–2B (buff)–2C (mauve)	1·50	1·50
10d.	3G (Prussian blue)–3D (green)–3A (turquoise)	2·50	2·50

The panes were transposed, the dot being on the left and the no dot on the right.

Minor Constant Flaws

2d. Cyls. 1A–1B–1C no dot
   6/4 Pale spot on neck below necklace (Th. F10)
  17/4 Dot in lower right pink horn (Th. F12)
  18/1 Diagonal dark brown patch across Queen's cheek. Later retouched (Th. E10)

2d. Cyls. 1A–1B–1C dot
   6/4 Small white dot to left of P
  18/6 Hairline from right-hand frame to sheet margin (Th. E13–14)

4d. Cyls. 2E–2B–2C dot
   5/3 Flaw at top right of E
  12/6 Dark patch above diadem (Th. A8)
  15/3 Flaw down Queen's forehead and nose (Th. C–D6)
  17/6 Pale patch on cheek (Th. D7)

10d. Cyls. 3G–3D–3A no dot
   4/6 White patch above Queen's right eye (Th. C10)
   6/1 Pale patch to right of Queen's neck (Th. E12–13, F12–13)
  10/3 White patch on Queen's forehead (Th. C10). Started during the run gradually becoming more
       prominent
  15/5 Small white patch at top centre of Queen's forehead (Th. C10)

10d. Cyls. 3G–3D–3A dot
   4/3 Break in loop of posthorn around P (Th. C7)
   4/6 Notch in frame at top right (Th. A13)
  14/2 Dark patch to right of lower right posthorn (Th. C8)

Sheet Details

Sheet size: 120 (6 × 20). Double pane reel-fed
Sheet markings:
   Cylinder numbers: Bottom margin below R. 20/5
   Guide holes: Opposite rows 14/15, at left (dot) or right (no dot), boxed
   Marginal arrow (hand engraved):
     "V" shaped at top and bottom; "W" shaped at both sides
   Marginal rule: At bottom of sheet
   Colour register marks:
   2d. Opposite rows 2/3 and 17/18 at left (dot) or right (no dot)
   4d. Opposite rows 2/3 and 18/19 at left (dot) or right (no dot)
   10d. None
   Autotron marks (solid):
   2d. Respectively brown, pink and orange opposite rows 18/20, at left (dot) or right (no dot)
   4d. Respectively ultramarine and mauve opposite rows 18/19, at left (dot) or right (no dot)
   10d. Respectively Prussian blue, green and turquoise opposite rows 18/20, at left (dot) or right
     (no dot)
   Colour designations:
   2d. "BROWN" in right margin reading upwards opposite rows 14/13 (no dot)
   4d. "YELLOW", "MAUVE", "BLUE" respectively in right margin opposite rows 11/12, 12/13 and
     13 (no dot)
   10d. None

Imprimaturs from the National Postal Museum Archives

Nos. W21/23 imperforate, watermark Type W.24
Watermark upright (*set of 3*) £3000

Quantities Sold   2d. 47,530,920; 4d. 7,614,480; 10d. 5,427,780

W21. Hammer Beam Roof,
Westminster Hall

W22. Palace of Westminster

(Des. Faith Jaques)

1961 (SEPTEMBER 25).   SEVENTH COMMONWEALTH PARLIAMENTARY CONFERENCE

The "Empire Parliamentary Association" was formed at the Coronation of King George V and in 1948 its name was changed to its present form.

The watermark is sideways on the 1s.3d.

				Mint	Used
W24 (=S.G.629) **W21**	6d.	purple and gold		25	25
	a.	Gold omitted		£800	
W25 (=S.G.630) **W22**	1s.3d.	green and blue		2·50	2·75
	a.	Blue (Queen's head) omitted		£12000	
	b.	Green omitted		—	

> First Day Cover (W24/5) . . . .   30·00

Cylinder Numbers (Blocks of Four)

	Cyl. Nos. (No dot)	Perforation Types	
		Type B	Type C
6d.	1B (gold)–1D (purple)	2·00 (E/P)	2·00 (I/P)
1s.3d.	2A (green)–2B (blue)	15·00 (P/I)	15·00 (P/E)

For Types B and C the 1s.3d. is with sheet orientated showing head to right.

Minor Constant Flaws

6d. Cyls. 1B–1D no dot
  3/4 Dot in middle bar of second E in CONFERENCE
  5/5 Enlarged white patch in Queen's hair (Th. C7)
  6/3 Two small retouches in neck above necklace (Th. F7–8)
  10/3 Patch of retouching below crossed maces (Th. G5–6)

1s.3d. Cyls. 2A–2B no dot
  5/4 White patch on Queen's forehead (Th. D4)
  6/2 Small white vertical line on Queen's forehead (Th. C–D4)

Sheet Details

Sheet sizes: 6d. 120 (6 × 20); 1s.3d. 120 (20 × 6). Single pane reel-fed
Sheet markings:
  Cylinder numbers: Bottom margin below R. 20/5 (6d.) or 6/19 (1s.3d.)
  Guide holes:
    6d. opposite rows 1 and 7/8, at both sides and boxed opposite rows 14/15, at both sides
    1s.3d. above and below vertical rows 1 and 7/8 and boxed above and below vertical rows 14/15
  Marginal arrows (hand engraved):
    6d. "V" shaped at top and bottom and "W" shaped at both sides
    1s.3d. "V" shaped at both sides and "W" shaped at top and bottom
  Marginal rule: 6d. at bottom of sheet; 1s.3d. at right side

Colour register marks:
  6d. Opposite both sides of rows 2/3 and 18/19
  1s.3d. Above and below vertical rows 2/3 and 18/19

Imprimaturs from the National Postal Museum Archives

Nos. W24/25 imperforate, watermark Type W.24

Watermark upright (6d.) or sideways (1s.3d.) (*set of 2*) £2000

Quantities Sold   6d. 16,680,000; 1s.3d. 5,760,000

W23. "Units of Productivity"

W24. "National Productivity"

W25. "Unified Productivity"

(Des. David Gentleman)

The National Productivity Year issue was the first commemorative series to appear with phosphor bands and presents a number of other interesting facets:

The watermark on the 2½d. and 3d. is inverted for the reason explained in the General Notes to this section.

There were several printings on the low values which are characterised by their distinct shades and confirmed by different states of some of the flaws and varieties. It is believed that the second printing of the 2½d. comes from sheets numbered between 439,000 and 450,000. Only the third printing was used for the phosphor stamps. There was considerable variation in the carmine-red during the printing and carmine-rose shades are quite common.

2½d. During the first printing both green cylinders were seriously damaged, hence the major repairs in the later printings.

3d. There were several printings of this value which fall into two shade groups. The violet cylinder 2A provided a number of minor flaws and was quickly replaced. It is believed that stamps from this cylinder were supplied only to Canterbury and Chelmsford.

1962 (NOVEMBER 14). NATIONAL PRODUCTIVITY YEAR

The stamps emphasised the need for greater productivity as an essential element in the continuing prosperity of Great Britain.

The watermark is inverted on the 2½d. and 3d.

A. Ordinary

					Mint	Used
W26 (=S.G.631) **W23**	2½d.	(1)	Myrtle-green and carmine-red		20	20
		(2)	Deep green and bright carmine-red		25	15
		(3)	Blackish olive and carmine-red		25	15
	a.		Emblem and arrows retouch (No dot, R. 3/3) (2)		4·00	
	b.		Ditto (3)		4·00	
	c.		Arrow head retouch (No dot, R. 4/4) (2)		3·00	
	d.		Ditto (3)		3·00	
	e.		Retouches, arrows 2 and 6 (No dot, R. 4/5) (2)		3·00	
	f.		Ditto (3)		3·00	
	g.		White nose (Dot, R. 2/6) (1)		3·00	

h.		Neck retouch (Dot, R. 15/4) (1)	4·00			
i.		Ditto (2)	4·00			
j.		Ditto (3)	4·00			
k.		Smudged red centre cube (Dot R. 18/3) (2)	3·50			
l.		Ditto (3)	3·50			
m.		Arrow head retouch (Dot, R. 19/6) (2)	4·00			
n.		Ditto (3)	4·00			

W27 (=S.G.632) **W24**	3d.	(1)	Light blue and violet	25	25
		(2)	Light blue and deep bluish purple	30	15
	a.		Light blue (Queen's head) omitted	£1200	
	b.		Lake in Scotland (Cyls. 2A–2B Dot, R. 1/3 . .	9·00	
	c.		"Kent" omitted (Cyls. 2C–2B No dot, R. 18/2)	7·00	
	d.		Lake in Yorkshire (Cyls. 2C–2B Dot, R. 19/1)	6·00	
	e.		Forehead line (Cyls. 2D–2B No dot, R. 17/6) .	7·50	
	f.		Ditto, removed	5·00	
	g.		Ditto, retouched	4·50	

W28 (=S.G.633) **W25**	1s.3d.	carmine, light blue and deep green	1·50	2·00
	a.	Light blue (Queen's head) omitted	£6500	

> First Day Cover (W26/8) . . . .   48·00

B. Phosphor
(2½d. has one band at left; others have three bands, all applied flexo.)

WP26 (=S.G.631P) **W23**	2½d.	blackish olive and carmine-red	60	50
	a.	Emblem and arrows retouch (No dot, R. 3/3) . . .	5·00	
	b.	Arrows head retouch (No dot, R. 4/4)	3·75	
	c.	Retouches, arrows 2 and 6 (No dot, R. 4/5)	3·75	
	d.	Neck retouch (Dot, R. 15/4)	3·75	
	e.	Smudged red centre cube (Dot, R. 18/3)	4·50	
	f.	Arrow head retouch (Dot, R. 19/6)	5·00	

WP27 (=S.G.632P) **W24**	3d.	light blue and violet	1·50	80
	a.	Left-hand band omitted		
	b.	Narrow band at left or right (stamp with vert. margin)	3·00	
	c.	Forehead line (Cyls. 2D-2B, No dot, R. 17/6) . . .	7·50	
	d.	Forehead line removed	5·50	

WP28 (=S.G.633P) **W25**	1s.3d.	carmine, light blue and deep green	35·00	22·00
	a.	Narrow band at left or right (stamp with vert. margin)	40·00	

> First Day Cover (WP26/8) £150

About 60 2½d., 350 3d. and 20 1s.3d. were pre-released at a Lewisham post office, London on 16 and 17 October, 1962.

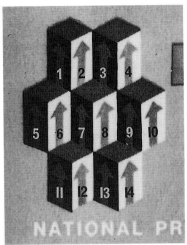

2½d. Arrows numbered for easy identification of varieties and flaws

W26*a/b*, WP26*a*

N and arrow head of emblem strongly shaded with diagonal cuts and dashes, also arrows 4, 10 and 14

W26*e/f*, WP26*c*

In W26*c/d*, WP26*b* the arrow head alone is retouched with diagonal lines and in W26*m/n*, WP26*f* with irregular dots

Less marked retouches occur in the same area on dot cyl., R. 19/2 and 19/4

W26*g*

W26*h/j*, WP26*d*

W26*k/l*, WP26*e*
This may not be fully constant

229

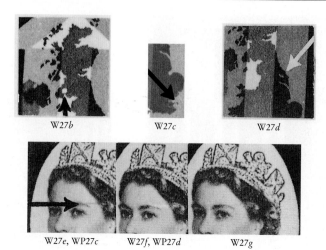

W27b   W27c   W27d

W27e, WP27c   W27f, WP27d   W27g

The original variety was a horizontal line from Queen's left eye to hair which was later removed, leaving a white gap and this was finally partly filled in by retouching

Cylinder Numbers (Blocks of Four)

(a) Ordinary

		Cyl. Nos.	Perforation No dot	Type A (E/I) Dot
2½d.	1D (red)–1B (green) (shade 1)		1·75	1·75
	1D–1B (shade 2)		2·50	5·50*
	1D–1B–(shade 3)		2·50	5·50*
3d.	2A (violet)–2B (blue)		30·00	30·00
	2C–2B		2·50	2·50
	2D–2B		3·25	3·25
1s.3d.	3C (carmine)–3B (blue)–3E (green)		8·00	†

			No dot Type B (E/P)	Type C (I/P)
1s.3d.	3C (carmine)–3B (blue)–3E (green)		18·00	18·00

(b) Phosphor

			Perforation No dot	Type A (E/I) Dot
2½d.	1D (red)–1B (green) (shade 3)		4·25	8·00*
3d.	2D (violet)–2B (blue)		4·25	4·25
1s.3d.	3C (carmine)–3B (blue)–3E (green)		£150	†

Minor Constant Flaws

2½d. Cyls. 1D–1B no dot
 1/2 Two small green dots right of arrow 2 (Th. B–C4) all shades, OP
 3/2 Scratch through top of bottom right cube (Th. F–E4) all shades, OP
 3/4 Minor retouches to face around mouth (Th. D–E10) shades 2/3, OP
 5/1 White scratch below Queen's nose and through mouth (Th. D–E10) all shades, OP
 17/5 Small retouch to cheek to right of mouth (Th. D10–11) all shades, OP

3d. Cyls. 2C–2B no dot
 1/4 Retouch in Scotland (Th. C3), O
 6/5 Dark patch above R of PRODUCTIVITY (Th. G6), O
 13/5 Line of retouching above blue sea of Ireland (Th. C2), O

3d. Cyls. 2C–2B dot
 7/1 Purple line across Solway Firth (Th. D3), O
 15/6 Row of dots from Queen's left eye to hair (Th. C11), O

3d. Cyls. 2D–2B no dot
13/5 Lines of retouching above blue sea of Ireland (Th. C2), OP

3d. Cyls. 2D–2B dot
1/3 Retouch in Yorkshire (Th. D4), OP

1s.3d. Cyls. 3C–3B–3E no dot
3/4 White flaw at back of Queen's hair (Th. D12), OP
6/2 Retouch on tail of large blue arrow (Th. D2), OP
13/4 White flaw left of earring (Th. E11), OP

Sheet Details

Sheet size: 120 (6 × 20)
2½d. and 3d. Double pane reel-fed on a Timson machine
1s.3d. Single pane reel-fed on a new Thrissell machine capable of using five colours
Sheet markings:
Cylinder numbers: Bottom row below R. 20/5
Guide holes:
2½d. and 3d. Opposite rows 14/15 (boxed), at left (no dot) or right (dot)
1s.3d. Opposite rows 1 and 7/8, at both sides and boxed opposite rows 14/15, at both sides
Marginal arrows (photo-etched): "W" shaped at top, bottom and sides
Marginal rule: At bottom of sheet
Colour register marks:
2½d. and 3d. Opposite rows 2/3 and 18/19, at left (no dot) or right (dot)
1s.3d. Opposite rows 2/3 and 18/19, at both sides
Autotron marks (stippled):
2½d. and 3d. Bottom margin in various positions
1s.3d. Respectively red, green, blue, green, red below vertical rows 4/6
Colour designations (usually trimmed off):
2½d. "G GREY" (not green) opposite rows 8/9 and "G RED" opposite row 13, right margin on the dot cylinder
3d. "G BLUE" opposite rows 8/9 and "G MAUVE" (Cyl. 2C) opposite row 13 or "G PURPLE" (Cyl. 2D) opposite rows 6/7, right margin on the dot cylinder
1s.3d. "G BLUE" opposite row 9 and "G GREEN" opposite rows 12/3, left margin
Traffic lights (boxed):
2½d. Green, red opposite R. 20/6 dot pane
3d. Blue, violet opposite R. 20/6 dot pane
1s.3d. Blue, red, green boxed opposite R. 20/6

Imprimaturs from the National Postal Museum Archives

A. Ordinary

Nos. W26/28 imperforate, watermark Type W.24

Watermark upright (*set of* 3) £3000

B. Phosphor

Nos. WP26/28 imperforate, watermark Type W.24

Watermark upright (*set of* 3) £3000

Quantities Sold

	Ordinary	Phosphor
2½d.	99,240,000	7,320,090
3d.	182,580,000	13,320,000
1s.3d.	8,832,000	1,320,000

Of the 2½d. ordinary it is estimated that about 62 million came from the first printing. 3 million from the second printing and 34 million from the third printing

W26. Campaign Emblem and Family   **W27.** Children of Three Races

(Des. Michael Goaman)

1963 (MARCH 21). FREEDOM FROM HUNGER

The stamps were part of a world-wide co-operative effort to focus attention on the problem of hunger and malnutrition.

The watermark is inverted

A. Ordinary

				Mint	Used
W29 (=S.G.634) **W26**	2½d.		crimson and pink	25	10
		a.	Line through MPA (Cyls. 1D–1H Dot, R. 7/2) ...	5·50	
		b.	Broken R in FREEDOM (Cyls. 1D–1H No dot, R. 16/2)	4·50	
W30 (=S.G.635) **W27**	1s.3d.		bistre-brown and yellow	1·75	1·90

> First Day Cover (WP29/30) .... 32·00

B. Phosphor (applied flexo.)

WP29 (=S.G.634p) **W26**	2½d.		One band	3·00	1·25
		a.	Line through MPA (Cyls. 1D–1H Dot, R. 7/2) ..	7·50	
		b.	Broken R in FREEDOM (Cyls. 1D–1H No dot, R. 16/2)	7·50	
WP30 (=S.G.635p) **W27**	1s.3d.		Three bands	30·00	23·00
		a.	Vert. pair, one stamp with phosphor omitted, the other with short bands		
		b.	Narrow band at left or right (stamp with vert. margin.)	35·00	

> First Day Cover (WP29/30) .... 52·00

The 2½d. value was pre-released at Chipping Norton on 20 March 1963.

W29*a*, WP29*a*
An unsuccessful attempt was
made to touch this out

W29*b*, WP29*b*

Cylinder Numbers (Blocks of Four)

(a) Ordinary

	Cyl. Nos.	Perforation Type A (E/I)	
		No dot	Dot
2½d.	1D (pink)–IG (crimson)	20·00	20·00
	1D–1H	2·50	2·50
1s.3d.	2E (yellow)–2G (brown)	10·00	10·00

(b) Phosphor

2½d.	1D (pink)–1H (crimson)	16·00	16·00
1s.3d.	2E (yellow)–2G (brown)	£150	£150

Only the lower halves of sheets from the 2½d. 1D–1G cylinders were released.

In the 1s.3d. the cylinder numbers are reversed, the dot pane being on the left and the no dot pane on the right of the printer's double pane sheet.

The 1s.3d. exists showing a single extension hole for alternate horizontal rows in the left margin. Cylinder blocks from the right-hand side of the sheets are identical to those from perforator Type A.

Minor Constant Flaws

2½d. Cyls. 1D–1H no dot
    9/6 Dot in upper part of second A of CAMPAIGN, OP
    15/2 Retouch from base of portrait to M of CAMPAIGN (Th. E11 and F12–13), OP

2½d. Cyls. 1D–1H dot
    8/1 and 7/1 Hairline extends from under GN on 8/1 to CAMPAIGN on 7/1, OP
    19/1 Retouch on left cheek and jawbone (Th. D10), OP

1s.3d. Cyls. 2E–2G no dot
    1/2 Small white line in extreme right wheatsheaf (Th. C6), OP

Sheet Details

Sheet size: 120 (6 × 20). Double pane reel-fed
Sheet markings:
    Cylinder numbers: Bottom row below R. 20/5
    Guide holes:
        2½d. Opposite rows 14/15 (boxed), at left (no dot) or right (dot)
        1s.3d. Opposite rows 14/15 (boxed), at left (dot) or right (no dot)
    Marginal arrows (photo-etched): "W" shaped at top, bottom and sides
    Marginal rule: At bottom of sheet
Colour register marks:
    2½d. Opposite rows 2/3 and 18/19, at left (no dot) or right (dot)
    1s.3d. Opposite rows 2/3 and 18/19, at left (dot) or right (no dot)
Autotron marks (stippled):
    2½d. Below vertical rows 2/3, no dot pane
    1s.3d. Below vertical rows 2/3, dot pane
Colour designation:
    1s.3d. "G2" in brown opposite row 7 at right, no dot, on wide cut margins
Traffic lights (boxed):
    2½d. Red, pink opposite R. 20/6, dot pane
    1s.3d. Brown, yellow opposite R. 20/6, no dot pane

Imprimaturs from the National Postal Museum Archives

A. Ordinary

Nos. W29/30 imperforate, watermark Type W. 24

Watermark upright (*set of 2*) £2000

B. Phosphor

Nos. WP29/30 imperforate, watermark Type W. 24

Watermark upright (*set of 2*) £2000

Quantities Sold

	Ordinary	Phosphor
2½d.	97,050,000	2,784,920
1s.3d.	9,009,000	624,960

Withdrawn   1.5.64

W28. "Paris Conference"

(Des. Reynolds Stone)

1963 (MAY 7). PARIS POSTAL CONFERENCE CENTENARY

A postal conference was held in Paris to commemorate the centenary of the first international meeting of postal authorities held in 1863.

The watermark is inverted

A. Ordinary

			Mint	Used
W31 (=S.G.636) **W28**	6d.	green and mauve	30	50
	a.	Green omitted £2700		
	b.	White spot in frame line (No dot, R. 19/3)	5·00	

First Day Cover (W31)	16·00

B. Phosphor (applied flexo.)

WP31 (=S.G.636p) **W28**	6d.	Three bands	6·00	7·00
	a.	Pair, with and without phosphor	60·00	
	b.	Horiz. pair; one stamp without phosphor, the other with two bands	70·00	
	c.	Narrow band at left or right (stamp with vert. margin)	8·00	
	d.	White spot in frame line (No dot, R. 19/3)	12·00	

First Day Cover (WP31)	37·00

W31*b*, WP31*d*

Cylinder Numbers (Blocks of Four)

	Cyl. Nos.	Perforation Type A (E/I)	
		No dot	Dot
6d.	2A (mauve)–1B (green) Ordinary	2·75	2·75
6d.	2A–1B Phosphor	30·00	30·00

The panes were reversed, the dot being on the left and the no dot on the right.

Minor Constant Flaws

6d. Cyls. 2A–1B no dot
- 1/1 Flaw in oval frame at 11 o'clock (Th. B9) and lack of definition in top right rose (Th. B13), OP
- 14/6 First N of CONFERENCE appears white, OP
- 19/5 Dot under R of CENTENARY, OP
- 20/5 White spot on ivy stem below first E of CONFERENCE and coloured dot in right frame near top (Th. A13), OP

6d. Cyls. 2A–1B dot
    14/2 White spot in R of CONFERENCE, OP

Sheet Details

Sheet size: 120 (6 × 20). Double pane reel-fed
Sheet markings:
    Cylinder numbers: Below R. 20/5
    Guide holes: Opposite row 15 (boxed), at left (dot) or right (no dot)
    Marginal arrows (photo-etched): "W" shaped at top, bottom and sides
    Marginal rule: At bottom of sheet
    Colour register marks: Opposite rows 2/3 and 18/19, at left (dot) or right (no dot)
    Autotron marks (stippled): Bottom margin, dot pane
    Traffic lights (boxed): Green, mauve opposite R. 20/6, no dot pane

Imprimaturs from the National Postal Museum Archives

A. Ordinary

No. W31 imperforate, watermark Type W.24

Watermark upright £1000

B. Phosphor

No. WP31 imperforate, watermark Type W.24

Watermark upright £1000

Quantities Sold   Ordinary 18,536,400; phosphor 1,430,800

Withdrawn   1.6.64

W29. Posy of Flowers

(Des. Stanley Scott)

W30. Woodland Life

(Des. Michael Goaman)

1963 (MAY 16).   NATIONAL NATURE WEEK

The Council for Nature organised a Nature Week from 18–25 May in order to draw attention to the natural history movement and the importance of wild life conservation.

The 4½d. value was the first stamp of Great Britain to be printed in five colours.

A. Ordinary

				Mint	Used
W32 (=S.G.637) **W29**	3d.	yellow, green, brown and black	15	15
	a.	"Caterpillar" flaw (Dot, R. 3/2)	5·00	
W33 (=S.G.638) **W30**	4½d.	black, blue, yellow, magenta and brown-red	25	35
	a.	Nose retouch (Cyl. 2E, R. 14/4)	5·00	

First Day Cover (W32/3) . . . .   22·00

B. Phosphor

				Mint	Used
WP32 (=S.G.637p) **W29**	3d.	Three bands, applied photo.	55	60
	a.	Narrow band at left or right (stamp with vert. margin)	2·00	
	b.	"Caterpillar" flaw (Dot, R. 3/2)	6·50	

WP33 (=S.G.638p) **W30** 4½d. Three bands, applied flexo. . . . . 2·75   3·00
        a.   Narrow band at left or right (stamp with vert.
          margin) . . . . 4·00
        b.   Nose retouch (Cyl. 2E. No dot, R. 14/4) . . . . . . 8·00
        c.   Error. Two bands . . . . †   —

> First Day Cover (WP32/3) . . . . 40·00

No. W32 is known pre-released on 15 May 1963 at Highbury, London.

W32*a*, WP32*b*
Several states exist,
later retouched

W33*a*, WP33*b*

Cylinder Numbers (Blocks of Six)

(a) Ordinary

	Cyl. Nos.	Perforation Type A (E/I)	
		No dot	Dot
3d.	1A (black)–3B (brown)–1C (green)–1D (yellow)	2·00	2·00
		No dot	
		Rows 12/13	Rows 18/19
4½d.	1A (brown-red)–1B (yellow)–1C (magenta)–1D (blue)–2E (black)	2·75	2·75
	1A–1B–1C–1D–3E	4·00	5·50

(b) Phosphor

		No dot	Dot
3d.	1A (black)–3B (brown)–1C (green)–1D (yellow)	4·75	4·75
		No dot	
		Rows 12/13	Rows 18/19
4½d.	1A (brown-red)–1B (yellow)–1C (magenta)–1D (blue)–2E (black)	22·00	22·00
	1A–1B–1C–1D–3E	25·00	27·00

In the 3d. the panes were reversed, the dot being on the left and the no dot on the right.

In the 4½d. there are two sets of cylinder numbers in the left-hand margin (perf. type E) opposite rows 12/13 and 18/19. In position 18/19 the "1D" is in grey-blue superimposed over an additional "1C" in magenta. Also in position 12/13 the black "2" is superimposed over a black "1". The cylinder numbers are engraved more boldly in position 12/13 and are boxed, the others being without boxes.

Minor Constant Flaws

3d. Cyls 1A–3B–1C–1D no dot
  2/1 Retouch to Queen's left jaw (Th. D–E11), OP
  2/5 Dot between top of A and T of NATURE, OP
  2/6 White line through top of 3 of value, OP

4/4 Green flaw at bottom right foot of I of NATIONAL, OP
5/4 First N of NATIONAL blurred at top left, OP
6/5 Diagonal green line crosses petals of left-hand daisy (Th. B–C3), OP
7/1 Retouch on Queen's left cheek (Th. D11), OP
9/1 Green dot near centre of N of NATURE, OP
9/2 White flaw at top of left-hand buttercup (Th. B2), OP
10/1 Patch of white to left of Queen's right eye (Th. C10), OP
10/4 Green dot at top right of 2, OP
12/6 White patch just above NA of NATIONAL, OP
13/6 Green spot above EK of WEEK, OP
14/1 White spot above 3 of value (Th. E8), OP
16/6 Dark spot to right of Queen's mouth (Th. E11–12), OP
18/3 Retouch above second A of NATIONAL, later retouched, appearing as a whitish blob (Th. F5), OP
18/5 White flaw under top left buttercup, at right (Th. C2), OP
19/3 Brown flaw to bottom right of T of NATURE, later retouched, OP
19/5 Large green blob above second A of NATIONAL, later touched out, OP
20/4 White dot between top of 3 of value and leaf (Th. E7–8), OP

3d. Cyls. 1A–3B–1C–1D dot
2/3 White dot just left of top of 3 of value, OP
6/6 Retouch under jaw extending to bottom of ear (Th. E10–11), OP
8/1 Brown dot under right leg of last A of NATIONAL, OP
8/3 Retouch by L of NATIONAL (Th. G6), OP
9/6 Brown dot under right leg of second N of NATIONAL, OP
14/1 Retouch above first E of WEEK, OP
14/4 Retouch left of 3 of value (Th. F7–8), OP
15/4 White flaw at bottom of oblique stroke in first N of NATIONAL, OP
15/5 Greyish smear over dot of value, OP
16/5 Retouch from mouth to ear (Th. D11), OP
18/4 Green dot above upper lip (Th. D10), OP
19/6 Small white retouch between 63 of 1963 and dark hairline between 3 of value and leaf (Th. F8), OP

4½d. Cyls. 1A–1B–1C–1D–2E no dot and 1A–1B–1C–1D–3E no dot
3/3 Dark spot under fawn (Th. G10), OP
7/1 Yellow patch above fawn's right ear (Th. E11), OP
14/1 Brown spot in second upper leaf from butterfly (Th. B3), OP
19/3 Retouch in background behind woodpecker (Th. E9), OP

Sheet Details

Sheet size: 120 (6 × 20). 3d. double pane reel-fed; 4½d. single pane reel-fed
Sheet markings:
  Cylinder numbers:
    3d. Below row 20/5
    4½d. Opposite rows 18/19 and boxed numbers opposite rows 12/13
  Guide holes:
    3d. Opposite rows 14/15 (boxed), at left (dot) or right (no dot)
    4½d. Opposite rows 14/15 (boxed), at both sides
  Marginal arrows (photo-etched): "W" shaped at top, bottom and sides
  Marginal rule: At bottom of sheet
  Colour register marks:
    3d. Opposite rows 2/3 and 17/19, at left (dot) or right (no dot)
    4½d. Opposite rows 3/4 and 17/18, at left (no dot) or right (dot)
  Autotron marks (stippled):
    3d. Between panes vertically, opposite rows 6/9 (seen either in right or left margin)
    4½d. Below vertical rows 1/3 and 4/6 but omitted from rows 1/3 in the first printing
  Colour designations (usually trimmed off):
    3d. "G BROWN" (rows 4/5), "G GREEN" (rows 6/7), "G YELLOW" (row; 8/9), "G ORANGE" (row 13), left margin dot pane reading downwards
    4½d. "G1 BROWN G2 YELLOW G3 RED G4 BLUE G5 BLACK" in left margin reading
downwards opposite rows 5/9
  Traffic lights (boxed):
    3d. Yellow, black, green, brown opposite R. 20/6, no dot pane
    4½d. Black, blue, magenta, yellow, brown-red opposite rows 19/20 at right

Imprimaturs from the National Postal Museum Archives

A. Ordinary

Nos. WP32/33 imperforate, watermark Type W.24

Watermark upright (*set of* 2) £2000

B. Phosphor

Nos. WP32/33 imperforate, watermark Type W.24

Watermark upright (*set of* 2) £2000

Quantities Sold

	Ordinary	Phosphor
3d.	148,560,000	8,640,000
4½d.	12,480,000	1,140,000

Withdrawn   1.6.64

W31. Rescue at Sea   **W32.** 19th-century Lifeboat

W33. Lifeboatmen

(Des. David Gentleman)

1963 (MAY 31).   NINTH INTERNATIONAL LIFEBOAT CONFERENCE
The International Lifeboat Conferences are held every four years. In 1963 the Conference was held at Edinburgh from 3 to 5 June.

A. Ordinary   Mint   Used
W34 (=S.G.639) **W31**   2½d.   blue, black and red   25   25
                        a.   Missing neckline (No dot, col. 1) . . . .   3·50
                        b.   Shaded diadem (Dot, R. 20/6) . . . .   3·50

W35 (=S.G.640) **W32**   4d.   red, yellow, brown, black and blue   50   50
                        a.   Spot on boom (R. 6/6) . . . .   4·25
                        b.   Spot under I (R. 13/3) . . . .   4·25

W36 (=S.G.641) **W33**   1s.6d.   sepia, yellow and grey-blue . . . .   3·00   3·25

> First Day Cover (W34/6) . . . .   35·00

B. Phosphor (applied flexo.)
WP34 (=S.G.639p) **W31**   2½d.   One band   50   60
                          a.   Missing neckline (No dot, col. 1) . . . .   5·00
                          b.   Shaded diadem (Dot, R. 20/6) . . . .   6·00
                          c.   White flaw in hair (No dot, R. 9/6) . . . .   3·50

WP35 (=S.G.640p) **W32**	4d.	Three bands	50	60

	a.	Narrow band at left or right (stamp with vert. margin)	2·00
	b.	Spot on boom (R. 6/6)	4·50
	c.	Spot under I (R. 13/3)	4·50

WP36 (=S.G.641p) **W33**	1s.6d.	Three bands	48·00	28·00
	a.	Narrow band at left or right (stamp with vert. margin)	50·00

> First Day Cover (WP34/6) . . . . 55·00

In the 1s.6d. the grey-blue is lighter on the phosphor stamps, presumably in order to show the phosphor more clearly.

All values are known pre-released on 30 May.

W34*a*, WP34*a*
Occurs on all stamps in
first vertical row in
varying degrees

W34*b*, WP34*b*
Occurred during the
course of printing

WP34*c*

W35*a*, WP35*b*

W35*b*, WP35*c*

Cylinder Numbers (Blocks of Six)

(a) Ordinary

		Cyl. Nos.	Perforation Type A (E/I)			
			No dot		Dot	
			Row 12	Row 19	Row 12	Row 19
2½d.		3A (red)–3B (black)–1C (blue)	2·00	2·75	2·00	2·75
4d.		1A (blue)–1B (black)–1C (red)–1D (brown)–1E (yellow)	4·50	4·50	†	†
				Row 18		
	1s.6d.	3A (blue)–1B (sepia)–1C (yellow)	21·00	21·00		

(b) Phosphor

			Row 12	Row 19		
2½d.		3A (red)–3B (black)–1C (blue)	4·50	4·50	4·50	4·50
4d.		1A (blue)–1B (black)–1C (red)–1D (brown)–1E (yellow)	4·50	4·50	†	†
				Row 18		
	1s.6d.	3A (blue)–1B (sepia)–1C (yellow)	£275	£275	†	†

In the 2½d. the cylinder numbers in row 12 are shown as A (red)–B (black)–1C (blue) in left margin (perf. type E) of left pane and the same in the right margin of right pane but without dot after C.

In the 1s.6d. the 1C is shown twice opposite row 18.

Minor Constant Flaws

2½d. Cyls. 3A–3B–1C no dot
   7/5 Scratch down Queen's face from hair to chin (Th. C–D11), OP
   8/5 Scratch continues from hair to shoulder (Th. C–D11), OP
   9/1 White scratch on dress above ENC (Th. F12), OP
 11/1 Scratch from hair to ear (Th. C–D12), OP
 14/3 Black dot below lower lip (Th. D10), OP

2½d. Cyls. 3A–3B–1C dot
   3/4 Retouch left of Queen's ear (Th. C11), OP
   9/6 Retouch on Queen's forehead (Th. C10), OP
 19/6 Pale grey patch over back of shoulder, normal in State 1 (Th. F12–13), OP

4d. Cyls. 1A–1B–1C–1D–1E no dot
   1/6 Retouch on Queen's nose (Th. B–C10), OP
   3/5 Vertical line of retouching on Queen's face down to shoulder (Th. C–E11), OP
   4/2 Vertical black line through shoulder to just above EN (Th. E–F12), OP
 13/1 Pale blue streak across top frame line at apex of sail (Th. A5), OP
 13/2 Yellow scratch across main sail from mast to rigging (Th. D6), OP
 18/2 Black dot over Queen's left eye (Th. C10), OP
 20/2 Blue dot on Queen's neck (Th. E11), OP
 20/3 Vertical red line down first N of CONFERENCE, OP

1s.6d. Cyls. 3A–1B–1C no dot
   6/5 Length of retouching on Queen's collar (Th. E11–12), OP
 15/6 Retouch over Queen's right eye (Th. B10), OP

Sheet Details

Sheet size: 120 (6 × 20). 2½d. double pane reel-fed; others single pane reel-fed
Sheet markings:
   Cylinder numbers:
      2½d. Boxed opposite R. 12/1 (no dot pane) or R. 12/6 (dot pane)
       Also opposite R. 19/1 on both panes without box
      4d. Boxed opposite R. 12/1 and without box in left margin opposite rows 17/20
      1s.6d. Boxed opposite rows 11/12, left margin and unboxed opposite R. 18/1
   Guide holes:
      2½d. Opposite rows 14/15 (boxed), at left (no dot) or right (dot)
      4d. and 1s.6d. Opposite rows 14/15 (boxed), at both sides
   Marginal arrows (photo-etched): "W" shaped, at top, bottom and sides
   Marginal rule: At bottom of sheet
   Colour register marks:
      2½d. Opposite rows 3/4 and 18/19. at left (no dot) or right (dot)
      4d. Opposite rows 2/3 and 17/18, at both sides
      1s.6d. Opposite rows 2/4 and 18/19, at both sides
   Autotron marks (stippled):
      2½d. Blue, black, red below vertical rows 4/6 on dot pane
      4d. Yellow. brown, black, red, blue below vertical rows 4/6
      1s.6d. Yellow, sepia, blue below vertical rows 4/6
   Colour designations (usually trimmed off):
      2½d. "G RED G BLACK G BLUE" opposite rows 6, 7 and 9 respectively reading upwards at left
       (no dot) or right (dot)
      4d. "G YELLOW G BROWN G BLACK G RED G BLUE" in right margin reading upwards
       opposite rows 14/10
      1s.6d. "G BLUE G BROWN G YELLOW" in left margin reading downwards opposite rows 6/9
   Traffic lights (boxed):
      2½d. Blue, black, red opposite R. 20/6, dot pane
      4d. Yellow, brown, black, red, blue opposite R. 20/6
      1s.6d. Yellow, sepia, blue opposite R. 20/6

Imprimaturs from the National Postal Museum Archives

A. Ordinary

Nos. W34/36 imperforate, watermark Type W.24

Watermark upright (*set of* 3) £3000

B. Phosphor

Nos. WP34/36 imperforate, watermark Type W.24

Watermark upright (*set of* 3) £3000

Quantities Sold

	Ordinary	Phosphor
2½d.	81,405,000	4,239,000
4d.	7,475,040	840,000
1s.6d.	7,484,780	886,000

Withdrawn   1.6.64

W34. Red Cross

W35. Red Cross

W36. Red Cross

(Des. H. Bartram)

1963 (AUGUST 15).   RED CROSS CENTENARY CONGRESS

The congress which opened in Geneva on 2 September marked the Centenary of the establishment of the Red Cross organisation.

A. Ordinary				**Mint**	**Used**
W37 (=S.G.642) **W34**	3d.	red and deep lilac		25	25
	a.	Red omitted		£6500	
	b.	Repaired cross (Cyls. 2A–2B, No. dot, R. 5/6)		7·00	
W38 (=S.G.643) **W35**	1s.3d.	red, blue and grey		3·00	3·00
W39 (=S.G.644) **W36**	1s.6d.	red, blue and bistre		3·00	3·00
	a.	Retouch in C of Cross (R. 14/4)		10·00	
	b.	Retouch over 1 of 1/6 (R. 16/4)		10·00	

First Day Cover (W37/9) . . . .   40·00

B. Phosphor (applied flexo.)

WP37 (=S.G.642p) **W34**	3d.	Three bands	1·10	1·00
	a.	Red omitted £12000		
	b.	Two bands only		
	c.	Narrow band at left or right (stamp with vert. margin)	2·00	

WP38 (=S.G.643p) **W35**	1s.3d.	Three bands	35·00	27·00
	a.	Narrow band at left or right (stamp with vert. margin)	42·00	

WP39 (=S.G.644p) **W36**	1s.6d.	Three bands	35·00	27·00
	a.	Narrow band at left or right (stamp with vert. margin)	38·00	
	b.	Retouch in C of Cross (R. 14/4)	40·00	
	c.	Retouch over 1 of 1/6 (R. 16/4)	40·00	

> First Day Cover (WP37/9) . . . .   90·00

W37*b*

W39*a*, WP39*b*

W39*b*, WP39*c*

Cylinder Numbers (Blocks of Four)

(a) Ordinary

	Cyl. Nos.	Perforation Types		
		A (E/I) No dot	A (E/I) Dot	E (AE/I) Dot
3d.	2A (lilac)–2B (red)	2·00	2·00	5·00
	3A–2B	2·00	2·00	†
	3A–3B	3·00	3·00	†
1s.3d.	1A (grey)–3B (blue)–1C (red)	18·00	†	†
1s.6d.	1A (blue)–1B (red)–1C (bistre)	18·00	†	†

(b) Phosphor

3d.	3A (lilac)–2B (red)	6·50	6·50	†
	3A–3B	6·50	6·50	†
1s.3d.	1A (grey)–3B (blue)–1C (red)	£160	†	†
1s.6d.	1A (blue)–1B (red)–1C (bistre)	£160	†	†

Perforation Type (AE/I) shows an alternate extension hole in the left margin.

Minor Constant Flaws

3d. Cyl. 3A no dot in combination with red cyls. 2B or 3B no dot
    2/3 Lilac coloured spot above t of Centenary. Retouched with cyl. 3B (Th. F10–11), OP

3d. Cyl. 2B no dot in combination with lilac cyls. 2A or 3A no dot
    4/1 Red retouch in top left centre of cross (Th. D4), OP
    7/3 Pale centre to cross (with cyl. 3A only), OP

3d. Cyl. 3A dot in combination with red cyls. 2B or 3B dot
  4/3 Coloured spur on C of Congress (Th. G9), OP
  15/2 Scratch above 3D. Retouched with cyl. 3B (Th. B8–C9), OP
  17/5 Retouching in and around D of 3D (Th. D9), OP

3d. Cyl. 2B dot in combination with lilac cyls. 2A or 3A dot
  16/1 Red retouches in left arm and top left centre of cross (Th. D3–4), OP
  19/1 Red retouch in lower arm of cross (Th. E4), OP

1s.3d. Cyls. 1A–3B–1C no dot
  11/4 Diagonal scratch from Queen's nose to jaw (Th. D7), OP
  12/1 White spot to left of Queen's earring (Th. D8), OP
  12/5 Dark patch to right of Queen's left eye (Th. C7), OP
  15/3 Line through words Red Cross, OP
  18/4 Large retouch on Queen's neck (Th. E7), OP

1s.6d. Cyls. 1A–1B–1C no dot
  15/3 Large retouch in right arm of cross (Th. C–D8), OP

Sheet Details

Sheet size: 120 (6 × 20). 3d. double pane reel-fed; others single pane reel-fed
Sheet markings:
  Cylinder numbers: Opposite R. 19/1, boxed
  Guide holes:
    3d. Opposite rows 14/15 (boxed), at left (no dot) or right (dot)
    1s.3d. and 1s.6d. Opposite rows 14/15 (boxed), at both sides
  Marginal arrows (photo-etched): "W" shaped, at top, bottom and sides
  Marginal rule: At bottom of sheet
  Colour register marks:
    3d. Opposite rows 2/3 and 18/19, at left (no dot) or right (dot)
    1s.3d. and 1s.6d. Opposite rows 17/19, at both sides
  Autotron marks (stippled):
    3d. Lilac, red below vertical rows 2/3 on no dot panes
    1s.3d. Grey, blue, red below vertical rows 1/3
    1s.6d. Blue, red, bistre below vertical rows 1/3 and 4/6
  Colour designations (usually trimmed off):
    3d. "G RED" in right margin opposite rows 5/6 (Cyls. 3A–3B dot)
    1s.3d. "G1 GREY G2 BLUE G3 YELLOW" in right margin reading downwards opposite rows 9/4
    1s.6d. None
  Traffic lights (boxed):
    3d. Lilac, red opposite R. 19/6
    1s.3d. Grey, blue, red opposite R. 19/6
    1s.6d. Blue, red, bistre opposite R. 19/6

Imprimaturs from the National Postal Museum Archives

A. Ordinary

Nos. W37/39 imperforate, watermark Type W.24

Watermark upright (*set of 3*) £3000

B. Phosphor

Nos. WP37/39 imperforate, watermark Type W.24

Watermark upright (*set of 3*) £3000

Quantities Sold

	Ordinary	Phosphor
3d.	157,277,800	10,349,280
1s.3d.	7,278,120	929,040
1s.6d.	6,995,160	1,038,840

Withdrawn 1.9.64

W37. "Commonwealth Cable"   B
(Des. Peter Gauld)

1963 (DECEMBER 3).   OPENING OF "COMPAC"

The Trans-Pacific Cable (COMPAC) was the first telephone cable to be laid across the Pacific Ocean. It links Canada with Australia and New Zealand by way of Hawaii and Fiji.

A. Ordinary

				Mint	Used
W40 (=S.G.645) **W37**	1s.6d.	blue and black	2·75	2·50
	a.	Black omitted	£4000	
	s.	"Cancelled", Type B, in red	30·00	

First Day Cover (W40)	28·00

B. Phosphor (applied flexo.)

WP40 (=S.G.645p) **W37**	1s.6d.	Three bands	16·00	15·50
	a.	Left band omitted	40·00	
	b.	Narrow band at left or right (stamp with vert. margin)	20·00	

First Day Cover (WP40)	40·00

The stamp handstamped "CANCELLED" was applied to Philatelic Bulletin No. 3 (November 1963) so that it only exists unused, no gum.

No. WP40 has a "blue" phosphor overprint but it is known with bands giving a short greenish after-glow after irradiation to ultra-violet light. It is probable that this was due to contaminated phosphor rather than the use of "green" phosphor.

Cylinder Numbers (Blocks of Four)

	Cyl. Nos.	Perforation Type F (P/E). No dot	
		Ordinary	Phosphor
1s.6d. 1A (blue)–1B (black)		15·00	75·00

Minor Constant Flaws

1s.6d. Cyls. 1A–1B no dot
  17/6 Bulge at top of figure 1 of value (Th. F10), OP
  19/1 Extra white dot on Queen's right eye (Th. C10), OP

Sheet Details

Sheet size: 120 (6 × 20). Single pane reel-fed
Sheet markings:
  Cylinder numbers: Opposite R. 19/1, boxed
  Guide holes: at top above R. 1/2 and at bottom below R. 20/4, cutting marginal arrow
  Marginal arrows (photo-etched): "W" shaped, at top, bottom and sides
  Marginal rule: At bottom of sheet
  Colour register marks: Opposite rows 1/2 and 17/8, at both sides
  Autotron marks (stippled): Below vertical rows 2/3
  Colour designations: "G1 BLUE" (row 9), "G2 BLACK" (row 12), left margin
  Traffic lights: Black, blue (boxed), opposite R. 19/6

Imprimaturs from the National Postal Museum Archives

A. Ordinary

No. W40 imperforate, watermark Type W.24

Watermark upright £1000

B. Phosphor

No. WP40 imperforate, watermark Type W.24

Watermark upright £1000

Quantities Sold   Ordinary 8,015,880; phosphor 824,280

Withdrawn   1.9.64

W38. Puck and Bottom   **W39.** Feste
(*A Midsummer Night's Dream*)   (*Twelfth Night*)

W40. Balcony Scene   **W41.** "Eve of Agincourt"
(*Romeo and Juliet*)   (*Henry V*)

(All the above des. David Gentleman)

W42. Hamlet contemplating
Yorick's Skull (*Hamlet*)

Des. Christopher and Robin Ironside. Recess printed, Bradbury, Wilkinson)

1964 (APRIL 23). SHAKESPEARE FESTIVAL

Issued on the occasion of the 400th Anniversary of the Birth of William Shakespeare. An additional feature of this issue was the introduction of Presentation Packs by the then, General Post Office. The packs include one set of stamps and details of the designs, the designer and the stamp printer. They were issued for this and almost all later commemorative issues.

The 2s.6d. is perf. 11 × 12, comb.

A. Ordinary

					Mint	Used
W41 (=S.G.646) **W38**	3d.	(1)	Yellow-bistre, black and deep violet-blue	. . . .	15	15
		(2)	Bistre-brown, black and deep violet-blue	. . . .	15	15
	a.		Black dots across Puck's head (Dot, R. 7/6)	. . .	6·00	
	b.		"Cancelled", Type B	. . . .	£140	

W42 (=S.G.647) **W39**	6d.	(1)	Yellow, orange, black and yellow-olive	30	30
		(2)	Yellow, orange, black and olive-green	40	30
	a.		Broken "H" (R. 12/3)	6·00	
	b.		Missing floorboards (R. 20/1 and 20/2)	5·50	
	c.		Olive spots by Queen's mouth (R. 9/6)	4·00	
	d.		"Cancelled", Type B		

W43 (=S.G.648) **W40**	1s.3d.	(1)	Cerise, blue-green, black and sepia	18·00	
		(2)	Cerise, turquoise, black and sepia	75	1·00
	a.		Watermark inverted	£600	
	b.		Large pearl (Dot, R. 13/2)	5·00	
	c.		"Cancelled", Type B (Shade (1))		

W44 (=S.G.649) **W41**	1s.6d.	(1)	Violet, turquoise, black and blue	1·00	85
		(2)	Pale violet, turquoise, black and blue	2·75	2·75
	a.		Watermark inverted	—	£1300
	b.		"Cancelled", Type B		

W45 (=S.G.650) **W42**	2s.6d.	(1)	Deep slate-purple	2·75	2·75
		(2)	Blackish brown	5·00	4·00
		(3)	Jet-black	£500	£200
	a.		Watermark inverted	£400	
	b.		"Cancelled", Type B (jet-black shade)	£450	

> First Day Cover (W41/5) . . . .   12·00
> Presentation Pack (W41/5) . . . .   22·00

B. Phosphor (Three bands) (3d. applied photo.; others flexo.)

WP41 (=S.G.646p) **W38**	3d.	(1)	Yellow-bistre, black and deep violet-blue . . .	25	30
		(2)	Bistre-brown, black and deep violet-blue . . .	30	25
	a.		Narrow band at left or right (stamp with vert. margin)	2·00	
	b.		Black dots across Puck's head (Dot, R. 7/6) . .	7·00	

WP42 (=S.G.647p) **W39**	6d.	Yellow, orange, black and yellow-olive	75	1·00
	a.	Narrow band at left or right (stamp with vert. margin)	2·75	
	b.	Broken "H" (R. 12/3)	7·00	
	c.	Missing floorboards (R. 20/1 and 20/2)	6·50	
	d.	Olive spots by Queen's mouth (R. 9/6)	5·00	

WP43 (=S.G.648p) **W40**	1s.3d.	Cerise, turquoise, black and sepia	4·00	6·50
	a.	Watermark inverted	£120	
	b.	Narrow band at left or right (stamp with vert. margin)	6·00	
	c.	Large pearl (Dot, R. 13/2)	9·00	

WP44 (=S.G. 649p) **W41**	1s.6d.	Violet, turquoise, black and blue	8·00	8·00
	a.	Narrow band at left or right (stamp with vert. margin)	10·00	

> First Day Cover (WP41/4) . . . .   17·00

Shades. The listed shades of the 6d. to 2s.6d. result from different printings. The 3d. and 6d. shades are quite distinct, the blue-green shade of the 1s.3d. comes from the scarce first printing from cylinder 1B, and although the pale violet in the 1s.6d. may only be due to under-inking, it came from part of the second printing. There were three printings of the 2s.6d. which produced a number of shades, but they fall into the two groups listed. The rare jet-black shade exists, possibly from proof sheets issued in error. Most examples have a "CANCELLED" overprint No. W45*b*.

The 3d. is known with yellow-bistre missing on the top two-thirds of the figures of Puck and Bottom. This occurred on the top row only of a sheet.

W41*a*, WP41*b*

W42*a*, WP42*b*
Also grey patch on Shakespeare's
right cheek. Both later retouched

W42*c*, WP42*d*

W42*b*, WP42*c*
Other less prominent states of missing
floorboards also occur on R. 19/1, 19/2,
19/6 and 20/6

W43*a*, WP43*c*

Cylinder Numbers (Blocks of Four)

(a) Ordinary

	Cyl. Nos.	Perforation Type A (E/I)	
		No dot	Dot
3d.	1A (violet-blue)–1B (black)–1C (bistre)	1·25	1·25
6d.	1A (olive-green)–1B (orange)–1C (yellow)–1D (black)	6·50*	†

		Perforation Type A(T) (E/P)	
		No dot	Dot
1s.3d.	3A (sepia)–1B (blue-green)–1C (cerise)–1D (black)	90·00	90·00
	3A–2B (turquoise)–1C–1D	4·50	4·50
1s.6d.	1A (blue)–1B (violet)–1C (black)–1D (turquoise)	7·00	7·00

(b) Phosphor

		Perforation Type A (E/I)	
		No dot	Dot
3d.	1A (violet-blue)–1B (black)–1C (bistre)	2·00	2·00
6d.	1A (olive-green)–1B (orange)–1C (yellow)–1D (black)	10·00*	†

		Perforation Type A(T) (E/P)	
		No dot	Dot
1s.3d.	3A (sepia)–2B (turquoise)–1C (cerise)–1D (black)	28·00	25·00
1s.6d.	1A (blue)–1B (violet)–1C (black)–1D (turquoise)	40·00	40·00

The 3d. no dot cylinders exist with a false dot after the 1B but this was later removed. In the dot cylinders of the 1s.6d. the dots appear to the left of 1C and 1D.

Plate Numbers (Blocks of Four)

Perforation Type A (E/I)

| 2s.6d. | Plate 1 . . . . | 15·00 | Plate 1A . . . . | 15·00 |

Minor Constant Flaws

3d. Cyls. 1A–1B–1C no dot
   9/5   White scratch on boards above AL (Th. 9/5), OP
   19/1   White line in floorboard division above S of FESTIVAL (Th. G8), OP
   20/1   White patch on Queen's collar, later retouched (Th. E12), OP

3d. Cyls. 1A–1B–1C dot
   2/5   White patch on floorboards above F (Th. G7), OP
   7/5   Retouches on Queen's left cheek, later partly retouched (Th. D11), OP
   11/5   Retouch below Queen's left eye (Th. C11), OP
   16/2   White spur to bottom arc of 3, OP
   20/1   Dark flaw in stage above VA, later retouched (Th. G9), OP

1s.3d. Cyls. 3A–2B–1C–1D no dot
   18/2   Outline of Shakespeare's nose cut short, later corrected (Th. C3), OP

1s.6d. Cyls. 1A–1B–1C–1D no dot
   1/6   White flaw on stage above EAR (Th. F4-G5), OP
   18/1   Black flaw at base of tent over last A of SHAKESPEARE (Th. F5), OP
   20/2   Vertical scratches on Queen's face (Th. B–D11), OP

1s.6d. Cyls. 1A–1B–1C–1D dot
   13/3   Flaw on stage above EA (Th. G4), OP

Sheet Details

Sheet sizes:
   3d. 120 (6 × 20). Double pane reel-fed
   6d. 120 (6 × 20). Single pane reel-fed
   1s.3d., 1s.6d. 120 (6 × 20). Double panes sheet-fed
   2s.6d. 40 (4 × 10). Double pane sheet-fed
   The 1s.3d. and 1s.6d. were printed by the Linotype and Machinery No. 4 machine, a rotary sheet-fed double pane machine.
Sheet markings:
   Cylinder numbers: Opposite R. 19/1, boxed
   Plate numbers (2s.6d.): Bottom margin below vertical rows 5/6
   Guide holes:
      3d. Opposite rows 14/15 (boxed), at left (no dot) or right (dot)
      6d. Opposite row 13 (boxed), at both sides
      1s.3d. Opposite rows 15/16 (boxes only, no holes), at left (no dot) or right (dot)
      1s.6d. Opposite rows 14/15 (boxes only, no holes), at left (no dot) or right (dot)
      2s.6d. Opposite row 6 (unboxed), at left (Plate 1) or right (Plate 1A)
   False boxes appear in both margins opposite rows 14/15 in the 6d. value and these are deleted by a
      diagonal black line.
   Marginal arrows (photo-etched): "W" shaped, at top, bottom and sides (none on 2s.6d.)
   Marginal rule: At bottom of sheet (except 2s.6d.)
Colour register marks:
   3d. Opposite rows 2 and 17/18, at left (no dot) or right (dot)
   6d. Opposite rows 1/3 and 17/18, at both sides (usually trimmed off)
   Others, none
Autotron marks:
   3d. In central gutter alongside rows 14/16
   6d. Below vertical rows 1/3: black (stippled), olive (solid), orange (stippled), yellow (solid)
   Others, none
Colour designations (usually trimmed):
   3d. "G BLUE" (rows 13/12), "G BLACK" (rows 9/8), "G YELLOW" (rows 5/4) reading upwards,
      right margin dot pane
   Others, none
Traffic lights (boxed): All R. 19/6
   3d. Violet-blue, black, bistre
   6d. Black, yellow, orange, olive
   1s.3d. Black, cerise, turquoise, sepia
   1s.6d. Turquoise, black, violet, blue

Imprimaturs from the National Postal Museum Archives

A. Ordinary

Nos. W41/45 imperforate, watermark Type W.24

Watermark upright (*set of* 5) £5000

B. Phosphor

Nos. WP41/44 imperforate, watermark Type W.24

Watermark upright (*set of* 4) £4000

Quantities Sold

	Ordinary	Phosphor		Ordinary	Phosphor
3d.	133,670,000	10,427,880	1s.6d.	6,910,120	657,120
6d.	19,238,200	1,318,560	2s.6d.	3,664,920	—
1s.3d.	7,067,200	727,800	Pack	108,541	—

Withdrawn   31.3.65 (3d. ordinary sold out earlier)

W43. Flats near Richmond Park ("Urban Development")

W44. Shipbuilding Yards, Belfast ("Industrial Activity")

W45. Beddgelert Forest Park, Snowdonia ("Forestry")

W46. Nuclear Reactor, Dounreay ("Technological Development")

(Des. Dennis Bailey)

1964 (JULY 1). 20TH INTERNATIONAL GEOGRAPHICAL CONGRESS

The first International Geographical Congress was held in 1871; since then one has normally been held at four-yearly intervals. London was chosen in 1964 and the Congress lasted from 20 to 28 July.

A. Ordinary

				Mint	Used
W46 (=S.G.651) **W43**	2½d.		black, olive-yellow, olive-grey and turquoise-blue . .	10	10
	a.		Short line under 2½d. (various)	4·00	
	b.		Line repaired (No dot, R. 18/5)	5·00	
	c.		Retouched lawn (No dot, R. 11/1 and 11/6)	4·50	
W47 (=S.G.652) **W44**	4d.		orange-brown, red-brown, rose, black and violet . . .	30	30
	a.		Violet (face value) omitted	£180	
	b.		Red-brown (dock walls) omitted	†	—
	c.		Violet and red-brown (dock walls) omitted	£300	
	d.		Watermark inverted	£600	
	e.		Scarred neck (R. 20/3)	5·50	
W48 (=S.G.653) **W45**	8d.		yellow-brown, emerald, green and black	75	85
	a.		Green (lawn) omitted	£9000	
	b.		Watermark inverted	£700	

W49 (=S.G.654) **W46**   1s.6d.   yellow-brown, pale pink, black and brown . . . . .   3·50   3·50
      a.   Watermark inverted . . . . 22·00
      b.   Neck flaw (R. 8/4) . . . . 10·00

> First Day Cover (W46/9) . . . .   22·00
> Presentation Pack (W46/9) £160

B. Phosphor (2½d. applied photo.; others flexo.)
WP46 (=S.G.651p) **W43**   2½d.   One band   40   50
      a.   Short line under 2½d. (various) . . . .   4·00
      b.   Line repaired (No dot, R. 18/5) . . . .   7·00
      c.   Retouched lawn (No dot, R. 11/1 and 11/6) . . .   6·00

WP47 (=S.G.652p) **W44**   4d.   Three bands . . . .   1·25   1·25
      a.   Narrow band at left or right (stamp with vert.
           margin) . . . .   2·25
      b.   Scarred neck (R. 20/3) . . . .   7·00

WP48 (=S.G.653p) **W45**   8d.   Three bands . . . .   2·50   2·75
      a.   Narrow band at left or right (stamp with vert.
           margin) . . . .   3·50

WP49 (=S.G.654p) **W46**   1s.6d.   Three bands . . . .   28·00   22·00
      a.   Narrow band at left or right (stamp with vert.
           margin) . . . .   30·00
      b.   Neck flaw (R. 8/4) . . . .   30·00

> First Day Cover (WP46/9) . . . .   40·00

A pair of No. WP47 exists with phosphor bands printed diagonally on the gum but omitted from the printed side. This was due to a paper fault which affected the corner of the sheet.
A used example of the 4d. (No. W47), is known with the red-brown omitted.

W46*a*, WP46*a*

The short lower line occurs on no dot R. 5/5, 9/5 (most marked) and 10/2 and on dot R. 3/4, 4/5 and 7/5 (short at left).
In No. W46*b* and WP46*b* the line has been repaired but there remains a short gap unfilled.

W46*c*, WP46*c*

The illustration shows the retouch on R. 11/1. On 11/6 it starts further over the line and is less extensive.

W47*e*, WP47*b*

W49*b*, WP49*b*
Later retouched

Cylinder Numbers (Blocks of Four)

(a) Ordinary

Cyl. Nos.		Perforation Types		
		A (E/I) No dot	A (E/I) Dot	F (P/E) No dot
2½d.	3D (black)–1C (yellow)–1B (grey)–1A (blue) .	1·00	1·00	†
4d.	1E (orange-brown)–1D (red-brown)–1C (rose) –1B (black)–1A (violet)	†	†	2·75
8d.	1D (brown)–1C (green)–1B (emerald)–1A (black)	9·00	†	5·00
1s.6d.	1D (yellow-brown)–1C (pink)–1B (black)–1A (brown)	20·00	†	†

(b) Phosphor

2½d.	3D (black)–1C (yellow)–1B (grey)–1A (blue) .	3·00	3·00	†
4d.	1E (orange-brown)–1D (red-brown)–1C (rose) –1B (black)–1A (violet)	†	†	7·00
8d.	1D (brown)–1C (green)–1B (emerald)–1A (black)	†	†	14·00
1s.6d.	1D (yellow-brown)–1C (pink)–1B (black)–1A (brown)	£150	†	£140

Minor Constant Flaws

2½d. Cyls. 3D–1C–1B–1A no dot
- 2/4 Black line from Queen's left eye to base of back of diadem, later retouched and showing as faint white line (Th. C12–13), O
- 4/1 Blue spot on Queen's collar, later retouched (Th. E12), OP
- 12/3 Green spot at foot of hills above second N of INTERNATIONAL (Th. F5), OP
- 15/2 Blue dot left of oval and above left end of upper value bar, later retouched (Th. E10), OP
- 19/3 Green blob above 2 of 20th (Th. E1), OP
- 20/3 White dot in portrait oval above right corner of central cross of crown (Th. A12), OP
- 20/5 White flaw in hair below central cross of crown (Th. B11), OP

2½d. Cyls. 3D–1C–1B–1A dot
- 7/5 Small retouch to right of Queen's nostril (Th. C11), OP
- 9/3 Retouch by Queen's left eye, later retouched on phosphor only (Th. B–C12), OP
- 12/3 White flaw in h of 20th, OP
- 12/5 Blue dot by grey panel opposite value (Th. G10), OP
- 13/5 Blue scratch on Queen's left cheek (Th. C11), OP
- 15/2 Two diagonal white lines above central cross of crown (Th. A12), OP
- 15/4 Blue patch in hills above black arrow (Th. D8) and slight retouch to right of L of GEO-GRAPHICAL, OP
- 15/5 White flaw in hair above Queen's left eye (Th. B12), OP
- 17/4 Retouch on Queen's neck above collar (Th. E12), OP

4d. Cyls. 1E–1D–1C–1B–1A no dot
- 1/1 Horizontal black line joining centre of 2 to left frame line, OP
- 1/2 Black spur on frame line below last S in CONGRESS, OP
- 1/5 White dot in panel to right of rear cross of crown (Th. B13), OP
- 1/6 Small flaw under right arm of N of CONGRESS (Th. H2), OP
- 3/5 White flaw on left of crown (Th. A11), OP
- 3/6 White spike projecting from back of neck (Th. D12), OP
- 6/1 Several small black dots on collar (Th. E11–12), OP
- 7/1 Horizontal line between Queen's lips and ear (Th. C11–12), OP
- 7/2 Similar retouch but lower down (Th. D11–12), OP
- 8/1 Violet dot to right of d in value (Th. G12), OP
- 14/2 Horizontal grey line through NATION, OP
- 16/5 Broken R in GEOGRAPHICAL, OP
- 18/1 Break in vertical lines above AT of INTERNATIONAL and small black dot to left of break (Th. E3), OP
- 20/2 Black dot above Queen's nostril (Th. D11), and break in vertical frame line to left of value, OP
- 20/5 Corner break in frame line left of value (Th. H9), OP
- Numerous other minor frame breaks are known

8d. Cyls. 1D–1C–1B–1A no dot
   1/1 Extensive retouching to back of Queen's collar (Th. E12–13), OP
   4/2 Dark patch in front of Queen's neck (Th. D–E11), OP
   4/6 Nick in final A of GEOGRAPHICAL, OP
   6/6 Retouch at back of Queen's collar (Th. E13), OP
   7/6 Shading on Queen's forehead, later retouched appearing as white patch (Th. B11–12), OP
 16/4–6 Green line runs through emerald field below brown area, OP
 17/5 Horizontal white line across Queen's face (Th. C11–12), OP
 18/5 Two horizontal white lines across face and chin (Th. C–D–11–12), OP

1s.6d. Cyls. 1D–1C–1B–1A no dot
   1/1 Dark flaw in front of Queen's collar (Th. E11), OP
   2/2 White scratch across necklace (Th. D12), OP
 13/3 White dot in panel below rear cross in crown (Th. B13), OP
 20/6 Dark spot below Queen's nose (Th. C12), OP

Sheet Details

Sheet size: 120 (6 × 20). 2½d. double pane reel-fed; others single pane sheet-fed
Sheet markings:
   Cylinder numbers: Opposite rows 19/20 at left, boxed
   Guide holes:
      2½d. Opposite rows 14/15 (boxed), at left (no dot) or right (dot)
      Others: Usually trimmed off
   Marginal arrows (photo-etched): "W" shaped, at top, bottom and sides
   Marginal rule: At bottom of sheet
   Colour register marks:
      2½d. Opposite rows 2/3 and 18/19, at left (no dot) or right (dot)
      Others: Above and below vertical rows 1 and 5/6
   Autotron marks (stippled):
      2½d. Black, blue, yellow, grey opposite rows 6/8, at right (no dot) or left (dot)
      Others: Trimmed off
   Colour designations (usually trimmed):
      2½d. "G1 GREY G2 DARK GREEN G3 YELLOW G4 BLACK" reading upwards, right margin dot pane
      Others: Trimmed off
   Traffic lights (boxed): All opposite rows 19/20 at right
      2½d. Black, yellow, blue, grey
      4d. Orange-brown, red-brown, rose, black, violet
      8d. Brown, green, black, emerald
      1s.6d. Order not known

Imprimaturs from the National Postal Museum Archives

A. Ordinary

Nos. W46/49 imperforate, watermark Type W.24

Watermark upright (*set of* 4) £4000

B. Phosphor

Nos. WP46/49 imperforate, watermark Type W.24

Watermark upright (*set of* 4) £4000

Quantities Sold

	Ordinary	Phosphor		Ordinary	Phosphor
2½d.	109,768,120	3,377,520	1s.6d.	10,154,040	519,000
4d.	15,241,680	577,800	Pack	29,952	—
8d.	8,226,800	465,720			

Withdrawn   2.7.65 (2½d. ordinary sold out earlier)

W47. Spring Gentian

W48. Dog Rose

W49. Honeysuckle

W50. Fringed Water Lily

(Des. Sylvia and Michael Goaman)

1964 (AUGUST 5). TENTH INTERNATIONAL BOTANICAL CONGRESS

Botanical Congresses are held every five years each alternate one taking place in Europe. The King of Sweden was Hon. President of the 1964 Congress, which took place in Edinburgh.

A. Ordinary

				Mint	Used
W50 (=S.G.655) **W47**	3d.		violet, blue and sage-green	25	25
	a.		Blue omitted	£5250	
	b.		Sage-green omitted	£8000	
	c.		Broken petal (Cyls. 3A–1B–1C Dot, R. 1/2)	6·00	
	s.		"Cancelled", Type B	20·00	
W51 (=S.G.656) **W48**	6d.		apple-green, rose, scarlet and green	50	50
	a.		Inverted watermark		
	b.		Rose hip flaw (No dot, R. 2/2)	6·00	
	s.		"Cancelled", Type B	20·00	
W52 (=S.G.657) **W49**	9d.		lemon, green, lake and rose-red	1·75	2·25
	a.		Green (leaves) omitted	£8000	
	b.		Watermark inverted	42·00	
	c.		Line through "INTER" (R. 1/1)	8·00	
	s.		"Cancelled", Type B	20·00	
W53 (=S.G.658) **W50**	1s.3d.		yellow, emerald, reddish violet and grey-green . .	2·50	2·50
	a.		Yellow (flowers) omitted	£20000	
	b.		Watermark inverted	£700	
	c.		Fruit flaw (R. 14/2)	10·00	
	s.		"Cancelled", Type B	20·00	

First Day Cover (W50/3)	24·00
Presentation Pack (W50/3)	£150

B. Phosphor (applied flexo.)

WP50 (=S.G.655p) **W47**	3d.		Three bands	40	40
	a.		Right band omitted		
	b.		Narrow band at left or right (stamp with vert. margin)	2·00	
	c.		Broken petal (Cyls. 3A–1B–1C Dot, R. 1/2) . . .	7·00	

WP51 (=S.G.656p) **W48**	6d.	Three bands	2·50	2·75
	a.	Four bands	15·00	
	b.	Narrow band at left or right (stamp with vert.		
		margin)	3·50	
	c.	Rose hip flaw (No dot, R. 2/2)	8·00	
WP52 (=S.G.657p) **W49**	9d.	Three bands	4·50	4·00
	a.	Narrow band at left or right (stamp with vert.		
		margin)	5·50	
	b.	Line through "INTER" (R. 1/1)	10·00	
WP53 (=S.G.658p) **W50**	1s.3d	Three hands	25·00	20·00
	a.	Narrow band at left or right (stamp with vert.		
		margin)	27·00	
	b.	Fruit flaw (R. 14/2)	30·00	

> First Day Cover (WP50/3) .... 40·00

Nos. W50s/53s have the "CANCELLED" handstamp as used on No. W40 applied in black spread over two values. It was used on sample first day covers distributed by the Post Office with the notice announcing the service.

All values were accidentally released before the official date of issue at several post offices and by the Philatelic Bureau. The earliest known date is 27 July.

The, possibly unique, example of No. W53*a* shows the yellow printed on the gummed side due to a paper fold.

Normal   W50*c*, WP50*c*
Petal is broken where the violet overlaps
the blue

W51*b*, WP51*c*
White flaw in rose hip

W52*c*, WP52*b*

W53*b*, WP53*b*
Grey-green overlaps centre of fruit

Cylinder Numbers (Blocks of Four)

(a) Ordinary

	Cyl. Nos.	Perforation Types		
		A (E/I) No dot	A (E/I) Dot	F (P/E) No dot
3d.	2A (violet)–1B (blue)–1C (sage-green)	2·00	2·00	†
	3A–1B–1C	2·00	2·00	†
6d.	1D (apple-green)–1C (rose)–1B (scarlet)–1A (green)	3·00	3·00	†
9d.	2D (lemon)–2C (green)–2B (lake)–2A (rose-red)	†	†	10·00
1s.3d.	1D (yellow)–1C (emerald)–1B (reddish violet)–1A (grey-green)	†	†	14·00

(b) Phosphor

		A (E/I) No dot	A (E/I) Dot	F (P/E) No dot
3d.	3A (violet)–1B (blue)–1C (sage-green)	2·50	2·50	†
6d.	1D (apple-green)–1C (rose)–1B (scarlet)–1A (green)	16·00	14·00	†
9d.	2D (lemon)–2C (green)–2B (lake)–2A (rose-red)	†	†	24·00
1s.3d.	1D (yellow)–1C (emerald)–1B (reddish violet)–1A (grey-green)	†	†	£120

Minor Constant Flaws

3d. Cyls. 2A–1B–1C and 3A–1B–1C no dot
   1/4 White dot between 3rd and 4th fruits below portrait (Th. E12), OP
   2/4 Curved white line across right petal of left Gentian (Th. C3), OP
   6/1 Small white vertical line on same petal as above (Th. C–D3), OP

3d. Cyl. 3A no dot
   2/5 Retouch on upper lip, OP
   7/5 Blue dash on small leaf pointing left below first flower (Th. F2), OP
  10/5 White dot below first S of CONGRESS, OP
  12/5 Line of damage extends from Queen's upper lip to base of ear (Th. C10–12), OP
  12/6 Line of damage extends from Queen's right cheek across nose to ear (Th. C10–12), OP
  13/1 Clear line of white dots joins SS of CONGRESS, OP
  19/3 White flaw at edge of petal under 3 (Th. C1), OP
  20/2 Retouch from Queen's left eye to ear (Th. B11–C12), OP

3d. Cyls. 2A–1B–1C and 3A–1B–1C dot
   1/4 Small patch of white on Queen's forehead (Th. B10), OP
   5/6 White dot in pod above R of CONGRESS (Th. F12), OP
  15/5 Green dots in leaves above OT of BOTANICAL (Th. E–F7), OP
  17/1 Retouch under necklace below earring (Th. D12), O but almost completely repaired on 3A phosphor
  19/1 White dot on right petal of partly opened bud (Th. B8), OP
  19/2 Retouch between Queen's left eyebrow and hair (Th. B11), OP

3d. Cyl. 2A dot
  10/6 Coloured line across Queen's neck (Th. D11), O

3d. Cyl. 3A dot
   6/4 Violet dot in Queen's forehead (Th. B10), OP
  12/5 Flaw in Queen's left eye, OP
  13/3 Thin white line from leaf to R of INTER (Th. G2), OP
  13/6 Small white dash above O of BOTANICAL and violet spot above middle of collar (Th. D12), OP
  19/6 Diagonal white line above ES of CONGRESS, and retouch from centre of cheek to earring (Th. C11–12), OP
  20/1 Light patch in background above 2nd N in INTERNATIONAL, OP

6d. Cyls. 1D–1C–1B–1A no dot
   2/6 Green flaws in T of INTER, OP
   5/4 Green spot between eyebrows (Th. B10), OP
   6/4 Retouch above necklace (Th. D11) and green dot on lower petal of flower nearest to portrait (Th. C–D9), OP
  10/1 White spot in hair below flowers of crown (Th. B12), OP

11/1 Retouch in Queen's collar (Th. D12), OP
17/2 Small retouch in front of Queen's ear (Th. C11), OP
18/2 Green indent in left side of seed pod (Th. F10), OP
20/1 Green spot in lowest leaf above TE of INTER (Th. F2), OP
20/4 Retouch on Queen's left cheek (Th. C11–12), OP

6d. Cyls. 1D–1C–1B–1A dot
2/6 Green flaws in T of INTER and line of yellow dots on middle leaf at left (Th. D1), OP
4/4 Three scarlet dots to right of Queen's left eye (Th. B11), OP
20/4 Retouch on Queen's left cheek (Th. C11–12), OP
20/5 Two green spots on seed pod (Th. F10), OP

9d. Cyls. 2D–2C–2B–2A no dot
4/4 ON of INTERNATIONAL joined by white line, OP
7/1 Red spot under jewel of necklace (Th. E11), OP
13/2 White dot between two left stamens of lower bloom (Th. F3), OP
14/2 Green dot above Queen's upper lip (Th. C11), OP
14/3 Red dot above Queen's right eye (Th. B10–11), OP

1s.3d. Cyls. 1D–1C–1B–1A no dot
5/1 White line through NI and above C of BOTANICAL, OP
8/3 Grey-green flaw at base of E of CONGRESS, OP
11/1 Retouch on Queen's jaw line and neck (Th. C11), OP
12/6 Horizontal dark line on left-hand bud (Th. B–C1–2), OP
13/2 Green spot on stem of largest bloom (Th. C5), OP
15/6 Pale patch in background adjoining Queen's lips (Th. C10), OP
18/3 Three dark horizontal dots above L of INTERNATIONAL (Th. G5–6), OP
19/1 Dark spot in leaf below left-hand flower (Th. D–E2), OP
20/1 Tops of IN of INTER joined, OP
20/6 White scratch through seed extending from above C of BOTANICAL to R of CONGRESS (Th. G8–12), OP

Sheet Details

Sheet size: 120 (6 × 20)
  3d., 6d. double pane reel-fed
  9d., 1s.3d. single pane sheet-fed
Sheet markings:
  Cylinder numbers: Boxed, opposite R. 20/1 3d., 19–20/1 others
  Guide holes:
    3d., 6d. Opposite rows 14/15 (boxed), at left (no dot) or right (dot)
    9d., 1s.3d. None
  Marginal arrows (photo-etched): "W" shaped, at top, bottom and sides
  Marginal rule: At bottom of sheet
  Colour register marks:
    3d., 6d. None
    9d., 1s.3d. Above and below vertical rows 1 and 6
  Autotron marks:
    3d. Solid, violet, blue, sage-green opposite rows 4/5 and 15/16 at right (no dot) or left (dot)
    6d. Stippled, green, scarlet, rose, apple-green opposite rows 4/6 at right (no dot) or left (dot) and again apple-green, rose, scarlet opposite rows 14/15 at right (no dot) or left (dot)
    9d., 1s.3d. None
  Coloured crosses (partly trimmed):
    1s.3d. Above and below vertical rows 1/2
    Others: None
  Colour designations (usually trimmed off):
    3d. "G1 GREEN G2 BLUE G3 MAUVE" in right margin of dot panes
  Traffic lights (boxed):
    3d. Violet, blue, sage-green opposite R. 20/6
    6d. Apple-green, rose, scarlet, green opposite R. 19–20/6
    9d. Lemon, green, lake, rose-red opposite R. 19–20/6
    1s.3d. Yellow, emerald, reddish violet, grey-green opposite R. 19–20/6

Imprimaturs from the National Postal Museum Archives

A. Ordinary

Nos. W50/53 imperforate, watermark Type W.24

Watermark upright (*set of* 4) £4000

B. Phosphor

Nos. WP50/53 imperforate, watermark Type W.24

Watermark upright (*set of* 4) £4000

Quantities Sold

	Ordinary	Phosphor		Ordinary	Phosphor
3d.	166,491,720	6,764,880	1s.3d.	15,664,600	650,920
6d.	25,361,120	996,720	Pack	16,140	—
9d.	11,896,060	498,460			

Withdrawn   2.7.65

W51. Forth Road Bridge

W52. Forth Road and
Railway Bridges

(Des. Andrew Restall)

1964 (SEPTEMBER 4).   OPENING OF FORTH ROAD BRIDGE

At that time the largest suspension bridge in Europe and the fourth largest in the world. Opened by Her Majesty The Queen.

A. Ordinary

				Mint	Used
W54 (=S.G.659) **W51**	3d.	black, blue and reddish violet		10	10
	a.	Imperforate between stamp and top margin		£700	
	b.	Dotted "3" (Cyl. 2A Dot, R. 15/1)		5·50	
W55 (=S.G.660) **W52**	6d.	blackish lilac, light blue and carmine-red		40	40
	a.	Light blue omitted		£2700	
	b.	Watermark inverted		2·00	

First Day Cover (W54/5)	7·00
Presentation Pack (W54/5)	£380

B. Phosphor (3d. applied photo., 6d. flexo.)

WP54 (=S.G.659p) **W51**	3d.	Three bands		1·00	1·50
	a.	Narrow band at left or right (stamp with vert. margin)		2·00	
	b.	Dotted "3" (Cyl. 2 A Dot, R. 15/1)		7·00	
WP55 (=S.G.660p) **W52**	6d.	Three bands		4·50	4·75
	a.	Watermark inverted		£750	
	b.	Narrow band at left or right (stamp with vert. margin)		5·50	

First Day Cover (WP54/5)	18·00

W54*b*, WP54*b*

Cylinder Numbers (Blocks of Four)

(a) Ordinary

		Cyl. Nos.	Perforation Type A (E/I)	
			No dot	Dot
3d.	1C (blue)–1B (black)–2A (violet)		1·25	1·25
	1C–1B–2A		15·00	15·00
	1C–1B–4A		1·50	1·50
	2C–1B–4A		2·00	2·00
6d.	1C (blue)–2B (blackish lilac)–2A (red)*		2·75	2·75

			Perforation Type A(T) (E/P)	
			No dot	Dot
6d.	1C (blue)–2B (blackish lilac)–2A (red)*		4·75	4·75

(b) Phosphor

			Perforation Type A (E/I)	
			No dot	Dot
3d.	1C (blue)–1B (black)–2A (violet)		5·50	5·00
	1C–1B–4A		24·00	24·00

			Perforation Type A(T) (E/P)	
			No dot	Dot
6d.	1C (blue)–2B (blackish lilac)–2A (red)*		24·00	24·00

*In the 6d. no dot pane the cylinder numbers are expressed in error thus: "1C–2.B.–2A"

Minor Constant Flaws

3d. Cyl. 1C no dot in combination with cyls. 1B–2A or 1B–4A no dot
    4/2 Blue spot to left and above B of BRIDGE, OP
    8/1 Blue spot below B of BRIDGE, OP
    13/6 Blue spot in sky S.W. of moon (Th. B1), O

3d. Cyl. 1C dot in combination with cyls. 1B–2A, 1B–3A or 1B–4A dot
    18/6 Blue dash to left of 3d. (Th. F–G11); also blue spot to left of tanker (Th. G3), latter coincident with a similar violet spot on cyl. 2A

3d. Cyl. 1B no dot in combination with cyls. 1C–2A, 1C–3A, 1C–4A or 2C–4A no dot
    1/3 Detail at rear of diadem is weak (Th. B–C10), OP
    2/3 Scratch on necklace and collar (Th. E9), OP
    4/4 Lack of detail at rear of diadem (Th. B–C10), OP
    8/4 Black flaw on Queen's neck above large jewel (Th. E9), OP
    9/2 White spot on Queen's nose (Th. D8), OP
    9/4 Black scratch on Queen's forehead (Th. C8–9), OP
    14/4 Black spot below Queen's left nostril (Th. D8), OP
    16/4 Loss of detail at back of Queen's neck and collar. Almost normal with cyl. 3A (Th. E10–F10–11), OP
    18/1 Black spots under G of BRIDGE (Th. A10), OP

3d. Cyl. 1B dot in combination with cyls. 1C–2A, 1C–3A, 1C–4A or 2C–4A dot
    2/2 White flaw in sea appears as extra wave (Th. G8), OP
    13/2 Weak top to O of FORTH, OP
    18/4 Small white flaw in hair above Queen's left eye (Th. B9), OP

3d. Cyls. 2A, 3A and 4A no dot (multipositive flaws)
    17/4 White patch at left side of moon (Th. B2), OP. Less pronounced on cyl. 3A
    19/4 Large retouch in sky left of bridge (Th. D1), OP. Most marked on cyl. 4A
    20/1 White tower on hill above funnel (Th. F3), OP. Retouched on cyls. 3A and 4A
    20/4 Large retouch in sky left of moon (Th. A–B1), OP. Most pronounced on cyls. 3A and 4A

3d. Cyls. 1C–1B–2A no dot
  10/6 Violet retouches below 1 and 4 of 1964 (Th. B11 and B13), OP
  18/5 White arc at top left of moon (Th. A–B2), OP

3d. Cyl. 4A no dot in combination with cyls. 1C–1B or 2C–1B no dot
  12/6 Faint acute accent over d of 3d (Th. F13), OP
  14/4 Small nick in left edge of value panel (Th. D11), OP
  16/2 Retouch in sky above funnel (Th. E–F3), OP

3d. Cyl. 4A dot in combination with cyls. 1C–1B or 2C–1B dot
  14/2 Violet coloured flaw in sky at left of pylon (Th. E2), OP

3d. Cyls. 2C–1B–4A dot
  17/3 Dark patch on skyline under bridge (Th. F5), O

6d. Cyls. 1C–2B–2A no dot
  5/1 Small nick in top of 9 of 1964, OP
  5/5 Red scratch over D of BRIDGE, OP
  7/1 Red scratch over 6 of 6d, OP
  7/3 Two small breaks in bridge below portrait (Th. G8), OP
  8/2 Black spot on Queen's collar (Th. E10), OP
  15/6 Dark red patch below 4 of 1964 (Th. B13), OP
  16/1 Black dot in front of D of ROAD, OP
  16/5 Mottled portrait, OP
  17/6 Mottled portrait, OP
  18/4 Black spot in water between left-hand towers of bridge (Th. F1), OP

6d. Cyls. 1C–2B–2A dot
  1/4 White scratch on Queen's cheek (Th. D9), OP
  15/5 Two small coloured flaws on Queen's forehead (Th. C9); also two small red spots below
       portrait by bridge (Th. G9), OP
  17/2 Diagonal red stroke by value panel (Th. D11), OP
  19/1 Queen's face is a mass of white dots (State 1) OP; later appears normal (State 2), O only. Other
       stamps in the sheet show a similar appearance but this is the most marked

Sheet Details

Sheet size: 120 (6 × 20). 3d. double pane reel-fed; 6d. double pane sheet-fed
Sheet markings:
  Cylinder numbers: Opposite R. 19/1, boxed
  Guide holes:
    3d. Opposite rows 14/15 (boxed), at left (no dot) or right (dot)
    6d. None
  Marginal arrows (photo-etched): "W" shaped, at top, bottom and sides
  Marginal rule: At bottom of sheet
  Colour register marks:
    3d. Opposite rows 2/3 and 17/18, at left (no dot) or right (dot)
    6d. Opposite rows 1/2 and 17/18, at left (no dot) or right (dot)
  Autotron marks (solid):
    3d. Black, blue, violet opposite rows 4/6 and violet, blue, black opposite rows 13/15 at right
       (no dot) or left (dot)
    6d. None
  Colour designations (usually trimmed off):
    3d. "G MAUVE G BLUE G BLACK" in right margin reading upwards opposite rows 8/4 on
       dot panes only
    6d. None
  Traffic lights (boxed):
    3d. Violet, blue, black opposite R. 19/6
    6d. Blue, red, blackish lilac opposite R. 19/6

Imprimaturs from the National Postal Museum Archives

A. Ordinary

Nos. W54/55 imperforate, watermark Type W.24

Watermark upright (*set of 2*) £2000

B. Phosphor

Nos. WP54/55 imperforate, watermark Type W.24

Watermark upright *(set of 2)* £2000

Quantities Sold

	Ordinary	Phosphor
3d.	108,098,480	8,020,920
6d.	12,055,960	1,240,800
Pack	11,450	—

Withdrawn 2.7.65

PHOSPHOR BANDS

From the Churchill issue onwards all phosphor bands were applied in photogravure, *unless otherwise stated.*

W53. Sir Winston Churchill   **W54.** Sir Winston Churchill

(Des. David Gentleman and Rosalind Dease, from photograph by Karsh)

1965 (JULY 8).   CHURCHILL COMMEMORATION

I. "REMBRANDT" Machine

Cyls. 1A–1B dot and no dot. Lack of shading detail on Churchill's portrait. Queen's portrait appears dull and coarse. This was a sheet-fed rotary machine.

A. Ordinary

			Mint	Used
W56 (=S.G.661) **W53**	4d.	black and olive-brown	10	10
	a.	Watermark inverted	2·25	
	b.	Vertical scratch (Dot, R. 20/3)	2·75	

B. Phosphor

			Mint	Used
WP56 (=S.G.661) **W53**	4d.	Three bands	25	25
	a.	Left band omitted	18·00	
	b.	Vertical scratch (Dot, R. 20/3)	5·00	

II. "TIMSON" Machine

Cyls. 5A–6B no dot. More detail on Churchill's portrait—furrow on forehead, his left eye-brow fully drawn and more shading on cheek. Queen's portrait lighter and sharper. This was a reel-fed, two-colour, 12-in. wide rotary machine. The differences in impression were due to the greater pressure applied by the cylinders.

Ordinary only

			Mint	Used
W57 (=S.G.661*a*) **W53**	4d.	black and pale olive-brown	35	35

III. "LINOTYPE AND MACHINERY NO. 4" Machine

Cyls. 1A–1B no dot. The "Linotype and Machinery No. 4" machine was a sheet-fed rotary press machine. Besides being used for printing the 1s.3d. stamps it was also employed to overprint the phosphor bands on both values.

A. Ordinary

			Mint	Used
W58 (=S.G.662) **W54**	1s.3d.	black and grey	30	40
	a.	Watermark inverted	75·00	

| First Day Cover (W56 and W58) . . . . .   7·00 |
| Presentation Pack (W56 and W58) . . . .   65·00 |

B. Phosphor

WP58 (=S.G.662p) **W54**	1s.3d.	Three bands	2·50	3·00
	a.	Narrow band at left or right (stamp with vert. margin)	4·50	

> First Day Cover (WP56 and WP58) . . .   9·00

These are known postmarked 7 July.

Two examples of the 4d. value exist with the Queen's head omitted, one due to something adhering to the cylinder and the other due to a paper fold. The stamp also exists with Churchill's head omitted, also due to a paper fold.

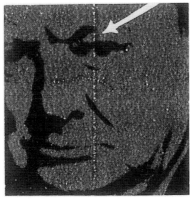

W56*b*, WP56*b*

Cylinder Numbers (Blocks of Four)

(a) Ordinary

	Cyl. Nos.	A(T) (E/P) No dot	A(T) (E/P) Dot	F (P/E) No dot
		Perforation Types		
4d.	1A (olive-brown)–1B (black) Rembrandt . . .	1·25	1·25	†
4d.	5A (olive-brown)–6B (black) Timson	†	†	2·50
1s.3d.	1A (black)–1B (grey) Linotype and Machinery No. 4	†	†	2·75

(b) Phosphor

		A(T) (E/P) No dot	A(T) (E/P) Dot	F (P/E) No dot
4d.	1A (olive-brown)–1B (black) Rembrandt . . .	2·50	2·50	†
1s.3d.	1A (black)–1B (grey) Linotype and Machinery No. 4	†	†	14·00

Minor Constant Flaws

4d. Cyls. 1A–1B no dot
- 1/1   Background retouch left of Churchill's right eye (Th. D2), scratch from Churchill's ear to Queen's chin (Th. D8–11), small background retouch to right of Churchill's left ear (Th. C9), OP
- 6/6   Queen's face mottled with white streaks (Th. B–D10–12), OP
- 14/1   Dark patch above Queen's left eye (Th. B11), OP

4d. Cyls. 1A–1B dot
- 1/6   Vertical line of white dots near hair above Churchill's right eye (Th. A–C3), OP
- 4/3   Disturbance under Churchill's left eye (Th. D6), OP
- 7/1   Queen's face mottled with white specks (Th. B–D10–12), OP
- 7/2   Queen's face mottled with white specks (Th. B–D10–12), OP
- 20/5   Brown diagonal line on bridge of Queen's nose (Th. C11), OP

The mottled face of the Queen varieties on no dot R. 6/6 and dot R. 7/1 and 7/2 are very marked and occur on ordinary and phosphor but only on some sheets. Many other stamps on this cylinder show signs of mottling

4d. Cyls. 5A–6B no dot (ordinary only)
    4/2 Retouch in background between portraits (Th. B9)
    6/4 Retouch at top of Churchill's nose (Th. D5)
  10/4 Two spots in vertical white line level with Churchill's shoulder (Th. E10)
  12/3 Small white flaw by Queen's right eye (Th. C10)
  14/5 Background retouch just above Churchill's right shoulder (Th. E–F2) and brown flaw in margin below Churchill's chin (Th. H5)
  15/5 Brown flaw left of Churchill's head (Th. A2)

1s.3d. Cyls. 1A–1B no dot
    1/4 Line of white dots in Queen's hair (Th. C12), OP
    7/1 Small white dot over Queen's left eyelid (Th. C11), OP
  15/4 White flaw at base of Queen's neck (Th. D2), OP
  19/4 Spur on top jewel of emblems in diadem (Th. A12), OP

Sheet Details

Sheet size: 120 (6 × 20)
    4d. Rembrandt double pane sheet-fed
        Timson single pane reel-fed
    1s.3d. L. & M. No. 4 single pane sheet-fed
Sheet markings:
    Cylinder numbers: Opposite R. 19/1, boxed
    Guide holes:
        4d. Timson above vertical row 2 (boxed) and below vertical rows 3/4 (unboxed and over arrow)
        Others: None
    Marginal arrows (photo-etched): "W" shaped, at top, bottom and sides; Rembrandt very small at bottom; others normal
    Marginal rule: At bottom of sheet
    Colour register marks:
        4d. Rembrandt, none
        4d. Timson, opposite rows 1/2 and 17/18, at both sides
        1s.3d. Above and below vertical rows 1/2 and 6
    Autotron marks (solid):
        4d. Timson: Brown, black above R. 1/2 and 1/3
        Others: None
    Colour designations: None
    Traffic lights (boxed): All R. 19/6
        4d. Black, brown; 1s.3d. Grey, black

Imprimaturs from the National Postal Museum Archives

A. Ordinary

Nos. W56, W58 imperforate, watermark Type W.24

Watermark upright (*set of 2*) £2000

B. Phosphor

Nos. WP56, WP58 imperforate, watermark Type W.24

Watermark upright (*set of 2*) £2000

Quantities Issued

		Ordinary	Phosphor		Ordinary	Phosphor
4d.	Rembrandt	103,217,520	10,322,760	1s.3d.	7,893,480	864,960
4d.	Timson	32,040,000	—	Pack	38,500	—

Withdrawn   4d. phosphor sold out Dec. 1965, remainder withdrawn 28.2.66

W55. Simon de Montfort's Seal

(Des. Stewart R. Black)

W56. Parliament Buildings
(after engraving by Hollar, 1647)

(Des. Prof. Richard Guyatt)

1965 (JULY 19).   700th ANNIVERSARY OF SIMON DE MONTFORT'S PARLIAMENT

Simon de Montfort summoned the first parliament representing many cities and shires and it met in various buildings at Westminster in January 1265.

A. Ordinary

				Mint	Used
W59 (=S.G.663) **W55**	6d.	olive-green		20	20
	a.	Imperforate between stamp and top margin		£1250	
W60 (=S.G.664) **W56**	2s.6d.	black, grey and pale drab		80	1·50
	a.	Watermark inverted		20·00	

First Day Cover (W59/60)	15·00
Presentation Pack (W59/60)	65·00

B. Phosphor

WP59 (=S.G.663p) **W55**	6d.	Three bands		60	1·00

First Day Cover (WP59)	26·00

Both values were accidentally released in several post offices in the London area on 8 July, the date of issue of the Churchill stamps. Covers are also known with both values, bearing the "First Day" cancellation of the Philatelic Bureau dated 8 July.

Cylinder Numbers (Blocks of Four)

Cyl. Nos.	Perforation	Type A (E/I)
	No dot	Dot
6d. 2 (olive-green). Ordinary	1·50	1·50
6d. 2 Phosphor	4·25	4·25

The 2s.6d. sheets had no cylinder numbers. Perforation is Type A(T) (E/P)

Minor Constant Flaws

6d. Cyl. 2 no dot
    1/1 Background scratch behind right cross of diadem (Th. C11–12), OP
    5/3 Small background blemish above jewels in diadem (Th. B11), OP
    9/4 Retouch at rear of horse's belly (Th. E4), OP
    15/2 Dot below e of Anniversary, OP
    17/3 Cut in m of Parliament, OP
    17/5 Background retouch to right of diadem (Th. C11), OP

6d. Cyl. 2 dot
    10/6 Spur to m of Parliament, OP
    14/5 White flaw on Queen's necklace (Th. E10), OP

2s.6d. No numbers
    4/1 Vertical line running through river wall and building in centre of stamp (Th. E–F9)
    4/6 Vertical line from left of steps at centre through Thames to frame line (Th. G–H7)
    6/3 Blemish between 5th and 6th windows of building in front of Westminster Hall (Th. E10)
    8/1 White scratches above V of ANNIVERSARY
    10/1 Nick in S of ANNIVERSARY

Sheet Details

Sheet sizes:
   6d. 120 (6 × 20). Double pane reel-fed
   2s.6d. 80 (8 × 10). Single pane sheet-fed
Sheet markings:
   Cylinder numbers: 6d. opposite R. 19/1, boxed; 2s.6d. none
   Guide holes:
      6d. In double photo-etched box opposite rows 14/15, at left (no dot) or right (dot). In the left
         margin the boxes are lettered "S O N", the "S" being in left box (usually trimmed off), the "O"
         below centre line and the "N" above right line. In the right margin the sequence is reversed. The
         letters are very small and denote respectively selvedge, off-side and near-side
      2s.6d. None
   Marginal arrows (photo-etched): "W" shaped, at top, bottom and sides
   Marginal rule: At bottom of sheet
   Colour register marks, Autotron marks, colour designations: None
   Traffic lights (boxed):
      6d. None
      2s.6d. Grey, drab and black opposite R. 9/8, boxed

This shows that the stamp was printed in three colours and accounts for misplacement of the
Queen's head downwards in some badly registered sheets

Imprimaturs from the National Postal Museum Archives

A. Ordinary

Nos. W59/60 imperforate, watermark Type W.24

Watermark upright (*set of 2*) £2000

B. Phosphor

No. WP59 imperforate, watermark Type W.24

Watermark upright £2000

Quantities Issued

	Ordinary	Phosphor
6d.	12,973,800	1,537,920
2s.6d.	4,055,120	—
Pack	24,450	—

Withdrawn   28.2.66

W57. Bandsmen and Banner
(Des. M. C. Farrar-Bell)

W58. Three Salvationists
(Des. G. Trenaman)

1965 (AUGUST 9).   SALVATION ARMY CENTENARY
   A religious militant movement, the Salvation Army was founded in 1865 by William Booth who
became its General in 1880.

A. Ordinary

			Mint	Used
W61 (=S.G.665) **W57**	3d.	indigo, grey-blue, cerise, yellow and brown	25	25
	a.	Diadem flaw (R. 16/6)	3·00	
	b.	Retouch to "V" (R. 19/3)	4·00	

W62 (=S.G.666) **W58** 1s.6d.   red, blue, yellow and brown . . . .   1·00   1·50
         a.   Extra pearl (R. 17/1) . . . .   5·50

> First Day Cover (W61/2) . . . .   23·00

B. Phosphor
WP61 (=S.G.665p) **W57** 3d.   One band   25   40
         a.   Diadem flaw (R. 16/6) . . . .   5·50
         b.   Retouch to "V" (R. 19/3) . . . .   4·50

WP62 (=S.G.666p) **W58** 1s.6d.   Three bands . . . .   2·50   2·75
         a.   Extra pearl (R. 17/1) . . . .   8·00

> First Day Cover (WP61/2) . . . .   33·00

W61*a*, WP61*a*   W61*b*, WP61*b*   W62*a* WP62*a*

Cylinder Numbers (Blocks of Six)

(a) Ordinary

	Cyl. Nos. (No dot)	Perforation Type A (E/I)
3d.	2A (blue)–2B (indigo)–1C (brown)–1D (cerise)–1E (yellow) .	2·00
1s.6d.	1A (red)–1B (brown)–1C (blue)–1D (yellow)	7·00

(b) Phosphor

3d.	2A (blue)–2B (indigo)–1C (brown)–1D (cerise)–1E (yellow) .	2·50
1s.6d.	1A (red)–1B (brown)–1C (blue)–1D (yellow)	20·00

Minor Constant Flaws

3d. Cyls. 2A–2B–1C–1D–1E no dot
  1/6 Pale area below D of 3D (Th. G13), OP
  2/1 Dark spot on Queen's chin (Th. D11), OP
  3/6 Vertical scratch below flag-bearer's collar (Th. D–E4), OP
  8/1 Spur at foot of T of SALVATION at bottom of stamp, OP
 11/2 Blue scratch in white vertical dividing line to left of Queen's lips (Th. D10); also blue spot to left of flag-bearer's lips (Th. D4), both OP
 15/6 Grey flaw protruding from collar under Queen's chin (Th. E11), OP
 16/1 Due to faulty registration on the multipositive, the cerise colour is positioned slightly to the right resulting in a white line at left of flag in sky, also cerise colour overlaps ear and face below ear (Th. B–C3 and C4), OP. *Note*—This variety is not an ordinary colour shift and is therefore best collected in a positional block. A similar variety, although much less marked, is found on R. 14/1, also OP
 17/4 White spot in lower part of V of SALVATION at bottom of stamp, OP

1s.6d. Cyls. 1A–1B–1C–1D no dot
  1/1 Retouch on right arm of left-hand man (Th. D1–2), OP
  1/4 White flaw on Queen's hair behind ear (Th. D12), OP
 15/6 Retouch on right leg of left-hand man (Th. G2), OP
 19/3 Diagonal scratch across Queen's forehead and nose (Th. B–C10), OP

20/1 White flaw on Queen's neck by necklace (Th. E11), OP
20/3 Small red flaw at back of Queen's hair (Th. D12), OP
20/5 A wispy line of blue dots by left leg of right-hand man (Th. F7), OP

Sheet Details

Sheet size: 120 (6 × 20). Single pane reel-fed
Sheet markings:
  Cylinder numbers:
    3d. Opposite rows 18/19 at left, boxed
    1s.6d. Opposite row 19 at left, boxed
  Guide holes: Opposite rows 14/15 (boxed), at both sides
  Marginal arrows (photo-etched): "W" shaped, at top, bottom and sides
  Marginal rule: At bottom of sheet
  Colour register marks:
    Opposite rows 1/2 and 17/18, at both sides
  Autotron marks (solid):
    3d. Blue, indigo, brown, cerise, yellow below vertical rows 1/3
    1s.6d. Red, brown, blue, yellow below vertical rows 1/3
  Colour designations:
    3d. "G1 YELLOW G2 RED G3 BROWN G4 BLUE BLACK G5 BLUE" in right margin
    reading upwards opposite rows 9/3 ("G1 YELLOW" is very faint on some sheets)
    1s.6d. "G1 YELLOW G2 BLUE G3 BROWN G4 RED" in right margin reading upwards
    opposite rows 9/3.
  Traffic lights (boxed):
    3d. Blue, indigo, brown, cerise, yellow opposite rows 18/19 at right
    1s.6d. Red, brown, blue, yellow opposite rows 18/19 at right

Imprimaturs from the National Postal Museum Archives

A. Ordinary

Nos. W61/62 imperforate, watermark Type W.24
Watermark upright (*set of 2*) £2000

B. Phosphor

Nos. WP61/62 imperforate, watermark Type W.24
Watermark upright (*set of 2*) £2000

Quantities Issued

	Ordinary	Phosphor
3d.	54,312,000	4,261,200
1s.6d.	5,244,120	652,320

Withdrawn   28.2.66 (3d. ordinary sold out Dec. 1965)

W59. Lister's Carbolic Spray
(Des. Peter Gauld)

W60. Lister and Chemical Symbols
(Des. Frank Ariss)

1965 (SEPTEMBER 1).   CENTENARY OF JOSEPH LISTER'S DISCOVERY OF ANTISEPTIC SURGERY

A. Ordinary

			Mint	Used
W63 (=S.G.667) **W59**	4d.	indigo, brown-red and grey-black	25	15
	a.	Brown-red (tube) omitted	£300	
	b.	Indigo omitted	£4000	
	c.	Corner scratch (No dot, R. 17/1)	5·50	
	d.	Face retouch (No dot, R. 18/1)	5·00	
	e.	Filled "e" (Dot, R. 20/4)	5·00	

| W64 (=S.G.668) **W60** | 1s. | black, purple and new blue . . . . | 1·00 | 1·10 |
| | *a.* | Watermark inverted . . . . | £325 | |

> First Day Cover (W63/4) . . . .   12·00

B. Phosphor

WP63 (=S.G.667p) **W59**	4d.	Three bands	25	25
	a.	Brown-red (tube) omitted	£2700	
	b.	Narrow band at left or right (stamp with vert.		
		margin)	1·50	
	c.	Error. Two broad bands	30·00	
	ca.	Error. One thin and one broad band	35·00	
	d.	Corner scratch (No dot, R. 17/1)	5·50	
	e.	Face retouch (No dot, R. 18/1)	5·00	
WP64 (=S.G.668p) **W60**	1s.	Three bands	2·00	2·50
	a.	Watermark inverted	£300	
	b.	Narrow band at left or right (stamp with vert.		
		margin)	3·00	
	c.	Error. Two broad bands	40·00	

> First Day Cover (W63/4) . . . .   15·00

Nos. W63/4 exist postmarked 1 August 1965 at Skeabost Bridge (Skye), and can also be found cancelled 31 August elsewhere.

Nos. WP63*c*/*ca* came from a sheet showing misplaced phosphor bands; No. WP63*ca* were from the left-hand vertical row only.

W63*c*, WP63*d*

W63*e*

"e" of "Antiseptic" nearly filled by white flaw (later retouched leaving malformed "e")

W63*d*, WP63*e*

Large grey retouch outlines face. Similar, but more minor flaws can be found on Row 19/2, 20/1

Cylinder Numbers (Blocks of Four)

	Cyl. Nos.	Perforation Types		
		A (E/I)	A (E/I)	F (P/E)
		No dot	Dot	No dot
4d.	4A (black)–1B (blue)–1C (red). Ordinary . . .	4·00	2·50	†
	4A–1B–1C. Phosphor	5·00	2·50	†
1s.	1A (black)–1B (purple)–1C (blue). Ordinary .	†	†	5·50
	1A–1B–1C. Phosphor	†	†	10·00

Minor Constant Flaws

4d. Cyls. 4A–1B–1C no dot
4/1 Line of white dots under apparatus (Th. H3–4), OP
4/4 Two dark flaws to lower right of apparatus (Th. G5–6), OP
5/6 Prominent retouch in front of Queen's dress (Th. E–F10), OP
6/6 Grey flaw hanging from rear jewel of tiara (Th. B12), OP
10/3 Grey flaw on Queen's forehead (Th. B10), OP

11/4 to 12/4 Grey line under g of Surgery extending across gutter joining frames, OP
11/6 Diagonal grey line from top left corner to apparatus (Th. A1–B2), OP
16/5 Retouch on Queen's forehead (Th. B10), OP
17/2 White flaw in loop of d of value, OP
19/6 Grey spots on Queen's forehead (Th. B10–11), OP
19/6 and 20/6 Grey line extends down right-hand margin, OP
20/3 Vertical grey line from lower left corner of stamp to gutter (Th. H1), OP
20/6 Base of 4 joined to tube by dark line (Th. B7), OP

4d. Cyls. 4A–1B–1C dot
  1/4 Blue spot between p and t of antiseptic, OP
  8/2 Retouch on Queen's collar (Th. E12), OP
10/2 Diagonal grey line above te of Lister and in front of Queen's collar (Th. F8–E10), OP
13/3 Retouch behind Queen's necklace (Th. D12), OP
18/1 Retouch on Queen's jaw close to ear (Th. D11), OP
19/2 White scratch above ur of Surgery, OP
20/1 Two dark spots at right of Queen's mouth (Th. D11), OP
20/6 Retouch in front of Queen's neck (Th. E10), OP

1s. Cyls. 1A–1B–1C no dot
  1/5 Large black spot at rear of Queen's collar (Th. E13), OP
  3/1 Retouch along Lister's right shoulder (Th. D3–C4), OP
  3/2 Broken frame line behind Queen's portrait was retouched by dots (Th. C13), OP
  6/1 Missing portions of jewels left of large cross on diadem heavily retouched (Th. A10), OP
  8/1 White retouch on Queen's throat (Th. D11), OP
11/2 Extra pearl half way up necklace (Th. D11), OP
11/3 Small retouch on Queen's left cheek (Th. D11), OP
14/2 Retouch on Queen's collar (Th. E12), OP
15/6 Line from Queen's left eyebrow into hair (Th. B11), OP
16/4 Retouch on back of Queen's collar (Th. E13), OP
17/6 Blue spot normally found by Lister's right wrist is missing (Th. E6), OP
19/1 Dark spot under Queen's nose (Th. C10), OP
20/3 Retouch below Queen's necklace (Th. D12), OP

Sheet Details

Sheet size: 120 (6 × 20). 4d. double pane reel-fed; 1s. single pane sheet-fed
Sheet markings:
  Cylinder numbers: Opposite R. 19/1, boxed
  Guide holes: Opposite rows 14/15 (boxed), at left (no dot) or right (dot)
  Marginal arrows (photo-etched): "W" shaped, at top, bottom and sides
  Marginal rule: At bottom of sheet
  Colour register marks:
    4d. Opposite rows 2/3 and 16/17, at left (no dot)
    1s. Above and below vertical rows 1/2 and 5/6
  Autotron marks (solid):
    4d. Black, indigo, brown-red opposite rows 3/5, at right (no dot) or left (dot)
    1s. None
  Colour designations: None
  Traffic lights (boxed):
    4d. Black, indigo, brown-red opposite R. 19/6
    1s. Black, purple, blue opposite R. 20/6

Imprimaturs from the National Postal Museum Archives

A. Ordinary

Nos. W63/64 imperforate, watermark Type W.24
Watermark upright (*set of 2*) £2000

B. Phosphor

Nos. WP63/64 imperforate, watermark Type W.24
Watermark upright (*set of 2*) £2000

Quantities Issued

	Ordinary	Phosphor
4d.	92,167,440	10,732,800
1s.	8,368,800	1,452,360

Withdrawn 15.4.66

W61. Trinidad Carnival Dancers   **W62.** Canadian Folk-dancers

(Des. David Gentleman and Rosalind Dease)

1965 (SEPTEMBER 1). COMMONWEALTH ARTS FESTIVAL

The Festival was aimed at promoting the cultural traditions of Commonwealth countries and was held in London and other centres between 16 September and 2 October.

A. Ordinary

				Mint	Used
W65 (=S.G.669) **W61**	6d.	black and orange	. . . .	20	20
W66 (=S.G.670) **W62**	1s.6d.	black and light reddish violet	. . . .	80	1·10

> First Day Cover (W65/6) . . . . 16·50

B. Phosphor

WP65 (=S.G.669p) **W61**	6d.	Three bands	. . . .	30	50
	a.	Narrow band at left or right (stamp with vert. margin)		1·50	
WP66 (=S.G.670p) **W62**	1s.6d.	Three bands		2·50	3·50
	a.	Narrow band at left or right (stamp with vert. margin)		3·50	
	b.	Error. Two broad bands		25·00	
	c.	Error. Two bands (9·5 and 6 mm.)		30·00	

> First Day Cover (WP65/6) . . . . 22·00

Nos. W65/6 are known postmarked 1 August 1965 at Skeabost Bridge (Skye).

No. WP66*c* come from the right-hand side of the sheet where the narrow band occurs on the stamp instead of the first vertical row of perforations.

Cylinder Numbers (Blocks of Four)

	Cyl. Nos.	Perforation Type F(L) (I/E) No dot
6d.	1A (orange)–1B (black). (Ordinary	. . . . 1·50
	1A–1B. Phosphor	2·75
1s.6d.	1A (violet)–1B (black). Ordinary	4·50
	1A–1B. Phosphor	14·00

Minor Constant Flaws

6d. Cyls. 1A–1B (no dot)

    1/2 Damaged right arm of v of Festival, OP

    1/6 Black spot at back of Queen's neck under hair (Th. C12), OP

11/2   S shaped line of white dots on Queen's neck (Th. D–E11), OP
17/1   Pale area in background by right sleeve of central figure (Th. D3–4), OP

1s.6d. Cyls. 1A–1B no dot
    2/3   White flaw under n of Commonwealth, OP
    3/4   Vertical scratch from Queen's ear to neck (Th. C–D12), OP
    5/6   Vertical line from diadem to Queen's neck (Th. B–D11), OP
    7/5   Pale area below C of Commonwealth, OP
    9/2   White triangle in Queen's hair (Th. B11), OP
   13/6   White spot between emblems and rear cross of diadem (Th. B12), OP
   15/1   Diagonal scratch to right of C of Commonwealth (Th. G1–2), OP
   20/6   Two dots to right of Queen's left eyebrow (Th. C11), OP

Sheet Details

Sheet size: 120 (6 × 20). Single pane reel-fed
Sheet markings:
    Cylinder numbers: Opposite R. 19/1, boxed
    Guide holes: Above vertical rows 3/4 and below vertical row 5, unboxed
    Marginal arrows (photo-etched): "W" shaped, at top, bottom and sides
    Marginal rule: At bottom of sheet
Colour register marks:
    6d. Opposite rows 1/2 and 18/19, at both sides and opposite rows 10/11 (orange only), at left
    1s.6d. Opposite rows 1/2, at both sides, rows 9/10 (violet only), at left and rows 18/19, at left and
       17/18 at right
Autotron marks (solid):
    6d. Orange, black above and below vertical rows 3/4
    1s.6d. Violet, black above and below vertical rows 3/4
Colour designations:
    6d. "G ORANGE G BLACK" reading upwards opposite rows 14/12, right margin
    1s.6d. "G MAUVE G BLACK" reading upwards opposite rows 15/13, right margin
Traffic lights (boxed):
    6d. Black, orange opposite R. 19/6
    1s.6d. Black, violet opposite R. 19/6

Imprimaturs from the National Postal Museum Archives

A. Ordinary

Nos. W65/66 imperforate, watermark Type W.24

Watermark upright (*set of 2*) £2000

B. Phosphor

Nos. WP65/66 imperforate, watermark Type W.24

Watermark upright (*set of 2*) £2000

Quantities Issued

	Ordinary	Phosphor
6d.	12,264,840	1,621,080
1s.6d.	5,003,000	788,880

Withdrawn   15.4.66

W63. Flight of Spitfires

W64. Pilot in Hurricane

W65. Wing-tips of Spitfire and Messerschmitt "ME-109"

W66. Spitfires attacking Heinkel "HE-111" Bomber

W67. Spitfires attacking Stuka Dive-bomber

W68. Hurricanes over Wreck of Dornier "DO-1722" Bomber

W69. Anti-aircraft Artillery in Action

W70. Air-battle over St. Paul's Cathedral

(Des. Andrew Restall (9d.), David Gentleman and Rosalind Dease (others))

1965 (SEPTEMBER 13). 25th ANNIVERSARY OF BATTLE OF BRITAIN

The "Battle of Britain" was the first major campaign in world history to be fought entirely between opposing air forces.

The 4d. values were issued together *se-tenant* in blocks of six (3 × 2) within the sheet

A. Ordinary

					Mint	Used
W67 (=S.G.671) **W63**	4d.	yellow-olive and black	. . . .		1·00	1·00
	a.	Block of 6. Nos. W67/72	. . . .		6·00	10·00
W68 (=S.G.672) **W64**	4d.	yellow-olive, olive-grey and black	. . . .		1·00	1·00
W69 (=S.G.673) **W65**	4d.	red, new blue, yellow-olive, olive-grey and black	. . .		1·00	1·00
	b.	Damaged wing (Cyl. 3D Dot, R. 19/3)	. . . .		4·50	
W70 (=S.G.674) **W66**	4d.	olive-grey, yellow-olive and black	. . . .		1·00	1·00

W71 (=S.G.675) **W67**	4d.	olive-grey, yellow-olive and black	1·00	1·00
	b.	Stuka retouch (Cyl. 1E No dot, R. 2/2)	5·50	
W72 (=S.G.676) **W68**	4d.	olive-grey, yellow-olive, new blue and black	1·00	1·00
	b.	New blue omitted	†	£4000
	c.	Damaged tailplane (Cyl. 3D Dot, R. 20/3)	4·50	
W73 (=S.G.677) **W69**	9d.	bluish violet, orange and slate-purple	1·75	2·00
	a.	Watermark inverted	50·00	
W74 (=S.G.678) **W70**	1s.3d.	light and deep grey, black and light and bright blue .	1·75	2·00
	a.	Watermark inverted	25·00	

> First Day Cover (W67/74) . . . . 25·00
> Presentation Pack (W67/74) . . . . 65·00

No. W72*b* is only known commercially used on cover from Truro.

B. Phosphor

WP67 (=S.G.671p) **W63**	4d.	Three bands	1·25	1·50
	a.	Block of 6. Nos. WP67/72	10·00	15·00
	b.	Narrow band at left (stamp with vert. margin) . .	2·50	
WP68 (=S.G.672p) **W64**	4d.	Three bands	1·25	1·50
WP69 (=S.G.673p) **W65**	4d.	Three bands	1·25	1·50
	b.	Narrow band at right (stamp with vert. margin) .	2·50	
	c.	Damaged wing (Cyl. 3D Dot, R. 19/3)	4·75	
	d.	Error. Two bands		
WP70 (=S.G.674p) **W66**	4d.	Three bands	1·25	1·50
	b.	Narrow band at left (stamp with vert. margin) . .	2·50	
WP71 (=S.G.675p) **W67**	4d.	Three bands	1·25	1·50
	b.	Stuka retouch (Cyl. 1E No dot, R. 2/2)	6·00	
WP72 (=S.G.676p) **W68**	4d.	Three bands	1·25	1·50
	b.	Narrow band at right (stamp with vert. margin) .	2·50	
	c.	Damaged tailplane (Cyl. 3D Dot, R. 20/3)	4·75	
WP73 (=S.G.677p) **W69**	9d.	Three bands	1·75	2·50
	a.	Narrow band at left or right (stamp with vert. margin)	3·50	
	b.	Error. Two bands		
WP74 (=S.G.678p) **W70**	1s.3d.	Three bands	1·75	2·50
	a.	Watermark inverted	3·00	
	b.	Narrow band at left or right (stamp with vert. margin)	3·50	

> First Day Cover (WP67/74) . . . . 28·00

W69*b*, WP69*c*

W71*b*, WP71*b*
This variety only occurs in combination with cyls. 3A–1B–1C–3D. With cyls. 2A–1B–1C–3D it is normal

W72*c*, WP72*c*

Cylinder Numbers (Blocks of Twelve (3 × 4) (4d.), Four (9d.), Six (1s.3d.))

(a) Ordinary

	Cyl. Nos.	Perforation Types		
		A (E/1) No dot	A (E/1) Dot	F (P/E) No dot
4d.	2A (black)–1B (blue)–1C (red)–3D (olive-grey)–1E (yellow-olive)	18·00	18·00	†
	3A–1B–1C–3D–1E	18·00	22·00*	†
9d.	1A (slate-purple)–1B (violet)–1C (orange) . . .	†	†	10·00
1s.3d.	1A (black)–1B (light blue)–1C (light grey)–1D (deep grey)–1E (bright blue)	†	†	14·00

(b) Phosphor

4d.	3A (black)–1B (blue)–1C (red)–3D (olive-grey)–1E (yellow-olive)	22·00	25·00*	†
9d.	1A (slate-purple)–1B (violet)–1C (orange) . . .	†	†	10·00
1s.3d.	1A (black)–1B (light blue)–1C (light grey)–1D (deep grey)–1E (bright blue)	†	†	14·00

Minor Constant Flaws

4d. Cyls. 1B–1C–3D–1E no dot in combination with black cyls. 2A or 3A no dot
  1/3 Horizontal scratch retouch under right of cross (Th. F5–7), OP
  1/6 Similar retouch under centre of cross (Th. F3–6), OP
 15/2 Nick in centre line of fuselage at left (Th. D1), OP
 20/1 Small dark area on left wing of bomber (Th. D2), OP

4d. Cyl. 3A no dot
  1/4 Nick in lower curve of B in BRITAIN, OP
  7/2 Black spot in front of Queen's ear (Th. C12), OP
 12/3 White scar across Queen's left cheek (Th. C12), OP
 13/2 Fine vertical line on Queen's left cheek (Th. C12), OP
 18/3 Extra white dot in Queen's hair behind earring (Th. C13), OP

4d. Cyls. 1B–1C–3D–1E dot in combination with black cyls. 2A or 3A dot
  5/3 Dark horizontal line below right arm of cross (Th. F5–6), OP
  8/1 Dark spot at left end of bomber's wing (Th. C1), OP
 11/2 Line of white dots on pilot's right shoulder (Th. E8–F10), OP
 16/1 Dark spot at right end of bomber's wing (Th. B9), OP
 16/3 Notch in bomber's tail under B of Battle (Th. A4), OP

9d. Cyls. 1A–1B–1C no dot
 11/2 Line across Queen's face under eyes (Th. C10–11), OP
 12/3 Retouch in sky behind hat of man with flag (Th. C1), OP
 20/5 White patch below where vapour trails cross (Th. C5–6), OP

1s.3d. Cyls. 1A–1B–1C–1D–1E no dot
   4/4 Scratch below 1 of 1940 (Th. H5), OP
   5/3 Horizontal bright blue line above building at right (Th. F8–10), OP
   5/4 Dark line between Br of Britain (Th. G–H5), OP
   9/5 Retouches in sky at lower right (Th. D–E9–10), OP
   14/4 Blue dot in front of Queen's ear (Th. C12), OP
   20/3 Line under value is shorter at right, OP

Sheet Details

Sheet size: 120 (6 × 20)
   4d. In *se-tenant* blocks of six, double pane reel-fed
   9d. and 1s.3d. Single pane sheet-fed
Sheet markings:
   Cylinder numbers:
      4d. and 1s.3d. Opposite rows 18/19 at left, boxed
      9d. Opposite R. 19/1, boxed
   Guide holes:
      4d. In double "S O N" box opposite rows 14/15, at left (no dot) or right (dot)
      Others: None
   Marginal arrows (photo-etched): "W" shaped, at top, bottom and sides
   Marginal rule: At bottom of sheet
   Colour register marks:
      4d. None
      9d. Above and below vertical rows 1/2 and 6
      1s.3d. Above and below vertical rows 1/2 and 5/6
         There is a large violet blob of colour under vertical rows 1/2 in the 9d. value
   Autotron marks (solid):
      4d. Black, red, blue, olive-grey, yellow-olive opposite rows 3/7, at right (no dot) or left (dot)
      Others: None
   Colour designations: None
   Traffic lights (boxed):
      4d. Olive-grey, red, black, blue, yellow-olive opposite rows 18/19 at right
      9d. Violet, orange, slate-purple opposite R. 19/6
      1s.3d. Deep grey, light blue, light grey, black, bright blue opposite rows 18/19 at right

Imprimaturs from the National Postal Museum Archives

   A. Ordinary

   Nos. W67/72 imperforate, watermark Type W.24

   Watermark upright (*se-tenant block of six*) £900

   Nos. W73/74 imperforate, watermark Type W.24

   Watermark upright (*2 values*) £2000

   B. Phosphor

   Nos. WP67/72 imperforate, watermark Type W.24

   Watermark upright (*se-tenant block of six*) £900

   Nos. WP73/74 imperforate, watermark Type W.24

   Watermark upright (*2 values*) £2000

Quantities Issued

	Ordinary	Phosphor
4d.	103,417,440	11,560,440
9d.	6,195,960	1,143,120
1s.3d.	6,469,440	1,239,840
Pack	28,524	—

Withdrawn   31.5.66

W71. Post Office Tower and
Georgian Buildings

W72. Post Office Tower and
"Nash" Terrace, Regent's Park

(Des. Clive Abbott)

1965 (OCTOBER 8). OPENING OF POST OFFICE TOWER

The tallest building in London, the Post Office Tower is 620 feet high and helps to provide more long distance telephone circuits and more television channels. An additional feature of this issue was the inclusion of the names of both the designer and printers at the foot of the stamps and this became the practice for many later issues until 1969.

Watermark sideways on 3d.

A. Ordinary				Mint	Used
W75 (=S.G.679) **W71**	3d.	olive-yellow, new blue and bronze-green		10	15
	a.	Olive-yellow (tower) omitted	£2000	£750
	b.	Extra window (Dot, R. 4/18)		4·50	
W76 (=S.G.680) **W72**	1s.3d.	bronze-green, yellow-green and blue		30	45
	a.	Watermark inverted		45·00	

First Day Cover (W75/6)	6·50
Presentation Pack (W75/6)	6·00

The one phosphor band on No. WP75 was produced by printing broad phosphor bands across alternate rows of vertical perforations. Individual examples show the band at right or left (*same prices either way*).

B. Phosphor					
WP75 (=S.G.679p) **W71**	3d.	One band at left		15	15
	a.	Band at right		15	15
	ab.	Nos. WP75/*a* (horiz. pair)		30	50
	ac.	Error. Broad band *se-tenant* with missing phosphor (horiz. pair)		50·00	
	b.	Extra window (Dot, R. 4/18)		4·50	
WP76 (=S.G.680p) **W72**	1s.3d.	Three bands		30	50
	a.	Watermark inverted		50·00	
	b.	Error. Left-hand band omitted		27·00	

First Day Cover (W75/6)	7·00
Presentation Pack* (WP75/6)	6·00

*See note under "Withdrawn" at end of listing.

The above are known pre-released on 4 October at Aish, South Brent (Devon).

W75*b*, WP75*b*

Cylinder Numbers (Blocks of Four)

(a) Ordinary

	Cyl. Nos.	Perforation Types		
		A (I/E) No dot	A (I/E) Dot	F (P/E) No dot
3d.	1A (blue)–1B (green)–1C (yellow)*	1·00	1·00	†
1s.3d.	1A (yellow-green)–1B (bronze-green)–1C (blue)	†	†	2·75

(b) Phosphor

3d.	1A (blue)–1B (green)–1C (yellow)*	1·25	1·25	†
1s.3d.	1A (yellow-green)–1B (bronze-green)–1C (blue)	†	†	2·75

*In the 3d. dot pane the dot after "1C" is omitted in error.
For perforation Type A the 3d. is with sheet orientated showing head to left.

Minor Constant Flaws

3d. Cyls. 1A–1B–1C dot
  1/20 White spot at base of tower (Th. L3), OP
  2/19 Olive-yellow spot below second ground floor window of building at base of tower at right (Th. M4), OP
  2/20 Blue spot below SO of HARRISON, OP
  5/2 White spot in O of OFFICE, OP
  5/8 Blue spot surrounded by pale area below T of TOWER, OP
  5/16 Pale spot in blue panel to left of 3d. (Th. J4), OP

1s.3d. Cyls. 1A–1B–1C no dot
  1/5 Pale area around lower tip of 3 of 1/3, OP
  3/1 Small retouch below T of TOWER (Th. C–D1), OP
  4/1 Horizontal line of retouching below 1/3 (Th. D11–12), OP
  6/2 Scratch in sky above roof of left-hand terrace (Th. E2), OP
  10/3 Dark spot to left of Queen's nose (Th. C8), OP
  10/4 Retouch to background at top right of 1 of 1/3, OP
  15/4 White scratch through E and over R of TOWER, OP

Sheet Details

Sheet sizes:
  3d. 120 (20 × 6). Double pane reel-fed
  1s.3d. 120 (6 × 20). Single pane sheet-fed
Sheet markings:
  Cylinder numbers:
    3d. Above vertical row 2, boxed
    1s.3d. Opposite R. 19/1, boxed
  Guide holes:
    3d. In double "S O N" box above vertical rows 6/7 (no dot) or below (dot)
    1s.3d. None
  Marginal arrows (photo-etched): "W" shaped, at top, bottom and sides
  Marginal rule: 3d. At left of sheet; 1s.3d. At bottom of sheet
  Colour register marks:
    3d. None
    1s.3d. Above and below vertical rows 1/2 and 5/6

Autotron marks (solid):
  3d Yellow, green, blue below vertical rows 15/17 (no dot) or above (dot)
  1s.3d. None
Colour designations: None
Traffic lights (boxed):
  3d. Yellow, green, blue reading left to right below vertical row 2
  1s.3d. Yellow-green, bronze-green, blue opposite R. 19/6

Imprimaturs from the National Postal Museum Archives

A. Ordinary

Nos. W75/76 imperforate, watermark Type W.24

Watermark upright (1s.3d.) or sideways (3d.) (*set of* 2) £2000

B. Phosphor

Nos. WP75/76 imperforate, watermark Type W.24

Watermark upright (1s.3d.) or sideways (3d.) (*set of* 2) £2000

Quantities Issued

	Ordinary	Phosphor
3d.	51,291,120	4,274,880
1s.3d.	5,722,320	1,107,480
Pack	25,060 (ordinary and phosphor)	

Withdrawn 30.6.66

When the Post Office Tower was opened on 19 May 1966 these stamps were issued from automatic machines giving a block of four of the 3d. and a pair of the 1s.3d. dispensed in envelopes, and packs were also issued from a machine. These continued to be available after the stamps had been withdrawn everywhere else and early in 1968 the ordinary stamps were replaced by phosphor stamps and packs. These were withdrawn on the introduction of decimal currency.

W73. U.N. Emblem   **W74.** I.C.Y. Emblem

(Des. Jeffery Matthews)

1965 (OCTOBER 25). 20th ANNIVERSARY OF THE UNITED NATIONS

Commemorating the 20th Anniversary of the formation of the United Nations in 1945. 1965 was also designated International Co-operation Year and the symbol of the clasped hands is shown on the 1s.6d. value.

A. Ordinary

				Mint	Used
W77 (=S.G.681) **W73**	3d.		black, yellow-orange and light blue	25	20
		a.	Broken circle (Dot, R. 11/4)	4·50	
		b.	Lake in Russia (Dot, R. 19/3)	4·00	
		c.	"Flying saucer" flaw (Dot, R. 18/3)	5·50	
		d.	Retouched	4·50	
		e.	Imperf. between stamp and top margin*	£1500	
W78 (=S.G.682) **W74**	1s.6d.		black, bright purple and light blue	1·00	80
		a.	Watermark inverted	—	£1750

First Day Cover (W77/8)	12·00

B. Phosphor

WP77 (=S.G.681p) **W73**	3d.		One centre band	25	30
		a.	Broken circle (Dot, R. 11/4)	4·75	
		b.	Lake in Russia (Dot, R. 19/3)	4·00	
		c.	"Flying saucer" flaw (Dot, R. 18/3)	5·50	
		d.	Retouched	4·50	
WP78 (=S.G.682p) **W74**	1s.6d.		Three bands	2·75	3·00
		a.	Error. Two bands	30·00	

> First Day Cover (WP77/8) .... 14·00

*No. W77*e* was caused by a paper fold.

W77*a*, WP77*a*	W77*b*, WP77*b*	W77*c*, WP77*c* Stroke over "S" of "ANNIVERSARY" and smudge	W77*d*, WP77*d* Retouched. Smudge removed

Cylinder Numbers (Blocks of Four)

(a) Ordinary

	Cyl. Nos.	Perforation Types		
		A (E/I) No dot	A (E/I) Dot	F (P/E) No dot
3d.	1A (black)–1B (blue)–1C (orange)*	2·00	2·00	†
1s.6d.	1A (black)–1B (blue)–1C (purple)	†	†	5·50

(b) Phosphor

3d.	1A (black)–1B (blue)–1C (orange)*	2·50	2·50	†
1s.6d.	1A (black)–1B (blue)–1C (purple)	†	†	15·00

*In the 3d. dot pane the dot is before instead of after the "1C".

Minor Constant Flaws

3d. Cyls. 1A–1B–1C no dot
    1/1 Diagonal scratch across Queen's face (Th. C11–12), OP
    1/4 Round pale grey flaw by Queen's left eye (Th. C11–12), OP
    2/2 Pale patch on Queen's neck (Th. E12), OP
    8/5 Dotted white scratch on right side of 0 of large 20 (Th. D8–9), OP
    9/2 Black flaw in lower loop of 3, OP
    10/4 Small break in middle of S of ANNIVERSARY, OP
    13/1 Curved white scratch in bottom right-hand corner of blue panel (Th. H9–10), OP
    14/4 Scratch on Queen's neck by necklace (Th. E12), OP
    15/6 Black spot on Queen's forehead (Th. C11), OP
    19/4 Horizontal white scratch over VERSARY, OP
    20/6 Black flaws between laurel leaves over middle of large 2 (Th. D3), OP

3d. Cyls. 1A–1B–1C dot
    20/1 White scratch through ARY U, OP

1s.6d. Cyls. 1A–1B–1C no dot
    2/1 White scratch behind Queen's neck (Th. D12–E12), OP
    5/1 Small patch of white dots to right of Queen's head (Th. B13), OP

6/2   Pale patch to left of top of large U (Th. B1), OP
10/1 Pale patch in background to left of Queen's mouth (Th. D10), OP
11/2 Pink spot central below large N (Th. F7), OP
15/1 White scratch in base of large U, (Th. E2), OP
20/1 Vertical white scratch in background behind Queen's head (Th. C–D13), OP
20/5 Retouch to background within upper thumb of symbol (Th. B5), OP

Sheet Details

Sheet size: 120 (6 × 20).3d. double pane reel-fed; 1s.6d. single pane sheet-fed
Sheet markings:
Cylinder numbers: Opposite R. 19/1, boxed
Guide holes:
   3d. In double "S O N" box opposite rows 14/15, at left (no dot) or right (dot). An unusual
      feature of this stamp is that there is an additional single box printed in orange beneath the
      double box which is in black
   1s.6d. None
Marginal arrows (photo-etched): "W" shaped, at top, bottom and sides
Marginal rule: At bottom of sheet
Colour register marks:
   3d. None
   1s.6d. Above and below vertical rows 1 and 6
Autotron marks (solid):
   3d. Black, blue, orange opposite rows 5/6 at right (no dot) or left (dot)
   1s.6d. None
Colour designations (usually trimmed off):
   3d. "G1 BROWN G2 BLUE G3 BLACK" in right margin reading upwards opposite rows 8/5
      on dot panes
   1s.6d. None
Traffic lights (boxed):
   3d. Black, blue, orange opposite R. 19/6
   1s.6d. Black, blue, purple opposite R. 19/6

Imprimaturs from the National Postal Museum Archives

A. Ordinary

Nos. W77/78 imperforate, watermark Type W.24

Watermark upright (*set of 2*) £2000

B. Phosphor

Nos. WP77/78 imperforate, watermark Type W.24

Watermark upright (*set of 2*) £2000

Quantities Issued

	Ordinary	Phosphor
3d.	50,598,720	4,488,240
1s.6d.	5,476,800	1,018,560

Withdrawn   30.6.66

W75. Telecommunications Network   **W76.** Radio Waves and Switchboard

(Des. Andrew Restall)

1965 (NOVEMBER 15).   I.T.U. CENTENARY

The aims of the Union created in 1865, then known as the International Telegraph Union, were to promote, maintain and extend international co-operation in telecommunications.

A. Ordinary

				Mint	Used
W79 (=S.G.683) **W75**	9d.	red, ultramarine, deep slate-violet, black and pink	..	50	40
	a.	Watermark inverted		14·00	
W80 (=S.G.684) **W76**	1s.6d.	red, greenish blue, indigo, black and light pink	..	1·50	1·25
	a.	Light pink omitted		£1500	
	b.	Watermark inverted		55·00	
	c.	Retouched arm (R. 1/4)		5·50	

First Day Cover (W79/80) . . . .   17·00

B. Phosphor

WP79 (=S.G.683p) **W75**	9d.	Three bands	1·00	75
	a.	Watermark inverted	70·00	
	b.	Error. Two bands	60·00	
	c.	Narrow band at left (stamp with vert. margin) ..	2·50	
WP80 (=S.G.684p) **W76**	1s.6d.	Three bands	4·25	5·25
	a.	Error. Two bands	25·00	
	b.	Narrow band at left (stamp with vert. margin)	6·00	
	c.	Red pin with arm (R. 1/4)	20·00	
	d.	Retouched	16·00	

First Day Cover (WP79/80) . . . .   20·00

Originally scheduled for issue on 17 May 1965, supplies from the Philatelic Bureau were sent in error to reach a dealer on that date and another dealer received his supply on 27 May. Ordinary and phosphor sets exist on cover postmarked Stretford on 18 May 1965.

On the phosphor printing the red pin has a projecting arm at right; this was later retouched leaving faint traces of red on the pink background and it is known only in the retouched state on the ordinary printing.

WP80*c*   W80*c*, W80*d*

Cylinder Numbers (Blocks of Six)

(a) Ordinary

		Cyl. Nos. (No dot)	Perforation Type F (P/E)
9d.		1A (ultram.)–1B (red)–1C (violet)–1D (pink)–2E (black)	4·50
1s.6d.		2A (blue)–1B (indigo)–1C (pink)–1D (red)–2E (black)	12·00

(b) Phosphor

9d.		1A (ultram.)–1B (red)–1C (violet)–1D (pink)–2E (black)	7·00
1s.6d.		2A (blue)–1B (indigo)–1C (pink)-1D (red)–2E (black)	27·00

The same black cylinder was used for both values.

Minor Constant Flaws

9d. and 1s.6d. Cyl. 2E
    2/4 Small white curl in hair behind Queen's ear (Th. C12), OP
    5/2 Small nick in diagonal stroke of first N of UNION, OP

9d. Cyls. 1A–1B–1C–1D–2E
    6/5 Small break in diagonal blue network line at right (Th. B8), OP
    9/5 Diagonal white scratch in blue background above ATIO of INTERNATIONAL (Th. E3), OP
   10/5 Damaged lower half of 1 of 1865, shows as white nick and white scratch, OP
   17/6 Small nick in right-hand stroke of first M of TELECOMMUNICATION, OP
   20/5 Wavy scratch in background over OMMUNI of TELECOMMUNICATION (Th. E7–9), OP

1s.6d. Cyls. 2A–1B–1C–1D–2E
    3/3 Retouches to background above first C of TELECOMMUNICATION, P

Sheet Details

Sheet size: 120 (6 × 20). Single pane sheet-fed
Sheet markings:
    Cylinder numbers: Opposite rows 18/19 at left, boxed
    Guide holes: None
    Marginal arrows (photo-etched): "W" shaped, at top, bottom and sides
    Marginal rule: At bottom of sheet
    Colour register marks: Above and below vertical rows 1/2 and 5/6
    Autotron marks: None
    Colour designations: None
    Traffic lights (boxed):
        9d. Ultramarine, red, violet, pink, black opposite rows 18/19 at right
        1s.6d. Blue indigo, pink, red, black opposite rows 18/19 at right

Imprimaturs from the National Postal Museum Archives

A. Ordinary

Nos. W79/80 imperforate, watermark Type W.24
Watermark upright (*set of 2*) £2000

B. Phosphor

Nos. WP79/80 imperforate, watermark Type W.24 . . . . £2000
Watermark upright (*set of 2*)

Quantities Issued

	Ordinary	Phosphor
9d.	5,321,880	556,080
1s.6d.	5,287,920	589,800

Withdrawn   30.6.66 (1s.6d. phosphor sold out December 1965)

W77. Robert Burns (after Skirving chalk drawing)

W78. Robert Burns (after Nasmyth portrait)

(Des. Gordon F. Huntly)

1966 (JANUARY 25). BURNS COMMEMORATION

Robert Burns (1759–1796), Scotland's celebrated national poet, was born in Alloway, near Ayr.

A. Ordinary

			Mint	Used
W81 (=S.G.685) **W77**	4d.	black, deep violet-blue and new blue	15	15
W82 (=S.G.686) **W78**	1s.3d.	black, slate-blue and yellow-orange	40	70

> First Day Cover (W81/2) . . . .   4·00
> Presentation Pack (W81/2) . . . .   55·00

B. Phosphor

WP81 (=S.G.685p) **W77**	4d.	Three bands	25	50
	a.	Narrow band at left or right (stamp with vert. margin)	2·00	
WP82 (=S.G.686p) **W78**	1s.3d.	Three bands	2·25	2·25

> First Day Cover (WP81/2) . . . .   6·00

These are known postmarked 24 January 1966.

Cylinder Numbers (Blocks of Four)

(a) Ordinary

	Cyl. Nos.	Perforation Types		
		A (E/I) No dot	A (E/I) Dot	F (P/E) No dot
4d.	1A (violet-blue)–1B (black)–1C (new blue) . .	1·25	1·25	†
	1A–2B–1C	1·25	1·25	†
1s.3d.	2A (slate-blue)–1B (black)–1C (orange)	†	†	2·50

(b) Phosphor

4d.	1A (violet-blue)–1B (black)–1C (new blue) . .	2·50	2·50	†
1s.3d.	2A (slate-blue)–1B (black)–1C (orange)	†	†	11·00

Minor Constant Flaws

4d. Cyls. 1A–1B–1C dot and 1A–2B–1C dot
    9/4 Small white flaw at front of diadem (Th. A10), OP
    18/1 Coloured spot above Queen's upper lip (Th. C10), OP
    19/3 White flaw on Queen's neck above centre of collar (Th. E11), OP

4d. Cyls. 1A–2B–1C dot only
    15/1 White spot at back of Burns's hair by parting (Th. A5), OP

1s.3d. Cyls. 2A–1B–1C no dot
    2/6 Pale background flaw in front of Queen's neck (Th. D9), OP
    3/6 Grey spot on Burns's nose near his right eye (Th. C5), OP
    4/6 Grey diagonal line through white line to panel at lower right (Th. E8–G9), OP
    6/5 White patch to right of Queen's left eyebrow (Th. B11), OP
    9/4 Large dark retouch in Burns's hair left of parting (Th. B4), OP

19/1 Flaw on Burns's right cheek (Th. D4), OP
19/5 Dark flaw on Burns's shirt touching left lapel (Th. F5), OP

Sheet Details

Sheet size: 120 (6 × 20). 4d double pane reel-fed: 1s.3d. single pane sheet-fed
Sheet marking:
   Cylinder numbers: R. 19/1, boxed
   Guide holes:
      4d. In double "S O N" box opposite rows 14/15, at left (no dot) or right (dot)
      1s.3d. None
   Marginal arrows (photo-etched): "W" shaped, at top, bottom and sides
   Marginal rule: At bottom of sheet
   Colour register marks:
      4d. None
      1s.3d. Above and below vertical rows 1 and 6
   Coloured crosses:
      4d. None
      1s.3d. Above and below vertical row 2
   Autotron marks (solid):
      4d. Violet-blue, black, new blue opposite rows 5/6, at right (no dot) or left (dot)
      1s.3d. None
   Colour designations: None
   Traffic lights (boxed):
      4d. New blue, black, violet-blue opposite R. 19/6
      1s.3d. Orange, black, slate-blue opposite R. 19/6

Imprimaturs from the National Postal Museum Archives

A. Ordinary

Nos. W81/82 imperforate, watermark Type W.24

Watermark upright (*set of 2*) £2000

B. Phosphor

Nos. WP81/82 imperforate, watermark Type W.24

Watermark upright (*set of 2*) £2000

Quantities Sold

	Ordinary	Phosphor
4d.	77,905,176	8,738,520
1s.3d.	5,685,096	1,226,160
Pack	38,968	—

Withdrawn 29.7.66 but later put on sale again in error for a short time at the Philatelic Counter in
London, the Philatelic Bureau in Edinburgh and at the Edinburgh Festival.

W79. Westminster Abbey
(Des. Sheila Robinson)

W80. Fan Vaulting, Henry VII Chapel
(Des. and eng. Bradbury, Wilkinson)

1966 (FEBRUARY 28). 900th ANNIVERSARY OF WESTMINSTER ABBEY
   Westminster Abbey, officially the Collegiate Church of St. Peter, Westminster, is the nation's
Coronation Church and a mausoleum for England's greatest men and women.
   The 2s.6d. is recess-printed on chalk-surfaced paper by Bradbury, Wilkinson and comb perf.
11 × 12.

A. Ordinary

			Mint	Used
W83 (=S.G.687) **W79**	3d.	black, red-brown and new blue	15	20
	a.	Diadem flaw (No dot, R.16/2)	3·00	
	b.	Retouch on Queen's cheek (Dot, R. 15/6)	3·00	
W84 (=S.G.688) **W80**	2s.6d.	black	55	80

First Day Cover (W83/4)	6·00
Presentation Pack (W83/4)	45·00

B. Phosphor

WP83 (=S.G.687p) **W79**	3d.	One band	20	25
	a.	Diadem flaw (No dot, R. 16/2)	4·50	
	b.	Retouch on Queen's cheek (Dot. R. 15/6)	4·00	
	c.	Error. Two bands	10·00	

First Day Cover (WP83)	14·00

W83*a*, WP83*a*   W83*b*, WP83*b*

Cylinder and Plate Numbers (Blocks of Four)

	Cyl. or Plate Nos.	Perforation Type A (E/I)	
		No dot	Dot
3d.	2A (blue)–1B (black)–1C (brown). Ordinary .	1·25	1·25
	2A–1B–1C. Phosphor	3·50	3·50
2s.6d.	Plate 1. Ordinary	5·00	†
	Plate 1A	7·00	†

Minor Constant Flaws

3d. Cyls. 2A–1B–1C no dot
    1/6 Vertical scratch to right of Queen's head and running through bottom frame of panel (Th. D–E12), OP
    15/1 Small white dots touching E and second A of ANNIVERSARY, OP

2s.6d. Plate 1
    2/2 Broken horizontal line in top margin over Y of ANNIVERSARY (Th. A1)
    6/1 Scratch in bottom margin below Y of ABBEY (Th. I13–14)
    10/2 Second 0 of 900 joined to t of th

2s.6d. Plate 1A
    5/3 Horizontal line in margin left of Y of ANNIVERSARY and vertical line in top margin at left (Th. A1 and A2)
    7/4 Scratch through Y of ANNIVERSARY

Sheet Details

Sheet sizes:
    3d. 120 (6 × 20). Double pane sheet-fed
    2s.6d. 40 (4 × 10). Double pane sheet-fed
Sheet markings:
    Cylinder numbers: 3d. R. 19/1, boxed
    Plate numbers: 2s.6d. Bottom margin below vertical rows 3/4

Guide holes:
  3d. In double "S O N" box opposite rows 14/15, at left (no dot) or right (dot)
  2s.6d. In circle opposite row 6, at left (Pl. 1) or right (Pl. 1A)
Marginal arrows (photo-etched): 3d. "W" shaped, at top, bottom and sides; 2s.6d. none
Marginal rule: 3d at bottom of sheet; 2s.6d. none.
Colour register marks: None
Coloured cross (black): 2s.6d. opposite row 6, at right (Pl. 1) or left (Pl. 1A)
Autotron marks (solid):
  3d. Blue, black, red-brown opposite rows 6/7, at right (no dot) or left (dot); 2s.6d. none
Colour designations: None
Traffic lights (boxed):
  3d. Blue, black, red-brown opposite R. 19/6

Imprimaturs from the National Postal Museum Archives

A. Ordinary

Nos. W83/84 imperforate, watermark Type W.24

Watermark upright (*set of* 2) £2000

B. Phosphor

No. WP83 imperforate, watermark Type W.24

Watermark upright £1000

Quantities Sold

	Ordinary	Phosphor
3d.	48,703,426	5,247,720
2s.6d.	2,819,056	—
Pack	24,272	—

Withdrawn   31.8.66 3d. (2s.6d. sold out in April 1966)

The 3d. was later put on sale again in error for a short time at the Philatelic Counter in London and at the Philatelic Bureau in Edinburgh.

W81. View near Hassocks, Sussex

W82. Antrim, Northern Ireland

W83. Harlech Castle, Wales

W84. Cairngorm Mountains, Scotland

(Des. Leonard Rosoman. Queen's portrait adapted by David Gentleman from coinage)

1966 (MAY 2).   LANDSCAPES

Britain's first special pictorial stamps featuring scenes in England, Northern Ireland, Wales and Scotland.

The Queen's profile design on this, and following special issues to 1967 Christmas, was taken from the coinage design by Mrs. Mary Gillick and adapted by David Gentleman.

A. Ordinary

				Mint	Used
W85 (=S.G.689) **W81**	4d.	black, yellow-green and new blue		10	15
	a.	Dash before "ENGLAND" (No dot, R. 20/5)		4·50	
	b.	Green flaw on tree trunk (Dot, R. 3/4)		4·50	
W86 (=S.G.690) **W82**	6d.	black, emerald and new blue		15	20
	a.	Watermark inverted		6·00	
	b.	"AN" for "AND" (R. 10/3)		16·00	
	c.	Retouched, with misaligned "D"		5·50	
W87 (=S.G.691) **W83**	1s.3d.	black, greenish yellow and greenish blue		25	35
	a.	Broken "D" (R. 14/2)		4·50	
W88 (=S.G.692) **W84**	1s.6d.	black, orange and Prussian blue		40	35
	a.	Watermark inverted		15·00	

> First Day Cover (W85/8) . . . . 7·00

B. Phosphor

				Mint	Used
WP85 (=S.G.689p) **W81**	4d.	Three bands		10	15
	a.	Narrow band at left or right (stamp with vert. margin)		2·00	
	b.	Green flaw on tree trunk (Dot. R. 3/4)		4·50	
WP86 (=S.G.690p) **W82**	6d.	Three bands		15	20
	a.	Watermark inverted		30·00	
	b.	"AN" for "AND" (R. 10/3)		8·00	
WP87 (=S.G.691p) **W83**	1s.3d.	Three bands		25	35
	a.	Broken "D" (R. 14/2)		4·50	
WP88 (=S.G.692p) **W84**	1s.6d.	Three bands		40	40

> First Day Cover (WP85/8) . . . . 8·50

These are known postmarked 26 April in Winchester.

No. W85 exists with Queen's head and value omitted, due to a paper fold, with the stamp above showing value only omitted. A vertical pair of No. W86 exists with the Queen's head and value omitted from the upper stamp and partial omission on the lower stamp, both due to a paper fold.

W86*b* and WP86*b*. 40,000 sheets, including all the phosphor stamps, were printed before this was discovered and the "D" was then added to the cylinder, forming W86*c*.

W85*a*
(Later retouched)

W85*b*, WP85*b*

W87*a*, WP87*a*

Cylinder Numbers (Blocks of Four)

(a) Ordinary

		Cyl. Nos.	Perforation Type A (E/I)	
			No dot	Dot
4d.	2A (blue)–1B (black)–1C (yellow-green)	. . .	1·25	1·25

	No dot	
	Type F (P/E)	Type F(L) (I/E)
6d. 1A (blue)–3B (black)–1C (green)	1·25	†
1s.3d. 2A (blue)–2B (black)–1C* (yellow)	2·50	†
1s.6d. 1A (blue)–1B (orange)–1C (black)	3·00	3·00

(b) Phosphor

	Perforation Types		
	A (E/I) No dot	A (E/I) Dot	F (P/E) No dot
4d. 2A (blue)–1B (black)–1C (yellow-green) . . .	1·25	1·25	†
6d. 1A (blue)–3B (black)–1C (green)	†	†	1·25
1s.3d. 2A (blue)–2B (black)–1C* (yellow)	†	†	2·50
1s.6d. 1A (blue)–1B (orange)–1C (black)	†	†	2·50

*The figure one of this cylinder is inverted

Minor Constant Flaws

4d. Cyls. 2A–1B–1C no dot
11/2 Pale area behind Queen's collar above value (Th. E–F12–13), OP
14/5 Dark spot in green field at top left corner (Th. A1–2), OP

4d. Cyls. 2A–1B–1C dot
2/4 Retouching in sky between clouds (Th. A2), OP

6d. Cyls. 1A–1B–1C no dot
2/2 Horizontal blue line across Queen's neck, later retouched on ordinary (Th. D11), OP
5/4 Green spot between N. and I, OP
17/2 Curved green flaw on trees opposite Queen's chin (Th. D9), OP
18/1 Blue mark in field left of cottage (Th. F5), OP
19/2 Green line running across Queen's head (Th. B10–12), OP
20/6 Diagonal black flaw below second R of HARRISON, OP

1s.3d. Cyls. 2A–2B–1C no dot
6/1 Pale diagonal white line above ES of WALES, OP
9/2 Pale area between 1 and 3 of value (Th. F11–12), OP
19/1 Dot before "M" of "ROSOMAN" (Th. H2), OP

1s.6d. Cyls. 1A–1B–1C no dot
1/6 Blurred area at back of Queen's hair (Th. B–C12), OP
4/6 Several blemishes in background between mountains which appear as italic figures 20 (Th. A4–5), OP
8/1 Retouch above d of value (Th. F13), OP
13/4 Retouch behind Queen's neck (Th. D12), OP
18/3 White spot between AN of SCOTLAND and foot of A is enlarged, OP

Sheet Details

Sheet size: 120 (6 × 20). 4d. double pane reel-fed; others single pane sheet-fed
Sheet markings:
Cylinder numbers: R. 19/1, boxed
Guide holes:
4d. In single "S O N" box opposite rows 14/15, at left (no dot) or right (dot). The centre bar of the double box has been erased
Others: None
Marginal arrows (photo-etched): "W" shaped, at top, bottom and sides
Marginal rule: At bottom of sheet
Colour register marks:
4d. None
Others: Above and below vertical rows 1/2 and 5/6
Autotron marks (solid):
4d. Blue, black, yellow-green opposite rows 5/6, at right (no dot) or left (dot); others, none
Colour designations: None
Traffic lights (boxed):
4d. Blue, black, yellow-green opposite R. 19/6
6d. Blue, black, green opposite R. 19/6
1s.3d. Blue, black, yellow opposite R. 19/6
1s.6d. Black, blue, orange opposite R. 19/6

Imprimaturs from the National Postal Museum Archives

A. Ordinary

Nos. W85/88 imperforate, watermark Type W.24

Watrmark upright (*set of* 4) £4000

B. Phosphor

Nos. WP85/88 imperforate, watermark Type W.24

Watermark upright (*set of* 4) £4000

Quantities Sold

	Ordinary	Phosphor		Ordinary	Phosphor
4d.	80,326,440	11,283,720	1s.3d.	5,286,000	1,242,720
6d.	11,531,760	2,459,280	1s.6d.	5,462,640	1,204,200

Withdrawn 1.5.67 but 6d. phosphor was sold out in January

W86. Goalmouth Mêlée
(Des. William Kempster)

W85. Players with Ball
(Des. David Gentleman)

W87. Goalkeeper saving Goal
(Des. David Caplan)

1966 (JUNE 1). WORLD FOOTBALL CUP CHAMPIONSHIP

Sixteen countries took part in the final stages of the World Football Championship for the Jules Rimet Cup in England during July, 1966. See also No. W96.

Watermark sideways on 4d.

A. Ordinary

				Mint	Used
W89 (=S.G.693) **W85**		4d.	red, reddish purple, bright blue, flesh and black	10	25
	a.		Patch on thigh (No dot, R. 3/20)	4·00	
	b.		Broken shadow (No dot, R. 5/17)	4·00	
W90 (=S.G.694) **W86**		6d.	black, sepia, red, apple-green and blue	15	25
	a.		Black omitted	£110	
	b.		Apple-green omitted	£3000	
	c.		Red omitted	£5000	
	d.		Watermark inverted	2·00	
W91 (=S.G.695) **W87**		1s.3d.	black, blue, yellow, red and light yellow-olive . . .	50	1·00
	a.		Blue omitted	£200	
	b.		Watermark inverted	£110	
	c.		Darned stocking (R. 19/2)	4·75	

> First Day Cover (W89/91) . . . . 20·00
> Presentation Pack (W89/91) . . . . 15·00

B. Phosphor

WP89 (=S.G.693p) **W85**	4d.	Two bands	10	25
	a.	Narrow band at left (stamp with vert. margin) . .	2·00	
	b.	Error. Extra phosphor band at right		
	c.	Error. One broad band	22·00	
	d.	Patch on thigh (No dot. R. 3/20)	4·00	
	e.	Red patch below ball (No dot, R. 4/16)	4·00	
	f.	Broken shadow (No dot, R. 5/17)	3·25	
WP90 (=S.G.694p) **W86**	6d.	Three bands	15	25
	a.	Black omitted	£700	
WP91 (=S.G.695p) **W87**	1s.3d.	Three bands	50	1·00
	a.	Watermark inverted	1·25	
	b.	Darned stocking (R. 19/2)	4·75	
	c.	Error. Two bands	14·00	

> First Day Cover (WP89/91) . . . . 22·00

The 4d. ordinary has been seen postmarked 31 May in Hereford.

W89*a*, WP89*d*, W96*a*

W89*b*, WP89*f*, W96*c*

WP89*e*, W96*b*

W91*c*, WP91*b*

Cylinder Numbers (Blocks of Six)

(a) Ordinary

	Cyl. Nos.	Perforation Type A (I/E)	
		No dot	Dot
4d.	1A (black)–1B (blue)–1C (red)–1D (purple)–1E (flesh)*	1·50	1·50
		Perforation Types	
		F (P/E)	F(L) (I/E)
		No dot	No dot
6d.	1A (blue)–1B (green)–1C (red)–1D (sepia)–1E (black)	1·50	†
	2A–1B–1C–1D–1E	3·00	†
1s.3d.	1A (black)–1B (yellow)–1C (yellow-olive)–1D (blue)–1E (red)	7·00*	8·50*
	1A–1B–1C–1D–2E	7·00*	7·50*

(b) Phosphor

		Perforation Types		
		A (I/E) No dot	A (I/E) Dot	F (P/E) No dot
4d.	1A (black)–1B (blue)–1C (red)–1D (purple)–1E (flesh)*	1·50	1·50	†
6d.	1A (blue)–1B (green)–1C (red)–1D (sepia)–1E (black)	†	†	1·50
1s.3d.	1A (black)–1B (yellow)–1C (yellow-olive)–1D (blue) –2E (red)	†	†	7·00*

*In the 4d. no dot pane the flesh cylinder is expressed in error thus: "1E.".
For perforation Type A the 4d. is with sheet orientated showing head to left.

Minor Constant Flaws

4d. Cyls. 1A–1B–1C–1D–1E no dot
    3/1 Horizontal scratch through top of ball (Th. K1–2), OP
    5/6 Blue patch below u of Cup, OP
    6/18 Blue spots over T of LTD, OP

4d. Cyls. 1A–1B–1C–1D–1E dot
    4/20 Red line joins head and left arm of player at left (Th. F3), OP
    5/10 Dark spot on ball (Th. K1), OP
    5/17 Grey coloured spur to top of l of World, OP

6d. Cyls. 1B–1C–1D–1E in combination with blue cyls. 1A or 2A no dot
    5/4 Diagonal scratch on barrier next to grass below crowd (Th. G5–7), OP

6d. Cyl. 1A no dot
    17/4 Pale area around top of 1 of 1966, OP

1s.3d. Cyls. 1A–1B–1C–1D no dot in combination with red cyls. 1E or 2E
    1/3 Patch on sock of central player (Th. G2), OP
    9/2 Black spur on head of right-hand player (Th. B7), OP
    14/5 Break in black frame line around players opposite U of CUP, OP
    18/1 Black spot to right of stroke of 1/3; also black spot below second R of HARRISON OP
    20/1 Black spot below second A of CAPLAN, OP

1s.3d. Cyl. 2E no dot
    1/6 Red scratch on face of central player, OP

Sheet Details

Sheet size:
    4d. 120 (20 × 6). Double pane reel-fed
    6d. and 1s.3d. 120 (6 × 20). Single pane sheet-fed
Sheet markings:
    Cylinder numbers:
        4d. Above vertical rows 2/3, boxed
        6d. and 1s.3d. Opposite rows 18/19 at left, boxed
    Guide holes:
        4d. In single photo-etched box above vertical rows 6/7 (no dot) or below (dot). On the no dot pane the box is now lettered "SN", the "S" being on the left in the box (usually trimmed off), and the "N" above the right line. On the dot pane the sequence is reversed.
        6d. and 1s.3d. None
    Marginal arrows (photo-etched): "W" shaped, at top, bottom and sides, except that early printings of the 6d. from cylinder 1A both ordinary and phosphor were without any arrow markings in the margins. These were later inserted by hand.
        Minimum price for marginal strip showing arrow omitted: £15 Ordinary or phosphor
    Marginal rule:
        4d. At left of sheet
        6d. and 1s.3d. At bottom of sheet
    Colour register marks:
        4d. Above vertical rows 3/4 and 18/19 (no dot) or below (dot)
        6d. and 1s.3d. Above and below vertical rows 1/2 and 6
    Coloured crosses:
        4d. None
        6d. Above and below vertical row 3
        1s.3d. Above and below vertical rows 3/4

Autotron marks (solid):
    4d. Red, purple, flesh, blue, black below vertical rows 15/18 (no dot) or above (dot)
    6d. and 1s.3d. None
Colour designations:
    4d. "5 BLACK G4 BLUE MAROON G3 G2 RED G1 LIGHT RED" below vertical rows 11/16
       on dot panes only
    6d. and 1s.3d. None
Traffic lights (boxed):
    4d. Black, blue, red, purple, flesh reading left to right below vertical rows 2/3
    6d. Blue, green, red, sepia, black opposite rows 18/19 at right
    1s.3d. Black, yellow, yellow-olive, blue, red opposite rows 18/19 at right

Imprimaturs from the National Postal Museum Archives

A. Ordinary

Nos. W89/91 imperforate, watermark Type W.24

Watermark upright (6d., 1s.3d.) or sideways (4d.) (*set of 3*) £3000

B. Phosphor

Nos. WP89/91 imperforate, watermark Type W.24

Watermark upright (6d., 1s.3d.) or sideways (4d.) (*set of 3*) £3000

Quantities Sold

	Ordinary	Phosphor
4d.	129,764,160	16,397,880
6d.	17,086,680	3,357,480
1s.3d.	7,026,240	1,761,240
Pack	48,732	—

Withdrawn   31.5.67

W88. Black-headed Gull

W89. Blue Tit

W90. Robin

W91. Blackbird

(Des. J. Norris Wood)

1966 (AUGUST 8). BRITISH BIRDS

    These were the first British stamps to be printed in eight colours. On the blackbird design the black was printed over the bistre.
    Issued together in *se-tenant* blocks of four within the sheet

				Mint	Used
A. Ordinary					
W92 (=S.G.696) **W88**	4d.	grey, black, red, emerald-green, bright blue, greenish yellow and bistre		20	20
	a.	Block of 4. Nos. W92/5		1·00	2·00
		Missing colours:			
	c.	Black, bright blue, bistre and reddish brown		£1750	

291

	d.	Greenish yellow	£575	
	e.	Red	£575	
	f.	Emerald-green	£110	
	g.	Bright blue	£400	
	h.	Bistre	£100	
	i.	Black (only)	£7500	
	j.	"HARRISO" omitted (No dot R. 15/5)* *Block of four*	25·00	
	k.	Watermark inverted	4·00	

W93 (=S.G.697) **W89**	4d.	black, greenish yellow, grey, emerald-green, bright blue and bistre		20	20
		Missing colours:			
	c.	Black, bright blue, bistre and reddish brown	£1750	
	d.	Greenish yellow	£575	
	e.	Emerald-green	£110	
	f.	Bright blue	£400	
	g.	Bistre	£100	
	k.	Watermark inverted	4·00	

W94 (=S.G.698) **W90**	4d.	red, greenish yellow, black, grey, bistre, reddish brown and emerald-green		20	20
		Missing colours:			
	c.	Black, bright blue, bistre and reddish brown	£1750	
	d.	Greenish yellow	£575	
	e.	Red	£575	
	f.	Emerald-green	£110	
	g.	Bistre	£100	
	h.	Reddish brown	90·00	
	i.	Black (only)	£7500	
	k.	Watermark inverted	4·00	

W95 (=S.G.699) **W91**	4d.	black, reddish brown, greenish yellow, grey and bistre		20	20
		Missing colours:			
	c.	Black, bright blue, bistre and reddish brown	£1750	
	d.	Greenish yellow	£575	
	e.	Reddish brown	90·00	
	f.	Bistre	£100	
	k.	Watermark inverted	4·00	

First Day Cover (W92/5)	8·00
Presentation Pack (W92/5)	10·00

B. Phosphor

WP92 (=S.G.696p) **W88**	4d.	Three bands		20	20
	a.	Block of 4. Nos. WP92/5	75	2·00
		Missing colours:			
	b.	Emerald-green	£110	
	c.	Bright blue	£3750	
	d.	Bistre	£2250	
	e.	Greenish yellow	£2500	
	i.	Watermark inverted	18·00	

WP93 (=S.G.697p) **W89**	4d.	Three bands		20	20
		Missing colours:			
	b.	Emerald-green	£110	
	c.	Bright blue	£3750	
	d.	Bistre	£2250	
	e.	Greenish yellow	£2500	
	i.	Watermark inverted	18·00	

WP94 (=S.G.698p) **W90**	4d.	Three bands		20	20
		Missing colours:			
	b.	Emerald-green	£110	
	c.	Bistre	£2250	

	d.	Reddish brown	90·00
	e.	Greenish yellow	£2500
	i.	Watermark inverted	18·00

WP95 (=S.G.699p) **W91**	4d.	Three bands	20		20
		Missing colours:			
	b.	Reddish brown	90·00		
	c.	Bistre	£2250		
	e.	Greenish yellow	£2500		
	i.	Watermark inverted	18·00		

> First Day Cover (WP92/5) . . . . 8·00

Prices for missing colour errors and inverted watermarks in blocks of four:

	Ordinary	Phosphor		Ordinary	Phosphor
Black, bright blue, bistre			Bright blue	£800	£7500
and reddish brown	£7000	†	Bistre	£400	£9000
Greenish yellow	£2300	£10000	Reddish brown	£180	£180
Red	£1150	†	Watermark inverted	17·00	75·00
Emerald green	£330	£330			

*"HARRISON" is omitted except for fragments of the "N" and on the stamp below (W94) the imprint is very faint, particularly "AND SO". The price is for a block containing both varieties. The damage was quickly discovered and repaired during the early stages of the printing.

Black only is not known in a block.

These are known postmarked at various places with dates from 17 July 1966 due to supplies prematurely released by the Philatelic Bureau.

Cylinder Numbers (Blocks of Eight)

	Cyl. Nos.	Perforation Type F (P/E). No dot	
		Ordinary	Phosphor
2A (black)–1B (grey)–1C (yellow)–1D (red)–1E			
(green)–2F (blue)–2G (bistre)–1H (Brown) . .		6·00	6·00
2A–1B–1C–1D–1E–2F–2G–2H		15·00	†

Minor Constant Flaws

4d. Cyls. 2A–1B–1C–1D–1E–2F–2G with 1H or 2H no dot
  1/2   Small brown dot under main twig (Th. B3), OP
  4/3   Small brown dot to right of Robin's tail (Th. B7), OP
  5/1   Small black dot in gull's wing (Th. D5), OP
  6/2   Red spot between blackbird's claws (Th. F6), OP
  7/1   Small black dot in gull's wing (Th. D6), OP
  7/4   Extension to main twig at right (Th. A6), OP
  9/6   Horizontal bistre line above main twig at left (Th. A–B3–4), O

Sheet Details

Sheet size: 120 (6 × 20). In *se-tenant* blocks of four, single pane sheet-fed
Sheet markings:
  Cylinder numbers: Opposite rows 17/19 at left, boxed
  Guide holes: None
  Marginal arrows (photo-etched): "W" shaped, at top, bottom and sides
  Marginal rule: At bottom of sheet
  Colour register marks: Above and below vertical rows 1/3 and 5/6
  Coloured crosses: Above and below vertical rows 3/4
  Autotron marks and colour designations: None
  Traffic lights (boxed): In same order as cylinder numbers opposite rows 18/19 at right

A number of sheets from the end of the printing run showed part of the design in the left-hand margin by row 20. This was caused by incomplete masking of the multipositive; touched out before printing, but then wearing through.

Imprimaturs from the National Postal Museum Archives

A. Ordinary

Nos. W92/95 imperforate, watermark Type W.24
Watermark upright (*se-tenant* block of 4) £6000

B. Phosphor

Nos. WP92/95 imperforate, watermark Type W.24
Watermark upright (*se-tenant* block of 4) £6000

Quantities Sold
Ordinary 88,047,742; phosphor 14,613,120; Pack (ordinary) 42,888

Withdrawn   7.8.57

W92. Cup Winners
(Des. David Gentleman)

1966 (AUGUST 18).   ENGLAND'S WORLD CUP FOOTBALL VICTORY
England won the World Cup Football Championship by defeating West Germany 4–2 at Wembley
on 30 July 1966.

Watermark sideways

Ordinary only				Mint	Used
W96 (=S.G.700) **W92**	4d.	red, reddish purple, bright blue, flesh and black		30	30
	a.	Patch on thigh (No dot, R. 3/20)		4·00	
	b.	Red patch below ball (No dot, R. 4/16)		4·00	
	c.	Broken shadow (No dot, R. 5/17)		4·00	

> First Day Cover (W96) . . . .   13·00

The above was only put on sale at post offices in England, the Channel Islands and the Isle of
Man, and the Philatelic Bureau in London and also, on August 22, in Edinburgh on the occasion of the
opening of the Edinburgh Festival as well as at Army post offices at home and abroad.
  It was also pre-released on 17 August at an Army Camp P.O. in Great Britain.
  An example of No. W89 with forged additional inscription on Edinburgh (22 August) first day
cover is known.
  For W96*a*, W96*b* and W96*c*. see illustrations after Nos. WP89/91.

Cylinder Numbers (Blocks of Six)

	Cyl. Nos.	Perforation Type A (I/E)	
		No dot	Dot
4d	1A (black)–1B (blue)–1C (red)–1D (purple)–1E		
	(flesh)*	4·00	4·00

*In the no dot pane the flesh cylinder is expressed in error thus: "1E." and on the dot pane the black
cylinder is shown as ".1A.".
  Perforation Type A is with sheet orientated showing head to left.

Minor Constant Flaws

4d. Cyls. 1A–1B–1C–1D–1E no dot
- 1/15   Black dot in second N of ENGLAND
- 2/9   Black spur on left player's right boot (Th. J–K5)
- 3/1   Horizontal scratch through top of ball (Th. K1–2)
- 5/6   Blue patch below u of Cup
- 6/13   White patch on heel of left player's left boot (Th. J3)
- 6/18   Blue spots over T of LTD

4d. Cyls. 1A–1B–1C–1D–1E dot
- 4/11   Black dot between W and I of WINNERS
- 5/10   Dark spot on ball (Th. K1)
- 5/17   Grey coloured spur to top of l of World

Sheet Details

Sheet size: 120 (20 × 6). Double pane reel-fed
Sheet markings:
    Cylinder numbers: Above vertical rows 2/3, boxed
    Guide holes: In single "S N" box above vertical rows 6/7 (no dot) or below (dot)
    Marginal arrows (photo-etched): "W" shaped, at top, bottom and sides
    Marginal rule: At left of sheet
    Colour register marks: Above vertical rows 3/4 and 18/19 (no dot) or below (dot)
    Autotron marks (solid): Red, purple, flesh, blue, black below vertical rows 15/18 (no dot) or above (dot)
    Colour designations: "5 BLACK G4 BLUE MAROON G3 G2 RED G1 LIGHT RED" below vertical rows 11/16 on dot panes only
    Traffic lights (boxed): Black, blue, red, purple, flesh reading left to right below vertical rows 2/3

Imprimatur from the National Postal Museum Archives

    Ordinary paper

    No. W96 imperforate, watermark Type W.24

    Watermark sideways £1000

Quantity Sold   12,452,640

Sold Out   Soon after issue

W93. Jodrell Bank Radio Telescope

W94. British Motor-cars

(Des. David and A. Gillespie)

W95. SRN 6 Hovercraft

W96. Windscale Reactor

(Des. Andrew Restall)

1966 (SEPTEMBER 19).   BRITISH TECHNOLOGY
The designs represent British Technological achievements.

				Mint	Used
A. Ordinary					
W97 (=S.G.701) **W93**	4d.	black and lemon		15	10
	a.	Struts flaw (No dot, R. 4/6)		4·50	
W98 (=S.G.702) **W94**	6d.	red, deep blue and orange		25	20
	a.	Red (Mini-cars) omitted		£7500	
	b.	Blue (Jaguar and inscr.) omitted		£5500	
	c.	Broken "D" (R. 19/6)		4·75	
W99 (=S.G.703) **W95**	1s.3d.	black, orange-red, slate and light greenish blue . . .		50	40
W100 (=S.G.704) **W96**	1s.6d.	black, yellow-green, bronze-green, lilac and deep blue		50	60

> First Day Cover (W97/100) . . . .   6·00
> Presentation Pack (W97/100) . . . .   9·00

				Mint	Used
B. Phosphor					
WP97 (=S.G.701p) **W93**	4d.	Three bands		10	10
	a.	Error. Pair, with and without phosphor		20·00	
	b.	Narrow band at left or right (stamp with vert. margin)		2·50	
	c.	Struts flaw (No dot, R. 4/6)		4·50	
WP98 (=S.G.702p) **W94**	6d.	Three bands		15	25
	a.	Narrow band at left or right (stamp with vert. margin)		2·50	
	b.	Broken "D" (R. 19/6)		5·00	
WP99 (=S.G.703p) **W95**	1s.3d.	Three bands		35	40
WP100 (=S.G.704p) **W96**	1s.6d.	Three bands		50	60
	a.	Narrow band at left or right (stamp with vert. margin)		2·50	
	b.	Error. Two broad bands		30·00	

> First Day Cover (WP97/100) . . . .   6·00

W97*a*, WP97*c*
Strong retouch consisting of three strong
black strokes in the form of an arrow

W98*c*, WP98*b*

Cylinder Numbers (Blocks of Six)

(a) Ordinary

		Cyl. Nos.	Perforation Type A (E/I)	
			No dot	Dot
4d.	1A (lemon)–1B (black)		1·50	1·50
6d.	1A (orange)–1B (red)–1C (blue)		2·00	†
1s.3d.	1A (blue)–1B (slate)–1C (orange)–1D (black) .		4·50	†
1s.6d.	1A (bronze-green)–1B (lilac)–1C (black)–1D			
	(yellow-green)–1E (blue)		4·50	†

(b) Phosphor

4d.	1A (lemon)–1B (black)		5·00	3·00
6d.	1A (orange)–1B (red)–1C (blue)		3·00	†
1s.3d.	1A (blue)–1B (slate)–1C (orange)–1D (black) .		4·00	†
1s.6d.	1A (bronze-green)–1B (lilac)–1C (black)–1D			
	(yellow-green)–1E (blue)		6·00	†

Minor Constant Flaws

4d. Cyls. 1A–1B no dot
    1/1 Lines of retouching above Queen's head resemble a thumb-print (Th. A9–12); also small pale
        area in left of telescope bowl (Th. C3–4), both OP
    1/2 Retouch to background right of value (Th. B3–4), OP
    1/6 Retouch to background top left corner of stamp (Th. A1), OP
    5/4 Retouch to background in front of Queen's neck (Th. E9), OP
    10/6 Horizontal line of retouching to background behind Queen's head (Th. D12–13), OP
    19/6 Horizontal white line above ON AND SONS of imprint, OP
    20/5 Horizontal white line below portrait (Th. F10–12), OP
    20/6 As 20/5 but stronger line, OP

4d. Cyls. 1A–1B dot
    3/3 Retouch to background in front of Queen's neck (Th. E10), OP
    5/5 White scratch in right of telescope bowl (Th. B6–7), OP
    9/3 Small white patch in background below portrait (Th. F–G12), OP
    9/5 Retouch to background at left of telescope bowl (Th. E–F1), OP
    13/4 Small white patch in background bottom left of portrait (Th. F–G9), OP

13/5   Pale patch in background to left of telescope bowl (Th. E–F2), OP
14/6   Yellow spot in right of telescope bowl (Th. D6), OP

6d. Cyls. 1A–1B–1C no dot
 5/6   Retouch to background above Queen's head (Th. A10–11), OP
10/3   Vertical blue line in Queen's portrait (Th. A–C10), OP
13/3   Pale area above value (Th. A2), OP
17/4   Spur of first S of SONS, OP

1s.3d. Cyls. 1A–1B–1C–1D no dot
 1/1   Retouch in background behind Queen's head (Th. C–D13), OP
 1/4   White spot below e of Hovercraft, OP
 1/6   Retouch in sea, bottom centre (Th. G7), OP
12/6   Horizontal orange coloured line extends from sea to sheet margin (Th. G13–15), OP

1s.6d. Cyls. 1A–1B–1C–1D–1E no dot
 1/3   Retouch in sky in front of Queen's neck (Th. C–D10), OP
 1/5   Grey coloured flaw in sky top right of Queen's head (Th. A13), OP
 2/2   Lower part of left stroke of n of Advanced is broken off, OP
16/3   Vertical blue line in gutter between design edge and perforation (Th. D–G13), OP
16/5   Wispy whitish line runs vertically above v of Advanced (Th. F–G2), OP
20/1   Small white flaw in large door of building (Th. F6), OP

Sheet Details

Sheet size: 120 (6 × 20). 4d. double pane reel-fed; others single pane reel-fed
Sheet markings:
  Cylinder numbers:
    4d., 6d., 1s.3d. Opposite R. 19/1, boxed
    1s.6d. Opposite rows 18/19 at left, boxed
  Guide holes:
    4d. In single "S N" box opposite rows 14/15, at left (no dot) or right (dot)
    Others. In single "S O N" box opposite rows 14/15, at both sides
  Marginal arrows (photo-etched): "W" shaped, at top, bottom and sides
  Marginal rule: None
  Colour register marks:
    4d. Opposite rows 1/2 and 20, at left (no dot) or right (dot)
    6d., 1s.3d. Opposite rows 2/3 and 17/18, at both sides
    1s.6d. Opposite rows 3/4 and 17/18, at both sides
  Autotron marks (solid):
    4d. Black, lemon, opposite row 5, at right (no dot) or left (dot)
    6d. Blue, red, orange below vertical rows 1/3
    1s.3d. Black, orange, blue, slate below vertical rows 1/3. Additional black below vertical row 3
    1s.6d. Black, lilac, bronze-green, yellow-green, blue below vertical rows 1/3 and additionally
      black below vertical row 1. During printing the correct sequence, black, blue, bronze-green,
      lilac, yellow-green, was engraved below vertical rows 4/6
  Colour designations:
    4d. "G1 YELLOW G2 BLACK" in right margin reading upwards opposite rows 8/5 on dot
      panes only
    6d. "G2 RED G3 BLUE" in right margin reading upwards opposite rows 7/6
    1s.3d. "G1 GREY G2 BLUE G3 RED G4 BLACK" in right margin reading upwards opposite
      rows 7/4
    1s.6d. "G1 BLUE G2 YELLOW G3 GREEN G4 MAUVE G5 BLACK" in right margin
      reading upwards opposite rows 9/5
  Traffic lights (boxed):
    4d. Lemon, black opposite R. 19/6
    6d. Orange, red, blue opposite R. 19/6
    1s.3d. Blue, slate, orange, black opposite rows 18/19 at right
    1s.6d. Black, lilac, bronze-green, yellow-green, blue opposite rows 18/19 at right

Imprimaturs from the National Postal Museum Archives

A. Ordinary

Nos. W97/100 imperforate, watermark Type W.24

Watermark upright (*set of* 4) £4000

B. Phosphor

Nos. WP97/100 imperforate, watermark Type W.24

Watermark upright (*set of* 4) £4000

Quantities Sold

	Ordinary	Phosphor		Ordinary	Phosphor
4d.	79,112,278	12,737,520	1s.6d.	5,284,069	1,414,320
6d.	11,087,516	2,388,720	Pack	35,437	—
1s.3d.	5,199,900	1,431,000			

Withdrawn   18.9.67 (6d. phosphor sold out earlier)

W97.   W98.

W99.   W100.

W101.   W102.

Types W97/102 show battle scenes and were issued together *se-tenant* in horizontal strips of six within the sheet

W103. Norman Ship   **W104.** Norman Horsemen attacking
Harold's Troops

(Des. David Gentleman)

(Printed in photogravure with the Queen's head die-stamped in gold 6d., 1s.3d.)

1966 (OCTOBER 14). 900th ANNIVERSARY OF BATTLE OF HASTINGS

The scenes depicted are all reproduced from the celebrated Bayeux Tapestry which records the Norman invasion of England.

Watermark sideways on 1s.3d. (normal is top of crown pointing to left when stamps are viewed from the *back*)

				Mint	Used
A. Ordinary					
W101 (=S.G.705) **W97**	4d.		black, olive-green, bistre, deep blue, orange, magenta, green, blue and grey	10	30
	a.	Strip of 6. Nos. W101/6	1·90	6·00
		Missing colours:		
	b.	Olive-green	60·00	
	c.	Bistre	60·00	
	d.	Deep blue	70·00	
	e.	Orange	60·00	
	f.	Magenta	60·00	
	g.	Green	60·00	
	h.	Blue	60·00	
	i.	Grey	60·00	
	j.	Watermark inverted	7·00	
W102 (=S.G.706) **W98**	4d.		black, olive-green, bistre, deep blue, orange, magenta, green, blue and grey	10	30
		Missing colours:		
	b.	Olive-green	60·00	
	c.	Bistre	60·00	
	d.	Deep blue	70·00	
	e.	Orange	60·00	
	f.	Magenta	60·00	
	g.	Green	60·00	
	h.	Blue	60·00	
	i.	Grey	60·00	
	j.	Watermark inverted	7·00	
W103 (=S.G.707) **W99**	4d.		black, olive-green, bistre, deep blue, orange, magenta, green, blue and grey	10	30
		Missing colours:		
	b.	Olive-green	60·00	
	c.	Bistre	60·00	
	d.	Deep blue	70·00	
	e.	Orange	60·00	
	f.	Magenta	60·00	
	g.	Green	60·00	
	h.	Blue	60·00	
	i.	Grey	60·00	
	j.	Watermark inverted	7·00	
W104 (=S.G.708) **W100**	4d.		black, olive-green, bistre, deep blue, magenta, green, blue and grey	10	30
		Missing colours:		
	b.	Olive-green	60·00	
	c.	Bistre	60·00	
	d.	Deep blue	70·00	
	f.	Magenta	60·00	
	g.	Green	60·00	
	h.	Blue	60·00	
	i.	Grey	60·00	
	j.	Watermark inverted	7·00	
W105 (=S.G.709) **W101**	4d.		black, olive-green, bistre, deep blue, orange, magenta, green, blue and grey	10	30
		Missing colours:		
	b.	Olive-green	60·00	
	c.	Bistre	60·00	

	d.	Deep blue	. . . .	70·00	
	e.	Orange	. . . .	60·00	
	f.	Magenta	. . . .	60·00	
	g.	Green	. . . .	60·00	
	h.	Blue	. . . .	60·00	
	i.	Grey	. . . .	60·00	
	j.	Watermark inverted	. . . .	7·00	

W106 (=S.G.710) W102   4d.   black, olive-green, bistre, deep blue, orange, magenta, green, blue and grey 10   30
Missing colours:

b.	Olive-green	. . . .	60·00	
c.	Bistre	. . . .	60·00	
d.	Deep blue	. . . .	70·00	
e.	Orange	. . . .	60·00	
f.	Magenta	. . . .	60·00	
g.	Green	. . . .	60·00	
h.	Blue	. . . .	60·00	
i.	Grey	. . . .	60·00	
j.	Watermark inverted	. . . .	7·00	

W107 (=S.G.711) W103   6d.   black, olive-green, violet, blue, green and gold . . .   10   30
a.	Watermark inverted	. . . .	42·00	
b.	Yellowish gold	. . . .	1·00	

W108 (=S.G.712) W104   1s.3d.   black, lilac, bronze-green, rosine, bistre-brown and gold 20   75
a.	Lilac omitted	. . . .	£650	
b.	Watermark sideways inverted (top of crown pointing to right)	35·00	
c.	Club flaw (R. 7/2)	5·50	

First Day Cover (W101/8)	8·00
Presentation Pack (W101/8)	9·00

B. Phosphor

WP101 (=S.G.705p) W97   4d.   Three bands 10   30
a.	Strip of 6. Nos. WP101/6	1·90	6·00

Missing colours:
b.	Olive-green	. . . .	60·00	
c.	Bistre	. . . .	60·00	
d.	Deep blue	. . . .	70·00	
e.	Orange	. . . .	60·00	
f.	Magenta	. . . .	60·00	
g.	Green	. . . .	60·00	
h.	Blue	. . . .	60·00	
i.	Grey	. . . .	60·00	
j.	Magenta and green	. . . .		
k.	Watermark inverted	. . . .	3·00	

WP102 (=S.G.706p) W98   4d.   Three bands 10   30
Missing colours:
b.	Olive-green	. . . .	60·00	
c.	Bistre	. . . .	60·00	
d.	Deep blue	. . . .	70·00	
e.	Orange	. . . .	60·00	
f.	Magenta	. . . .	60·00	
g.	Green	. . . .	60·00	
h.	Blue	. . . .	60·00	
i.	Grey	. . . .	60·00	
j.	Magenta and green	. . . .		
k.	Watermark inverted	. . . .	3·00	

WP103 (=S.G.707p) **W99**	4d.	Three bands		10	30
		Missing colours:			
	b.	Olive-green	60·00		
	c.	Bistre	60·00		
	d.	Deep blue	70·00		
	e.	Orange	60·00		
	f.	Magenta	60·00		
	g.	Green	60·00		
	h.	Blue	60·00		
	i.	Grey	60·00		
	j.	Magenta and green			
	k.	Watermark inverted	3·00		

WP104 (=S.G.708p) **W100**	4d	Three bands		10	30
		Missing colours:			
	b.	Olive-green	60·00		
	c.	Bistre	60·00		
	d.	Deep blue	70·00		
	f.	Magenta	60·00		
	g.	Green	60·00		
	h.	Blue	60·00		
	i.	Grey	60·00		
	j.	Magenta and green			
	k.	Watermark inverted	3·00		

WP105 (=S.G.709p) **W101**	4d.	Three bands		10	30
		Missing colours:			
	b.	Olive-green	60·00		
	c.	Bistre	60·00		
	d.	Deep blue	70·00		
	e.	Orange	60·00		
	f.	Magenta	60·00		
	g.	Green	60·00		
	h.	Blue	60·00		
	i.	Grey	60·00		
	j.	Magenta and green			
	k.	Watermark inverted	3·00		

WP106 (=S.G.710p) **W102**	4d.	Three bands		10	30
		Missing colours:			
	b.	Olive-green	60·00		
	c.	Bistre	60·00		
	d.	Deep blue	70·00		
	e.	Orange	60·00		
	f.	Magenta	60·00		
	g.	Green	60·00		
	h.	Blue	60·00		
	i.	Grey	60·00		
	j.	Magenta and green			
	k.	Watermark inverted	3·00		

WP107 (=S.G.711p) **W103**	6d.	Three bands		10	30
	a.	Watermark inverted	55·00		
	b.	Yellowish gold	1·00		

WP108 (=S.G.712p) **W104**	1s.3d.	Four bands		20	75
	a.	Lilac omitted	£650		
	b.	Error. Three bands	7·00		
	c.	Watermark sideways inverted			
		(top of crown pointing to right)	35·00		
	d.	Club flaw (R. 7/2)	5·50		

First Day Cover (WP101/8) . . . .   9·00

4d. *Prices for missing colour errors and inverted watermarks in strips of six*:

	Ordinary	Phosphor		Ordinary	Phosphor
Olive-green	£360	£360	Green	£360	£360
Bistre	£360	£360	Blue	£360	£360
Deep blue	£425	£425	Grey	£360	£360
Orange (on five stamps)	£300	£300	Magenta and green	†	—
Magenta	£360	£360	Watermark inverted	45·00	20·00

Nos. W101 and W105 with grey and blue omitted have been seen commercially used, posted from Middleton-in-Teesdale.

The 6d. and 1s.3d. were also issued with the die-stamped gold head omitted but as these can also be removed by chemical means we are not prepared to list them unless a way is found of distinguishing the genuine stamps from the fakes which will satisfy the Expert Committees. However, three examples of No. W108 in a right-hand top corner block of 10 (2 × 5) are known with the Queen's head omitted as a result of a double paper fold prior to die-stamping. The perforation is normal. Of the other seven stamps, four have the Queen's head misplaced and three are normal.

W108*c*, WP108*d*

The fallen knight has what appears to be a
large black club at his right hand

Cylinder Numbers (Blocks of Twenty-Four (4d.), Six (6d.), Eight (1s.3d.))

	Cyl. Nos	Perforation Types			
		F (P/E)		No dot	
		Ordinary		Phosphor	
4d.	1A (black)–1B (olive-green)–1C (bistre)–1D (deep blue)–1E (orange)–1F (magenta)–1G (green)–1H (blue)–1J (grey)	12·00		10·00	
	2A–1B–1C–1D–1E–1F–1G–1H–1J	10·00		†	

			G (P/P)			
		No dot	Dot	No dot	Dot	
		Ordinary		Phosphor		
6d.	1A (black)–1B (olive-green)–1C (violet)–1D (blue)–1E (green)	1·00	1·00	1·00	1·00	

		A (T) (E/P) No dot	
		Ordinary	Phosphor
1s.3d.	1A (black)–1B (lilac)–1C (bronze-green)–1D (rosine)–1E (bistre-brown)	7·00*	7·00*

Minor Constant Flaws

4d. Cyls. 1B–1C–1D–1E–1F–1G–1H–1J no dot in combination with black cyls. 1A or 2A
  3/4   Spur on second S of HASTINGS, OP
  4/1   Horizontal black line to left of Queen's forehead (Th. A10–11), OP (1A only)
  4/5   Black line under Queen's chin (Th. C11), OP (1A only)
  9/1   Right hind leg of dark horse is paler than normal (Th. F–G8), OP
  9/2   Second S of SONS pale and distorted, possibly hand drawn (OP) (1A only)
  19/4   White spot on horseman's leg (Th. F7), OP (1A only)
  20/3   LTD heavier than normal, OP (1A only)
  20/4   HARRISON AND heavier than normal, OP (1A only)

4d. Cyl. 2A no dot
  10/1   H of HARRISON is indistinct, O
  11/1   Hastings 1066 weaker than normal, O

6d. Cyls. 1A–1B–1C–1D–1E no dot
　1/1　Blue patch on hull due to lack of black shading (Th. F9), OP
　4/1　Small dot after final s of Hastings, OP
　6/1　Diagonal black line through figures in small boat (Th. C3–B5), OP
　8/4　diagonal spur on first t of Battle, OP

6d. Cyls. 1A–1B–1C–1D–1E dot
　1/1　Partial break in main left-hand rigging of main vessel (Th. D3), OP
　3/1　Extra gold enlarges Queen's throat at both sides (Th. C–D12), P
　8/5　Horizontal black line in upper part of first 6 of 1966, OP
　8/6　Horizontal black line through HAR of HARRISON, OP

1s.3d. Cyls. 1A–1B–1C–1D–1E no dot
　6/2　Dot in g of Hastings, OP
　8/1　Diagonal hairline runs from bottom of red shield of second soldier through toes of right foot
　　　to bottom of stamp (Th. E–H12), O
　9/1　Line continues to right-hand arm of first soldier (Th. A12), O
　10/4　Bronze-green dot upper left of 1 of 1/3 (Th. F8), OP

Sheet Details

Sheet sizes:
　4d. 120 (6 × 20). In *se-tenant* strips of six, single pane sheet-fed
　6d. 60 (6 × 10). Double pane reel-fed
　1s.3d. 60 (6 × 10). Single pane reel-fed
Sheet markings:
　Cylinder numbers:
　　4d. Opposite rows 17/19 at left, boxed
　　6d. Opposite rows 8/9 at left, boxed
　　1s.3d. Opposite rows 7/8 at left, boxed
　Guide holes: None
　Marginal arrows (photo-etched): "W" shaped, at top, bottom and sides
　Marginal rule: None
　Colour register marks:
　　4d. Above and below vertical rows 1 and 5/6
　　6d. Above vertical rows 1 and 5/6 (no dot) or below them (dot)
　　1s.3d. Opposite rows 1/2 and 9/10, at both sides
　Coloured crosses:
　　4d. Above and below vertical rows 3/4
　　6d. Above vertical rows 3/4 (no dot) or below them (dot)
　　1s.3d. Opposite rows 5/6, at both sides
　Autotron marks and colour designations: None
　Traffic lights (boxed and in same order as cylinder numbers):
　　4d. Opposite rows 17/19 at right
　　6d. Opposite rows 8/9 at right
　　1s.3d. Opposite rows 7/8 at right

Imprimaturs from the National Museum Archives

A. Ordinary

Nos. W101/106 imperforate, watermark Type W.24
Watermark upright (*se-tenant* strip of six) £9000
Nos. W107/108 imperforate, watermark Type W.24
Watermark upright (6d.) or sideways (1s.3d.) . . . . (*Each*) £1000

B. Phosphor

Nos. WP101/106 imperforate, watermark Type W.24
Watermark upright (*se-tenant* strip of six) £9000
No. WP107 imperforate, watermark Type W.24
Watermark upright (6d.) £1000

Quantities Sold　Ordinary. 4d. 89,197,226; 6d. 12,012,328; 1s.3d. 5,721,426; Pack 51,332
　Phosphor. 4d. 15,861,960; 6d. 2,820,360; 1s.3d. 1,646,280

Withdrawn　13.10.67 (6d. phosphor sold out in September)

W105. King of the Orient   **W106.** Snowman

(Des. Miss Tasveer Shemza)   (Des. James Berry)

(Printed in photogravure with the Queen's head die-stamped in gold)

1966 (DECEMBER 1). CHRISTMAS

These designs, executed by two six-year-old children, were chosen from nearly 5,000 entries in a Post Office competition for Britain's first adhesive Christmas stamps.

Watermark sideways on 3d.

A. Ordinary   Mint   Used

W109 (=S.G.713) **W105**	3d.	black, blue, green, yellow, red and gold	10	25
	a.	Queen's head double	£550	†
	ab.	Queen's head double, one albino	£550	
	b.	Green omitted	£6500	
	c.	Missing "T" (No dot, R. 6/2)	4·00	
W110 (=S.G.714) **W106**	1s.6d.	blue, red, pink, black and gold	30	50
	a.	Pink (hat) omitted	£1300	
	b.	Watermark inverted	15·00	

> First Day Cover (W109/10) . . . .   2·50
> Presentation Pack (W109/10) . . . .   12·00

The one phosphor band on No. WP109 was produced by printing broad phosphor bands across alternate vertical rows of perforations. Individual examples show the band at right or left (*same prices either way*).

B. Phosphor

WP109 (=S.G.713p) **W105**	3d.	One band at left	10	10
	a.	Band at right	10	25
	ab.	Nos. WP109/*a* (horiz. pair)	20	20
	ac.	Error. Pair, with and without phosphor	15·00	
	b.	Missing "T" (No dot. R. 6/2)	4·00	
WP110 (=S.G.714p) **W106**	1s.6d	Two bands	30	50
	a.	Watermark inverted	42·00	

> First Day Cover (WP109/10) . . . .   2·00

W109*c*, WP109*b*

Both values were also issued with the die-stamped gold head omitted but as these can also be removed by chemical means we are not prepared to list them unless a way is found of distinguishing the genuine stamps from the fakes which will satisfy the Expert Committees. However, the gold head and embossing omitted also occurred on the last vertical row of a sheet of the 3d. ordinary due to a major displacement to the left. Examples in horizontal marginal pairs can be considered to be genuine. Another example shows two gold head omissions, due to a paper fold, with three partial gold heads on the gummed side.

No. WP109 exists with a horizontal phosphor band across the top of the stamp. This was caused by phosphor spillage under the doctor blade and occurred on the top horizontal row of a sheet.

Cylinder Numbers (Blocks of Six)

(a) Ordinary

		Cyl. Nos	Perforation Types	
			A (I/E) No dot	A (I/E) Dot
3d.	1A (blue)–2B (black)–1C (green)–1D (yellow)– 1E (red)		20·00	20·00
	1A–3B–1C–1D–1E		1·00	1·00
	1A–4B–1C–1D–1E		1·00	1·00
			A (I/E) No dot	A(T) (P/E) No dot
1s.6d.	1A (blue)–1B (black)–2C (red)–1D (pink) . . .		4·00	4·00

(b) Phosphor

		Cyl. Nos.	Perforation Types	
			A (I/E) No dot	A (I/E) Dot
3d.	1A (blue)–3B (black)–1C (green)–1D (yellow)– 1E (red)		1·00	1·00
	1A–4B–1C–1D–1E		1·00	1·00
			A (I/E) No dot	A(T) (P/E) No dot
1s.6d.	1A (blue)–1B (black)–2C (red)–1D (pink) . . .		4·00	4·00

Perforation Types A and A(T) are with sheets orientated showing head to left.
In the dot panes of the 3d. the dot is missing after B in the black colour.

Minor Constant Flaws

3d. Cyls. 1A–1C–1D–1E no dot in combination with black cyls. 3B or 4B
  2/1 During the course of printing a diagonal cut developed at base of Queen's neck and later the piece of gold foil separated and dropped downwards (Th. C–D5), OP
  2/3 Blue dot in front of H of HARRISON, OP
  2/8 A of AND in imprint shorter than normal, OP
  3/4 White patch at top left corner of panel is larger than normal (Th. A1), OP
  3/8 Extra stop after T. of T. SHEMZA, OP
  7/1 Damaged top to A of AND, OP
  8/8 Red dot under first leg of H of HARRISON, OP

3d. Cyls. 1A–1C–1D–1E dot in combination with black cyls. 3B or 4B
  1/5 Two red dots in the yellow above red circle in crown (Th. F–G3), OP (3B only)
  2/1 As for no dot cyls.
  4/6 Background retouch between points of crown at right (Th. F5), OP
  4/7 First S of SONS incomplete, OP
  5/5 Red spot in white area below Queen's portrait (Th. D5), OP (3B only)
  8/1 Top of S of HARRISON incomplete, OP

1s.6d. Cyls. 1A–1B–2C–1D no dot
  3/1 White spot normally found in red scarf is filled in (Th. E4), OP
  6/7 Dark blue spot inside 6 of 1/6, OP
  8/2 Small blue projection into right-hand margin (Th. L7), OP
  9/1 Second R of BERRY is damaged, OP

Sheet Details

Sheet size: 80 (8 × 10)
  3d. double pane reel-fed, with dot pane above no dot pane
  1s.6d. single pane sheet-fed

Sheet markings:
  Cylinder numbers:
    3d. Above vertical rows 2/3, boxed
    1s.6d. Opposite R. 8/1, boxed
  Guide holes: 3d. Boxed above vertical rows 6/7; 1s.6d. none
  Marginal arrows (photo-etched): "W" shaped, at top, bottom and sides
  Marginal rule: None
  Colour register marks:
    3d. None; 1s.6d. above and below vertical rows 1/2 and 7/8
  Coloured crosses: 3d. None; 1s.6d. above and below vertical rows 4/5
  Autotron marks (solid):
    3d. Green, yellow, red, black, blue opposite rows 8/10, left margin (dot); 1s.6d. none
  Colour designations: None
  Traffic lights (boxed):
    3d. Black, blue, green, yellow, red below vertical rows 2/3
    1s.6d. Blue, red, pink, black opposite R. 8/10

Imprimaturs from the National Postal Museum Archives

A. Ordinary

Nos. W109/110 imperforate, watermark Type W.24

Watermark upright (1s.6d.) or sideways (3d.) *(set of 2)* £2000

B. Phosphor

Nos. WP109/110 imperforate, watermark Type W.24

Watermark upright (1s.6d.) or sideways (3d.) *(set of 2)* £2000

Quantities Sold

	Ordinary	Phosphor
3d.	153,318,160	20,774,000
1s.6d.	8,756,960	2,109,280
Pack	33,672	—

Withdrawn

The 3d. phosphor was sold out in January, the 3d ordinary and 1s.6d. phosphor were sold out in October, and the 1s.6d. ordinary was withdrawn on 30.11.67

W107. Sea Freight

W108. Air Freight

(Des. Clive Abbott)

1967 (FEBRUARY 20). EUROPEAN FREE TRADE ASSOCIATION

Issued to commemorate the movement of trade between Austria, Denmark, Norway, Portugal, Sweden, Switzerland and the United Kingdom. Finland was an associate member.

A. Ordinary

				Mint	Used
W111 (=S.G.715) **W107**	9d.		deep blue, red, lilac, green, brown, new blue, yellow and black	25	20
			Missing colours:		
		a.	Black (Queen's head), brown, new blue and yellow	£750	
		b.	Lilac	60·00	
		c.	Green	60·00	
		d.	Brown (rail trucks) omitted	45·00	
		e.	New blue	60·00	
		f.	Yellow	60·00	

g.	Watermark inverted	45·00	
h.	Quay flaw (R. 8/3)	4·50	

W112 (=S.G.716) **W108**   1s.6d.   violet, red, deep blue, brown, green, blue-grey,
new blue, yellow and black   50   45
Missing colours:

a.	Red	—	£3500
b.	Deep blue	£375	
c.	Brown	60·00	
d.	Blue-grey	60·00	
e.	New blue	60·00	
f.	Yellow	60·00	
g.	Green		
h.	Broken ribbon (R. 11/3)	4·75	
i.	Broken strut (R. 13/6)	4·50	
j.	Break in frame (R. 20/1)	4·50	

> First Day Cover (W111/12) ....   3·00
> Presentation Pack (W111/12) ....   3·50

B. Phosphor (9d. applied flexo.; 1s.6d. applied typo.)
WP111 (=S.G.715P) **W107**   9d.   Three bands   25   20
Missing colours:

a.	Lilac	£140
b.	Green	60·00
c.	Brown (rail trucks) omitted	45·00
d.	New blue	60·00
e.	Yellow	£110
f.	Watermark inverted	12·00
g.	Quay flaw (R. 8/3)	4·00

WP112 (=S.G.716p) **W108**   1s.6d.   Three bands   25   40
Missing colours:

a.	Red	
b.	Deep blue	£375
c.	Brown	50·00
d.	Blue-grey	60·00
e.	New blue	60·00
f.	Watermark inverted	25·00
g.	Broken ribbon (R. 11/3)	4·75
h.	Broken strut (R. 13/6)	4·50
j.	Break in frame (R. 20/1)	4·50
k.	"All over" phosphor	

> First Day Cover (WP111/12) ....   3·00

No. WP112*k* came from the first vertical column of a sheet. It was due to a weak mixture of the phosphor ink which leaked under the phosphor doctor blade.

W111*h*, WP111*g*
Black protuberance on
quay between trucks

Normal   W112*h*, WP112*g*

W112*i*, WP112*h*
Broken strut below wing

W112*j*, WP112*j*
Break in the frame
of Portuguese flag

Cylinder Numbers (Blocks of Eight)

| | Cyl. Nos. | Perforation Type | |
		F (P/E) Ordinary	No dot Phosphor
9d.	1A (deep blue)–1B (red)–1C (lilac)–1D (green)– 1E (brown)–1F (new blue)–1G (yellow)–1H (black)	3·00	3·00
1s.6d.	2A (violet)–1B (red)–1C (deep blue)–1D (green)–1E (brown)–1F (new blue)–1G (yellow)–2H (blue-grey)–2J (black)	5·50*	5·00*

Minor Constant Flaws

9d. Cyls. 1A–1B–1C–1D–1E–1F–1G–1H no dot
  6/5 Black colour on roof of bridge is smudged (Th. D8–9), OP
 11/5 Small blue dot in base of letter E (Th. B–C2), OP
 12/5 White spot in lilac superstructure (Th. E11), OP

1s.6d. Cyls. 2A–1B–1C–1D–1E–1F–1G–2H–2J no dot
 10/1 Small violet dot in top of letter E (Th. A2), OP
 19/1 White spur in 6 of 1/6, OP

Sheet Details

Sheet size: 120 (6 × 20). Single pane sheet-fed
Sheet markings:
  Cylinder numbers:
    9d. Opposite rows 17/19 at left, boxed
    1s.6d. Opposite rows 17/20 at left, boxed
  Guide holes: None
  Marginal arrows (photo-etched): "W" shaped, at top, bottom and side.
  Marginal rule: At bottom of sheet
  Colour register marks: Above and below vertical rows 1/2 and 5/6
  Coloured crosses: Above and below vertical rows 4/5
  Autotron marks and colour designations: None
  Traffic lights (boxed):
    9d. Opposite rows 17/19 at right, in same order as cylinder numbers
    1s.6d. Violet, red, deep blue, brown, green, blue-grey, new blue, yellow, black opposite rows
      17/19 at right

Imprimaturs from the National Postal Museum Archives

A. Ordinary

Nos. W111/112 imperforate, watermark Type W.24
Watermark upright (*set of 2*) £2000

B. Phosphor

Nos. WP111/112 imperforate, watermark Type W.24
Watermark upright (*set of 2*) £2000

Quantities Sold

	Ordinary	Phosphor
9d.	6,553,738	5,557,104
1s.6d.	6,363,483	4,237,944
Pack	42,906	—

Withdrawn 19.2.68

W109. Hawthorn and Bramble

W110. Larger Bindweed and Viper's Bugloss

W111. Ox-eye Daisy, Coltsfoot and Buttercup

W112. Bluebell, Red Campion and Wood Anemone

The above were issued together *se-tenant* in blocks of four within the sheet
(Des. Rev. W. Keble Martin)

W113. Dog Violet

W114. Primroses

(Des. Mary Grierson)

1967 (APRIL 24). BRITISH WILD FLOWERS

A. Ordinary

				Mint	Used
W113 (=S.G.717) **W109**	4d.		grey, lemon, myrtle-green, red, agate and slate-purple	20	20
		a.	Block of 4. Nos. W113/16	80	3·00
		b.	Grey double*	£1500	
		c.	Red omitted	£2750	
		d.	Watermark inverted	2·00	
		e.	Slate-purple omitted	£4500	
W114 (=S.G.718) **W110**	4d.		grey, lemon, myrtle-green, red, agate and violet . .	20	20
		b.	Grey double*	£1500	
		d.	Watermark inverted	2·00	

W115 (=S.G.719) **W111**   4d.   grey, lemon, myrtle-green, red and agate   20   20
       b.   Grey double* £1500
       d.   Watermark inverted . . . .   2·00

W116 (=S.G.720) **W112**   4d.   grey, lemon, myrtle-green, reddish purple, agate and
            violet   20   20
       b.   Grey double* £1500
       c.   Reddish purple omitted £1100
       d.   Watermark inverted . . . .   2·00
       e.   Value omitted (see note) . . . .

W117 (=S.G.721) **W113**   9d.   lavender-grey, green, reddish violet and orange-
            yellow   20   25
       a.   Watermark inverted . . . .   1·25
       b.   Notch in leaf (R. 20/2) . . . .   7·00

W118 (=S.G.722) **W114**   1s.9d.   lavender-grey, green, greenish yellow and
            orange   25   35

First Day Cover (W113/18)	5·00
Presentation Pack (W113/18)	5·25

B. Phosphor
WP113 (=S.G.717p) **W109**   4d.   Three bands   10   15
       a.   Block of 4. Nos. WP113/16   50   2·75
       b.   Agate omitted £3000
       c.   Slate-purple omitted £275
       d.   Watermark inverted . . . .   2·00

WP114 (=S.G.718p) **W110**   4d.   Three bands   10   15
       b.   Agate omitted £3000
       c.   Violet omitted £5500
       d.   Watermark inverted . . . .   2·00

WP115 (=S.G.719p) **W111**   4d.   Three bands   10   15
       b.   Agate omitted £3000
       c.   Watermark inverted . . . .   2·00

WP116 (=S.G.720p) **W112**   4d.   Three bands   10   15
       b.   Agate omitted £3000
       c.   Violet omitted £5500
       d.   Watermark inverted . . . .   2·00

WP117 (=S.G.721p) **W113**   9d.   Three bands   15   25
       a.   Notch in leaf (R. 20/2) . . . .   7·00

WP118 (=S.G.722p) **W114**   1s.9d.   Three bands   20   30

First Day Cover (WP113/18)	6·00
Presentation Pack (WP113/18)	5·25

4d. *Prices for missing colour errors and inverted watermarks in blocks of four:*

	Ordinary	Phosphor		Ordinary	Phosphor
Red	£2750	†	Slate purple	£4500	£275
Reddish purple	£1100	†	Watermark inverted	9·00	9·00
Agate	†	£12000	Grey double	£6000	†
Violet	†	£11000			

*The double impression of the grey printing affects the Queen's head, value and inscription.

The 1s.9d. is known postmarked 20 April in the Bristol area.

No. W116*e* (Bluebell etc.) was caused by something obscuring the face value on R. 14/6 during the printing of one sheet.

W117*b*, WP117*a*

Cylinder Numbers (Blocks of Eight (4d.) or Six (others))

	Cyl. Nos.	Perforation Types	
		F (P/E) Ordinary	No dot Phosphor
4d.	3A (grey)–1B (lemon)–2C (myrtle-green)–1D (reddish purple)–1E (red)–1F (agate)–2G (violet)–1H (slate-purple)	3·25	3·00
	3A–1B–3C–1D–1E–1F–2G–1H	†	22·00
		A (E/I) No dot	
9d.	2A (lavender-grey)–3B (green)–3C (reddish violet)–2D (orange-yellow)	8·00*	8·00*
1s.9d.	2A (lavender-grey)–2B (green)–2C (greenish yellow)–2D (orange)	2·50	2·25

Minor Constant Flaws

4d. Cyls. 3A–1B–2C–1D–1E–1F–2G–1H no dot
    1/4 Green flaw in large leaf above flower (Th. A4), OP
    4/6 Yellow spot by Queen's chin (Th. C10), P
    8/6 Small spot by upper leaf of wood anemone (Th. A6), OP
    10/2 Small green spot in lower wood anemone (Th. D9), OP
    15/6 Style on left-hand flower of right-hand plant is incomplete (Th. A6), OP
    16/2 Green spot at left of bluebell leaf (Th. E1), P

9d. Cyls. 2A–3B–3C–2D no dot
    9/6 Diagonal hairline running down from small right-hand leaf (Th. F10), OP
    13/5 Green spot between left leaf and centre violet flower (Th. D3), OP
    14/1 Fine vertical yellow line at right of right-hand leaf on top left-hand stamen (Th. B–C3), OP
    20/6 Green spot in lower left-hand leaf (Th. G1), OP

1s.9d. Cyls. 2A–2B–2C–2D no dot
    1/2 Diagonal yellow hairline in the white portion from Queen's neck to top of value (Th. C–E11), OP
    1/6 Retouch between top of stroke and 9 of value (Th. F12), OP
    2/2 Retouch over 9 of value (Th. F13), OP
    10/1 M of MARY is weak, OP
    15/1 Line of green dots between two right-hand primroses (Th. E9), OP
    19/4 Dotted green line projecting left from top left-hand leaf (Th. C–D1), OP
    19/5 Horizontal green hairline on central primrose (Th. D4), OP
    19/6 N of HARRISON is weak, OP
    20/1 Break in outline of petals in topmost primrose (Th. B7), OP

Sheet Details

Sheet size: 120 (6 × 20)
    4d. In *se-tenant* blocks of four, single pane sheet-fed
    9d. and 1s.9d. Single pane reel-fed
Sheet markings:
    Cylinder numbers:
        4d. Opposite rows 17/19 at left, boxed
        9d., 1s.9d. Opposite rows 18/19 at left, boxed
    Guide holes:
        4d. None
        9d., 1s.9d. Opposite row 15 (boxed), at both sides

Marginal arrows (photo-etched): "W" shaped at top, bottom and sides
Marginal rule: At bottom of sheet
Colour register marks:
    4d. Above and below vertical rows 1/2 and 5/6
    9d., 1s.9d. Opposite rows 1/2 and 20, at both sides
Coloured crosses:
    4d. Above and below vertical rows 3/4
    9d., 1s.9d. None
Autotron marks (solid):
    4d. None
    9d. Lavender-grey, green, reddish violet, green over orange, below vertical rows 1/3
    1s.9d. Lavender-grey, orange, green, greenish yellow, below vertical rows 1/3
Colour designations:
    4d. None
    9d. "G1 GREEN G2 MAUVE G3 ORANGE G4 GREY" in right margin reading upwards
        opposite rows 9/3
    1s.9d. "G1 YELLOW G2 GREEN G3 ORANGE G4 GREY" in right margin reading upwards
        opposite rows 13/7
Traffic lights (boxed and in same order as cylinder numbers):
    4d. Opposite rows 17/19 at right
    9d., 1s.9d. Opposite rows 18/19 at right

Imprimaturs from the National Postal Museum Archives

A. Ordinary

Nos. W113/116 imperforate, watermark Type W.24
Watermark upright (*se-tenant* block of four) £6000

Nos. W117/118 imperforate, watermark Type W.24
Watermark upright (2 *values only*) . . . . (*Each*) £1000

B. Phosphor

Nos. WP113/116 imperforate, watermark Type W.24
Watermark upright (*se-tenant* block of four) £6000

Nos. WP 117/118 imperforate, watermark Type W.24
Watermark upright (2 *values only*) . . . . (*Each*) £1000

Quantities Sold

	Ordinary	Phosphor
4d.	78,331,778	37,133,952
9d.	5,873,042	5,701,608
1s.9d.	3,259,521	4,929,648
Pack (including ordinary and phosphor)	53,446	

Withdrawn   23.4.68

PHOSPHOR BANDS. All the following commemorative issues were normally issued with phosphor bands only; however, most also exist with phosphor omitted in error.

W115. "Master Lambton"
(Sir Thomas Lawrence)

W116. "Mares and Foals in a
Landscape" (George Stubbs)

W117. "Children Coming Out of
School" (L. S. Lowry)

(Des. Stuart Rose)

1967 (JULY 10). BRITISH PAINTINGS

This is the first issue of British Paintings for which Harrisons made photographs from the originals.

No watermark. Two phosphor bands, applied by flexography

				Mint	Used
W119 (=S.G.748) **W115**	4d.	rose-red, lemon, brown, black, new blue and gold .		10	10
	a.	Gold omitted (value and Queen's head)	£200	
	b.	New blue omitted	£6500	
	c.	Phosphor omitted	7·00	
W120 (=S.G.749) **W116**	9d.	Venetian red, ochre, grey-black, new blue, greenish yellow and black	15	15
	a.	Black omitted (Queen's head and value)	£450	
	ab.	Black (Queen's head only) omitted	£750	
	b.	Greenish yellow omitted	£1500	
	c.	Phosphor omitted	£450	
	d.	Error. One broad band	15·00	
W121 (=S.G.750) **W117**	1s.6d.	greenish yellow, grey, rose, new blue, grey-black and gold	25	35
	a.	Gold omitted (Queen's head)	£7500	
	b.	New blue omitted	£180	
	c.	Grey (clouds and shading) omitted	95·00	
	d.	Phosphor omitted	£300	
	e.	Error. One broad band	8·00	
	f.	Extra window (No dot, R. 9/1)	4·75	

> First Day Cover (W119/21) . . . . 4·00
> Presentation Pack (W119/21) . . . . 8·00

No. W120*ab* with Queen's head only omitted, was due to a major colour shift. A similar shift caused the face value to be misplaced to the right of the Queen's head.

All values were put on sale in error on 30 June 1967 at the Lincoln head post office.

W121*f*

Cylinder Numbers (Blocks of Four (4d.) or Six (others))

		Cyl. Nos.	Perforation Type A(T) (I/E)	
			No dot	Dot
4d.	3A (gold)–1B (lemon)–1C (rose-red)–1D (new blue)–1E (brown)–1F (black)	1·00	1·00
	3A–1B–2C–1D–1E–1F	1·00	1·00
	4A–1B–1C–1D–1E–1F	1·00	1·00
	4A–1B–2C–1D–1E–1F	1·00	1·00
	5A–1B–2C–1D–1E–1F	1·00	1·00

			Perforation Type A(T) (E/P)	
			No dot	Dot
9d.	2A (black)–1B (greenish yellow)–1C (Venetian red)–1D (ochre)–1E (new blue)–3F (grey-black)	2·00	2·00
1s.6d.	2A (grey-black)–1B (greenish yellow)–1C (rose)–1D (new blue)–1E (grey)–1F (gold) . .	2·75	2·75

Perforation Type A(T) on the 4d. is with sheet orientated showing head to right. In the 4A dot pane the dot is omitted for the gold cylinder and it appears before the C in the rose-red cylinder.

In the 9d. the greenish yellow 1B is very faint in the dot pane and is sometimes almost invisible. Also in the dot pane the dot appears before the 2A.

In the 1s.6d. dot pane the dot appears before the 1F.

Minor Constant Flaws

4d. Cyls. 1B–2C–1D–1E–1F in combination with gold cyls. 3A, 4A or 5A no dot
    2/1 Two small dots on boy's left leg (Th. K6, L6)
    3/1 Gold dot on boy's right collar (Th. F5)
    5/4 Dark spot on right leg of boy's breeches (Th. 14)

4d. Cyls 1B–2C–1D–1E–1F in combination with gold cyls. 3A, 4A or 5A dot
    1/11 Red spot in left gutter, sometimes lost in perforations (Th. JO)
    2/11 Small red spot on boy's right collar (Th. E5)
    3/4 Small spot in the "V" of boy's collar (Th. F5)
    5/3 Dark spot on inside of boy's left elbow (Th. F7)

9d. Cyls. 2A–1B–1C–1D–1E–3F no dot
    3/1 Break in first S of STUBBS
    4/3 Dark spot in foliage of lower centre branch (Th. C5)
    7/1 Dark spot between right-hand foal's forelegs (Th. G7) and another in the grass just below (Th. H7)

9d. Cyls. 2A–1B–1C–1D–1E–3F dot
    2/5 Slight nick in upright stroke of d of value
    9/3 Small retouch in sky above white horse (Th. D10)
    10/1 Break in first R of HARRISON
    11/1 Dark dot below horse's hind hoof in bottom left corner (Th. H1)

1s.6d. Cyls. 2A–1B–1C–1D–1E–1F no dot
   1/1 Circular patch in building below 1 of value (Th. C2)
   1/5 Small dot by leg of foreground figure left of centre (Th. I6)
   9/4 Small spot above roof of small house in side street (Th. E9)
1s.6d. Cyls. 2A–1B–1C–1D–1E–1F dot
   1/1 Break in Y of LOWRY
   1/4 Lack of colour on second red door from right (Th. F–G11)
   12/1 Line of small dots in top gutter

Sheet Details

Sheet size: 4d. 60 (12 × 5), others (5 × 12). All double pane sheet-fed
Sheet markings:
   Cylinder numbers:
      4d. Opposite R. 4/1, boxed
      Others, Opposite rows 10/11 at left, boxed
   Guide holes: None
   Marginal arrows (photo-etched): "W" shaped, at top and bottom (4d.) or at both sides (others)
   Marginal rule: At bottom of sheet
   Colour register marks, coloured crosses, autotron marks and colour designations: None
   Traffic lights (boxed and in same order as cylinder numbers):
      4d. Opposite R. 4/12
      Others. Opposite rows 10/11 at right

Imprimaturs from the National Postal Museum Archives

Nos. W119/121 imperforate
No watermark (*set of* 3) £3000

Quantities Sold

4d. 102,443,229; 9d. 9,568,991; 1s.6d. 9,660,509; Pack 46,017

Withdrawn

9.7.68 (4d. sold out October 1967, 9d. sold out January 1968)

W118. *Gipsy Moth IV*
(Des. Michael and Sylvia Goaman)

1967 (JULY 24).   SIR FRANCIS CHICHESTER'S WORLD VOYAGE
Sir Francis Chichester voyaged single-handed from England to Australia and back in *Gipsy Moth IV*
and was knighted by the Queen on his return.

No watermark. Three phosphor bands, applied by flexography

				Mint	Used
W122 (=S.G.751) **W118**	1s.9d.	black, brown-red, light emerald and blue	. . . . .	20	20
	a.	Broken ribbon (R. 19/3)	. . . .	4·00	

First Day Cover (W122)	1·25

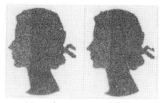

Normal   W122*a*

Cylinder Numbers (Blocks of Six)

	Cyl. Nos.	Perforation Type A (E/I)
		No dot
1s.9d.	2A (black)–1B (light emerald)–1C (blue)–1D (brown-red)	2·25

Minor Constant Flaws

1s.9d. Cyls. 2A–1B–1C–1D no dot
    1/6 Dark flaw in Queen's hair below ribbon (Th. B12–13)
    2/1 Grey flaw at top of main sail (Th. A7) and flaw in rear sail (Th. C8–9)
    6/5 Diagonal line running across main sail (Th. D6–7)
    13/1 Line of small blue dots in rear sail (Th. D–E8)
    14/4 White flaw in figure 1 of value (Th. G12)
    16/2 Break in rigging near main-mast (Th. D5)
    17/6 Line of blue dots on hull below main sail (Th. E4–5)
    18/5 Scratch through rear sail to grey clouds (Th. E8–D11)
    18/6 Same scratch extends to foresail (Th. C1–B5)
    19/1 Small spur protrudes from top right of rear sail (Th. B–C9)
    20/1 Curved dotted blue line between rear sail and Queen's portrait (Th. C9)
    20/2 Diagonal blue line in top gutter (Th. 9–13 in gutter)
    20/3 Vertical white line at bottom left of main sail (Th. D–E5)
    20/4 Blue flaw at top of main sail (Th. A7)
    20/6 Dot between ON of HARRISON

Sheet Details

Sheet size: 120 (6 × 20). Single pane reel-fed
    Sheet markings:
    Cylinder numbers: Opposite rows 18/19 at left, boxed
    Guide holes: Boxed, opposite row 14, at both sides. Boxes without holes also appear opposite row
      15, at both sides
    Marginal arrows (photo-etched): "W" shaped, at top, bottom and sides
    Marginal rule: At bottom of sheet
    Colour register marks: Opposite rows 1/2 and 20, at both sides
    Autotron marks (solid):
      Black, blue, emerald, brown-red, below vertical rows 1/3
    Coloured crosses and colour designations: None
    Traffic lights (boxed): Blue, brown-red, black, emerald, opposite rows 18/19 at right

Imprimatur from the National Postal Museum Archives

No. W122 imperforate
No watermark (*single*) £1000

Quantity Sold 10,060,867

Withdrawn 23.7.68

W119. Radar Screen

W120. Penicillin Mould

(Des. Clive Abbott)

W121. "VC-10" Jet Engines

W122. Television Equipment

(Des. Negus and Sharland team)

1967 (SEPTEMBER 19). BRITISH DISCOVERY AND INVENTION

Watermark Multiple Crowns, sideways on 1s.9d. This was the last commemorative issue to bear a watermark.

Three phosphor bands (4d.) or two phosphor bands (others)

				Mint	Used
W123 (=S.G.752) **W119**	4d.	greenish yellow, black and vermilion	....	10	10
	a.	Phosphor omitted	....	5·00	
	b.	Major scale break (R. 10/2)	....	2·75	
W124 (=S.G.753) **W120**	1s.	blue-green, light greenish blue, slate-purple and bluish violet	....	10	20
	a.	Phosphor omitted	....	9·00	
	b.	Watermark inverted	....	12·00	
W125 (=S.G.754) **W121**	1s.6d.	black, grey, royal blue, ochre and turquoise-blue		20	25
	a.	Phosphor omitted	....	£500	
	b.	Watermark inverted	....	33·00	
	c.	Cowling flaw (R. 1/2)	....	3·25	
W126 (=S.G.755) **W122**	1s.9d.	black, grey-blue, pale olive-grey, violet and orange	....	20	30
	a.	Pale olive-grey omitted	....	£4500	
	b.	Orange (Queen's head)			
	c.	Phosphor omitted	....	£500	

First Day Cover (W123/6)	....	2·50
Presentation Pack (W123/6)	....	4·00

All values are known on a special cover prepared by the Edinburgh G.P.O. Philatelic Bureau but postmarked 8 August 1967.

W123*b*   W125*c*

Cylinder Numbers (Blocks of Six)

	Cyl. Nos. (No dot)	Perforation Types	
		A (E/I)	F (P/E)
4d.	1A (vermilion)–1B (greenish yellow)–1C (black)	1·00	†
1s.	1A (bluish violet)–1B (blue-green)–1C (light greenish blue)–1D (slate-purple)	†	1·00
1s.6d.	1A (black)–1B (ochre)–1C (royal blue)–1D (grey)–1E (turquoise-blue)	†	2·25
		F (E/P)	
1s.9d.	1A (black)–1B (violet)–1C (pale olive-grey)–1D (grey-blue)–1E (orange)	2·25	

Perforation Type F on the 1s.9d. is with sheet orientated showing head to right.

Minor Constant Flaws

4d. Cyls. 1A–1B–1C
    2/2 Break in outer ring of radar screen at top centre (Th. A6)
    8/5 Break in scale division of radar screen just to left of centre bottom mark (Th. G5)
    14/5 Break in scale division of radar screen in centre left mark (Th. D3)

1s. Cyls. 1A–1B–1C–1D
    19/3 Retouch to background at right of value (Th. F12–13)
    19/6 Violet coloured flaw in bottom right of white outer ring (Th. G6)

1s.6d. Cyls. 1A–1B–1C–1D–1E
    12/3 Small break in outer frame-line to right of 1/6 (Th. G13)
    13/2 Pale area in background above first e of engine (Th. F8)
    19/5 White scratch to background—extends to next stamp (Th. G3–10)
    19/6 White scratch to background—extending from previous stamp (Th. G4–10)
    20/3 The small grey coloured projection of the tailplane at right of the engines is malformed (Th. C8)

1s.9d. Cyls. 1A–1B–1C–1D–1E
    1/18 Two of the holes of the disc at left are joined (Th. E1)
    5/1 One of the slits in grey-blue disc below portrait is joined to hub by white flaw (Th. E5)

Sheet Details

Sheet sizes:
    4d. 120 (6 × 20). Single pane reel-fed
    1s. and 1s.6d. 120 (6 × 20). Single pane sheet-fed
    1s.9d. 120 (20 × 6). Single pane sheet-fed
Sheet markings:
    Cylinder numbers:
       4d. and 1s. Opposite R. 19/1, boxed
       1s.6d. Opposite rows 18/19 at left, boxed
       1s.9d. Opposite rows 5/6 at left, boxed
    Guide holes:
       4d. Opposite rows 14/15 (boxed), at both sides; others, none
    Marginal arrows (photo-etched): "W" shaped, at top, bottom and sides
    Marginal rule: At bottom of sheet

Colour register marks:
  4d. Opposite rows 3/4 and 17/18, at both sides
  1s. and 1s.6d. Above and below vertical rows 1 and 6
  1s.9d. Opposite rows 1 and 6 bottom margin, at both sides
Coloured crosses:
  4d. None
  1s. and 1s.6d. Above and below vertical rows 2/3
  1s.9d. Opposite rows 4/5, at both sides
Autotron marks (solid):
  4d. Black, yellow, vermilion below vertical rows 1/3. An additional semi-solid mark in red appears below vertical row 1; others, none
Colour designations: None
Traffic lights (boxed):
  4d. and 1s. In same order as cylinder numbers opposite R. 19/6
  1s.6d. In reverse order to cylinder numbers opposite rows 18/19 at right
  1s.9d. Violet, black, olive-grey, grey-blue, orange opposite rows 5/6 at right

Imprimaturs from the National Postal Museum Archives

Nos. W 123/126 imperforate, watermark Type W.24

Watermark upright (4d., 1s., 1s.6d.) or sideways (1s.9d.) (*set of* 4) £4000

Quantities Sold

4d. 104,165,625; 1s. 10,718,389; 1s.6d. 10,380,413; 1s.9d. 7,469,585; Pack 59,117

Withdrawn   18.9.68

NO WATERMARK. All commemorative stamps from here onwards were printed on paper without watermark.

W123. "The Adoration of the Shepherds" (School of Seville)

W124. "Madonna and Child" (Murillo)

W125. "The Adoration of the Shepherds" (Louis Le Nain)

(Des. Stuart Rose)

1967. CHRISTMAS

The 4d. was issued on 18 October and the others were put on sale on 27 November.
One phosphor band (3d.) or two phosphor bands (others), applied by flexography

				Mint	Used
W127 (=S.G.756) **W123**	3d.		olive-yellow, rose, blue, black and gold	10	15
		a.	Gold omitted (value and Queen's head)	75·00	
		ab.	Gold (value only) omitted	£2500	
		b.	Rose omitted	£2750	
		c.	Imperforate between stamp and left margin	£650	
		d.	Phosphor omitted	1·00	
		e.	Printed on the gummed side	£400	
		f.	Olive-yellow omitted	—	£400
W128 (=S.G.757) **W124**	4d.		bright purple, greenish yellow, new blue, black and gold	10	15
		a.	Gold omitted (value and Queen's head)	60·00	
		b.	Gold ("4D" only) omitted	£1500	
		c.	Greenish yellow (Child, robe and Madonna's face) omitted	£6750	
		d.	Phosphor omitted	£125	
		da.	Error. Right-hand band omitted		
		e.	Error. One broad band	35·00	
		f.	Brown flaw (Dot, R. 2/3)	4·50	
		g.	Greenish yellow and gold omitted	£6500	
W129 (=S.G.758) **W125**	1s.6d.		bright purple, bistre, lemon, black, orange-red, ultramarine, gold	15	50
		a.	Gold omitted (value and Queen's head)	£5500	
		ab.	Gold (Queen's head only) omitted	£1500	
		b.	Ultramarine omitted	£450	
		c.	Lemon omitted	£10000	
		d.	Phosphor omitted	12·00	
		e.	Error. One broad band	40·00	

> First Day Covers (2)(W127/29) . . . . . . 2·00

There is a wide variation on shades of the 3d. and 4d. but they are not listed as there are a number of intermediate shades. For the 4d. value, stamps from one machine show a darker background and give the appearance of the greenish yellow being omitted, but this is not so and these should not be confused with the true missing greenish yellow, No. W128*c*.

The 3d. and 4d. are known with value omitted resulting from colour shifts. No. W128*b* comes from first vertical row of a sheet on which the gold cylinder was stopped so that it printed the head only.

No. W129 *ab* comes from stamps in the first vertical row of a sheet.

No. W127 *ab* was caused by a paper fold.

No. W128*f*. This marked variety on the 4d. consists of a large brown area in the lower right corner (Th. J–K 8–9) which can be clearly seen by the naked eye but which would not show up in an enlarged illustration. It occurs on cylinders 2B–2C–2D–2E dot in conjunction with gold cylinders 2A or 3A.

Cylinder Numbers (Blocks of Six)

	Cyl. Nos.	Perforation Types A (P/E)	
		No dot	Dot
3d.	1A (gold)–1B (olive-yellow)–1C (rose)–1D (blue)–1E (black)	1·00	†
	2A–1B–1C–1D–1E	1·00	†
		(I/E)	(I/E)
4d.	2A (gold)–1B (bright purple)–1C (new blue)– 1D (greenish yellow)–1E (grey-black)	1·00	1·00
	2A–2B–2C–2D–2E	4·00	4·00
	3A–2B–2C–2D–2E	1·00	1·00
	6A–3B–3C–3D–3E	6·00	†
	8A–3B–3C–3D–3E	6·00	†

A(T) (E/P) No dot

1s.6d. 2A (gold)–1B (ultramarine)–1C (bright purple)–1D
(orange-red)–1E (lemon)–1F (bistre)–2G (black) . . . . 4·00

Perforation Type A on the 3d. and 4d. are with the sheet orientated showing the head to right.
The gold of the Queen's portrait and the value is normally further to the left on the 6A and 8A
cylinders.

Minor Constant Flaws

3d. Cyls. 1B–1C–1D–1E in conjunction with gold cyls. 1A or 2A no dot
  1/7 Black horizontal line across triangle of red above Mary's head (Th. E2–3)
3d. Cyls. 1A–1B–1C–1D–1E no dot
  1/11 Break in upright wall of building shows against sky (Th. D6)
3d. Cyls. 2A–1B–1C–1D–1E no dot
  3/10 Small black spot in Joseph's cloak (Th. D5)
  4/9 Background retouch in left pillar (Th. D2)
4d. Cyls. 2B–2C–2D–2E in conjunction with gold cyls. 2A or 3A no dot
  1/5 Prominent pale area in background at bottom right (Th. K–L 8–9)
4d. Cyls. 3A–2B–2C–2D–2E no dot
  2/12 A cut at top of diagonal of 4 of value
  7/5 Dark spot in Mother's right hand (Th. E5)
4d. Cyls. 2B–2C–2D–2E in conjunction with gold cyls. 2A or 3A dot
  4/5 Line of pale dots over 4 of value (Th. J1)
4d. Cyls. 3A–2B–2C–2D–2E dot
  2/12 Black dot over first R of HARRISON
  3/6 Black dot on Child's forehead (Th. C6)
  4/9 Spot on lower left margin of stamp (Th. K1)
  7/2 Small spot just beyond little finger of Madonna's right hand (Th. E6)
  7/12 Two small red dots over H of HARRISON
1s.6d. Cyls. 2A–1B–1C–1D–1E–1F–2G no dot
  1/2 Background disturbance above ll of shilling
  3/6 Curved green flaw left of cow's tail (Th. E1)
  4/9 Background disturbance below n of One

Sheet Details

Sheet sizes:
  3d. 120 (12 × 10). Single pane sheet-fed
  4d. 120 (12 × 10). Double pane reel-fed for gold cyls. 2A and 3A and single pane reel-fed for gold
    cyls. 6A and 8A
  1s.6d. 60 (10 × 6). Single pane sheet-fed
Sheet markings:
  Cylinder Numbers:
    3d. Opposite R. 9/1, boxed
    4d. Below vertical row 11, boxed
    1s.6d. Opposite rows 4/5 at right, boxed
  Guide holes:
    3d. and 1s.6d None
    4d. Above and below vertical row 8
  Marginal arrows (photo etched): "W" shaped, at top, bottom and sides
  Marginal rule: None
  Colour register marks:
    3d. Above and below vertical rows 1/2 and 11/12
    4d. Above and below vertical rows 1/3 (dot) and 8/10 (no dot)
    1s.6d. Opposite rows 1/2 and 6, at both sides
  Coloured crosses:
    3d. Above and below vertical rows 3/4
    4d. None
    1s.6d. Next to cylinder numbers at left and traffic lights at right
  Autotron marks (solid):
    3d. and 1s.6d. None
    4d. Greenish yellow, bright purple, new blue, grey-black, gold opposite rows 6/8, right margin
      (dot) with the 3A–2B–2C–2D–2E cylinders but the order of the colours is reversed with the
      2A–1B–1C–1D–1E cylinders

Colour designations:

3d. and 1s.6d. None

4d. "G1 YELLOW" above vertical row 12 on the dot pane and "G2 GREY G3 GREEN G4 RED G5 GOLD" above vertical rows 1/4 on the no dot pane, the whole inscription being upside down. The "G3 GREEN" is printed in blue

Traffic lights (boxed):

3d. In the same order as the cylinder numbers opposite R. 9/12

4d. Greenish yellow, bright purple, gold, new blue, grey-black above vertical rows 10/11

1s.6d. Lemon, bright purple, orange-red, ultramarine, black, bistre, gold opposite rows 4/5 at right

In the case of the 4d. value all the above information relates to the stamps printed from gold cylinders 2A and 3A in double panes. We have not been able to examine full sheets from the single pane cylinders 6A and 8A on which some of the markings may well be different. However, we have seen part of the top which showed the following differences: colour register marks above row 1/1 and 1/12 and colour designations inverted but reading "G1 YELLOW G2 RED G3 GREEN (printed in blue) G4 GREY G5 GOLD" above vertical rows 1/6, with the yellow above row 6 and the gold above row 1. There was no perforation guide hole.

Imprimaturs from the National Postal Museum Archives

Nos. W127/129 imperforate

No watermark (*set of* 3) £3000

The 3d. (missing phosphor) and 4d. (normal and missing gold) are known imperforate and were not issued. Care should be taken not to confuse these with NPM imprimaturs.

Quantities Sold   3d. 270,349,845; 4d. 287,827,440; 1s.6d. 17,913,209

Withdrawn   3d. Sold out July 1968; 4d. 17.10.68; 1s.6d. 26.11.68

1967 (NOVEMBER 27).   GIFT PACK 1967

WGP1 Comprising Nos. WP111/18 and W119/29 . . . . 3·00

Quantity Sold   105,577

PVA GUM. All commemorative issues from here onwards printed by Harrisons are on paper with PVA gum. For further particulars about this gum see notes at the beginning of Section UA on the Machin definitive issues.

W126. Tarr Steps, Exmoor
(Des. Jeffery Matthews)

W127. Aberfeldy Bridge
(Des. Andrew Restall)

W128. Menai Bridge
(Des. Leonard Rosoman)

W129. M4 Viaduct
(Des. Jeffery Matthews)

1968 (APRIL 29). BRITISH BRIDGES

Two phosphor bands, applied by flexography (4d., 1s.9d.) or photogravure (others)

				Mint	Used
W130 (=S.G.763) **W126**	4d.		black, bluish violet, turquoise-blue and gold	10	10
		a.	Printed on the gummed side	25·00	
		b.	Phosphor omitted	5·00	
		c.	"O" retouch (R. 20/6)	4·00	
		d.	No curve to slab (R. 10/6)	6·00	
W131 (=S.G.764) **W127**	9d.		red-brown, myrtle-green, ultramarine, olive-brown, black and gold	10	15
		a.	Gold (Queen's head) omitted	£160	
		b.	Ultramarine omitted	†	£4250
		c.	Phosphor omitted	15·00	
		d.	Phosphor bands diagonal	25·00	
		e.	Error. One broad band	20·00	
		f.	"HARRISON" redrawn (R. 18/3)	7·00	
		g.	"RESTALL" redrawn (R. 18/4)	7·00	
W132 (=S.G.765) **W128**	1s.6d.		olive-brown, red-orange, bright green, turquoise-green and gold	15	25
		a.	Gold (Queen's head) omitted	£180	
		b.	Red-orange omitted	£200	
		c.	Phosphor omitted	50·00	
		d.	Broken corner stones (R. 15/1)	8·00	
W133 (=S.G.766) **W129**	1s.9d.		olive-brown, greenish yellow, dull green, deep ultramarine and gold	20	30
		a.	Gold (Queen's head) omitted	£180	
		b.	Gold (Queen's head) and phospor omitted	£4000	£1600
		c.	Phosphor omitted	10·00	
		d.	Error. One broad band		

First Day Cover (W130/3)	2·00
Presentation Pack (W130/3)	3·00

No. W131*b* is only known on first day covers posted from Canterbury, Kent or the Philatelic Bureau, Edinburgh.

Used examples of the 1s.6d are known with both the gold and the phosphor omitted.

W130*c*

W130*d*
No curve at left to central slab

W132*d*

W131*f*   W131*g*

Inscriptions redrawn by hand. Normal above varieties

Cylinder Numbers (Blocks of Eight)

	Cyl. Nos.	Perforation Type F (P/E) No dot
4d.	3A (black)–1B (turquoise-blue)–2C (bluish violet)–2D (gold)	1·50
9d.	1A (black)–1B (red-brown)–1C (ultramarine)–1D (olive-brown)–1E (myrtle-green)–1F (gold)	1·50
1s.6d.	2A (olive-brown)–1B (red-orange)–1C (bright green)–2D (turquoise-green)–3E (gold)	2·50
1s.9d.	2A (olive-brown)–1B (gold)–IC (dull green)–1D (deep ultramarine)–1E (greenish yellow)	3·00

Minor Constant Flaws

4d. Cyls. 3A–1B–2C–2D no dot
   4/1 Diagonal dotted line across top of bridge near far end (Th. C10)
   9/1 Lack of screening dots in left of pale green patch left of Tarr (Th G4–5)
   11/1 Similar variety but more pronounced (Th. G4–5)
   12/2 Broken tip to horizontal bar of T of Tarr
   14/2 Scratch across lower stones near far end of bridge (Th. D10–C12)
   17/2 Weakness behind and below hi of Prehistoric (Th. G11)
   19/4 Damaged H in HARRISON

9d. Cyls. 1A–1B–1C–1D–1E–1F no dot
   9/4 Break in olive-brown line at left of ultramarine area under main arch (Th. F6)
   20/4 Small dark spot under r of Bridge

1s.6d. Cyls. 2A–1B–1C–2D–3E no dot
   5/5 Two diagonal lines in sky at right (Th. B–C13)
   5/6 Diagonal line in sky extending to base of Queen's neck (extension of one of the lines in 5/5) (Th. C1)
   6/1 Small curved flaw in front of H of HARRISON
   6/2 White flaw in first arch beyond the far tower (Th. E12)
   14/5 Small white flaw at top right of near tower (Th. B8)
   19/1 Green spot on near tower above right-hand arch (Th. D7–8)

1s.9d. Cyls. 2A–1B–1C–1D–1E no dot
   2/5 Retouch in centre lane (Th. C–D8)
   10/4 Disturbance at right of pale green area below Queen (Th. D3–4)
   14/5 Vertical line appears as radio mast above building on skyline (Th. A6)
   15/1 Retouch between buildings at bend in motorway (Th. C10)
   17/4 Break at foot of s in value

Sheet Details

Sheet size: 120 (6 × 20). Single pane sheet-fed
Sheet markings:
   Cylinder numbers: Opposite rows 17/18 at left, boxed
   Guide holes: None
   Marginal arrows (photo-etched): "W" shaped, at top, bottom and sides
   Marginal rule: At bottom of sheet

Colour register marks:
    4d. and 1s.9d. Above and below vertical rows 1/2 and 6
    9d. and 1s.6d. Above and below vertical rows 1 and 5/6
Coloured crosses:
    4d. and 1s.6d. Above and below vertical row 3
    9d. Above and below vertical rows 3/4
    1s.9d. Above and below vertical rows 2/3
Autotron marks and colour designations: None
Traffic lights (boxed):
    4d. Gold, bluish violet turquoise-blue, black above vertical row 5
    9d. Black, red-brown, ultramarine, myrtle-green, gold, olive-brown above vertical rows 4/5
    1s.6d. Gold, turquoise-green, bright green, red-orange, olive-brown above vertical row 5
    1s.9d. Gold, dull green, olive-brown, deep ultramarine, greenish yellow above vertical row 5

Imprimaturs from the National Postal Museum Archives

Nos. W130/133 imperforate
No watermark (*set of* 4) £4000

Quantities Sold

4d. 97,458,120; 9d. 8,773,080; 1s.6d. 9,451,400; 1s.9d. 5,924,800; Pack 69,646

Withdrawn   28.4.69

W130. "T U C" and
Trade Unionists

W131. Mrs. Emmeline
Pankhurst (statue)

W132. Sopwith "Camel" and
"Lightning" Fighters

W133. Captain Cook's
Endeavour and Signature

(Des. David Gentleman (4d.), Clive Abbott (others))

1968 (MAY 29). BRITISH ANNIVERSARIES

Four famous anniversaries, with the events described on the stamps.

Two phosphor bands, applied by flexography (1s., 1s.9d.) or photogravure (others)

					Mint	Used
W134 (=S.G.767)	**W130**	4d.		emerald, olive, blue and black	10	10
		a.		Phosphor omitted*	12·00	
		b.		Retouch on large "C" (No dot, R. 3/2)	4·00	
W135 (=S.G.768)	**W131**	9d.		reddish violet, grey and black	10	15
		a.		Phosphor omitted	7·00	
		b.		Error. One broad band	30·00	
W136 (=S.G.769)	**W132**	1s.		olive-brown, blue, red, slate-blue and black	15	15
		a.		Phosphor omitted	10·00	

W137 (=S.G.770) **W133**   1s.9d.   ochre, brownish ochre and blackish brown   35   35
          a.   Phosphor omitted† £175
          b.   Broken bulwarks (R. 8/2) . . . .   6·00

> First Day Cover (W134/7) . . . .   3·00
> Presentation Pack (W134/7) . . . .   3·00

*The phosphor bands are normally faint and difficult to see and care is needed in identifying the phosphor omitted on the 4d. value.

†The 1s.9d. is known with phosphor removed by chemical means. These can be detected, but care is needed in identifying genuine examples.

This issue is known postmarked at Netheravon, Salisbury, Wiltshire on 28 May.

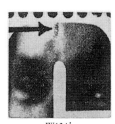 

         W134*b*   W137*b*

Cylinder Numbers (Blocks of Eight (4d., 1s.), Four (9d.), Six (1s.9d.))

	Cyl. Nos.	Perforation Types	
		A (E/I) No dot	A (E/I) Dot
4d.	1A (black)–1B (blue)–1C (olive)–1D (emerald)	1·60	1·60
		F (P/E) No dot	
9d.	1A (black)–1B (reddish violet)–1C (grey) . . .	1·25	
1s.	1A (black)–1B (olive-brown)–1C (blue)–1D (slate-blue)–1E (red)	2·00	
1s.9d.	2A (blackish brown)–1B (brownish ochre)–1C (ochre)	4·00	

Minor Constant Flaws

4d. Cyls. 1A–1B–1C–1D no dot
    1/1 Small retouch in right cross bar of large T
    2/2 Stop between Union and Congress
    4/1 Retouch at top of large C (not as prominent as No. W134*b*)
    10/6 Small retouch at top left of large U
    11/3 Small flaw in 6 of 1968
    11/6 Vertical green line from right cross bar of large T (Th. B–E3)

4d. Cyls. 1A–1B–1C–1D dot
    2/6 Small spot right of 4 of value
    4/5 Green spots by d of Trades (Th. F–G1)
    5/5 Dotted line across back of Queen's hair (Th. B–C12)
    19/1 Retouch on cheek of face shown in large T (Th. D1–2)
    20/5 Two tiny dots above g of Congress

9d. Cyls. 1A–1B–1C no dot
    9/4 Spur at top right of Queen's head (Th. A13)
    14/6 Dark flaw on collar (Th. D10/11) and small flaw on left sleeve (Th. F11)

1s. Cyls. 1A–1B–1C–1D–1E no dot
    3/1 Dot over O of ROYAL
    4/4 Extension of wing joining it to last T of ABBOTT

1s.9d. Cyls. 2A–1B–1C no dot
10/3 Small flaws in background above Y of DISCOVERY level with value (Th. F10–11)
11/2 Small cut in Y of VOYAGE
13/2 Flaw in lower part of S of DISCOVERY
16/2 Sliced F in FIRST
20/5 Tail of 9 of 1968 slightly shortened

Sheet Details

Sheet size: 120 (6 × 20). 4d. double pane reel-fed; others single pane sheet-fed
Sheet markings:
Cylinder numbers:
4d. and 1s. Opposite rows 17/18 at left, boxed
9d. Opposite R. 19/1, boxed
1s.9d. Opposite R. 18/1, boxed
Guide holes:
4d. In double "S O N" box opposite rows 14/15, at left (no dot) or right (dot)
Others: None
Marginal arrows (photo-etched): "W" shaped, at top, bottom and sides
Marginal rule: 4d. None; others at bottom of sheet
Colour register marks:
4d. Opposite rows 2/4 and 18/20 at left (no dot) or right (dot)
Others: Above and below vertical rows 1 and 6
Coloured crosses:
4d. None
9d. and 1s.9d. Above and below vertical row 3
1s. Above and below vertical rows 2/3
Autotron marks (solid):
4d. Black, blue, olive, emerald opposite rows 4/6, at right (no dot) or left (dot); others, none
Colour designations: None
Traffic lights (boxed):
4d. In same order as cylinder numbers opposite rows 1/2, at right
9d. Black, grey, reddish violet above vertical row 5
1s. Olive-brown, blue, slate-blue, red, black above vertical row 5
1s.9d. Brownish ochre, blackish brown, ochre above vertical row 5

Imprimaturs from the National Postal Museum Archives

Nos. W134/137 imperforate
No watermark (*set of* 4) £4000

Quantities Sold

4d. 97,757,920; 9d. 9,135,240; 1s. 9,872,160; 1s.9d. 6,217,440; Pack 67,639

Withdrawn   28.5.69

W134. "Queen Elizabeth I" (Unknown Artist)

W135. "Pinkie" (Sir Thomas Lawrence)

W136. "Ruins of St. Mary Le Port" (John Piper)

W137. "The Hay Wain" (John Constable)

(Des. Stuart Rose)
(Printed in photogravure with the Queen's head embossed in gold)

1968 (AUGUST 12). BRITISH PAINTINGS

This is the second issue of British Paintings for which Harrisons made photographs from the originals.

Two phosphor bands applied by photogravure (1s.9d.) or flexography (others)

				Mint	Used
W138 (=S.G.771) **W134**	4d.		black, vermilion, greenish yellow, grey and gold . .	10	10
		a.	Gold omitted (value and Queen's head)	£180	
		b.	Gold (value and Queen's head) and phosphor omitted	£180	
		c.	Vermilion omitted*	£350	
		d.	Phosphor omitted	1·50	
		e.	Embossing omitted	80·00	
		f.	Blister on hand (No dot, R. 2/8)	4·50	
W139 (=S.G.772) **W135**	1s.		mauve, new blue, greenish yellow, black, magenta and gold	10	20
		a.	Gold omitted (value and Queen's head)	£3000	
		b.	Gold (value and Queen's head), embossing and phosphor omitted	£250	
		c.	Embossing omitted	£225	
		d.	Phosphor omitted	7·00	
W140 (=S.G.773) **W136**	1s.6d.		slate, orange, black, mauve, greenish yellow, ultramarine, and gold	20	25
		a.	Gold omitted (value and Queen's head)	£110	
		b.	Phosphor omitted	10·00	
		c.	Embossing omitted		

329

W141 (=S.G.774) **W137**   1s.9d.   greenish yellow, black, new blue, red and gold   ..   25   40
       a.   Gold (value and Queen's head), embossing and
          phosphor omitted £500
       b.   Red omitted £10000
       c.   Phosphor omitted . . . . 20·00
       d.   Embossing omitted £140

First Day Cover (W138/41)	2·00
Presentation Pack (W138/41)	1·75
Pack also exists with a Japanese insert card.	
Presentation Pack (German) (W138/41)	12·00

*No. W138*c* shows the face and hands white, and there is more yellow and olive in the costume.
The 4d. also exists with the value only omitted resulting from a colour shift.
This issue is known pre-released on a first day cover postmarked 10 August from Vauxhall Bridge
P.O., S.W.1.

W138*f*

Cylinder Numbers (Blocks of Six)

	Cyl. Nos.	Perforation Type A(T) (I/E)	
		No dot	Dot
4d.	2A (gold)–1B (embossing)–3C (black)–2D (grey)–3E (vermilion)–2F (greenish yellow) . .	1·00	1·00
1s.	2A (gold)–1B (embossing)–2C (black)–2D (new blue)–2E (mauve)–2F (magenta)–2G (greenish yellow)	1·25	1·25
	2A–2B–2C–2D–2E–2F–2G	1·25	1·25
1s.6d.	1A (gold)–1B (embossing)–1C (black)–1D (ultramarine)–1E (slate)–1F (mauve)–1G (orange)–1H (greenish yellow)	1·75	1·75

		Perforation Type A(T) (E/P)	
1s.9d.	2A (gold)–1B (embossing)–1C (black)–1D (new blue)–1E (red)–1F (greenish yellow)	3·00	3·00

Perforation Type A(T) on the 4d., 1s. and 1s.6d. are with sheet orientated showing head to right.
In each value the 1B cylinder number appears in colourless embossing; it is difficult to see but can often be discerned with the aid of a magnifying glass.

Minor Constant Flaws

4d. Cyls. 2A–1B–3C–2D–3E–2F no dot
    6/8 Thick A in HARRISON

4d. Cyls. 2A–1B–3C–2D–3E–2F dot
    4/2 Black flaw on dress above Queen's right hand (Th. J4–5)

1s. Cyls. 2A–1B–2C–2D–2E–2F–2G no dot
    2/4 Diagonal black line across Pinkie's shoulder (Th. D4)
    5/1 Black spur to A of HARRISON
    6/1 Thin diagonal black line across dress (Th. H3–5)

1s.6d. Cyls. 1A–1B–1C–1D–1E–1F–1G–1H no dot
    6/1 Dark coloured spot in top right corner of dark blue area (Th. A8–9)

1s.6d. Cyls. 1A–1B–1C–1D–1E–1F–1G–1H dot
    1/8 ? shaped black flaw in doorway (Th. J5)
    6/6 Extra patch at upper left corner of yellow wall (Th. E8)

1s.9d. Cyls. 2A–1B–1C–1D–1E–1F no dot
    9/2 Blue spot after HARRISON
    10/1 Green instead of brown bush in bottom left-hand corner

Sheet Details

Sheet size: 1s.9d. 60 (6×10), others 60 (10×6). All double pane sheet-fed
Sheet markings:
    Cylinder numbers:
        4d. Opposite row 5, left margin, boxed
        1s. and 1s.6d. Opposite rows 4/5, left margin, boxed
        1s.9d. Opposite rows 8/9, left margin, boxed
    Guide holes: None
    Marginal arrows (photo-etched): "W" shaped, at top, bottom and sides
    Marginal rule: None
    Colour register marks:
        4d., 1s. and 1s.6d. Above vertical rows 1/2 and 9/10 (no dot) or below (dot)
        1s.9d. Opposite rows 1/2 and 9/10, left margin (no dot) or right margin (dot)
    Coloured crosses:
        4d. and 1s. Above vertical rows 6/7 (no dot) or below (dot)
        1s.6d. Above vertical rows 7/8 (no dot) or below (dot)
        1s.9d. Opposite rows 7/8, left margin (no dot) or right margin (dot)
    Autotron marks, colour designations: None
    Traffic lights (boxed):
        4d., 1s. and 1s.6d. In same order as cylinder numbers, except that on the 1s.6d. the gold and embossing "lights" are transposed, reading left to right above vertical rows 8/9
        1s.9d. In same order as cylinder numbers, except that the gold and embossing "lights" are transposed, reading left to right above vertical row 5

Imprimaturs from the National Postal Museum Archives

Nos. W138/141 imperforate
No watermark (*set of* 4) £4000

Quantities Sold

4d.	185,034,000	English Pack	93,829
1s.	17,953,440	German Pack	7,880
1s.6d.	8,878,440		
1s.9d.	5,739,000		

Withdrawn 11.8.69

1968 (SEPTEMBER 16). GIFT PACK 1968

WGP2 Comprising Nos. W130/41 . . . . 6·00
              a. German text . . . . 28·00

Quantities Sold Ordinary 41,308; German 1,650

1968 (SEPTEMBER 16). COLLECTORS PACK 1968

WCP1 Comprising Nos. W123/41 . . . . 7·00

Quantity Sold 26,284

W139. Girl with
Doll's House

W138. Boy and Girl with
Rocking Horse

W140. Boy with
Train Set

(Des. Rosalind Dease)

(Printed in photogravure with the Queen's head embossed in gold)

1968 (NOVEMBER 25). CHRISTMAS

The joy of giving is emphasised on this Christmas issue; all three designs show children playing with their Christmas toys.

One centre phosphor band (4d.) or two phosphor bands (others), applied by flexography

				Mint	Used
W142 (=S.G.775) **W138**	4d.	black, orange, vermilion, ultramarine, bistre and gold	10	15
	a.	Gold omitted	£4000	
	b.	Vermilion omitted*	£300	
	c.	Ultramarine and phosphor omitted	£250	
	d.	Embossing omitted	6·00	
	e.	Phosphor omitted	5·00	
	f.	Retouched dapples (Cyl. 1A. R. 12/4)	4·00	
	g.	Bistre omitted	—	£3000
W143 (=S.G.776) **W139**	9d.	yellow-olive, black, brown, yellow, magenta, orange, turquoise-green and gold	15	25
	a.	Yellow omitted	65·00	
	b.	Turquoise-green (dress) omitted	£10000	
	c.	Embossing and phosphor omitted	10·00	
	d.	Embossing omitted	6·00	
	f.	Phosphor omitted	10·00	
W144 (=S.G.777) **W140**	1s.6d.	ultramarine, yellow-orange, bright purple, blue-green, black and gold	15	50
	a.	Embossing omitted		
	b.	Phosphor omitted	15·00	

First Day Cover (W142/4)	1·20	
Presentation Pack (W142/4)	5·00	
Presentation Pack (German) (W142/4) .	14·00	

*The effect of the missing vermilion is shown on the rocking horse, saddle and faces which appear orange instead of red.

No. W142 is known pre-released on 24 November at Edinburgh.

A single used example of No. W142*g* has been seen with the bistre omitted from the mane of the rocking horse and the girl's hair. No. W142*a* also exists with a single complete omission and three partial gold heads on the gummed side due to a paper fold.

Two machines were used for printing the 4d. value:

Stamps from cylinders 1A–1B–2C–1D–1E in combination with 1F, 2F or 3F (gold) were printed entirely on the Rembrandt sheet-fed machine. They invariably have the Queen's head level with the top of the boy's head and the sheets are perforated through the left side margin (perforation type F).

Stamps from cylinders 2A–2B–3C–2D–2E in combination with 1F, 2F, 3F or 4F (gold) were printed on the reel-fed Thrissell machine in five colours (its maximum colour capacity) and subsequently
sheet-fed on the Rembrandt machine for the gold the Queen's head and the embossing. The position of
the Queen's head is generally lower than on the stamps printed at one operation but it varies in different parts of the sheet and is not, therefore, a sure indication for identifying single stamps. Another
small difference is that the boy's grey pullover is noticeably "moth-eaten" in the Thrissell printings and
is normal on the Rembrandt. The Thrissell printings are perforated through the top margin (perforation type A).

Marginal copies can usually be identified by the characteristics of the perforation (if any) in the sheet
margin. Ideally, cylinder blocks of six are required to show examples of the two printing machines used.

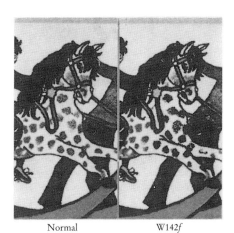

Grey dapples on the horse nearest to the
boy and extending to the boy's belt and
trousers, are heavily retouched

Normal   W142*f*

Cylinder Numbers (Blocks of Six)

			Perforation Types	
	Cyl. Nos. (No dot)		A (E/I)	F (P/E)
A.	"Rembrandt" only printings			
	4d.	1A (black)–1B (orange)–2C (vermilion)–1D (ultramarine)–1E (bistre)–1F (gold)	†	2·00
		1A–1B–2C–1D–1E–2F	†	2·00
		1A–1B–2C–1D–1E–3F	†	3·00
				(E/P)
	9d.	1A (black)–1B (brown)–1C (yellow)–2D (magenta)–1E (orange)– 1F (turquoise-green)–1G (yellow-olive)–1H (gold)	†	3·00
	1s.6d.	1A (black)–1B (ultramarine)–1C (yellow-orange)–1D (bright purple)–1E (blue-green)–1F (gold)	†	4·00
B.	"Thrissell" and "Rembrandt" printings			
	4d.	2A (black)–2B (orange)–3C (vermilion)–2D (ultramarine)–2E (bistre)–1F (gold)	2·00	†
		2A–2B–3C–2D–2E–2F	3·00	†
		2A–2B–3C–2D–2E–3F	5·00	†
		2A–2B–3C–2D–2E–4F	5·00	†

Perforation Type F on the 9d. and 1s.6d. are with sheet orientated showing head to right. The 1s.6d.
has cyl. nos. 1B–1E unboxed.

Minor Constant Flaws

4d. Cyls. 1A–1B–2C–1D–1E in combination with gold cyls. 1F, 2F, 3F, or 4F
    3/6 Small black flaw in m of Christmas
    12/5 Small nick on right edge of upright stroke of 4 of value

4d. Cyls. 2A–2B–3C–2D–2E in combination with gold cyls. 1F, 2F, 3F or 4F
    16/4 Small black flaw above horse's left foreleg by boy's waist (Th. D9)
    20/4 Break in outline at top centre of near rocker (Th. F4–5)

9d. Cyls. 1A–1B–1C–2D–1E–1F–1G–1H
   4/3 Small black flaw between a and s of Christmas
   6/18 Break in middle of final s of Christmas

1s.6d. Cyls. 1A–1B–1C–1D–1E–1F
   2/18 Pale patch on boy's left shoulder (Th. F4)
   3/8 Thick horizontal spur on left of lower central purple slotted plate (Th. D–E4)
   5/2 Black flaws in background lower right of Queen's head (Th. C–D7)
   5/3 Two black dots between 1 and stroke of 1/6
   6/20 Purple coloured flaws in background below boy's foot (Th. J7)

Sheet Details

	Rembrandt	Thrissell/Rembrandt
Sheet sizes:		
4d. 120 (6 × 20)	Single pane sheet-fed	Single pane reel-fed for five colours, and then single pane sheet fed for the gold and embossing
9d. and 1s.6d. 120 (20 × 6)	Single pane sheet-fed	
Sheet markings:		
Cylinder numbers:		
4d.	Opposite rows 18/19, left margin, boxed	Opposite rows 18/19, left margin, boxed
9d. and 1s.6d.	Opposite rows 4/5, left margin, boxed	
Guide holes:		
4d.	None	Opposite rows 14/15 (boxed), at both sides
9d. and 1s.6d.	None	
Marginal arrows (photo-etched):		
4d.	"W" shaped, at top, bottom and sides	"W" shaped, at top, bottom and sides
9d. and 1s.6d.	As 4d.	
Marginal rule:	None	None
Colour register marks:		
4d.	Above and below vertical rows 1/2 and 6	Opposite rows 2/3 and 19/20 at both sides
9d. and 1s.6d.	Opposite rows 1/2 and 5/6 at both sides	
Coloured crosses:		
4d.	Above and below vertical row 3	Gold only below vertical row 3
9d. and 1s.6d.	Opposite rows 3/4 at both sides	
Autotron marks (solid):		
4d.	None	Black, bistre, ultramarine, vermilion, orange below vertical rows 4/6
9d. and 1s.6d.	None	
Colour designations:	None	None
Traffic lights (boxed):		
4d.	Orange, vermilion, ultramarine, bistre, black, gold, embossing opposite rows 18/19, right margin; also above vertical row 5 reading left to right	Orange, vermilion, ultramarine, bistre, black, gold, embossing opposite rows 18/19, right margin; also gold and embossing (unboxed) above vertical row 5 reading left to right
9d.	Gold, olive, green, orange, magenta, yellow, brown, black opposite rows 4/5, right margin; also embossing, gold, olive, green, orange, magenta, yellow, brown, black above vertical rows 17/19 reading left to right	

1s.6d.	Embossing, gold, green, purple, orange, ultramarine, black opposite rows 4/5, at right; also gold, green, purple, orange, ultramarine, black, above vertical rows 18/19 reading left to right

Although the Traffic Light box in the right margin on the 9d. and the upper margin on the 1s.6d. were designed to accommodate an embossing "light" the space was not in fact used.

Imprimaturs from the National Postal Museum Archives

Nos. W142/144 imperforate

No watermark (*set of 3*) £3000

Quantities Sold

4d. 326,078,360, 9d. 17,102,520, 1s.6d. 21,344,760, English Pack 72,474, German Pack 7,298

Withdrawn   24.11.69

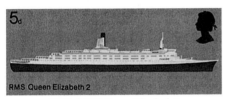

W141. R.M.S. *Queen Elizabeth 2*

W142. Elizabethan Galleon

W145. S.S. *Great Britain*

W143. East Indiaman

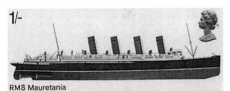

W146. R.M.S. *Mauretania*

W144. *Cutty Sark*

(Des. David Gentleman)

1969 (JANUARY 15).   BRITISH SHIPS

Issued as a tribute to British shipbuilders and seamen, these stamps depict five famous ships of the past and the *Queen Elizabeth 2*, which sailed on her maiden voyage to New York on 2 May 1969.

The 9d. values were issued together *se-tenant* in strips of three throughout the sheet and the 1s. values were issued together *se-tenant* in pairs throughout the sheet.

Two phosphor bands at right (1s.), one horizontal phosphor band (5d.) or two phosphor bands (9d.), applied by flexography

335

				Mint	Used
W145 (=S.G.778) **W141**	5d.		black, grey, red and turquoise	10	15
		a.	Black omitted (Queen's head, value, hull and inscr.)	£1200	
		b.	Grey omitted (decks, etc.)	90·00	
		c.	Red (inscription) omitted	50·00	
		d.	Red and phosphor omitted	90·00	
		e.	Phosphor omitted	5·00	
W146 (=S.G.779) **W142**	9d.		red, blue, ochre, brown, black and grey	10	25
		a.	Strip of 3.Nos. W146/48	1·50	3·00
		b.	Red, blue and phosphor omitted	£1600	
		c.	Blue omitted	£1600	
		d.	Phosphor omitted	12·00	
		da.	Phosphor omitted. (*strip of three*)	40·00	
W147 (=S.G.780) **W143**	9d.		ochre, brown, black and grey	10	25
		b.	Phosphor omitted	12·00	
W148 (=S.G.781) **W144**	9d.		ochre, brown, black and grey	10	25
		b.	Phosphor omitted	12·00	
W149 (=S.G.782) **W145**	1s.		brown, black, grey, green and greenish yellow . . .	40	35
		a.	Pair, Nos. W149/50	1.25	2·50
		b.	Greenish yellow omitted	£2750	
		c.	Phosphor omitted	28·00	
		ca.	Phosphor omitted. (*pair*)	65·00	
W150 (=S.G.783) **W146**	1s.		red, black, brown, carmine and grey	40	35
		a.	Carmine (hull overlay) omitted	£20000	
		b.	Red (funnels) omitted	£14000	
		c.	Carmine and red omitted	£14000	
		d.	Phosphor omitted	30·00	

> First Day Cover (W145/50) . . . .   6·00
> Presentation Pack* (W145/50) . . . .   4·00
>   Pack also exists with a Dutch or
>   Japanese insert card.
> Presentation Pack (German) (W145/50)   40·00

*In addition to the generally issued Presentation Pack (inscribed "RMS Queen Elizabeth 2 ... she sailed on her maiden voyage to New York on 17 January 1969") a further pack (inscribed "RMS Queen Elizabeth 2 ... she sails on her maiden voyage early in 1969") was issued for sale exclusively on board the Q.E.2 during her maiden voyage which had been postponed. (*Price* £8).

9d. *Prices for missing colour errors in strips of three*:
>   Red, blue and phosphor £1600
>   Blue £1600

1s. *Price for missing colour error in pair*:
>   Greenish yellow £2750

First Day covers are known postmarked 14 January, Buckley, Flintshire. The year date shown as 1968 instead of 1969 exists postmarked at Brighton, Sussex.

Cylinder Numbers (Blocks of Six (5d. and 1s.) or Twelve (9d.))

		Perforation Types	
	Cyl. Nos. (No dot)	A(T) (E/P)	F (P/E)
5d.	1A (black)–1B (grey)–1C (red)–1D (turquoise)	3·00	†
9d.	1A (black)–2B (brown)–1C (ochre)–1D (grey)– 1E (red)–1F (blue)	†	5·50
1s.	2A (black)–1B (grey)–1C (green)–1D (red)–1E (carmine)–1F (brown)-1G (yellow)	7·00	†

Minor Constant Flaws

5d. Cyls. 1A–1B–1C–1D
    2/5 Disturbance in sea over liz of Elizabeth
    3/2 Blue flaw on superstructure halfway between funnel and stern (Th. E6) (later removed)
    4/5 Weak patch in hull directly below funnel (Th. F9)

9d. Cyls. 1A–2B–1C–1D–1E–1F
    16/2 Rope between second and third masts is broken (Th. D5)

1s. Cyls. 2A–1B–1C–1D–1E–1F–1G
    1/6 Small brown flaw lower right of stern mast (Th. D6)
    2/8 Curved black flaw just above third funnel (Th. C10)
    4/2 Weak patch in hull directly below fore mast (Th. E17)
    10/1 Wispy black flaw in front of Queen's chin (Th. B–C17)

Sheet Details

Sheet sizes:
    All single pane sheet-fed
    5d. 72 (8 × 9)
    9d. 120 (6 × 20). In *se-tenant* strips of three
    1s. 80 (8 × 10). In *se-tenant* pairs
Sheet markings:
    Cylinder numbers:
        5d. Opposite rows 7/8, left margin, boxed
        9d. Opposite rows 17/18, left margin, boxed
        1s. Below vertical row 7, boxed
    Guide holes: None
    Marginal arrows (photo-etched); "W" shaped, at top and bottom (5d.); "W" shaped, at top, bottom and sides (others)
    Marginal rule: None
    Colour register marks:
        5d. Opposite rows 1/2 and 8/9 at both sides
        9d. Above and below vertical rows 1 and 6
        1s. Opposite rows 1/2 and 10 at both sides
    Coloured crosses:
        5d. Opposite rows 5/6 at both sides
        9d. Above and below vertical rows 3/4
        1s. Opposite rows 5/7 at both sides
    Autotron marks, colour designations: None
    Traffic lights (boxed):
        5d. In same order as cylinder numbers opposite rows 7/8, right margin; also above vertical row 7 reading left to right
        9d. In same order as cylinder numbers opposite rows 18/19, right margin; also above vertical rows 5/6 but in reverse order to cylinder numbers reading left to right
        1s. In reverse order to cylinder numbers opposite rows 8/9, right margin; also above vertical row 8 in reverse order to cylinder numbers reading left to right

Imprimaturs from the National Postal Museum Archives

Imperforate, no watermark
No W145 single £1500
Nos. W146/8 *se-tenant* strip of three £4500
Nos. W149/50 *se-tenant* pair £3000

Quantities Sold

5d. 67,584,528, 9d. 14,351,160, 1s. 10,784,480, English Pack 116,526, German Pack 4.416

Withdrawn   14.1.70

W147. "Concorde" in Flight
(Des. Michael and Sylvia Goaman)

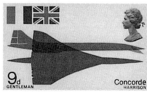 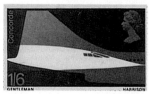

W148. Plan and Elevation Views   **W149.** "Concorde's" Nose and Tail
(Des. David Gentleman)

1969 (MARCH 3).   FIRST FLIGHT OF "CONCORDE"

Issued to commemorate the first flight of the "Concorde" supersonic airliner developed and produced jointly by Britain and France.

Two phosphor bands

				Mint	Used
W151 (=S.G.784) **W147**	4d.	yellow-orange, violet, greenish blue, blue-green and pale green	25	25
	a.	Violet omitted (value, etc.)	£350	
	b.	Yellow-orange and phosphor omitted	£350	
	c.	Yellow-orange omitted	£350	
	d.	Phosphor omitted	1·00	
	e.	Error. Left-hand band omitted	50·00	
	f.	"Oil slick" flaw (R. 13/2)	4·00	
W152 (=S.G.785) **W148**	9d.	ultramarine, emerald, red and grey-blue	55	75
	a.	Phosphor omitted	£100	
	b.	Grey-blue (Face value and inscr. omitted) £25000*		£1500
W153 (=S.G.786) **W149**	1s.6d.	deep blue, silver-grey and light blue	75	1·00
	a.	Silver-grey omitted*	£350	
	b.	Phosphor omitted	9·00	

First Day Cover (W151/3)	4·00
Presentation Pack* (W151/3)	12·00
Pack also exists with a Dutch or Japanese insert card.	
Presentation Pack (German) (W151/3) .	40·00

No. W153a affects the Queen's head which appears in the light blue colour.

*This exists as a complete sheet with guide marks and sheet markings in grey-blue affecting the remaining five stamps of top row.

A cover with all three values is known postmarked 2 March 1969, at Hindon, Salisbury.

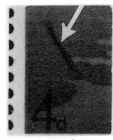

Dark flaw in Atlantic Ocean appears as an oil slick

W151*f*

Cylinder Numbers (Blocks of Six)

	Cyl. Nos. (No dot)	Perforation Type F (P/E at left and I/E at right)

4d.   1A (violet)–1B (orange)–1C (greenish blue)–1D (pale green)–1E (blue-green) . . . .   3·00
9d.   2A (grey-blue)–1B (red)–1C (emerald)–1D (ultramarine) . .   5·50
1s.6d.   1A (deep blue)–1B (silver-grey)–3C (light blue) . . . .   7·00

In this issue cylinder blocks exist at the left or right of the sheets.

Minor Constant Flaws

4d. Cyls. 1A–1B–1C–1D–1E
   1/2 Disturbance in background below tail (Th. F–G11)
   2/2 Disturbance in background below tail (Th. F–G12)

9d. Cyls. 2A–1B–1C–1D
   11/2 Flaw on Queen's hair below ribbons (Th. B13)

1s.6d. Cyls. 1A–1B–3C
   18/2 Small white patch below tip of Concorde's nose (Th. F13)

Sheet Details

Sheet size: 120 (6 × 20). Single pane sheet-fed
Sheet markings:
   Cylinder numbers:
      4d. Opposite rows 1/2 and 18/19, at both sides, boxed
      9d. Opposite rows 2/3 and 18/19, at both sides, boxed
      1s.6d. Opposite rows 2 and 19, at both sides, boxed
   Guide holes: None
   Marginal arrows (photo-etched): "W" shaped, at top, bottom and sides
   Marginal rule: At bottom of sheet
   Colour register marks:
      4d. Above and below vertical rows 1/2 and 6
      9d. Above and below vertical rows 1 and 5/6
      1s.6d. Above and below vertical rows 1/2 and 6
   Coloured crosses: Above and below vertical rows 2/3
   Autotron marks, colour designations: None
   Traffic lights (boxed):
      4d. Blue-green, orange, violet, greenish blue, pale green reading left to right above vertical row 5
      9d. Ultramarine, emerald, red, grey-blue reading left to right above vertical row 5
      1s.6d. Deep blue, light blue, silver-grey reading left to right above vertical row 5

Imprimaturs from the National Postal Museum Archives

Nos. W151/153 imperforate
No watermark (*set of* 3) £3500

Quantities Sold

4d.	91,551,720	English Pack	100,608
9d.	9,488,520	German Pack	2,827
1s.6d.	9,874,560		

Withdrawn   2.3.70

W150. Page from *Daily Mail*
and Vickers "Vimy" Aircraft

(Des. Philip Sharland)

W151. Europa and CEPT
Emblems

(Des. Michael and Sylvia Goaman)

W152. ILO Emblem

(Des. Philip Sharland)

W153. Flags of NATO Countries

(Des. Philip Sharland)

W154. Vickers "Vimy" Aircraft and
Globe showing Flight

(Des. Michael and Sylvia Goaman)

1969 (APRIL 2).   NOTABLE ANNIVERSARIES

Five famous anniversaries, with the events described on the stamps.
Two phosphor bands, applied by photogravure (5d.) or flexography (others)

				Mint	Used
W154 (=S.G.791) **W150**	5d.	black, pale sage-green, chestnut and new blue . . .		10	15
	a.	Phosphor omitted			
	b.	Missing windshield (R. 3/4)		4·50	
W155 (=S.G.792) **W151**	9d.	pale turquoise, deep blue, light emerald-green and black		15	25
	a.	Uncoated paper*	£1500		
	b.	Phosphor omitted	18·00		
W156 (=S.G.793) **W152**	1s.	bright purple, deep blue and lilac		15	25
	a.	Phosphor omitted	10·00		

W157 (=S.G.794) **W153** 1s.6d. red, royal blue, yellow-green, black, lemon and new

		blue	15	30
a.	Black omitted	60·00	
b.	Yellow-green (from flags) omitted	50·00	
c.	Yellow-green and phosphor omitted	55·00	
d.	Phosphor omitted	9·00	
e.	Shadow variety (R. 18/6)	4·50	
f.	Lemon (from flags) omitted	†	£3500

W158 (=S.G.795) **W154** 1s.9d. yellow-olive, greenish yellow and pale turquoise-

		green	20	40
a.	Uncoated paper*	£200	
b.	Phosphor omitted	6·00	

First Day Cover (W154/8)	3·00
Presentation Pack (W154/8)	3·50
Pack also exists with a Japanese	
insert card.	
Presentation Pack (German) (W154/8) .	55·00

*Uncoated paper–see General Notes for Section UA also below Nos. W159/64.
No. W154 is known postmarked 1 April.
No. W157*f* is only known used on a first day cover from Liverpool.

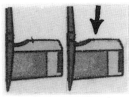

Normal	W154*b*	W157*e*
		Deficient shading in shadow
		by fold

Cylinder Numbers (Blocks of Six (5d., 1s., 1s.9d.) or Eight (9d., 1s.6d.))

		Cyl. Nos. (No dot)	Perforation Types	
			A (E/I)	F (P/E)
5d.	1A (blue)–1B (chestnut)–1C (sage-green)–1D (black)		1·75	†
9d.	1A (blue)–1B (green)–1C (black)–1D (turquoise)		†	2·75
1s.	1A (blue)–1B (purple)–1C (lilac)		†	2·50
1s.6d.	1A (new blue)–1B (lemon)–1C (red)–1D (royal blue)–1E (black)–1F (green)		†	4·00
1s.9d.	2A (yellow-olive)–2B (green)–1C (yellow) . .		†	4·50

Minor Constant Flaws

5d. Cyls. 1A–1B–1C–1D
   3/4 Black horizontal line extending through the engine and fuselage (Th. E9–12)
   4/6 Vertical black scratch top left of photograph of Alcock (Th. A–B3)
   15/3 Retouch to base of engine (Th. E10)
   15/5 White flaw on Brown's cap (Th. B6). Later retouched

9d. Cyls. 1A–1B–1C–1D
   14/1 Retouch to background below O of EUROPA (Th. F–G4)
   15/3 Weak patch in background to left of CEPT symbol (Th. E11)
   19/3 Retouch to background below EU of EUROPA (Th. F2)
   20/2 Weak patch in background above O of EUROPA (Th. B–C4)

1s. Cyls. 1A–1B–1C
  19/1 Dark patch in upper jaw of spanner (Th. F1)
1s.9d. Cyls. 2A–2B–1C
  17/4 Horizontal scratch through value (Th. A1–3)
  20/6 Pale patch in East Asia on globe (Th. B12)

Sheet Details

Sheet size: 120 (6× 20). 5d. single pane reel-fed; others single pane sheet-fed
Sheet markings:
  Cylinder numbers:
    5d. Opposite rows 18/19, left margin, boxed
    9d. Opposite rows 17/18, left margin, boxed
    1s. Opposite row 18, left margin, boxed
    1s.6d. Opposite rows 17/18, left margin, boxed
    1s.9d. Opposite row 18, left margin, boxed
  Guide holes:
    5d. Opposite rows 14/15 (boxed), at both sides
    Others: None
  Marginal arrows (photo-etched): "W" shaped, at top, bottom and sides
  Marginal rule: None
  Colour register marks:
    5d. Opposite rows 1/2 and 19/20 at both sides
    Others: Above and below vertical rows 1 and 6
  Coloured crosses:
    5d. None
    9d., 1s. and 1s.9d. Above and below vertical row 3
    1s.6d. Above and below vertical rows 3/4
  Autotron marks (solid):
    5d. Black, sage-green, blue, chestnut below vertical rows 1/3
    Others: None
  Colour designations:
    5d. "G1 BROWN G2 BLUE G3 (blank) G4 BLACK" in right margin reading upwards opposite
      rows 14/9
    Others: None
  Sheet values: Opposite rows 4/7 and 14/17 reading upwards in left margin and downwards in right
    margin
  Traffic lights (boxed):
    5d. Black, sage-green, blue, chestnut opposite rows 18/19, right margin; also in same order opposite
      rows 1/2, left margin
    9d. Black, green, blue, turquoise opposite rows 17/18, right margin; also in reverse order reading
      left to right above vertical row 5
    1s. In same order as cylinder numbers opposite row 18, right margin; also in reverse order
      reading left to right above vertical row 5
    1s.6d. In same order as cylinder numbers opposite rows 17/18, right margin; also in reverse order
      reading left to right above vertical row 5
    1s.9d. In same order as cylinder numbers opposite row 18, right margin; also in reverse order
      reading left to right above vertical row 5

Imprimaturs from the National Postal Museum Archives

Nos. W154/158 imperforate
No watermark (*set of* 5) £5000

Quantities Sold

5d.	82,285,680	English Pack	90,282
9d.	9,823,200	German Pack	4,539
1s.	10,302,360		
1s.6d.	10,512,480		
1s.9d.	6,155,760		

Withdrawn 1.4.70

W155. Durham Cathedral

W156. York Minster

W157. St. Giles', Edinburgh

W158. Canterbury Cathedral

W159. St. Paul's Cathedral

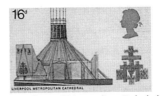

W160. Liverpool Metropolitan Cathedral

(Des. Peter Gauld)

1969 (MAY 28). BRITISH ARCHITECTURE (CATHEDRALS)

The designs show six famous British Cathedrals dating from medieval times to the present, the Liverpool Metropolitan Cathedral being completed in 1967.

The 5d. values were issued together *se-tenant* in blocks of four throughout the sheet

Two phosphor bands, applied by flexography (5d.) or photogravure (others)

				Mint	Used
W159 (=S.G.796) **W155**	5d.		grey-black, orange, pale bluish violet and black	10	20
		a.	Block of 4. Nos. W159/62	75	2·50
		ac.	Uncoated paper* *(block of four)*	£1000	
		b.	Pale bluish violet omitted	£3750	
		c.	Uncoated paper*	£250	
		d.	Missing "d"	£300	
W160 (=S.G.797) **W156**	5d.		grey-black, pale bluish violet, new blue and black	10	20
		b.	Pale bluish violet omitted	£3750	
		c.	Uncoated paper*	£250	
W161 (=S.G.798) **W157**	5d.		grey-black, purple, green and black	10	20
		b.	Green omitted*	55·00	
		c.	Uncoated paper*	£250	
		d.	Missing "d"	£300	
W162 (=S.G.799) **W158**	5d.		grey-black, green, new blue and black	10	20
		c.	Uncoated paper*	£250	
W163 (=S.G.800) **W159**	9d.		grey-black, ochre, pale drab, violet and black	25	50
		a.	Black (value) omitted.	£100	
		b.	Black (value) and phosphor omitted	£150	
		c.	Phosphor omitted	45·00	

W164 (=S.G.801) **W160**   1s.6d.   grey-black, pale turquoise-blue, pale reddish
violet, pale yellow-olive and black   25   50

     a.   Black (value) omitted £2000

     b.   Black (value) double ....

     c.   Phosphor omitted ....   20·00

     ca.   Error. Phosphor omitted and one stamp with
diagonal phosphor band (*pair*) ....   40·00

First Day Cover (W159/64)	3·00
Presentation Pack* (W159/64)	3·25
Pack also exists with a Dutch or	
Japanese insert card.	
Presentation Pack (German) (W159/64)	30·00

*Uncoated paper. This does not respond to the chalky paper test, and may be further distinguished from the normal chalk-surfaced paper by the fibres which clearly show on the surface, resulting in the printing impression being rougher, and by the screening dots which are not so evident.

For this issue hand stamped "Cancelled" see Special Issues – Notes, "Specimen".

5d. *Prices for missing colour errors in blocks of four:*

         Pale bluish violet £7500

         Green ....   55·00

*The missing green on the roof top is known on R. 2/5, R. 8/5 and R. 10/5 but all from different sheets and it only occurred in part of the printing, being "probably caused by a batter on the impression cylinder". Examples are known with the green partly omitted.

Nos. W159*d* and W161*d* missing "d" affects stamps R. 1/1 and R. 2/1 in a block; the stamps at right were normal.

Cylinder Numbers (Blocks of Eight (5d.) or Six (9d., 1s.6d.))

	Cyls. Nos.	Perforation Types		
		A (E/I) No dot	A (E/I) Dot	F (P/E) No dot
5d.	1A (black)–1B (purple)–1C (blue)–1D (orange)–2E (green)–2F (grey-black)–1G (violet)*	3·00	3·00	†
	1A–1B–2C–1D–2E–2F–1G*	3·00	3·00	†
9d.	1A (black)–1B (grey-black)–2C (violet)–1D (drab)–1E (ochre)**	†	†	4·00
1s.6d.	1A (black)–1B (violet)–1C (turquoise-blue)–1D (yellow-olive)–1E (grey-black)	†	†	4·00

*In the 5d. dot panes the violet cylinder is expressed in error thus: "1.G" and the black cylinder "1.A".

**In the 9d. the violet "2C" often appears battered, the "2" sometimes being hardly discernible.

Minor Constant Flaws

5d. Cyls. 1A–1B–1D–2E–2F no dot in combination with blue cyls. 1C or 2C no dot
    12/4 Thin diagonal green line joins portrait to inset design (Th. C-E2)

5d. Cyls. 1A–1B–1D–2E–2F dot in combination with blue cyls. 1C or 2C dot
    1–4/3 Green coloured scratch extends from bottom of third stamp in row 1 to top of third stamp in
       row 4.
       Most noticeable in the sky of R. 3/3
    4/1 Damaged first S of ST. GILES'
    10/3 Grey-black coloured spur at right of angel (Th. F13)

9d. Cyls. 1A–1B–2C–1D–1E
    8/5 Dark spot in window on first floor just to right of centre of St. Paul's (Th. F7)
    9/1 Dot left of ground floor window next to entrance columns (Th. G3)

1s.6d. Cyls. 1A–1B–1C–1D–1E
    1/1 Retouch on Queen's head (Th. A11)
    15/1 Spur at left of third spike of central tower (Th. A5); also dot before C of CATHEDRAL

Sheet Details

Sheet sizes:
    5d. 72 (6 × 12). In *se-tenant* blocks of four, double pane reel-fed, with dot pane above no dot pane
    9d. and 1s.6d. 120 (6 × 20). Single pane sheet-fed

Sheet markings:
    Cylinder numbers:
        5d. Opposite rows 10/11, left margin, boxed
        9d. and 1s.6d. Opposite rows 18/19, left margin, boxed
    Guide holes:
        5d. Opposite rows 6/7 (boxed), at both sides
        Others: None
    Marginal arrows (photo-etched): "W" shaped, at top, bottom and sides
    Marginal rule: None
    Colour register marks:
        5d. Opposite rows 10/12, left margin, although usually trimmed off
        9d. and 1s.6d. Above and below vertical rows 1 and 6
    Coloured crosses:
        5d. None
        9d. and 1s.6d. Above and below vertical rows 3/4
    Autotron marks:
        5d. Normally trimmed off
        9d. and 1s.6d. None
    Colour designations: None
    Sheet values:
        5d. Opposite rows 2/5 and 8/11 reading upwards in left margin and downwards in right margin
        9d. and 1s.6d. Opposite rows 5/6 and 15/16 reading upwards in left margin and downwards in right margin
    Traffic lights (boxed):
        5d. In same order as cylinder numbers opposite rows 10/11, right margin; also in same order reading left to right above vertical rows 4/5
        9d. In reverse order to cylinder numbers opposite rows 18/19, right margin; also above vertical row 5 but in same order as cylinder numbers reading left to right
        1s.6d. Black, yellow-olive, turquoise-blue, violet, grey-black opposite rows 18/19, right margin; also grey-black, yellow-olive, turquoise-blue, violet and black reading left to right above vertical row 5

Imprimaturs from the National Postal Museum Archives

Imperforate, no watermark

Nos. W159/62 *se-tenant* block of four £6000
Nos. W163 single £1500
Nos. W164 single £1000

Quantities Sold

5d.	65,344,176	English Pack	119,828
9d.	11,065,920	German Pack	7,200
1s.6d.	11,414,280		

Withdrawn   27.5.70

W161. The King's Gate,
Caernarvon Castle

W162. The Eagle Tower,
Caernarvon Castle

W163. Queen Eleanor's Gate,
Caernarvon Castle

Types **W161/63** were issued together *se-tenant* in horizontal strips of three within the sheet

W164. Celtic Cross,
Margam Abbey

W165. H.R.H. The Prince of Wales
(after photograph by G. Argent)

(Des. David Gentleman)

1969 (JULY 1).   INVESTITURE OF H.R.H. THE PRINCE OF WALES

The ceremony of Investiture dates back to 1284 when King Edward I presented his son to the people of Caernarvon as the first Prince of Wales.

Two phosphor bands, applied by flexography, the phosphor being printed between two groups of colour units.

				Mint	Used
W165 (=S.G.802)	**W161**	5d.	deep olive-grey, light olive-grey, deep grey, light grey, red, pale turquoise-green, black and silver ..	10	15
		a.	Strip of 3. Nos. W165/7	30	1·50
		b.	Black (value and inscr.) omitted	£250	
		c.	Red omitted*	£400	
		d.	Deep grey omitted**	£180	
		e.	Pale turquoise-green omitted	£400	
		f.	Phosphor omitted	5·00	
		fa.	Phosphor omitted (strip of three)	15·00	
W166 (=S.G.803)	**W162**	5d.	deep olive-grey, light olive-grey, deep grey, light grey, red, pale turquoise-green, black and silver ..	10	15
		b.	Black (value and inscr.) omitted	£250	
		c.	Red omitted*	£400	
		d.	Deep grey omitted**	£180	
		e.	Pale turquoise-green omitted	£400	
		f.	Light grey (marks on walls, window frames, etc.) omitted (see footnote)	—	£7500
		g.	Phosphor omitted	5·00	

W167 (=S.G.804) **W163**	5d.	deep olive-grey, light olive-grey, deep grey, light grey, red, pale turquoise-green, black and silver . .	10	15
	b.	Black (value and inscr.) omitted	£250
	c.	Red omitted*	£400
	d.	Deep grey omitted**	£180
	e.	Pale turquoise-green omitted	£400
	f.	Phosphor omitted	5·00
W168 (=S.G.805) **W164**	9d.	deep grey, light grey, black and gold	15	30
	a.	Phosphor omitted	22·00
	b.	Error. One broad band	40·00
W169 (=S.G.806) **W165**	1s.	blackish yellow-olive and gold	15	30
	a.	Phosphor omitted	15·00
	b.	Error. One broad band	35·00
	c.	Error. Diagonal broad band	45·00

> First Day Cover (W165/9) . . . .   1·50
> Presentation Pack† (W165/9) . . . .   2·50
>   Pack also exists with a Dutch or
>   Japanese insert card.
> Presentation Pack (German) (W165/9) .   28·00

5d. *Prices for missing colour errors in strips of three:*

Black	£750	Pale turquoise-green	£1200
Red	£1200	Light grey	£30000
Deep grey	£550		

The light grey is unique in a mint strip of three and one. No. W166*f* commercially used on cover.

*The 5d. is also known with the red misplaced downwards and where this occurs the red printing does not take very well on the silver background and in some cases is so faint that it could be mistaken for a missing red. However, the red can be seen under a magnifying glass and caution should therefore be exercised when purchasing examples of W165/7*c*.

**The deep grey affects the dark portions of the windows and doorways.

†In addition to the generally issued Presentation Pack a further pack in different colours and with all texts printed in both English and Welsh was made available exclusively through Education Authorities for free distribution to all schoolchildren in Wales and Monmouthshire. (*Price* £6).

First Day Covers are known postmarked in error "1 JUL 1968" at London N.W.1.

Cylinder Numbers (Blocks of Nine (5d.) or Four (9d., 1s.))

	Cyl. Nos.	Perforation Type F (E left margin) No dot
5d.	1A (black)–1B (red)–1C (silver)–1D (green)–E (deep 1 olive-grey)–1F (light olive-grey)–1G (deep grey)–1H (light grey)	3·00

		A (P/E) No dot	A (P/E) Dot	A(T) (I/E) No dot	A(T) (I/E) Dot
9d.	1A (black)–1B (gold)-1C (deep grey)–1D (light grey)	2·50	2·50	†	†
1s.	1A (gold)–2B (blackish yellow-olive)	2·50	2·50	–	–

The above are with sheets orientated showing head to right.

Minor Constant Flaws

9d. Cyls. 1A–1B–1C–1D dot
  5/9 yw of Tywysog are joined together

1s. 1A–2B no dot
  1/10 Retouch to right of Prince's lower lip (Th. J–K6)
  3/4 Small retouch below Prince's left eye (Th. G6)
  1A–2B dot
  3/9 Dark patch below Prince's left eye (Th. G6)

Sheet Details

Sheet sizes:
    5d. 72 (12 × 6). In *se-tenant* strips of three, single pane sheet-fed
    9d. and 1s. 60 (10 × 6). Double pane sheet-fed, with no dot pane above dot pane
Sheet markings:
    Cylinder numbers:
        5d. Opposite rows 4/5, left margin, boxed
        9d. and 1s. Opposite row 6, left margin, boxed
    Guide holes: None
    Marginal arrows (photo-etched):
        5d. None
        9d. and 1s. "W" shaped, at top, bottom and sides
    Marginal rule: None
    Colour register marks:
        5d. Opposite rows 1 and 6, at both sides
        9d. Above (no dot) or below (dot) vertical rows 1/2 and 10
        1s. Above (no dot) or below (dot) vertical rows 1/2 and 9/10
    Coloured crosses:
        5d. Opposite rows 3/4, at both sides
        9d. and 1s. Above (no dot) or below (dot) vertical row 4
    Autotron marks, colour designations: None
    Sheet values:
        5d. Above and below vertical rows 2/5 and 8/11 reading left to right in top margin and right to left (upside-down) in bottom margin
        9d. and 1s. Opposite rows 1/3 and 4/6 reading upwards in left margin and downwards in right margin
    Traffic lights (boxed):
        5d. In same order as cylinder numbers opposite rows 4/5, right margin; also in same order reading left to right above vertical rows 10/11
        9d. In same order as cylinder numbers opposite row 6, right margin; also in same order reading left to right above vertical row 9
        1s. In reverse order to cylinder numbers opposite row 6, right margin; also in reverse order reading left to right above vertical row 9

Imprimaturs from the National Postal Museum Archives

Imperforate, no watermark

Nos. W165/7 *se-tenant* strip of three £4500
Nos. W168 and W169 . . . . *(Each)* £1500

Quantities Sold

    5d. 99,467,496; 9d. 13,384,380; 1s.12,972,720; English Pack 256,709; German Pack 9,360; Welsh Schoolchildren's Pack 146,958

Withdrawn   30.6.70

W166. Mahatma Gandhi
(Des. Biman Mullick)

1969 (AUGUST 13).   GANDHI CENTENARY YEAR

    This stamp marking the Gandhi Centenary Year was also the first United Kingdom postage stamp to commemorate an overseas leader and the first to be designed by an overseas artist.
    Two phosphor bands, applied by flexography

W170 (=S.G.807) **W166**   1s.6d.   black, green, red-orange and grey   30   30
                       a.   Printed on the gummed side £400
                       b.   Phosphor omitted . . . .   4·00
                       c.   Tooth Flaw (R. 20/3) . . . .   4·50

> First Day Cover (W170) . . . .   1·00

The above is known pre-released on 12 August at Penyfai (Bridgend), Glamorgan and also post-marked Paisley, Renfrewshire 13 July 1969, the latter being due to the use of an incorrect date-stamp on a first day cover.

White patch in Gandhi's mouth appears as tooth. Later retouched to near normal

W170c

Cylinder Numbers (Blocks of Six)

	Cyl. Nos. (No dot)	Perforation Type F (P/E)
1s.6d.	2A (black)–1B (grey)–2C (green)–1D (orange)	5·00

Minor Constant Flaws

1s.6d. Cyls. 2A–1B–2C–1D
    1/6 Second white spot in Gandhi's right eye (Th. D6). Later retouched; also small nick in left arm
      of Y of Year
    3/4 Dark patch on arm of spectacles (Th. C4)
    3/5 Retouch on Gandhi's nose (Th. E6)
    5/3 Dark spot in front of Gandhi's right ear (Th. D3)
    8/2 Dark spot on Gandhi's temple (Th. C4). Later retouched
    12/4 White patch on Gandhi's right lapel (Th. G2)
    16/1 Retouched G of Gandhi

Sheet Details

Sheet size: 120 (6×20). Single pane sheet-fed
Sheet markings:
    Cylinder numbers: Opposite rows 18/19, left margin, boxed
    Guide holes: None
    Marginal arrows (photo-etched): "W" shaped, at top, bottom and sides
    Marginal rule: None
    Colour register marks: Above and below vertical rows 1 and 6
    Coloured crosses: Above and below vertical row 3
    Autotron marks and colour designations: None
    Sheet values: Opposite rows 4/7 and 14/17 reading upwards in left margin and downwards in right
      margin
    Traffic lights (boxed): Black, grey, green, orange opposite rows 19/20, right margin; also in reverse
      order reading left to right above vertical row 5

Imprimatur from the National Postal Museum Archives

No. W170 imperforate
No watermark (single) £1000

Quantity Sold   10,804,920

Withdrawn   12.8.70

1969 (SEPTEMBER 15).   COLLECTORS PACK

	Mint	Used
WCP2 Comprising Nos. W142/70	20·00	

This pack also exists with a German or Japanese insert card.

Quantity Sold   63,890

W167. National Giro
"G" Symbol

W168. Telecommunications—
International Subscriber Dialling

W169. Telecommunications—
Pulse Code Modulation

W170. Postal Mechanisation—
Automatic Sorting

(Des. David Gentleman)

(Lithography by De La Rue)

1969 (OCTOBER 1).   POST OFFICE TECHNOLOGY COMMEMORATION

Issued on the day the Post Office became a public corporation, these stamps depict some of its technological achievements. This issue in itself was a technical departure for the Post Office being the first British stamps to be printed by lithography.

Comb perforation 13½ × 14. Two phosphor bands applied by typography

				Mint	Used
W171 (=S.G.808) **W167**	5d.		new blue, greenish blue, pale lavender and black .	10	10
		a.	Phosphor omitted	5·00	
		b.	Error. One broad band	15·00	
W172 (=S.G.809) **W168**	9d.		emerald, violet-blue and black	15	20
		a.	Error. One broad band	15·00	
W173 (=S.G.810) **W169**	1s.		emerald, lavender and black	15	20
		a.	Phosphor omitted	£300	
		b.	Error. One broad band	15·00	
W174 (=S.G.811) **W170**	1s.6d.		bright purple, light turquoise-blue, grey-blue and black	15	35
		a.	Error. One broad band	18·00	

> First Day Cover (W171/4) . . . .   1·50
> Presentation Pack (W171/4) . . . .   2·75
>   Pack also exists with a Dutch,
>   German or Japanese insert card.

No. W171*a* can be found with or without a "dry" impression of the typography plate.

The 1s. is known postmarked at Gloucester on 29 September and the 1s.6d. at Gutcher Yell (Shetland Isles) on 26 September.

For advance publicity the Post Office produced sample sets of stamps sealed in a sheet of perspex (size 4 × 6 in.) together with details of the designs, and names of the stamp designer and printer.

For examples with "Cancelled" handstamp, see Special Issues—Notes, "Specimens".

Plate Numbers (Blocks of Four)

	Pl. Nos. (all Dot)	Perforation Type F (L) (I/E)
5d.	2A (new blue)–2B (greenish blue)–2C (lavender)–2D (black)	1·25
	2A–3B–2C–2D	1·00
	2A–3B–2C–3D	1·00
	3A–4B–3C–4D	1·50
9d.	2A (emerald)–2B (violet-blue)–2C (black)	1·50
1s.	1A (emerald)–1B (lavender)–1C (black)	3·00
	1A–1B–2C	2·50
	1A–1B–3C	2·50
1s.6d.	1A (purple)–1B (light turquoise-blue)–1C (grey-blue)–1D (black)	3·00

Although all the plate numbers are followed by a dot they were in fact only printed in single panes.

Minor Constant Flaws

Numerous minor flaws caused by specks of dust settling on the printing plate and preventing the ink from reaching the area appear as white inkless rings and are known as litho "ring" flaws. Minor flecks of colour are similarly caused. As such flaws only affect part of a printing and cannot be regarded as constant we have decided not to record them.

Sheet Details

Sheet size: 120 (10 × 12). Single pane sheet-fed

Sheet markings:
Plate numbers: Opposite rows 1/2, left margin, unboxed
Guide holes: Above and below vertical row 6 in crossed box. Reserve guide-hole boxes appear above and below vertical row 4 but these were not used
Marginal arrows (solid): "W" shaped, at top, bottom and sides
Marginal rule: None
Colour register marks:
5d., 9d. and 1s. Below vertical rows 1 and 10 and opposite rows 1 and 12, at both sides
1s.6d. Above and below vertical rows 1 and 10 and opposite rows 1 and 12, at both sides
Coloured crosses, autotron marks, colour designations: None
Sheet values: Above and below vertical rows 2/4 and 7/9 reading left to right in top margin and right to left (upside-down) in bottom margin
Traffic lights (unboxed):
5d. Opposite rows 8/10, right margin
9d. and 1s. Opposite rows 9/10, right margin
1s.6d. Opposite rows 9/11, right margin

Imprimaturs from the National Postal Museum Archives

Nos. W171/174 imperforate
No watermark (*set of* 4) £4000

Quantities Sold   5d. 72,405,720; 9d. 8,472,000; 1s. 10,296,120; 1s.6d. 10,757,040; Pack 104,230

Withdrawn   30.9.70

W171. Herald Angel

W172. The Three Shepherds   **W173.** The Three Kings

(Des. Fritz Wegner)

(Printed in photogravure with the Queen's head (and stars 4d., 5d. and scroll-work
1s.6d. embossed in gold)

1969 (NOVEMBER 26). CHRISTMAS

Traditional religious themes are featured on these stamps by Austrian-born designer Fritz Wegner.

One 7 to 8 mm. centre phosphor band (4d.) or two phosphor bands (others), applied by photogravure (W175*b*) or flexography (others)

				Mint	Used
W175 (=S.G.812) **W171**	4d.		vermilion, new blue, orange, bright purple, light green, bluish violet, blackish brown and gold . . .	10	10
		a.	Gold (Queen's head etc.) omitted	£4000	
		b.	Centre band 3·5 mm	30	20
W176 (=S.G.813) **W172**	5d.		magenta, light blue, royal blue, olive-brown, green, greenish yellow, red and gold	15	15
		a.	Light blue (sheep, etc.) omitted	60·00	
		b.	Red omitted*	£675	
		c.	Gold (Queen's head etc.) omitted	£450	
		d.	Green omitted	£200	
		e.	Olive-brown, red, gold and phosphor omitted . .	£9000	
		f.	Embossing omitted	22·00	
		g.	Phosphor omitted	5·00	
		h.	Olive-brown omitted	—	£3500
		i.	Greenish yellow (tunic at left) omitted	—	£3500
W177 (=S.G.814) **W173**	1s.6d.		greenish yellow, bright purple, bluish violet, deep slate, orange, green, new blue and gold	20	20
		a.	Gold (Queen's head etc.) omitted	90·00	
		b.	Deep slate (value) omitted	£250	
		c.	Greenish yellow omitted	£250	
		e.	New blue omitted	60·00	
		f.	Embossing omitted	10·00	
		g.	Embossing and phosphor omitted	10·00	
		h.	Phosphor omitted	6·00	
		i.	Broken arch (R. 1/6)	4·50	

First Day Cover (W175/7) . . . .   1·00
Presentation Pack (W175/7) . . . .   2·50
    Pack also exists with a Dutch,
    German or Japanese insert card.

*The effect of the missing red is shown on the hat, leggings and purse which appear as dull orange. The 4d. is known postmarked at Dudley, Worcs. on 25 November.

No. W175 has one centre band 8 mm. wide but this was of no practical use in the automatic facing machines and after about three-quarters of the stamps had been printed the remainder were printed with a 3·5 mm. band (No. W175*b*). The wide band is sometimes difficult to see. Stamps have also been seen with a very wide "phantom" band measuring about 20 mm. which only reacts very faintly under the lamp and with a clear 3·5 mm. band over it.

No. W176*e* was caused by a paper fold.

No. W177*d* bluish violet has been deleted as examples showed only a partial omission.

Break in the arch above the crown of King at right

W 177*i*

Cylinder Numbers (Blocks of Six (4d.) or Eight (5d., 1s.6d.))

Cyl. Nos.		Perforation Types A (E/I)			
		7–8 mm. band		3·5 mm. band	
		No dot	Dot	No dot	Dot
4d.	1A (brown)–1B (vermilion)–2C (orange)–1D (purple)–1E (new blue)–1F (green)–1G (violet)–1H (gold)	2·00	2·00	†	†
	1A–1B–2C–1D–1E–2F–1G–1H	4·00	4·00	4·00	4·00
		F (P/E) No dot		F(L) (I/E) No dot	
5d.	1A (royal blue)–1B (yellow)–1C (magenta)–1D (green)–2E (brown)–1F (light blue)–1G (red)–1H (gold)	3·00		15·00	
1s.6d.	3A (slate)–1C (gold)–1D (blue)–1E (yellow)–1F (green)–1G (violet)–1H (purple)–1J (orange)	5·00		†	

On the 4d. cylinder numbers 1A and 1H often appear as "1A1" and "1H1" on the dot and no dot panes respectively; the 1B and 1E have what appear to be small letters "IN" in place of dot, whilst the 2C is an alteration from "1C", all on the dot panes.

Minor Constant Flaws

4d. Cyls. 1A–1B–2C–1D–1E–2F–1G–1H dot
    5/3 White flaw in hem of angel's gown (later corrected) (Th. E1)
    11/1 A break in the pattern of the pillar on the right (Th. E13)
    11/4 White flaw in the pattern of the arch over the Queen's head (Th. A11)

Sheet Details

Sheet sizes:
    4d. 72 (6 × 12). Double pane reel-fed (one pane above the other) for four colours and phosphor, and then single pane sheet-fed for remaining four colours and embossing
    5d. and 1s.6d. 120 (6 × 20). Single pane sheet-fed
Sheet markings:
    Cylinder numbers:
        4d. Opposite rows 10/12, left margin, boxed
        5d. and 1s.6d. Opposite rows 17/19, left margin, boxed
    Guide holes:
        4d. Opposite rows 6/7 (boxed), at both sides
        5d. and 1s.6d. None
    Marginal arrows (photo-etched): "W" shaped, at top, bottom and sides
    Marginal rule: None
    Colour register marks:
        4d. None
        5d. and 1s.6d. Above and below vertical rows 1/2 and 5/6
    Coloured crosses:
        4d. Usually trimmed off
        5d. and 1s.6d. Above and below vertical rows 3/4

Autotron marks, colour designations: None
Sheet values:
    4d. Opposite rows 3/4 and 9/10 reading upwards in left margin and downwards in right margin
    5d. Opposite rows 4/7 and 14/17 reading upwards in left margin and downwards in right margin
    1s.6d. Opposite rows 5/6 and 15/16 reading upwards in left margin and downwards in right margin
Traffic lights (boxed):
    4d. Vermilion, orange, purple, new blue, green, brown, violet, gold and embossing opposite rows 9/11, right margin; also in same order reading left to right above vertical rows 4/5
    5d. Embossing and then as cylinder numbers but in reverse order opposite rows 17/19, right margin; also in same order as cylinder numbers followed by embossing above vertical rows 4/5
    1s.6d. Embossing, gold, blue, yellow, slate, green, violet, purple and orange opposite rows 17/19, right margin; also in reverse order reading left to right above vertical rows 4/5

Imprimaturs from the National Postal Museum Archives

Nos. W175/177 imperforate
No watermark (*set of* 3) £3000

Quantities Sold   4d. 271,244,808; 5d. 139,845,600; 1s.6d. 19,136,520; Pack 121,454

Withdrawn   25.11.70

W174. Fife Harling

W175. Cotswold Limestone

(Des. David Gentleman)

W176. Welsh Stucco

W177. Ulster Thatch

(Des. Sheila Robinson)

1970 (FEBRUARY 11). BRITISH RURAL ARCHITECTURE

The designs feature typical cottage architecture in Scotland, England, Wales and Northern Ireland respectively.

Two phosphor bands

				Mint	Used
W178 (=S.G.815)	**W174**	5d.	grey, grey-black, black, lemon, greenish blue, orange-brown, ultramarine and green	10	10
	a.		Lemon omitted	80·00	
	b.		Lemon omitted from chimney at left (R. 12/2) . .	2·50	
	c.		Grey (Queen's head and cottage shading) omitted	£5000	
	d.		Greenish blue (door) omitted	†	£3500
	e.		Grey-black omitted £12000		
	f.		Phosphor omitted	2·00	
	g.		Nick in hair (R. 15/6)	4·50	

W179 (=S.G.816) **W175** 9d. orange-brown, olive-yellow, bright green, black,
grey-black and grey 10   25
    a. Phosphor omitted . . . . 10·00

W180 = S.G. 817) **W176** 1s. deep blue, reddish lilac, drab and new blue 15   25
    a. New blue omitted . . . . 80·00
    b. Phosphor omitted . . . . 15·00
    c. Error. One broad band . . . .

W181 (=S.G.818) **W177** 1s.6d. greenish yellow, black, turquoise-blue and lilac . 20   40
    a. Turquoise-blue omitted £5000
    b. Phosphor omitted . . . . 5·00
    c. Broken panes in middle window (No dot, R. 3/2) 4·75

> First Day Cover (W178/81) . . . . 1·50
> Presentation Pack (W178/81) . . . . 3·25
> Pack also exists with a Dutch,
> German or Japanese insert card.

Examples showing "Fife harling" (No. W178) omitted were due to a partial omission of the grey-black (*Price mint* £475). The listed example of No.W178*d* is used and tied on piece, with the greenish blue colour omitted. No. W178*e* is a total omission and should only be purchased with certificate.

First Day covers are known postmarked 11 January (Doncaster) or 1969 (Farnham).

No. W178*b*. The lemon is omitted from the chimney at left once in every sheet (later added to cylinder and appearing normal).

      W178*g*   W181*c*

Cylinder Numbers (Blocks of Eight (5d.), Six (9d.), Four (1s., 1s.6d.))

	Cyl. Nos.	Perforation Types		
		F (P/E)	A(T)	(E/P)
		No dot	No dot	Dot
5d.	1A (black)–1B (grey-black)–1C (brown)–1D (ultramarine)–1E (greenish blue)–1F (green)–1G (grey)–1H (lemon)	2·00	†	†
9d.	1A (grey-black)–1B (yellow)–1C (brown)–1D (black)–IE (green)–1F (grey)	3·00	†	†
1s.	1A (deep blue)–2B (lilac)–1C (new blue)–1D (drab)	†	4·00	4·00
1s.6d.	1A (black)–1B (yellow)–1C (turquoise-blue)–1D (lilac)	†	5·00	5·00

Minor Constant Flaws

5d. Cyls. 1A–1B–1C–1D–1E–1F–1G–1H no dot
   4/2 Right leg of h of harling is broken
   9/6 Pale patch on wall above left-hand first-floor window of building at right (Th. D8)
   20/6 Pale patch on wall by top of upright at the bottom of the banisters and similar patch with grey spot in it just above (Th. F1); coloured spur to centre chimney (Th. A7); and orange-brown flaw below F of Fife (Th. A2)

9d. Cyls. 1A–1B–1C–1D–1E–1F no dot
   19/1 Dark flaw on gate at left (Th. G2)

1s.6d. Cyls. 1A–1B–1C–1D no dot
   2/3 Pale flaw on left stroke of U of ULSTER and two yellow dots in front of Queen's neck

1s.6d. Cyls. 1A–1B–1C–1D dot
   5/5 White flaw to right of sixth brick from bottom (Th. G7)

Sheet Details

Sheet sizes:
   5d. and 9d. 120 (6 × 20). Single pane sheet-fed
   1s. and 1s.6d. 60 (6 × 10). Double pane sheet-fed (etched sideways on the cylinder)
Sheet markings:
   Cylinder numbers:
      5d. Opposite rows 17/19, left margin, boxed
      9d. Opposite rows 18/19, left margin, boxed
      1s. and 1s.6d. Opposite rows 9/10, left margin, boxed
   Guide holes: None
   Marginal arrows (photo-etched): "W" shaped, at top, bottom and sides
   Marginal rule: None
   Colour register marks:
      5d. and 9d. Above and below vertical rows 1/2 and 6
      1s. Opposite rows 1/2 and 6, at left (no dot) or right (dot)
      1s.6d. Opposite rows 1 and 6, at left (no dot) or right (dot)
   Coloured crosses:
      5d. and 9d. Above and below vertical rows 3/4
      1s. Opposite row 7, at left (no dot) or right (dot)
      1s.6d. Opposite rows 6/7, at left (no dot) or right (dot)
   Autotron marks, colour designations: None
Sheet values:
   5d. and 9d. Opposite rows 4/7 and 14/17 reading upwards in left margin and downwards in right
      margin
   1s. Opposite row 2/4 and 7/9 reading upwards in left margin and downwards in right margin
   1s.6d. As 1s. but reading downwards in left margin and upwards in right margin
Traffic lights (boxed):
   5d. In same order as cylinder numbers opposite rows 18/19, right margin; also in reverse order
      reading left to right above vertical rows 4/6
   9d. In reverse order to cylinder numbers opposite rows 18/19; also in same order as cylinder
      numbers above vertical row 5
   1s. In same order as cylinder numbers opposite rows 6/7, right margin; also in same order
      reading left to right above vertical row 5
   1s.6d. In same order as cylinder numbers opposite rows 7/8 at both sides; also in reverse order
      above vertical row 5

Imprimaturs from the National Postal Museum Archives

Nos. W178/181 imperforate
No watermark (*set of* 4) £4000

Quantities Sold   5d. 81,581,880; 9d. 11,723,160; 1s. 10,258,320; 1s.6d. 8,969,280; Pack 116,983

Withdrawn   10.2.71

SALES QUANTITIES. The figures quoted for quantities actually sold of the 1970 issues are according to the best estimates available from the Post Office, as exact records of unsold returns could not be made in the circumstances following the postal strike, and the change to decimal issues. In particular the estimates for the Philympia and Christmas issues cannot be guaranteed.

W178. Signing the Declaration
of Arbroath

W179. Florence Nightingale
attending Patients

(Des. Fritz Wegner)

W180. Signing the International
Co-operative Alliance

(Des. Marjorie Saynor)

W181. Pilgrims and *Mayflower*

(Des. Fritz Wegner)

W182. Sir William Herschel, Francis Baily,
Sir John Herschel and Telescope

(Des. Marjorie Saynor)

(Printed in photogravure with the Queen's head embossed in gold)

1970 (APRIL 1). GENERAL ANNIVERSARIES

Five famous anniversaries, with the events described on the stamps.

An additional feature of this issue was the introduction of cylinder numbers for the cylinders printing the phosphor bands. They are not easy to see but are printed below the ordinary cylinder numbers.

Two phosphor bands

				Mint	Used
W182 (=S.G.819) **W178**	5d.	black, yellow-olive, blue, emerald, greenish yellow, rose-red, gold and orange-red		10	10
	a.	Gold (Queen's head) omitted		£700	
	b.	Emerald omitted		£225	
	c.	Phosphor omitted		£300	
	d.	White flaw in desk (R. 2/6)		4·00	
	e.	White spot in hem (R. 5/5)		4·00	
	f.	Missing portions of desk and foot (R. 20/4)		4·75	

W183 (=S.G.820) **W179**   9d.   ochre, deep blue, carmine, black, blue-green,
                               yellow-olive, gold and blue   15   15
                         a.   Ochre omitted £180
                         b.   Embossing omitted . . . .   15·00
                         c.   Phosphor omitted . . . .   5·00

W184 (=S.G.821) **W180**   1s.   green, greenish yellow, brown, black, cerise, gold
                               and light blue   20   25
                         a.   Gold (Queen's head) omitted . . . .   50·00
                         b.   Green and embossing omitted . . . .   80·00
                         c.   Green omitted . . . .   85·00
                         d.   Brown and phosphor omitted £150
                         e.   Brown omitted £150
                         f.   Embossing and phosphor omitted . . . .   22·00
                         g.   Embossing omitted . . . .   12·00
                         h.   Phosphor omitted . . . .   5·00

W185 (=S.G.822) **W181**   1s.6d.   greenish yellow, carmine, deep yellow-olive,
                               emerald, black, blue, gold and sage-green   20   30
                         a.   Gold (Queen's head) omitted £140
                         b.   Emerald omitted . . . .   75·00
                         c.   Embossing omitted . . . .   6·00
                         d.   Phosphor omitted . . . .   5·00
                         e.   Flag flaw (R. 20/5) . . . .   5·50

W186 (=S.G.823) **W182**   1s.9d.   black, slate, lemon, gold and bright purple   25   30
                         a.   Lemon (trousers and document) omitted £7500
                         b.   Phosphor omitted . . . .   5·00
                         c.   Embossing omitted . . . .   75·00
                         d.   Error. One broad band . . . .   9·00

> First Day Cover (W182/6) . . . .   2·00
> Presentation Pack (W182/6) . . . .   3·00
>   Pack also exists with a Dutch,
>   German or Japanese insert card.

The 5d. is known with the gold partly omitted, possibly due to under-inking. Of a complete sheet seen the cylinder number did not show, the traffic lights appeared smaller and the back of the Queen's head on every stamp was rounded with no ribbons.

The 1s.9d. (No. W186*a*) is also known used on first day cover postmarked London WC.

Nos. W182/6 were pre-released at Dorking on 25 March.

Two dies were used to emboss the presentation pack coat of arms. The designer's name was spelt as "Majorie" instead of "Marjorie", used on the later version.

W182*d*

W182*f*
Large part of base of
desk and front of shoe
missing

W182*e*
Amount of white varies
with the registration
of colours

All the above are multipositive flaws which appear on no dot and dot panes

Portion of blue in bottom right-hand corner of Union Jack is missing

W185*e*

Cylinder Numbers (Blocks of Eight (5d., 9d., 1s., 1s.6d.) or Six (1s.9d.))

Cyl. Nos.		Perforation Types			
		A (T) (E/P)		F (P/E)	F(L) (I/E)
		No dot	Dot	No dot	No dot
5d.	1A (black)–1B (gold)–1C (blue)–1D (emerald)–IE (olive)–1F (rose-red)–1G (yellow)–1H (orange-red)– P1 (phosphor)	2·00	2·00	†	†
9d.	2A (blue)–1B (ochre)–1C (deep blue)–1D (green)–1E (gold)–2F (black)–1G (olive)–1H (carmine)–P2 (phosphor)	†		3·00	†
1s.	1A (black)–1B (blue)–1C (yellow)–1D (brown)–IE (gold)–2F (cerise)–1G (green)–P2 (phosphor)	†		4·00	20·00
1s.6d.	1A (black)–1B (sage-green)–1C (yellow)–1D (carmine)–1E (gold)–2F (blue)–1G (deep yellow-olive)–1H (emerald)–P2 (phosphor)	†		6·00	†
1s.9d.	1A (black)–1E (gold)–1B (slate)–1C (lemon)–2D (bright purple)–P2 (phosphor)	†		6·00	†

The phosphor cylinder numbers appear below the ordinary cylinder numbers opposite R. 20/1. In the 5d. the "P1" is indented into the phosphor band but in the other values the "P2" is to the left of the phosphor band.

In the 5d. the "1" of "1C" and the bar below it are sometimes missing.

The 9d. is known without phosphor cylinder number.

In the 1s.9d. the cylinder numbers are always out of sequence.

Minor Constant Flaws

5d. Cyls. 1A–1B–1C–1D–1E–1F–1G–1H–P1 no dot
    2/1 Weak patches in background below r and t of Declaration
    6/1 Vertical scratch in background, through and below th of Arbroath (Th. A10 to C11)
    7/1 As 6/1

9d. Cyls. 2A–1B–1C–1D–1E–2F–1G–1H–P2 no dot
    8/6 Pale area surrounds final e of Florence
    19/4 Dark patch in background below second g of Nightingale

1s. Cyls. 1A–1B–1C–1D–1E–2F–1G–P2 no dot
    3/4 Missing top to t in Co-operative
    8/3 Dark flaw by top of first l of Alliance

1s.6d. Cyls. 1A–1B–1C–1D–1E–2F–1G–1H–P2 no dot
    8/3 Letters flo of Mayflower have hazy appearance

1s.9d. Cyls 1A–1E–1B–1C–2D–P2 no dot
    2/3 Pale patch in background above on of Astronomical
    2/6 Small break in t of Astronomical
    19/1 Dark patch on left leg of figure at right (Th. F6)
    19/5 Bright purple coloured flaw on left sleeve of man at left due to lack of screening dots on black cylinder (Th. D3)
    20/4 Black dot on e of Society

Sheet Details

Sheet sizes: 120 (6 × 20). 5d. double pane reel-fed with no dot pane above dot pane; others single pane sheet-fed

Sheet markings:
Cylinder numbers:
1s.9d. Opposite rows 18/19, left margin, boxed. Others: Opposite rows 17/19, left margin, boxed.
Guide holes: 5d. Opposite rows 6/7 (boxed), at both sides. Others: None
Marginal arrows (photo-etched): "W" shaped, at top, bottom and sides
Marginal rule: None
Colour register marks:
5d. Opposite rows 9/12 at right (no dot) or left (dot). Others: Above and below vertical rows 1 and 6
Coloured crosses: 5d. None. Others: Above and below vertical rows 3/4
Autotron marks (solid):
5d. Gold, black, blue, emerald, olive, rose-red, yellow, orange-red above left margin and above vertical rows 1/4. Others: None
Colour designations: None
Sheet values:
1s. Opposite rows 5/6 and 15/16 reading upwards in left margin and downwards in right margin
Others: Opposite rows 4/7 and 14/17 reading upwards in left margin and downwards in right margin
Traffic lights (boxed):
5d. Embossing, gold, black, blue, emerald, olive, rose-red, yellow and orange-red opposite rows 16/18, right margin; also in same order reading left to right above vertical rows 4/5
9d. Blue, ochre, deep blue, green, gold, embossing, black, olive and carmine opposite rows 17/19, right margin; also in reverse order reading left to right above vertical rows 4/5
1s. Green, black, cerise, gold, embossing, brown, yellow and blue opposite rows 18/19, right margin; also blue, yellow, embossing, gold, brown, cerise, black and green reading left to right above vertical rows 4/5
1s.6d. Sage-green, yellow, carmine, blue, gold, embossing, deep yellow-olive, black and emerald opposite rows 17/19, right margin; also in reverse order reading left to right above vertical rows 4/5
1s.9d. Black, gold, embossing, slate, lemon and bright purple opposite rows 18/19, right margin; also embossing, gold, black, slate, lemon and bright purple reading left to right above vertical row 5

Imprimaturs from the National Postal Museum Archives

Nos. W182/186 imperforate
No watermark *(set of 5)* £5000

Quantities Sold   5d. 71,259,000; 9d. 10,590,120; 1s. 10,287,840; 1s.6d. 11,388,960; 1s.9d. 6,120,600; Pack 120,564

Withdrawn   31.3.71

W183. "Mr. Pickwick and Sam Weller"
(Pickwick Papers)

W184. "Mr. and Mrs. Micawber"
(David Copperfield)

W185. "David Copperfield
and Betsy Trotwood"
(David Copperfield)

W186. "Oliver asking
for more"
(Oliver Twist)

W187. "Grasmere"
(from engraving by
J. Farington, R.A.)

(Des. Rosalind Dease. 5d. based on etchings by "Phiz" and George Cruickshank)

(Printed in photogravure with the Queen's head embossed in gold)

1970 (JUNE 3). LITERARY ANNIVERSARIES

The four 5d. stamps, commemorating the death centenary of Charles Dickens, feature popular characters from his novels. The 1s.6d. stamp commemorates the birth bicentenary of Lakeland poet William Wordsworth.

The 5d. values were issued together *se-tenant* in blocks of four throughout the sheet.

Two phosphor bands

				Mint	Used
W187 (= S.G.824) **W183**	5d.		black, orange, silver, gold and magenta	10	25
		a.	Block of 4. Nos. W187/90	75	2·00
		ab.	Imperf. (*block of four*)	£850	
		ac.	Silver (inscr) omitted (*block of four*)	£20000	
		ad.	Error. One broad band (*block of four*)	30·00	
W188 (=S.G.825) **W184**	5d.		black, magenta, silver, gold and orange	10	25
W189 (=S.G.826) **W185**	5d.		black, light greenish blue, silver, gold and yellow-bistre	10	25
		b.	Yellow-bistre (value) omitted	£2000	
W190 (=S.G.827) **W186**	5d.		black, yellow-bistre, silver, gold and light greenish blue	10	25
		b.	Yellow-bistre (background) omitted	£4250	
		c.	Light greenish blue (value) omitted*	£500	
		d.	Light-greenish blue and silver (inscription at foot) omitted	£8000	

W191 (=S.G.828) **W187**   1s.6d.   light yellow-olive, black, silver, gold and bright

		blue	25	50
a.	Gold (Queen's head) omitted	£2700	
b.	Silver ("Grasmere") omitted	£110	
c.	Bright blue (value) omitted	£8000	
d.	Embossing and phosphor omitted	22·00	
e.	Embossing omitted	6·00	
f.	Phosphor omitted	5·00	
g.	Retouch in slope (R. 1/18)	4·75	
h.	Extra road (R. 6/8)	6·00	
i.	Bright blue and silver omitted	£12000	

> First Day Cover (W187/91) . . . .   2·00
> Presentation Pack (W187/91) . . . .   3·00
>   Pack also exists with a Dutch,
>   German or Japanese insert card.

*No. W190*c* (unlike No. W189*b*) results from a partial missing colour. Although it is completely missing on No. W190, it is only partially omitted on No. W189.

5d. *Prices for missing colour errors in blocks of four:*

Yellow-bistre	£6250
Light greenish blue	£500
Light greenish blue and silver	£25000

The light greenish blue and silver error in block of four is unique.

Nos. W187/91 also exist on black card printed in white describing the issue with designer and printer's name at foot. The stamps were affixed and embedded in plastic on both sides. It was supplied with press releases sent to journalists.

W191*g*
Retouch consists of diagonal
black lines over triangular
green patch N.E. of Grasmere

Normal   W191*h*
Green line gives the impression of an extra
road leading up the foothill

Cylinder Numbers (Blocks of Eight (5d.) or Four (1s.6d.))

	Cyl. Nos.	Perforation Types		
		A (P/E)		F (E/P)
		No dot	Dot	No dot
5d.	1A (orange)–1B (magenta)–3C (bistre)–1D (blue)–1E (black)–1F (silver)–1G (gold)–P4 (phosphor)	3·00	3·00	†
1s.6d.	1A (blue)–1B (gold)–1C (silver)–1D (black)–1E (olive)–P3 (phosphor)		†	3·50

Perforation Type A on 5d. have the sheets orientated showing head to right.
In the 5d. the 1F is printed over a figure "2" in both panes.

Minor Constant Flaws

5d. Cyls. 1A–1B–3C–1D–1E–1F–1G dot
  5/17 Extra "button" on Sam's coat under armpit (Th. B6)
  5/19 Dot by 7 of 1870 level with centre of 8

Sheet Details

Sheet size: 120 (20 × 6)
   5d. In *se-tenant* blocks of four, double pane reel-fed with no dot pane above dot pane
   1s.6d. Single pane sheet-fed
Sheet markings:
   Cylinder numbers:
     5d. above vertical rows 1/3, boxed
     1s.6d. Opposite row 5, left margin, boxed
   Guide holes:
     5d. In single box above and below vertical rows 14/15
     1s.6d. None
   Marginal arrows (photo-etched): "W" shaped, at top, bottom and sides
   Marginal rule: None
   Colour register marks:
     5d. None
     1s.6d. Opposite rows 1 and 6 at both sides
   Coloured crosses:
     5d. None
     1s.6d. Opposite rows 3/4 at both sides
   Autotron marks (solid):
     5d. Opposite rows 1/4 at right on no dot pane only
     1s.6d. None
   Sheet values: Above and below vertical rows 4/7 and 14/17
   Traffic lights (boxed):
     5d. Embossing, gold, silver. blue, bistre, magenta, orange and black opposite rows 5/6, right margin; also in reverse order below vertical rows 3/4
     1s.6d. Embossing, gold, silver, blue, black and olive opposite row 5, right margin; also in same order above vertical rows 18/19

Essays. Nos. W187/90 exist as a block of four, each design $22\frac{1}{2} \times 38\frac{1}{2}$ mm. (larger than issued). The Queen's head is printed in silver and the Copperfield stamps are in olive-green. The four inscriptions read: "Mr. Pickwick & Sam", "Mr. & Mrs. Micawber", "David Copperfield & Aunt Trotwood" and "Oliver asks for more".

Imprimaturs from the National Postal Museum Archives

   Imperforate, no watermark

   Nos. W187/90 *se-tenant* block of four £6000

   Nos. W191 single £1000

Quantities Sold   5d. 83,472,440; 1s.6d. 10,913,360; Pack 113,770

Withdrawn   3.6.71

W188. Runners

W189. Swimmers

W190. Cyclists

(Des. Andrew Restall)

(Lithography by De La Rue)

1970 (JULY 15).   BRITISH COMMONWEALTH GAMES

These were issued on the eve of the Ninth British Commonwealth Games which were held in Edinburgh. Like the Post Office Technology issue these were printed in lithography by De La Rue.

Comb perforation 13½ × 14. Two phosphor bands applied by typography

			Mint	Used
W192 (=S.G 832) **W188**	5d.	pink, emerald, greenish yellow and deep yellow-green	25	25
	a.	Greenish yellow omitted	£7500	
	b.	Phosphor omitted	£200	
	c.	Error. One diagonal broad band at right	55·00	
W193 (=S.G.833) **W189**	1s.6d.	light greenish blue, lilac, bistre-brown and Prussian blue	50	50
	a.	Phosphor omitted	60·00	
W194 (=S.G.834) **W190**	1s.9d.	yellow-orange, lilac, salmon and deep red-brown	50	50

> First Day Cover (W192/4) . . . .   1·20
> Presentation Pack (W192/4) . . . .   3·00
>   Pack also exists with a Dutch,
>   German or Japanese insert card.

Plate Numbers (Blocks of Four)

	Pl. Nos.	Perforation Type F (L) (I/E) No dot	Dot
5d.	1A (yellow)–1B (emerald)–1C (pink)–1D (green)	2.50	2.50
	2A–1B–1C–1D	2·50	2·50
1s.6d.	1A (bistre-brown)–1B (greenish blue)–1C (lilac)–1D (indigo)	3·00	3·00
	2A–2B–2C–2D	3·00	3·00
1s.9d.	1A (salmon)–1B (lilac)–1C (yellow-orange)–1D (red brown)	3·00	3·00
	1A–2B–1C–1D	3·00	3·00

Minor Constant Flaws

The notes relating to minor flaws in lithographed stamps under the 1969 Post Office Technology issue also apply here.

Sheet Details

Sheet size: 120 (10 × 12). Double pane sheet-fed with no dot pane at top and dot pane below
Sheet markings:
  Plate numbers: Opposite rows 1/2, left margin, unboxed
  Guide holes: Above and below vertical row 4 in crossed box on no dot pane and below vertical row 4 in crossed box on dot pane; the reserve box in top margin was not used. In addition reserve guide-hole boxes appear above and below vertical row 6 in both panes but these were not used
  Marginal arrows (solid): "W" shaped, at top, bottom and sides
  Marginal rule: None
  Colour register marks: Below vertical rows 1 and 12 and in right-hand margin opposite rows 1 and 12 in both panes; in addition, they occur in the left-hand margin opposite row 12 in the no dot pane
  Coloured crosses, autotron marks, colour designations: None
  Sheet values: Above and below vertical rows 2/4 and 7/9 reading left to right in top margin and right to left (upside down) in bottom margin
  Traffic lights (unboxed): Opposite rows 9/10, right margin in same order as plate numbers

Imprimaturs from the National Postal Museum Archives

Nos. W192/194 imperforate
No watermark (*set of 3*) £3000

Quantities Sold 5d. 75,255,440; 1s.6d. 10,909,760; 1s.9d. 6,303,800; Pack 114,209

Withdrawn 15.7.71

1970 (SEPTEMBER 14).   COLLECTORS PACK 1970

WCP3 Comprises Nos. W171/94 . . . . 20·00
  This pack also exists with a German or Japanese insert card.

Quantity Sold 54,768

Withdrawn 13.9.71

W191. 1d. Black (1840)   **W192.** 1s. Green (1847)   **W193.** 4d. Carmine (1855)

(Des. David Gentleman)

1970 (SEPTEMBER 18).   "PHILYMPIA 70" STAMP EXHIBITION

Issued for the opening of the International Philatelic Exhibition held at the Olympia Exhibition Hall, London. The 5d. depicts the first adhesive postage stamp ever issued, the famous Penny Black. This is shown with the check letters "P" and "L" for "Philympia" and "London". The 9d. and 1s.6d. show the first Great Britain stamps using the embossed and surface-printed processes respectively.
  Two phosphor bands

				Mint	Used
W195 (=S.G.835) **W191**	5d.	grey-black, brownish bistre, black and dull purple		25	10
	a.	Grey-black (Queen's head) omitted	£12000		
	b.	Phosphor omitted*		5·00	
	c.	Error. One broad phosphor band	25·00		
	d.	White blob (No dot, R. 5/6)	5·50		
	e.	Weak entry (Dot, R. 1/2)	4·50		
W196 (=S.G.836) **W192**	9d.	light drab, bluish green, stone, black and dull purple		25	30
	a.	Phosphor omitted	11·00		
W197 (=S.G.837) **W193**	1s.6d.	carmine, light drab, black and dull purple		25	45
	a.	Phosphor omitted	4·00		
	b.	Missing dot over "i" (R. 6/12)	5·50		

First Day Cover (W195/7)	1·50
Presentation Pack (W195/7)	2·75
Pack also exists with a German or Japanese insert card.	

The 5d. is known postmarked at Boughton, King's Lynn on 17 September.

*The phosphor is sometimes difficult to see on the 5d. due to "dry" prints so care is needed in iden-tifying true missing phosphors.

W195*d*
Large white blob between "OS" of
"POSTAGE" (later retouched)

W195*e*
Weak entry of frameline
in top left corner

In No. W197*b* the dot is missing over the "i" of "printed"

Cylinder Numbers (Blocks of Four)

		Cyl. Nos.	Perforation Types		
			A (T) No dot	(I/E) Dot	A (P/E) No dot
5d.	1A (black)–1B (dull purple)–1C (brownish bistre)–1D (grey-black)–P6 (phosphor)		2·00	2·00	†
9d.	1A (black)–1B (bluish green)–2C (stone)–1D (dull purple)–1E (light drab)– P10 (phosphor)		†		2·00
1s.6d.	1A (black)–1B (light drab)–1C (dull purple)–1D (carmine)–P5 (phosphor)			†	2·00

Perforation Types A and A (T) of the above are with sheets orientated showing head to right.

Minor Constant Flaw

1s.6d. Cyls. 1A–1B–1C–1D–P5 no dot
1/1 Frame flaw below N of PENCE

Sheet Details

Sheet size: 120 (12 × 10). 5d. double pane reel-fed with no dot pane above dot pane; others single pane sheet-fed

Sheet markings:
   Cylinder numbers: Opposite row 9, left margin, boxed but the phosphor number is opposite row 10, left margin
   Guide holes: 5d. Above and below vertical row 6 (boxed). Others: None
   Marginal arrows (photo-etched): "W" shaped, at top, bottom and sides
   Marginal rule: None
   Colour register marks:
     5d. None. Others: Above and below vertical rows 1 and 10/11
   Coloured crosses: 5d. None. Others: Above and below vertical rows 3/4
   Autotron marks and colour designations: None
   Sheet values: Opposite rows 2/4 and 7/9 at both sides, reading up at left and down at right
   Traffic lights (boxed):
     5d. Dull purple, black, brownish bistre, grey-black opposite row 10 right margin; also in same order reading from left to right above vertical rows 11/12
     9d. Bluish green, stone, dull purple, black, light drab opposite row 10 right margin; also in same order reading from left to right above vertical rows 11/12
     1s.6d. Light drab, dull purple; carmine, black opposite 9/10 right margin; also in reverse order reading from left to right above vertical row 12

Imprimaturs from the National Postal Museum Archives

Nos. W195/197 imperforate
No watermark (*set of* 3) £3000

Quantities Sold   5d. 72,211,000; 9d. 16,330,000; 1s.6d. 15,203,836

Withdrawn   18.9.71

W194. Shepherds and   **W195.** Mary, Joseph and   **W196.** The Wise Men
Apparition of the Angel   Christ in the Manger   bearing Gifts
                         (Des. Sally Stiff)

(Printed in photogravure with the Queen's head in gold and then embossed)

1970 (NOVEMBER 25). CHRISTMAS
   The designs depict traditional Nativity scenes taken from the De Lisle Psalter in the Arundel Collection at the British Museum.
   The 4d. stamps were printed by the Wood machine which has a capacity for ten cylinders. Eight were used for the colours and the others for simultaneous application of the embossing and phosphor bands.
   One central 4 mm. phosphor band (4d.) or two phosphor bands (others)

				Mint	Used
W198 (=S.G.838)	**W194**	4d	brown-red, blue, turquoise-green, pale chestnut, brown, grey-black, gold and vermilion	15	10
		a.	Embossing omitted	50·00	
		b.	Phosphor omitted	60·00	
		c.	Error. Two side bands		
		ca	Error. Band at left		
		d.	Imperf, between stamp and left margin	£160	
		e.	Thinned frame (No dot, R. 4/6)	4·00	

W199 (=S.G.839) **W195**   5d.   emerald, gold, blue, brown-red, ochre, grey-black

		and violet	15	15
	a.	Gold (Queens head) omitted	†	£3500
	b.	Emeraid omitted	60·00	
	c.	Imperforate (pair)	£275	
	d.	Embossing omitted	15·00	
	e.	Phosphor omitted	5·00	

W200 (=S.G.840) **W196**   1s.6d.   gold, grey-black, pale turquoise-green, salmon,

		ultramarine, ochre, red and yellow-green	25	30
	a.	Salmon omitted	80·00	
	b.	Ochre omitted	55·00	
	c.	Embossing and phosphor omitted		
	d.	Embossing omitted	35·00	
	e.	Phosphor omitted	5·00	
	f.	Error. One broad band		

> First Day Cover (W199/200) . . . .   1·50
> Presentation Pack (W199/200) . . . .   2·75
> Pack also exists with a German or
> Japanese insert card.

A red slip-in wallet bearing the Royal Arms and inscribed "Christmas 1970" was issued with the "Scandinavia 71" special pack produced for sale during a visit to six cities in Denmark, Sweden and Norway by a mobile display unit between 15 April and 20 May 1971. Due to the moratorium on commemoratives at the time of the introduction of decimal issues, these 1970 £.s.d. Christmas stamps were the only recent commemoratives on sale at Special counters etc. which could be offered for sale in Scandinavia alonside the decimal definitives.

Gold frame at right by shepherd's arm is thinned and has been strengthened by two parallel chestnut lines

W198*e*

Cylinder Numbers (4d. Blocks of Ten; Others Blocks of Six)

	Cyl. Nos.	Perforation Type A (P/E)	
		No dot	Dot
4d.	1A (vermilion)–1B (grey-black)–1C (brown)–1D (brown-red)–1E (turquoise-green)–1F (blue)–1G (pale chestnut)–1J (gold)– P9 (phosphor)	2·75	2·75
5d.	1A (violet)–1B (brown-red)–1C (blue)–1D (ochre)–3E (grey-black)–1F (emerald)–1G (gold)–P7 (phosphor)	1·50	†
1s.6d.	1A (yellow-green)–1B (grey-black)–1D (red)–1E (salmon)–1F (pale turquoise-green)–1G (gold)–1J (ochre)–1C (ultramarine)–P7 (phosphor)	4·50	†

Perforation Type A on the above are with sheets orientated showing head to right. On some sheets of the 4d. the J is completely omitted.

Minor Constant Flaws

4d. Cyls. 1A–1B–1C–1D–1E–1F–1G–1J–P9 no dot
   5/5 Dotted line across central shepherd's temple and through hair (Th. G6–7)

5d. Cyls. 1A–1B–1C–1D–3E–1F–1G–P7 no dot
   8/8 Diagonal line over Mary's left hand (Th. J3)

1s.6d. Cyls. 1A–1B–1D–1E–1F–1G–1J–1C–P7 no dot
   1/12 Horizontal scratch across cloaks of Three Wise Men (Th. K2–6)

The Thirkell Position Finder readings are taken with the finder over the perforations.

Sheet Details

Sheet size: 120 (12 × 10). 4d. double pane reel-fed with no dot pane above dot pane; others single pane
    sheet-fed

Sheet markings:

    Cylinder numbers:

        4d. Bottom margin, unboxed, reading down below vertical rows 5/2

        5d. Opposite rows 8/9, left margin, boxed but the phosphor number is opposite row 10, left margin

        1s.6d. Opposite rows 8/10, left margin, boxed. The 1C was added at the bottom opposite row 10

    Guide holes: 4d. Above and below vertical row 6 (boxed). Others: None

    Marginal arrows (photo-etched): "W" shaped, at top, bottom and sides

    Marginal rule: None

    Colour register marks:

        4d. Above and below vertical rows 2/5. Others: Above and below vertical rows 1/2 and 12

    Autotron marks and colour designations: None

    Coloured crosses: 4d. None. Others: Above and below vertical rows 3/4

    Sheet values: Opposite rows 2/4 at both sides and rows 7/8 at left and 7/9 at right, reading up at left
        and down at right

    Traffic lights (boxed):

        4d. Vermilion, grey-black, brown, brown-red, turquoise-green, blue, pale chestnut, gold,
        embossing* opposite rows 9/10 right margin; also in same order reading from left to right above
        vertical rows 11/12

        5d. Violet, brown-red, blue, ochre, grey-black, emerald, gold, embossing opposite rows 9/10
        right margin; also in same order reading from left to right above vertical rows 10/11

        1s.6d. Yellow-green, grey-black, ultramarine; red, salmon, pale turquoise-green, gold, ochre,
        embossing; also in same order reading from left to right above vertical rows 9/11

*The embossing is usually very faint on the 4d. traffic lights.

Imprimaturs from the National Postal Museum Archives

    Nos. W198/200 imperforate

    No watermark (*set of* 3) £3000

Quantities Sold   4d. 360,016,216; 5d. 181,161,720; 1s.6d. 22,598,520

Withdrawn   25.11.71

SECTION XA
Regional £.s.d. Issues
1958–70. Photogravure

General Notes

INTRODUCTION. On 18 August 1958 the first Great Britain Regional issues were put on sale for use in Northern Ireland, Scotland and Wales and Monmouthshire and in the islands of Guernsey, Jersey and the Isle of Man. The ordinary postage stamps of Great Britain in the same values are not on sale at post offices in these regions except at the Philatelic Counters in Belfast, Cardiff, Edinburgh and Glasgow, apart from Monmouthshire where the Welsh Regionals and Great Britain postage stamps were on sale concurrently.

Although specifically issued for regional use, these issues were initially valid for use throughout Great Britain. However, they ceased to be valid in Guernsey and Jersey from 1 October 1969 when these islands each established their own independent postal administrations and introduced their own stamps. Guernsey and Jersey Regionals were withdrawn locally on 30 September 1969 but remained on sale at British Philatelic Counters until 30 September 1970.

Following the practice set by Great Britain, these issues do not bear the names of the regions, these being indicated by various devices and symbols which relate to them. The three island issues are inscribed "Postage" only and have no usage as revenue stamps as they have their own Parliaments.

The portrait used is by Dorothy Wilding, Ltd.

PRINTERS. All the Regional issues were printed in photogravure by Harrison & Sons on continuous reels of paper "on the web". The 3d., 4d. and 5d. values of Northern Ireland, Scotland and Wales and Monmouthshire were printed in double pane width, i.e. 480 stamps consisting of two panes (no dot and dot) each of 240 stamps arranged in twenty rows of twelve stamps, the panes being guillotined before issue. All the island issues and the 6d., 9d., 1s.3d. and 1s.6d. values from the other regions were made from single cylinders printing sheets of 240 stamps (i.e. no dot panes only).

PAPER AND WATERMARK. As with the Wilding definitives, for the first few years the Regional issues were printed on a creamy paper but starting in February 1962 a whiter paper was gradually introduced as new printings were made. See the General Notes for Section S for further information. Exceptionally, a chalk-surfaced paper was used for a printing of the Isle of Man 3d. in 1963.

Crowns
W.24

Only the Crowns watermark, type **W.24** was used for the Regional issues. From 1967 new printings of a number of values were on the chalk-surfaced paper without watermark, as used for the Machin definitives.

GUM. Gum arabic was used from 1958 to 1968 after which PVA gum was introduced.

The distinction between gum arabic and PVA gum is explained in the General Notes to Section U. It is worth noting that gum arabic was used on the creamy, white and unwatermarked chalk-surfaced papers but that PVA gum exists only on the last of these.

PERFORATION. Harrisons used the same 15×14 comb perforation as for the Wilding definitives. A number of different perforators were used and these are described and illustrated in Appendix G. The following listings include abbreviations for the side and horizontal margins of the listed block so that the first letter refers to the left margin and the second to the bottom margin. See page 2 under Notes in Section S.

PHOSPHOR BANDS.   See the General Notes for Section S for a detailed description of these. In the Regional issues it is sufficient to state that these were applied as follows:
"Blue" 8 mm. bands: 1963–64
"Violet" 8 mm. bands: 1965–66
"Violet" 9·5 mm. bands: 1967–70
The one centre band stamps in the "violet" period were always 4 mm. bands.

Phosphor omitted.   A number of values have appeared with the phosphor bands omitted in error and these are listed separately. All values are believed to have the bands applied in photogravure.

Misplaced Bands.   The instances of misplaced bands in the regionals is unusual. One broad (9·5mm.) instead of two bands are listed and one (No. XG8*b*) with horizontal band is recorded under Guernsey.

DATES OF ISSUE.   Conflicting dates of issue have been announced for some of the issues, partly explained by their being released on different dates by the Philatelic Bureau in Edinburgh or the Philatelic Counter in London and in the regions. We give the earliest date, since once released the stamps could have been used anywhere in the U.K.

FIRST DAY COVERS.   Prices for these are only quoted where there was a specific service provided by the Post Office. These are listed at the end of each region.

PRESENTATION PACKS.   The pack containing stamps from the six regions is listed after Wales and Monmouthshire. The other packs are listed at the end of each region.

SHEET MARKINGS.   Reference should be made to the descriptions of sheet markings given in the General Notes for Sections S and U, as most of them apply to this Section and the information given there is not repeated here. Additional information is given below.

Cylinder Numbers.   In the Regional issues these appear in the left-hand margin opposite Row 18 No. 1 (R. 18/1) in the style as illustrated in Section S.

Phosphor Cylinder Numbers.   The notes in the General Notes for Section U £.s.d. Low Values also apply here but they are only found on the Scottish 5d. No. XS15 and Welsh 5d. No. XW10.

Marginal Arrows.   In the Regional issues these are "W" shaped (photo-etched) at top, bottom and sides, except for the Jersey and Isle of Man 3d. and the Northern Ireland, Scotland and Wales and Monmouthshire 3d., 6d. and 1s.3d. which are all "V" shaped (hand engraved) at top and bottom of the sheet and "W" shaped (photo-etched) at both sides (only cyl. 4 Scotland 1s.3d.).

Perforation Guide Holes.   Perforation guide holes which relate to the perforator employed appear in the sheet margins. Refer to the descriptions given for Section U at the end of the General Notes where an illustration of the box associated with perforator type F(L)* appears. Perforator types are given under Cylinder Block listings and further details will be found under Appendix G.

"CANCELLED" OVERPRINT.   No. XW5 exists overprinted "CANCELLED" as part of the test programme carried out by the Forensic Department of the Post Office.

WITHDRAWAL DATES.   All £.s.d. Regional issues, not previously withdrawn, were taken off sale at the Post Office Philatelic Counters on 25 November 1971 and were invalidated as from 1 March 1972.

---

*PRICES FOR CYLINDER BLOCKS WITH ASTERISKS
These denote cylinder blocks containing a listed variety and the price includes the variety.

A. Guernsey

XG1   XG2

(Des. E. A. Piprell)

2½d., Type XG1 (1964)

1964 (JUNE 8). 2½d. WATERMARK CROWNS

				Mint	Used
XG1 (=S.G.6)	2½d.	(1)	Pale rose-red (Cyl. 1)	1·50	1·50
		(2)	Rose-red (Cyl. 3)	35	40

Cylinder Numbers (Blocks of Six)

Single pane cylinders. Perforation Type F (L) (I/E)

Cyl. Nos.	No dot
1	12·00
3	4·00

Minor Constant Flaws

Cyl. 1   1/4 Small retouch over TA
    1/5 White patch over left part of diadem to left of central cross (Th. A3)
    17/12 Background disturbance in top loop of left-hand ribboning (Th. B1)
    19/2 White patch below left leg of R
Cyl. 3   17/5 Dark spot under topmost tip of ribboning at right (Th. B6)
    17/12 and 19/2. As on cyl. 1 (multipositive flaws)

Quantity Sold   3,485,760 including 10,100 on First Day Covers

Withdrawn   31.8.66

3d., Type XG2 (1958–62)

1958 (AUGUST 18).   3d. WATERMARK CROWNS

A. Cream Paper

			Mint	Used
XG2	3d.	Deep lilac	1·50	50

B. White Paper (5 July 1962)

			Mint	Used
XG3 (=S.G.7)	3d.	Deep lilac	30	30

Cylinder Numbers (Blocks of Six)

Cream Paper (No. XG2)				Whiter Paper (No. XG3)			
Cyl. No.	(No dot)	Perf. Types		Cyl. No.	(No dot)	Perf. Types	
		B (I/P)	C (E/P)			B (I/P) C (E/P) F (L) (I/E)	
4		15·00	15·00	4		4·50 4·50	4·50
				5		† †	4·25

372

Minor Constant Flaws

Cyl. 5   4/1 Background scratch above right-hand petal (Th. C–D2)
     7/10 Dark spot in left-hand margin (opposite Th. C1)
     9/10 Pale scratch in background from petal at far right down to Queen's chin (Th. D–E3)
     11/11 Diagonal background scratch from base of lily's stem to base of Queen's neck (Th. F3–E4)
     13/1 Flaw in background above centre stamen of lily (Th. C2)
     18/6 Smudge in background near Queen's mouth (Th. D3)

Quantity Sold   25,812,360

Sold Out   6.3.68

1967 (MAY 24). 3d. ONE CENTRE PHOSPHOR BAND REACTING VIOLET. WATERMARK CROWNS

			Mint	Used
XG4 (=S.G.7p)	3d.	(1) Deep lilac	15	20
		(2) Deep reddish lilac	60	30

Cylinder Number (Block of Six)

Single pane cylinder. Perforation Type F (L) (I/E)

Cyl. No.   No dot
  5   . . . .   2·25

Minor Constant Flaws

As for flaws on Cyl. 5 of No. XG3

Sold Out   11.68

4d., Type XG2 (1966–69)

1966 (FEBRUARY 7). 4d. WATERMARK CROWNS

			Mint	Used
XG5 (=S.G.8)	4d.	Ultramarine	25	30
	a.	Stem flaw (R. 12/8)	4·75	

Coloured line across top of stem

XG5a, XG6a, XG7b, XG8c

Cylinder Number (Block of Six)

Single pane cylinder. Perforation Type F (L) (I/E)

Cyl. No.   No dot
  1   . . . .   3·50

Minor Constant Flaws

Cyl. 1   1/1 Small spot above centre stamen of lily (Th. C2)
          9/5 White dot between two stamens on left-hand side (Th. D2)
      13/4 White spot on right-hand petal (Th. D3)
   20/12 Pale flaw in background to right of central diadem (Th. A5)

These are generally more marked on later issues from this cylinder.

Quantity Sold   4,415,040 including 12,350 on First Day Covers

Sold Out   6.3.68

1967 (OCTOBER 24). 4d. TWO 9·5 mm. PHOSPHOR BANDS REACTING VIOLET. WATERMARK CROWNS

			Mint	Used
XG6 (=S.G.8p)	4d.	Ultramarine	15	20
	a.	Stem flaw (R. 12/8)	4·75	

For illustration of No. XG6a, see No. XG5a.

Cylinder Number (Block of Six)

Single pane cylinder. Perforation Type F (L) (I/E)

Cyl. No.	No dot
1	2·25

Minor Constant Flaws

Cyl. 1   5/10 Circular background retouch below Queen's chin (Th. E4)
   16/12 Break in centre stamen (Th. C–D2)
   17/10 Break in second stamen from left (Th. C2)

Others: As on No. XG5

Sold Out   10.68

1968 (APRIL 16*). 4d. NO WATERMARK. CHALKY PAPER. PVA GUM. TWO 9·5 mm PHOSPHOR BANDS REACTING VIOLET

			Mint	Used
XG7 (=S.G.9)	4d.	Pale ultramarine	10	20
	a.	Phosphor omitted	45·00	
	b.	Stem flaw (R. 12/8)	5·00	

*This was not issued in Guernsey until 22 April.
For illustration of No. XG7b, see No. XG5a.

Cylinder Number (Block of Six)

Single pane cylinder. Perforation Type F (L) (I/E)

Cyl. No.	No dot
1	1·90

Minor Constant Flaws

Cyl. 1   2/8 Weak patch in background at upper left (Th. A1)
   19/6 Small retouch between A and G

Others: As on Nos. XG5 and XG6

Sold Out   3.69

1968 (SEPTEMBER 4).   4d. CHANGE OF COLOUR. NO WATERMARK. CHALKY PAPER. PVA GUM. ONE CENTRE PHOSPHOR BAND REACTING VIOLET

				Mint	Used
XG8 (=S.G.10)	4d.	Olive-sepia	10	15
	a.	Phosphor omitted	45·00	
	b.	Error. Phosphor horizontal	90·00	
	c.	Stem flaw (R. 12/8)	7·00	
	d.	Retouched "4" (R. 16/10)	6·00	

For illustration of No. XG8*c*, see No. XG5*a*.

Spot over "4" has been retouched
Corrected on No. XG9

XG8*d*

Cylinder Number (Block of Six)

Single pane cylinder. Perforation Type F (L) (I/E)

Cyl. No.	No dot
1	1·90

Minor Constant Flaws

As for No. XG7 except that flaw on R. 5/10 does not show

Withdrawn   30.9.70

1969 (FEBRUARY 26).   4d. FURTHER CHANGE OF COLOUR. NO WATERMARK. CHALKY PAPER. PVA GUM. ONE CENTRE PHOSPHOR BAND REACTING VIOLET

			Mint	Used
XG9 (=S.G.11)	4d.	Bright vermilion	20	25
	a.	Stem flaw retouched (R. 12/8)	5·75	

The stem flaw has been retouched but still shows as a
smudge to right of stem

XG9*a*

Cylinder Number (Block of Six)

Single pane cylinder. Perforation Type F (L) (I/E)

Cyl. No.	No dot
1	2·75

Minor Constant Flaws

As for No. XG8

Withdrawn   30.9.70

5d., Type XG2 (1968)

1968 (SEPTEMBER 4).　5d. NO WATERMARK. CHALKY PAPER. PVA GUM. TWO 9·5 mm. PHOSPHOR BANDS REACTING VIOLET

			Mint	Used
XG10 (=S.G.12)	5d.	Royal blue	20	30
	a.	Stamen flaw (R. 12/1)	5·75	
	b.	Retouched	5·75	

XG10*a*　　　　　　　　　XG10*b*

Still visible after retouch on late printing

Cylinder Number (Block of Six)

Single pane cylinder. Perforation Type F (L) (I/E)

Cyl. No.	No dot
1	2·75

Minor Constant Flaw

Cyl. 1　12/6 Small white flaw to left of Queen's mouth (Th. D3)

Withdrawn　30.9.70

First Day Covers

XGFC1	(8.6.64)	10,100 posted	2½d.		30·00
XGFC2	(7.2.66)	12,350 posted	4d.	Ultramarine	8·00
XGFC3	(4.9.68)	52,449 posted	4d.	Olive-sepia, 5d.	3·00

INVALIDATION.　The regional issues for Guernsey were invalidated for use in Guernsey and Jersey on 30 September 1969 but remained valid for use in the rest of the United Kingdom. Those still current remained on sale at philatelic sales counters until 30 September 1970.

B. Jersey

XJ1   **XJ2**

(Des. Edmund Blampied)   (Des. William M. Gardner)

2½d., Type XJ1 (1964)

1964 (JUNE 8). 2½d. WATERMARK CROWNS

			Mint	Used
XJ1 (=S.G.9)	2½d.	Carmine-red	30	45
	a.	Imperf. three sides (pair)	£2000	
	b.	Thin "POSTAGE" (R. 18/1)	9·00	

Letters of "POSTAGE" are thinner, resulting in more white showing in the "O" and "G"

Normal   XJ1*b*

Cylinder Number (Block of Six)

Single pane cylinder. Perforation Type F (L) (I/E)

Cyl. No.   No dot
1 . . . . 12·00*

Minor Constant Flaws

Cyl. 1   11/1 Two tiny dots on Queen's nose
18/2 Spot to right of mace level with O of POSTAGE

Quantity Sold   4,770,000 including 12,800 on First Day Covers

Withdrawn   31.8.66

3d., Type XJ2 (1958–67)

1958 (AUGUST 18). 3d. WATERMARK CROWNS

A. Cream Paper

			Mint	Used
XJ2	3d.	Deep lilac	1·50	40
	a.	Joined tomato (Cyl. 1, R. 19/9)	8·00	
	b.	"Halberd" flaw (Cyl. 1, R. 20/3)	8·00	

B. Whiter Paper (23 September 1962)

			Mint	Used
XJ3 (=S.G.10)	3d.	Deep lilac	30	25
	a.	Scratched collar (Cyl. 2, R. 9/8)	4·75	

XJ2*a*   XJ2*b*   XJ3*a*, XJ4*a*

Both these varieties were later retouched to normal

Cylinder Numbers (Blocks of Six)

Cyl. No.	Cream Paper (No. XJ2) (No dot)	Perf. Types B (I/P)	C (E/P)	Cyl. No.	Whiter Paper (No. XJ3) (No dot)	Perf. Types B (I/P)	C (E/P)	F (L) (I/E)
1		15·00	15·00	1		4·25	4·25	4·25
				2		†	†	27·00

Minor Constant Flaws

Cyl. 1   20/4 Short white line extends below left of D
Cyl. 2   3/7 Weak background below left-hand berry of middle pair on right-hand plant (Th. E5)
          14/12 Dot in left-hand margin (Opposite Th. D1)
           16/1 Dot on top left leaf of right-hand plant (Th. C5–6)
          16/12 Dot in top margin (Above Th. A4)
          20/3 Dot in top margin (Above Th. A4)

Quantity Sold   35,169,720

Sold Out   10.67

1967 (JUNE 9). 3d. ONE CENTRE PHOSPHOR BAND REACTING VIOLET. WATER-MARK CROWNS

					Mint	Used
XJ4 (=S.G.10p)	3d.	(1)	Deep lilac		15	15
		(2)	Dull reddish lilac		45	30
	a.		Scratched collar (Cyl. 2, R. 9/8)		5·50	

For illustration of No. XJ4*a*, see No. XJ3*a*.

Cylinder Numbers (Blocks of Six)

Single pane cylinder. Perforation Type F (L) (I/E)

Cyl. No.	Deep Lilac (No. XJ4(1)) No Dot	Cyl. No.	Dull reddish lilac (No. XJ4(2)) No dot
2	2·75	2	6·00

Minor Constant Flaws

As for flaws on Cyl. 2 of No. XJ3

Sold Out   10.68

4d., Type XJ2 (1966–69)

1966 (FEBRUARY 7).   4d. WATERMARK CROWNS

			Mint	Used
XJ5 (=S.G.11)	4d.	Ultramarine	25	30
	a.	Leaf flaw (R. 3/6)	4·50	
	b.	Neck flaw (R. 18/9)	4·50	

Arrow-like flaw over top leaf at left. Later retouched and only exists retouched on phosphor issues

XJ5*a*   XJ5*b*, XJ6*a*, XJ7*b*, XJ8*a*

Cylinder Number (Block of Six)

Single pane cylinder. Perforation Type F (L) (I/E)

Cyl. No.	No dot
1	3·50

Minor Constant Flaws

Cyl. 1   3/4 Diagonal scratch under Queen's chin (Th. E2–3)
         3/11 Spot in top margin (close to perf. hole) (Above Th. A4)
         9/10 Slight dent in left-hand frame line (Opposite Th. D-E1)
        11/10 White flaw in background behind Queen's hair (Th. C5)
        15/1 Dark patch in background to left of top leaf on left-hand side of sceptre (Th. D1). This varies in intensity and is particularly strong on No. XJ7.
        15/12 Two small white flaws in front of Queen's collar (Th. F2–3)
        18/8 Break in top frame line (Above Th. A5)
        20/8 Diagonal scratch to right of Queen's left eye (Th. C3–4)

Quantity Sold   6,623,040 including 14,487 on First Day Covers

Sold Out   11.67

1967 (SEPTEMBER 5).   4d. TWO 9·5 mm. PHOSPHOR BANDS REACTING VIOLET. WATERMARK CROWNS

			Mint	Used
XJ6 (=S.G.11p)	4d.	Ultramarine	15	25
	a.	Neck flaw (R. 18/9)	4·50	

For illustration of No. XJ6*a*, see No. XJ5*b*.

Cylinder Number (Block of Six)

Single pane cylinder. Perforation Type F (L) (I/E)

Cyl. No.	No dot
1	2·50

Minor Constant Flaws

As for No. XJ5

Sold Out   10.68

1968 (SEPTEMBER 4). 4d. CHANGE OF COLOUR. NO WATERMARK. CHALKY PAPER. PVA GUM. ONE CENTRE PHOSPHOR BAND REACTING VIOLET

			Mint	Used
XJ7 (=S.G.12)	4d.	Olive-sepia	15	25
	a.	Phosphor omitted	£1000	
	b.	Neck flaw (R. 18/9)	4·50	

For illustration of No. XJ7*b*, see No. XJ5*b*.

Cylinder Number (Block of Six)

Single pane cylinder. Perforation Type F (L) (I/E)

Cyl. No.	No dot
1	2·50

Minor Constant Flaws

As for No. XJ5

Withdrawn 30.9.70

1969 (FEBRUARY 26). 4d. FURTHER CHANGE OF COLOUR. NO WATERMARK. CHALKY PAPER. PVA GUM. ONE CENTRE PHOSPHOR BAND REACTING VIOLET

			Mint	Used
XJ8 (=S.G.13)	4d.	Bright vermilion	15	25
	a.	Neck flaw (R. 18/9)	5·00	

For illustration of No. XJ8*a*, see No. XJ5*b*.

Cylinder Number (Block of Six)

Single pane cylinder. Perforation Type F (L) (I/E)

Cyl. No.	No dot
1	2·50

Minor Constant Flaws

As for No. XJ5

Withdrawn 30.9.70

5d., Type XJ2 (1968)

1968 (SEPTEMBER 4). 5d. NO WATERMARK. CHALKY PAPER. PVA GUM. TWO 9·5 mm. PHOSPHOR BANDS REACTING VIOLET

			Mint	Used
XJ9 (=S.G.14)	5d.	Royal blue	15	50
	a.	Leaf dot (R. 16/6)	4·50	
	b.	Shield flaw (R. 19/12)	4·00	

XJ9*a*
White dot above lowest leaf

XJ9*b*
Leaf joined to shield

Cylinder Number (Block of Six)

Single pane cylinder. Perforation Type F (L) (I/E)

Cyl. No.	No Dot
1	2·50

Minor Constant Flaws

Cyl. 1   5/1   Dot in top margin (Above Th. A2)
          6/5   White scratch from back of Queen's collar to back of neck (Th. E–F4)
          9/11   Flaw in background above middle right-hand jewel of sceptre (Th. A2)
          10/4   White scratch extending from Queen's chin to top of P
          11/1   Tiny break in left-hand frame line (Th. C1)
          14/12   Small white flaw on Queen's collar (Th. F3–4)
          17/12   Dotted line extending from right of top leaf below flower at right of sceptre across
               Queen's face and plant at right (Th. E2–6)

Withdrawn   30.9.70

First Day Covers

XJFC1	(8.6.64)	12,800 posted	2½d.	30·00
XJFC2	(7.2.66)	14,487 posted	4d. Ultramarine	10·00
XJFC3	(4.9.68)	57,500 posted	4d. Olive-sepia, 5d.	3·00

INVALIDATION.   The regional issues for Jersey were invalidated for use in Jersey or Guernsey on 30 September 1969 but remained valid for use in the rest of the United Kingdom. Those still current remained on sale at philatelic sales counters until 30 September 1970.

C. Isle of Man

XM1 XM2

(Des. J. H. Nicholson)

2½d., Type XM1 (1964)

1964 (JUNE 8). 2½d. WATERMARK CROWNS

			Mint	Used
XM1 (=S.G.1)	2½d.	Carmine-red	50	1·25

Cylinder Number (Block of Six)

Single pane cylinder. Perforation Type F (L) (I/E)

Cyl. No.	No Dot
1	7·50

Minor Constant Flaw

Cyl. 1 11/1 Red dot to right of lower cross of crown (Th. C5)

Quantity Sold   4,298,160 including 9,237 on First Day Covers

Withdrawn   31.8.66

3d., Type XM2 (1958–68)

1958 (AUGUST 18). 3d. WATERMARK CROWNS

A. Cream Paper

			Mint	Used
XM2	3d.	Deep lilac	1·50	35

B. Chalky Paper (17 May 1963)

XM3 (=S.G.2a)	3d.	Deep lilac	12·00	10·00

C. Whiter Paper (1963)

XM4 (=S.G.2)	3d.	Deep lilac	50	20

No. XM3 was released in London sometime after 17 May 1963.

The paper used for No. XM3 was the residue of the heavy chalk-surfaced paper remaining from the 1961 Post Office Savings Bank Centenary issue.

Cylinder Numbers (Blocks of Six)

	Cream Paper (No. XM2)			Chalky Paper (No. XM3)	
Cyl. No.	(No dot)	Perf. Types		Cyl. No. (No dot)	Perf. Type
		B (I/P)	C (E/P)		J (I/P)
1		15·00	15·00	1	£125

	Whiter Paper (No. XM4)	
Cyl. No.	(No dot)	Perf. Types
		F(L) (I/E)
1		7·50

Minor Constant Flaw

Cyl. 1   19/6 Fine curved line to right of second link from bottom at left (Th. G1)

Imprimatur from the National Postal Museum Archives

Cream paper. Imperforate, watermark Type W.24
Watermark upright

Quantity Sold   35,959,420 up to 31.3.68 and including 1,080,000 on chalky paper (No. XM3)

Sold Out   12.68

1968 (JUNE 27). 3d. ONE CENTRE PHOSPHOR BAND REACTING VIOLET. WATER-MARK CROWNS

				Mint	Used
XM5 (=S.G.2p)	3d.	Deep lilac		20	50

This issue is known postmarked at Douglas, Isle of Man, on 19 June 1968.

Cylinder Number (Block of Six)

Single Pane cylinder. Perforation Type F (L) (I/E)

Cyl. No.	No dot
1	2·75

Minor Constant Flaws

As for Nos. XM2/4

Sold Out   4.69

4d., Type XM2 (1966–69)

1966 (FEBRUARY 7). 4d. WATERMARK CROWNS

				Mint	Used
XM6 (=S.G.3)	4d.	Ultramarine		1·50	1·50

Cylinder Number (Block of Six)

Single pane cylinder. Perforation Type F (L) (I/E)

Cyl. No.	No dot
1	15·00

Minor Constant Flaws

Cyl. 1   7/12 Fine line from top of diadem to inner frame at right (Th. B3–5)
        8/7 Coloured dot left of inner frame line at right (Th. C5–6)
        17/1 Coloured scratches below Queen's left eye (Th. D3–4)
        19/1 Coloured scratch behind Queen's neck (Th. F5)

Quantity Sold   4,353,840 including 7,553 on First Day Covers

Sold Out   11.67

1967 (JULY 5).   4d. TWO 9·5 mm. PHOSPHOR BANDS REACTING VIOLET. WATER-MARK CROWNS

			Mint	Used
XM7 (=S.G.3p)	4d.	Ultramarine	20	30

Cylinder Number (Block of Six)

Single pane cylinder. Perforation Type F (L) (I/E)

Cyl. No.	No dot
1	2·75

Minor Constant Flaws

As for No. XM6

Sold Out   12.68

1968 (JUNE 24).   4d. NO WATERMARK. CHALKY PAPER. PVA GUM. TWO 9·5 mm. PHOSPHOR BANDS REACTING VIOLET

			Mint	Used
XM8 (=S.G.4)	4d.	Blue	25	30

Cylinder Number (Block of Six)

Single pane cylinder Perforation Type F (L) (I/E)

Cyl. No.	No dot
1	3·50

Minor Constant Flaws

Cyl. 1   6/7 Flaw behind lower cross of diadem (Th. D5)
14/2 White background spot just above Queen's right eye (Th. C–D2)
Others as for No. XM6

Sold Out   16.7.69

1968 (SEPTEMBER 4).   4d. CHANGE OF COLOUR. NO WATERMARK. CHALKY PAPER. PVA GUM. ONE CENTRE PHOSPHOR BAND REACTING VIOLET

			Mint	Used
XM9 (=S.G.5)	4d.	Olive-sepia	25	40
	a.	Phosphor omitted	22·00	

Cylinder Number (Block of Six)

Single pane cylinder. Perforation Type F (L) (I/E)

Cyl. No.	No dot
1	2·75

Minor Constant Flaws

As for No. XM8

1969 (FEBRUARY 26). 4d. FURTHER CHANGE OF COLOUR. NO WATERMARK. CHALKY PAPER. PVA GUM. ONE CENTRE PHOSPHOR BAND REACTING VIOLET

			Mint	Used
XM10 (=S.G.6)	4d.	Bright vermilion	45	75

Cylinder Number (Block of Six)

Single pane cylinder. Perforation Type F (L) (I/E)

Cyl. No.	No dot
1	6·00

Minor Constant Flaws

As for No. XM8

5d., Type XM2 (1968)

1968 (SEPTEMBER 4). 5d. NO WATERMARK. CHALKY PAPER. PVA GUM. TWO 9·5 mm. PHOSPHOR BANDS REACTING VIOLET

				Mint	Used
XM11 (=S.G.7)	5d.		Royal blue	45	75
		a.	Phosphor omitted	£175	
		b.	Error. Single broad band	45·00	
		c.	Frame flaw (top right) (R. 20/1)	4·75	
		d.	Frame flaw (bottom left) (R. 20/12)	4·50	

XM11*c*

XM11*d*

Cylinder Number (Block of Six)

Single pane cylinder. Perforation Type F (L) (I/E)

Cyl. No.	No dot
1	10·00*

First Day Covers

XMFC1	(8.6.64)	9,237 posted	2½d.	45·00
XMFC2	(7.2.66)	7,553 posted	4d. Ultramarine	15·00
XMFC3	(4.9.68)	42,910 posted	4d. Olive-sepia, 5d.	4·00

D. Northern Ireland

XN1

(Des. W. Hollywood)

XN2

(Des. L. Pilton)

XN3

(Des. T. Collins)

3d., Type XN1 (1958–67)

1958 (AUGUST 18).   3d. WATERMARK CROWNS

A. Cream Paper

			Mint	Used
XN1	3d.	Deep lilac	1·50	25

B. Whiter Paper (21 May 1962)

			Mint	Used
XN2 (=S.G.NI1)	3d.	Deep lilac	15	10

Cylinder Numbers (Blocks of Six)

Cream Paper (No. XN1)
Perforation Type A (E/I)

Cyl. No.	No dot	Dot
3	15·00	15·00

White Paper (No. XN2)
Perforation Type A (E/I)

Cyl. No.	No dot	Dot
3	2·50	2·50

Perf. Type F (L)* (I/E no dot and P/E dot)

3**	—	—

**This is probably No. XN3 with the phosphor omitted.

Minor Constant Flaw

Cyl. 3   4/9 White flaw on edge of lowest flax flower (Th. G2)

Imprimatur from the National Postal Museum Archives

Cream paper. Imperforate, watermark Type W.24
Watermark upright

Quantity Sold   375,417,400

Sold Out   10.67

1967 (JUNE 9).   3d. ONE CENTRE PHOSPHOR BAND REACTING VIOLET. WATER-MARK CROWNS

			Mint	Used
XN3 (=S.G.NI1p)	3d.	Deep lilac	15	15

Cylinder Numbers (Blocks of Six)

Perforation Type A (E/I)

Cyl. No.	No dot	Dot
3	2·50	2·50

Perforation Type F (L)*

Cyl. No.	No dot (I/E)	Dot (P/E)
3	2·50	2·50

Minor Constant Flaws

As for flaw on Nos. XN1/2

4d., Type XN1 (1966–69)

1966 (FEBRUARY 7).   4d. WATERMARK CROWNS

				Mint	Used
XN4 (=S.G. NI2)	4d.	Ultramarine		15	15
	a.	Dot on leaf (No dot, R. 3/12)		4·50	
	b.	Flower flaw (No dot, R. 7/7)		4·75	
	c.	Dot under "S" of "POSTAGE" (Dot R. 2/4)		6·00	

XN4*a*, XN5*a*, XN6*a*, XN7*a*, XN8*b*	XN4*b*	XN4*c*
White dot on leaf of plant. Retouched on No. XN9	White spot on top flower. The above only exists on No. XN4. It was retouched and shows as a dark patch on Nos. XN5*b*, XN6*b*, XN7*b*, XN8*c* and XN9*b*	White dot under "S" of "POSTAGE". Retouched on No. XN5

Cylinder Numbers (Blocks of Six)

Perforation Type A (E/I)

Cyl. No.	No dot	Dot
1	2·50	2·50

Cylinder number: Opposite R.18/1. In addition, early printings of both no dot and dot panes bore a trace of cylinder numbers reading "1A" and "1A." with two sides of a box opposite R.19/1. These had been inserted in error. Attempts to remove them were only partially successful, so that they exist in varying degrees of faintness.

Minor Constant Flaws

Cyl. 1   16/5 Small white spot to right of second leaf down on upright flax plant (Th. B6)
Cyl. 1.   2/1 Small coloured projection above upper frame line (Th. A2)
          3/12 Small white dot below lower right leaf of flax plant (Th. G4)
          10/6 Coloured flaw in lower left of badge (Th. E1)
     `   12/1 Pale patch below P of POSTAGE (Th. F1)

Quantity Sold   61,449,360

Sold Out   11·68

1967 (OCTOBER 2).   4d. TWO 9·5 mm. PHOSPHOR BANDS REACTING VIOLET. WATERMARK CROWNS

				Mint	Used
XN5 (=S.G. NI2p)	4d.	Ultramarine		15	15
	a.	Dot on leaf (No dot, R. 3/12)		4·75	
	b.	Flower flaw retouch (No dot, R. 7/7)		4·75	

For illustration of No. XN5*a* and for description of No. XN5*b*, see Nos. XN4*a*/*b*.

Cylinder Numbers (Blocks of Six)

Perforation Type F (L)*

Cyl. No.	No dot (I/E)	Dot (P/E)
1	2·50	2·50

Minor Constant Flaws

Cyl. 1 16/5 Small white spot to right of second leaf down on upright flax plant (Th. B6)
Cyl. 1. 2/1 Small coloured projection above upper frame line (Th. A2)
2/4 Dark patch below S of POSTAGE where former white dot, No. XN4a, existed (Th. F2)
3/12 Small white dot below lower right leaf of flax plant (Th. G4)
10/6 Coloured flaw in lower left of badge (Th. E1)
12/1 Pale patch below P of POSTAGE (Th. F1)

Sold Out 1.70

1968 (JUNE 27). 4d. NO WATERMARK. CHALKY PAPER. TWO 9·5 mm. PHOSPHOR BANDS REACTING VIOLET

A. Gum Arabic

			Mint	Used
XN6 (=S.G. NI7)	4d.	Ultramarine	15	15
	a.	Dot on leaf (No dot, R. 3/12)	4·75	
	b.	Flower flaw retouch (No dot, R. 7/7)	4·75	

B. PVA Gum* (23 October 1968)

XN7 (=S.G.NI7Ev)	4d.	Ultramarine . . . . 13·00
	a.	Dot on leaf (No dot, R. 3/12) . . . . 20·00
	b.	Flower flaw retouch (No dot, R. 7/7) . . . . 20·00

For illustration of Nos. XN6a and XN7a and for description of Nos. XN6b and XN7b, see Nos. XN4a/b respectively.

*No. XN7 was never issued in Northern Ireland. After No. XN6 (gum arabic) had been withdrawn from Northern Ireland but whilst still on sale at the philatelic counters elsewhere, about fifty sheets with PVA gum were sold over the London Philatelic counter on 23 October 1968, and some were also on sale at the British Philatelic Exhibition Post Office.

Cylinder Numbers (Blocks of Six)

	Gum Arabic (No. XN6)			PVA Gum (No. XN7)		
	Perforation Type A (E/I)			Perforation Type A (E/I)		
Cyl. No.		No dot	Dot	Cyl. No.	No dot	Dot
1		2·50	2·50	1	£125	†

Minor Constant Flaws

Cyl. 1 16/5 Small white spot to right of second leaf down on upright flax plant (Th. B6)
Cyl. 1. 2/1 Small coloured projection above upper frame line (Th. A2)
2/4 Dark patch below S of POSTAGE where former white dot, No. XN4a, existed (Th. F2)
3/12 Small white dot below lower right leaf of flax plant (Th. G4)
6/12 Small coloured flaws on leaf above NU of REVENUE
10/6 Coloured flaw in lower left of badge (Th. E1)
12/1 Pale patch below P of POSTAGE (Th. F1)

Sold Out No. XN6, 4.70

Withdrawn No. XN7 on the same day as released

1968 (SEPTEMBER 4). 4d. CHANGE OF COLOUR. NO WATERMARK. CHALKY PAPER. PVA GUM. ONE CENTRE PHOSPHOR BAND REACTING VIOLET

			Mint	Used
XN8 (=S.G. NI8)	4d.	Olive-sepia	15	15
	a.	Phosphor omitted		
	b.	Dot on leaf (No dot, R. 3/12)	4·75	
	c.	Flower flaw retouch (No dot, R. 7/7)	4·75	

For illustration of No. XN8b and for description of No. XN8c, see Nos. XN4a/b respectively.

Cylinder Numbers (Blocks of Six)

Perforation Type A (E/I)

Cyl. No.		No dot	Dot
1	. . . .	2·50	2·50

Cylinder number: Opposite R.18/1. In addition both no dot and dot panes bear traces of cylinder numbers reading "1A" and "1A." with two sides of a box opposite R. 19/1. These exist in varying degrees of faintness.

Minor Constant Flaws

As for Nos. XN6/7

1969 (FEBRUARY 26). 4d. FURTHER CHANGE OF COLOUR. NO WATERMARK. CHALKY PAPER. PVA GUM. ONE CENTRE PHOSPHOR BAND REACTING VIOLET

			Mint	Used
XN9 (=S.G. NI9)	4d.	Bright vermilion	20	20
	a.	Phosphor omitted	4·50	
	b.	Flower flaw retouch (No dot, R. 7/7)	4·00	

For description of No. XN9b, see No. XN4b.

Cylinder Numbers (Blocks of Six)

Perforation Type A (E/I)

Cyl. No.		No dot	Dot
1	. . . .	2·75	2·75

Cylinder number: Opposite R. 18/1. In addition both no dot and dot panes bear traces of cylinder numbers reading "1A" and "1A". with two sides of a box opposite R. 19/1. These exist in varying degrees of faintness.

Minor Constant Flaws

Cyl. 1.	2/4	Dark patch below S of POSTAGE where former white dot, No. XN4a, existed (Th. F2)
	6/12	Small coloured flaws on leaf above NU of REVENUE
	10/6	Coloured flaw in lower left of badge (Th. E1)
	12/1	Pale patch below P of POSTAGE (Th. F1)

5d., Type XN1 (1968)

1968 (SEPTEMBER 4). 5d. NO WATERMARK. CHALKY PAPER. PVA GUM. TWO 9·5 mm. PHOSPHOR BANDS REACTING VIOLET

			Mint	Used
XN10 (=S.G. NI10)	5d.	Royal blue	20	20
	a.	Phosphor omitted	25·00	
	b.	"Extra leaf" (No dot, R. 13/2)	5·00	

XN10*b*

White flaw near junction of flax plant stalks appears as an extra leaf

Cylinder Numbers (Blocks of Six)

Perforation Type A (E/I)

Cyl. No.	No dot	Dot
1	2·75	2·75

6d., Type XN2 (1958–62)

1958 (SEPTEMBER 29). 6d. WATERMARK CROWNS

A. Cream Paper

			Mint	Used
XN11	6d.	Deep claret	2·25	50

B. Whiter Paper (4 June 1962)

XN12 (=S.G. NI3)	6d.	Deep claret	20	25

Cylinder Numbers (Blocks of Six)

	Cream Paper (No. XN11)			Whiter Paper (No. XN12)			
Cyl. No.	(No dot)	Perf. Types		Cyl. No. (No dot)	Perf. Types		
		B (I/P)	C (E/P)		B (I/P)	C (E/P)	F (L) (I/E)
1		30·00	30·00	1	4·00	4·00	2·75

Minor Constant Flaws

Cyl. 1 1/12 Flaw in background to right of diadem (Th. A4)
2/11 White coloured spur on lowest leaf of left flax plant (Th. F1)
3/9 Dot in diamond to right of 6D (Th. F4); also similar dot in diamond to right of Queen's collar (Th. E–F5)
3/10 "Ring" on little finger of hand at left (Th. F2)
3/12 Dark spot in centre of central cross of diadem (Th. B3)
4/2 Coloured line in background to right of 6D (Th. G4)
10/2 White bulge half way down stalk at left (Th. D1)
12/2 Coloured spot in background to right of Queen's hair (Th. D5)

Imprimatur from the National Postal Museum Archives

Cream paper. Imperforate, watermark Type W.24
Watermark upright

Quantity Sold 28,531,180 up to 31.3.68

Sold Out 11.68

9d., Type XN2 (1967)

1967 (MARCH 1). 9d. WATERMARK CROWNS. TWO 9·5 mm. PHOSPHOR BANDS REACTING VIOLET

			Mint	Used
XN13 (=S.G. NI4)	9d.	Bronze-green	30	70

Cylinder Number (Block of Six)

Single pane cylinder. Perforation Type F (L) (I/E)

Cyl. No.	No dot
1	4·25

Imprimatur from the National Postal Museum Archives

Imperforate, watermark Type W.24
Watermark upright

1s.3d., Type XN3 (1958–62)

1958 (SEPTEMBER 29). 1s.3d. WATERMARK CROWNS

		Mint	Used
A. Cream Paper			
XN14	1s.3d. Green	5·00	1·25

		Mint	Used
B. Whiter Paper (9 November 1962)			
XN15 (=S.G. NI5)	1s.3d. Green	30	70

Cylinder Numbers (Blocks of Six)

Cream Paper (No. XN14)			Whiter Paper (No. XN15)			
Cyl. No.	(No dot)	Perf. Types	Cyl. No.	(No dot)	Perf. Types	
		B (I/P) C (E/P)			B (I/P) C (E/P) F (L) (I/E)	
1	50·00 50·00		1	4·75 4·75 4·00		

Minor Constant Flaws

Cyl. 1   1/1 White dot in upper loop of S of POSTAGE; also small area of retouching above emblems in diadem (Th. A4)
   3/7 White spur to O of POSTAGE (Th. E1)

Imprimatur from the National Postal Museum Archives

Cream paper. Imperforate, watermark Type W.24
Watermark upright

Quantity Sold   14,060,520 up to 31.3.68

1s.6d., Type XN3 (1967–69)

1967 (MARCH 1). 1s.6d. WATERMARK CROWNS. TWO 9·5 mm. PHOSPHOR BANDS REACTING VIOLET

			Mint	Used
XN16 (=S.G. NI6)	1s.6d.	Grey-blue	30	70
	a.	Phosphor omitted	£200	

Cylinder Number (Block of Six)

Single pane cylinder. Perforation Type F (L) (I/E)

Cyl. No.	No dot
1	4·50

Minor Constant Flaws

Cyl. 1   4/12 Small area of retouching behind Queen's head. Consists of several small dark coloured dots (Th. E5)
   14/1 Dark coloured spot on Queen's cheek (Th. D4)
   15/12 A multitude of tiny coloured spots over the Queen's face, neck and collar, and in the background behind her neck
   17/8 Coloured spot to right of Queen's left eye (Th. D3–4)

Imprimatur from the National Postal Museum Archives

Imperforate, watermark Type W.24
Watermark upright

1969 (MAY 20). 1s.6d. NO WATERMARK. CHALKY PAPER. PVA GUM. TWO 9·5 mm. PHOSPHOR BANDS REACTING VIOLET

			Mint	Used
XN17 (=S.G. NI11)	1s.6d.	Grey-blue	2·25	2·50
	a.	Phosphor omitted	£500	

It is believed that only three examples exist of No. XN17a.

Cylinder Number (Block of Six)

Single pane cylinder. Perforation Type F (L) (I/E)

Cyl. No.	No dot
1	30·00

Minor Constant Flaws

Cyl. 1   4/12 Small area of retouching behind Queen's head. Consists of several small dark coloured dots (Th. E5)

11/12 Small dark coloured flaw on Queen's neck, just above necklace (Th. E4)

14/1 Small dark coloured flaw on Queen's cheek (Th. D4)

15/12 A multitude of tiny dark coloured spots over the Queen's face, neck and collar, and in the background behind her neck

17/8 Area of retouching to right of Queen's left eye (Th. D3–4)

Imprimatur from the National Postal Museum Archives

Chalky paper, imperforate
No watermark

Presentation Pack

XNPP1 (9.12.70)   Seven stamps   3·50

Comprises Nos. XN3, 8/10, 13, and 15/16

Quantity Sold   28,944

Withdrawn   25.11.71

First Day Covers

XNFC1	(1.3.67)	9d., 1s.6d.	4·00
XNFC2	(4.9.68)	4d., 5d.	3·00

E.   Scotland

XS1

(Des. Gordon F. Huntly)

XS2

(Des. J. B. Fleming)

XS3

(Des. A. B. Imrie)

3d., Type XS1 (1958–68)

1958 (AUGUST 18).   3d. WATERMARK CROWNS

A. Cream Paper   Mint   Used

XS1   3d.   Deep lilac   70   35
             a.   Spot on "U" of "REVENUE" (Cyl. 3 No dot,
                    R. 19/8) . . . .   5·50
             b.   Dot in "d" of "3d" (Cyl. 3 Dot, R. 20/12) . . . .   4·50

B. Whiter Paper (9 July 1962)

XS2 (=S.G. S1)   3d.   Deep lilac   15   15
                  a.   Spot after last "E" of "REVENUE" (Cyl. 5 No dot,
                         R. 20/2) . . . .   4·50

XS1*a*

XS1*b*
Later retouched

XS2*a*, XS3*a*, XS4
XS5*b*, XS7*b* X

Cylinder Numbers (Blocks of Six)

Cream Paper (No. XS1)			Whiter Paper (No. XS2)		
Perforation Type A (E/I)			Perforation Type A (E/I)		
Cyl. No.	No dot	Dot	Cyl. No.	No dot	Dot
3	10·00	10·00	4	2·75	2·75
4	10·00	10·00	5	2·75	5·50*

Perforation Type H

	(E/I)	(P/I)
4	.10·00**	—

**Same price as perforation type A with extension holes in left margin.

Imprimatur from the National Postal Museum Archives

Cream paper. Imperforate, watermark Type W.24
Watermark upright.

Quantity Sold   1,487,481,480

Sold Out   18.3.68

1962. Miniature Sheet. On the occasion of Scotex the 1962 Scottish Stamp Exhibition, a miniature sheet, size 105 × 60 mm., was produced comprising Types **XS1/3** printed *se-tenant* in black, imperforate and surrounded by a decorative frame and inscription in blue on white chalk-surfaced gummed paper watermarked "HARRISON AND SONS LTD" sideways. The sheet was printed by Harrison & Sons with the use of actual stamp positives. It had no franking value. 15,000 printed.

1963 (JANUARY 29). 3d. PHOSPHOR BANDS REACTING BLUE. WATERMARK CROWNS

A. Two 8 mm. Bands

			Mint	Used
XS3 (=S.G.S1p)	3d.	Deep lilac	13·00	2·75
	a.	Spot after last "E" of "REVENUE" (Cyl. 5 Dot, R. 20/2)	25·00	

B. One Side Band* (30 April 1965)

XS4	3d.	Deep lilac (band at left)	4·00	70
	a.	Band at right	4·00	70
	ab.	Nos. XS4/a (horiz. pair)	8·00	
	b.	Spot after last "E" of "REVENUE" (Cyl. 5 Dot, R. 20/2)	8·00	

*The one side band stamps were produced by an 8 mm. band applied down alternate vertical rows of the sheets over the perforations so that alternate stamps have the band at left (No. XS4) or right (No. XS4a). In theory the width of the band on a single stamp should be 4 mm. but this will vary if the bands have not been perfectly positioned.

For illustration of Nos. XS3a and XS4b, see No. XS2a.

Cylinder Numbers (Blocks of Six)

Two Bands (No. XS3) Perforation Type A (E/I)			One Side Band (No. XS4) Perforation Type A (E/I)		
Cyl. No.	No dot	Dot	Cyl. No.	No dot	Dot
4	£130	£130	5	35·00	40·00*
5	£130	£140*			

Imprimatur from the National Postal Museum Archives

Imperforate, watermark Type W.24. Two 8 mm. bands
Watermark upright

Sold Out   No. XS3, 1968

1965 (DECEMBER 16). 3d. PHOSPHOR BANDS REACTING VIOLET. WATERMARK CROWNS

A. One Side Band*

			Mint	Used
XS5 (=S.G.S1pa)	3d.	Deep lilac (band at left)	20	25
	a.	Band at right	20	25
	ab.	Nos. XS5/a (horiz. pair)	50	
	b.	Spot after last "E" of "REVENUE" (Cyl. 5 Dot, R. 20/2)	4·75	

B. One 4 mm. Centre Band (9 November 1967)

XS6 (=S.G.S1pb)	3d.	Deep lilac	15	15

*The note *re* one side band stamps after No. XS4b also applies here.
For illustration of No. XS5b, see No. XS2a.

Cylinder Numbers (Blocks of Six)

One Side Band (No. XS5) Perforation Type A (E/I)			One Centre Band (No. XS6) Perforation Type A (E/I)		
Cyl. No.	No dot	Dot	Cyl. No.	No dot	Dot
5	2·75	7·00*	4	2·50	2·50

Sold Out   No. XS5, 15.7.68; No. XS6, 11.68

1968 (MAY 16). 3d. NO WATERMARK. CHALKY PAPER. ONE CENTRE PHOSPHOR BAND REACTING VIOLET

A. Gum Arabic			Mint	Used
XS7 (=S.G.S7)	3d.	Deep lilac	10	15
	a.	Phosphor omitted	7·00	
	b.	Spot after last "E" of "REVENUE" (Cyl. 5 Dot, R. 20/2)	4·00	

B. PVA Gum (11 July 1968)				
XS8 (=S.G.S7Ev)	3d.	Deep lilac	10	
	a.	Phosphor omitted	4·00	
	b.	Spot after last "E" of "REVENUE" (Cyl. 5 Dot, R. 20/2)	4·00	

For illustration of Nos. XS7*b* and XS8*b*, see No. XS2*a*.

Cylinder Numbers (Blocks of Six)

Gum Arabic (No. XS7)			PVA Gum (No. XS8)		
Perforation Type F (L)*			Perforation Type F (L)*		
Cyl. No.	No dot (I/E)	Dot (P/E)	Cyl. No.	No dot (I/E)	Dot (P/E)
5	1·90	4·00*	5	1·90	4·00*

Minor Constant Flaws

Cyl. 5   8/6   Retouching on Queen's forehead, nose and around lips (Th. B–D3)
             13/3   Pale patch on Queen's collar (Th. E–F4)
             15/3   Small dark flaw surrounded by white area on right side of thistle (Th. G6)
             17/7   Area of retouching on Queen's neck (Th. E4–5)
             18/1   Horizontal coloured line through G of POSTAGE

4d., Type XS1 (1966–69)

1966 (FEBRUARY 7). 4d. WATERMARK CROWNS

			Mint	Used
XS9 (= S.G.S2)	4d.	Ultramarine	15	15
	a.	Dot before second "E" of "REVENUE" (Dot, R. 10/9)	4·50	
	b.	Spot on "T" (Dot, R. 4/4)	4·75	

XS9*a*, XS10*a*   XS9*b*, XS10*b*
Later retouched
on No. XS10

Cylinder Numbers (Blocks of Six)

Perforation Type A (E/I)

Cyl. No.	No dot	Dot
2	2·50	2·50

Minor Constant Flaws

Cyl. 2   7/11 White spot to left of crown at right (Th. F5)
         8/6 Small blue flaw on top left-hand leaf of thistle (Th. F5)
        20/5 Small dark flaw in background to right of d of 4d (Th. F4–5)
Cyl. 2.   8/12 Blue spot below Queen's left eye (Th. C3)
       11/7 Small blue spot on Queen's forehead (Th. B2)
       12/8 Small dark flaw in background to left of EV of REVENUE (Th. B5); also
            retouching on Queen's temple and cheek (Th. C3–4)
       20/3 Small coloured flaw above Queen's left eye (Th. B3); also small blue spot on top left-
            hand leaf of thistle (Th. F5)

Sold Out   7.70.

1966 (FEBRUARY 7). 4d. TWO 8 mm. PHOSPHOR BANDS REACTING VIOLET. WATER-MARK CROWNS

				Mint	Used
XS10 (=S.G.S2p)	4d.	Ultramarine		15	15
	a.	Dot before second "E" of "REVENUE" (Dot, R.10/9)		4·50	
	b.	Spot on "T" (Dot, R. 4/4)		4·50	

For illustrations of Nos. XS10*a*/*b*, see Nos. XS9*a*/*b*.

Cylinder Numbers (Blocks of Six)

Perforation Type A (E/I)

Cyl. No.	No dot	Dot
2	2·50	2·50

Minor Constant Flaws

Cyl. 2   As for flaws on No. XS9 except that flaw on R. 20/5 was later retouched
Cyl. 2.   As for flaws on No. XS9

Sold Out   7.70.

1967 (NOVEMBER 28). 4d. NO WATERMARK. CHALKY PAPER. TWO 9·5 mm. PHOSPHOR BANDS REACTING VIOLET

A. Gum Arabic

			Mint	Used
XS11 (=S.G.S8)	4d.	Ultramarine	10	15
	a.	Phosphor omitted	10·00	

B. PVA Gum (25 July 1968)

			Mint
XS12 (= S.G.S8Ev)	4d.	Ultramarine	10

Cylinder Numbers (Blocks of Six)

Gum Arabic (No. XS11)				PVA Gum (No. XS12)		
Perforation Type F (L)*				Perforation Type A (E/I)		
Cyl. No.	No Dot	Dot		Cyl. No.	No dot	Dot
	(I/E)	(P/E)				
2	2·00	2·00		2	2·00	2·00

Minor Constant Flaws

Cyl. 2   1/7 Retouch on Queen's forehead (Th. B3). PVA only
       3/7 Retouch on Queen's collar (Th. E4–5). PVA only
      5/10 White patches on Queen's nose and forehead
       8/6 Small blue flaw on top left-hand leaf of thistle (Th. F5)
     10/11 Retouch to right of Queen's mouth (Th. D3). PVA only
     12/12 White spot at rear tip of diadem (Th. C5)
     14/10 Retouch on Queen's forehead (Th. B3). Less pronounced on PVA
     15/4 Retouch on Queen's cheek (Th. C–D3)
     19/7 White spot on Queen's cheek (Th. C3). Retouched on PVA where it shows as three
          dark spots

Cyl. 2 continued

20/5 Small dark flaw in background to right of d of 4d (Th. F4–5). Less pronounced on PVA but can be confirmed by additional retouches on Queen's nose and forehead (Th. C2 and B3)

20/6 Small blue flaw on Queen's cheek (Th. C3). On PVA there is an additional white flaw on Queen's right cheek (Th. C2)

Cyl. 2.   1/5 Coloured spot above Queen's left eye (Th. B3).

2/6 Retouch on Queen's collar (Th. E4)

6/11 White spot on Queen's cheek (Th. C–D3). Retouched on PVA where it shows as a dark spot

8/12 White spot below Queen's left eye where former blue spot appeared (Th. C3). Further retouched on PVA

11/7 Small blue spot on Queen's forehead (Th. B2)

12/8 Small dark flaw in background to left of EV of REVENUE (Th. B5); also retouching on Queen's temple and cheek, the latter much more pronounced on PVA (Th. C3–4)

15/1 Small retouch on Queen's temple (Th. C3–4). PVA only

15/2 Small retouch on Queen's forehead (Th. B2). PVA only

18/4 Weak patches on Queen's chin (Th. D2–3).

18/6 Blue spot on Queen's collar (Th. E4). Retouched on PVA but a scratch now appears across Queen's neck and collar (Th. E4)

19/3 White spot on Queen's left cheek (Th. D3). Shows larger on PVA

20/3 Small coloured flaw above Queen's left eye (Th. B3); also small blue spot on top left-hand leaf of thistle (Th. F5)

20/4 Coloured spots around Queen's eyes and nose (Th. C2–3)

1968 (SEPTEMBER 4).   4d. CHANGE OF COLOUR. NO WATERMARK. CHALKY PAPER. PVA GUM. ONE CENTRE PHOSPHOR BAND REACTING VIOLET

			Mint	Used
XS13 (=S.G.S9)	4d.	olive-sepia	10	10
	a.	Phosphor omitted	3·00	

Cylinder Numbers (Blocks of Six)

Perforation Type A (E/I)

Cyl. No.	No dot	Dot
2	2·00	2·00

Minor Constant Flaws

Cyl. 2 12/12 White spot at rear tip of diadem (Th. C5)

Cyl. 2.   1/5 Coloured spot above Queen's left eye (Th. B3)

2/6 Retouch on Queen's collar (Th. E4)

6/11 Retouch on Queen's cheek (Th. C–D3)

8/12 Retouch below Queen's left eye (Th. C3)

11/7 Coloured spot on Queen's forehead (Th. B2)

12/8 Small dark flaw in background to left of EV of REVENUE (Th. B5); also retouching on Queen's temple and cheek (Th. C3–4)

15/1 Small retouch on Queen's temple (Th. C3–4)

15/2 Small retouch on Queen's forehead (Th. B2)

18/4 Weak patches on Queen's chin (Th. D2–4)

18/6 Retouch on Queen's collar and also scratch across her neck and collar (Th. E4)

19/3 Large white spot on Queen's left cheek (Th. D3)

20/3 Small coloured flaw above Queen's left eye (Th. B3); also small coloured spot on top left-hand leaf of thistle (Th. F5)

20/4 Coloured spots around Queen's eyes and nose (Th. C2–3)

1969 (FEBRUARY 26).   4d. FURTHER CHANGE OF COLOUR. NO WATERMARK. CHALKY PAPER. PVA GUM. ONE CENTRE PHOSPHOR BAND REACTING VIOLET

			Mint	Used
XS14 (=S.G.S10)	4d.	Bright vermilion	10	10
	a.	Phosphor omitted	2·50	

Cylinder Numbers (Blocks of Six)

Perforation Type A (E/I)				Perforation Type A (E/I)		
Cyl. No.	No dot	Dot		Cyl. No.	No dot	Dot
2	2·00	2·00		4	2·00	2·00

Minor Constant Flaws

Cyl. 2   1/7 Retouch on Queen's forehead (Th. B3)
        3/7 Retouch on Queen's collar (Th. E4–5)
        5/10 Retouching on Queen's nose and forehead where former white patches appeared
        8/11 Retouch by Queen's ear (Th. C–D4)
      12/12 White spot at rear tip of diadem (Th. C5)
      10/11 Retouch to right of Queen's mouth (Th. D3)
      14/10 Heavy retouching on Queen's forehead (Th. B3)
      15/4 Retouch on Queen's cheek (Th. C–D3)
      19/7 Retouch on Queen's cheek where former white spot appeared (Th. C3)
      20/5 Retouches on Queen's nose and forehead (Th. C2 and B3). Small dark flaw in background to right of d of 4d now hardly shows (Th. F4–5)
      20/6 Retouches on both of the Queen's cheeks where former flaws appeared (Th. C2–3)

Cyl. 2.   1/5 Coloured spot above Queen's left eye (Th. B3)
       2/6 Retouch on Queen's collar (Th. E4)
      6/11 Heavy area of retouching on Queen's cheek (Th. C–D3)
      8/12 Retouch below Queen's left eye (Th. C3)
      10/5 Extensive area of retouching on Queen's temple and cheek (Th. B3 and C3–4)
      11/7 Area of retouching on Queen's forehead where former coloured spot appeared (Th. B2)
      12/8 Small dark flaw in background to left of EV of REVENUE (Th. B5) is now less noticeable but retouches on Queen's temple and cheek remain (Th. C3–4)
      15/1 Small retouch on Queen's temple (Th. C3–4)
      15/2 Small retouch on Queen's forehead (Th. B2)
      18/4 Weak patches on Queen's chin (Th. D2–4)
      18/6 Retouch on Queen's collar and also scratch across her neck and collar (Th. E4)
      20/3 Small coloured flaw above Queen's left eye (Th. B3); also small coloured spot on top left-hand leaf of thistle (Th. F5)
      20/4 Coloured spots around Queen's eyes and nose (Th. C2–3)

5d., Type XS1 (1968)

1968 (SEPTEMBER 4). 5d. NO WATERMARK. CHALKY PAPER. PVA GUM. TWO 9·5 mm. PHOSPHOR BANDS REACTING VIOLET

			Mint	Used
XS15 (=S.G.S11)	5d.	Royal blue	20	10
	a.	Phosphor omitted	55·00	
	b.	Shoulder retouch (Cyl. 2., R. 16/6)	4·75	

Large retouch on Queen's shoulder

XS15*b*

Cylinder Numbers (Blocks of Six)

Perforation Type A (E/I)

Cyl. No.		No dot	Dot
2	. . . .	2·75	2·75
3	. . . .	10·00	10·00

Phosphor cylinder number: "Ph 1" found on cyl. 3 dot, right margin

6d., Type XS2 (1958–66)

1958 (SEPTEMBER 29).   6d. WATERMARK CROWNS

						Mint	Used
A. Cream Paper							
XS16		6d.	Reddish purple			2·75	90
		a.	Broken "V" of "REVENUE" (Cyl. 1, R. 11/12) . . .			12·00	
		b.	Curled leaf (Cyl. 1, R. 7/7)			8·00	
B. Whiter Paper (28 May 1962)							
XS17 (=S.G.S3)		6d.	Deep reddish purple			20	15
		a.	Broken "V" of "REVENUE" (Cyl. 1, R. 11/12) . . .			6·00	
		b.	Curled leaf (Cyl. 1, R. 7/7)			4·75	
		c.	Cut leaf (Cyl. 4, R. 2/10)			4·75	

XS16*a*, XS17*a*

This is a multipositive flaw. It was later retouched on Cyl. 1. On Cyls. 2 and 4 it is only known retouched and it shows as a much thicker "V" than normal

XS16*b*, XS17*b*

Later retouched

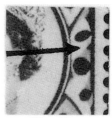

XS17*c*, XS18*a*

Leaf half-way down at right has V-shaped cut in solid colour

Cylinder Numbers (Blocks of Six)

	Cream Paper (No. XS16)			Whiter Paper (No. XS17)			
Cyl. No.	(No dot)	Perf.Types		Cyl. No.	(No dot)	Perf. Types	
		B(I/P)	C(E/P)			B (I/P) C (E/P) F (L) (I/E)	
1	. . . .	35·00	35·00	1	. . . .	† † 3·50	
				2	. . . .	2·75 2·75 †	
				4	. . . .	† † 2·75	

Marginal rule:

    Cylinder 1: Instead of the usual "stamp width" rule below each stamp in the bottom row the rules on this cylinder are shorter (approx. 17 mm.) and are arranged alternately with a 1 mm. wide rectangular rule, the latter being perforated through. The rules below vertical rows 9/12 are damaged Cylinders 2 and 4: As given in General Notes

Minor Constant Flaws

Cyl. 1	5/8	Small white flaw by left thistle just outside oval frame (Th. B2)
Cyl. 2	11/12	V of REVENUE retouched. It is thicker than normal and has a fuzzy appearance
Cyl. 4	11/12	As for Cyl. 2

Imprimatur from the National Postal Museum Archives

Cream paper. Imperforate, watermark Type W.24
Watermark upright

1963 (JANUARY 29). 6d. TWO 8 mm. PHOSPHOR BANDS REACTING BLUE. WATER-MARK CROWNS

			Mint	Used
XS18	6d.	Deep reddish purple	2·75	90
	a.	Cut leaf (Cyl. 4, R. 2/10)	8·00	

Cylinder Number (Block of Six)

Single pane cylinder. Perforation Type F (L) (I/E)

Cyl. No.	No dot
4	35·00

Minor Constant Flaw

Cyl. 4 11/12 V of REVENUE retouched. It is thicker than normal and has a fuzzy appearance

Imprimatur from the National Postal Museum Archives

Imperforate, watermark Type W.24
Watermark upright

1966 (FEBRUARY 2). 6d. TWO 8 mm. PHOSPHOR BANDS REACTING VIOLET. WATERMARK CROWNS

			Mint	Used
XS19 (=S.G.S3p)	6d.	Deep reddish purple	20	20

Cylinder Number (Block of Six)

Single pane cylinder. Perforation Type F (L) (I/E)

Cyl. No.	No dot
4	3·00

Quantity Sold   26,758,320 (including No. XS18) up to 31.3.68

Sold Out   10.68

9d., Type XS2 (1967–70)

1967 (MARCH 1). 9d. WATERMARK CROWNS. TWO 9·5 mm. PHOSPHOR BANDS REACTING VIOLET

			Mint	Used
XS20 (=S.G.S4)	9d.	Bronze-green	35	40

Cylinder Number (Block of Six)

Single pane cylinder. Perforation Type F (L) (I/E)

Cyl. No.	No dot
1	4·00

Imprimatur from the National Postal Museum Archives

Imperforate, watermark Type W.24
Watermark upright

1970 (SEPTEMBER 28).   9d. NO WATERMARK. CHALKY PAPER. PVA GUM. TWO 9·5 mm. PHOSPHOR BANDS REACTING VIOLET

			Mint	Used
XS21 (= S.G. S12)	9d.	bronze-green	5·50	5·50
	a.	Phosphor omitted	£250	

Cylinder Number (Block of Six)

Single pane cylinder. Perforation Type F (L) (I/E)

Cyl. No.	No dot
1	. . . . 50·00

Imprimatur from the National Postal Museum Archives

Chalky paper, imperforate
No watermark

1s.3d., Type XS3 (1958–65)

1958 (SEPTEMBER 29).   1s.3d. WATERMARK CROWNS

A. Cream Paper

			Mint	Used
XS22	1s.3d.	Green	4·50	90
	a.	Broken oblique in value (Cyl. 4, R. 15/2)	8·00	
	b.	Broken hinge (Cyl. 4, R. 19/2)	8·00	

B. Whiter Paper (31 July 1962)

			Mint	Used
XS23 (=S.G.S5)	1s.3d.	Green	40	40
	a.	Broken oblique in value (Cyl. 4, R. 15/2)	4·50	
	b.	Broken hinge (Cyl. 4, R. 19/2)	4·50	

XS22*a*, XS23*a*,
XS24*a*, XS25*a*

XS22*b*, XS23*b*, XS24*b*, XS25*b*

Lowest "hinge" of the flag is incomplete. A multipositive flaw, (Cyls. 4 and 8, R. 19/2)

Cylinder Numbers (Blocks of Six)

Cyl. No.	Cream Paper (No. XS22) (No dot)			Cyl. No. (No dot)	Whiter Paper (No. XS23)		
		Perf Types				Perf. Types	
		B (I/P)	C (E/P)			B (I/P)	C (E/P)	F (L) (I/E)
4	. . . .	45·00*	45·00*	4	. . . . . .	8·00*	8·00*	7·00*

Marginal arrows: "V" shaped, hand engraved at top and bottom; "W" shaped, photo-etched at both sides. Early printings have the arrows omitted from the top and bottom of the sheet. *Price for marginal strip of 7 stamps* £60.

Minor Constant Flaws

Cyl. 4	3/7	Green spot on shoulder of right-hand unicorn (Th. D6)
	11/12	Small break in inner frame line at right of value tablet (Th. G4)
	15/2	Hind leg of lion on standard is severed (Th. B1)

Imprimatur from the National Postal Museum Archives

Cream paper. Imperforate, watermark Type W.24
Watermark upright

1963 (JANUARY 29). 1s.3d. TWO 8 mm. PHOSPHOR BANDS REACTING BLUE. WATERMARK CROWNS

			Mint	Used
XS24	1s.3d.	Green	4·50	90
	a.	Broken oblique in value (Cyl. 4. R. 15/2)	12·00	
	b.	Broken hinge (Cyl, 4, R. 19/2)	16·00	

For illustration of Nos. XS24*a/b*, see Nos. XS22*a/b*.

Cylinder Number (Block of Six)

Single pane cylinder. Perforation Type F (L) (I/E)

Cyl. No.	No dot
4	45·00*

Minor Constant Flaws

As for Nos. XS22/3

Imprimatur from the National Postal Museum Archives

Imperforate, watermark Type W.24
Watermark upright

1965 (NOVEMBER 26). 1s.3d. TWO 8 mm. PHOSPHOR BANDS REACTING VIOLET. WATERMARK CROWNS

			Mint	Used
XS25 (=S.G.S5p)	1s.3d.	Green	40	40
	a.	Broken oblique in value (Cyl. 4, R. 15/2)	5·00	
	b.	Broken hinge (Cyls. 4, 8, R. 19/2)	5·00	

For illustration of Nos. XS25*a/b*, see Nos. XS22*a/b*.

Cylinder Numbers (Blocks of Six)

Single pane cylinders. Perforation Type F (L) (I/E)

Cyl. No.	No dot	Cyl. No.	No dot
4	8·00*	8	15·00*

Minor Constant Flaws

Cyl. 4 As for Nos. XS22/3

1s.6d., Type XS3 (1967–68)

1967 (MARCH 1). 1s.6d. WATERMARK CROWNS. TWO 9·5 mm. PHOSPHOR BANDS REACTING VIOLET

			Mint	Used
XS26 (=S.G.S6)	1s.6d.	Grey-blue	45	50

Cylinder Number (Block of Six)

Single pane cylinder. Perforation Type F (L) (I/E)

Cyl. No.	No dot
1	6·00

Minor Constant Flaw

Cyl. 1   1/11   Coloured spot in background to right of Queen's neck, below her hair (Th. E4)

Imprimatur from the National Postal Museum Archives

Imperforate, watermark Type W.24
Watermark upright

1968 (DECEMBER 12). 1s.6d. NO WATERMARK. CHALKY PAPER. PVA GUM. TWO 9·5 mm. PHOSPHOR BANDS REACTING VIOLET

			Mint	Used
XS27 (=S.G.S13)	1s.6d.	Grey-blue	1·75	1·50
	a.	Phosphor omitted	£125	

Cylinder Number (Block of Six)

Single pane cylinder. Perforation Type F (L) (I/E)

Cyl. No.	No dot
1	20·00

Minor Constant Flaw

As for No. XS26

Imprimatur from the National Postal Museum Archives

Chalky paper, imperforate
No watermark

Presentation Pack

XSPP1 (9.12.70)   Eight stamps   8·00
    Comprises Nos. XS8, 13/15, 17, 21, 25 and 27.

Quantity Sold   31,476

Withdrawn   25.11.71

First Day Covers

XSFC1	(1.3.67)	9d., 1s.6d.	6·00
XSFC2	(4.9.68)	4d., 5d.	3·00

F. Wales and Monmouthshire

XW1 **XW2** **XW3**

(Des. Reynolds Stone)

3d., Type XW1 (1958–67)

1958 (AUGUST 18). 3d. WATERMARK CROWNS

			Mint	Used
A. Cream Paper				
XW1	3d.	Deep lilac	70	35
	a.	Bulge on oval value tablet (Cyl. 1 No dot, R. 6/3) . .	4·50	
	b.	Wing-tail flaw (Cyl. 2 No dot, R. 16/1)	4·50	

B. Whiter Paper (30 April 1962)				
XW2 (=S.G.W1)	3d.	Deep lilac	15	15
	a.	Wing-tail flaw (Cyl. 2, No dot, R. 16/1)	4·00	

XW1*a*
Later retouched

XW1*b*, XW2*a*
White flaw joins spine
of dragon's wing to its tail

Cylinder Numbers (Blocks of Six)

Cream Paper (No. XW1)				Whiter Paper (No. XW2)			
Perforation Type A (E/I)				Perforation Type A (E/I)			
Cyl. No.		No dot	Dot	Cyl. No.		No dot	Dot
1	. . . .	32·00	32·00	2	. . . .	2·50	2·50
2	. . . .	9·00	9·00	3	. . . .	2·50	2·50

Minor Constant Flaws

Multipositive flaws
No dot 1/12 Small coloured flaw on dragon's neck (Th. F–G3)
    17/10 Known in three states:
        Cyl. 1 Two pale coloured dots on back of Queen's neck just below hair (Th. D4)
        Cyl. 2 Cylinder retouched to almost normal
        Cyl. 3 Cylinder retouched but still leaving one coloured dot on back of neck
Cyl. 1 15/7 White flaw in middle of central cross of diadem (Th. A3)
Cyl. 2 6/11 White spot on end of top horizontal bar of first E of REVENUE

Imprimatur from the National Postal Museum Archives

Cream paper. Imperforate, watermark Type W.24
Watermark upright

Quantity Sold 902,289,240

Sold Out 12.67

1967 (MAY 16). 3d. ONE CENTRE PHOSPHOR BAND REACTING VIOLET. WATER-MARK CROWNS

		Mint	Used
XW3 (=S.G.W1p)	3d. Deep lilac	20	15

Cylinder Numbers (Blocks of Six)
Perforation Type A (E/I)

Cyl. No.	No dot	Dot
3	3·00	3·00

Minor Constant Flaws

Multipositive flaws
No dot	1/12	Small coloured flaw on dragon's neck (Th. F–G3)
	17/10	Pale coloured dot on back of Queen's neck just below hair (Th. D4)
Cyl. 3	1/7	Coloured spot on oval frame line opposite R of REVENUE (Th. A5)
	1/8	Small coloured flaw just inside oval frame opposite G of POSTAGE (Th. E2)
	7/11	Small coloured flaw on Queen's collar (Th. E5)
	10/11	Small dot on leaf to right of final E of REVENUE (Th. E6)
	11/10	Small dot on leaf to left of second E of REVENUE (Th. C6)
Cyl. 3.	1/6	Small retouch to right of Queen's mouth (Th. D3)
	1/8	Retouch on Queen's cheek (Th. C–D4)
	3/5	Small dot on leaf above E of POSTAGE (Th. E1)
	3/9	Coloured flaw on Queen's neck just above collar (Th. E4)
	4/9	Coloured diagonal flaw in front of Queen's neck (Th. E3)
	5/9	Coloured spot inside lower loop of 3 of right-hand 3D
	8/1	Two white flaws on dragon's front left foot (Th. G–H2)
	10/2	Coloured spot on Queen's collar (Th. E4)
	11/6	Small retouch on back of Queen's collar (Th. E4–5)
	18/10	Retouch to background within oval to right of O of POSTAGE (Th. A–B2)
	18/11	Small dot on leaf to right of T of POSTAGE (Th. C1–2)
	20/6	Pale patch on Queen's shoulder (Th. E4)

Sold Out   1.68

1967 (DECEMBER 6). 3d. NO WATERMARK. CHALKY PAPER. ONE CENTRE PHOS-PHOR BAND REACTING VIOLET

		Mint	Used
XW4 (=S.G.W7)	3d. Deep lilac	20	10
	a. Phosphor omitted	50·00	

Cylinder Numbers (Blocks of Six)
Perforation Type F (L)*

Cyl. No.	No dot (I/E)	Dot (P/E)
3	3·00	3·00

Minor Constant Flaws

As for multipositive and cylinder flaws on No. XW3 with the addition of the following cylinder flaws:
Cyl. 3	5/9	Retouch on Queen's cheek (Th. D3–4)
Cyl. 3.	5/8	Retouch on Queen's chin (Th. D3)
	14/1	Retouch on Queen's cheek (Th. D4)
	20/5	Retouch on Queen's chin (Th. D3–4) and several dark spots on her forehead, cheek and neck

4d., Type XW1 (1966–69)

1966 (FEBRUARY 7). 4d. WATERMARK CROWNS

		Mint	Used
XW5 (=S.G.W2)	4d. Ultramarine	20	15

Cylinder Numbers (Blocks of Six)

Perforation Type A (E/I)

Cyl. No.	No dot	Dot
1	3·00	3·00

Quantity Sold   148,137,600

Sold Out   7.2.68

1967 (OCTOBER).   4d. TWO 9·5 mm. PHOSPHOR BANDS REACTING VIOLET. WATER-MARK CROWNS

				Mint	Used
XW6 (=S.G.W2p)	4d.	Ultramarine		20	15

Cylinder Numbers (Blocks of Six)

Perforation Type F (L)*

Cyl. No.	No dot (I/E)	Dot (P/E)
1	3·00	3·00

Sold Out   4.70

1968 (JUNE 21).   4d. NO WATERMARK. CHALKY PAPER. PVA GUM. TWO 9·5 mm. PHOSPHOR BANDS REACTING VIOLET

			Mint	Used
XW7 (=S.G.W8)	4d.	Ultramarine	20	10
	a.	White spot before "E" of "POSTAGE" (No dot, R. 17/12)	4·50	
	b.	White spot after "E" of "POSTAGE" (No dot, R. 18/10)	4·50	
	c.	Bump on dragon's head (No dot, R. 19/2)	4·50	
	d.	White spot above dragon's hind leg (No dot, R. 20/1)	4·50	

XW7a, XW8a
Later retouched on No. XW8

XW7b, XW8b
Later retouched on No. XW8

XW7c, XW8c,
XW9b

XW7d, XW8c
Retouched on No. XW9

Cylinder Numbers (Blocks of Six)

Perforation Type A (E/I)

Cyl. No.	No dot	Dot
2	6·00*	3·00

Minor Constant Flaws

Cyl. 2	6/9	Small dot on leaf to left of second E of REVENUE (Th. C6)
	12/6	Coloured flaw on Queen's left eye-brow (Th. C4)
	13/2	Small dot on leaf above U of REVENUE (Th. D6)
	18/5	Coloured spots over Queen's face and background
	20/12	Coloured flaw over D of left-hand 4D.
Cyl. 2.	1/6	Small dot on leaf above U of REVENUE (Th. D6)
	3/12	Small dot on leaf to left of N of REVENUE (Th. D6)
	4/3	Small dot on leaf to right of T of POSTAGE (Th. C1–2)
	4/6	White spot in background of oval frame opposite R of REVENUE (Th. A4)
	4/9	White spot on right-hand frame line by first E of REVENUE (Th. B6–7)
	7/2	Small dot on leaf to right of E of POSTAGE (Th. E2)
	7/11	Small coloured flaw in background of oval frame opposite VE of REVENUE (Th. C5)
	8/6	Small white flaw to right of dragon's left hind foot (Th. H5)
	11/7	Coloured spot in left-hand margin opposite P of POSTAGE (opposite Th. A1)
	12/2	Retouch on Queen's chin (Th. D3)
	12/6	White flaw over Queen's upper lip (Th. D3)
	16/10	Small coloured flaw on Queen's shoulder just above collar (Th. E4)

Sold Out 4.70

1968 (SEPTEMBER 4). 4d. CHANGE OF COLOUR. NO WATERMARK. CHALKY PAPER. PVA GUM. ONE CENTRE PHOSPHOR BAND REACTING VIOLET

			Mint	Used
XW8 (=S.G.W9)	4d.	Olive-sepia	20	10
	a.	White spot before "E" of "POSTAGE" (No dot, R. 17/12)	4·50	
	b.	White spot after "E" of "POSTAGE" (No dot, R. 18/10)	4·50	
	c.	Bump on dragon's head (No dot, R. 19/2)	4·50	
	d.	White spot above dragon's hind leg (No dot, R. 20/1)	4·50	

For illustrations of Nos. XW8a/d, see Nos. XW7a/d.

Note. Varieties XW8a/b were later retouched.

Cylinder Numbers (Blocks of Six)

Perforation Type A (E/I)

Cyl. No.	No dot	Dot
2	6·00*	3·00

Minor Constant Flaws

As for No. XW7

1969 (FEBRUARY 26). 4d. FURTHER CHANGE OF COLOUR. NO WATERMARK. CHALKY PAPER. PVA GUM. ONE CENTRE PHOSPHOR BAND REACTING VIOLET

			Mint	Used
XW9 (=S.G.W10)	4d.	Bright vermilion	20	20
	a.	Phosphor omitted	1·75	
	b.	Bump on dragon's head (No dot, R. 19/2)	4·50	

Cylinder Numbers (Blocks of Six)

Perforation Type A (E/I)

Cyl No.	No dot	Dot
2	6·00*	3·00

Minor Constant Flaws

Cyl. 2 As for flaws on No. XW7 except that flaw on R. 13/2 has been retouched
Cyl. 2. As for flaws on No. XW7 except that the following were retouched, R. 7/2, 8/6 and 12/6

5d., Type XW1 (1968)

1968 (SEPTEMBER 4). 5d. NO WATERMARK. CHALKY PAPER. PVA GUM. TWO 9·5 mm. PHOSPHOR BANDS REACTING VIOLET

			Mint	Used
XW10 (=S.G.W11)	5d.	Royal blue	20	10
	a.	Phosphor omitted	2·25	

Cylinder Numbers (Blocks of Six)

Perforation Type A (E/I)

Cyl. No.	No dot	Dot
2	3·00	3·00

Phosphor cylinder number: "Ph 1" found on cyl. 2 dot, right margin

Minor Constant Flaws

Cyl. 2 2/3 Coloured spot in background of oval frame just above central cross of diadem (Th. A3)
16/5 Coloured flaws in background of oval frame to left of Queen's nose (Th. C–D2)
20/4 White flaw on bottom frame line below dragon's left hind foot (Th. H4)

6d., Type XW2 (1958–62)

1958 (SEPTEMBER 29). 6d. WATERMARK CROWNS

A. Cream Paper

			Mint	Used
XW11	6d.	Deep claret	1·75	70

B. Whiter Paper (18 July 1962)

XW12 (=S.G.W3)	6d.	Reddish purple	35	30

Cylinder Numbers (Blocks of Six)

	Cream Paper (No. XW11)				Whiter Paper (No. XW12)		
Cyl. No.	(No dot)	Perf. Types		Cyl. No.	(No dot)	Perf. Types	
		B (I/P)	C (E/P)			B (I/P) C (E/P) F (L) (I/E)	
2		16·00	16·00	3		6·00 6·00 4·50	

Minor Constant Flaw

Cyl. 3 16/4 Coloured spot on dragon's tail (Th. F5)

Imprimatur from the National Postal Museum Archives

Cream paper. Imperforate, watermark Type W.24
Watermark upright

Quantity Sold 66,754,200

Sold Out 3.68

9d., Type XW2 (1967)

1967 (MARCH 1). 9d. WATERMARK CROWNS. TWO 9·5 mm. PHOSPHOR BANDS REACTING VIOLET

			Mint	Used
XW13 (=S.G.W4)	9d.	Bronze-green	40	35
	a.	Phosphor omitted	£350	

Cylinder Number (Block of Six)

Single pane cylinder. Perforation Type F (L) (I/E)

Cyl. No.	No dot
1	4·50

Imprimatur from the National Postal Museum Archives

Imperforate, watermark Type W.24
Watermark upright

1s.3d., Type XW3 (1958–64)

1958 (SEPTEMBER 29). 1s.3d. WATERMARK CROWNS

				Mint	Used
A. Cream Paper					
XW14	1s.3d.		Green	5·00	1·75
B. Whiter Paper (11 May 1964)					
XW15 (=S.G.W5)	1s.3d.	(1)	Myrtle-green	5·00	90
		(2)	Deep dull green	40	40
		(3)	Deep myrtle-green	2·00	75

Cylinder Numbers (Blocks of Six)

Cream Paper (No. XW14)			Whiter Paper (No. XW15)	
Cyl. No. (No dot)	Perf. Types B (I/P)	C (E/P)	Cyl. No. (No dot)	Perf. Type F (L)(I/E)
2 . . . . 45·00		45·00	2 . . . . 10·00	
			3 . . . . 4·75	

Imprimatur from the National Postal Museum Archives

Cream paper. Imperforate, watermark Type W.24
Watermark upright

Sold Out 7.70.

1s.6d., Type XW3 (1967–69)

1967 (MARCH 1). 1s.6d. WATERMARK CROWNS. TWO 9·5 mm. PHOSPHOR BANDS REACTING VIOLET

			Mint	Used
XW16 (=S.G.W6)	1s.6d.	Grey-blue	40	40
	a.	Phosphor omitted	50·00	

Cylinder Number (Block of Six)

Single pane cylinder. Perforation Type F (L) (I/E)

Cyl. No.	No dot
1	4·75

Minor Constant Flaws

Cyl. 1   3/11 Small dot in top of left fork of V of REVENUE
       6/7 Coloured flaw in base of second E of REVENUE
      10/1 Small dot on upper right-hand leaf of leek (Th. F6)
      10/3 Small coloured flaw on Queen's neck (Th. D4)
      15/9 Retouch on Queen's shoulder just above collar (Th. E4)

Imprimatur from the National Postal Museum Archives

Imperforate, watermark Type W.24
Watermark upright

1969 (AUGUST 1). 1s.6d. NO WATERMARK. CHALKY PAPER. PVA GUM. TWO 9·5 mm. PHOSPHOR BANDS REACTING VIOLET

		Mint	Used
XW17 (=S.G.W12) 1s.6d. Grey-blue		3·50	3·50

Cylinder Number (Block of Six)

Single pane cylinder. Perforation Type F (L) (1/E)

Cyl. No.	No dot
1	40·00

Minor Constant Flaws

As for No. XW16

Imprimatur from the National Postal Museum Archives

Chalky paper, imperforate
No watermark

Presentation Pack

XWPP1 (9.12.70)		
Comprises Nos. XW4, 8/10, 13 and 16.	Six stamps	4·00

Quantity Sold   32,964

Withdrawn   25.11.71

First Day Covers

XWFC1	(1.3.67)	9d., 1s.6d.	4·00
XWFC2	(4.9.68)	4d., 5d.	3·00

Presentation Pack (Six Regions)

XPP1 (issued 1960)	Twelve values	£100

The issued pack contained one each of the ordinary 3d., 6d. and 1s.3d. stamps from Northern Ireland, Scotland and Wales and Monmouthshire and one each of the ordinary 3d. stamps from Guernsey, Jersey and the Isle of Man together with 6-page printed leaflet describing the stamps.
Two forms of the pack exist:
(a) Inscribed "7s. 3d." for sale in the U.K. and
(b) Inscribed "$1.20" for sale in the U.S.A.

SECTION ZA
Postage Due Stamps
1954–69 (Typographed) and 1968–1971 (Photogravure)

General Notes

INTRODUCTION. These stamps generally fulfilled two functions: the lower values, inscribed "POSTAGE DUE", were affixed to understamped and unstamped correspondence by the Post Office, to indicate to the postman and to the addressee the amount which was to be collected on delivery (usually twice the excess). The higher values, inscribed "TO PAY", were affixed to mail from abroad for the collection of customs charges. The same basic stamp design was in continual use from 1914 until 1971.

PRINTERS. All the Postage Due stamps were typographed by Harrison & Sons with the exception of the 4d. and 8d. values of 1969 and 1968 respectively which were printed in photogravure.

They were printed on sheet-fed machines in single panes of 240 each arranged in twelve rows of twenty stamps and this applies to both printing processes.

PAPER. As with the Wilding definitives, for about the first ten years the Postage Due stamps were printed on a creamy paper but starting in 1964 a whiter paper was gradually introduced as new printings were made. See the General Notes for Section S for further information. Exceptionally, the 2s.6d. to £1 values were always printed on a yellow paper which did not change its appearance.

From 1968 unwatermarked chalk-surfaced paper, as used for the Machin definitives, was introduced for a number of values.

WATERMARKS. These were used as follows:

W.22 Tudor Crown		Nos. Z1/6 (1954–55)
W.23 St. Edward's Crown		Nos. Z7/16 (1955–57)
W.24 Crowns		Nos. Z17/37 (1959–64)
No watermark		No. Z38 onwards (1968–69)

See the General Notes for Section S for illustrations of these.

The watermarks are *always* sideways and *when seen from the front of the stamp* the normal watermark has the top of the Crowns pointing to left. In cases where the sheets were fed into the press the wrong way round (sideways inverted), the watermark appears as sideways with the Crowns pointing to right *when seen from the front of the stamp.*

GUM. This was used as follows:

Gum Arabic	Nos. Z1/39 (1954–68)
PVA Gum	No. Z40 onwards (1968–69)

The distinction between gum arabic and PVA gum is explained in the General Notes relating to Section UA.

PERFORATION. All values are comb perforated 14 × 15. The perforation types used are given following each issue, and are described and illustrated in Appendix G. In the photogravure-printed values the cylinder numbers are listed and priced according to the type of perforator used. The typographed issues do not have plate numbers.

DATE OF ISSUE. The dates given are those on which the stamps were first issued by the Supplies Dept. to postmasters except in the case of dates for changes to chalky paper or to PVA gum when we have usually quoted dates of release by the Philatelic Bureaux.

SHEET MARKINGS. Compared with other stamps the Postage Due stamps show very few markings.

Cylinder Numbers. These only occur on the photogravure-printed stamps, opposite Row 11 No. 1 (4d.) or opposite Row 10 No. 1 (8d.). They are similar in style to the illustration in Section S.

Marginal Arrows. These are "W" shaped at top and bottom of the sheet only. They appear solid (typographed issues) or photo-etched (photogravure issues) as illustrated in Section S.

Marginal Rule. This occurs on all four sheet margins in the typographed issues only. It is similar in style to the "Narrow Rule" illustration in Section S. In the 1½d., 6d., 5s., 10s. and £1 values an additional 1 mm. square appears at each corner of the sheet thus giving a neater appearance.

"Morse Code" marking   Cross

Other Markings. On the typographed issues "Morse Code" markings as illustrated appear opposite rows 6/7 at both sides of the sheet. These are possibly allied to the way in which the printing plate is fixed to the press.

In photogravure issues the "Morse Code" markings are replaced by a cross as illustrated. These are often trimmed off.

WATERMARK. The normal sideways watermark *when seen from the front of the stamp* has the top of the Crowns pointing to left.

Z1. "POSTAGE DUE"   Z2. "TO PAY"

1954–55. TYPE Z1 AND Z2 (2s.6d.). TYPOGRAPHED. WATERMARK TUDOR CROWN, TYPE W.22, SIDEWAYS

				Mint	Used
Z1 (=S.G.D40)	**Z1**	½d.	Bright Orange (8.6.55)	4·75	5·25
		a.	Wmk. Crown to right	12·00	
Z2 (=S.G.D41)	**Z1**	2d.	Agate (28.7.55)	22·00	18·00
		a.	Wmk. Crown to right		
Z3 (=S.G.D42)	**Z1**	3d.	Violet (4.5.55)	62·00	52·00
Z4 (=S.G.D43)	**Z1**	4d.	Blue (14.7.55)	26·00	26·00
		a.	Imperf. (pair)	£250	
Z5 (=S.G.D44)	**Z1**	5d.	Yellow-brown (19.5.55)	20·00	15·50
Z6 (=S.G.D45)	**Z2**	2s.6d.	Purple/*yellow* (–.11.54)	£135	5·75
		a.	Wmk. Crown to right		

Perforation Type

Type A, all values

Imprimaturs from the National Postal Museum Archives

Imperforate, watermark Type W.22 (sideways)
½d., 2d., 3d., 4d., 5d.
Perf. 14 × 15, watermark Type W.22 (sideways)
2s.6d.

1955–57. TYPE Z1 AND Z2 (2s.6d., 5s.). TYPOGRAPHED, WATERMARK ST. EDWARD'S CROWN, TYPE W.23, SIDEWAYS

				Mint	Used
Z7 (=S.G.D46)	**Z1**	½d.	Orange (16.7.56)	2·75	3·25
		a.	Wmk. Crown to right	12·00	
Z8 (=S.G.D47)	**Z1**	1d.	Violet-blue (7.6.56)	5·00	1·50
Z9 (=S.G.D48)	**Z1**	1½d.	Green (13.2.56)	8·50	7·00
		a.	Wmk. Crown to right	15·00	
		b.	Stop after "THREE" (Row 1)	15·00	
Z10 (=S.G.D49)	**Z1**	2d.	Agate (22.5.56)	45·00	3·50
Z11 (=S.G.D50)	**Z1**	3d.	Violet (5.3.56)	6·00	1·50
		a.	Wmk. Crown to right	30·00	
Z12 (=S.G.D51)	**Z1**	4d.	Blue (24.4.56)	25·00	6·00
		a.	Wmk. Crown to right	35·00	
Z13 (=S.G.D52)	**Z1**	5d.	Brown-ochre (23.3.56)	26·00	20·00
Z14 (=S.G.D53)	**Z1**	1s.	Ochre (22.11.55)	65·00	2·25
		a.	Wmk. Crown to right		
Z15 (=S.G.D54)	**Z2**	2s.6d.	Purple/yellow (28.6.57)	£200	8·25
		a.	Wmk. Crown to right		
Z16 (=S.G.D55)	**Z2**	5s.	Scarlet/yellow (25.11.55)	£150	32·00
		a.	Wmk. Crown to right		

Stamps from the above issue are known bisected and used for half their face value at the following sorting offices:

1d. Huddersfield (1956), London S.E.D.O. (1957), Beswick, Manchester (1958)
2d. Eynsham, Oxford (1956), Garelochhead, Helensburgh (1956), Harpenden (1956), Hull (1956), Kingston on Thames (1956), Leicester Square, London W.C. (1956), London W.C. (1956)
3d. London S.E. (1957)
4d. Poplar, London E. (1958)

Stop after "THREE". Occurs on most stamps in row 1

Z9b Z19a

Perforation Types

Type A, all values, except that in the case of the 5s. the left-hand sheet margin is perforated through, possibly due to the use of a wider comb-head

Imprimaturs from the National Postal Museum Archives

Imperforate, watermark Type W.23 (sideways)
½d., 1d., 1½d., 2d., 3d., 4d., 5d., 1s., 2s.6d., 5s.

1959–70. TYPE Z1 AND Z2 (2s.6d. to £1). TYPOGRAPHED. WATERMARK CROWNS, TYPE W.24, SIDEWAYS

A. Cream Paper

				Mint	Used
Z17	**Z1**	½d.	Orange (18.10.61)	50	80
Z18	**Z1**	1d.	Violet-blue (9.5.60)	50	20
Z19 (=S.G.D58)	**Z1**	1½d.	Green (5.10.60)	2·50	2·50
		a.	Stop after "THREE" (Row 1)	10·00	

Z20	**Z1**	2d.	Agate (14.9.59)	2·75	1·00
Z21	**Z1**	3d.	Violet (24.3.59)	75	25
Z22	**Z1**	4d.	Blue (17.12.59)	75	30
Z23	**Z1**	5d.	Yellow-brown (6.11.61)	90	70
		a.	Wmk. Crown to right	28·00	
Z24	**Z1**	6d.	Purple (29.3.62)	1·00	1·25
Z25	**Z1**	1s.	Ochre (11.4.60)	3·00	50
Z26 (=S.G.D65)	**Z2**	2s.6d.	Purple/*yellow* (11.5.61)	3·00	50
		a.	Wmk. Crown to right	9·00	
Z27 (=S.G.D66)	**Z2**	5s.	Scarlet/*yellow* (8.5.61)	8·25	1·00
		a.	Wmk. Crown to right	15·00	
Z28 (=S.G.D67)	**Z2**	10s.	Blue/*yellow* (2.9.63)	11·00	5·75
		a.	Wmk. Crown to right (4.70)	35·00	
Z29 (=S.G.D68)	**Z2**	£1	Black/*yellow* (2.9.63)	45·00	8·25

Whilst the 2s.6d. and 5s. already existed with watermark Crown to right further printings were issued in 1970, as also of the 10s., on highly fluorescent paper and with watermark Crown to right. These can only be distinguished by the use of a. u.v. lamp and so are not listed separately.

B. Whiter Paper

Z30 (=S.G.D56)	**Z1**	½d.	Orange (22.9.64)	10	1·25
		a.	Wmk. Crown to right	2·00	
Z31 (=S.G.D57)	**Z1**	1d.	Violet-blue (1.3.65)	15	50
		a.	Wmk. Crown to right	16·00	
Z32 (=S.G.D59)	**Z1**	2d.	Agate (1.3.65)	1·10	50
		a.	Wmk. Crown to right	50·00	
Z33 (=S.G.D60)	**Z1**	3d.	Violet (1.6.64)	30	30
		a.	Wmk. Crown to right	12·00	
Z34 (=S.G.D61)	**Z1**	4d.	Blue (3.3.64)	30	30
		a.	Wmk. Crown to right	35·00	
Z35 (=S.G.D62)	**Z1**	5d.	Yellow-brown (9.6.64)	45	60
		a.	Wmk. Crown to right	5·00	
Z36 (=S.G.D63)	**Z1**	6d.	Purple (30.1.64)	50	30
		a.	Wmk. Crown to right	45·00	
Z37 (=S.G.D64)	**Z1**	1s.	Ochre (28.8.64)	90	30
		a.	Wmk. Crown to right	10·00	

Stamps from the above issue are known bisected and used for half their face value at the following sorting offices:

1d. Chieveley, Newbury (December 1962, March 1963), Henlan, Llandyssil (1961), Mayfield (1962), St. Albans (1964)

2d. Doncaster (?)

For illustration of No. Z19*a*, see No. Z9*b*.

Perforation Types

Type A, all values; 2s.6d. also Type A (T)

Imprimaturs from the National Postal Museum Archives

Imperforate, watermark Type W.24 (sideways)
Cream paper
½d., 1d., 1½d., 2d., 3d., 4d., 5d., 6d., 1s., 2s.6d., 5s., 10s., £1

Sold Out 1s. 11.68; 2d. 1.69; 4d. 11.69; 3d. 9.71; 6d. 10.71

Withdrawn. The 1½d. was withdrawn from sale to the public on 26.4.65. It had ceased to be issued on 31.1.65 but post offices continued to use existing stocks until exhausted.

1968–69. TYPE Z1. TYPOGRAPHED. NO WATERMARK. CHALKY PAPER

				Mint	Used
A. Gum Arabic					
Z38 (=S.G.D69)	**Z1**	2d.	Agate (11.4.68)	75	1·00
Z39 (=S.G.D71)	**Z1**	4d.	Blue (25.4.68)	1·00	1·00
B. PVA Gum					
Z40 (=S.G.D69Ev)	**Z1**	2d.	Agate (26.11.68)	75	
Z41 (=S.G.D70)	**Z1**	3d.	Violet (5.9.68)	1·00	1·00
Z42 (=S.G.D71Ev)	**Z1**	4d.	Blue (See footnote)	£1500	
Z43 (=S.G.D72)	**Z1**	5d.	Orange-brown (3.1.69)	8·00	11·00
Z44 (=S.G.D73)	**Z1**	6d.	Purple (5.9.68)	2·25	1·75
Z45 (=S.G.D74)	**Z1**	1s.	Ochre (19.11.68)	4·00	2·50

A copy of No. Z42 has been confirmed using infra-red attenuated total reflection spectroscopy, there is no date of issue.

Perforation Types

4d., 6d. Type A (T); other values Type A (T), except that in the case of the 2d. the right-hand sheet margin is perforated through and in the 4d. the left-hand sheet margin is perforated through, both possibly due to the use of a wider comb-head

1968–69. TYPE Z1. SMALLER FORMAT. 21½ × 17½ mm. PHOTOGRAVURE. NO WATERMARK. CHALKY PAPER. PVA GUM

				Mint	Used
Z46 (=S.G.D75)	**Z1**	4d.	Blue (12.6.69)	7·00	6·75
Z47 (=S.G.D76)	**Z1**	8d.	Red (3.10.68)	50	1·00

Cylinder Numbers (Block of Four (4d.) or Six (8d.))

Perforation Type A (T) (E/P)

	Cyl. No.	No dot
4d.	1	. . . . 35·00
8d.	1	. . . . 5·00

On the 8d. the cylinder number appears as "I".

Imprimaturs from the National Postal Museum Archives

Chalky paper, imperforate. No watermark
2d., 3d., 4d., 5d., 6d., 8d., 1s.
Stamps from the above issue are known bisected and used for half their face value at the following sorting offices:
4d.   Northampton (1970)
6d.   Kilburn, London N.W. (1968)

APPENDIX G
Perforators

General Notes

INTRODUCTION. Basically, two kinds of perforating machines were used for British stamps listed in this catalogue, 1952–70: sheet-fed and reel-fed. The sheet-fed machines generally employ a two-row comb and the reel-fed machines a three-row comb. Both kinds are full width, i.e. they are able to perforate two panes side by side.

Types A to H and J are the different *sheet perforation types* recorded in this catalogue, produced either by the sheet-fed or the reel-fed machines but they should not be regarded as representing the use of ten different machines, rather they are ten different sheet perforation types produced by various perforating machines.

Types E, E ($\frac{1}{2}$v) (from sheets), I, I ($\frac{1}{2}$v), AP and P relate to booklet panes.

GUIDE HOLES. Perforation guide holes can be an indication of the type of perforator used and these are recorded, where known, following the sheet perforation characteristics for each type. For reasons unknown these may not always appear in the sheet margins.

ORDER. This Appendix is divided into four sections:
1. Low Value Definitive Stamps (including Regionals and Postage Due Stamps)
2. High Value Definitive Stamps
3. Special Issues
4. Booklet Panes

ILLUSTRATIONS. The illustrations are all from definitive stamps but they are equally representative of the High Value and Special issues where the same types occur.

TABLE OF PERFORATION TYPES. The useful tabulated list of Perforation Types at the end of this Appendix is primarily designed to be used for Special issues, although, the first part may also be used in conjunction with the Low and High Value definitive stamps for Types A, A (T), B, C, E (no dot panes only).

1. Low Value Definitive Stamps

This section deals with the small size Wilding and Machin definitives, the Regionals and the Postage Due Stamps.

Type A. Horizontal two-row comb. Sheet-fed.

No dot and dot panes—		
	Top margin	Perforated through
	Bottom margin	Imperforate
	Left margin	A single extension hole
	Right margin	A single extension hole
	Guide holes	Opposite rows 14/15, at left (no dot panes) or right (dot panes)

In this machine an appropriate number of sheets (usually six to eight) are impaled through the guide holes and they go forward together under the comb. The imperf. margin (at the bottom) indicates the point of entry.

Type A (T). Horizontal two-row comb. Sheet-fed.

Single pane printing—		
	Top margin	Imperforate
	Bottom margin	Perforated through
	Left margin	A single extension hole
	Right margin	A single extension hole
	Guide holes	None

This is simply a top (T) instead of a bottom feed of Type A. In the definitive stamps it only occurs in the Postage Due Stamps. Cylinder blocks are identical in appearance with Type C.

Types B and C. Horizontal three-row comb. Reel-fed.

Type B. No dot panes—	Top margin	Perforated through
	Bottom margin	Perforated through
	Left margin	Imperforate
	Right margin	A single extension hole
	Guide holes	Usually opposite rows 1, 7/8 and 14/15 at both sides of pane

Type C. No dot and dot panes—	Top margin	Perforated through
	Bottom margin	Perforated through
	Left margin	A single extension hole
	Right margin	Imperforate
	Guide holes	As Type B, above

Type B is the left and Type C the right halves of the same reel-fed perforator. The outer ends of the comb are without extension pins, there being only single extension pins in the interpane margin. In this machine the continuous web of paper advances under the comb in a single thickness and without interruption, hence both top and bottom margins are perforated through.

It often happened that two narrow reels were perforated together by placing them side by side on the machine so that single pane printings (i.e. no dot panes only) occur perforated with Type B and also Type C. It is only when double pane printings are perforated on this machine that no dot panes will always be Type B and dot panes will always be Type C, except that in the Special issues, the 4d. Scout Jamboree stamp from Cyl. 1 dot is known with perforation Type B and Type C.

Type E. Horizontal two-row comb. Sheet-fed.

No dot panes—	Top margin	Perforated through
	Bottom margin	Imperforate
	Left margin	A single extension hole on alternate rows only
	Right margin	A single extension hole
	Guide hole	Opposite rows 14/15, at left

Dot panes—	Top margin	Perforated through
	Bottom margin	Imperforate
	Left margin	A single extension hole
	Right margin	A single extension hole on alternate rows only
	Guide hole	Opposite rows 14/15, at right

This is a simple variation of Type A (*q.v.*) that may result from the removal of a perforating pin or a repair to a comb-head. Therefore, no dot cylinder blocks are as Type A but left margin has the single extension hole missing on alternate rows.

Cylinder blocks from the dot pane would be indistinguishable from Type A, hence only no dot cylinder blocks are recorded with Type E.

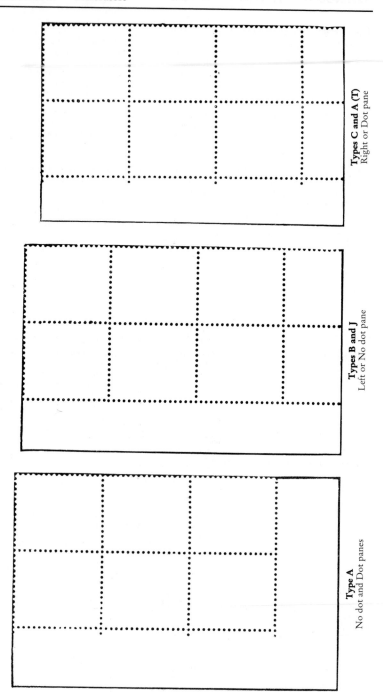

Types C and A (T)
Right or Dot pane

Types B and J
Left or No dot pane

Type A
No dot and Dot panes

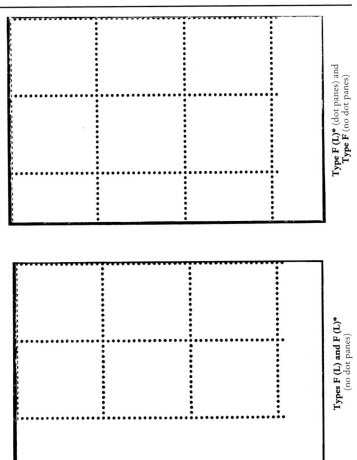

Type F (L). Vertical two-row comb. Sheet-fed.

No dot panes—	Top margin	A single extension hole
	Bottom margin	A single extension hole
	Left margin	Imperforate
	Right margin	Perforated through
	Guide holes	Through marginal arrow above vertical rows 6/7 and below vertical row 10

This type perforates from the left (L) through to the right side of the sheet. In this catalogue the use of this type has been restricted to single pane printings (i.e. no dot panes only).

Type F (L)*. Vertical two-row comb. Sheet-fed.

No dot panes—	Top margin	A single extension hole
	Bottom margin	A single extension hole
	Left margin	Imperforate
	Right margin	Perforated through
	Guide holes	Above and below eighth vertical row

Type F(L)* Contd.

Dot panes—

Top margin	A single extension hole
Bottom margin	A single extension hole
Left margin	Perforated through
Right margin	Perforated through
Guide holes	None (occur on no dot panes *only*)

This is the same perforator as used for Type F (L) and it is given in this catalogue when double pane printings (i.e. no dot and dot panes) have been perforated together prior to their being guillotined into single sheets. This gives no dot cylinder blocks exactly as Type F (L) but because the vertical comb has perforated horizontally from left to right across *both* panes the interpane margin is also perforated and, therefore, the dot cylinder blocks are perforated through the left margin.

Type H. Horizontal two-row comb. Sheet-fed.

No dot panes—

Top margin	Perforated through
Bottom margin	Imperforate
Left margin	A single extension hole
Right margin	Perforated through
Guide hole	Opposite rows 14/15, at left

Dot panes—

Top margin	Perforated through
Bottom margin	Imperforate
Left margin	Perforated through
Right margin	A single extension hole
Guide hole	Opposite rows 14/15, at right

This is a further variation of Type A (*q.v.*) differing by the fact that the interpane margin is perforated through instead of there being single extension holes at the end of every row at right on the no dot pane and at the end of every row at left on the dot pane. Therefore, dot cylinder blocks are as Type A but left margin is perforated through. Cylinder blocks from the no dot pane would be indistinguishable from Type A, hence only dot cylinder blocks are recorded with Type H.

Type J. Vertical two-row comb. Sheet-fed.

Single pane printing—

Top margin	A single extension hole
Bottom margin	Perforated through
Left margin	Imperforate
Right margin	Perforated through
Guide holes	Through marginal arrow above vertical rows 6/7 and below vertical row 10

This is similar to Type F (L) (*q.v.*), except that the bottom sheet margin is perforated through instead of there being only a single extension hole at the end of every row. Cylinder blocks are identical in appearance with Type B.

2. High Value Definitive Stamps

This section deals with the Wilding and Machin High Value stamps.

Wilding High Values

Perforation Type A, as described at the beginning of this Appendix, was used exclusively for these stamps. Waterlow and De La Rue both used a single-row comb and Bradbury, Wilkinson a two-row comb.

The guide holes appear opposite row 6, at left on left-hand panes and at right on right-hand panes. For diagram showing printer's guide marks see the General Notes for Section T.

Machin £.s.d. High Values

The printer's sheet was perforated with Type A prior to being guillotined into four panes, so that the characteristics of each individual Post Office pane are different and this has, therefore, been described as perforation Type A*. The description of Type A, given at the beginning of this Appendix, applies equally to Type A*, except that Bradbury, Wilkinson used a single-row comb.

For diagram showing the printer's sheet, the method of perforation and the position of plate numbers and guide holes see the General Notes for Section UC.

3. Special Issues

Type A. In the special issues this type is exactly as described at the beginning of this Appendix except that with single pane printings (i.e. no dot panes only) the guide holes are opposite rows 14/15, at both sides of the sheet.

Type A (T). In the special issues this type is exactly as described at the beginning of this Appendix and it applies equally to both no dot and dot panes. Guide holes very rarely appear in the sheet margins but where they do this is given under "Sheet Details" in Section W.

Type B and C. In the special issues these types are exactly as described in the first part of this Appendix.

Type E. Horizontal two-row comb. Sheet-fed.

Right-hand panes—		
	Top margin	Perforated through
	Bottom margin	Imperforate
	Left margin	A single extension hole on alternate rows only
	Right margin	A single extension hole
	Guide hole	Opposite rows 14/15, at right

This is a variation of Type A that may result from the removal of a perforating pin or a repair to a comb-head. Therefore, cylinder blocks are as Type A but left margin has the single extension hole missing on alternate rows.

This type is only known on the 1s.3d. Freedom from Hunger and the 3d. Red Cross on the right-hand panes only (i.e. dot cylinder pane of 3d. Red Cross). The left-hand panes in both cases are believed to be Type A.

Perforation Type E did not affect the cylinder blocks of the 1s.3d. Freedom from Hunger issue as the cylinder numbers were placed at bottom right corner of each pane, at the opposite side of the left margin perforated with alternate extension holes.

Types F and F (L). Vertical single-row comb. Sheet-fed.

Single pane printings.

Type F. Right feed—		
	Top margin	A single extension hole
	Bottom margin	A single extension hole
	Left margin	Perforated through
	Right margin	Imperforate
Type F (L). Left feed—		
	Top margin	A single extension hole
	Bottom margin	A single extension hole
	Left margin	Imperforate
	Right margin	Perforated through

Type F perforates from the right through to the left side of the sheet and Type F (L) perforates from the left through to the right side of the sheet. Both types are used for single pane printings (i.e. no dot panes only). Guide holes very rarely appear in the sheet margins but where they do this is given under "Sheet Details" in Section W.

Type G. Vertical single-row comb. Sheet-fed.

No dot and dot panes—		
	Top margin	Perforated through
	Bottom margin	Perforated through
	Left margin	Perforated through
	Right margin	Imperforate
	Guide holes	None

This was a special perforator used exclusively for the 6d. Battle of Hastings issue. The cylinder block is perforated through in both the bottom and left margins.

TABLE OF SPECIAL ISSUE PERFORATION TYPES

The table below combines a list of the different *sheet perforation types* recorded in Section W, together with the characteristics of the four sheet margins. Following the basic perforation type the characteristics given relate to the sheet viewed with the stamps the right way up.

The identification of a particular perforation type from a cylinder block (or any corner block) can easily be established by referring to this table in conjunction with the recorded types under "Cylinder Numbers" in Section W.

Whilst this table is mainly designed to be used for the special stamps, the first part may also be used in conjunction with the Low and High Value definitive stamps for Types A, A (T), B, C, E (no dot panes only) and F (L).

I. HORIZONTAL FORMAT STAMPS

Perforation Type	Top margin	Bottom margin	Left margin	Right margin
Type A (*bottom feed*)	Perforated through	Imperforate	Single extension hole	Single extension hole
Type A (T) (*top feed*)	Imperforate	Perforated through	Single extension hole	Single extension hole
Type B	Perforated through	Perforated through	Imperforate	Single extension hole
Type C	Perforated through	Perforated through	Single extension hole	Imperforate
Type E	Perforated through	Imperforate	Single extension hole alternate rows only	Single extension hole
Type F (*right feed*)	Single extension hole	Single extension hole	Perforated through	Imperforate
Type F (L) (*left feed*)	Single extension hole	Single extension hole	Imperforate	Perforated through
Type G	Perforated through	Perforated through	Perforated through	Imperforate

II. VERTICAL FORMAT STAMPS*

Perforation Type	Top margin	Bottom margin	Left margin	Right margin
Type A (*head to right*)	Single extension hole	Single extension hole	Perforated through	Imperforate
Type A (*head to left*)	Single extension hole	Single extension hole	Imperforate	Perforated through
Type A (T) (*head to right*)	Single extension hole	Single extension hole	Imperforate	Perforated through
Type A (T) (*head to left*)	Single extension hole	Single extension hole	Perforated through	Imperforate
Type B (*head to right*)	Single extension hole	Imperforate	Perforated through	Perforated through
Type C (*head to right*)	Imperforate	Single extension hole	Perforated through	Perforated through
Type F (*head to right*)	Imperforate	Perforated through	Single extension hole	Single extension hole

*The position of the head on vertical format stamps is determined by viewing the sheet with the marginal rule (normally on a short side) at the bottom. In most instances the head (or top of the stamp) is to the right; the head to the left occurring on the 3d. Post Office Tower, 4d. World Football Cup, 4d. World Cup Victory and the 3d. and 1s.6d. 1966 Christmas issue, although the latter does not in fact bear marginal rules and it should be regarded as being "head to left".

From the 1966 Christmas issue onwards many sheets did not bear marginal rules. Where this is the case with vertical format designs the correct orientation of the sheets to determine the perforation type is given below the "Cylinder Numbers" in the listings.

Exceptionally, the 1967 British Paintings 4d. and the British Discovery and Inventions 1s.9d. show the marginal rule on a *long* side and this should be orientated to the left-hand side to show perforation Types A (T) (head to right) and F (head to right) respectively.

4. Booklet Panes

(a) Panes of Four

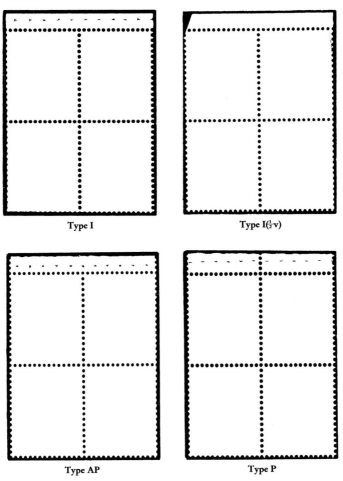

Type I	Type I($\frac{1}{2}$v)
Type AP	Type P

Type I.   Margin imperforate

Type I($\frac{1}{2}$v).   Ditto but with slanting cut at left or right (left illustrated)

Type AP.   Margin perforated through but alternate rows imperforate

Type P.   Margin fully perforated through

In order to facilitate access to the bottom selvedge, which has to be torn off by hand, a slanting scissor cut is made in the trimmed margin. This pane is termed "I($\frac{1}{2}$v)". The vertical perforations below the cut should have been torn, and not guillotined, apart.

Panes of four from the Wilding series on Crowns watermark paper exist as Type AP, but with only two extension holes at each side of the binding margin. It is believed that this was caused by a perforator with a pin missing from the bottom line of the comb.

(b) Panes of Six

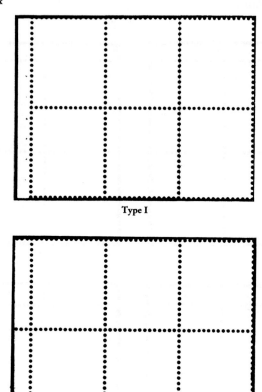

Type I

Type P

Type I. Margin imperforate

Type P. Margin fully perforated through

All panes of six are perforated Type I except for UB3 which also exists Type P and UB4 which only exists Type P.

Both the 20-row and the 21-row cylinders perforated with Type I come with pairs of extension holes in the margin between the no dot and dot panes. The 20-row cylinders were perforated with a three-line comb, so that panes can be found with traces of the inter-pane extension hole at the top, in the middle or at the bottom of the binding margin. After the change to 21-row cylinders a four-row comb was used, and on these panes the extension hole can be found at the top or at the bottom of the margin. We do not distinguish these sub-types of perforation.

On 21-row cylinders the perforated web is cut at every 20th row to make sheets of 480 (two panes of 240 (12 × 20)). Consequently on successive sheets the cylinder number appears one row lower so that a pane can have it adjoining the top or bottom row. In the listing of cylinder blocks for stamps from the 4s.6d., 5s., 6s., and 10s. booklets the letter "T" after the cylinder number indicates that it is a pane with the cylinder number adjoining the top row.

(c) Panes of Fifteen

These come from the £1 "Stamps for Cooks" booklet and are all perforated Type I.

(d) Panes of Two

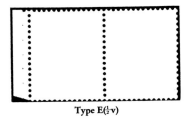

Type E($\frac{1}{2}$v)

Type E.   Extension hole in the margin in each row

Type E($\frac{1}{2}$v).   Ditto but with slanting cut

Type I.   Margin imperforate

Type I($\frac{1}{2}$v).   Ditto but with slanting cut

The panes of two stamps were made up from vertical rows 1 and 2 from sheets. The horizontal sheet margin was removed leaving a narrow vertical binding margin which was either imperforate or showed an extension hole at the top and bottom of the binding margin. In addition, both types exist with the slanting scissor cut already described under section (a) of these notes. Panes with this form of separation should show torn and not guillotined perforations below the cut. The stamps were separated towards the slanting cut ensuring that the binding margin would remain intact.

APPENDIX HA
Post Office Booklets of Stamps

General Notes

This appendix is divided into the following sections:

A. Wilding Issues in Non-pictorial Types of Booklet Covers (1953–68)

B. Machin Pre-decimal Issues with Violet Phosphor Bands. Non-pictorial and Pictorial Covers (1968–70)

The booklets are listed in value order except for the 2 shilling booklets for Holiday Resorts (1963/64) and Christmas Cards (1965) which follow the ordinary 2s. booklets The £1 booklet "Stamps for Cooks" containing Machin issues is at the end of the section. All booklets, except No. ZP1 which was stapled, had stitched panes. Some of the £1 booklets were stitched and these are listed under No. ZP1a.

BOOKLET SHEET ARRANGEMENT. Booklets are made up from specially printed sheets which are differently arranged from normal Post Office sheets in order to facilitate economic manufacture. The arrangement of the sheet varies according to the size and format of the booklet pane required. For example, in the case of booklet panes of six, the printer's sheet of 480 stamps, consisting of two panes (no dot and dot) each of 240 stamps arranged in twenty rows of twelve stamps, has additional gutters provided between the 6th and 7th vertical rows in both panes, and the stamps in the 4th, 5th and 6th, and 10th, 11th and 12th vertical rows in both panes are inverted in relation to the others (i.e. tête-bêche). Two horizontal rows of the sheet (producing eight booklets) would be arranged thus:

	No dot pane		Dot pane	
↑	12395Þ	GUTTER 12395Þ	GUTTER 12395Þ	GUTTER 12395Þ	←
Watermark	456£ZI	456£ZI	456£ZI	456£ZI	←
	↑ ↑ ↑ ↑ ↑ ↑ ↑

The sheets of stamps, interleaving sheets and covers are stitched vertically, once at the two outer edges of the double pane and twice in each of the gutters as shown by the vertical rules in the diagram. Finally, the booklets are guillotined both horizontally and vertically as indicated by the arrows.

INVERTED WATERMARKS. From the diagram it is easy to see how 50% of Wilding booklets have stamps with inverted watermarks.

WATERMARK POSITIONS. Although 50% of booklet panes have the watermark inverted, in describing the contents of the booklets reference is made to the catalogue numbers of the basic stamps with normal watermark throughout the list. This is to avoid continual reference to the catalogue numbers of the inverted watermarks, etc.

WHITER PAPER. During the changeover period cream and whiter paper stamps could occur in the same booklet and we make no attempt to distinguish these.

TÊTE-BÊCHE ERRORS. These occur in booklets due to faulty manufacture, usually the result of a corner of the sheet being folded over.

ERRORS OF MAKE-UP. Such errors exist but we do not list them as it is not difficult to break up booklets and remake them to agree with known errors.

BOOKLET COVERS. All covers are printed in black except where otherwise stated.

BOOKLET CYLINDER NUMBERS. These occur in the left-hand margin of both panes (i.e no dot and dot) as normal Post Office sheets. They are illustrated in Section S except that they always have prefix letters, e.g. E4, F5, G3, but the letters are liable to be partly or completely trimmed off.

Booklet panes of six printed from 20-row cylinders always have the cylinder number adjoining the bottom row of stamps but in the case of 21-row cylinders, the perforated web is cut at every 20th row to make sheets of 480. Consequently, on successive sheets the cylinder number appears one row lower and thus a pane can have it adjoining the top or bottom row.

Booklet panes of four and fifteen usually have the cylinders trimmed off completely.

DATES.   The month and year dates are those found printed on the booklets, either on the outer back cover or on the white leaves. No dates are given on the 1s. booklets, the 2s. booklets Nos. N1/3, the 5s. "Philympia" booklet No. HP34 and the £1 booklet No. ZP1. The dates of issue of every booklet in a new cover design or composition are given in brackets where known.

QUANTITIES.   The quantities given are of the numbers manufactured, but some of the figures are shared by two or more booklets and this is indicated in the listing.

PATTERN BOOKS.   These were dummy books, including the postal rates panel dated December 1952, with "SPACE AVAILABLE FOR COMMERCIAL ADVERTISING" printed on the reverse of the front cover, reverse of second end leaf and on both sides of the back cover. The panes of stamps were represented by perforated and gummed labels. In the 2s.6d. booklet the third pane had the three labels in the upper row inscribed "1d." and "SPACE AVAILABLE FOR COMMERCIAL ADVERTISING" printed across the lower row.

These pattern books were produced prior to the re-introduction of commercial advertising and were distributed to potential advertising contractors.

The contractor was responsible for selling the advertising space and for the provision of copy to the printer. The printed material, both commercial and official matter, was then submitted to the Post Office in galley form for approval. These proofs were then used to prepare paste-up examples of each book, so that the make-up could be checked.

ADVERTISERS' VOUCHER COPIES.   With the introduction of commercial advertising in 1953 the Post Office began to supply voucher copies of the various booklets to the firms whose advertisements appeared in them.

In 1953 the 2s.6d. September, October, and November editions, together with the 5s. September, were supplied as voucher copies with the stamps torn out. Subsequent editions of the 2s., 2s.6d., 3s.9d., 4s.6d., 5s., 6s., 10s. and £1 (sewn, and without black binding) booklets were made up as voucher copies without the stamp panes.

Of particular interest are the 2s.6d. booklets containing the *se-tenant* pane of three 1d. stamps and three labels. Between January 1954 and January 1955 voucher copies of these booklets come with these *se-tenant* labels shown, but not the stamps. In the January 1954 edition the labels were printed on ungummed paper, imperforate, but on subsequent occasions they come perforated on gummed paper with the Harrison "house" watermark.

CATALOGUE NUMBERS.   In order to avoid confusion we have used the same booklet numbers as in the *Concise Catalogue.* Many of these booklets bear the same prefix letters as other stamps listed in the *Great Britain* Specialised Catalogues so that when quoting numbers in this Appendix it should be made clear that booklets are being referred to.

Varieties shown thus "(*a*)" are those listed in the *Great Britain* Specialised Catalogues only.

ILLUSTRATIONS.   The illustrations of the covers are ¾ size except where otherwise stated.

BOOKLET PRICES.   Prices in this Appendix are for booklets containing panes with "average" perforations (i.e. full perforations on two edges of the pane only). Booklets containing panes with complete perforations are worth more.

NON-PICTORIAL TYPES OF BOOKLET COVERS

Type A
Circular GPO Cypher

Type B
Oval Type GPO Cypher

Type C
Oval Type GPO Cypher 15 *mm* wide

Type D
Larger Oval GPO Cypher 17 *mm* wide

Section A. Wilding Issues

1s. BOOKLETS FOR USE IN SLOT MACHINES

Booklet Series "D"
Contents: 4 × 1½d., 4 × ½d. in panes of two

I. WHITE UNPRINTED COVER. Not interleaved. For use in experimental machines
Watermark Tudor Crown (Nos. S1, S13, S25)

E1 No date (issued 2.9.53)	56,650	7·00

Watermark St. Edward's Crown (Nos. S2, S14, S26)

E2 No date (issued 11.57)	7,180	18·00

These booklets were made up from vertical rows 1 and 2 from sheets and so do not have inverted watermarks. "D" booklet machines were withdrawn in November 1960.

Booklet Series "E"
Contents: 4 × 1½d., 4 × 1d., 4 × ½d. in panes of four

II. WHITE PRINTED COVER AS TYPE B. Not interleaved. For use in "F1" machines.
Watermark Tudor Crown (Nos. S1, S13, S25)

K1 No date (Back cover "MINIMUM FOREIGN LETTER RATE FOUR PENCE") (issued 22.7.54)	180,360	6·00
K1*a* No date (Back cover "MONEY BY POST") (issued 11.54)	572,900	6·00

Watermark St. Edward's Crown (Nos. S2, S14, S26)

K2 No date (Back cover "£5 only"). (issued 5.7.56)	373,000	6·00
K2*a* No date (Back cover "£10 only". Inland letter rate 2½d.) (issued 6.57) .	532,000	6·00
K2*b* No date (Back cover "£10 only". Inland letter rate 3d.) (issued 8.58) . .	541,000	7·00

Watermark Crowns (Nos. S4, S16, S28)

K3 No date (Back cover "£10 only". Overseas letter rate 6d.) (issued 13.8.59)	623,500	6·00
K3a No date (Back cover "£10 only". Overseas letter rate 4d.) (issued 10.60)	250,000	9·00

1s. booklets continued to be available until 1964. The machines were then converted to issue the thicker 2s. booklets.

2s. BOOKLETS

Contents: 4 × 3d., 4 × 1½d., 4 × 1d., 4 × ½d. in panes of four

I. Salmon Cover as Type B. Fully interleaved
  Watermark St. Edward's Crown (Nos. S2, S14, S26, S68)

N1 No date (issued 22.4.59)	452,470	5·00

II. Salmon Cover as Type C. Fully interleaved
  Watermark Crowns (upright) (Nos. S4, S16, S28, S70)

N2 No date (issued 2.11.60)	300,500	7·00

III. Lemon Cover as Type C. Fully interleaved
  Watermark Crowns (upright) (Nos. S4, S16, S28, S70)

N3 No date (issued 9.2.61)	1,330,750	7·00

Watermark Crowns (sideways) (Nos. S4d or S5a, S16e or S17a, S28a or S29a, S70d or S71a) or blue phosphor (Nos. S10b or S11a, S21b or S22a, S33b or S34a, S75b or S76a)

N 4	APR 1961 (issued 26.5.61)	1,381,440	25·00
	p. With blue phosphor bands (issued 14.7.61)	171,400	60·00
N 5	SEPT 1961	889,000	38·00
N 6	JAN 1962	911,600	40·00
N 7	APR 1962	958,600	42·00
N 8	JULY 1962	935,600	40·00
	p. With blue phosphor bands	51,600	80·00
N 9	NOV 1962	975,000	50·00
	p. With blue phosphor bands	56,000	85·00
N10	JAN 1963	1,105,400	40·00
	p. With blue phosphor bands	58,390	£120
N11	MAR 1963	1,090,800	40·00
N12	JUNE 1963	1,014,800	40·00
	p. With blue phosphor bands	57,800	75·00
N13	AUG 1963	989,000	40·00
	p. With blue phosphor bands	56,400	75·00
N14	OCT 1963	1,018,800	40·00
	p. With blue phosphor bands	11,200	£120
N15	FEB 1964	1,122,400	40·00
	p. With blue phosphor bands	76,600	75·00
N16	JUNE 1964	386,570	40·00
	p. With blue phosphor bands	63,400	£100
N17	AUG 1964	122,300	50·00
	p. With blue phosphor bands	58,800	£100
N18	OCT 1964	1,179,800	40·00
	p. With blue phosphor bands	94,200	65·00
N19	DEC 1964	109,170	45·00
	p. With blue phosphor bands	34,000	65·00
N20	APR 1965	1,435,400	38·00
	p. With blue phosphor bands	40,800	60·00

2s. booklets in this composition were withdrawn from sale on 31 August 1965

Contents changed: 4 × 4d. in pane of four, 2 × 1d. and 2 × 3d. in pane of four arranged *se-tenant* horizontally

Orange-Yellow Cover as Type C. Printed in black. Fully interleaved
  Watermark Crowns (sideways) (Nos. S17a, S71a, S85d) and blue or violet phosphor with one band on 3d. (Nos. S22a, S23d, or S24b; S77b or S78c; S90c, S91b or S92b)

N21	JULY 1965 (issued 16.8.65)	2,671,800	3·00
	p. With blue phosphor bands (issued 16.8.65)	109,600	15·00

N22 OCT 1965	1,852,800	3·50
p. (a) With blue phosphor bands . . . .⎫		24·00
p. (b) With violet 8 mm. phosphor bands . . . .⎭	223,200	14·00
N23 JAN 1966	1,633,200	5·00
p. (a) With blue phosphor bands . . . .⎫		24·00
p. (b) With violet 8 mm. phosphor bands . . . .⎭	350,600	20·00
N24 APR 1966	2,125,200	5·00
p. With violet 8 mm. phosphor bands	240,000	9·00
N25 JULY 1966	1,981,800	4·00
p. With violet 8 mm. phosphor bands	97,400	55·00
N26 OCT 1966	1,787,400	5·00
p. With violet 8 mm. phosphor bands	471,400	12·00
N27 JAN 1967	644,200	6·00
p. With violet 8 mm. phosphor bands	2,100,400	6·50
N28p APR 1967 . . . . (a) With violet 8 mm. phosphor bands .⎫		7·50
(b) With violet 9·5 mm. phosphor bands ⎭	2,330,200	—
N29p JULY 1967. With violet 8 mm. phosphor bands	3,209,800	5·00
N30p OCT 1967 (issued 15.9.67) (a) With violet 8 mm. phosphor bands .⎫		5·00
(b) With violet 9·5 mm. phosphor bands ⎭	3,924,600	32·00

For illustration showing how the *se-tenant* stamps with one phosphor band on the 3d. are printed, see listing of No. SB36.

Watermark Crowns (sideways), 3d. with two violet phosphor bands (Nos. S23d or S24b; S78c or S80; S91b or S92b)

N31p JAN 1968 (issued early 11.67) . .	(a) Violet 9·5 mm. ⎫		3·00
	(b) 8 mm. bands on 4d. pane ⎬ 1,864,800		18·00
	(c) 8 mm. bands on *se-tenant* pane ⎭		18·00
N32p MAR 1968 (issued mid 1.68) . .	(a) Violet 9·5 mm. ⎫		3·50
	(b) 8 mm. bands on 4d. pane ⎬ 3,078,800		18·00
	(c) 8 mm. bands on *se-tenant* pane ⎭		18·00

Nos. N31p(c) and N32p(c) have one band on 3d.

2s. booklets were withdrawn on 11 February 1971 prior to decimalisation on 15 February.

2s. BOOKLETS FOR HOLIDAY RESORTS

Contents: 8 × 2½d. in panes of four and 3 × ½d. and 1 × 2½d. in pane of four arranged
  se-tenant

LEMON COVER AS TYPE C. Printed in red. Fully interleaved
  Watermark Crowns. Chalky paper (Nos. S6, S58)

A. Black stitching

NR1 No date (issued 15.7.63)	415,000	3·50

B. White stitching

NR1a No date (issued 3.9.63)	50,000	4·00

Contents changed: 8 × ½d. and 8 × 2½d. in panes of four arranged sideways, vertically
  se-tenant

LEMON COVER AS TYPE C. Printed in red. Fully interleaved
  Watermark Crowns (sideways) (No. S5a/b, S57b/c)

NR2 1964 (issued 1.7.64)	827,800	1·60

These replaced the normal 2s. booklets in the resort towns to which they were issued.

2s. BOOKLET FOR CHRISTMAS CARDS

Contents: 8 × 3d. in two panes of four arranged sideways

ORANGE-YELLOW COVER AS TYPE C. Printed in red. Fully interleaved
  Watermark Crowns (sideways) (No. S71a)

NX1 1965 (issued 6.12.65)	1,208,000	80

The above was withdrawn on 3.1.66 but reissued on 16.5.66 as a holiday resort booklet.

2s.6d. BOOKLETS

Contents: 6 × 2½d., 6 × 1½d., 3 × 1d. (page completed by three perforated labels), 6 × ½d.
in panes of six

> LABELS. The wording printed on the labels differs as follows:—
> "PPR" = "MINIMUM INLAND PRINTED PAPER RATE 1½d." Two types exist:
>   (*a*) 17 mm. high. Printed in photogravure
>   (*b*) 15 mm. high. Printed by typography
> "SHORTHAND" = "SHORTHAND IN 1 WEEK" (covering all three labels)
> "POST EARLY" = "PLEASE POST EARLY IN THE DAY"
> "PAP" = "PACK YOUR PARCELS SECURELY" (1st label), "ADDRESS YOUR
> LETTERS CORRECTLY" (2nd label) "AND POST EARLY IN THE DAY" (3rd label)

I. Composite Booklets containing Stamps of King George VI and Queen Elizabeth II

A. GREEN COVER AS TYPE A. Not interleaved

K.G. VI ½d. (No. Q3), 1d. (No. Q6) and Q.E. II 1½d. (No. S25), 2½d. (No. S51)

F 1 MAY 1953 PPR 17 mm.	2,272,000	25·00
b. Date error "MAY 195" for "MAY 1955"		70·00
F 2 JUNE 1953 PPR 17 mm.	2,751,000	28·00
F 3 JULY 1953 PPR 17 mm.	2,199,000	32·00
F 4 AUG 1953 PPR 17 mm.	2,464,000	28·00

B. GREEN COVER AS TYPE A, but with the addition of two interleaving pages, one at each end

K.G. VI ½d. (No. Q3), 1d. (No. Q6) and Q.E. II 1½d. (No. S25), 2½d. (No. S51)

F 5 SEPT 1953 PPR 17 mm.	} 2,386,000	£160
F 6 SEPT 1953 PPR 15 mm.		£100

C. GREEN COVER AS TYPE B. Contents as Nos. F 5/6

K.G. VI ½d. (No. Q3), 1d. (No. Q6) and Q.E. II 1½d. (No. S25), 2½d. (No. S51)

F 7 OCT 1953 PPR 17 mm.	} 2,532,000	40·00
F 8 OCT 1953 PPR 15 mm.		90·00
F 9 NOV 1953 PPR 17 mm.	} 4,308,000	40·00
F10 NOV 1953 PPR 15 mm.		£140
F11 DEC 1953 PPR 17 mm.	2,918,000	45·00
F12 JAN 1954 SHORTHAND	2,199,000	70·00
F13 FEB 1954 SHORTHAND	2,202,000	70·00

D. GREEN COVER AS TYPE B with contents as Nos. F 5/6 but Q.E. II ½d. in place of K.G. VI ½d.

K.G. VI 1d. (No. Q6) and Q.E. II ½d. (No. S1), 1½d. (No. S25), 2½d. (No.S51)

F14 MAR 1954 PPR 17 mm.	139,000	£425
F14*a* MAR 1954 SHORTHAND		

II. Booklets containing only Queen Elizabeth II Stamps

GREEN COVER AS TYPE B.
Watermark Tudor Crown (Nos. S1, S13, S25, S51)

A. Two interleaving pages, one at each end

F15 MAR 1954 PPR 15 mm.	2,085,000	£250
F16 APR 1954 POST EARLY	3,176,000	40·00
F17 MAY 1954 POST EARLY	2,435,000	40·00
F18 JUNE 1954 POST EARLY	2,419,000	40·00
F19 JULY 1954 POST EARLY	2,876,000	40·00
F20 AUG 1954 POST EARLY	2,871,000	40·00
F21 SEPT 1954 POST EARLY	2,799,000	40·00
F22 OCT 1954 POST EARLY	2,803,000	40·00
F23 NOV 1954 POST EARLY	3,739,000	40·00
F24 DEC 1954 POST EARLY	2,813,000	40·00

B. Fully interleaved

F25 JAN 1955 POST EARLY	(*a*) (original setting)	} 2,551,000	50·00
	(*b*) (modified setting)		45·00

F26 JAN 1955 PAP	....	160,000	£100
F27 FEB 1955 PAP	....	2,694,000	40·00
F28 MAR 1955 PAP	....	2,530,000	40·00
F29 APR 1955 PAP	....	2,522,000	40·00
F30 MAY 1955 PAP	....	2,530,000	40·00
F31 JUNE 1955 PAP	....	2,522,000	40·00
F32 JULY 1955 PAP	....	2,431,000	40·00
F33 AUG 1955 PAP	....		

$$\left.\begin{array}{l}(a)\ \text{Combination TTET}\\(b)\ \text{Combination TEET}\end{array}\right\}\ 2{,}563{,}000 \qquad 40\cdot00$$

In the modified setting the distance between "IN THE" is 1 mm. and this is only found on the majority of the Jan. 1955 edition (Booklet F25). The normal spacing is 1½ mm.

> MIXED WATERMARKS. Nos. F33/8 and F42/3 exist with mixed Tudor Crown and St. Edward's Crown watermarks. The mixed watermarks are indicated by the code letters "T" (Tudor) and "E" (Edward) starting with the first pane of the booklet, i.e. 2½d., 1½d., 1d., ½d.
>   We only quote one price for each booklet and this is the minimum price. Some combinations are scarcer and worth more.

Tudor Crown, St. Edward's Crown and mixed watermarks. All have PAP labels.

F34 SEPT 1955 (TTTT) ....

$$\left.\begin{array}{l}(a)\ \text{Combination TTET}\\(b)\ \text{Combination TEET}\\(c)\ \text{Combination TEEE}\\(d)\ \text{Combination ETET}\\(e)\ \text{Combination EEET}\\(f)\ \text{Combination EEEE}\end{array}\right\}\ 2{,}275{,}000 \qquad 45\cdot00$$

F35 OCT 1955 (TTTT) ....

$$\left.\begin{array}{l}(a)\ \text{Combination TEET}\\(b)\ \text{Combination EEET}\\(c)\ \text{Combination TEEE}\\(d)\ \text{Combination EEEE}\end{array}\right\}\ 2{,}289{,}000 \qquad 30\cdot00$$

F36 NOV 1955 (TTTT) ....

$$\left.\begin{array}{l}(a)\ \text{Combination TEEE}\\(b)\ \text{Combination EEET}\\(c)\ \text{Combination EEEE}\end{array}\right\}\ 4{,}125{,}000 \qquad 30\cdot00$$

Watermark St. Edward's Crown (Nos. S2, S14, S26, S53). All have PAP labels

F37 DEC 1955			F44 JULY 1956	2,279,400	30·00
(a) Combination TEET .	2,789,000	30·00	F45 AUG 1956	2,264,400	20·00
(b) Combination EEET .			F46 SEPT 1956	2,533,000	35·00
F38 JAN 1956	2,001,000	30·00	F47 OCT 1956	2,536,000	30·00
(a) Combination EEET .			F48 NOV 1956	4,165,800	30·00
F39 FEB 1956	2,031,000	30·00	F49 DEC 1956	2,724,600	30·00
F40 MAR 1956	2,289,000	30·00	F50 JAN 1957	2,212,800	30·00
F41 APR 1956	2,283,000	35·00	F51 FEB 1957	2,772,790	30·00
F42 MAY 1956	2,275,000	30·00	F52 MAR 1957	2,497,800	22·00
(a) Combination EEET .					
(b) Combination TEEE .					
F43 JUNE 1956	2,293,000	30·00			
(a) Combination EEET					
(b) Combination TEEE					

Contents changed: 6 × 2½d., 6 × 2d., 6 × ½d. in panes of six

Watermark St. Edward's Crown (Nos. S2, S38, S53)

F53 APR 1957	2,451,800	30·00	F58 SEPT 1957	2,482,200	25·00
F54 MAY 1957	2,062,400	30·00	F59 OCT 1957	2,505,600	25·00
F55 JUNE 1957	1,843,000	25·00	F60 NOV 1957	3,085,600	20·00
F56 JULY 1957	2,305,000	25·00	F61 DEC 1957	281,000	35·00
F57 AUG 1957	2,265,000	25·00			

The 2s.6d. booklets were withdrawn from sale on 27 July 1958.

3s. BOOKLETS

Contents: 6 × 3d., 6 × 1½d., 6 × 1d., 6 × ½d. in panes of six

I. RED COVER AS TYPE B. Fully interleaved

Watermark St. Edward's Crown (Nos. S2, S14, S26, S68)

M1 JAN 1958	1,815,000	18·00	M9 NOV 1958
M2 FEB 1958	2,224,000	18·00	(a) Combination EEEC
M3 MAR 1958	2,271,000	18·00	(b) Combination EECE
M4 APR 1958	2,654,000	18·00	(c) Combination EECC
M5 MAY 1958	2,146,000	18·00	(d) Combination CECE
M6 JUNE 1958	2,222,000	18·00	(e) Combination CCCE
M7 JULY 1958	885,000	18·00	
M8 AUG 1958	896,000	20·00	

M9 NOV 1958 (a)–(e) 1,367,000   20·00

> MIXED WATERMARKS. See notes above No. F34. The mixed watermarks here are indicated by the code letters "E" (Edward) and "C" (Crowns) starting with the first pane of the booklet, i.e. 3d., 1½d., 1d., ½d.

Watermark Crowns (Nos. S4, S16, S28, S70), or graphite lines (Nos. S7, S18, S30, S72)

M10 DEC 1958			
(a) Combination ECEC			
(b) Combination CEEE			
(c) Combination CECE	886,000	25·00	
(d) Combination CEEC			
(e) Combination CECC			
M11 JAN 1959			
(a) Combination CECC	1,145,000	20·00	
M12 FEB 1959	1,125,000	22·00	
M13 AUG 1959	1,038,000	25·00	
g. With graphite lines (issued 4.8.59)	47,000	£200	
M14 SEPT 1959	1,542,000	25·00	
g. With graphite lines	74,000	£260	

II. BRICK-RED COVER AS TYPE C. Fully interleaved

Watermark Crowns (Nos. S4, S16, S28, S70), graphite lines (Nos. S7, S18, S30, S72) or green phosphor (Nos. S9, S20, S32, S74)

M15 OCT 1959	1,016,000	25·00
g. With graphite lines	74,000	£250
M16 NOV 1959	2,287,000	25·00
M17 DEC 1959	1,027,000	25·00
M18 JAN 1960	752,000	25·00
M19 FEB 1960	750,000	25·00
g. With graphite lines	37,600	£250
M20 MAR 1960	966,000	25·00
g. With graphite lines	39,600	£300
M21 APR 1960	941,000	25·00
g. With graphite lines	38,200	£260
M22 MAY 1960	911,000	25·00
M23 JUNE 1960	982,000	25·00
M24 JULY 1960	989,200	25·00
M25 AUG 1960	897,000	25·00
p. With green phosphor bands (issued 14.8.60)	39,800	50·00
M26 SEPT 1960	1,326,600	25·00
M27 OCT 1960	1,343,400	25·00
M28 NOV 1960	2,068,200	25·00
p. With green phosphor bands	11,900	55·00

III. BRICK-RED COVER AS TYPE D. Fully interleaved

Watermark Crowns (Nos. S4 or S5, S16 or S17, S28 or S29, S70 or S71), green or blue phosphor (Nos. S9 or S10, S20 or S21, S32 or S33, S74 or S75)

M29 DEC 1960	905,200	25·00
p. With green phosphor bands	31,800	60·00

M30	JAN 1961	731,800	25·00
M31	FEB 1961	727,000	25·00
M32	MAR 1961	754,600	22·00
M33	APR 1961	760,800	25·00
	p. With blue phosphor bands	142,600	50·00
M34	MAY 1961	738,000	25·00
M35	JUNE 1961	768,000	25·00
M36	JULY 1961	783,400	25·00
	p. With blue phosphor bands	7,800	50·00
M37	AUG 1961	747,400	25·00
	p. (a) With green phosphor bands	54,400	60·00
	p. (b) With blue phosphor bands		50·00
M38	SEPT 1961	513,600	25·00
	p. With blue phosphor bands	19,200	50·00
M39	OCT 1961	494,600	25·00
	p. With blue phosphor bands	18,800	50·00
M40	NOV 1961	467,600	25·00
M41	DEC 1961	356,800	25·00
M42	JAN 1962	447,000	25·00
M43	FEB 1962	654,200	25·00
	p. With blue phosphor bands	11,800	50·00
M44	MAR 1962	655,200	25·00
	p. With blue phosphor bands	19,400	50·00
M45	APR 1962	569,600	25·00
	p. With blue phosphor bands	19,600	50·00
M46	MAY 1962	475,000	25·00
	p. With blue phosphor bands	27,000	48·00
M47	JUNE 1962	468,400	25·00
	p. With blue phosphor bands	27,200	48·00
M48	JULY 1962	729,400	22·00
M49	AUG 1962	691,200	22·00
	p. With blue phosphor bands	28,800	50·00
M50	SEPT 1962	687,400	25·00
	p. With blue phosphor bands	11,800	50·00
M51	OCT 1962	864,600	26·00
	p. With blue phosphor bands	35,200	48·00
M52	NOV 1962	1,125,600	25·00
	p. With blue phosphor bands	51,800	50·00
M53	DEC 1962	1,035,000	25·00
	p. With blue phosphor bands	19,200	50·00
M54	JAN 1963	499,400	25·00
M55	FEB 1963	462,400	22·00
	p. With blue phosphor bands	39,400	48·00
M56	MAR 1963	512,800	22·00
	p. With blue phosphor bands	39,200	48·00
M57	APR 1963	512,800	22·00
	p. With blue phosphor bands	39,600	48·00
M58	MAY 1963	520,800	22·00
	p. With blue phosphor bands	19,400	£200
M59	JUNE 1963	532,400	22·00
	p. With blue phosphor bands	19,800	36·00
M60	JULY 1963	712,000	22·00
	p. With blue phosphor bands	17,800	50·00
M61	AUG 1963	698,600	22·00
	p. With blue phosphor bands	19,800	50·00
M62	SEPT 1963	503,000	22·00
M63	OCT 1963	660,400	22·00
M64	NOV 1963	670,000	22·00
	p. With blue phosphor bands	39,400	48·00
M65	DEC 1963	711,400	30·00
	p. With blue phosphor bands	19,350	85·00
M66	JAN 1964	619,600	30·00
	p. With blue phosphor bands	67,000	40·00
M67	MAR 1964	666,600	25·00
	p. With blue phosphor bands	30,400	50·00

M68 MAY 1964	636,600	25·00
p. With blue phosphor bands	46,600	65·00
M69 JULY 1964	865,800	25·00
p. With blue phosphor bands	27,400	50·00
M70 SEPT 1964	915,600	30·00
p. With blue phosphor bands	39,800	50·00
M71 NOV 1964	2,157,600	30·00
p. With blue phosphor bands	99,200	40·00
M72 JAN 1965	1,009,800	30·00
p. With blue phosphor bands	50,000	40·00
M73 MAR 1965	944,600	20·00
p. With blue phosphor bands	38,200	40·00
M74 MAY 1965	765,600	20·00
p. With blue phosphor bands	58,200	40·00

3s. booklets were withdrawn from sale on 31 August 1965.

3s.9d. BOOKLETS

Contents: 18 × 2½d. in panes of six

RED COVER AS TYPE B.

A. Two interleaving pages, one at each end
  Watermark Tudor Crown (No. S51)

G1 NOV 1953	1,446,000	28·00	G5 FEB 1955	925,000	30·00
G2 JAN 1954	1,572,000	30·00	G6 APR 1955	1,112,000	30·00
G3 MAR 1954	1,474,000	30·00	G7 JUNE 1955	675,000	30·00
G4 DEC 1954	1,477,000	30·00	G8 AUG 1955	636,000	30·00

  Tudor Crown, St. Edward's Crown and mixed watermarks

G9   OCT 1955 (TTT) . . . .
           (*a*) Combination TET ⎫
           (*b*) Combination EET ⎬ 1,661,000   28·00
           (*c*) Combination EEE ⎭

G10   DEC 1955 (TTT) . . . .
           (*a*) Combination TET ⎫ 616,000   30·00
           (*b*) Combination EEE ⎭

B. Fully interleaved
  Watermark St. Edward's Crown (No. S53)

G12 FEB 1956	638,000	20·00	G17 DEC 1956	1,065,800	20·00
G13 APR 1956	642,000	20·00	G18 FEB 1957	1,376,000	20·00
G14 JUNE 1956	634,000	20·00	G19 APR 1957	1,139,600	20·00
G15 AUG 1956	747,200	20·00	G20 JUNE 1957	1,115,200	12·00
G16 OCT 1956	1,762,800	20·00	G21 AUG 1957	39,600	28·00

3s.9d. booklets were withdrawn from sale on 30 September 1957.

4s.6d. BOOKLETS

Contents: 18 × 3d. in panes of six

I. PURPLE COVER AS TYPE B. Fully interleaved
  Watermark St. Edward's Crown (No. S68)

L1 OCT 1957	2,249,000	20·00	L5 JUNE 1958	1,096,000	22·00
L2 DEC 1957	4,539,000	20·00	L6 OCT 1958	1,796,000	22·00
L3 FEB 1958	1,789,000	24·00	L7 DEC 1958	1,808,000	22·00
L4 APR 1958	2,691,000	20·00			

  Watermark Crowns (No. S70)

L8 DEC 1958	(*incl. above*)	70·00

II. PURPLE COVER AS TYPE C. Fully interleaved
  Watermark Crowns (No. S70) or graphite lines (No. S72)

L 9 FEB 1959	(*with* L14)	2,260,000	22·00
L10 JUNE 1959	(*with* L16)	2,195,000	22·00

435

L11	AUG 1959	1,710,000	22·00
	g. With graphite lines	97,600	28·00
L12	OCT 1959	1,852,000	30·00
L13	DEC 1959 . . . . (*with* L17)	1,409,000	24·00

III. Violet Cover as Type C. Fully interleaved
Watermark Crowns (No. S70), graphite lines (No. S72) or green phosphor (No. S74)

L14	FEB 1959 . . . . (*incl. in* L9)		30·00
L15	APR 1959	2,137,000	24·00
	g. With graphite lines	99,200	20·00
L16	JUNE 1959 . . . . (*incl. in* L10)		24·00
	g. With graphite lines	99,400	20·00
L17	DEC 1959 . . . . (*incl. in* L13)		24·00
L18	FEB 1960	1,801,000	24·00
	g. With graphite lines	79,600	24·00
L19	APR 1960	1,730,000	24·00
	g. With graphite lines	78,800	24·00
L20	JUNE 1960	1,832,000	24·00
L21	AUG 1960	1,771,600	24·00
	p. With green phosphor bands	39,800	40·00
L22	OCT 1960	2,723,600	24·00

IV. Violet Cover as Type D. Fully interleaved
Watermark Crowns (No. S70 or S71), green or blue phosphor (Nos. S74, S75 or S76)

L23	DEC 1960	1,772,000	40·00
L24	FEB 1961	1,982,200	40·00
	p. With green phosphor bands	27,200	30·00
L25	APR 1961	3,428,400	28·00
	p. With blue phosphor bands	297,400	30·00
L26	JUNE 1961	1,825,600	28·00
L27	AUG 1961	2,679,800	28·00
	p. (*a*) With green phosphor bands	} 63,120	48·00
	p. (*b*) With blue phosphor bands		36·00
L28	OCT 1961	3,061,000	25·00
	p. With blue phosphor bands	31,400	36·00
L29	DEC 1961	1,942,800	25·00
L30	FEB 1962	2,405,200	36·00
	p. With blue phosphor bands	43,600	36·00
L31	APR 1962	1,985,000	36·00
	p. With blue phosphor bands	75,400	36·00
L32	JUNE 1962	2,190,600	36·00
	p. With blue phosphor bands	74,600	45·00
L33	AUG 1962	2,533,800	25·00
	p. With blue phosphor bands	83,600	50·00
L34	OCT 1962	3,525,400	25·00
	p. With blue phosphor bands	83,200	£140
L35	DEC 1962	1,822,000	25·00
	p. With blue phosphor bands	82,200	36·00
L36	FEB 1963	2,352,600	25·00
	p. With blue phosphor bands	117,000	36·00
L37	APR 1963	2,390,200	25·00
	p. With blue phosphor bands	119,000	36·00
L38	JUNE 1963	2,873,600	25·00
	p. With blue phosphor bands	178,600	36·00
L39	AUG 1963	2,474,200	25·00
	p. With blue phosphor bands	111,000	36·00
L40	OCT 1963	1,829,200	25·00
	p. With blue phosphor bands	99,400	36·00
L41	NOV 1963	1,821,000	25·00
	p. With blue phosphor bands	99,600	36·00
L42	DEC 1963	2,431,400	25·00
	p. With blue phosphor bands	46,400	£130
L43	JAN 1964	1,043,800	55·00

L44	FEB 1964	1,069,000	25·00
	p. With blue phosphor bands	87,000	36·00
L45	MAR 1964	1,014,200	55·00
	p. With blue phosphor bands	82,800	70·00
L46	APR 1964	1,006,600	55·00
	p. With blue phosphor bands	62,400	36·00
L47	MAY 1964	1,028,800	25·00
	p. With blue phosphor bands	105,200	36·00
L48	JUNE 1964	1,067,400	25·00
	p. With blue phosphor bands	70,400	36·00
L49	JULY 1964	1,673,600	25·00
	p. With blue phosphor bands	56,200	36·00
L50	AUG 1964	1,622,600	30·00
	p. With blue phosphor bands	78,200	24·00
L51	SEPT 1964	1,561,200	36·00
	p. With blue phosphor bands	98,000	24·00
L52	OCT 1964	1,781,800	25·00
	p. With blue phosphor bands	197,800	36·00
L53	NOV 1964	1,686,000	25·00
	p. With blue phosphor bands	138,000	36·00
L54	DEC 1964	1,684,000	25·00
	p. With blue phosphor bands	119,200	36·00
L55	JAN 1965	1,519,200	20·00
	p. With blue phosphor bands	95,000	36·00
L56	FEB 1965	1,504,600	20·00
	p. With blue phosphor bands	94,200	35·00
L57	MAR 1965	1,479,600	22·00
	p. With blue phosphor bands	18,800	£275
L58	APR 1965	1,438,400	18·00

An edition dated MAY 1965 was prepared, but not issued. Advertisers' voucher copies are known (*Price* £90).

Contents changed: 12 × 4d., 6 × 1d. in panes of six

SLATE-BLUE COVER AS TYPE D

Watermark Crowns (Nos. S17, S85), blue or violet phosphor (Nos. S22, S23 or S24; S90, S91 or S92)

L59	JULY 1965 (issued 26.7.65)	2,191,600	18·00
	p. With blue phosphor bands (issued 26.7.65)	75,400	24·00
L60	SEPT 1965	1,839,600	18·00
	p. (*a*) With blue phosphor bands . . . . }	200,800	24·00
	p. (*b*) With violet 8 mm. phosphor bands . . . . }		24·00
L61	NOV 1965	2,005,000	18·00
	p. (*a*) With blue phosphor bands . . . . }	165,800	26·00
	p. (*b*) With violet 8 mm. phosphor bands . . . . }		24·00
L62	JAN 1966	1,671,000	18·00
	p. (*a*) With blue phosphor bands . . . . }	334,600	26·00
	p. (*b*) With violet 8 mm. phosphor bands . . . . }		24·00
L63	MAR 1966	1,201,600	18·00
	p. With violet 8 mm. phosphor bands	153,200	20·00
L64	JAN 1967	98,800	15·00
	p. With violet 8 mm. phosphor bands	396,600	15·00
L65	MAR 1967	97,200	24·00
	p. (*a*) With violet 8 mm. phosphor bands . . . . }	255,400	15·00
	p. (*b*) With violet 9·5 mm. phosphor bands . . . . }		15·00

Watermark Crowns, violet 9·5 mm. phosphor (Nos. S24, S92)

L66p	MAY 1967	697,200	9·00
L67p	JULY 1967	569,000	10·00
L68p	SEPT 1967	750,800	10·00
L69p	NOV 1967	1,802,600	9·00
L70p	JAN 1968	729,400	9·00
L71p	MAR 1968	729,400	8·00

5s. BOOKLETS

Contents: 12 × 2½d., 6 × 2d., 6 × 1½d., 6 × 1d., 6 × ½d. in panes of six

I. Composite Booklets containing Stamps of King George VI and Queen Elizabeth II

A. Buff Cover as Type A. Not interleaved
K.G. VI ½d. (No. Q3), 1d. (No. Q6), 2d. (No. Q12) and Q.E. II 1½d. (No. S25), 2½d. (No. S51)

H1 MAY 1953	. . . .	1,309,000	35·00
H2 JULY 1953	. . . .	1,716,000	38·00

B. Buff Cover as Type A but with the addition of two interleaving pages, one at each end
K.G. VI ½d. (No. Q3), 1d. (No. Q6), 2d. (No. Q12) and Q.E. II 1½d. (No. S25), 2½d. (No. S51)

H3 SEPT 1953	. . . .	1,070,000	38·00

C. Buff Cover as Type B. Contents as No. H3
K.G. VI ½d. (No. Q3), 1d. (No. Q6), 2d. (No. Q12) and Q.E. II 1½d. (No. S25), 2½d. (No. S51)

H4 NOV 1953	. . . .	2,126,000	36·00
H5 JAN 1954	. . . .	692,000	36·00

D. Buff Cover as Type B. Contents as Nos. H4/5 but ½d. Q.E. II in place of K.G. VI ½d.
K.G. VI 1d. (No. Q6), 2d. (No. Q12) and Q.E. II ½d. (No. S1), 1½d. (No. S25), 2½d. (No. S51)

H6 MAR 1954	. . . .	16,000	£250

E. Buff Cover as Type B. Contents as No. H6 but 1d. Q.E. II in place of K.G. VI 1d.
K.G. VI 2d. (No. Q12) and Q.E. II ½d. (No. S1), 1d. (No. S13), 1½d. (No. S25), 2½d. (No. S51)

H7 MAR 1954	. . . .	160,000	£140
a. Extra 1½d. pane	. . . . .		

II. Booklets containing only Queen Elizabeth II Stamps

A. Buff Cover as Type B
Watermark Tudor Crown (Nos. S1, S13, S25, S36, S51)

A. Two interleaving pages, one at each end

H 8 MAR 1954	. . . .	1,092,000	£120	H11 SEPT 1954	. . . .	1,357,000	35·00
H 9 MAY 1954	. . . .	1,884,000	60·00	H12 NOV 1954	. . . .	2,309,000	60·00
H10 JULY 1954	. . . .	1,351,000	70·00				

B. Fully interleaved

H13 JAN 1955	. . . .	1,349,000	60·00	H15 MAY 1955	. . . .	1,461,000	50·00
H14 MAR 1955	. . . .	1,450,000	50·00	H16 JULY 1955	. . . .	1,460,000	50·00

MIXED WATERMARKS. Nos. H17/19 and H21 exist with mixed Tudor Crown and St. Edward's Crown watermarks. The mixed watermarks are indicated by the code letters "T" (Tudor) and "E" (Edward), starting with the first pane of the booklet, i.e. 2½d. (2), 2d., 1½d., 1d., ½d.

We only quote one price for each booklet and this is the minimum price. Some combinations are scarcer and worth more.

H17   SEPT 1955 . . . .

(a) Combination TTTETT		
(b) Combination TTTEET		
(c) Combination TTTETE		
(d) Combination TTEETT		
(e) Combination TTEEET		
(f) Combination TTEEEE		
(g) Combination TETETT		
(h) Combination TETEET		
(i) Combination TEEETT		
(j) Combination TETETE		
(k) Combination TEEETE		
(l) Combination ETTETT		
(m) Combination ETTEET	1,328,000	28·00
(n) Combination ETEETT		
(o) Combination ETEEET		
(p) Combination EETETT		
(q) Combination EETEET		
(r) Combination EETETE		
(s) Combination EETEEE		
(t) Combination EEETTT		
(u) Combination EEETET		
(v) Combination EEETEE		
(w) Combination EEEETT		
(x) Combination EEEEET		
(y) Combination EEEEEE		

Watermark St. Edward's Crown (Nos. S2, S14, S26, S37, S53)

H18 NOV 1955			H20 MAR 1956	1,403,000	40·00
(a) Combination TTEEEE			H21 MAY 1956		
(b) Combination EETEEE			(a) Combination EETETT	1,572,000	36·00
(c) Combination TEEEEE	2,147,000	30·00	(b) Combination EEEEET		
(d) Combination EEEETE			H22 JULY 1956	1,465,190	36·00
(e) Combination EEEEET			H23 SEPT 1956	1,589,000	35·00
(f) Combination ETEEEE			H24 NOV 1956	2,430,600	36·00
H19 JAN 1956			H25 JAN 1957	100,000	40·00
(a) Combination TTTEET					
(b) Combination EETETT	1,337,000	35·00			
(c) Combination EEEEET					

Introduction of 2d. light red-brown (No. S38) in place of No. S37

H26 JAN 1957	1,417,800	36·00	H29 JULY 1957	1,453,600	30·00
H27 MAR 1957	1,435,400	36·00	H30 SEPT 1957	2,104,600	30·00
H28 MAY 1957	1,375,200	35·00	H31 NOV 1957	1,708,400	30·00

Contents changed: 12 × 3d., 6 × 2½d., 6 × 1d., 6 × ½d. in panes of six

Watermark St. Edward's Crown (Nos. S2, S14, S53, S68)

H32 JAN 1958	1,528,000	30·00	H36 NOV 1958		
H33 MAR 1958	442,000	30·00	(a) Combination EEECE .		
H34 MAY 1958	795,000	30·00	(b) Combination EECEE .		
H35 JULY 1958 (11.58) . .			(c) Combination ECCEE .	1,235,000	22·00
(a) Combination EEEEC			(d) Combination CCEEE		
(b) Combination EEECE	1,313,000	22·00	(e) Combination CCCEE		
(c) Combination EEECC					

MIXED WATERMARKS. See notes above No. H17. The mixed watermarks here are indicated by the code letters "E" (Edward) and "C" (Crowns) starting with the first pane of the booklet, i.e. 3d. (2), 2½d., 1d., ½d.

II. BLUE COVER AS TYPE C. Fully interleaved
Watermark Crowns (Nos. S4, S16, S55, S70), graphite lines (Nos. S7, S18, S59, S72) or green phosphor (Nos. S9, S20, S61, S74)

H37	JAN 1959	. . . .		
		(a) Combination CCCCE		
		(b) Combination CCCEC	1,330,000	25·00
		(c) Combination CCCEE		
		(d) Combination CCECC		
H38	MAR 1959	. . . .		
H39	JULY 1959		895,000	30·00
			1,122,000	30·00
	g. With graphite lines (issued 21.8.59)	46,200	£120
H40	SEPT 1959		1,541,000	30·00
H41	NOV 1959		1,340,000	30·00
H42	JAN 1960		1,092,000	30·00
H43	MAR 1960		1,042,000	30·00
	g. With graphite lines	38,000	£130
H44	MAY 1960		1,023,000	35·00
H45	JULY 1960		1,104,000	35·00
H46	SEPT 1960		1,158,800	40·00
	g. With graphite lines	65,999	£130
	p. With green phosphor bands	39,600	95·00
H47	NOV 1960	. . . .	1,308,400	40·00

III. BLUE COVER AS TYPE D. Fully interleaved
Watermark Crowns (Nos. S4, S16, S55, S70) or blue phosphor with two bands on 2½d. (Nos. S10, S21, S62, S75)

H48	JAN 1961	1,344,600	40·00
H49	MAR 1961	2,382,800	40·00
	p. With blue phosphor bands	97,400	£120
H50	MAY 1961	1,219,200	42·00
H51	JULY 1961	1,148,200	42·00
	p. With blue phosphor bands	7,200	£130
H52	SEPT 1961	1,728,600	42·00
	p. With blue phosphor bands	15,200	£130
H53	NOV 1961	1,367,000	42·00
H54	JAN 1962	963,800	42·00
	p. With blue phosphor bands	38,600	£130

Several examples of booklet No. H50 exist with pane 3 comprising No. S62 blue phosphor.

Watermark Crowns (Nos. S4 or S5, S16 or S17, S55 or S57, S70 or S71) or blue phosphor with one phosphor band on 2½d. (Nos. S10 or S11, S21 or S22, S63 or S65, S75 or S76)

H55	MAR 1962	1,006,200	42·00
	p. With blue phosphor bands	23,600	£135
H56	MAY 1962	1,120,800	42·00
	p. With blue phosphor bands	50,800	£120
H57	JULY 1962	1,309,600	42·00
	p. With blue phosphor bands	16,600	£120
H58	SEPT 1962	1,523,800	42·00
	p. With blue phosphor bands	49,800	£130
H59	NOV 1962	1,543,200	42·00
	p. With blue phosphor bands	51,000	£130
H60	JAN 1963	1,024,600	42·00
	p. With blue phosphor bands	38,800	£400
H61	MAR 1963	1,116,800	42·00
	p. With blue phosphor bands	15,800	£135
H62	MAY 1963	1,102,200	42·00
	p. With blue phosphor bands	78,600	£130
H63	JULY 1963	1,456,400	42·00
	p. With blue phosphor bands	44,600	£130
H64	SEPT 1963	1,402,200	42·00
	p. With blue phosphor bands	36,200	£150
H65	NOV 1963	1,400,000	42·00
	p. With blue phosphor bands	78,800	£130

H66 JAN 1964	831,600	42·00
p. With blue phosphor bands	43,000	90·00
H67 MAR 1964	760,200	42·00
p. With blue phosphor bands	55,800	90·00
H68 MAY 1964	760,200	42·00
p. With blue phosphor bands	66,000	£130
H69 JULY 1964	1,647,200	42·00
p. With blue phosphor bands	29,400	£120
H70 SEPT 1964	1,574,000	42·00
p. With blue phosphor bands	38,400	£120
H71 NOV 1964	1,152,400	42·00
p. With blue phosphor bands	98,600	90·00
H72 JAN 1965	1,119,000	42·00
p. With blue phosphor bands	55,200	90·00
H73 MAR 1965	657,600	36·00
p. With blue phosphor bands	19,000	£120
H74 MAY 1965	1,076,600	36·00
p. With blue phosphor bands	56,800	95·00

5s. booklets were withdrawn from sale on 31 August 1965.

6s. BOOKLETS

Contents: 18 × 4d. in panes of six

CLARET COVER AS TYPE D. Fully interleaved
Watermark Crowns (No. S85), blue or violet phosphor (Nos. S90, S91 or S92)

Q 1 JUNE 1965 (issued 21.6.65)	1,166,800	24·00
p. With blue phosphor bands (issued 21.6.65)	101,800	24·00
Q 2 JULY 1965	1,718,000	24·00
p. With blue phosphor bands	136,200	24·00
Q 3 AUG 1965	1,192,400	28·00
p. With blue phosphor bands	87,600	32·00
Q 4 SEPT 1965	1,907,800	24·00
p. (a) With blue phosphor bands . . . . ⎫	244,400	30·00
p. (b) With violet 8 mm. phosphor bands . . . . ⎭		30·00
Q 5 OCT 1965	1,889,600	24·00
p. (a) With blue phosphor bands . . . . ⎫	263,600	30·00
p. (b) With violet 8 mm. phosphor bands . . . . ⎭		30·00
Q 6 NOV 1965	1,788,800	24·00
p. (a) With blue phosphor bands . . . . ⎫	98,200	30·00
p. (b) With violet 8 mm. phosphor bands . . . . ⎭		30·00
Q 7 DEC 1965	1,662,000	24·00
p. (a) With blue phosphor bands . . . . ⎫	93,000	30·00
p. (b) With violet 8 mm. phosphor bands . . . . ⎭		30·00
Q 8 JAN 1966	1,114,800	24·00
p. (a) With blue phosphor bands . . . . ⎫	349,200	30·00
p. (b) With violet 8 mm. phosphor bands . . . . ⎭		30·00
Q 9 FEB 1966	1,448,600	24·00
p. With violet 8 mm. phosphor bands	116,800	30·00
Q10 MAR 1966	1,038,000	24·00
p. With violet 8 mm. phosphor bands	122,400	30·00
Q11 APR 1966	1,124,200	24·00
p. With violet 8 mm. phosphor bands	119,600	50·00
Q12 MAY 1966	1,099,000	24·00
p. With violet 8 mm. phosphor bands	121,000	34·00
Q13 JUNE 1966	1,070,400	24·00
p. With violet 8 mm. phosphor bands	121,000	30·00
Q14 JULY 1966	667,600	28·00
p. With violet 8 mm. phosphor bands	46,800	42·00
Q15 AUG 1966	1,503,200	28·00
p. With violet 8 mm. phosphor bands	42,400	£100
Q16 SEPT 1966	1,402,400	24·00
p. With violet 8 mm. phosphor bands	227,200	24·00

Q17 OCT 1966	986,600	28·00
p. With violet 8 mm. phosphor bands	227,200	60·00
Q18 NOV 1966	1,078,000	28·00
p. With violet 8 mm. phosphor bands	271,200	24·00
Q19 DEC 1966	1,069,400	24·00
p. With violet 8 mm. phosphor bands	270,500	28·00
Q20 JAN 1967	231,400	35·00
p. With violet 8 mm. phosphor bands	622,400	35·00
Q21 FEB 1967	253,800	35·00
p. With violet 9·5 mm. phosphor bands	566,200	24·00
Q22 MAR 1967	395,000	28·00
p. With violet 9·5 mm. phosphor bands	580,800	24·00
Q23 APR 1967	395,400	24·00
p. With violet 9·5 mm. phosphor bands	632,200	25·00

Watermark Crowns, violet 9·5 mm. phosphor (No. S92)

Q24p MAY 1967		
Q25p JUNE 1967	1,612,600	24·00
Q26p JULY 1967	1,596,800	24·00
Q27p AUG 1967	776,600	30·00
	750,600	36·00

10s. BOOKLETS

Contents: 30 × 3d., 6 × 2d., 6 × 1½d., 6 × 1d., 6 × ½d. in panes of six

I. GREEN COVER AS TYPE D. Fully interleaved
  Watermark Crowns (Nos. S4, S16, S28, S40, S70)

X1 No date (issued 10.4.61)	902,000	£110
X2 OCT 1961	483,200	£125

Contents changed: 30 × 3d., 6 × 2½d., 6 × 1½d., 6 × 1d. in panes of six
  Watermark Crowns (Nos. S17, S29, S57, S71)

X3 APR 1962	524,680	90·00
X4 AUG 1962	474,600	£120
X5 MAR 1963	493,200	£115
X6 JULY 1963	620,600	£115
X7 DEC 1963	606,600	£115
X8 JULY 1964	599,400	£115
X9 DEC 1964	415,200	£225

10s. booklets in this composition were withdrawn from sale on 31 August 1965.

Contents changed: 24 × 4d., 6 × 3d., 6 × 1d. in panes of six

II. OCHRE COVER AS TYPE D. Fully interleaved
  Watermark Crowns (Nos. S17, S71, S85)

X10 AUG 1965		
(issued 23.8.65)	854,200	24·00
X11 DEC 1965	658,800	35·00
X12 FEB 1966	663,600	35·00
X13 AUG 1966	686,800	24·00
X14 NOV 1966	796,000	24·00

Watermark Crowns, violet phosphor with one side band on 3d. (Nos. S23 or S24, S78, S91 or S92)

X15p FEB 1967	(a) With violet 8 and 4 mm. phosphor bands ⎱	301,800	8·00
	(b) With violet 9·5 and 4 mm. phosphor bands ⎰		8·00

Watermark Crowns, violet 9·5 mm. phosphor with one centre 4 mm. band on 3d. (Nos. S24, S79, S92)

X16p AUG 1967	1,488,800	6·00
X17p FEB 1968	474,400	6·75

Section B. Machin £.s.d. Issues with Violet Phosphor Bands

> NOTE. All booklets in this Section are fully interleaved

2s. BOOKLETS

Contents: 4 × 4d. in pane of four and 2 × 1d. and 2 × 3d. in pane of four arranged *se-tenant* horizontally

ORANGE-YELLOW COVER AS TYPE C
PVA gum (Nos. U2, U10, U12)

NP27 MAY 1968 (issued 6.4.68)	3,112,400	1·25
NP28 JULY 1968	1,971,685	1·00
NP29 AUG 1968		4·00

 2s. booklets containing 3d. stamps were withdrawn on 14 September 1968.

Contents changed: 6 × 4d. in pane of four and in pane of two plus two printed labels *se-tenant* vertically

GREY COVER AS TYPE C
 One centre phosphor band on *se-tenant* pane. PVA gum (Nos. U12, U13)

NP30 SEPT 1968 (issued 16.9.68)	2,497,400	90
NP31 JAN 1969	2,247,600	£200

 Change to one centre phosphor band on 4 × 4d. pane. PVA gum (No. U13)

NP31a . . . . SEPT 1968 (issued 16.9.68)		(*incl. in*
NP30) £500		
NP32 NOV 1968	2,397,400	90
NP33 JAN 1969	(*incl. in* NP31)	90

 Change to 4d. bright vermilion with one centre phosphor band. PVA gum (No. U14)

NP34 MAR 1969			NP39 JAN 1970	1,172,000	2·00
(issued 3.3.69)	1,952,000	1·25	NP40 MAR 1970	1,168,600	2·00
NP35 MAY 1969	2,092,000	1·50	NP41 MAY 1970	1,390,800	2·00
NP36 JULY 1969	436,000	2·00	NP42 JULY 1970	1,023,800	2·25
NP37 SEPT 1969	1,612,400	1·50	NP43 AUG 1970	1,037,800	2·00
NP38 NOV 1969	1,470,400	1·50	NP44 OCT 1970	2,544,600	2·00
b. Imprint error "HARRISOU" for			NP45 DEC 1970	2,273,400	2·00
"HARRISON"					

4s.6d. BOOKLETS

Contents: 12 × 4d., 6 × 1d. in panes of six

I. SLATE-BLUE COVER AS TYPE D
 PVA gum (Nos. U2, U12)

LP45 MAY 1968 (issued 1.5.68)	742,600	6·00

Type E. With GPO Cypher   Type F. With Post Office Crown Symbol

(Des. Stuart Rose)

(In Types E/F the design subject is changed from time to time and this is indicated in brackets after the date)

443

II. BLUE COVER AS TYPE E showing Ships
PVA gum (Nos. U2, U12)
LP46 JULY 1968 *(Cutty Sark)*   427,600   1·50

Change to one centre phosphor band on 4d. PVA gum (Nos. U2, U13)
LP47 SEPT 1968 *(Golden Hind)* (issued 16.9.68)   1,052,800   2·00
LP48 NOV 1968 *(Discovery)*   1,009,000   2·00

Change to 4d. bright vermilion with one centre band. PVA gum (No. U14)
LP49 JAN 1969 *(Queen Elizabeth 2)* (issued 6.1.69)   775,200   3·25
LP50 MAR 1969 *(Sirius)*   1,105,800   3·00
LP51 MAY 1969 *(Sirius)*   993,200   2·50
LP52 JULY 1969 *(Dreadnought)*   932,000   3·00
LP53 SEPT 1969 *(Dreadnought)*   1,318,600   5·00
LP54 NOV 1969 *(Mauretania)*   1,469,400   3·50
LP55 JAN 1970 *(Mauretania)*   1,046,600   5·00
LP56 MAR 1970 *(Victory)*   872,400   4·00
LP57 MAY 1970 *(Victory)*   515,800   10·00

III. BLUE COVER AS TYPE F showing Ships
PVA gum (Nos. U2, U14)
LP58 AUG 1970 *(The Sovereign of the Seas)*   412,600   3·75
LP59 OCT 1970 *(The Sovereign of the Seas)*   746,600   10·00

5s. BOOKLETS

Type E. With GPO Cypher   Type F. With Post Office Crown Symbol
(Des. Stuart Rose)

Contents: 12 × 5d. in panes of six
I. CINNAMON COVER AS TYPE E showing English Homes
PVA gum (No. U17)
HP26 DEC 1968 (Ightham Mote) (issued 27.11.68)   978,000   2·40
HP27 FEB 1969 (Little Moreton Hall)   1,510,200   2·40
HP28 APR 1969 (Long Melford Hall)   1,963,200   2·50
HP29 JUNE 1969 (Long Melford Hall)   1,821,000   2·50
HP30 AUG 1969 (Long Melford Hall)   1,660,800   4·00

II. CINNAMON COVER AS TYPE F showing English Homes
PVA gum (No. U17)
HP31 OCT 1969 (Mompesson House)   2,251,200   2·50
HP32 DEC 1969 (Mompesson House)   960,200   3·00
HP33 FEB 1970 (Cumberland Terrace)   910,800   2·50

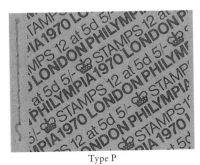

Type P

(Des. Peter Gauld)

Issued to publicise the "Philympia" International
Philatelic Exhibition, London, September 1970

III. CINNAMON COVER AS TYPE P. Stitched in red
PVA gum (No. U17)
HP34 (no date) (issued 3.3.70)   1,019,800   2·50

IV. CINNAMON COVER AS TYPE F showing English Homes
PVA gum (No. U17)
HP35 JUNE 1970 (The Vineyard, Saffron Walden)   1,814,400   3·00
HP36 AUG 1970 (The Vineyard, Saffron Walden)   2,076,800   4·00
HP37 OCT 1970 (Mereworth Castle)   3,301,400   3·75
HP38 DEC 1970 (Mereworth Castle)   5,517,680   4·00

6s. BOOKLETS

Contents: 18 × 4d. in panes of six

I. CLARET COVER AS TYPE D
Gum arabic (No. U11 (1))
QP28 SEPT 1967 (issued 21.9.67)   1,345,000   38·00
QP29 OCT 1967   1,487,400   38·00
QP30 NOV 1967   1,522,200   38·00
QP31 DEC 1967   1,531,000   38·00
QP32 JAN 1968   1,251,400   36·00

Change to 4d. deep olive-brown. Gum arabic (No. U11 (2))
QP33 FEB 1968   1,314,400   34·00
QP34 MAR 1968   1,090,600   34·00
QP35 APR 1968   1,127,800   30·00
QP36 MAY 1968   1,398,000   15·00

Change to PVA gum (No. U12 (2))
QP37 MAY 1968 . . . .   (incl. in QP36)   £400

Type E. With GPO Cypher   Type F. With Post Office Crown Symbol

(Des. Stuart Rose)

II. ORANGE-RED COVER AS TYPE E showing Birds
   PVA gum (No. U12 (2))

QP38 JUNE 1968 (Kingfisher) (issued 4.6.68)   1,212,000   1·80
QP39 JULY 1968 (Kingfisher)   1,195,000   11·00
QP40 AUG 1968 (Peregrine Falcon)   1,223,800   1·50

   Change to one centre phosphor band. PVA gum (No. U13)

QP41 SEPT 1968 (Peregrine Falcon) (issued 16.9.68)   1,010,200   1·80
QP42 OCT 1968 (Pied Woodpecker)   1,277,800   1·80
QP43 NOV 1968 (Pied Woodpecker)   1,006,200   1·90
QP44 DEC 1968 (Great Crested Grebe)   975,600   1·90
QP45 JAN 1969 (Barn Owl)   1,017,000   3·00

   Change to 4d. bright vermilion with one centre phosphor band. PVA gum (No. U14)

> MIXED GUMS. Nos. QP46/7 exist with gum arabic and PVA panes in the same
> booklet. The mixed gums are indicated by the code letters "G" (Gum arabic) and "P"
> (PVA), starting with the first pane of the booklet.

QP46 FEB 1969 (Barn Owl) (issued 20.2.69) (PPP) . . . .   3·50
    (*a*) Combination GGP   £125
    (*b*) Combination GPG   £125
    (*c*) Combination GPP   60·00
    (*d*) Combination PGG   1,035,200   £125
    (*e*) Combination PGP   60·00
    (*f*) Combination PPG   60·00
    (*g*) Combination GGG   £160

QP47 MAR 1969 (Jay) (PPP) . . . .   3·00
    (*a*) Combination GGP   £125
    (*b*) Combination PGP   60·00
    (*c*) Combination PPG   1,424,400   60·00
    (*d*) Combination GPP   60·00
    (*e*) Combination GPG   £125
    (*f*) Combination GGG   £160

QP48 MAY 1969 (Jay)   533,800   3·50
QP49 JULY 1969 (Puffin)   498,400   3·00
QP50 SEPT 1969 (Puffin)   506,200   5·00

III. ORANGE-RED COVER AS TYPE F showing Birds
   PVA gum (No. U14)

QP51 NOV 1969 (Cormorant)   472,600   3·50
QP52 JAN 1970 (Cormorant)   487,800   4·00
QP53 APR 1970 (Wren)   512,800   3·50
QP54 AUG 1970 (Golden Eagle)   570,600   3·50
QP55 OCT 1970 (Golden Eagle)   754,800   3·50

10s. BOOKLETS

Type E I   Type E II

Pictorial Cover with GPO Cypher

(Des. Stuart Rose)

Two types of Cypher:
Type I. GPO in clear letters. 10s. Booklets XP4/5
Type II. GPO in black letters. 10s. Booklets XP6/10

Contents: 24 × 4d., 6 × 3d., 6 × 1d. in panes of six

BRIGHT PURPLE COVER AS TYPE E I showing Explorers
PVA gum (Nos. U2, U9, U12)

XP4 MAY 1968 (Livingstone) (issued 25.3.68)	713,200	5·00
XP5 AUG 1968 (Livingstone)	39,497	5·00

Contents changed: 12 × 5d., 14 × 4d., 4 × 1d., in panes of six and one horizontally *se-tenant* pane of 2 × 4d., and 4 × 1d.

YELLOW-GREEN COVER AS TYPE E II showing Explorers
PVA gum (Nos. U3, U13, U17)

XP6 SEPT 1968 (Scott) (issued 16.9.68)	1,513,400	4·00

Change to 4d. bright vermilion but *se-tenant* pane comprises 1d. with two phosphor bands and 4d. with one left side phosphor band. PVA gum (Nos. U2, U14, U16, U17). For booklets with mixed gum, see note above No. QP46

XP 7 FEB 1969 (Mary Kingsley) (issued 6.1.69)		3·00
XP 8 MAY 1969 (Mary Kingsley) (PPPPP)		4·00
(a) Combination PPPGP	1,165,200	55·00
(b) Combination PPGPP		£150
XP 9 AUG 1969 (Shackleton)	1,765,600	4·00
XP10 NOV 1969 (Shackleton)	1,176,000	6·00

(Note: XP 7 FEB 1969 value 2,338,200)

Type F

(Des. Stuart Rose)

Pictorial Cover with Post Office
Corporation Crown Symbol

YELLOW-GREEN COVER AS TYPE F showing Explorers
   PVA gum (Nos. U2, U14, U16, U17)
XP11 FEB 1970 (Frobisher) (issued 2.2.70)   490,200   6·00
XP12 NOV 1970 (Captain Cook)   737,400   6·50

£1 BOOKLET ('STAMPS FOR COOKS')

Type X

Contents: 18 × 5d., 36 × 4d., 6 × 1d., in panes of fifteen and one horizontally *se-tenant* pane
of 3 × 5d., 6 × 4d., and 6 × 1d. There are 12 recipes on interleaving pages and on *se-tenant*
labels attached to each pane.

FULL COLOUR COVER AS TYPE X size 6 × 2⅞ in. showing "Baked Stuffed Haddock"

Pane of fifteen 5d. has two phosphor bands, panes of fifteen 4d. have one centre phosphor band but
se-tenant pane has two phosphor bands on 1d. and 5d. and one side band on 4d. (three stamps with
band at left and three stamps with band at right)
ZP1   (no date) (issued 1.12.69) (stapled)   10,848   £250
ZP1a As last but booklet is sewn with thread   374,902   9·00
            (s)   Each stamp overprinted "Specimen". Stapled   £2000
            (sa) Each stamp cancelled with Philatelic Bureau
                  postmark of 8 June 1971. Stitched   £1800

Examples of this booklet are known with one or two colours omitted from the cover.
   Examples of No. ZP1sa were issued as specimens to firms and organizations interested in sponsoring
similar booklets.

APPENDIX HB
Postage Rates

Postage rates from 1635 have been researched from official records and the following extract is reproduced with kind permission of the Post Office. The rates given apply only to the period covered by this Catalogue.

Letter Post

The Treasury was empowered to regulate rates of postage, and subsequent changes were made by Treasury Warrant

Date	Rates of Charge		Date	Rates of Charge	
1 May 1952	2oz	2½d.	**17 May 1965**	2oz	4d.
	4oz	3d.	Each additional 2oz. up to 1lb. 2d.		
Then 1d. for each additional 2oz.			Each additional 2oz. thereafter 3d.		
1 January 1956	2oz	2½d.	**3 October 1966**	2oz.	4d.
Then 1½d. for each additional 2oz.			Each additional 2oz up to 1lb. 2d.		
			Each additional 2oz. up to 1lb. 8oz. 3d.		
1 October 1957	1oz	3d.	Over 1lb. 8oz. up to 2lb. 3s.6d.		
	2oz	4½d.	Each additional 1lb. 2s.		

Then 1½d. for each additional 2oz.

Introduction of the first and second class services for letters and cards.

Date	Weight not exceeding	First Class	Second Class
16 September 1968	4oz	5d.	4d.
	6oz	9d.	6d.
	8oz	1s. 0d.	8d.
	10oz	1s. 3d.	10d.
	12oz	1s. 6d.	1s. 0d.
	14oz	1s. 9d.	1s. 2d.
	1lb. 0oz	2s. 0d.	1s. 4d.
	1lb. 2oz	2s. 3d.	1s. 6d.
	1lb. 4oz	2s. 6d.	1s. 7d.
	1lb. 6oz	2s. 9d.	1s. 8d.
	1lb. 8oz	3s. 0d.	1s. 9d.
	2lb. 0oz	4s. 0d.	Not admissible over 1½lbs.

Each additional 1lb. 2s.

Postcards

From 1925 the maximum size allowed was $5\frac{7}{8}'' \times 4\frac{1}{8}''$ and the minimum size was $4'' \times 2\frac{3}{4}''$.

Date	Charge
1 May 1940	. . . . 2d.
1 October 1957	. . . . 2½d.
17 May 1965	. . . . 3d.

Printed Papers

Date	Rates of Charge		Date	Rates of Charge	
1 June 1951	4oz	1½d.	**1 October 1961**	2oz	2½d.
Then ½d. for each additional 2oz. up to 2lb.				4oz.	4d.
1 January 1956	2oz	1½d.	**17 May 1965**		
Then 1d. for each additional 2oz.			Not over 2oz.		3d.
			Not over 4oz.		5d.
1 June 1956	4oz.	2d.	Each additional 2oz.		1d.
Then 1d. for each additional 2oz.					
1 October 1957	2oz.	2d.			
	4oz.	4d.			
Then 1d. for each additional 2oz.					

Newspaper Post

From 1870 the charge had been ½d. per copy irrespective of weight, but from 1 November 1915 the maximum weight permitted was 2lb.

Date	Charge Per Copy not exceeding	
1 July 1940	4oz.	1½d.

Then ½d. for each additional 4oz.

Date		
1 June 1956	6oz.	2d.

Then 1d for each additional 6oz.

Date		
1 October 1957	6oz.	2½d.

Then 1½d. for each 6oz.

Date	Charge Per Copy not exceeding	
1 October 1961	6oz.	3d.

Then 1½d. for each additional 6oz.

Date		
17 May 1965	2oz.	3d.
	4oz.	5d.

Then 1d. for each additional 2oz. Per copy regulation abolished

Articles for the Blind

This service was made free of charge from 17 May 1965 (maximum weight 15lb.).

Date	Rates of Charge		Date	Rates of Charge	
1 July 1940	2lb.	½d.	**12 April 1954**	2lb.	½d.
	5lb	1d.		5lb.	1d.
	8lb.	1½d.		8lb.	1½d.
	11lb.	2d.		11lb.	2d.
	15lb.	2½d.		15lb.	2½d.

Express Service

Service 1.   Express by special messenger all the way.

Date	Charges	Notes
1934	6d. per mile plus cost of special conveyance if used. Weight fee (for packets over 1lb.) 3d.	Charge for additional articles 1d. per article after the first. Waiting fee 2d. for each 10 minutes after the first 10 minutes
1 January 1956	1s. per mile plus cost of special conveyance if used	Additional articles 2½d. for each item beyond the first. Waiting fee 4d. for each 10 minutes after the first 10 minutes
1 October 1957	As above	Additional articles 3d. for each item beyond the first
17 May 1965	3s. per mile plus cost of special conveyance if used	Each additional article 4d. for each item beyond the first. Waiting fee 1s. for each 10 minutes after the first 10 minutes

Service 2. Special Delivery at the request of the sender. Post Office messenger from the delivery office after transmission by post.

Date	Charges	Notes
1 January 1956	Full postage plus special fee of 1s. (from 1934 6d.).	If a special conveyance was used the actual cost, or if that was unknown, 1s. per mile
17 May 1965	Full postage plus special fee of 3s.	As above but 6s. per mile
16 September 1968	As above but only for first class service.	

There was also a Limited Sunday Special Delivery Service. Charges were as for Service 2 except the special fee was 1s.6d. in 1934; 3s. from 1 January 1956 and 9s. from 17 May 1965 in addition to full postage.

The service providing for the express delivery of a message received by telephone was withdrawn on 30 December 1955.

Service 3. Express delivery all the way at the request of the addressee. Charges were the same as for Service 1. Additional articles 2d. for every ten beyond the first (from 1934 1d.). From 17 May 1965 this charge was increased to 6d. for every ten after the first.

Railex

This service was introduced on 1 January 1934. It provided for the conveyance of a postal packet to a railway station by Post Office messenger for despatch on the first available train, and for its immediate delivery by Post Office messenger from the station of destination.

Date	Charge	
1 July 1940	Not exceeding 2oz	3s. 0d.
	Over 2oz. and up to 1lb . . .	3s. 6d.
1 January 1956	Not over 2oz	6s. 0d.
	Not over 1lb	7s. 0d.
17 May 1965	Charge per packet	20s. 0d.
	(irrespective of weight but not exceeding 1lb.)	

Official Parcel Post

This service had first been introduced on 1 August 1883.

Date	Rates of Postage		Date	Rates of Postage	
31 March 1952	2lb.	11d.		7lb.	2s. 6d.
	3lb. . . . . . 1s.	1d.		8lb.	2s. 9d.
	4lb. . . . . . 1s.	3d.		15lb.	3s. 0d.
	5lb. . . . . . 1s.	5d.			
	6lb. . . . . . 1s.	7d.	**1 October 1957**	2lb.	1s. 6d.
	7lb. . . . . . 1s.	9d.		3lb.	1s. 9d.
	8lb. . . . . . 1s.	10d.		4lb.	2s. 0d.
	11lb. . . . . . 1s.	11d.		5lb.	2s. 3d.
	15lb. . . . . . 2s.	0d.		6lb.	2s. 6d.
				7lb.	2s. 9d.
7 April 1953	2lb. . . . . . 1s.	0d.		8lb.	3s. 0d.
	3lb. . . . . . 1s.	2d.		11lb.	3s. 3d.
	4lb. . . . . . 1s.	4d.		15lb.	3s. 6d.
	5lb. . . . . . 1s.	6d.			
	6lb. . . . . . 1s.	8d.	**1 October 1961**	2lb.	2s. 0d.
	7lb. . . . . . 1s.	10d.		3lb.	2s. 3d.
	8lb. . . . . . 1s.	11d.		4lb.	2s. 6d.
	11lb. . . . . . 2s.	0d.		5lb.	2s. 9d.
	15lb. . . . . . 2s.	1d.		6lb.	3s. 0d.
				7lb.	3s. 3d.
12 April 1954	2lb. . . . . . 1s.	1d.		8lb.	3s. 6d.
	3lb. . . . . . 1s.	3d.		11lb.	3s. 9d.
	4lb. . . . . . 1s.	6d.		15lb.	4s. 0d.
	5lb. . . . . . 1s.	8d.			
	6lb. . . . . . 1s.	10d.	**29 April 1963**	2lb.	2s. 0d.
	7lb. . . . . . 2s.	0d.		3lb.	2s. 3d.
	8lb. . . . . . 2s.	1d.		4lb.	2s. 6d.
	11lb. . . . . . 2s.	3d.		5lb.	2s. 9d.
	15lb. . . . . . 2s.	4d.		6lb.	3s. 0d.
				8lb.	3s. 6d.
1 January 1956	2lb. . . . . . 1s.	3d.		10lb.	4s. 0d.
	3lb. . . . . . 1s.	5d.		12lb.	4s. 6d.
	4lb. . . . . . 1s.	8d.		15lb.	5s. 0d.
	5lb. . . . . . 1s.	11d.		18lb.	5s. 9d.
	6lb. . . . . . 2s.	1d.		22lb.	6s. 6d.
	7lb. . . . . . 2s.	3d.	Increased weight limit of 22 lbs. introduced		
	8lb. . . . . . 2s.	6d.	18 February 1963		
	11lb. . . . . . 2s.	8d.			
	15lb. . . . . . 2s.	9d.	**17 May 1965**	2lb.	2s. 9d.
				3lb.	3s. 0d.
1 June 1956	2lb. . . . . . 1s.	4d.		4lb.	3s. 3d.
	3lb. . . . . . 1s.	6d.		6lb.	3s. 6d.
	4lb. . . . . . 1s.	9d.		8lb.	4s. 0d.
	5lb. . . . . . 2s.	0d.		10lb.	4s. 6d.
	6lb. . . . . . 2s.	3d.		14lb.	5s. 6d.

Date   *Rates of Postage*
                                18lb. . . . . . 6s. 6d.
                                22lb. . . . . . 7s. 6d.

3 October 1966   (Ordinary Rate)
                                1½lb. . . . . 2s. 6d.
                                2lb. . . . . . 3s. 0d.
                                6lb. . . . . . 4s. 6d.
                                10lb. . . . . . 6s. 0d.
                                14lb. . . . . . 7s. 6d.
                                18lb. . . . . . 9s. 0d.
                                22lb. . . . . . 10s. 6d.
(Local delivery) As for ordinary less 1s.0d.
at each step.

The Local Parcel Delivery Area comprised all places which had, in their local address, the same post town name as that of the office of posting.

Further Reading

The following list is representative of the major works relating to Queen Elizabeth II pre-decimal issues, stamp booklets, postmarks and postal history. Originally culled in part from *A List of Books on the Postal History, and Adhesive Postage and Revenue Stamps of Great Britain*, compiled by Arnold M. Strange (2nd edition, 1971, Great Britain Philatelic Society, London). Later publications have been included.

GENERAL

Alderfer, David and Rosenblum, Larry. *Introduction to the Stamps of Great Britain* (2004, Amos Press, Sidney, Ohio, USA)

Allen, Giles. *Special Stamp History: 1953 Coronation Issue* (1997, National Postal Museum, London.)

Allen, Giles. *The Wildings: The First Elizabeth II Definitives* (2002, British Philatelic Bulletin Publication No 9, Royal Mail, London)

Allen, Giles. *The First Elizabeth II Castle High Value Definitives* (2005, British Philatelic Bulletin Publication No 11, Royal Mail, London)

Bater, Gerry and The Lord Spens. *The Queen Elizabeth II Waterlow "Castle" High Values, 1955–1958.* (1990. The G.B. Overprints Society.)

Furfle, Michael. *British Postage Due Mail, 1914–1971.* (1993. The Author, Middx.)

Gentleman, David. *Artwork* (2002, Ebury Press, London)

Hine, I. S. and Loveland, R. A. *Great Britain, Queen Elizabeth II. Check List of Photogravure Cylinder Numbers, 1952–1963.* (1964, A. L. Bert.)

J.L. *Shelley Simplified Catalogue of Varieties on Queen Elizabeth II Postage Stamps.* (11th Edn. 1968. Shelley Stamps, London. Supplement 1969/70.)

Langston, Colin M. *Catalogue of Flaws on Q.E. G.B. Sheet Stamps.* (1966. The Author, London.)

Langston, Colin M. *A Priced Catalogue and Guide to Collecting Queen Elizabeth Great Britain Stamp Booklets. March 1953 to December 1963.* (1964. The Author, London.)

Langston, Colin M. *The Complete List of Flaws on Queen Elizabeth Great Britain (1st Design) Stamps from Booklets and Coils.* (1969. The Author, London.)

Langston, Colin M. and Corliss, H. C. *Stamps of Great Britain Issued in Rolls and the Machines which Use Them. An Historical Survey including a Check List of the Rolls issued since 1938.* (1961. The Authors, London.)

Mackay, James A. *British Stamps.* (1985. Longman Group Ltd., London.)

Machin, Arnold. *Artist of an Icon: The Memoirs of Arnold Machin* (2002, Frontier Publishing, Kirstead, Norfolk)

Morgan, Glenn H. *British Stamp Exhibitions* (1995, The Author, London.)

Myall, D. G. A. *The Deegam Se-tenant Catalogue of G.B. Elizabethan Definitives.* (1979. The Author, Bridport, Dorset.)

Myall, D. G. A. *The Deegam Catalogue of Elizabethan Coil Leaders.* (1987. The Author, Bridport, Dorset.)

Myall, D.G.A. *The Complete Deegam Machin Handbook* (2003, 3rd edition, The Author, Bridport, Dorset. Published in printed & electronic versions. Supplement published 2005)

Pierron, Tom. *The 2005 Catalogue of Great Britain Errors & Varieties* (2005, 2nd edition, Baccic Multimedia. No place stated. Published in printed and electronic versions)

Potter, David. *British Elizabethan Stamps.* (1971. B.T. Batsford, London.)

Rigo de Righi, A. G. *The Stamps of Royalty; British Commemorative Issues for Royal Occasions, 1935–1972.* (1973. The National Postal Museum, London.)

Rose, Stuart. *Royal Mail Stamps.–A Survey of British Stamp Design.* (1980. Phaidon Press, Oxford.)

The Shalan Catalogue. A Guide to the Missing Phosphor Lines Issues of Queen Elizabeth II Great Britain. (3rd. Edn. 1971. Shelley Stamps, and B. Alan Ltd., London.)

Sweet, Fay. *Queen Elizabeth II: A Jubilee Portrait in Stamps* (2002, Royal Mail & The British Library, London).

West, Richard and Muir, Douglas N. *The Story of Definitive Stamps* (1993, Royal Mail, London)

Wijman, J. J. *Postage Stamps of Great Britain and their History.* (1986. The Author, Netherlands.)

Williams, L. N. and M. *Commemorative Postage Stamps of Great Britain.* (1967. Arco Publications, London.)

POST OFFICE BOOKLETS OF STAMPS

Alexander, Jean and Newbery, Leonard F. *British Stamp Booklets. Part 1, Series 1: Part 2, Series 1/2; Part 3, Series 3/5; Part 4, Series 6: Part 5, Series 7; Part 6, Series 8/9: Part 7, Series 10/11, Part 8, Appendix A and B, Part 9, Appendix C, Addenda & Corrigenda and Index* (1987–97 in nine parts. The Great Britain Philatelic Society, London.) Parts 4/7 contain information on booklets issued from 1951/70.

POSTAL HISTORY AND POSTMARKS

Awcock, P. G. *Automatic Letter Sorting in the United Kingdom.* (7th. Edn. 1985. The Author, Haywards Heath.)

Bennett, J. Bruce, Parsons, Cyril, R. H., and Pearson, G. R. *Current Machine Postmarks of the United Kingdom.* (1963. British Postmark Society, London.)

Dagnall, H. *The Mechanised Sorting of Mail.* (1976. The Author, Leicester.)

Daunton, M. J. *Royal Mail: The Post Office since 1840.* (1985. The Athlone Press, London.)

Farrugia, Jean. *A Guide to Post Office Archives.* (1986. The Post Office, London.)

Holland, F. C. *Introduction to British Postmark Collecting.* (1971.)

Langston, Colin M. *Surcharge and Explanatory Dies of Great Britain.* (1964. The Author.)

Mackay, James A. *The Parcel Post of the British Isles.* (1982. The Author, Dumfries.)

Mackay, James A. *Registered Mail of the British Isles.* (1983. The Author, Dumfries.)

Mackay James A. *Scottish Postmarks 1693–1978.* (1978. The Author, Dumfries.)

Mackay James A. *English and Welsh Postmarks since 1840.* (1980. The Author, Dumfries.)

Mackay, James A. *British Post Office Numbers 1924–1969.* (1981. The Author, Dumfries.)

Mackay, James A. *Surcharged Mail of the British Isles.* (1984. The Author, Dumfries.)

Mackay, James A. *Official Mail of the British Isles.* (1983. The Author, Dumfries.)

Mackay, James A. *Machine Cancellations of Scotland.* (1986. The Author, Dumfries.)

Mackay, James A. *Postal History Annual.* (From 1979. The Author, Dumfries.)

Mackay, James A. *Scotland's Posts* (2000. The Author, Glasgow)

Muir, Douglas N. and Robinson Martin. *An Introduction to British Postal Mechanisation.* (1980. Postal Mechanisation Study Circle, Henley-on-Thames, Oxon. Supplements 1981, 1983 and 1992.)

Parsons, Cyril R. H., Peachey, Colin G. and Pearson, George R. *Local Publicity Slogan Postmarks 1963–1969.* (1981. 2nd edn. The Authors, Herts.)

Parsons, Cyril R. H., Peachey, Colin G. and Pearson, George R. *Slogan Postmarks of the Seventies.* (1980. The Authors, London.)

Parsons, Cyril R.H., Peachey, Colin G. and Pearson, George. *Collecting Slogan Postmarks 1917–69.* (1986. The Authors, Aylesbury.)

Pask, Brian and Peachey, Colin, G. *Twenty Years of First Day Postmarks.* (1983. British Postmark Society, Herts.)

Peach, Jack. *U.K. Machine Marks.* (1982. 2nd Edn. Vera Trinder Ltd., London.)

Peachey, Colin G. *In-depth U.K. Slogan Postmark Listings: Details of All Towns Using Multi-Town Slogan Postmarks in the U.K. Over Four Decades 1960–1999.* (1996. The Author, Hemel Hempstead.)

Pearson, George R. *Special Event Postmarks of the United Kingdom, Vol. II 1963–1983.* (1996. British Postmark Society, Hemel Hempstead, Herts.)

Pearson, George R. *Special Event Postmarks of the United Kingdom. Vol. I "The Early Years" 1851–1962* (1991 4th. Edn. British Postmark Society, Hemel Hempstead, Herts.)

Reynolds, Paul. *The Machine Cancellations of Wales 1905–1985.* (1985. Welsh Philatelic Society, Swansea.)

Swan, V. *British Slogan Cancellations, 1917–1960.* (1960. The Author, Alton.)

Wellsted, Hilary. *Express Service 1891–1971.* (1986. Postal History Society, Tonbridge.)

Whitney, Dr. J. T., Peachey, Colin G. and Crookes, V. Brian. *Collect British Postmarks.* (1997 7th Edn. British Postmark Society, Hemel Hempstead, Herts.)

POSTAL RATES

Johnson, Robert and Peet, Gordon. *British Postal Rates 1937 to 2000.* (2000)

Stanley Gibbons
Investment Department

Celebrating
150 years

Minimum Guaranteed Return
Investment Contracts.

An interesting, secure way to achieve growth on your savings.

The combination of a low inflation, low interest environment, with the consistent annual increases in pricing experienced over 100 plus years, enables Stanley Gibbons to provide a unique investment product, offering minimum returns significantly in excess of current bank interest rates.

Up to **7%** guaranteed return per annum*

*Subject to terms and conditions

Contract Length	Minimum Guaranteed Annual Return	Min value at end of term £5,000 Invested	Min value at end of term £25,000 Invested	Min value at end of term £100,000 Invested	Min value at end of term £250,000 Invested
3 Years	5%	£5,750	£28,750	£115,000	£287,500
5 Years	6%	£6,500	£32,500	£130,000	£325,000
10 Years	7%	£8,500	£42,500	£170,000	£425,000

Key terms

Take out a Stanley Gibbons rare stamp or autograph investment contract for a set period of between 3 and 20 years, to enjoy a guaranteed minimum annual return on completion of the contract. At the end of the contract term, the investor has the following options, subject to conditions:

1) Retain the stamps or autographs
2) Sell items privately
3) Auction them – sell through Stanley Gibbons auctions, commission free
4) Sell to Stanley Gibbons directly at a minimum guaranteed price, either: initial purchase price plus percentage return per annum* or 75% of listed catalogue price*
   *whichever is greater
5) Roll over the contract for an additional period of 3 to 20 years.

Advantages

Fixed term contracts benefit from potential high returns based on rising market prices, whilst providing peace of mind and security from the guaranteed minimum rate annual returns. Advantages include:
· Free storage in a secure vault, with free insurance during contract term
· No additional management fees or hidden administration charges
· Beneficial for budgeting purposes such as school fees, career breaks and future major asset purchases

Do not delay -
Contact us via one of
the methods below.

399 Strand, London WC2R 0LX
Adrian Roose: Tel: +44 (0) 20 7557 4454 Email: aroose@stanleygibbons.co.uk
Geoff Anandappa: Tel: +44 (0)20 7557 4442 Email: ganandappa@stanleygibbons.co.uk
Fax: +44 (0) 20 7557 4499
www.stanleygibbons.com/investment

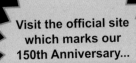

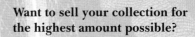
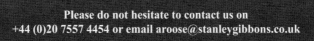

COLLECT
GREAT BRITAIN STAMPS
From Stanley Gibbons, THE WORLD'S LARGEST STAMP STOCK
Priority order form
Four easy ways to order

Phone:
020 7836 8444
Overseas: +44 (0)20 7836 8444

Fax:
020 7557 4499
Overseas: +44 (0)20 7557 4499

Email:
lmourne@stanleygibbons.co.uk

Post:
Lesley Mourne, Stamp Mail Order
Department Stanley Gibbons Ltd,
399 Strand London, WC2R 0LX

Customer Details
Account Number_____

Name _____

Address_____

_____ Postcode _____

Country _____ Email _____

Tel No_____ Fax No _____

Registered Postage & Packing £3.60

I enclose my cheque/postal order for £............ in full payment. Please make cheques/postal orders payable to Stanley Gibbons Ltd. Cheques must be in £ sterling and drawn on a UK bank

Please debit my credit card for £.......... in full payment. I have completed the credit card section below.

Card Number

☐ ☐ ☐ ☐ ☐ ☐ ☐ ☐ ☐ ☐ ☐ ☐ ☐ ☐ ☐ ☐

Start Date (Switch & Amex)   Expiry Date   Issue No (Switch)

☐ ☐ ☐ ☐   ☐ ☐ ☐ ☐   ☐ ☐

Signature_____ Date_____

COLLECT

GREAT BRITAIN STAMPS

From Stanley Gibbons, THE WORLD'S LARGEST STAMP STOCK

Priority order form
Four easy ways to order

Condition (mint/ UM/used)	Country	SG No.	Description	Price	Office use only
			Postage & Packing	£3.60	
			Grand Total	£	

Minimum price. The minimum catalogue price quoted is 10p. For individual stamps, prices between 10p and 95p are provided as a guide for catalogue users. The lowest price charged for individual stamps or sets purchased from Stanley Gibbons Ltd is £1

Please complete payment, name and address, details overleaf